Proceedings of the International and Interdisciplinary Symposium
Colombo, Sri Lanka, 12-26 March 1990

As-6-II-7-17

ECOLOGY AND LANDSCAPE MANAGEMENT IN SRI LANKA

Edited by

W. Erdelen, C. Preu, N. Ishwaran, C.M. Madduma Bandara

 **Margraf Verlag**

Proceedings of the International and Interdisciplinary Symposium
ECOLOGY AND LANDSCAPE MANAGEMENT IN SRI LANKA
W. Erdelen, C. Preu, N. Ishwaran, C.M. Madduma Bandara (eds.)
Colombo, Sri Lanka, 12-26 March 1990

Editors:

Inv.-Nr. 94/A35356

Dr. Walter Erdelen
Dept. of Biogeography
University of the Saarland
Postfach 151150
D-66041 Saarbrücken
Germany

Dr. Christian Preu
Dept. of Physical Geography
University of Augsburg
Universitätsstr. 10
D-86159 Augsburg
Germany

Dr. Natarajan Ishwaran
Regional Office for Science and Technology
for Southeast Asia (ROSTSEA)
UNESCO
Jl. M.H. Thamrin 14
Tromol Pos 1273/Jkt
Jakarta 10012
Indonesia

Prof. Dr. C.M. Madduma Bandara
Dept. of Physical Geography
University of Peradeniya
Peradeniya
Sri Lanka

CIP-Titelaufnahme der Deutschen Bibliothek

Ecology and landscape management in Sri Lanka: proceedings
of the international and interdisciplinary symposium,
Colombo, Sri Lanka; 12 - 26 march 1990 / ed. by W. Erdelen...
- Weikersheim: Margraf, 1993
  ISBN 3-8236-1182-8
NE: Erdelen, Walter [Hrsg.]

Cover Photo:
   W. Erdelen

Typesetting and Layout:
   Sonya Hetherington
   Sabine Hilpmann

Printing and Binding:
   F. & T. Müllerbader
   Germany

© **Verlag Josef Margraf**, 1993
   P.O. Box 105
   D-97985 Weikersheim
   Germany

ISBN 3-8236-1182-8

Dedicated to the late

Prof. H. Crusz

and

Prof. S. Balasubramaniam

CONTENTS

Page

i

II. IMPACT STUDIES AND CONSERVATION ASPECTS

SUMMARIZING REMARKS

LIST OF CONTRIBUTORS

ABEYWICKRAMA, B.A., Prof. Dr.
Dept. of Botany, University of Colombo, Thurstan Rd. Colombo 3, Sri Lanka

ASHTON, P.M.S., Prof. Dr.
School of Forestry and Environmental Studies, Marsh Hall, Yale University, 360 Prospect Street, New Haven, Connecticut 06511, USA

BERUGODA, S.
Survey Department, P.O. Box 506, Colombo 5, Sri Lanka

BRAND, K.
Dept. of Physical Geography, University of Augsburg, Universitätsstr. 10, D-86159 Augsburg, Germany.

COORAY, P.G., Prof. Dr.
Dept. of Geography, University of Peradeniya, Peradeniya, Sri Lanka

DASSANAYAKE, M.D., Prof. Dr.
Dept. of Botany, University of Peradeniya, Peradeniya, Sri Lanka

De ALWIS, A.
National Aquatic Resources Agency, Crow Island, Colombo 15, Sri Lanka

De SILVA, J.A.
National Aquatic Resources Agency, Crow Island, Colombo 15, Sri Lanka

De SILVA, S.H.C.
Irrigation Department, Bauddhaloka Mawatha, Colombo 7, Sri Lanka

DERANIYAGALA, S.U., Dr.
Archaeological Department, M. Fernando Rd. Colombo 7, Sri Lanka

DISSANAYAKE, C.B., Prof. Dr.
Institute of Fundamental Studies, Hantana Rd. Kandy, Sri Lanka

DUNCAN, A., Dr.
Dept. of Biology, University of London, Royal Holloway and Bradford New College, Egham, Surrey, TW20 OEX, UK

ERDELEN, W., Dr.
Dept. of Biogeography, University of the Saarland, Postfach 151150, D-66041 Saarbrücken, Germany

FERNANDO, C.H., Prof. Dr.
Dept. of Biology, University of Waterloo, Waterloo, Ontario N2L 3G1, Canada

FERNANDO, S.B.U.
National Zoological Gardens, Dehiwela, Sri Lanka

GANGODAWILA, C.D., Dr.
Sri Lanka Department of Agriculture, Land and Water Use Division, Sarasavi Mawatha, Peradeniya, Sri Lanka

GANS, C., Prof. Dr.
Dept. of Biology, University of Michigan, 2127 Nat. Sci. Bldg, Ann Arbor, Michigan 48109, USA

GÖLTENBOTH, F., Dr.
Universitas Kristen Satya Wacana,, Jl. Diponegoro 52-60, Salatiga/Java, 50711 Indonesia

GRELLER, A.M., Dr.
Dept. of Botany, Queens College and Graduate Center, City University of New York, 65 Kissena Boulevard, Flushing, New York 11367, USA

GUNASEKERA, J.S.
Mahaweli Authority of Sri Lanka, Upper Mahaweli Watershed Management Project, 64, Sangaraja Mawatha, Kandy, Sri Lanka

GUNATILAKA, A., Dr.
Dept. of Limnology, Institute of Zoology, University of Vienna, Althanstr. 14, A-6020 Vienna, Austria

GUNATILLEKE, C.V.S., Prof. Dr.
Dept. of Botany, University of Peradeniya, Peradeniya, Sri Lanka

GUNATILLEKE, I.A.U.N., Prof. Dr.
Dept. of Botany, University of Peradeniya, Peradeniya, Sri Lanka

HUMBEL, R., Dr.
Geostat, Bundesamt für Statistik, Fellerstr. 21, 3003 Bern, Switzerland

ISHWARAN, N., Dr.
Regional Office for Science and Technology for Southeast Asia (ROSTSEA), UNESCO, Jl. M.H. Thamrin 14, Tromol Pos 1273/Jkt. Jakarta 10012, Indonesia

JAYASINGAM, T., Dr.
Dept. of Botany, Eastern University, Chenkaladi, Sri Lanka

JAYASINGHE, J.M.P.K.
National Aquatic Resources Agency, Crow Island, Colombo 15, Sri Lanka

JAYASURIYA, A.H.M., Prof. Dr.
National Herbarium, P.O. Box 15, Peradeniya, Sri Lanka

JAYATILAKA, S.
Survey Department, Centre for Remote Sensing, P.O. Box 506, Colombo 5, Sri Lanka

JAYAWARDENE, I.F.W.
Sri Lanka Subaqua Club, 58 Maya Ave, Colombo 5, Sri Lanka

KIRCHHOF, W.M., Dr.
DLR, Remote Sensing, Optoelectronics, Münchener Str. 20, Oberpfaffenhofen, D-82234 Weßling, Germany

LIMAYE, S.D., Dr.
Ground Water Institute and South and West Asian Geoscience Newsletter, 2050 Sadashiv Peth, Poona - 411030, India

MADDUMA BANDARA, C.M., Prof. Dr.
Dept. of Geography, University of Peradeniya, Peradeniya, Sri Lanka

MATHES, J.A.P., Dr.
CISIR, 363 Bauddhaloka Mawatha, Colombo 7, Sri Lanka

MITHTHAPALA, S.
National Zoological Park, Smithsonian Institution, Washington DC 20008, USA

MOTHA, M.S.
CISIR, 363 Bauddhaloka Mawatha, Colombo 7, Sri Lanka

PINTO, L., Dr.
Dept. of Zoology, Open University of Sri Lanka, Nawala, Nugegoda, Sri Lanka

PREU, C., Dr.
Dept. of Physical Geography, University of Augsburg, Universitätsstr. 10, D-86159 Augsburg, Germany

PUNCHIHEWA, N.N., Dr.
Dept. of Zoology, Open University of Sri Lanka, Nawala, Nugegoda, Sri Lanka

RAJASURIYA, A.
National Aquatic Resources Agency, Crow Island, Colombo 15, Sri Lanka

RATNAYEKE, S.
Dept. of Botany, University of Peradeniya, Peradeniya, Sri Lanka

SARATH KUMARA, A.A.D.
National Aquatic Resources Agency, Crow Island, Colombo 15, Sri Lanka

SCHIEMER, F., Prof. Dr.
Dept. of Limnology, University of Vienna, Althanstr. 14, A-1090 Vienna, Austria

SEIDENSTICKER, J., Dr.
National Zoological Park, Smithsonian Institution, Washington DC 20008, USA

SENANAYAKE, F.R., Dr.
Faculty of Agriculture and Forestry, University of Melbourne, Parkville, Victoria, Australia

SILVA, E.I.L., Dr.
Dept. of Life Sciences, Institute of Fundamental Studies, Hantana Road, Kandy, Sri Lanka

SRI BHARATHIE, K.P.
Forest Department, Rajamalwatta Road, Battaramulla, Sri Lanka

STARMÜHLNER, F., Prof. Dr.
Dept. of Zoology, University of Vienna, Althanstr. 14, A-1090 Vienna, Austria

UDAYA, W.V.F.,
National Aquatic Resources Agency, Crow Island, Colombo 15, Sri Lanka

VITANAGE, P.W., Prof. Dr.
Dept. of Geology, University of Peradeniya, Peradeniya, Sri Lanka

WANNINAYAKE, W.M.T.B., Dr.
National Aquatic Resources Agency, Crow Island, Colombo 15, Sri Lanka

WHITE, R., Dr.
ODA, Upper Mahaweli Catchment, Development Unit 64, Sangaraya Mawatha, Kandy, Sri Lanka

WICKRAMASINGHE, R.H., Dr.
Institute For Tropical Environmental Studies, 41 Flower Rd. Colombo 7, Sri Lanka

WIENEKE, F., Prof. Dr.
Dept. of Geography, University of Munich, Luisenstr. 37, D-80333 Munich, Germany

FOREWORD

The international and interdisciplinary symposium "Ecology and Landscape Management in Sri Lanka" was held at the Hotel Taj Samudra, Colombo, Sri Lanka. Participants were from countries like Sri Lanka, Maldives, Indonesia, the USA, Canada, Norway, Sweden, the UK, the Netherlands, Belgium, France, Switzerland, Austria and the Federal Republic of Germany. The first five days were devoted to the presentation of papers, paralleled with a poster presentation and an exhibition which illustrated the most relevant environmental issues. These presentations covered (1) the ecological context, (2) impact studies and conservation aspects, (3) methodological approaches, (4) the organizational framework, and (5) special evening lectures. The presentations were followed by field excursions to sites of natural and man-made landscapes and major development project sites in Sri Lanka. The field excursions lasted eight days. The symposium ended with a final session in which the major findings were discussed and summarized, and recommendations for the future were made.

The realization of this symposium would have been impossible without the support of many individuals, national and international companies and organizations whom we wish to thank. First of all we thank the Natural Resources, Energy and Science Authority (NARESA) of Sri Lanka, the sponsoring and coordinating Sri Lankan agency. Dr. R.P. Jayewardene, Director-General, and Mr. D.E.F. Ferdinandez, Director of Scientific Affairs, of NARESA, have both been particularly encouraging and supporting in our efforts. Moreover, the members of the organizing committee have continuously helped us in many ways. We deeply regret the loss of Prof. Dr. H. Crusz, a member of the organizing committee, and Prof. Dr. S. Balasubramanian. They were not only teachers and friends to many of us but had always strongly supported the idea of having this symposium. We are grateful for the cooperation received from Her Excellency, The Ambassador of the Democratic Socialist Republic of Sri Lanka in the Federal Republic of Germany, Mrs. M. Abeysekera, and from His Excellency, The Ambassador of the Federal Republic of Germany in Sri Lanka, Mr. K. Franke, and the staff members of the German Embassy in Colombo. We thank Mr. L.A. Coulter, Director and General Manager, Hotel Taj Samudra, and members of his staff who have made special efforts to host this symposium. For support we have received from our universities, we are particularly grateful to the heads of our departments Prof. Dr. K. Fischer, Dept. of Physical Geography, University of Augsburg, and Prof. Dr. Dr. h.c. mult. P. Müller, Dept. of Biogeography, University of the Saarland. We thank the German Research Foundation (Deutsche Forschungsgemeinschaft) and our Sri Lankan colleagues for supporting our research in Sri Lanka.

W. Erdelen
C. Preu

PREFACE

Sri Lanka in 1990 turned out to be a challenging venue for the International Symposium on Ecology and Landscape Management for several reasons. It followed a period of civil turmoil which virtually wrecked the economy and normal social life in most parts of the country. Therefore, after many months, the scholars in tropical ecology interested in the mountains and plateaus, forests and grasslands, gemming areas and beaches could visit these sites in relative peace and discuss many issues with the local people at ease. The panoramic view of the Adam's Peak over the Horton Plains, the rain forests of Sinharaja, the massive dams of the Mahaweli, the gem pits, coral gardens and turtle hatcheries have undoubtedly left lasting impressions of the landscape of Sri Lanka in the minds of the participants.

During the working sessions of the symposium, many critical and sensitive issues pertaining to the landscape ecology of Sri Lanka were discussed in an atmosphere of free exchange and cordiality in the salubrious precincts of the Taj Samudra Hotel. The participants had the opportunity to meet and discuss landscape management issues with both the present and past Ministers of Lands and Land Development. Similarly, the leading institutions responsible for environmental and natural resource management in Sri Lanka such as the Natural Resources, Energy and Science Authority (NARESA) and the Central Environmental Authority (CEA), provided much support and extended much cooperation for the symposium. On the other hand, many of Sri Lanka's prominent environmentalists participated in the discussions and aired their views without fear or favor. An opportunity was afforded to all parties in the debate on ecological issues to gain a multi-dimensional perspective of the problems of landscape management. For instance, the Ceylon Tobacco Company not only supported the symposium but also took much interest in taking the participants on a conducted tour to its nurseries and development sites.

There is hardly any doubt that Sri Lanka had much to gain from an international and interdisciplinary symposium of this nature. The rapid economic growth in the early 1980s, the increasing population pressure on land and unemployment has led to an acceleration in the exploitation of natural resources. The rate of resource exploitation has also been enhanced by the burgeoning demand of the construction industry, facilitated by political support for free enterprise afforded by the liberal economic policies of the government.

The symposium also followed a period of accelerated development programs such as the Mahaweli Project, housing development endeavours like the village re-awakening (Udagam) programs and efforts towards industrialization as witnessed in the development of the Free Trade Zone. It is well known that such leading development programs were largely supported by international assistance, as in the case of the Mahaweli Ganga Development Project, where Germany, the UK, Sweden, Canada, Japan and many other countries and funding agencies became involved. Investments in some of these projects were the biggest undertakings for some countries in the field of international assistance in recent years. Nevertheless, in many of these activities it is not certain whether environmental and ecological considerations have received their desired attention. It was, therefore, obviously useful and timely at this juncture to organize an international symposium on ecology and landscape management in Sri Lanka.

The need for interdisciplinarity in landscape management was well demonstrated at the symposium by the variety of disciplines involved as well as by the participation of a wide range of professionals from universities and state agencies. It is true that there had been symposia related to ecological issues in Sri Lanka in the past under the sponsorship of various local institutions and organizations. However, they were often dominated by mono-disciplinary approaches and narrowly defined themes. The present symposium has undoubtedly broken such barriers and opened the subject for a wider audience. In this context, it is necessary to draw our attention to the observation made by Schutze (1985) in a paper on this subject that:

"Environment spreads horizontally across the conventional academic divisions of knowledge into natural sciences and humanities. Should it seek a new unity of knowledge which expresses an authentic interdisciplinarity, or a unity of social purpose and action which cannot be sustained by any one existing profession or discipline.....?"

It is our conviction that the symposium has certainly contributed much towards solving this dilemma, though in a modest way. I am confident that this symposium publication will carry this message further.

Prof. Dr. C.M. Madduma Bandara,
Dept. of Physical Geography
University of Peradeniya
Peradeniya
Sri Lanka

EMBASSY OF THE DEMOCRATIC SOCIALIST
REPUBLIC OF SRI LANKA

ROLANDSTRASSE 52
5300 BONN 2
TELEPHONE: (0228) 33 20 55 / 56 / 57
TELEX: 885 612 LANKA D

4th January 1990

Message from the Ambassador

An international and interdisciplinary Symposium being held
in Sri Lanka is most welcome and this one is more so as it relates
directly to ecology and landscape management in Sri Lanka.

While ecological and environmental concerns are recognised
today as being of high priority, they present a dilemma, especially
to developing countries, of how to strike the right balance between
preservation of the ecology and acceleration of development : how to
combat the 'pollution of poverty' within ecological and environmental
constraints. Obviously, ecological and environmental issues must be
integrated into the development process, but the question is what
the combined strategies should be and how they can be applied without
adverse impact on either aspect of an acute human need.

The highly researched content of the Symposium and its
interdisciplinary approach will no doubt be of great value in
suggesting conflict management, compromise and adjustment between
these two aspects, while the international nature of the Symposium
is very apt, since the problem is a global one and must receive a
global response in which the developed world, with its technical
know-how and resources, would be better equipped to tackle it.

I am happy that the embassy of Sri Lanka in the Federal
Republic of Germany has provided even a small link in the admirable
venture of this Symposium which is yet another example of the close
co-operation between the two countries in many areas which are of
relevance to the topics of the Symposium.

I have great pleasure in wishing the Symposium success in
the achievement of its objectives.

Mrs. I.M.Abeysekera
Ambassador

Botschaft
der Bundesrepublik Deutschland
Embassy
of the Federal Republic of Germany

MESSAGE

from His Excellency Mr. K. FRANKE

Ambassador of the Federal Republic of Germany

In recent years scientists all over the world have increasingly
warned of environmental problems due to certain landscape management and land-use planning in various parts of the world. Their
research as well as growing public awareness of the value of a
balanced environment have paved the way for important environmental policy decisions by a number of governments. The symposium
on "Ecology and Landscape Management in Sri Lanka" is a further
attempt to combine scientific research and practical benefit in
order to find solutions to the problems of landscape management in
Sri Lanka. International input from reputed scientists from Asia,
Australia, Europe, the United States and Canada and an interdisciplinary approach might help to broaden the approach to problem
solution.

Dr. habil. Chr. Preu, Dept. of Physical Geography at the University of Augsburg and Dr. W. Erdelen, Dept. Biogeography at the
University of the Saarland, have started to prepare this symposium
already a long time ago. As they are regularly coming to Sri Lanka
on study visits they have designed the seminar in such a way that
it integrates various interests and experiences, including a profound knowledge of Sri Lanka, of which participants might be able
to profit during the excursion, which is part of the symposium.

I wish all participants of the symposium stimulating and fruitful
discussions and I hope that this joint effort to find solutions to
burning environmental problems by an interdisciplinary scientific
approach will be crowned with success, thus benefitting the people
of Sri Lanka and elsewhere.

Klaus Franke
Ambassador of the Federal Republic of Germany

ශ්‍රී ලංකා ස්වාභාවික සම්පත්, බලශක්ති හා විද්‍යා අධිකාරිය
இலங்கை இயற்கைவள, சக்தி விஞ்ஞான அதிகாரசபை
NATURAL RESOURCES, ENERGY & SCIENCE AUTHORITY OF SRI LANKA

දුරකථන අංකය
தொலைபேசி இல. } 596771-3
Telephone No.

47/5 { මේට්ලන්ඩ් පෙදෙස, කොළඹ 7.
මෙයිත්லන්ட பிளேஸ், கொழும்பு 7.
Maitland Place, Colombo 7

මගේ අංකය
எனது இல. }
My No.

ඔබේ අංකය
உமது இல. }
Your No.

දිනය
திகதி }
Date
13 December 1989

I am happy to welcome the participants to the International
Symposium on "Ecology and Landscape Management in Sri Lanka:
Conflict or Compromise?" to be held in Colombo, 12–26 March
1990. We are very pleased to be able to host the Symposium
in Colombo immediately following a period of intensive agricultural development activity in the country. The participants
would then get an excellent opportunity to analyse scientifically the changes that have been brought about to the landscape in the country and to search for solutions to issues and
problems in Landscape Management as conservationists, developers
and managers. By participating in the Symposium and taking part
in its deliberations you will develop new concepts and strategies
applicable to problems in Landscape Management in Sri Lanka.
These will not only be of benefit to this country but will also
serve as guidelines for Landscape Management in all developing
countries and thus contribute substantially towards sustainable
development of natural resources of this planet.

I wish you all luck and hope that the Symposium will be a great
success.

Dr. R.P. Jayewardene
Director-General

Director-General - 94781
Dr. R. P. Jayewardene
Office: 596771 - 3

Additional Director-General - 94754
Administrative Secretary   - 91691

INAUGURAL SESSION

INAUGURAL ADDRESS

by the Chief Guest

Mr. P. DAYARATNE

Minister of Lands, Irrigation and Mahaweli Development

In a recent issue of a draft report on "World Conservation Strategy for the 1990s" prepared by the International Union for the Conservation of Nature, the United Nations Environment Program and the Worldwide Fund for Nature, four principles which form the core of sustainable development were identified. They are (a) ecological sustainability, (b) social sustainability, (c) cultural sustainability and (d) economic sustainability. In the past, development projects have been formulated looking more at economic sustainability and ignoring or giving lesser emphasis to ecological, social and cultural sustainability, each of which is applicable in one way or another. We in Sri Lanka have an ancient civilization, a civilization based on a highly advanced system of irrigation which has a history of over 2000 years. Our forefathers, in their quest for improvement of the quality of life of our people, developed this system of irrigation which took into account the four principles of sustainable development that I mentioned earlier. They did not look at the irrigation system as a source of economic sustainability of a community of people bent on agriculture. They looked at the totality of the system and understood very clearly that the sustainability of such a system needed attention to ecological considerations. The conservation of the watershed of the country was their prime concern. They knew that whoever tampered with the watershed would bring irreparable loss by way of affecting the resource of water - the life-saving resource that provides continuity and economic advancement to an agrarian community. They knew very clearly the need to conserve streams, tanks, forests and other reservations. They knew the importance of wildlife, the fauna and flora of a country and the importance of maintaining genetic diversity and its endemism. They knew very well that the degradation of the ecosystem would deteriorate the ecosystem's ability to meet human needs. That is why we have a rich heritage of a people who maintained a stable ecosystem and used the natural resources wisely in the long and illustrious history of our nation.

Economic Sustainability

I do not intend to place before you the numerous historical records that we are in a position to cite. They clearly indicate the heritage of conservation brought about through religion and the culture of a community of people who were tolerant towards every form of life. Conditions have changed over the years with the so-called advent of the new civilization which brought about emphasis to material advancement of the individual as against the welfare of a community of people concerned and conscious of the environment, social imperatives, cultural values and the economic sustainability that are basic for any human development. So at the present juncture, Sri Lanka like all other developing as well as developed countries faces challenges in regard not only to the physical environment but also to the fauna and flora and the natural resources that keep them vibrant in our land.

Having recognized the concerns regarding the management of the natural resources of land, water and forests including wildlife, an approach was made regarding the conservation and management of natural resources by placing the policy framework on a scientific and rational basis. The Government for the first time spelt out the concepts and rationale for natural resource management. The principles identified to form the basis of the strategy were (a) that the resources of the natural environment must be seen to belong ultimately to the whole nation and must be devoted to national welfare, (b) that there is an obligation on the part of the social democratic state to erect an institutional structure by virtue of which such resources may be located, evaluated, conserved and distributed so that they may be utilized on a sustainable basis and to the greatest national advantage, (c) that, as land provides the conceptual and operational plane of contact between national and environmental resources, this institutional structure should be framed in terms of land policy and land use planning, (d) that land policy planning should be rooted in scientific knowledge of biophysical processes and in a deep understanding of economic progress and of sociopolitical change; they should be supported by reliable data; they should have a positive development orientation; they should be comprehensive and closely integrated but sufficiently flexible to permit and promote the operation of state, corporate and private sectors in a mixed economy, and (e) that the objective must be that the nation should learn to live in productive equilibrium with natural resources and that access to resources should be widely and equitably distributed and that basic needs should be safeguarded for all citizens.

This policy framework was adopted in the management of natural resources. I wish to highlight few of the projects and programs undertaken in recent times to bring about the policies that we have identified into an implementation program. In June 1986, we embarked on a project to strengthen the land use planning capability, firstly, in both quality and quantity. The collection, management and application of basic data for planning, and, secondly, by developing the institutional base for land use planning at the national, provincial and district level by a project funded by the Asian Development Bank, which expects to undertake this task through (a) increasing the land data base which is essential to all land based exercise, (b) strengthening the soil data base and the land evaluation system which is central to the identification of land use opportunities and conservation, and (c) strengthening the land use planning system without which rational planning cannot take place.

Geological Data System

This project has subcomponents which would enhance the aerial photographic capability, establish a digital mapping and geological data system, support a cadastral data base, expand the soil survey and land evaluation capability, improve the soil analytical capability and finally strengthen the Land Use Policy Planning Division of my Ministry and establish provincial, district and divisional land use planning units. This project, which is ongoing, will help us to formulate the national policy on land use that would help resolve the conflict in demands for land use between forestry, wildlife, agriculture, industrial and urban use and the need for conservation and would give clear guidelines to strengthen the process of soil conservation and watershed management.

In the forestry sector we developed a master plan, which was completed in 1986, and a five-year investment program was also developed to identify an implementation strategy for the forestry sector. This project has now commenced with the assistance of the World Bank, ODA, Finnida and the UNDP. One of the most important features of this project is the emphasis provided for environmental management. Adequate care has been taken to ensure environmental protection and stability during the implementation of the project. The environmental protection units have been established both in the Forest Department and my Ministry and will take care of environmental protection in specific areas. Forest plantations, development of management plans and release of areas for felling, logging operations will come under the scrutiny of these units.

The management of existing forests is vital for forest sector development. Both forest plantations and natural forests will be managed on a carefully prepared plan and all environmentally critical areas such as watersheds, steep slopes, river and stream reservations will be put under permanent conservation. Necessary action will be taken to declare such areas as strict natural reserves. People's participation is essential for the success of any forestry program. Public awareness of the importance of forestry for life and of the programs that are implemented to conserve and manage forests for posterity are essential. My Ministry has, therefore, negotiated a parallel project with the Asian Development Bank for the funding of the implementation of a participatory forestry project.

On the conservation of wildlife we have accepted a policy which is in keeping with the objectives of the World Conservation Strategy. The objectives of the Sri Lanka National Conservation Strategy are (a) to maintain essential ecological processes and life-support systems on which human survival and development depend (b) to preserve genetic diversity on which the functioning of many of the above processes and life-support systems depend, and (c) ensure the sustainable utilization of species and ecosystems. We are therefore in the process of complete reassessment of all protected areas for wildlife conservation, where we will introduce management of wildlife which will be undertaken with a "hands on" policy which recognizes the need to maintain resource potential at its natural level.

The Goverment has also taken the following steps to ensure the conservation of tropical forest ecosystems: (a) the prevention of the loss and/or degradation of natural forests on steep and erodible sites by designating them as protection forests, (b) the promotion of sustainable use for the production of timber and fuelwood of tropical forest ecosystems in a few selected areas in such a way that the genetic resources they contain are safeguarded; technical and operational plans for the management of these forests have already been prepared and are in operation, and (c) the promotion of the conservation and management of critical ecosystems as reservoirs of genetic diversity.

Pursuant to this policy the Government has taken various initiatives to conserve critical ecosystems. Particular attention is paid to Sinharaja and Knuckles in view of their environmental significance, and national heritage values. Sinharaja has also been nominated to be inscribed on the World Heritage List of UNESCO. The Government enacted the National Heritage Wilderness Act in January 1988 to confer special status to critical ecosystems that should be conserved for posterity. The Sinharaja and Knuckles forests are declared as protected areas under the provisions of this act. In 1987, the Government requested the International Union for Conservation of Nature, assistance to develop and implement sustainable management programs for Sinharaja and Knuckles. The goals of these projects are to design and implement the sustainable management of these critical ecosystems and to thereby contribute to the overall watershed management plans of Sri Lanka and to conserve an ecosystem of outstanding economic importance, environmental significance and national heritage value.

I have made an attempt to place the policy initiatives taken by the Goverment and also to refer to some of the development plans that we have embarked on for the long-term management of natural resources in Sri Lanka. Natural forest covers over 27 per cent of the land area and over 12 per cent of the island's area is set aside for the conservation of natural ecosystems. As you are aware, these systems contain an important pool of genetic resources for the entire world.

The conservation of such an important pool of genetic resources is not only the responsibility of our people but a responsibility cast on the world community. Developing countries with innumerable problems and priorities need the support of the world community in regard to the conservation efforts that they undertake. Unless and until such support is given without reservation, it would be near impossible task for developing countries such as ours to embark on this exercise out of our own resources.

In Sri Lanka, we have a population of approximately 16.9 million people at the present moment. 78 per cent of our population live in rural areas and are engaged in agriculture. The other sectors of the economy have not developed to absorb the large percentage of unemployed and under-employed persons, and over a million people are now in the category of the unemployed. We have a literacy rate of over 85 per cent and nearly 67 per cent of the population is below 30 years of age. So, with this background and the socioeconomic conditions that I mentioned earlier, the majority of our population turn to land for survival.

When we approach the subject of ecology and landscape management in Sri Lanka we should not forget these socioeconomic conditions under which the people struggle for survival. I am stressing this point for the reason that any deliberation devoid of human considerations will be of no use and will only be an exercise confined to paper. Whatever proposals that we make should promote the continued survival of man, beast and plant.

Lord Buddha, in one of his early sermons, did very clearly mention that one should not attempt to lead a man who is hungry on the path of salvation for he would refuse to understand the glory of "Nirvana" (salvation) for his immediate need would be the salvation from hunder. Unless we bring a better quality of life to our people, it would be a futile effort to make them more conscious of the need for environmental conservation. We understand very well that sustained productivity and conservation of natural resources can be guaranteed only through scientific evaluation and rational allocation of land. The rational allocation of land can only be made possible, if the basic human needs of the community at large are met.

WELCOME ADDRESS

by H.E. Dr. K. FRANKE

Ambassador of the Federal Republic of Germany

I deem it an honor to have been invited to address you on this occasion but must at the same time confess that I am unqualified to do so - at least when I consider the expertise on the subject matter of this symposium concentrated here in the persons of its learned participants. But then, I have to remind myself that ambassadors often talk - and have to about matters of which they know very little and that they are being paid to be a sort of jack-of-all-trades. And in this role let me just throw in a few thoughts for what they are worth.

First why another seminar or symposium? There are so many of them now that it can truely be said that over the last twenty years or so the holding of seminars has developed into a major international industry whose output in terms of tangible benefit to others than the participants themselves is hard to ascertain in quite a few cases. But while there are, to my conviction, a host of superfluous seminars, this does not, I think, apply to this syposium. At any rate, its subject matter is a very important one. If I have grasped it correctly it is about whether and to what extent this country will succeed in harmonizing its development needs with a need to protect its ecology. That indeed is the key question which will decide Sri Lanka's very future. That of course applies to also to my country and to all other countries. There is no use shutting one's eyes to the fact that development will inevitably go at the cost of the natural environment and, very often, at the cost of its beauty. When I compare what I have seen since since my arrival last November with what I saw in the early seventies when I repeatedly came here as a tourist, I note that some of the beauty I saw then has disappeared. Again, that applies also to my country which in my youth was decidedly more beautiful than it is now.

But to state this does not mean to have arrived at the simple conclusion henceforth to put a stop to all activities which further reduce the natural environment and its beauty. For economic and social development is necessary to feed, house, provide jobs for people and to give them education and generally, material and spiritual propects of life. People will insist upon getting that and it would be futile to think they would ever accept anything else. So, there will, for need's sake, be further economic and technical development and it will "eat up" landscape.

Now, while acknowledging this as a fact, one has again not arrived at the simple answer that we cannot but go on with pushing ahead with developmental efforts irrespective of what they do to the environment. For, it is equally a fact that the natural environment and natural resources - and now I am not just talking of beauty and esthetics - are the basis of development itself. If rivers cease to flow because forests have been destroyed, if you get large-scale erosion because of harmful land use - to name but two examples out of possible dozens - development will become self-defeating and will itself grind to a halt.

All this is commonplace but, sometimes, the commonplace needs to be stated so as to avoid that it is being overlooked and disregarded because it is so commonplace.

Having said all that the answer to the question which is the subtitle of this symposium, "conflict or compromise?", can be that there must be compromise, not conflict between ecology and landscape management. And as the two factors between which a compromise is to be acheived are of great importance, the compromise must be a balanced one - one that does not harm the substance of either of the two.

That is, of course, very much easier said than done. But that is why you the experts and the scientists are here to set your brain and expertise to this task to which I cannot contribute in a meaningful way.

Only one thing I cannot resist saying although it may not be entirely topical in our context and that is, that the great and world famous natural beauty of this island of Sri Lanka is a danger unto itself - a danger, because it invites its own destruction through overutilization. While fully recognizing the great advantages of tourism and its contribution to the nation's income and welfare, mass tourism also has its dark side and it will bring with it the temptation to use every bit of the country's beauty for the purpose of turning it into money and that may in the end kill the goose that lays the eggs and then there will just be damage and no more profit. Because we have seen in the southern Europe that if, for example, all beautiful beaches are dotted with a string of hotels, tourists will one day say that that is not what they have come to see and go elsewhere. But I think or at least hope, Sri Lanka is aware of such a danger.

The symposium has set itself the task of reaching an overall synthesis out of which new concepts for long-term landscape management strategies in Sri Lanka can be developed. This is a formidable challenge - but at the same time there are factors that should make the task of harmonizing development needs with ecological needs easier in this country than elsewhere.

- One is that the predominant religion of Sri Lanka, Buddhism, is not centered around man alone and does not regard him as the absolute lord of creation to do with it as he pleases but, in a comprehensive view, regards all life as sacred and to be protected;

- The other prehaps originating in the first, is that large areas have already been set aside by Sri Lanka for the protection of natural ecosystems amounting to over 10% of its territory. A fact, by the way, that sets a shining example to other countries who could do more and have done so much less;

- And last, that population growth is, in Sri Lanka, fortunately no longer the frightening problem that it is for so many other countries so that pressure on land resources, while it is perhaps not likely to assume such proportions as to make nonsense of even the best concepts of balanced land use.

What comes out of undertakings like the present symposium will eventually have to be translated into reality by governments acting with wisdom, responsibility and foresight, with taking an interest as first step. And that is why I think it is most gratifying that the honorable P. Dayaratne, as Minister in charge of land and land development, is here today and by his presence shows this interest and underlines the importance he attaches to the topic of this symposium.

I am, of course, also happy that so many scientists and experts from my country played a leading role in organizing this symposium and in contributing to its deliberations to such a great extent.

Let me conclude by wishing the symposium fruitful discussions and a good and practical result.

WELCOME ADDRESS

by the Organizers

W. ERDELEN and C. PREU

Objectives and Scope of the International and Interdisciplinary Symposium on "Ecology and Landscape Management in Sri Lanka"

After planning and organizing for almost two years, the international and interdisciplinary symposium "Ecology and Landscape Management in Sri Lanka" is now a reality. Starting from an earlier estimate of a meeting with some 50 participants the massive response received in the course of organizing this symposium clearly indicated the interest of both, Sri Lankans and non-Sri Lankans, to discuss environmental issues related to landscape management in Sri Lanka. It also indicates the importance that is now attributed to managing ecological problems along with the socioeconomic development of Sri Lanka.

The realization of this symposium would have been impossible without the support of many individuals, national and international companies and organizations whom we wish to thank. First of all, we thank the Natural Resources, Energy and Science Authority (NARESA) of Sri Lanka, the sponsoring and coordinating Sri Lankan agency. Dr. R.P. Jayewardene, Director General, NARESA, and Mr. D.E.F. Ferdinandez, Director Scientific Affairs, NARESA, have been particularly helpful and supported our efforts. Moreover, the members of the organizing committee have continuously helped us in many ways and we sincerely thank Prof. Madduma Bandara and Dr. Ishwaran. We are grateful for the cooperation received from Her Excellency, the Ambassador of the Democratic Socialist Republic of Sri Lanka in the Federal Republic of Germany, Mrs. M. Abeysekera, and from His Excellency, the Ambassador of the Federal Republic of Germany in Sri Lanka, Mr. K. Franke, and his members of staff. We thank Mr. L.A. Coulter, Director and General Manager of Hotel Taj Samudra, and members of his staff, particularly Mr. P. Perera, who have done their utmost to make the stay of participants of this symposium a pleasant one. Moreover, for support received in Sri Lanka, we sincerely thank Mr. S.K. Wickremesinghe, Chairman of Ceylon Tobacco Co Ltd, Mr. A.R. Pandithage, Managing Director of DIMO Co Ltd, Mr. N. Nanayakkara, Managing Director of N-Car Travels and Tours Ltd, our operating agent, and particularly Mr. E.W. Coll, General Manager of Deutsche Bank, Colombo. Invaluable logistic support we have received from Nixdorf Colombo and IBM Colombo. In addition to these, many German firms and companies have sponsored this symposium.

We gratefully appreciate the efforts of all who are contributing papers to the symposium and who have agreed to join us as "experts in charge" in the excursion. We express our sincere thanks to UNESCO for sponsoring this symposium and to our students who spent many hours of their free time on the preparatory work. We are grateful to all who contributed to the exhibition which not only underscores the multi-facetted nature of environmental issues to be covered in this symposium, but also stresses the significant activities of various important departments, authorities and non-governmental organizations of Sri Lanka.

The idea of having this symposium grew out of our experiences in Sri Lanka. During this period we got to know many colleagues of ours, have made friends, and got to know and love this tropical island. For this reason being in Sri Lanka is like being at home for us. This has shaped our lives both as private persons and as scientists. As a result of our experienes during years spent in Sri Lanka and many discussions with colleagues from Sri Lanka and abroad we felt that an overall synthetic analysis of the environmental situation of this tropical island was not only feasible but worth trying. Of specific importance in this regard was our national and international contact with colleagues, experts, and representatives of various governmental authorities and non-governmental agencies.

Sri Lanka is characterized by a mosaic of different ecosystems with high floristic and faunistic diversity, embedded in landscape units ranging from natural to totally man-made. Natural forest still covers about 20%-25% of the land area of Sri Lanka. 10%-12% of the island's area is set aside for the conservation of wildlife and natural ecosystems such as tropical rain forests, mangroves and coral reefs. These systems contain an important pool of genetic resources for South Asia. Sri Lanka's natural environment has undergone changes since those times when human intervention rose to meet needs above subsistence levels. Significant impacts on the natural environment have reached new dimensions since the last century. Due to increasing population growth and increasing interest conflicts among user-groups, drastic changes have particularly occurred in the last few decades, changes which are definitely closely linked to overall quality of life on the island. Natural forests have been cleared, mangroves have been removed, agricultural land has been extended, and land use has been intensified through the application of chemicals. Rivers have been dammed for irrigation schemes and for production of hydroelectricity. Coral reefs have been mined and wetlands have been filled. The process of urbanization has been intensified and new settlements have been established. The degree of industrialization has increased. This development has led to increasing degradation of the environment, as exemplified by soil erosion, coastal erosion, water and air pollution. Moreover, human pressure on the remaining natural ecosystems, which are already fragmented and restricted to small areas, is increasing.

However, particularly since independence, in 1948, substantial amounts of information and knowledge, regarding the environmental changes in Sri Lanka, have been gathered by Sri Lankan and foreign scientists and experts. In the environmental sector of the country many activities have been initiated and carried out, encompassing legislative, executive, educational measures, by public as well as private agencies. Sufficient experience, to identify conflicts between development and conservation efforts in landscape management strategies is dispersed among such specialists. Exceptions to this are publications like the "National Conservation Strategy", the "Environmental Study of Sri Lanka", and the Sector Report of the Science and Technology Policy.

An overall synthesis, based on consideration of the landscape mosaic of the whole island and on available information, knowledge, experience, and insights to facilitate decision making processes in landscape management has not yet been attempted within the framework of a symposium like this for Sri Lanka. Therefore, this symposium attempts at such a synthesis and hopes to provide a forum for developing new concepts for long-term landscape management strategies in Sri Lanka. More specifically, the objectives of the symposium are (1) to bring together resident and expatriate Sri Lankan as well as foreign specialists with recognized research and management experience in Sri Lanka, (2) to highlight and demonstrate the environmental dimension in landuse planning and landscape management in Sri Lanka, (3) to provide a forum for the identification of important issues and problems of landscape management in Sri Lanka, and (4) to stimulate the international scientific and management community to develop new concepts and strategies for the future.

The structure of this two-week symposium consists of three units, the paper and poster presentations paralleled by an exhibition documenting relevant environmental issues, the excursion and the final session. In the papers, important aspects and a wide range of topics related to the environmental situation in Sri Lanka will be illustrated and discussed. More specifically, an overview of the ecological context in Sri Lanka will be given, impact studies will demonstrate positive as well as negative consequences of human interference with the natural environment, conservation issues will be highlighted within the socioeconomic framework in which environmental questions and problems are embedded. Methodological approaches will be discussed, and the organizational framework needed for the development of appropriate environmental management regimes will be outlined. Because of the complexity and diversity of the environmental situation in Sri Lanka, an interdisciplinary approach is used. Accordingly all important groups, i.e. scientists, planners and decision makers, are represented at this symposium. The second unit is a 1-week excursion to sites at which representative significant environmental questions and problems will be introduced and discussed. These sites are Naulla Reafforestation Project, Kotamale, Upper Mahaweli Water Management Project at Kandapola, Horton Plains National Park, Sinharaja, a World Hertitage site, Hikkaduwa Marine Sanctuary, Kalutara, a coastal ecosystem, with tourism and the lagoon at Negombo. In the final session, the third unit, not only the major findings of the paper presentations and the excursion will be summarizied and the conclusions will be formulated but also the coordination of further activities related to the topics of the symposium will be discussed.

We consider the symposium a first step towards a working basis and impulse for further activities with regard to the environmental situation in Sri Lanka. The proceedings, to be published after the symposium, will document the innovative approach used for this symposium. It will not only be available to the Sri Lankan community but it may also initiate similar activities with regard to the environmental situation in other tropical countries.

However, as everybody knows - let us in this context refer to the two special lectures incorporated into the program, on Tropical Ecology in Papua New Guinea, by Dr. Göltenboth, and on Forest Damage in the Federal Republic of Germany, by Dr. Kirchhof - environmental questions and problems do not exist in Sri Lanka only.

We do hope you will enjoy participation in the symposium and make use of the opportunities for discussion and exchange of ideas.

PAPER PRESENTATIONS

I. THE ECOLOGICAL CONTEXT

Proceedings of the International and Interdisciplinary Symposium
ECOLOGY AND LANDSCAPE MANAGEMENT IN SRI LANKA
W. Erdelen, C. Preu, N. Ishwaran, C.M. Madduma Bandara (eds.)
Colombo, Sri Lanka, 12-26 March 1990
© 1993
Margraf Scientific Books, D-97985 Weikersheim
ISBN 3-8236-1182-8

Integrated Conservation for Human Survival in Sri Lanka

B.A. ABEYWICKRAMA

Abstract

Integrated conservation means living in a state of equilibrium with our environment. This involves a proper understanding of man's place in nature, an appreciation and respect for nature, and the use of resources for satisfying our need rather than our greed. Development is for man, but man is not an independent entity by himself. Man is part of nature. We can live and enjoy life, because countless other organisms have built up and are now maintaining our life support systems. Heedless destruction of these organisms or systems will inevitably result in our own demise. Sri Lanka is primarily an agricultural country. An essential prerequisite for agriculture is ecological security. The latter is best provided in the humid tropics by forests in the right places and in adequate extents. Our forefathers recognized this. They integrated forestry with agriculture, demarcated villages on a watershed basis and adopted land use systems essentially in harmony with nature. Resource overexploitation and large-scale deforestation began during the colonial period, and have continued since then. We now have only about a fifth of the land area under forest, and much of even that extent is degraded and not situated where it is most wanted. Extensive deforestation has resulted in severe soil degradation, large-scale disturbances in water balance and a steady decline in land productivity. With a limited land area and an increasing population we can ill afford any further misuse. Fortunately, the land degradation over many areas is still not irreversible. Land use in accordance with ecological potentials and strict enforcement of integrated conservation measures could once again make Sri Lanka a paradise.

Introduction

Our landscapes are a very special heritage. They are dynamic systems where patterns and processes as well as values can be destroyed by disruption no less than by depletion. For our survival man's role should at least not be a disruptive one. Management and conservation are both man-centered, but man is not an entity by himself. Landscapes and man are products of evolution; landscapes came first, man much later. The primeval landscapes were no home for man. They were rough and desolate and marked by turbulence and disorder. With the advent of life millions of years ago the earth transcended her surface. Microbes and plants enriched the air with oxygen, regulated winds and the flow of water, meliorated climates, stabilized the crust, and created the life supporting atmosphere and the productive soil. It was to this environment that man came a million or so years ago. By being alive we are united to all life. We are dependent not only on our fellow members and our physical surroundings but also on all other forms of life that have evolved along with us. We can now live and enjoy life only because numberless millions of other organisms have been created and are now maintaining our life support systems. Thoughtless destruction of these organisms can easily trigger processes that may endanger our own selves.

Conservation should be the preservation of our environment in a condition that will not only provide for our present and future needs but also make life pleasant and rewarding for all nature. To make conservation effective, it should be integrated with our way of life and involve a realistic knowledge of man's place in nature, an awareness of the services other organisms render to us and our obligations to them and a self-discipline that would enable us to be content and happy with satisfying our need rather than our greed.

Our traditional teaching recognized man as a part of nature. Religion enjoined us to respect and revere the world around us, and to aim at maximum well-being with minimum use of resources and the least possible violence to nature. Property was regarded as a social trust and the higher a man was, the fewer were his rights and the more numerous his duties (Radhakrishnan, 1948).

Environmental Issues - A Historical Perspective

Sri Lanka is primarily an agricultural country. Our prosperity has been and will always be dependent on the productivity of the land. To us the land is a priceless resource. The care of the land is a prerequisite for our survival. We have a diversity of landscapes; each has its own character, but within this diversity there is a basic unity. We cannot develop the croplands in the plains, if we ignore the mountains and their forest cover. We must respect the integrity of landscapes, if we want to ensure good and sustainable agricultural production. Early man in Sri Lanka recognized this integrity. All delicate and fragile ecosystems were left practically undisturbed. Development activities were concentrated on the dry zone plains where climate and physical conditions created immense problems for both agriculture and human settlement. Still for seventeen centuries or longer this was the center of Sri Lanka's civilization (Abeywickrama 1956, Brohier and Paulusz 1951; Fig. 1).

There, they transformed natural ecosystems into essentially similar agroecosystems. Wetlands in valleys and floodplains were made into rice fields, and clearings on high land into multilayered home gardens with a diversity of species (Abeywickrama, 1964). They stored all the water from the short seasonal rains and devised elaborate gravity-fed systems for leading it to the fields. Sri Lanka is reputed to have had "one of the most wonderful systems of irrigation that ever existed" with practically no water reaching the sea until it had done the maximum of work (Willis, 1914).

The dry zone villages of the past were physically well-defined natural units with socially homogeneous populations and agriculturally sustainable practices. Ancient boundaries between villages are said to be still visible in some places (Abeyratna, 1956). The demarcation of the villages is reported to have been done about 437 B.C. (Geiger, 1912). Each village had all the land and water vital for its existence, viz. the water reservoir (or tank), its catchment, the irrigated fields and the settlement with its temple, homesteads and home gardens. Very light shifting cultivation in the catchment forest supplemented the produce from the fields. Such villages formed integral ecosystems which provided moderate but sustained yields with no input of minerals or energy (Fig. 2).

In the catchment forest, a good vegetation cover protected the soil. There was good infiltration and no erosion. Clear water was slowly released to the tanks. Sedimentation was minimal and the water stored was sufficient for the fields. The home gardens had permanent

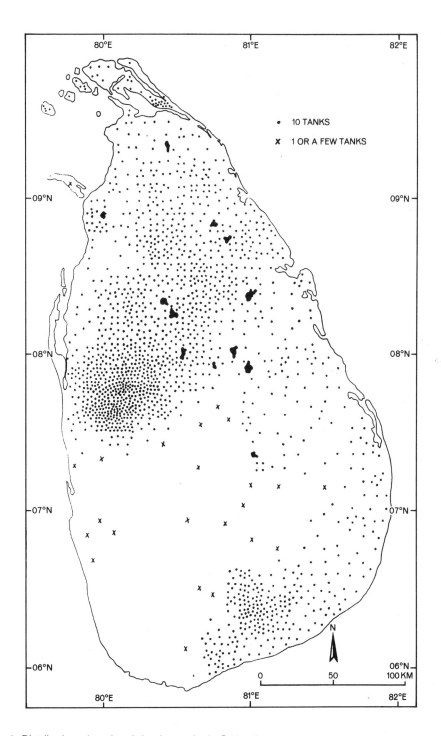

Figure 1. Distribution of ancient irrigation tanks in Sri Lanka.

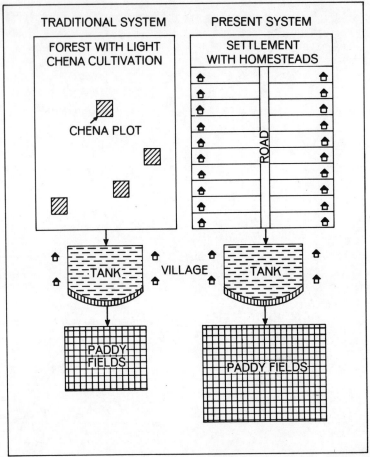

Figure 2. Schematic representation of approximate proportions of land reserved for catchments, water reservoir (= tank), settlements and rice fields in 2500-year-old traditional systems and in present day systems. Based on data from Weerakoon and Schall (1987).

fruit crops and other trees, various shrubs, and some annual crops (Weerakoon and Schall, 1987). Contrary to popular opinion the chena system, as practiced formerly does not appear to have had much of an adverse effect on species diversity. The small size of the plot, the partial clearing, the short cultivation period and the long fallow would in fact have increased both diversity as well as biomass production.

From about 1200 A.D. onwards, invasions from India forced a partial population shift to the central highlands. There, too, essentially similar village settlements were established. The main difference was that, where rainfall was seasonal, the perennial mountain streams provided the water, and the chenas were on the lower slopes of the hills. On ridges, hill tops and the upper slopes, forest cover was left undisturbed. In fact many of them were protected and preserved as sacred forests.

Maps produced by a Dutch surveyor, Boomgart, in 1720 give us a good idea of a chena cultivation as it was then practiced in Sri Lanka (Boomgart, 1720). The chena covered about 1.7 hectares. One map shows the distribution of woody plants before clearing, the second the trees left uncut, and the third the natural regeneration after the clearing had been planted with cinnamon. Apparently the objective has been to enrich the forest with cinnamon rather than to grow the latter in a monoculture. The surveyor has given exact figures for each species before and after cultivation (Fig. 3). All species except Kekuna, *Canarium zeylanicum,* are present in much larger numbers than before the land was cleared. Chena cultivation would undoubtedly have caused changes in the relative abundance of species but it seems to have done little or nothing to destroy any species.

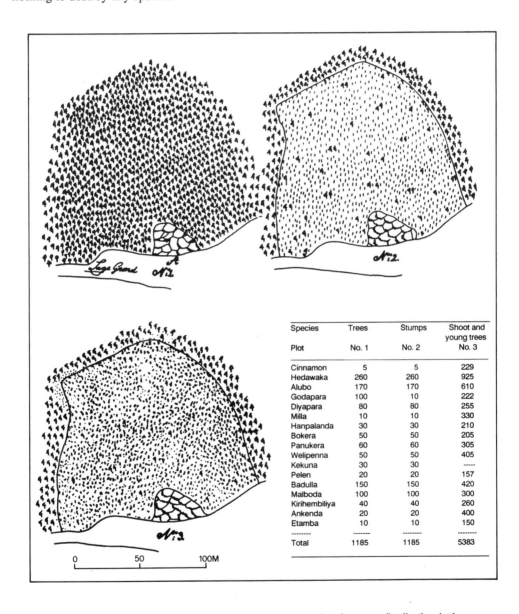

Species	Trees	Stumps	Shoot and young trees
Plot	No. 1	No. 2	No. 3
Cinnamon	5	5	229
Hedawaka	260	260	925
Alubo	170	170	610
Godapara	100	10	222
Diyapara	80	80	255
Milla	10	10	330
Hanpalanda	30	30	210
Bokera	50	50	205
Panukera	60	60	305
Welipenna	50	50	405
Kekuna	30	30	-----
Pelen	20	20	157
Badulla	150	150	420
Malboda	100	100	300
Kirihembiliya	40	40	260
Ankenda	20	20	400
Etamba	10	10	150
Total	1185	1185	5383

Figure 3. Land used for chena cultivation. No. 1. Land area showing tree distribution before clearing. No. 2. Same area after clearing showing stumps of cut trees, and the larger trees left undisturbed. No. 3. Same area a few years after the planting of cinnamon showing positions of new growth of shoots and young trees (after Boomgart, 1720).

Before the advent of colonial power, agriculture in Sri Lanka was essentially rice cultivation. This was always a cooperative enterprise where the entire village worked together for the common interest. A Council of Elders or a Gan-sabhawa dealt with the coordination of all activities pertaining to agriculture, irrigation and other matters. With the introduction of alien practices and customs, both the cohesion of the villages and the integrated use of landscapes were completely destroyed (Brohier, 1975).

The Portuguese first came to the island in 1505 at a time when the country was much weakened by internal dissension. Shortly afterwards, they and later the Dutch and the British took control over the coastal areas. The interior, however, retained its independence and traditional land use practices for a further 300 years until the entire island went under foreign rule in 1815.

Within two decades, in 1832, on the recommendations of a Royal Commission an ancient practice of service to the Crown in respect of land tenure was abolished. According to Brohier (1975), a leading authority on land use and irrigation in Sri Lanka, "by beat of tom-toms it was proclaimed that no community of labor was required, and that any headmen who called out the working men of this district for the purpose of repairing dams or keeping up the banks of the irrigation canals would be dismissed. It destroyed the power of cooperation among the people by which alone irrigation works could be kept in working order; it abolished the power to compel the owner of a share in a communal property to contribute his quota of work for the maintenance and protection of that property. Thus, what was everybody's business became nobody's business, and the industrious majority were placed at the mercy of the indolent few." Many of the tanks steadily deteriorated, and a few years later a flood made most of them victims of neglect, and consigned them to the jungle tide (Brohier, 1975).

Much worse was to follow. In 1840, laws were passed giving the Crown powers for summary eviction of any person who had not continually occupied or worked on a piece of land for a continuous period of thirty years. A later amendment reduced the thirty to five, but still no chenas had then been worked continuously for five years. Very large extents of village forests, protected forests and those on river catchments were then taken over by the British Crown (Brohier and Paulusz, 1951). What had once been the common resources of the people of the country were then given over to foreigners for nominal payments for establishing coffee plantations. "The rush for land was only paralleled by the movement towards the mines of California and Australia. Capitalists from England arrived by every packet. The glory of an illimitable sea of forest-topped hillsides fell to the axe and became a memory of the past. Then followed the burn, and wreaths of blue smoke curling from among the blackened ruins, hung over the scene for days, to tell of the mad conflagration" (Tennent, 1859).

Vast areas of forests on steep slopes were cleared. Some plantations became degraded and unproductive within two decades. The planters then moved over to other areas leaving wastelands behind. In the dry zone, climatic conditions were not suitable for plantation crops. The cutting of timber was allowed, on payment of nominal royalties, to clear-fell forests in blocks of about 200-300 acres (i.e. about 100 ha) to extract all valuable timber. These areas were than brought under chena for two to three years and then abandoned (Tennent 1859, Tisseverasinghe 1956). The official sales of ebony alone in 1881 amounted to 2600 tons (Gamble, 1922). These clearings were one of the main causes of the degradation of the dry zone forests.

Dr. G.H.K. Thwaites, Superintendent of the Peradeniya Botanic Gardens from 1849 to 1880, realized the serious consequences of the indiscriminate land alienation and the very severe erosion in plantations. Locally his was a voice in the wilderness, but representation made by him to London resulted in an order in 1873 from the then Colonial Secretary banning all land alienation above 5000 ft. Still little meaningful action was taken till about the end of the British Period. In 1927, the Governor, Sir Hugh Clifford, indicated in an address to an agricultural conference that the prosperity of the country could be maintained not by stimulating large estates but by bringing into existence "a prosperous, self-supporting and self-respecting multitude of peasant proprietors". Shortly afterwards, the economic depression made it very clear that the development of the country depended on the better use of land and the production of crops which provided a direct means of subsistence for the people (Brohier and Paulusz, 1951). A Land Commission was then appointed and on its recommendations the laws of 1840 were repealed by the State Council and replaced by the Land Development Ordinance of 1935. This has been referred to as the magna charta of the peasantry of Sri Lanka (Brohier and Paulusz, 1951).

After independence was regained in 1948 successive governments, while supporting the plantation sector, have attempted to give very high priority to food production in the country. Small farmers have been given various financial incentives ranging from guaranteed prices for produce, crop insurance, subsidies for inputs, easy credit terms and even pension schemes. One of the major objectives of several larger state projects has been to make the island self-sufficient in rice and agricultural research has been geared to providing high yielding rice varieties suitable for local conditions. For a time there was some success. Productivity and production of rice both increased. Productivity rose from about 1.5 mt/ha per season in the mid-1950s to about 3.5 mt per season in the mid-1980s but now it has more or less peaked (Agricultural Statistics of Sri Lanka, 1988). Production of plantation crops during the period 1977-1987 showed little increase. In rubber it actually declined (Sri Lanka's Economy, 1988). Rice production increased till 1984 when we were nearly self-sufficient. It has since declined. In 1989, the total production was about two million tons, the lowest for over a decade, and our requirements were an additional one million tonnes of cereals which had to be imported (FAO, December 1989). All the time the input of fertilizers and agrochemicals has progressively increased.

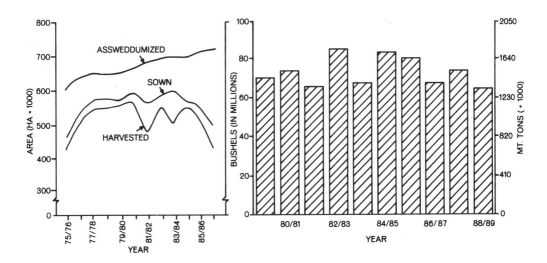

Figure 4. Paddy statistics for areas (left) up to Maha 1986/87 and production (right) up to Maha 1988/89.

What is more disturbing, however, is the fact that for rice the land made ready for cultivation increased by 81,745 ha (about 200,000 acres) during the period 1977-1987 but the harvested area in the main cultivation season, Maha, of 1987 was well below that of 1977. In the 1987 Maha season, only about 70 per cent of the paddy lands were sown, and only 85 per cent of the sown area was harvested (Agricultural Statistics of Sri Lanka 1988; Fig. 4).

Various factors were responsible for the noncultivation and the harvest failures: drought, salinity, floods, diseases, pest attacks and more recently civil unrest. But, are these independent and natural factors by themselves? Are they not the symptoms of a much deeper disease, viz. the disruption of environmental security to agriculture resulting from landscape fragmentation, massive deforestation, misuse of land, and our attempts to tamper with unit processes independently, with a multiplicity of organizations, rather than treating the environment as a whole? Is it just a coincidence that most countries which had major crop failures in recent years due to droughts or floods are those where forests had been razed to the ground without replacing them with an adequate woody vegetation cover (CERES, 1973)? "Good and permanent agriculture depends on good and permanent forestry. It is a dangerous and indeed a fatal delusion to imagine that the prime essential of land use - for food production - can survive unless government and farmer alike give zealous attention to the non-farm lands which support or destroy farm enterprises" (FAO, 1952).

Deforestation has been the most important single factor which makes land unproductive and unfit for human use. In the humid tropics, the forests are the guardians of agricultural soils. They regulate water supply, serve as wind breaks to prevent desiccation of crops and soil, prevent salinity development, and even control the spread of pests and diseases. They also generally ameliorate the local climates.

The planting of broad shelter belts in Canada, USA and Russia were not for wood production but purely for agricultural purposes (Orr, 1949). In Sri Lanka in the Uva Basin we once had a deserted village called Palugama. Drying winds made it almost impossible for people to live there. Carefully planned plantings of forest shelter belts transformed the place into a very prosperous vegetable growing townlet (Wijesinghe, 1962). It has now been named Keppetipola, after a national hero.

In 1900, about 70 per cent of our land area was under forest cover. Now a little over 20 per cent is under forest cover. Even these forests are present not where they are most needed and much of them are badly degraded. The percentage of forest is expected to drop to 10 per cent within the next decade (CIDA, 1986). This deforestation, some say, is inevitable and is the result of increasing population. Much of past deforestation however had nothing to do with population increases. The clearing of forests from 1840 onwards was purely for short-term economic gains. Even the recent rape of Sinharaja and the adjacent forests was not to meet any needs of the people but to feed an ill-conceived woodwork complex. Now we do have a population problem. To conserve our resources we have to stabilize them at a sustainable level. We, especially the more affluent among us, must also reduce our resource consumption to a reasonable level.

In 1815, after 2300 years of settled agriculture with integrated use of landscapes, our environments were fully intact. Over the last 100 years with foreign practices the landscapes are fragmented and the ecosystems disrupted. The damage caused during the latter period is well documented (Brohier, 1975). In 1821, Captain Davy referred to the "beautifully transparent" waters of the Kelani Ganga. A hundred years later, even after a two-month drought "the rivers ran mud, not water" (Report of the Committee on Soil Erosion, 1931). Today, after such droughts in most rivers there is no run at all.

With a limited land area and an increasing population, we can no longer afford the prodigal waste of our lands. Over 80 per cent of our farmers are smallholders owning less than one hectare of land. However well managed their lands may be, they cannot protect themselves from the actions or inaction of others. With land misuse in catchments above them, some have abandoned cultivation because of heavy silt deposits; others suffer crop failures due to floods or water shortages. They can be given protection only by the integrated management of landscapes.

The challenge before us is to restore the productivity of our landscapes. Fortunately the land degradation in many areas of Sri Lanka is still not irreversible. Restoration is a difficult and slow process, but it can be done. Now we cannot return directly to our traditional practices, but there is much we can learn from them. A judicious mix of such practices and technology relevant to us can pay very high dividends (Abeywickrama *et al.* 1983, Greval *et al.* 1990). With such practices the Coconut Research Institute registered an output of 10,878 nuts per acre from a 5-acre block in 1985 (CRI, 1987). These are normal tall palms, and I think this is a world record for such palms. This land, I understand, is continuing to give high yields.

Management and conservation practices in order to be effective and sustainable must be organic developments resulting from close associations between man and his land. Planners should take note of this and involve people's participation at all levels. Land use should be complementary and not competetive, and there should be a harmonious balance between the uses. Production alone cannot go on without adequate protective support for the maintenance of ecological systems. On the other hand we cannot maintain strict natural reserves in isolation, if people have no access to basic needs. Landscape management with integrated conservation within the framework of a rational land use policy for the whole country, and in accordance with the land potentials, if introduced now, can still make Sri Lanka the grain bowl and the paradise that it once was.

Literature Cited

Abeyratna, E.L.F. 1956. Dry land farming in Ceylon. *Trop. Agricult.* 112: 191-229.

Abeywickrama, B.A. 1956. The origin and affinities of the flora of Ceylon. *Proc. 11th Ann Sess. CAAS.* 11:99-121.

Abeywickrama, B.A. 1964. Natural history and national planning. *Proc. 46th Ann. Gen. Meeting of the Ceyl. Nat. Hist. Soc.* pp. 1-9. Luxman Press, Colombo.

Abeywickrama, B.A. 1978. Development and the Environment. *Report of the Citizens' Task Force (April 1978)* : 26-27.

Abeywickrama, B.A., D.V. Liyanage and P.R. Wijewardena. 1983. *Measures to Minimise Drought Damage in Coconut Plantations.* Coconut Research Institute, Lunuwila.

Agricultural Statistics of Sri Lanka. 1988. Department of Census and Statistics. Colombo.

Boomgart, L. 1720. Three charts of a plot of land situated in Hewagam Korale. *In* R.L. Brohier and J.H.O. Paulusz, eds. *Lands, Maps and Surveys. Vol. 2.* pp. 89-91. Ceyl. Govt. Press. Colombo.

Brohier, R.L. 1975. *Food and the People.* Lake House Investments Ltd. Colombo.

Brohier, R.L. and J.H.O. Paulusz. 1951. *Lands, Maps and Surveys.* Ceyl. Govt. Press. Colombo.

CERES. 1973. *The Nurturing Forest.* CERES 44, FAO, Rome

CIDA. 1986. *Project Identification Mission.* Mahaweli Environment Rehabilitation Report.

CRI (Coconut Research Institute). 1987. *The Isolated Seed Garden and its Irrigation System.* CRI, Lunuwila.

Deraniyagala, P.E.P. 1946. Some phases of the evolution of Ceylon. *Proc. 2nd Sess. Ceyl. Ass. Sc.* 3: 69-88.

Ministry of Agricultural Development and Research. 1984. *Development Strategy - Crop Agriculture.* Ministry of Agricultural Development and Research, Colombo.

Ministry of Lands and Land Development. 1984. *Development Strategy - Irrigation, Land and Forestry.* Ministry of Lands and Land Development, Colombo.

FAO. 1952. *Soil Conservation*. FAO. - Agricultural Studies No. 4. FAO, Rome.

FAO. 1989. *Food Crops and Shortages*. FAO, Rome.

Land Comission. 1985. *First Interim Report of the Land Commission*. Govt. Publications Bureau. Colombo.

Gamble, J.S. 1922. *A Manual of Indian Timbers*. Sampson Low, Marston & Co, London.

Geiger, W. 1912. *The Mahawamsa*. Ceyl. Govt. Information Department, Colombo.

Greval, S.S., S.P. Mittal and G. Singh. 1990. Rehabilitation of degraded lands in the Himalayan foothills: People's participation. *Ambio* 19: 45-48.

Orr, J. B. 1949. Forestry today. *In* T. I. Williams, ed. *The Soil and the Sea*. The Saturn Press, London.

Radhakrishnan, S. 1948. *The Hindu View of Life*. Allen & Unwin Ltd, London.

Committee on Soil Erosion. 1931. *Report of the Committee on Soil Erosion*. Sessional Paper III - 1931. Ceyl. Govt. Press, Colombo.

Sri Lanka's Economy. 1988. *Econ. Rev.* 14: 3-24.

Stockdale, F.A. 1923. Soil erosion. *Trop. Agricult.* 61: 131-140.

Stocking, M.A. 1986. *Land Use Planning - Phase II*. UNDP/FAO Consultant's Report. Colombo.

Tennent, J.S. 1859. *Ceylon*. Vols. 1 and 2. Longman Publ, London.

Tisseverasinghe, A.E.K. 1956. Land tenure and forest in ancient Ceylon. *The Ceylon Forester* 11: 124-130.

Weerakoon, W.L. and R. Schall. 1987. *Proposed Workplan for Conservation Farming Project. Mahailluppalama*. Sri Lanka.

Weil, R.R. 1981. Soil conservation needs in the Upper Mahaweli Catchment Watershed Management Project. *The Sri Lanka Forester* 15: 37-53.

Wijesinghe, L.C.A. 1962. Some aspects of land use in the dry zone grasslands. *The Ceylon Forester* 5: 128-138.

Willis, J.C. 1914. *Agriculture in the Tropics*. Cambridge Univ. Press, Cambridge.

Proceedings of the International and Interdisciplinary Symposium
ECOLOGY AND LANDSCAPE MANAGEMENT IN SRI LANKA
W. Erdelen, C. Preu, N. Ishwaran, C.M. Madduma Bandara (eds.)
Colombo, Sri Lanka, 12-26 March 1990
© 1993
Margraf Scientific Books, D-97985 Weikersheim
ISBN 3-8236-1182-8

Pleistocene Human Ecology in Sri Lanka

S.U. DERANIYAGALA

Abstract

Archeological deposits have been dated in Sri Lanka from about 125,000 B.P. and possible occurrences extended into the Middle Pleistocene. Sedimentological data suggest increased atmospheric circulation, and hence increased seasonality of precipitation, during certain Pleistocene altithermals, particularly in the dry zone. It is postulated that altithermals were characterized by increased aridity in the dry zone and a concomitant increase in human carrying capacity. The converse has been proposed for glacial episodes when atmospheric circulation was considered to have been depressed. In the wet zone, these climatic oscillations were not thought to have registered markedly on prehistoric carrying capacity. Available faunal and floral evidence for the wet zone did not indicate an environment significantly different from that of the present for the last 30,000 years. Man's adaption to this more or less constant environment, in terms of subsistence strategy and technology, had also been consistent during the last 30,000 years. Subsistence strategy comprised the non-specialized exploitation of a broad spectrum of plants and animals, with an accent on small game. Technologically, the cultures were characterized by microtithic stone tool industries (Mesolithic) from about 30,000 B.P. onwards, with small-flake industries preceding these at least up to 125,000 B.P. Carrying capacities of Sri Lanka's environment had presumably been low, and human settlements seemed to have been small, with a modal extent suggesting occupation by no more than one or two nuclear families. Hypotheses, regarding patterns of Pleistocene man/environment interactions in Sri Lanka, which might serve as a model for equatorial monsoonal environments in general, are formulated for future testing.

Introduction

Climatologically, Sri Lanka, located some 50 km off the southern tip of India between 05°54'-09°52'N and 79°39'-81°53'E, is dominated by the tropical SW monsoon regime. The annual rainfall distribution is distinctly seasonal and reaches an annual amount of precipitation varying from about 600 mm to over 5000 mm according to locality. The average annual temperatures range from about 18°C in the central highlands, which reach an elevation of slightly over 2400 m, to about 26°C in the lowlands; the annual fluctuations in temperature are negligible. The natural vegetation comprises tropical rain forest and its variants.

On the basis of the seasonal rainfall distribution Sri Lanka may be divided into the wet zone and dry zone and six ecozones (Gaussen *et al.* 1968, Mueller-Dombois 1968; Fig. 1). Ecozone D covering the wet zone is characterized by heavy SW monsoonal precipitation during the summer and a drier period during the winter. It comprises one-fourth of the island and is confined to western and southwestern Sri Lanka. This ecozone can be subdivided into three areas; ecozone D_1, the lowlands below 900 m with an annual rainfall of about 2000-5000 mm, ecozone D_2, the uplands between 900 m and 1500 m with an annual rainfall of about 2000-5000 mm, and ecozone D_3, the highlands between 1500 m and 2400 m with an annual rainfall of about 2000-4000 mm. The remaining three-fourths of Sri Lanka are assignable to the dry zone which is characterized by rainfall during the winter and droughts during the summer. Between the dry zone and wet zone, there is a zone of transition which is predominantly dry in character. It comprises ecozone C, the intermediate dry lowlands below 900 m with annual rainfall of 1250-2000 mm, and ecozone E, the intermediate dry uplands between 900 m and 1500 m with an annual rainfall of about 2000-2500 mm. Considering increasing aridity the area of the dry zone itself may be subdivided into ecozone B, the dry lowlands below 900 m with an annual rainfall of about 1150-2000 mm, ecozone A, the semi-arid lowlands below 900 m with an annual rainfall of about 750-1150 mm, and ecozone F, the arid lowlands below 900 m with annual rainfall similar to ecozone A but with a characteristically prolonged drought period (Deraniyagala, 1992).

During the Pleistocene, man evolved from advanced ape-like forms to his present state. The Pleistocene is defined as a geological epoch that commenced at about 2.5 million years B.P. and ended at about 10,000 B.P. and is distinguishable into the Lower Pleistocene (2.5-0.7 million B.P.), the Middle Pleistocene (700,000-150,000 B.P.) and the Upper Pleistocene (150,000-10,000 B.P.). This geological epoch may be subdivided into at least four major glacial periods when continental ice sheets expanded over the land masses of the northern hemisphere. These cold glacial periods are conveniently refered to as Günz, Mindel, Riss and Würm. Due to the water trapping in the ice sheets the sea level dropped eustatically and the land was emergent. It is estimated that the mean sea level during the last peak of the Würm maximum at about 15,000 B.P. was more than 100 m below the present sea level (Fairbridge, 1976). The warm interglacial periods, i.e. Cromerian (Günz/Mindel), Holstein (Mindel/Riss) and Eem (Riss/Würm), which were interspersed among the glacial periods, were characterized by high sea levels because melted water caused an eustatic rise in sea level. The changes in the global climate accompanying these Pleistocene phases were reflected in the biomes and ecozones and, naturally, had a direct impact on the genus *Homo*. The cultural paleoecology, which may be defined as a subdiscipline of ecology, investigates the systemic interaction of man and environment in time. This involves four major steps, first establishing a chronological framework, second observing environmental configurations within this framework and isolating elements that would have had a direct impact on "core" activities such as settlement, subsistence and technology, termed "effective environment", third observing biological and cultural changes with reference to the chronological framework, and fourth observing the systemic interactions between man and environment through the time span under investigation and formulating hypotheses on the basis of these observations.

Pleistocene Chronology of Sri Lanka

The Pleistocene chronology of Sri Lanka has primarily been delineated from three sets of sediment bodies, from deposits in caves of the lowland area in the wet zone, i.e. ecozone D_1, from the fluviatile Ratnapura Beds in the lowland area of the wet zone, and from the alluvial gravels and overlying dune sands of the Iranamadu Formation (IFm) in the coastal zone of the semi-arid zone, i.e. ecozone A (Fig. 2). The term Iranamadu Formation has been introduced by Deraniyagala (1976, 1992) to supersede the term Red Earth Formation as it was employed by

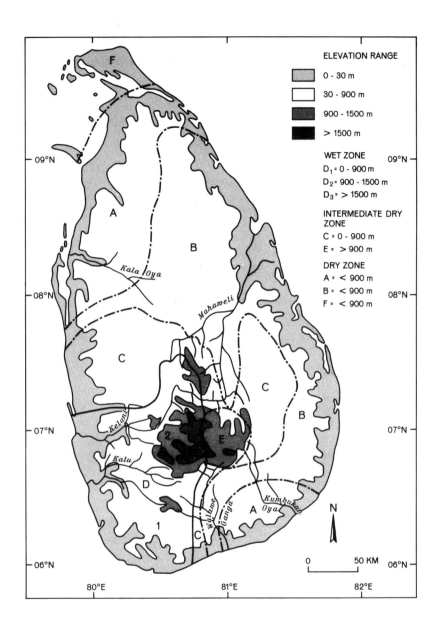

Figure 1. Sri Lanka's ecozones: A = semi-arid lowlands; B = dry lowlands; C = intermediate dry lowlands; D_1 = wet lowlands; D_2 = wet uplands; D_3 = wet highlands; E = dry uplands; F = arid lowlands;. Adapted from Gaussen *et al.* (1968) and Mueller-Dombois (1968).

Cooray (1967). The term Red Earth Formation can be misleading because these beds are frequently buff-colored (where the associated soil is a yellow latosol) and because the basal layer of this formation consists of gravels that are distinct from the overlying "earth" derived from weathered dune sands.

The sediments of the Ratnapura Beds have still to be adequately studied chronologically. Despite the occurrence of Upper (but perhaps Middle) Pleistocene faunistic elements in these

27

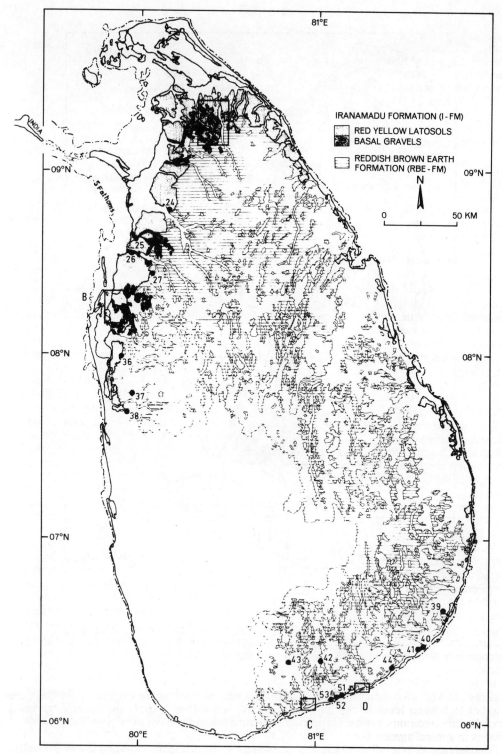

Figure 2. Distribution of Iranamadu (IFm) and Reddish Brown Earth Formations (Deraniyagala, 1992).

gravels, the chrono-stratigraphy of the Ratnapura Beds is complicated because they show evidence of repeated redeposition. In contrast, the sediments of the Iranamadu Formation have been dated more securely. The coastal dune sands from two sites near Bundala (Hambantota District), which are separated by over 6 km, have a thermoluminescence age of about 74,000-64,000 B.P. and 28,000 B.P. (Singhvi *et al.* 1986; Fig. 2 inset D). The associated basal gravels have been assigned dates of about 125,000 B.P. and 75,000 B.P. respectively, if the eustatic sea level altimetry is considered and if the height of these "thalasso-static" coastal gravels above the present sea level is determined by a contemporaneous sea level. The basal gravels are correlated with a sea level of about 15 m high during the main Monastirian (main Eem interglacial), with a sea level of 8 m high during late Monstirian (final Eem). While it is possible to estimate the age of a wide array of occurrences of the Iranamadu Formation through eustatic altimetry, it is hypothesized that some of the raised coastal gravel terraces have a minimum age of 300,000 B.P. (Holstein interglacial). Reliable data are also available from dated cave sediments. The caves of Fa Hien, Batadomba, Kitulgala Beli-lena and Attanagoda Alu-lena have been radiocarbon dated between 34,000 B.P. and 3000 B.P.

Pleistocene Environment

Since the sediments of the Ratnapura Beds are chronologically amorphous, they may be discounted from further consideration, whereas the sediments of the Iranamadu Formation can be used for the reconstruction of environmental changes during the Pleistocene. The basal gravels were deposited during interglacial periods, or "altithermal" episodes, under climatic conditions when greater seasonal extremes of drought and rainfall prevailed in the dry zone area than at present (Deraniyagala, 1992). This evidence may be interpreted as a function of increased atmospheric circulation during such altithermals (e.g. at about 125,000 B.P. and 75,000 B.P.) which caused katabatic Föhn winds during the SW monsoon desiccating the area of the dry zone much more than under present conditions. Based on Thambyahpillay (1958, 1967) who observed a positive correlation between the intensity of the SW monsoon and the occurrence of cyclones and convectional rainfall at present in the area of the dry zone, increased atmospheric circulation could also have caused increased occurrences of cyclones and convectional precipitation during the interglacial periods. This had led to massive denudation processes in the hinterland because this area has been parched by extended summer droughts as postulated above, and hence the protective vegetational cover was decreased. The denuded sediments were thalasso-statically deposited as gravels in the coastal plain. The sediments which had been left behind and constitute the basal gravels of the terrestrial Reddish Brown Earth Formation in the hinterland (Fig. 2) seem to have had a similar origin (Deraniyagala 1976). This hypothesis about the correlation between altithermal and pluvial conditions has recently been corroberated by radiocarbon dated deposits of basal gravels at Gedige in Anuradhapura at an age of about 5900 B.P. These data correlate with the Atlantic altithermal's older Peron high sea level dated 6300-5300 B.P. which was contemporaneous with a humid period in the southern Sahara and high water levels in Lake Victoria, East Africa as well as along part of the Nile. Moreover, the data of about 5900 B.P. coincides almost exactly with the period of high rainfall in Rajasthan, India (Fairbridge 1976, Deraniyagala 1990). Another altithermal period with a sea level of 1 m high is radiocarbon dated at about 3800 B.P. from charcoal which was found at Matota near the island of Mannar in a prehistoric habitation located presently in the intertidal zone. This age correlates with the younger Peron high sea level at about 4900-3600 B.P. and coincides with increased monsoonal activity in Africa with a maximum at about 3700 B.P. represented by humid conditions in the southern Sahara and a period of high water level of the Lake Victoria, East Africa as well as the Nile. Based on these data, pluvial conditions can be also postulated for Sri Lanka during this altithermal period, which is in general agreement with the correlation between interglacials and pluvial conditions outlined above. Since altithermal periods were characterized by increased atmospheric circulation and hence by an intensification of weather phenomena over Sri Lanka, it is a corollary to propose that cool glacial periods, i.e. "hypothermal" episodes, would have experienced opposite climatic patterns, in particular a depressed SW monsoonal, cyclonic and convectional circulation which caused a decreasing range of extremes between the hydroclimatic zones of Sri Lanka.

Molluscan and botanical data derived notably from the gastropod species *Acavus* and the tree species *Artocarpus nobilis* and *Canarium zeylanicum* in caves of the lowland area of the wet zone (ecozone D_1) indicate that the annual average temperature was not lower than about 5°C compared to the present one, even at the Würm maximum at about 15,000 B.P. It is likely, however, that the fluvial regimes and, consequently, the surface runoff in the wet zone area fluctuated to a marked degree due to the rainfall oscillations. These fluctuations could conceivably be assessed by the analysis of remains of fluviatile molluscs, notably of the *Paludomus* genus.

The data derived from the analysis of the cave deposits indicate that the "effective environment" (as above) of the lowland area in the wet zone has not significantly changed in Sri Lanka over the last 34,000 years. However, a gradation of the natural environment would have occurred during the Pleistocene ranging from highly differentiated zonal configurations which can be synchronized with certain altithermal episodes such as the Holstein interglacial to environmental conditions with a medium differentiation such as during the present times to pronounced glacial periods such as the Mindel glacial period in the higher latitudes which probably was characterized by an only minimal zonal climatic and hence biotic differentiation in Sri Lanka. This gradation of the island's zonal differentiation would have reflected the respective carrying capacities, and hence the densities of human population in Sri Lanka.

The altitudinal boundary of the ecozone D_3, which is presently at about 1500 m, would have been lowered due to the temperature decrease which may be estimated at least partly taking into consideration the present vertical lapse-rate of 0.65°C per 100 m altitudinal difference (Domrös, 1974). Thus, a hypothesized 5°C drop in temperature during the Würmian glacial maximum, which could have lowered the altitudinal boundary of ecozone D_3 by about 770 m, would have resulted in an almost trebling of its present extension because the wet highlands would have also included the area of the present ecozone D_2 and more. On the other hand, the discontinuous distribution of uropeltid burrowing snakes in Sri Lanka and Southern India (Gans, 1990) convincingly indicates that rainfall conditions characterizing the area of the wet zone have not prevailed in the dry zone area for the last several million years. Since the climatic patterns in the dry zone area, in particular its relative dryness, are only a direct function of the interaction between the SW monsoon regime and the relief of Sri Lanka causing a luff and lee effect for the rain-bearing SW monsoonal air masses (Deraniyagala, 1992), it can be said beyond any doubt that the SW monsoon has been the dominant climatic regime controlling the climatic patterns in South Asia over the last several million years without any significant break. This is an important advance in our knowledge about the paleoclimate in this region.

The cave deposits dated (as above) suggest that the wet zone area did not experience any significant changes in the human carrying capacity throughout the Upper Pleistocene and perhaps during the Middle Pleistocene as well as between about 700,000 B.P. and 150,000 B.P.

Culture and Environment during the Pleistocene

Since seafaring prehistoric man could not reach Sri Lanka from the very distant southeast and west Asian region, the Pleistocene colonization of Sri Lanka had obviously its source in the subcontinent of India. A eustatic drop in sea level of only 10 m would have been sufficient to create a landbridge across the Palk Strait between Southern India and Sri Lanka. According to sea level curves (Fairbridge 1976), it is suggested that the most recent evidence of such a landbridge was at about 7000 B.P. The penultimate landbridge may possibly be dated at about 30,000 B.P. Therefore, the prehistoric human ecology of Sri Lanka has to be seen as part of the situation in India. These prehistoric bands would have interacted between the ecozonal mosaic of Sri Lanka and its counterparts in Southern India and probably further afield too.

Bearing this caveat in mind, however, this paper focuses on Sri Lanka and not on the situation within the "wider Indian scene" as this would be beyond its scope.

It is possible that *Homo erectus (Pithecanthropus)*, whose existence since the Middle Pleistocene is proved for the Indian subcontinent, had also inhabited Sri Lanka during this period. Anatomically modern *Homo sapiens* is recorded from Batadomba cave dated about 28,000 B.P. (Kennedy and Deraniyagala, 1989) and perhaps also from Fa Hien cave dated at about 31,000 B.P. These records are the oldest evidence of the anatomically modern man in South Asia.

The question now is how these humans had interacted with their environment in Sri Lanka. By means of ethnographic analogy and based on data derived from the Kadar of Kerala (India) and Semang (Malaysia), it is hypothesized that the population densitity in the wet zone area of Sri Lanka was about 0.1 individuals per km^2 through much of the late Quaternary, at least since about 34,000 B.P. Since the dry zone area with its higher rainfall variability (Domrös 1974) had experienced much more pronounced oscillations in the "effective environment", it is hypothesized that the population density in this area ranged between about 0.8 individuals per km^2 and 0.25 individuals per km^2 (e.g. Vaddas in Sri Lanka, Chenchu in India), but that a exceptionally high population density rising to about 1.5 individuals per km^2 had occurred along the resource-rich prograding coastal belt (e.g. Andaman Islanders).

Data of the settlement history suggest that the communities in Sri Lanka were primarily based on the effective subsistence procurance unit of the nuclear family (Deraniyagala, 1992). The carrying capacities of the different ecozones were apparently never conducive to bigger agglomerations of individuals constituting their basic subsistence units, except perhaps in the coastal belt of the dry zone area. Vadda (Sri Lanka) and Semang (Malaysia) ethnography provide valuable insights into how these communities had functioned in the hinterland; similar data from the Andaman Islands may be relevant for the cultural facies in the coastal belt.

Records of prehistoric faunal elements from caves indicate a non-specialized exploitation strategy involving a wide spectrum of forms concentrating on small game. This strategy had obviously not been changed since at least 34,000 B.P. This has also been the case with the foodplants such as the nut species *Canarium zeylanicum* and the wild breadfruit *Artocarpus nobilis* which probably supplemented the yam species (*Dioscorea*) known as a staple among the Vaddas. Records from the Fa Hien cave give evidence that the ability of fire-making applied since at least about 34,000 B.P. and may be dated much further back. In Sri Lanka, the grasslands of the Horton Plains, for instance, would have experienced periodic burning since at least 34,000 B.P. This proposition may be verified by radiocarbon dating combined with the analysis of pollen from swamps of the Horton Plains. The grasslands of ecozone D_3 and E (Fig. 1) seem to be anthropogenic, created in order to facilitate hunting efficiency in prehistoric times.

The technology employed in the subsistence strategy had comprised not only the use of quartz and, occasionally, of chert tools, but had also been supplemented by artefacts of bone and antler since at least 28,000 B.P. Deposits of quartz raw material are almost ubiquitous in Sri Lanka and are absent only in the extreme north where Miocene limestone forms the basement and alluvial gravels are lacking. Therefore, the availability of raw material for manufacturing tools had apparently not been a limiting factor for settlements. Over the period from the Middle Paleolithic to the Mesolithic technological phase (125,000-3000 B.P.), which is documented by the sediments of the Iranamadu Formation and the cave deposits, the tools had progressively become smaller and more refined. This progression had been a general pattern throughout most areas of the Old World, but the occurrence of one of the earliest known instances of the techno-tradition, termed "geometric microlithic", is documented from Sri Lanka (Fig. 3). This evolutionary stage in lithic technology, which is the hallmark of the European Mesolithic, has long been assumed to have appeared in Europe at about 10,000 B.P. at the end of the Pleistocene. But records from Sri Lanka from the four widely separated sites of Bundala-Patirajawela, Bundala-Wellagangoda, Batadomba and Kitulgala have provided unequivocal evidence that microlithic tools had been used as early as 28,000 B.P.

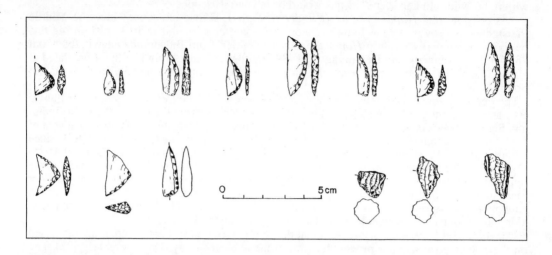

Figure 3. Geometric microliths from Bundala: 28,000 years old.

Microlithic tools of a similar age have been discovered in Zaire (Noten, 1977) and in Southern Africa (Sampson, 1974). Apart from the fact that it may be tempting to see the natural environment of the low latitudinal Asian and African regions as 'catalysts' for this technological phenomenon occurring in these regions about 18,000 years earlier than in Europe, the causative factors can only be surmised. It can be postulated, however, that the human animal had developed by 28,000 B.P. to such a degree of complexity that his expression, which is documented by the form of stone tools, could have been almost entirely a matter of cultural choice rather than a product of the environment as prime mover. Towards the beginning of lithic technology a couple of million years ago, the facility of cultural choice increasingly diminishes during the Pleistocene. During the Acheulian techno-tradition which is roughly dated at about 400,000 B.P. and documented by stylized stone "handaxes" and "cleavers" in India, the cultural choice over environmental pressures had already been ascendant. This distinctive tradition ranged from Western Europe to the southernmost part of Africa and then to India, but its manifestation in the extreme south of India, particularly south of the Kaveri River, and in Sri Lanka had been checked. The question is what this "barrier" had resulted from. Deraniyagala (1990) assumes that a combination of two environmental factors had formed this "barrier". First, these areas lack suitable sedimentary quartzites which were preferred as raw material for handaxe manufacture. Second, the ecozones of Sri Lanka are characterized by a relatively low faunal carrying capacity in terms of exploitable herbivores throughout the Pleistocene, whereas the Acheulian tradition had been invariably represented in regions where a high density of usually large or medium-sized herbivores had been maintained. These factors could have been sufficient to relegate Sri Lanka to a "cultural backwater" which the "sophisticated2 bearers of the Acheulian tradition eschewed. But several hundred millennia thereafter, when the stage of the geometric microlithic technology commenced, the Sri Lankan environment had provided not only an abundance of appropriate raw material in the form of quartz deposits but also a fauna (mostly small game) that had been exploitable with the new technology at an adequate cost effectiveness in terms of labor input. Based on the factor that anatomically modern man had occupied Sri Lanka already at about 28,000 B.P. the island rose above the status of a cultural backwater. However, the studies by Kennedy (1974) provide evidence for a remarkable continuity in the physical traits of the humans between approximately 16,000 B.P. and 6500 B.P. presently preserved in the relict Vadda hunter-gatherers. This seems to signify a marked lack of fresh intrusions into the Sri Lankan gene pool during this period from diverse groups with different genetic characters from any considerable distant areas of India. Despite the occurrence of several hundreds or perhaps thousands of stone age sites in Sri Lanka, there is the strange anomaly between the dry zone and the wet zone in terms of habitations. In the dry zone, open air habitations prevail and very few were found in otherwise eminently habitable, large and well-ventilated caves but located in close proximity to open-air sites; this is in contrast to the habitations in the wet zone where practically every cave has rich deposits of late Quaternary cultural material. It may be assumed that the former natural environment in the dry zone did not require the shelter of caves and that an open air habitation provided a degree of flexibility in the procurement of food which, hence, offset the advantage accruing from living in caves. But in the wet zone with its incessant rains, the shelter of a cave was of prime importance. However, on the one hand, those speculations indicate the enormous complexity of the interaction between man and his natural environment in prehistoric times. On the other hand, those speculations clearly demonstrate that the study of the human paleoecology of Sri Lanka has already been started, but much more research activities on that subject are needed in future times.

Epilogue

Sri Lanka is an ideal "laboratory" for paleoecological research in South Asia. Environmental studies are greatly facilitated by the predictable interaction between relief and climate. This is dramatically exemplified by the hygroclimatic zonation of the island which results from the luff and lee effect of the central mountains for the SW monsoonal air masses and causes a particular configuration of ecozones. A complementary asset is the great richness of prehistoric sites with well-preserved cultural and ecofactual remains of considerable antiquity. Considering this situation, there is a wide field of research activities for the future.

Literature Cited

Cooray, P.G. 1967. An Introduction to the Geology of Ceylon. *Spol. Zeylan.* 31: 1-324.

Deraniyagala, S.U. 1976. The geomorphology and pedology of three sedimentary formations containing a mesolithic industry in the lowlands of the dry zone of Sri Lanka (Ceylon), 1972. *In* K.A.R. Kennedy and G.l. Possehl, eds. *Ecological Backgrounds of South Asian Prehistory,* pp. 11-27. Cornell University: South Asia Program.

Deraniyagala, S.U. 1992. *The Prehistory of Sri Lanka: an Ecological Perspective.* Archeological Dept. Sri Lanka.

Domrös, M. 1974. *The Agroclimate of Ceylon.* Franz Steiner, Wiesbaden.

Fairbridge, R.W. 1976. Effects of Holocene climatic change on some tropical geomorphic processes. *Quaternary Research* 6: 529-556.

Gans, C. This volume. *Fossorial Amphibian and Reptiles: Their Distributions as Environmental Indicators.*

Gaussen, H., P. Legris, M. Viart and L. Labroue. 1968. *Explanatory Notes on the Vegetation Map of Ceylon.* Govt. Press, Sri Lanka.

Kennedy, K.A.R. 1974. The paleodemography of Ceylon: a study of the biological continuum of a population from prehistoric times. *In* A.K. Ghosh, ed. *Perspectives in Paleoanthropology*, pp. 95-113. Mukhopadhyay, Calcutta.

Kennedy, K.A.R. and S.U. Deraniyagala. 1989. Fossil remains of 28,000 year-old hominids from Sri Lanka. *Current Anthropology* 30: 394-99.

Mueller-Dombois, D. 1968. Ecogeographic analysis of a climate map of Ceylon with particular reference to vegetation. *The Ceylon Forester* 8: 39-58.

Noten, F. van, 1977. Excavations at Matupi cave. *Antiquity* 51: 35-40.

Sampson, C.G. 1974. *The Stone Age Archaeology of Southern Africa*. Academic Press, New York.

Singhvi, A.K., S.U. Deraniyagala and D. Sengupta. 1986. Thermoluminescence dating of Quaternary Red Sand Beds in Sri Lanka. *Earth and Planetary Science Letters* 80: 139-44.

Thambyahpillay, G.G.R. 1958. Secular fluctuations in the rainfall climate of Colombo. *University of Ceylon Review* 16: 3-106.

Thambyahpillay, G.G.R. 1967. Climatological research and agricultural development in the dry zone, *In* O.S. Peries, ed. *Proceedings of a Symposium on the Development of Agriculture in the Dry Zone,* pp. 18-28. Ceylon Assoc. Advancement of Science, Colombo.

Proceedings of the International and Interdisciplinary Symposium
ECOLOGY AND LANDSCAPE MANAGEMENT IN SRI LANKA
W. Erdelen, C. Preu, N. Ishwaran, C.M. Madduma Bandara (eds.)
Colombo, Sri Lanka, 12-26 March 1990
© 1993
Margraf Scientific Books, D-97985 Weikersheim
ISBN 3-8236-1182-8

The Geoecological Landscape Units of Sri Lanka

System Interactions, Human Impact and Consequences

C. PREU

Abstract

Landscapes comprise geoecological units, shaped by the interactions between atmosphere, reliefsphere, pedosphere, hydrosphere and biosphere. These landscape units are interconnected by the transfer of energy and matter. The dominant ruling factors, shaping the quality and quantity of these interactions, are tectonics and climate. Using the climatic differentiation within Sri Lanka as a framework distribution of abiotic and biotic components of the natural environment are described and the interdependencies between different geoecological landscape units are illustrated. Examples for long-distance interrelations between landscape units and the temporal character of their interdependencies are given for coastal and riverine systems in Sri Lanka. Human impacts are identified and changes in the systems are outlined. The study shows that these impacts not only affect the interactions among the geoecological factors of the system where human interference actually takes place, but may also influence the interactions in neighboring or even distant systems. For this reason, all landscape management activities should take into account the possibility of the occurrence of long-distance effects, often coupled with time lags.

Introduction

Sri Lanka (05°54'-09°52'N and 79°39'-81°53'E) is a mesotop tropical island located off the southern tip of the Indian Peninsula. Within the island's area of 65.610 km², different geological formations, types of weathering, morphographic features and morphodynamic processes can be separated, different types of sediments, soils and vegetation can be distinguished, and different hydrological and climatological patterns are found. Based on the horizontal, vertical and seasonal variation of the climatic parameters "temperature" and "amount and seasonal distribution of rainfall", Mueller-Dombois (1968) has subdivided Sri Lanka into ecozones, each of which is characterized by a particular type of potential natural vegetation. Using this approach the effect of climatic changes on the type of vegetation can be studied. When taking the abiotic factors, "reliefsphere", "pedosphere" and "hydrosphere" as well as the factors above into consideration, it is also possible to find out the way how changes in climate and vegetation impinge on other environmental factors of a particular ecozone and how those environmental changes may affect neighboring ecozones. It is also possible to determine the consequences which result from human impact on the natural environment of a particular ecozone and how this human interference affects the interrelations between ecozones. Using this geoecological approach, Mueller-Dombois's (1968) "ecozones" become "geoecological landscape units" forming characteristic spatial units on the basis of their location, outward appearance and combined action of abiotic and biotic factors within these units.

Geoecological landscape units are in a state of dynamic equilibrium which results from the continuous exchange of matter and energy between the units' abiotic and biotic components. In order to balance this internal cycle, matter and energy are exchanged with surrounding units. Consequently this external cycle interconnects landscape units and, hence, influences the units' internal dynamic cycles through feedback. Especially coastal and riverine units show that these interrelations can result in long-distance interconnections and interdependencies which are governed by the dominant ruling factors "tectonics" and "climate".

Due to climatic changes, both the internal and external cycle, and hence the quality of the units' interrelations have experienced natural changes during the Quaternary. But since man started utilizing the island's natural environment, about 25 centuries ago, the dynamic of the these cycles has been affected at an increasing rate. As human impacts have led to modifications of the internal cycle, the external cycle has been also affected. From man's point of view, "environmental problems" have arisen which make the implementation of countermeasures necessary in order to ensure further utilization of the "natural environment". This, however, has often led to a spatial transfer of the "environmental problem", a process which has resulted from the dynamic of the external cycle.

In this paper, (1) the conceptual framework, (2) the main geoecological features of the natural environment and their morphoclimatic dynamic during the Quaternary are presented, and (3) the main human impacts and geoecological consequences are described and discussed.

Conceptual Framework

Defined by location, outward appearance and combined action of their abiotic and biotic geofactors, landscapes form homogenous spatial units which comprise different geoecological systems (Fig. 1). Considering their areal dimension, those systems range from the global-regionic "zonobiomes" (Walter, 1976) or "landscape belts" (Müller-Hohenstein, 1981) to the topic "geo-ecotop" (Leser, 1991) or "bio-ecotop" (Schubert, 1991). Geoecological landscape units representing the choric dimension compose different topic units.

Despite the spatial dimension, the abiotic and biotic components of ecosystems are vertically and horizontally interrelated by an internal cycle of matter and energy transfer. These processes result in mutual interaction between the components and entail a dynamic equilibrium. As in most cases the internal cycle is not balanced, the state of equilibrium can be only reached by the exchange of matter and energy with neighboring ecosystems. This external cycle, however, not only interconnects ecosystems but also leads to their mutual interdependency, as the quality of the internal cycle of the contributing ecosystems are correlated with the quality of their external cycle.

Considering the mode of operation, the factors controlling the interaction of ecosystems can be subdivided into (1) the primary factors, "energy" and "matter" and (2) the secondary factors "energy supply", "availability of transport medium", "spatial relationship" and "time".

The existence of energy is the fundamental precondition for the operation of both the internal and external cycle. Solar radiation being the extraterrestrial energy source drives the hydrological cycle and, hence, controls the dynamic processes in the marine-littoral and

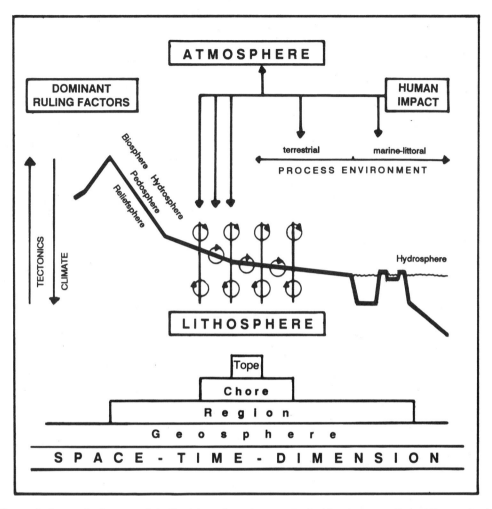

Figure 1. Conceptual approach to the interaction of geoecological landscape units and the mode of interference through human impact.

terrestrial environment, both of which are governed by the cycle's atmospheric components. The earth's geothermal heat flow represents the endogenic energy source. Resulting from geotectonic processes, such as horizontal and vertical crust movements, it provides the relief's potential energy by which, in combined action with solar radiation, all exogenic processes such as removal and transport of material are governed.

"Matter" can be subdivided into organic and anorganic matter. Its mobility and transport probability are mainly controlled by its physical property, whereas its chemical and biological property determines its effects. As matter can experience physical and biochemical transformation, it can trigger other processes after it has been deposited. Of all the types of matter, water possesses the highest geoecological significance due to its global availability and contribution to all processes within the internal and external cycle.

As initiation and intensity of the internal and external cycle are bound to it, the supply of energy is the predominant secondary factor. For instance, the transformation of the relief's potential energy into kinetic energy can result in a mass movement and hence in a direct interaction; as in addition this process makes the operation of a mobile transport medium such as running water possible, an indirect interaction has been caused too. Therefore, the availability of a transport medium represents the second secondary factor. Due to its global availability and high transport capacity, water again is the most important factor. The quality of its interacting effect, however, not only depends on the water's state of aggregation, magnitude and velocity, at which it circulates through the storage systems of the hydrological cycle but also depends on the spatial relationship of ecosystems. As far-reaching interactions caused by water result from repeated interactions between neighboring ecosystems, the energy and matter transferred are subject to partial modification. In addition, however, the factor, "time", has to be taken into account. This means that qualitative and quantitative changes of the primary and secondary factors also affect the quality of the interaction. These are characterized by changes in the dynamic processes as a result of changes in the transfer of matter and energy. The processes triggered last until a new state of equilibrium has been reached.

The processes of interaction result from the exchange of energy and matter between ecosystems. Matter mobilized in a "source system" is transferred by a suitable transport medium to a "target system" where it is demobilized or respectively deposited. Mobilization and demobilization are dominated by the property of matter, whereas its transfer depends on the transport medium and/or energy.

During mobilization, matter becomes movable after a physical and/or chemical transformation. The various types of weathering and erosion are the dominant processes of mobilization in the reliefsphere; mineralization of organic matter and transpiration of plants represent such processes in the biosphere. After it has reached the "target system" matter is demobilized and deposited for a certain period of time during which it is either transformed further or during which it triggers other processes.

Being a process of physical displacement, the transport of matter and energy takes place in two ways. Either, matter is self-mobile or it is displaced by a mobile transport medium. Its transport capability and importance for the interaction between ecosystems depend on (1) the medium's availability and the frequency of the transport process, (2) the velocity of the transport medium and the transport process, and (3) the transport capacity and the amount of matter to be displaced.

In the biosphere, the transport of matter is of only minor importance due to the limited action radius and transport capacity of organisms. By contrast, the transfer of matter in the reliefsphere is much more significant and results mainly from fluvial erosion. Although large amounts of debris can be transported, the interacting effect of gravitational transfer processes, such as rockfalls and landslides, is of only local significance.

Summarizing, it can be stated that the processes of matter and energy transfer in both the internal and external cycle and in both the terrestrial and the marine-littoral environment, are predominantly controlled by climatic patterns and/or relief. Therefore, the factors "climate" and "tectonics" are the dominant factors ruling the interaction between ecosystems.

Human impact has become an important factor in the interaction between geoecological landscape units, beginning with the first fires which burnt vegetation and left the soil more vulnerable to erosion. Since the Industrial Revolution in particular, this factor has increasingly affected the internal and external cycle of the natural ecosystems at an accelerating rate. Above all, this has been caused by a drastic reduction of forests in order to meet the increasing demand for timber, agricultural land and new settlements. More recent human interference results from industrialization, colonization schemes, modern technology in agriculture and forestry, the introduction of new business sectors and the extension of the infrastructure.

Human impact has resulted in an interference with the abiotic and biotic components of the natural ecosystems. As this has caused alterations in the ecosystems' internal cycle, particularly in regard to its quality and velocity, the processes within the external cycle have also been affected. This in turn has led to an alteration in the interaction between ecosystems, as a result of which the "natural environment" has, in many cases, been changed to such an extent, that - from man's point of view - "environmental problems" have arisen. As human impact not only affects the interactions between the geoecological factors of a ecosystem where human interference actually takes place but also affects the interrelations between different systems, the implementation of countermeasures aiming at further utilization of the "natural environment" has often resulted in medium to long-distance effects with important geoecological consequences in other areas. As a result the "environmental problem" has been spatially transferred and/or new "environmental problems" have arisen.

Natural Environment of Sri Lanka

Geoecological Setting

Sri Lanka morphographically consists of the central highlands in the south central part, which is subdivided into midlands (300-900 m) and uplands (900 m to about 2500 m), from which most of the rivers radiate coastwards (Fig. 2). The central highlands are surrounded by an extensive lowland (0-300 m) which is narrow in the west and south but widens towards the north and east. The 1920 km long coastline is characterized by numerous bays and headlands, lagoons, estuaries, salt marshes and mangrove swamps. In the northwest and southeast, sand dunes and spits are well developed. Coral reefs are found off the southern, southwestern, and eastern coasts. Geologically, nine-tenths of Sri Lanka is composed of highly metamorphosed crystalline rocks of Pre-Cambrian and Cambrian age; the remainder includes limestone, sandstones and shales of Tertiary and Quaternary age (Cooray, 1984).

The climate of Sri Lanka is characterized by seasonal changes in wind direction and rainfall patterns. During the SW monsoon (mid-May to September), westerly to southwesterly winds prevail and heavy convectional rains occur in the southwest when average precipitation is between 1500 mm and 3000 mm. In the remaining parts of the island, rainfall is less and droughts are a common feature. During the NE monsoon (December to February), the relatively dry and stable air masses of northeasterly winds predominate and lead to rainfall maxima in the north and east. Thus, with the intermonsoonal periods between the SW monsoon and the NE monsoon (October to November, March to mid-May), Sri Lanka's climate comprises four seasons. Based on seasonal and spatial rainfall patterns, Domrös (1974) subdivides Sri Lanka into two main hygroclimatic zones, viz. the wet zone (mean annual rainfall greater than 1904 mm) in the southwest, including the western and southwestern slopes of the central highlands, and the dry zone (mean annual rainfall less than 1904 mm) covering the remaining parts of the island. The boundary of the hygroclimatic zones coincides with the climatic shed in the central highlands. Average temperatures vary little from month to month. Mean annual temperatures are about 27°C at sea level, 24°C at 500 m, and 15°C at 1900 m (Domrös, 1974). Humidity is generally high throughout the year; annual averages are between 80% and 85%.

The spatial rainfall patterns reflect the distribution of the major vegetational communities, which can be subdivided into four zones (Mueller-Dombois 1968; Fig. 2): (A) monsoon scrub jungle; (B) semi-evergreen forest; (C) intermediate forest; (D) rain forest and grassland. Whereas zones A to C are comparatively uniform in floral composition, zone D is differentiated into lowland forest (sea level to approx. 900 m), montane forests (900-1500 m), and cloud forest (above 1500 m). Area D is more or less congruent with the wet zone, the remaining areas belong to the dry zone.

The hygroclimatic differentiation is also reflected in the timing of the annual water and sediment discharge of the rivers. Rivers debouching at the southwest and west coast have their headwaters in the wet zone and reach runoff maximum during the SW monsoon, whereas rivers of the dry zone debouch at the south, east and north coasts and reach highest runoff during the NE monsoon. The Mahaweli Ganga is the only river showing discharge patterns characteristic of both hygroclimatic zones. In it headwaters, the runoff is dominated by the SW monsoon, whereas the runoff at the river mouth reflects NE monsoonal climatic patterns.

Also the spatial distribution of soils shows the hygroclimatic zonation of the island. In the wet zone, soils developed on the Pre-Cambrain and Cambrain rocks are red-yellow podzolic soils, reddish brown latosolic soils, immature brown loams and laterite, the latter mainly along

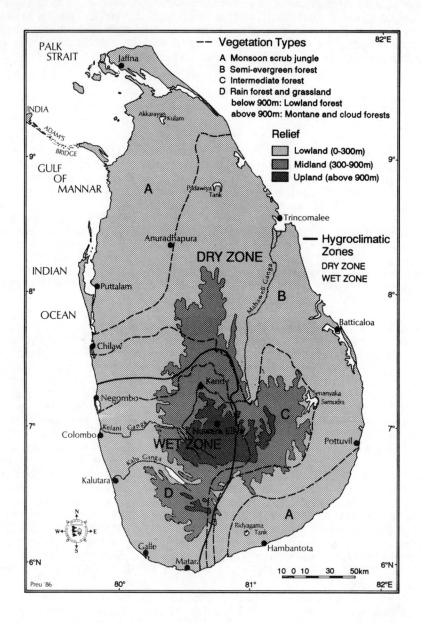

Figure 2. Relief, hygroclimatic zones and vegetation types of Sri Lanka.

the coastal belt, whereas reddish brown earths predominate in the dry zone. In the coastal belt of the dry zone, regosols have developed on unconsolidated coastal sands and sand dunes; lagoonal flats, estuaries and marshes are dominated by solonetz and solonchaks.

Morphoclimatic Development during the Quaternary

During the Quaternary the island's ecosystems and their mutual interaction have experienced repeated changes due to changes in climate and sea level (Preu, 1991).

Data available on Quaternary climatic fluctuations are from the last glacial and the Holocene. For the last glacial maximum, Kuhle (1987) postulates a maximum lowering in temperature of 11°C in Tibet and lowering of the snow line by 1100-1500 m and extended glaciation in the Himalayan region. The concomitant changes in the large-scale heating-pressure patterns on the Tibetan Plateau prevented the Inner Tropical Convergence Zone (ITCZ) reaching the northern extension as it had during the previous interglacial (125,000 B.P.). Aridity in Sri Lanka increased due to the weakening of the southwest airflow, and northeastern trade winds prevailed. Based on calculations of changes in rainfall (Gates 1976a, 1976b), Verstappen (1980) estimates precipitation to have been approximately 30% below recent values. The tropical dry climate predominating even in the wet zone (Späth, 1981) coincided with horizontal shrinkage and depression of the vegetation zones (Ashton and Gunatilleke, 1989). After the glacial maximum the climate gradually became warmer, and humidity increased. According to Van Campo (1986), precipitation reached a maximum at about 10,000 B.P. and an interglacial tropical wet climate prevailed on the island. This higher precipitation resulted from a northward shift of the ITCZ, which was caused by the melting of the Himalayan glaciers, coupled with an increase in the importance of the SW monsoon. Following this phase, there was a gradual transition of precipitation, temperature, and the ITCZ position towards present conditions. Preu (1991) postulates that these changes in climatic patterns had been similar during earlier glacial-interglacial cycles of the Quaternary.

Sedimentological and geomorphological studies give evidence for repeated eustatic sea level changes. Based on raised beach levels, Preu (1991) andPreu and Weerakkody (1987) postulate three transgression phases with maxima at 5-6 m, 3 m and 1-1.5 m above present mean sea level. Radiocarbon datings of shells and corals suggest ages of 6200-5100 B.P. for the 3 m, and 3200-2300 B.P. for the 1-1.5 m level (Katupotha and Fujiwara, 1987); the 5-6 m maximum supposedly originates from the last interglacial (Preu, 1991). Terrestrial sediments of the coastal hinterland, such as gravel remains and pisolith deposits, show that additional maxima must have existed, but there are no corresponding marine deposits.

The evaluation and dating of the glacial regression phases is much more complicated. As the seismic surveys of Sarathchandra et al. (1986), Wickremaratne et al. (1986) and Wijeyananda et al. (1986) show the island's shelf consists of a tropical inselberg relief, which is of Tertiary age (Preu, 1991) and is covered with three Quaternary sediment bodies of terrestrial origin (Preu, 1985); the sediments having mainly been transported while the shelf was dry (Preu, 1991). As these sediments are at a depth of 70 m on the outer fringe of the shelf, sea level lowering was at least of the same magnitude. The three-layered composition of the sediment body substantiates three regression phases. Most likely, however, more regression phases occurred (Preu 1991, Shackleton and Updyke 1976). Datings for the sediment bodies are not available. Generally, the onset of the global drop in sea level during the last interglacial-glacial transition phase took place a short time after 125,000 B.P. (Denton and Hughes, 1983) and reached its lowest level for the Indian Ocean at approximately 15,000 B.P. (Emeryet al. 1971). The sea level began to rise again at approximately 13,000 B.P. (Verstappen, 1980).

These climatic and sea level fluctuations have had effects not only on the vegetation but also on weathering, soils, slope processes, river runoff and coastal development. During the interglacial, chemical weathering dominated and dense tropical vegetation imposed linear river work carrying off mainly clays in suspension. Due to both the vertical lowering in the central highlands and the southward shift of the vegetation zones, the morphodynamics changed and monsoon forest and savanna vegetation prevailed during the glacial. Physical weathering increased, and soils tended to be thinner and coarser or were replaced by dry zone soil types. As the glacial climate was drier than of the previous interglacial a more pronounced river runoff resulted. During the wet season, large amounts of debris were transported from the central highlands to the lowland by a high water discharge. Due to a sudden decrease in slope gradient at the highland's mountain front, the debris was deposited either in fan-like patterns or was temporarily deposited in the river bed until it was transported further towards the "glacial coastline". As the sea level had dropped, the material transported was partly deposited on the continental shelf which had fallen dry.

During the transition to the following interglacial or Holocene the climatic change has led to an increase in chemical weathering, a rise in altitude or respectively a northward shift of the vegetation zones and a return of interglacial river runoff patterns. Due to the rise of the eustatic sea level, the terrestrial sediments covering the continental shelf were drowned and a new beach level was formed at the interglacial or Holocene coastline. Based on sedimentological and geomorphological studies, Preu (1991) postulates three such interglacial-glacial-interglacial cycles with marked changes in climate and sea level for the Pleistocene, whereas the three Holocene cycles were characterized by minor oscillations only.

Human Impact and Geoecological Consequences

Although human interference with the island's natural ecosystems and their interactions began when man came first to Sri Lanka, about 25 centuries ago, human impact have increasingly gained in importance for the landscapes of the island (Tab. 1). According to the methodological approach (Fig. 1), human impact and their geoecological consequences are assigned to that environment in which the human impact has taken place.

Terrestrial Environment - Human Impact

Human impact in the terrestrial environment on the island's forest cover are of greatest significance. When man first came to Sri Lanka, about 25 centuries ago, most of the island was covered to a varying extent by either natural forest or grassland (Silva, 1986). Up to the "Kandyan Period" (1509-1815), "chena cultivation" was practised only in some restricted areas of virtually all the provinces and therefore human impacts on the forests were negligible. Except where village settlements existed and shifting cultivation was practised, the watersheds of the central highlands remained largely in their natural state (Tennent, 1859). Due to the small population shifting cultivation was only practised around the villages located in valley bottoms, and fallow periods were undoubtedly much longer at that time. In the east where the density of settlements was higher, an irrigation system had evolved in which the central highlands functioned as a "reservoir" feeding the irrigation ditches providing water for the paddy fields in the valleys (Panabokke, 1988).

With the introduction of plantations, after the arrival of the British in 1815, much of the forests in the central highlands were cleared and very little remained in regions below 1500 m (Preu and Erdelen, 1992). In 1900, when the population was 3.5 million, Sri Lanka had an approximate forest cover of 70%. This diminished to 50% in 1953, while the population had grown to 8.1 million. In 1982 with a population of nearly 15 million the natural forest cover was estimated to be 25% (Nanayakkara, 1982) and fell to 23% in 1985 (Governmental Land Commission, 1985). By 1988, when the population of Sri Lanka had reached the 18 million mark, forest cover was reduced to about 20%. Both lowland and montane forests have been cleared for the extension of settled agriculture and cash crop cultivation, for expansion and intensification of shifting cultivation with cycles shortened from over 10 years to less than 3 years, for the planting of tobacco, for tea and rubber plantations and for timber and fuel. Colonization schemes, urbanization and expansion of agricultural land within the scope of large-scale development projects, such as "The Accelerated Mahaweli Development Programme" (TAMS, 1980), have reduced the remaining natural forest cover even further and is estimated at only approximately 9%, especially in the upper watershed areas (Governmental Land Commission, 1989). In addition, reforestation of grasslands, which partly covered previously deforested steep slopes in the central highlands, with exotic tree species such as *Pinus* and *Eucalyptus* has qualitatively changed the forest cover.

Table 1. Three main types of land use, their impacts and consequences for the natural environment in Sri Lanka.

Land Use	Human Impact on Terrestrial Environment	Human Impact on Marine-Littoral Environment
Agriculture and Forestry	Deforestation and qualitative alterations of natural vegetation Intensification and modification of agricultural and forest systems	Removal and qualitative alterations of coastal vegetation Intensification and modification of agricultural, forest and fishery land land use systems
	Consequences	
	Changes in runoff patterns and sediment budget in rivers Water pollution (e.g. fertilizer)	Changes in marine-littoral sediment budget Changes in marine-littoral current and wave patterns
Water Economy	Construction of irrigation schemes Construction of water reservoirs for drinking water and the production of hydroelectricity Measures for river bed regulation Measures for runoff regulation of rivers	Construction of port facilities Construction of coastal protection measures (e.g. groynes, revetments) Construction of flood protection and salt water intrusion measures at river mouths Removal of fringing reefs for navigation
	Consequences	
	Changes in runoff patterns and sediment budget in rivers	Changes in marine-littoral sediment budget Changes of marine-littoral current and wave patterns
Engineering and Industry	Removal of sand from rivers Construction of infrastructure (e.g. roads, settlements) Construction of industrial plants	Removal of sand from beaches and shelf Removal of coral reefs for lime production Construction of infrastructure (e.g. roads, settlements, tourism) Construction of industrial plants Land reclamation measures
	Consequences	
	Changes in runoff patterns and sediment budget in rivers Water pollution (e.g. waste from industry and households)	Changes in marine-littoral sediment budget Changes of marine-littoral current and wave patterns Water pollution (e.g. from industry, households, tourism)

There are few studies showing how climatic patterns are modified by this human impact. Based on daily rainfall data from the Horton Plains, a plateau at an altitude of approximately 2000 m in the central highlands, Mueller-Dombois (1968) and Mueller-Dombois and Ellenberg (1974) demonstrated that forests received more precipitation during March and April compared to the open grasslands adjacent to the forests. The authors explain the difference by the fact that clouds moving across the Horton Plains do not always result in precipitation during March and April, but that the trees comb out the supersaturated air masses and droplets precipitate on tree branches and leaves. Hamamori (1967) comes to the same conclusion in his study on the decrease in the average annual rainfall of Nuwara Eliya since the last quarter of the 19th century. He says that "this tendency seems to be common to most of the places in the upstream areas of the Upper Mahaweli Ganga and that this phenomenon is more or less coincident with the intensification of tea plantation in its extent and period as well". In addition, there is much evidence that deforestation in the central highlands has frequently resulted in the occurrence of stronger winds in cleared areas (Nanayakkara, 1982). Tree planting experiments show that the average wind velocity can be reduced and, as an additional effect, humidity increases and rates of evapotranspiration are reduced (Governmental Land Commission, 1985).

Indeed, there is only a limited number of studies conducted on the modification of hydrological patterns due to human impact, but they indicate that water yields from many catchments increased after deforestation and led to a steady increase in the runoff/rainfall ratio of the river catchment areas. According to studies by Abernathy (1976) and Madduma Bandara (1977) studies the average annual increase in runoff/rainfall ratio between 1953 and 1974 was about 0.75% in dry zone catchments, whereas the increase in runoff/rainfall ratio in wet zone catchments reached nearly 1.4%. Based on these data the authors concluded that the increase in runoff/rainfall ratios over the years is a direct consequence of increased deforestation and land degradation in the upper catchment areas. Ponnadurai *et al.* (1979), who studied the effects of selective logging in two catchment areas in the Sinharaja Forest, concluded that peak flows are significantly higher and tend to occur at shorter intervals in "exploited" catchment areas compared to "unexploited" ones.

The modification of geomorphological processes, viz. erosion and sedimentation, is a more drastic and obvious geoecological consequence. Although the problem of soil erosion caused by deliberate deforestation was recognized soon after the introduction of plantation agriculture at the beginning of the 19th century, few systematic and detailed studies on the loss of soil under natural forest or in areas where forest has been removed for the extension of agricultural land have been undertaken. According to Krishnarajah (1984), the areas with highest soil erosion are the midlands and uplands in the wet zone area of the central highlands in which 30 cm of the top soil has been lost since the beginning of the century.

More detailed studies on soil erosion were conducted in the Nuwara Eliya District where, with the arrival of the British in 1815, vast areas were cleared for the cultivation of coffee, later partly substituted by tea. The areas left fallow developed into grasslands, where, even after a period of 100 years, forests have not established themselves and remaining forests were removed to extend tea plantations even into the peak regions of the mountains. The increased demand for land for food production and infrastructure measures has led to further deforestation (Zijlstra, 1989a). The specific geomorphological situation together with poor management in some of the tea plantations, and inappropriate agricultural methods have led to serious soil erosion. Stocking (1986) estimates that in tea lands about 30 cm of the topsoil, corresponding to 40 /ha/yr, has been lost during the past century. Panabokke's (1988) estimates range between 100 /ha/yr and 150 t/ha/yr in poorly managed seedling tea plantations and 0.3 /ha/yr in well-managed vegetatively propagated (VP) tea plantations. In contrast soil erosion rates in areas under "dense forest" are very low and range between 0.1 /ha/yr and 1.0 /ha/yr (Zijlstra, 1989b).

Although no quantitative empirical studies have investigated the relation between changes in forest cover and the occurrence of earthslips and landslides in Sri Lanka (Preu, 1986), it is generally agreed that such mass movements are less frequent in forested areas than in areas cleared of forests (Goudie 1988, Morgan 1986). The extension of human settlements and the opening up of forests for agriculture and tea plantation, particularly in steep terrain and geologically vulnerable areas have led to an increase in earthslips and landslides. The records available (Nanayakkara 1982, Geological Survey Department 1987) indicate that over 60% of earthslips and landslides can be attributed to changes in forest cover in steep terrain (Preu, 1986). Some of the worst earthslips and landslides were recorded in wet zone areas of the central highlands in January 1986. The Governmental Land Commission (1989) reported that "there is hardly any doubt that the immediate cause ... was the spell of unusually heavy rain and continued rainfall in the areas concerned". However, if other conditions favorable for landsliding are not met, heavy rainfall alone cannot cause earthslips and landslides of devastating dimensions. In addition to the natural factors - such as the geological, structural, geomorphological and topographical features which favor the occurrence of earthslips and landslides - the human impact on the forest and subsequent improper land use over the past 100 years were the main reasons for these mass movements.

Soil erosion in the central highlands has led to changes in sedimentation processes in catchments as it is indicated by the siltation of Lake Gregory in Nuwara Eliya, Kandy Lake, Polgolla and Norton reservoirs and several irrigation canals such as Waduwawela Ela, Bodi Ela and Murapola Ela and others in the area of Walapane, Hanguranketa and Hewaheta. Joachim and Pandithasekera (1930) estimated that the bed load carried by the Upper Mahaweli Ganga (above Peradeniya/Kandy) ranges from about 130,000-820,000 t/yr. At Weragantota (located off the central highlands' eastern slope), the bed load of the Mahaweli Ganga was estimated at 618,000 t in 1975 and 1,540,000 t in 1982 (Lauterjung and Platz, 1985). However, the Water Resources Board (1985) maintains that the increase in the sediment transport figures tend to be underestimated.

Due to increased runoff and soil erosion in catchments, human impact on forests have led to modifications of the coastal development. Siltation of lagoons and related problems have altered the physical and chemical characteristics of the Valachchenai Lagoon (east coast) and Negombo Lagoon (west coast). The accumulation of fine sediments has caused excessive oxygen reduction both within the sediments and the overlying water (Preu, 1991). In some lagoons, high quantities of sediment also increased water temperatures beyond critical levels for aquatic species (Wickramaratne, 1985).

Although the formation of seasonal sand bars across mouths of rivers and lagoons is a natural phenomenon, their size and continuity have increased in recent decades due to increased soil erosion and sediment transport in rivers. Such closures not only cause downstream flooding (Preu, 1991) but also affect the productivity of estuaries through decreased salinity levels, siltation, concentration of pollutants beyond minimum acceptable levels and insufficient flushing and water exchange (Swan, 1987) as seen in Mundel Lake (west coast) and the Batticaloa Lagoon (east coast) (Preu, 1991). In some cases, where water of estuarine areas has been used for agriculture and irrigation the opening of outlets by artifical means has caused an increase in salinity thus creating ecological problems in soils of nearby areas under cultivation (Preu et al. 1989).

Marine-Littoral Environment - Human Impact

Although Sri Lanka boasts a culture dating back 2500 years, its inhabitants had very little use for its surrounding ocean and coastal zone resources in the precolonial era. Therefore, even at the beginning of British colonization, vast areas of the coastal zone were covered with mangroves and "littoral woodland" (Tennent, 1859). At present, Sri Lanka's coastal land, especially in the southwest, is densely populated and most of the natural vegetation has been removed for various kinds of high density land use systems and for infrastructure (Preu, 1991).

In terms of traditional land use, fisheries are very important, which the beaches and nearshore areas are used for. Although centralization of these activities has taken place with the establishment of fishing harbors in some areas, fishing activities have been generally extended along a narrow strip of coastal land. The intensity of the activities has increased most markedly in key fishing areas such as Negombo, Ambalangoda and Dondra, and has led to a significant reduction in natural vegetation cover. Further disturbance and pollution pose a threat to the remaining patches of natural coastal vegetation. In many areas natural coastal vegetation has been replaced by coconut plantations or has been cleared for construction or fuel. More recently, urbanization has become a threat with the establishment of shanty housing such as south of Colombo between Dehiwala and Panadura, as well as industrial plants, power stations and tourist facilities, even up to the high water mark (Preu, 1989). Along the east coast the demand for fuelwood has resulted in the denudation of mangrove areas (Pinto, this volume). Denudation of coastal vegetation and increased runoff and sediment load of rivers have radically altered the natural rhythm of organisms typical of coastal ecosystems, especially their breeding, feeding and migration, and thereby affecting the overall productivity of coastal waters.

Other common direct human impacts are the extraction of sediments from beaches and nearshore areas to facilitate mining of minerals and materials for construction, or the construction of hard maritime structures such as sea walls, breakwaters, groynes and revetments, or replenishment of sediment from nearshore or offshore areas, or planting of vegetation.

Indirect human impacts are often less easy to recognize as they tend to induce processes which would not otherwise occur or to accelerate morphodynamic processes as a result of modification of natural processes. Moreover, the effects of indirect human impacts include those resulting from direct human impacts such as structural works in one place, but which affect and modify coastal morphodynamics in another. Engineering structures or the removal of fringing reefs, for instance, not only create changes in the nearshore topography but also modify wave and current patterns as well as sediment transport in the coastal zone.

The most important indirect impact results from human activities in the coastal hinterland. Rivers transport sediment from the catchments to the coastal zone where it is incorporated into beaches through longshore drift. Any changes in the quality and quantity of river sediments result in changes in the sediment budget of connected beaches. Accelerated soil erosion, caused by deforestation or other land use changes, increases the sediment yield of rivers and siltation of river mouths or coastal accretion may follow (Preu, 1988a). When sediment loads are reduced, e.g. as a result of the construction of dams or the extraction of sediment, severe coastal erosion problems in neighboring beaches may result. In these cases, nearshore currents passing a river mouth are not provided with sufficent river sediment, and hence they are "undernourished" compared to their energy and transport capacity. Consequently, sediment supply has to be met by unconsolidated beach sediment from coastal stretches connected to the river mouth.

In addition to these, there is a great variety of human impact which can act either indirectly or directly. Above all, this impact includes water pollution not only caused by the discharge of bilge water and oil slicks from ships but also caused by the discharge of untreated industrial effluence and sewage as well as waste water into the coastal zone. A third source of sea water pollution stems from the excessive application of pesticides and insecticides in agriculture of the river catchment

Marine-Littoral Environment - Geoecological Consequences

Some 970 km of the island's 1920 km long coastline are subject to varying degrees of coastal erosion, whereas only some 300 km show evidence of accretion (Preu, 1991). The southwest coast between Negombo and Dondra Head, in particular, faces intense coastal retreat averaging about 1.1m/yr, amounting to an annual loss of about 1km^2 of land for the last 25 years. Coastal accretion proceeds only at an average of only 0.50m/yr, resulting in a gain of about 15 ha of land/yr during the same period. "By far the largest contribution to the problems of erosion of the island's shoreline has been made by the interference by man with the natural processes" (Gerritsen and Amarasinghe, 1976).

The most obvious modifications to the marine-littoral environment caused by indirect human impact is sand mining. The island's river basins are the major sources of sand supply for the formation and stability of beaches. The sediment load delivered at the river mouths is picked up, transported and distributed by waves and currents depending upon seasonally prevailing setting direction in the nearshore zone. It can be assumed that presently 50% of the beaches are supplied by 70% or more of sand contributed from the catchments (Swan, 1983). Because rivers deliver sand to the coastal area continuously throughout the year, with maximum delivery being at the beginning and the end of the SW monsoon or respectively NE monsoon, sand-mining agencies of different scales have been established in the lower reaches of rivers, on the southwest coast in particualar. At present sand mining in some locations has reached such a dimension that the amount of sand extracted in the lower reaches of the rivers exceeds the annual supply from the upper catchments (Preu, 1987a). In the case of the Kelani Ganga, for instance, due to the prevailing longshore drift setting northwards, the sediment delivered to the river mouth is the main source of supply for the beaches north of the mouth between Hendala and Negombo. This coastal stretch is subject to erosion mainly due to the lack of material supplied by the Kelani Ganga. The nearshore currents off the mouth of the Kelani Ganga are "undernourished" and therefore, pick up sediment from the beaches located in the setting direction. Similar situations prevail on coastal stretches adjacent to the outfalls of all other major rivers, especially along the southwest coast.

The application of insecticides, fungicides, weedicides and fertilizers for agricultural and epidemic eradication programs has increased in almost all catchments. As rain partly washes off these chemicals they reach the drainage network of the catchment and leads to an increased stress on the coastal vegetation and to marine pollution in the nearshore zone. Although there is no recorded evidence in Sri Lanka of damage to mangrove communities, coral reefs and other marine communities due to excess nutrient flow and the resulting eutrophication, the increased use of chemicals since the mid-sixties can lead to similar coastline changes reported from other countries (Goudie, 1983). Another source of marine pollution is the discharge of industrial effluents. Several large-scale fish kills in the Kelani Ganga estuary and in the Bolgoda Lake (CCD, 1986) have demonstrated that the potential for widespread environmental damage in the coastal zone from this source exists.

Especially in the coastal hinterland between Ambalangoda and Dondra Head fossil coral deposits are found in abundance. Miners have opened up large pits and removed the coral debris. As the pits were refilled after exploitation most of the mined areas experience major environmental problems. First, the pits ran full of water and form large swamps and brakish water pools resulting in breeding places for mosquitoes, decreasing quality of the ground water, and reduction in fertile agricultural land. Second, since some of the pits are located very near to the present coastline they have destabilized the morphological "buffer" between the mining areas and the beach to such an extent that a breakage of this buffer due to unusually strong waves has to be feared. In Madampagama, near Akurala, several revetments have been set up along the coast not only to protect the road between Colombo and Galle but also to prevent the sea breaching into coral mining areas.

The most obvious modifications in the marine-littoral environment caused by direct human impact is coral mining throughout the 80-km long stretch between Ambalangoda and Dondra Head, predominantly concentrated between Akurala and Hikkaduwa, where a significant percentage of the population are dependent on mining for their livelihood (Preu, 1987b). "Miners" break off chunks of coral reefs to manufacture "limepowder". The miners have already created deep pools in the reefs located close to the coastline and are now extending their activities towards the outer reef edges, where it is still live and growing. In addition, reefs have been also destroyed by the extraction of ornamental corals for export, dynamiting of fish or coral reefs and dragging of anchor chains.

Apart from the damage and depletion of coral resources such activities have seriously influenced the marine-littoral factors and exacerbated coastal erosion due to the removal of the "natural wave breakers". Between Akurala and Hikkaduwa, for instance, a stretch of land of about 200 m width has been eroded within the last 50 years.

Coral reefs and beachrock platforms act as barriers preventing direct wave attack to beaches and, hence, reduce the intensity of wave action. Since the introduction of mechanized crafts, navigation channels have been formed by blasting passages through fringing reefs. However, blasting actually destroys a much larger area than that part which is blasted. Strong waves can enter these gaps and reach the coast. Since strong rip currents are an additional consequence of this human impact the stability of beaches is significantly decreased resulting in drastic coastal changes. In Hikkaduwa, for instance, a part of the fringing reef northeast of Waal Islet was blasted at the end of the 50s. Since that time, waves and rip currents have retreated the coastline some 150 m and formed a small "bay". As this coastal erosion has also affected the Colombo-Galle Road and some hotels located around this site, the construction of revetments became necessary.

The geoecological consequences of human impacts on coastal vegetation are illustrated with two representative examples below. In the case of Negombo, a tourist resort north of Colombo (west coast), about 95% of the tourist hotels built in and around Negombo are located in close proximity of the coast and Negombo Lagoon. These hotels are located on a 100-150 m wide strip of land between Negombo town and Kuda Paduwa. Hoteliers have cleared the coastal vegetation and have built hotels very close to the beach considering the tourists' preference for the beach. More than 50% of the hotels are located less than 20 m from the high water mark. Only 10% of the hotels are more than 30 m away. Presently, some 80% of these hotels facing the coastal strip are confronted with the problem of coastal erosion (Preu, 1991). In addition to various protective structures which the government has built to protect these hotels from erosion, the hoteliers themselves have undertaken coast protection measures. All these protection efforts, while providing only a temporary solution, have destroyed the scenic attraction of the coastal stretch. Apart from this, the hotels are faced with an enormous financial burden as the destruction of the scenic value has reached such an extent that tourists are no longer attracted to the area.

A second example is to be found on the coast near Hikkaduwa, 20 km north of Galle, an area representative of the coastal zone in the southwest of Sri Lanka outside towns and larger settlements. The coastal section may be subdivided into (1) raised beach with main road and various types of land use, (2) present beach, and (3) the nearshore zone. During the NE monsoon low waves 0.5-1.5 m high and the southeast setting swell cause a southward sand drift resulting in accumulation and increasing width of the present beach. During the SW monsoon, however, strong southwesterly to westerly winds prevail and high waves of 1.0-3.0 m occur. The oncoming waves reach up to the front of the raised beach and reform its edge by erosion. Mainly in places, where the vegetation was removed and destroyed, the swash runs in canal-like footpaths further landwards, reaches the raised beach and washes over it. Subsequently, the receding water removes unconsolidated raised beach sand, widens the "canals", and lateraly erodes the raised beach (Preu, 1991). Although the beach profile seems to show a similar appearance in the following NE monsoon period as in the preceding one, the annual net sediment balance is negative and, therefore, poses an increasing threat to settlements and public installations in years to come.

The third group of modifications caused by direct human impacts comprises the construction of buildings and other structures, within the dynamic zone of the coast, in order to prevent the continuation of coastal retreat and protect the infrastructure and land use systems. After independence in 1948, investment programs aiming at developing fisheries, commerce and agriculture resulted in the construction of a series of maritime structures ranging from breakwaters and quay walls for fishery harbors and ports, river draining schemes for flood protection and salt water extrusion schemes for cultivation. Most of these activities were carried out without adequate prior studies thus causing a series of new and negative effects to the marine-littoral environment. Numerous examples of such human impacts can be seen along almost all parts of the coast. Two representative cases shall be mentioned in more detail here.

The first case in point is the construction of a long groyne to stabilize the south bank of the outlet of the Panadura Ganga debouching into the sea about 30 km south of Colombo. Due to a lower runoff during the period between October and April the river mouth is closed by the formation of a seasonal sand bar. The intention was to keep the river mouth open throughout the year, to drain the waters of Bolgoda Lake, and to prevent seasonal flooding of the adjacent paddy lands. An additional objective was to provide access for fishing boats to the river for mooring. Although these objectives were met, the construction of the groyne has caused serious erosion problems in the area north of the river mouth due to the interruption of the predominant longshore drift setting from south to north. The entire coastline from Panadura to Ratmalana has been subject to intense coastal retreat, numerous houses have been washed away and the beaches of Egodauyana and Lunawa have been completely wiped out (CCD, 1986).

The second example is from Hikkaduwa, one of the most crowded beach resorts in Sri Lanka. The low-lying coast is underlain by beachrock and fringed with a coral reef. Virtually the entire coastal stretch of about 3 km is lined with maritime structures, such as revetments, groynes and a fishing harbor, causing drastic changes in the coast's morphodynamic. The oncoming waves break directly against these constructions, are then reflected by the wall and accelerate scouring. The groynes have effected a considerable accretion of beach sediment in luff of the structures, but have also caused coastal retreat in its lee position. The jetty of the fishing harbor, built in 1974, has induced wave refraction in such a way that the sand-bearing nearshore currents turn towards the harbor and deposit their sediment there. This process, causing an unintended and unexpected siltation, has resulted in the accumulation of sand. This has affected the function of the harbor, and has reduced the amount of sediment available for the formation and stabilization of the beaches located towards the predominant direction of the longshore drift, i.e. north of the harbor.

Apart from the faecal pollution of beaches the discharge of sewage is perhaps the largest source of pollution. Besides land-borne pollutants, such as settlements and tourist resorts, another source of marine pollution stems from discharges from ships. All these discharges contribute to the pollution of coastal waters and beaches. In many cases both oil slicks and remnants of waste water and sewage have been deposited on the coral reefs and have stimulated the spread of blue algae. Therefore, the growth rates of coral polyps and even the number of living corals (Mergner and Scheer, 1974) have declined in some spots to such an extent that coral reefs are unable to withstand the force of the oncoming waves and their destructive action. Consequently, either a total collapse of the reef or large gaps in the reef could emerge and modify nearshore currents and wave patterns. This would result in a "disequilibrium" and therefore initiate and cause alterations and changes in the morphodynamics of the coast.

Conclusion

As indicated the internal cycle of ecosystems resulting from the interaction between their abiotic and biotic components is very complex. Even more complex are the interrelations between ecosystems which are interconnected by the external dynamic cycle. The quality and intensity of both cycles are governed by the dominant ruling factors "tectonics" and "climate" in the terrestrial and marine-littoral environment. As Sri Lanka has not experienced significant tectonic movements during the Quaternary and hence represents a tectonically stable island (Bremer, 1981), climatic conditions have been the dominant factor for the transfer of energy and matter within and between the ecosystems during that period. This is indicated by two facts. First, the present spatial distribution of the natural landscape units and the factors and processes interrelating them reflect the present distribution of the climatic patterns, viz. "rainfall" and "temperature". Second, changes in these climatic patterns along with fluctuations in the sea level, both of which have been caused by global changes in climate, have caused changes in the internal cycle. The subsequent changes in the external cycle have led to modifications in the morphodynamic processes.

As man has utilized the natural environment, his activities have resulted in a modification of the quality and intensity of the natural controlling factors and have changed the internal cycle of energy and matter transfer of ecosystems. Therefore, the external cycle of the interrelated ecosystems as well as the processes of interaction have also been affected and have led to modifications in the interaction between ecosystems. This means that human-induced disturbances of the natural relationship have led to changes within landscape units and to phenomena such as soil degradation and coastal erosion. As demonstrated, this can lead to long-distance effects as human impact not only affects the interactions between the geoecological factors of a unit where human interference actually takes place but also affects the interrelations between different units. Therefore, it is the responsibility of landscape management to take into consideration local human impact may cause long-distance effects, often coupled with time lags.

The human impact on the ecosystems of Sri Lanka have caused land degradation which has reached serious dimensions, particularly in the central highlands and the coastal zone. If present trends continue irreversible changes in the availability and quality of natural resources may occur in the near future. Present management activities should focus on the landscape mosaic of Sri Lanka as a whole rather than on units which, as shown above, may be situated very far apart but are in fact interlinked through the flow of energy and matter. Understanding long-distance and often delayed effects may be crucial for the formulation of integrated management plans in Sri Lanka.

Sri Lanka like many other developing countries faces a more or less paradoxical situation in the attempt in so far as, on the one hand, to improve the economic situation and to meet increasing demands for food, shelter, clothing and employment and, on the other hand, to conserve the natural resources which form the basis of the economy. A "solution" to this dilemma can only be reached, if the coordinated planning and implementation of human interference take into account the dynamic processes of the natural environment. Any kind of planned activity has therefore to consider whether and how impacts can affect the natural morphodynamic of landscape units.

Our poor understanding of patterns and processes that characterize these highly complex systems, requires detailed basic and applied research programs which have not been formulated to date. Within its environmental programs and activities conservation and management of natural resources in different landscape units should be given higher priority by the decision-making community of Sri Lanka.

Literature Cited

Abernathy, C.L. 1976. *Report on a visit in Sri Lanka*. Unpublished report. National Committee for the IHP Irrigation Department, Colombo.

Ashton, P.S. and C.V.S. Gunatilleke. 1987. New light on the plant geography of Ceylon. I. Historical plant geography. *J. Biogeogr.* 14: 249-285

Bremer, H. 1981. Reliefformen und reliefbildende Prozesse in Sri Lanka. *In* H. Bremer, A. Schnütgen and H. Späth, eds. Zur Morphogenese in den feuchten Tropen. Verwitterung und Reliefbildung am Beispiel von Sri Lanka. *Relief, Boden, Paläoklima* 1: 7-184.

Coast Conservation Department (CCD) 1986. *Coast protection masterplan*. Unpublished report. Ministry of Fisheries, Colombo.

Cooray, P.G. 1984. *An introduction to the geology of Sri Lanka*. National Museums of Sri Lanka.

Denton, G.H. and T.J. Hughes. 1983. Milankovitch theory on ice ages: Hypothesis of ice-age linkage between regional insolation and global climate. *Quaternary Research* 20: 125-144.

Domrös, M. 1974. *The agroclimate of Ceylon*. Geoecological Research 2. Franz Steiner Verlag, Wiesbaden.

Emery, K.O., H. Niino and B. Sullivan. 1971. Postpleistocene levels of the East China Sea. *In* K.K. Turekian, ed. *The Late Cenozoic Glacial Ages*, pp. 381-390. Yale Univ. Press.

Erdelen, W. and C. Preu. 1990. Quaternary coastal and vegetation dynamics in the Palk Strait Region, South Asia - The evidence and hypotheses. *In* J.B. Thornes, ed. *Vegetation and Erosion,* pp. 491-504. John Wiley & Sons Ltd, New York.

Gates, W.L. 1976a. Modeling the ice-age climate. *Science* 191: 1138-1144.

Gates, W.L. 1976b. The numerical simulation of ice-age climate with a global general circulation model. *J. Atmospheric Sciences* 33: 1844-1873.

Geological Survey Department (Colombo). 1987. *Disaster in the Hills.* Unpublished report. Colombo.

Gerritsen, F., and S.R. Amarasinghe. 1976. Coastal Problems in Sri Lanka. *Proc. Coastal Engineering Conference (Honolulu, Hawaii)* 15: 3487-3505.

Goudie, A.S. 1983. *Environmental change.* (2nd Ed.). Oxford Univ. Press, Oxford.

Goudie, A.S. 1988. *The Human Impact on the Natural Environment.* Basil Blackwell, Oxford.

Governmental Land Commission. 1985. *First interim report of the land commission.* Ministry of Agriculture, Colombo.

Governmental Land Commission. 1989. *Second interim report of the land commission.* Ministry of Agriculture, Colombo.

Hamamori, A. 1967. *Mahaweli Ganga irrigation and hydropower survey.* FAO and Irrigation Department, Colombo.

Jacobeit, J. 1991. Climatic impacts of tropical land use practices. *In* W. Erdelen, N. Ishwaran and P. Müller, eds. *Tropical Ecosystems. Systems Characteristics, Utilization Patterns, and Conservation Issues,* pp. 65-82. Margraf Scientific Books, Weikersheim.

Joachim, A.W.R., and D.G. Pandithasekera. 1930. Sediment transport in the Mahaweli Ganga. *Trop. Agricult.* 74: 203-209.

Katupotha, J. and K. Fujiwara. 1987. *Holocene sea level change of the southwest and south coast in Sri Lanka.* Final Field Symposium on the Late Quaternary sea level corelations and applications, NATO Advanced Study Institute.

Krishnarajah, P. 1984. *Erosion and degradation of the environment.* Unpublished paper presented at the annual session of the Soil Science Society.

Kuhle, M. 1987. Subtropical mountain and highland glaciation as the ice-age trigger and the waning of the glacial periods in the Pleistocene. *Geo Journal* 14: 393-421.

Lauterjung, H., and H. Platz. 1985. *Watershed management project for the Upper Mahaweli Ganga.* Unpublished report. Irrigation Department, Colombo.

Leser, H. 1991. *Landschaftsökologie. UTB 521.* Ulmer Publishers, Stuttgart.

Madduma Bandara, C.M. 1977. *Water resources of SE Sri Lanka.* Asian regional meeting of the national committee of the IHP, Colombo.

Morgan, R.P.C. 1986. *Soil erosion and conservation.* Longman, London.

Müller-Dombois, D. 1968. Ecogeographic analysis of a climate map of Ceylon with special reference to vegetation. *The Ceylon Forester* 8: 39-58.

Müller-Dombois, D. and H. Ellenberg. 1974. *Aims and methods of vegetation ecology.* John Wiley & Sons Ltd, New York.

Müller-Hohenstein, K. 1981. *Die Landschaftsgürtel der Erde.* Teubner Studienbücher, Stuttgart.

Nanayakkara, V.R. 1982. Forests: Policies and strategies for conservation and development. *The Sri Lankan Forester* 15: 32-47.

Panabokke, C.R. 1988. *Land use planning for Sri Lanka.* Unpublished report. Ministry of Agriculture, Colombo.

Ponnadurai, D.K., G.E.M Gomez, and A. Kandiah. 1979. Effect of selective felling on hydrological parameters of a wet zone catchment. Asian regional meeting of IHP national committee, Colombo, 41pp.

Pinto, L. and N.N. Punchihewa. This volume. Short-term effects of denudation of mangroves on the fish crustacean communities of the Negombo Lagoon.

Preu, C. 1985. Erste Forschungsergebnisse quartärmorphologischer Untersuchungen an den Küsten Sri Lankas. *Kieler Geographische Schriften* 62: 115-125.

Preu, C. 1986. Geomorphological observations in the tea-growing areas of the wet zone of Sri Lanka's uplands with special regard to the problem soil erosion. *The Sri Lankan Forester* 17: 157-162.

Preu, C. 1989a. Zur Problematik der rezenten Morphodynamik an den Küsten Sri Lankas - Ursachen und Auswirkungen der Küstenabrasion an der W- und SW-Küste zwischen Negombo und Dondra Head. *Forschungen auf Ceylon* III: 23-42.

Preu, C. 1991a. *Zur Küstenentwicklung Sri Lankas im Quartär - Untersuchung der Steuerungsmechanismen und ihrer Dynamik im Quartär zur Ableitung eines Modells der polygenetischen Küstenentwicklung einer Insel in den wechsel-feuchten Tropen.* Augsburger Geographische Hefte 10.

Preu, C. 1991b. Human impact on the morphodynamics of coasts: A case study of the SW coast of Sri Lanka. *In* W. Erdelen, N. Ishwaran and P. Müller, eds. *Tropical Ecosystems. Systems Characteristics, Utilization Patterns, and Conservation Issues,* pp. 121-138. Margraf Scientific Books, Weikersheim.

Preu, C. and W. Erdelen. 1992. Geoecological consequences of human impacts on forests in Sri Lanka. *In* J.G. Goldammer, ed. *Tropical Forests in Transition,* pp. 147-164. Birkhäuser Verlag, Basel.

Preu, C. and U. Weerakkody. 1987. Mapping of geomorphology of estuarine coasts using remote sensing techniques. *Berliner Geographische Studien* 25: 389-401.

Preu, C., H. Sterr, F. Wieneke and W-D. Zumach. 1988. "Low Altitude Photography" (LAP) - a balloon-borne mobile remote sensing technique for geoscientific surveys on present-day environments and their dynamic processes. *International Archives of Photogrammetry and Remote Sensing, Kyoto (Japan)* 27: 501-512.

Preu, C., H. Sterr and W-D. Zumach. 1989. Monitoring of the coastal environments by means of a remote controlled balloon-borne camera (LAP-technique) - Examples of application from the SW coast of Sri Lanka and the Kiel Bay (Baltic Sea, West Germany). *Proc. 6th Symposium on Coastal and Ocean Management/ASCE, Charleston, SC.* 4847-4861.

Sarathchandra, M.J., W.S. Wickremeratne, N.P. Wijeyananda and N.G. Ranatunga. 1986. *Preliminary results of seismic reflection and bathymetric studies off Dondra and Matara.* Unpublished report.

Schubert, R. 1991. *Lehrbuch der Ökologie.* Gustav Fischer Publishers, Stuttgart.

Shackleton, N.J. and N.D. Updyke. 1976. Oxygen-isotope and paleomagnetic stratigraphy of Pacific core, V28-239, late Pliocene to latest Pleistocene. *Mem. Geol. Soc. Amer.* 145: 449-464.

Silva, P. 1986. *The need for land use planning in Sri Lanka.* Sri Lanka Foundation Institute.

Späth, H. 1981. Bodenbildung und Reliefentwicklung in Sri Lanka. *In* H. Bremer, A. Schnütgen, H. Späth, eds. Zur Morphogenese in den feuchten Tropen: Verwitterung und Reliefbildung am Beispiel von Sri Lanka. *Relief, Boden, Paläoklima* 1: 185 -238.

Stocking, M.A. 1986. *Land use planning - Phase II.* UNDP/FAO Project SRL/84/032.

Swan, S.B.St.C. 1983. *An introduction to the coastal geomorphology of Sri Lanka.* National Museum, Colombo.

Swan, S.B.St.C. 1987. *Sri Lanka mosaic: environment, man, continuity and change.* Marga Institute, Colombo.

TAMS. 1980. *Environmental Assessment: Accelerated Mahaweli Development Programme.* Unpublished report. Ministry of Mahaweli Development.

Tennent, E. 1859. *Ceylon: An account of the island.* London.

Van Campo, E. 1986. Monsoon fluctuations in two 20,000-yr B.P. oxygen-isotope/pollen records off southwest India. *Quaternary Research* 26: 376-388.

Verstappen, H. Th. 1980. Quaternary climatic changes and natural environment in Southeast Asia. *Geo Journal* 4: 45-54.

Walter, H. 1976. *Die ökologischen Systeme der Kontinente und Prinzipien ihrer Gliederung.* Gustav Fischer Publishers, Stuttgart.

Werner, W.L. 1984. Die Höhen- und Nebelwälder auf der Insel Ceylon (Sri Lanka). *Tropisch-subtropische Pflanzenwelt* 46: 467-504.

Wickramaratne, H.J.M. 1985. Environmental problems of the coastal zone in Sri Lanka. *Econ. Rev.*: 8-16.

Wickremeratne, W.S., N.P. Wijeyananda, M.J. Sarathchandra and N.G. Ranatunga. 1986. *Quaternary geological research of the continental shelf and slope off Panadura.* Unpublished report.

Wijeyananda, N.P., W.S. Wickremeratne and M.J. Sarathchandra. 1986. *Geophysical, sedimentological studies around Great Basses Ridge, Southeast Coast of Sri Lanka.* Unpublished report.

Zijlstra, P.J. 1989a. *Erosion hazard and suitability of the present land use.* Unpublished report. Integrated Rural Development Project, Ministry of Agriculture, Colombo.

Zijlstra, P.J. 1989b. *The need for land use improvement in the Nuwara Eliya District.* Integrated Rural Development Project, Ministry of Agriculture, Colombo.

Proceedings of the International and Interdisciplinary Symposium
ECOLOGY AND LANDSCAPE MANAGEMENT IN SRI LANKA
W. Erdelen, C. Preu, N. Ishwaran, C.M. Madduma Bandara (eds.)
Colombo, Sri Lanka, 12-26 March 1990
© 1993
Margraf Scientific Books, D-97985 Weikersheim
ISBN 3-8236-1182-8

Physiognomic, Floristic and Bioclimatological Characterization of the Major Forest Types of Sri Lanka

A.M. GRELLER AND S. BALASUBRAMANIAM

Abstract

Using the H. Walter Zonobiome System, we recognize two zonobiomes (ZB I, ZB II) and two orobiomes (OB I-1, OB I-2), each with two subzones encompassing the forests of Sri Lanka. We classify them vegetationally by reference to physiognomy and floristics of the arborescent layers. For ZB I we recognize two subzones: ZB I/1, mesophyllous evergreen dipterocarp rain forest and ZB I/2, mesophyllous evergreen mixed families rain forest. In the mountains of ZB I/1 we recognize two altitudinal belts of rain forest: OB I/1-1, the lower montane notophyllous evergreen dipterocarp and OB I/1-2, the upper montane microphyllous evergreen dipterocarp. In the mountains of ZB I/2 we also recognize two altitudinal belts of rain forests: OB I/2-1, the lower montane notophyllous evergreen mixed and OB I/2-2, the upper montane microphyllous evergreen mixed. For ZB II we recognize two subzones: ZB II/1, semi-deciduous forest and ZB II/2, semi-deciduous woodland/thornshrub. Climatic differences can be recognized between the two zonobiomes as well as between subzones of each zonobiome or orobiome; these involve effective precipitation. Using nomenclature developed by H.P. Bailey for his system of bioclimatology, we characterize the climate of ZB I as "torrid/subtemperate/humid". The climate of ZB II is "torrid/subtemperate/subhumid". OB I-1 (lower montane) and OB I-2 (upper montane) have cooler, more equable climates than ZB I, and they show higher amounts of effective precipitation.

Introduction

Ceylon (Sri Lanka) has long interested vegetation geographers such as DeRosayro (1950), Domrös (1971), Gaussen *et al.* (1968), Holmes (1958), Kerner (1916), Koelmeyer (1958a, 1985b); Mueller-Dombois (1968), Perera (1975), and more recently, Ashton and Gunatilleke (1987), Werner (1984), Gunatilleke and Gunatilleke (1980), as well as the present authors

(Greller and Balasubramaniam 1980, 1988, Balasubramaniam and Greller 1981). The early plant taxonomic studies of Ceylon by Linnaeus, culminating in Trimen's "Handbook to the Flora of Ceylon," no doubt propelled interest in and prepared the way for the earlier vegetation studies. The floristic overview by Abeywickrama (1959) and Dassanayake and Fosberg's (1980-1991) multivolumed series, "A Revised Handbook to the Flora of Ceylon" have encouraged futher work to advance the earlier vegetation studies. We (Greller and Balasubramaniam 1980) briefly reviewed the historical classifications of Ceylon forests and presented a "preliminary floristic-climatic classification" of historical classifications. Here we attempt to classify the forests of Ceylon using Walter's (1985) world zonobiome systems, and to incorporate more detailed analyses of bioclimatology using Bailey's system (Bailey 1958, 1960).

Methods

Walter's (1985) Zonobiome System

Walter classified major types of world vegetation within "zonobiomes" which reflected macroclimate, and "orobiomes" which described climate-vegetation belts on mountains within each zonobiome. Zonal vegetation, according to Walter, developed where soils are "not too heavy and not too light so that the rainfall does not flow off the surface or sink too rapidly into the ground water, but rather stands fully at the disposal of the vegetation". The regional unit of vegetation was the "biome". Walter presented a physiognomic classification for world vegetation correlated with climate regime. He gave only a "simplified" classification of vegetation within his zonobiomes.

Walter recognized two zonobiomes (ZB) for the India-Sri Lanka portion of South Asia. These are ZB I and ZB II. He defined these as follows: ZB I had an "equatorial with diurnal climate, humid" and is characterized by "evergreen tropical rain forest. ZB II had a climate that was "tropical with summer rains, humido-arid" and supported "tropical deciduous forests or savannas". Orobiomes (OB) represented the vertical division of the geobiosphere. He stated that "mountains differ climatically from the climate of the zone from which they rise and must be considered separately. Such mountainous environments are termed orobiomes (OB) and can be vertically subdivided into altitudinal belts." He noted that mean annual temperatures of all orobiomes decreased with altitude. Further, he stated that "orobiomes are distinguished according to the zonobiome to which they belong, e.g. Orobiome I, Orobiome II, and so on."

Walter (1985) recognized only one zonobiome for Ceylon (Sri Lanka), ZB I. However, ZB II was found throughout central India including the southwestern Malabar coast. He indicated the presence of mountains on Ceylon, implying orobiomes, as well. For the present study, we have accepted two of Walter's zonobiomes for Ceylon: ZB I for the southwestern part of the island and ZB II for the rest of the island. This followed long-accepted practice in Sri Lanka of recognizing a wet zone and a dry zone. Further, we applied the designation OB I to the three ranges of mountains: Central, Knuckles and Deniyaya, for they all arise in the ZB I region and are well supplied with rain.

Bailey's (1958, 1960) System of Bioclimatology

We use Bailey's system of bioclimatology for the present study of zonal climates. This system has been extensively applied to modern arborescent vegetation both in midlatitudes (Axelrod 1965, 1968, Greller 1980, 1989, 1990) and also previously in Ceylon (Greller and Balasubramaniam, 1988). Bailey (1960) proposed the statistic effective temperature (ET or W), as a measure of warmth of climate. It is the "one thermal level which best characterizes a temperature regime...[the temperature] at which the growing season begins and ends." For example, the ET of Colombo, in the lowlands, is 24.7°C, whereas Nuwara Eliya, in the Central mountains, has an ET of 15.1°C. Bailey's statistic t_d is the number of days with an average temperature greater than the effective temperature. It is a measure of the length of the growing season. Bailey used the value f_0 (in °C) as an estimation of the frost frequency. It is the number of hours at or below 0°C. Bailey introduced the statistic M as a measure of temperateness (equability). M measures the departure of the annual range of average monthly temperatures from 0°C, and also the departure of the earth's surface. Bailey rated temperateness on a scale from 0-100 with 100 being "supertemperate". He produced a nomograph (Fig. 1, annexed) on which climate stations can be plotted, so that values for ET, M, t_d, and f_0 could easily be derived. Bailey (1958) also developed a simple statistic based on a primary law of evaporation to describe the moisture regime. He called that statistic effective precipitation (EP or S). He defined the "humid" climate as having a range of S between 8.7 inches (22.1 cm) and 16.2 inches (41.1 cm). Above S = 16.2 inches, the moisture regime is rated as "perhumid;" below S = 8.7 inches, it is "subhumid" or drier. Figure 2 (annexed) shows Bailey's nomograph for different moisture regimes. Only the categories "perhumid", "humid" and "subhumid" appear to occur in Ceylon. The reader is referred to Bailey's original papers for formulae and their derivations.

Results

Floristic and Vegetational Descriptions of Major Forest Zones of Sri Lanka

Following Walter's (1985) description of zonobiomes (ZB) and orobiomes, we recognize two ZBs, ZB I and ZB II. ZB I is the zonobiome of the "equatorial humid diurnal climate with evergreen tropical rain forest." ZB II is the zonobiome of the "humido-arid tropical summer-rain region with deciduous (sic) forests." ZB I includes the traditional wet zone and intermediate zone, and ZB II includes the dry zone (Sri Lanka Department of Agriculture, 1976).

We recognize two subzones of ZB I and designate these as ZB I/1, the region of the mesophyllous evergreen dipterocarp (rain forest) and ZB I/2, the region of the mesophyllous evergreen mixed (rain forest). In the mountains of ZB I/1 we recognize two altitudinal belts of rain forests: OB I/1-1, the lower montane, Notophyllous Evergreen Dipterocarp; and OB I/1-2, the upper montane, Microphyllous Evergreen Dipterocarp. In the mountains of ZB I/2 we also recognize two altitudinal belts of rain forests: OB I/2-1, the lower montane notophyllous evergreen mixed and OB I/2-2, the upper montane microphyllous evergreen mixed. In an earlier paper we presented a detailed physiognomic analysis of the altitudinal series of evergreen mixed rain forests: ZB I/2, OB I/2-1, OB I/2-2 (Greller and Balasubramaniam 1988; also Fig. 1).

For ZB II we also recognize two subzones: ZB II/1, semi-deciduous forest and ZB II/2, semi-deciduous woodland/thornshrub (Manilkara woodland/thornshrub of Greller and Balasubramaniam 1980). There are no mountains high enough to bear distinct orobiomes in ZB II. The present classification is summarized in Table 1 (annexed) where it is compared to previous classifications.

Detailed descriptions of each of the eight subzones of forests that we recognize are presented in Tables 2-9 (annexed). These descriptions are based on published data, especially Perera (1975), Greller and Balasubramaniam (1980), and Balasubramaniam and Greller (1981), as well as subsequent extensive personal observations and the paper published in this volume on the lower montane mixed rain forest (Jayasuriya et al. this volume). Because verbal description is often insufficient to gain a true picture of vegetation, a number of original photographs (Figs. 3-13, annexed) have been included as supplements to the tables of data.

Bioclimatology of the Forest Zones

Parameters of standard statistics, as well as for Bailey's statistics for warmth, temperateness and effective moisture, are given in Table 1 (annexed). Nomographs for selected forest zones are presented in Figure 1 (warmth and temperateness of the altitudinal sequence of evergreen mixed rain forest) and Figure 2 (effective precipitation and moisture province for six forest zones). To summarize all of these briefly, both lowland forest zones, ZB I and ZB II, develop in hot to torrid warmth conditions. To distinguish between them it is necessary to refer to effective precipitation, listed as S in Table 10; the forest zones in ZB I develop in a humid to perhumid regime, whereas those in ZB II develop in a subhumid regime. Within the subhumid regime of ZB II, the semi-deciduous forest develops in a wetter climate than the semi-deciduous woodland/thornshrub.

Orobiomes within ZB I are cooler and more equable with increasing elevation, as follows: ZB I, OB I-1, OB I-2. In comparing the dipterocarp-dominated altitudinal sequence of rain forests: ZB I/1 > OB I/1-1 > OB I/1-2 with that of the mixed dominants: ZB I/2 > OB I/2-1 > OBI/2-2, it is clear that each subzone of the dipterocarp-dominated sequence (ZB or OB I/1) exhibits higher effective precipitation (S) than its mixed-families counterpart (ZB or OB I/2). In Tables 2-9 (annexed) parameters for Bailey's warmth, temperateness and moisture province are given for each subzonal forest.

Discussion and Summary

We recognize eight zonal (subzonal) forest types related to macroclimate. We classify these eight forests in two zonobiomes (ZB, Walter 1985) and one orobiome (OB). ZB I forest types are characterized by hot to torrid warmth, subtemperate equablity and by a humid moisture province in which effective precipitation (S) is greater than 10 inches (25cm). ZB II forest types exhibit the same parameters of warmth and temperateness, but differ in their moisture province which is subhumid, with S below 10 inches. Three forest types compose an altitudinal sequence of evergreen dipterocarp-dominated forests. These are: mesophyllous evergreen dipterocarp (ZB I/1), notophyllous evergreen dipterocarp (OB I/1-1) and microphyllous evergreen dipterocarp (OB I/1-2). The second subzone is dominated by the endemic genus *Doona*. The third subzone is dominated by either *Doona* or by the genus *Stemonoporus*, which is also endemic. This sequence develops under the highest regimes of effective precipitation at their respective warmth levels. Three other types compose an altitudinal sequence of evergreen forests dominated by a wide mixture of families. They are mesophyllous evergreen mixed (ZB I/2), notophyllous evergreen mixed (OB I/2-1) and microphyllous evergreen mixed (OB I/2-2). These occur under lower regimes of effective precipitation than their respective altitudinal counterparts in the dipterocarp-dominated sequence. Two forest types, in addition, compose a semi-deciduous group that occurs under mainly subhumid regimes. These two are semi-deciduous forest (ZB II/1) and semi-deciduous woodland/thornshrub (ZB II/2). Floristically, ZB I forests are characterized by the following dominant families: Dipterocarpaceae, Moraceae, Sapindaceae, Anacardiaceae, Lauraceae, Clusiaceae and many others. ZB II forest are dominated by Meliaceae, Sapotaceae, Euphorbiaceae, Tiliaceae and a few other families.

Acknowledgments

The authors gratefully acknowledge the assistance of A.H.M. Jayasuriya, I.A.U.N. Gunatilleke and C.V.S. Gunatilleke, M.D. Dassanayake and Odile Garcia who collaborated in collecting vegetation, provided photographs and/or helped in compiling data. Others who assisted with logistical support are also gratefully acknowledged: H.W. Dias, Bogoda Premaratne, Osman Shinaishin, Dorothy Robbins-Mowry, Pat Sharp, Donna Culpepper, Y.D.A. Senanayake and H.P.M. Gunasena. Special thanks go to U. Pethiyagoda for unpublished climate data for Bandirippuwa Estate and for his encouragement of our work. This work was supported by a Fulbright Senior Lectureship and by grants NSF/INT 8317600, NSF/INT 861184 and NSF/INT 8820119, all to A.M. Greller. That author wishes to express his gratitude for the generous support provided by agencies of the Government of the United States, and for the whole-hearted cooperation of the many officials involved.

Literature Cited

Abeywickrama, B.A. 1959. A provisional check list of the flowering plants of Ceylon. *Ceyl. J. Sci. (Biol. Sci.)* 2: 119-240.

Ashton, P.S. and C.V.S. Gunatilleke. 1987. New light on the plant geography of Ceylon. I. Historical plant geography. *J. Biogeogr.* 14: 249-285.

Axelrod, D.I. 1965. A method for determining the altitudes of tertiary floras. *The Palaeobotanist* 14: 144-171.

Axelrod, D.I. 1968. Tertiary floras and topographic history of the Snake River Basin, Idaho. *Geol. Soc. Amer. Bull* 79: 713-734.

Bailey, H.P. 1958. A simple moisture index based upon a primary law of evaporation. *Geografiska Annaler* 40: 196-215.

Bailey, H.P. 1960. A method of determining the warmth and temperateness of climate. *Geografiska Annaler* 42: 1-16.

Balasubramaniam, S. and A.M. Greller. 1981. Floristic analysis of the eight zonal forest types of Sri Lanka. *Phyta (Univ. of Peradeniya, Sri Lanka)* 2: 13-20.

Chapman, V.J. 1947. The application of aerial photography to ecology as exemplified by the natural vegetation of Ceylon. *The Indian Forester* 73: 287-314.

Dassanayake, M.D. and F.R. Fosberg. 1980-1991. *A Revised Handbook to the Flora of Ceylon*, Vol. I-VII. Smithsonian Institution and the National Science Foundation, Washington DC.

DeRosayro, R.A. 1950. Ecological conceptions and vegetational types with special reference to Ceylon. *Trop. Agricult.* 56: 108-121.

DeRosayro R.A. 1957. Afforestation for protection and conservation in the upcountry patanas. *The Ceylon Forester* 3: 50-68

Domrös, M. 1976. An agro-climatological land classification of Sri Lanka (Ceylon) for tea, rubber and coconut palms. *Plant Res. and Developm.* 4: 87-113

Gaussen, H.P. Legris, M. Viart and L. Labroue. 1968. *Explanatory Notes on the Vegetation Map of Ceylon*. Govt. Press, Colombo.

Greller, A.M. 1980. Correlation of some climate statistics with distribution of broadleaved forest zones in Florida, USA. *Bull. Torrey Bot. Club* 107: 189-219.

Greller, A.M. 1989. Correlation of warmth and temperateness with distributional limits of zonal forests in eastern North America. *Bull. Torrey Bot. Club* 116: 145-163.

Greller, A.M. and S. Balasubramaniam. 1980. A preliminary floristic-climatic classification of the forests of Sri Lanka. *The Sri Lanka Forester* 14: 163-170.

Greller, A.M. and S. Balasubramaniam. 1988. Vegetational composition, leaf size and climate warmth in an altitudinal sequence of evergreen forests in Sri Lanka (Ceylon). *Trop. Ecol.* 29: 121-145.

Greller, A.M., I.A.U.N. Gunatilleke, A.H.M. Jayasuriya, C.V.S. Gunatilleke, S. Balasubramaniam and M.D. Dassanayake. 1987. *Stemonoporus* (Dipterocarpaceae)-dominated montane forests in the Adam's Peak Wilderness, Sri Lanka. *J. Trop. Ecol.* 3: 243-253.

Gunatilleke, C.V.S. and I.A.U.N. Gunatilleke. 1980. The floristic composition of Sinharaja - a rain forest in Sri Lanka with special reference to endemics. *The Sri Lanka Forester* 14: 171-179.

Holmes, C.H. 1958. The broad pattern of climate and vegetational distribution in Ceylon, pp. 99-114. *Study of Tropical Vegetation: Proceeding of the Kandy Symposium.* UNESCO, Paris.

Jayasuriaya, A.H.M., A.M. Greller, S. Balasubramanian, I.A.U.N. Gunatilleke, C.V.S. Gunatilleke and M.D. Dissanayake. This volume. Phytosociological Studies of Mid-Elevational (Lower Montane) Evergreen Forests in Sri Lanka.

Kerner, A. 1916. *Pflanzenleben, Dritter Band: Die Pflanzenarten als Floren und Genossenschaften.* Bibliographisches Institut, Leipzig und Wien.

Koelmeyer, K. O. 1958a. Climatic classification and the vegetational distribution in Ceylon. *The Ceylon Forester* 3: 144-163.

Koelmeyer, K.O. 1958b. Climatic classification and the vegetational distribution in Ceylon. *The Ceylon Forester* 3: 265-288.

Mueller-Dombois, D. 1968. Ecogeographic analysis of a climate map of Ceylon, with particular reference to vegetation. *The Ceylon Forester* 8: 39-58.

Nisbet, R.H. McD. 1961. *A Forest Inventory of the Peak Wilderness - Agra Bopats Forest Area and Part of the Kelani Valley Forest Area, Ceylon.* Govt. Press, Colombo.

Perera, N.P. 1975. A physiognomic vegetation map of Sri Lanka (Ceylon) *J. Biogeogr.* 2: 185-203.

Sri Lanka Department of Agriculture. 1976. *Agro-Ecological Regions of Sri Lanka (map).*

Sri Lanka Department of Meteorology. 1971. *Report for 1971.* Sri Lanka Dept. Meteorol. Colombo.

Walter, H. 1985. *Vegetation of the Earth.* Springer Verlag, Heidelberg.

Werner, W.L. 1984. *Die Höhen- und Nebelwälder auf der Insel Ceylon (Sri Lanka).* Franz Steiner Verlag, Wiesbaden.

Table 1. Forest classification in Sri Lanka.

Chapman (1947)	De Rossayro (1950)	Holmes (1958a, 1958b)	Koelmeyer (1961)	Andrews (1964)	Gaussen et al. (1975)	Perera (1980)	Greller and Balasubramanian (1980)	Present study (Walter 1985 categories)
Dipterocarp forest	Wet evergreen forest climax	Wet tropical evergreen forest	Tropical wet evergreen forest	Lowland wet evergreen forest	Doona-Dipterocarpus-Mesua Series	Tropical lowland rain forest	1. *Doona, Dipterocarpus, Mesua* Zone	1. (ZBI/1) Meso-phyllous evergreen dipterocarp
Moist tropical semi-evergreen forest	Intermediate wet evergreen forest ecotone	Wet tropical evergreen forest (Dry Facies)	Wet semi-evergreen	Tropical lowland semi-evergreen forest	Filicium-Euphoria-Artocarpus-Myristica Series		2. *Artocarpus, Pometia, Filicium* Zone	2. (ZB/2) Meso-phyllous evergreen mixed
			Moist semi-evergreen					
Western tropical evergreen forest		Wet tropical evergreen forest (Midland)	Submontane evergreen forest	Highland wet evergreen	Doona-Calophyllum-Syzygium Series	Tropical sub-montane rain forest	3. *Doona, Calophyllum, Syzygium* Zone	3. (OBI/1-1) Noto-phyllous evergreen dipterocarp
							4. *Myristica, Cullenia, Aglaia Litsea* Zone	4. (OBI/2-1) Noto-phyllous evergreen mixed
							5. *Stemonoporus* Zone	5. (OBI/1-2) Micro-phyllous evergreen dipterocarp
Montane temperate forest	Montane ever-green forest climax	Wet subtropical montane forest forest	Montane temperate forest	Tropical montane forest	*Michelia-Elaeo-carpus-Syzygium-Gordonia* Series	Tropical montane rain forest	6. *Calophyllum* Zone	6. (OBI/2-2) Micro-phyllous evergreen mixed
Tropical dry evergreen forest	Dry mixed evergreen forest climax	Dry tropical evergreen forest	Dry evergreen forest	Tropical dry mixed evergreen forest	*Chloroxylon-Vitex-Berrya-Schleichera* Series	Tropical lowland rain forest	7. *Vitex, Berrya, Schleichera, Drypetes* Zone	7. (ZBII/1) Semi-deciduous forest
South tropical moist deciduous forest		Wet tropical evergreen forest (typical)	Moist deciduous forest					
Southern thorn forest			Tropical thorn forest	Tropical thorn forest	*Manilkara-Chloroxylon* Series	Tropical thorn forest	8. *Manilkara-Randia Dichro-stachys* Zone	8. (ZBII/2) Semi-deciduous wood-land/thornshrub

Table 2. Lowland mesophyllous evergreen dipterocarp rain forest.[1]W = effective temperature, M = equability, S = effective precipitation, Bailey (1958, 1960); [2]Perera (1975), Holmes (1958); [3]Koelmeyer (1958a, 1985b); [4]De Rosayro (1950), Holmes (1958), Nisbet (1961), Greller *et al.* (1987), Gunatilleke and Gunatilleke (1980).

Characteristic	Description
Sri Lanka Forest Type (Walter 1985 equivalent)	Mesophyllous Evergreen Dipterocarp (ZB I/1)
Location	Widespread in wet zone at elevations of or below 900 m, e.g. Galle, Ratnapura, Kanneliya, Morapitiya
Climate[1]	Torrid (W = 25.0-42.2°C) Subtemperate (M = 42) Humid/perhumid (S = 13.0-20.6 inches)
Physiognomy[2]	3 Tree Layers A. Emergent (38-38 m,interrupted) B. Canopy (20-24 m, continuous) C. Subcanopy (15-20 m, interrupted) Shrub Layer (2-5 m, interrupted) Ground Layer (0.1-0.5 m, interrupted) Lianas Epiphytes
Dominant or Characteristic Flora[3]	Emergents *Dipterocarpus hispidus Doona congestiflora, Doona macrophylla, Shorea oblongifolia, Canarium zeylanicum, Palaquium petiolare* Canopy *Mesua ferrea, Doona affinis, Doona disticha, Anisophyllea cinnamomoides, Bhesa ceylanica, Calophyllum thwaitesii, Chaetocarpus castanocarpus, Cullenia zeylanica, Dillenia(Wormia) triquetra, Myristica dactyloides, Syzygium firmum, Syzygium makul* Subcanopy *Garcinia hermonii, Xylopia championii, Hopea juncunda, Schumacheria castanefolia, Timonius jambosella, Agrostistachys hookeri, Desmos elegans* Lianas and climbers *Uncaris elliptica, Connarus championii, Dalbergia pseudo-sisso, Freycinetia pycnophylla, Ficus diversiformis, Psychotria sarmentosa* Shrubs *Gaertnera vaginans, Lasianthus strigosus, Apama siliquosa, Litsea longifolia* Herbs *Acrotrema* spp. *Neurocalyx* spp. *Acranthera ceylanica, Schizostigma hirsutum, Zingiberaceae*
Plant Communities[4]	(i) *Mesua-Doona* (ii) *Dipterocarpus zeylanicus* (iii) *Doona congestiflora*

Table 3. Lowland mesophyllous evergreen mixed rain forest. [1]W = effective temperature, M = equability, S = effective precipitation, Bailey (1958, 1960); [2]Perera (1975), Holmes (1958); [3]Koelmeyer (1958a, 1985b); [4]De Rosayro (1950), Holmes (1958), Nisbet (1961), Greller *et al.* (1987), Gunatilleke and Gunatilleke (1980).

Characteristic	Description
Sri Lanka Forest Type (Walter 1985 equivalent)	Mesophyllous Evergreen Mixed (ZB I/2)
Location	Widespread in intermediate zone at or below 900 m, e.g. Badulla, Bandirippuwa Est., Kandy, Kurunegala
Climate[1]	Hot/very warm (W = 20.5-24.8°C) Subtemperate (M = 41-50) Humid/perhumid (S = 10.3-12.4 inches)
Physiognomy[2]	3 Tree Layers A. Emergent (> 20 m, poorly developed) B. Canopy (15-20 m, continuous) C. Subcanopy (6-9 m) Shrub Layer Ground Layer Lianas (well developed) Epiphytes
Dominant or Characteristic Flora[3]	Emergents — *Mangifera zeylanica, Pometia eximia* Canopy — *Artocarpus nobilis, Filicum decipiens* Subcanopy — *Turpinia malabarica, Rejoua dichotoma, Neolitsea cassia* Lianas and climbers — *Anamirta cocculus, Artabotrys uncinatus, Paramignya monophylla, Anodendron manubriatum, Entada sp. Pothos scandens* Shrubs — *Micromelum ceylanicum, Goniothalamus gardneri, Thraulococcus erectus, Pavetta blanda* Herbs — *Dracaena thwaitesii, Ophiorrhiza mungos, Scleria lithosperma* (According to Koelmeyer 1958a, 1958b, the following trees are best represented in this subzone: *Filicum decipiens, Bombax malabaricum, Melia composita*)
Plant Communities[4]	(i) *Artocarpus nobilis-Filicum decipiens-Mangifera zeylanica-Pometia exima* (ii) *Scutinanthe brunnea-Tetrameles nudiflora*

Table 4. Lower montane notophyllous evergreen dipterocarp rain forest. [1]W = effective temperature, M = equability, S = effective precipitation, Bailey (1958, 1960); [2]Perera (1975), Holmes (1958); [3]Koelmeyer (1958a, 1985b); [4]De Rosayro (1950), Holmes (1958), Nisbet (1961), Greller *et al.* (1987), Gunatilleke and Gunatilleke (1980).

Characteristic	Description		
Sri Lanka Forest Type (Walter 1985 equivalent)	Notophyllous evergreen dipterocarp (OB I/1-1)		
Location	Elevations between 900-1525 m in the wet zone, especially on the southern escarpment of the Peak Wilderness, e.g. Dolosbage, Norton Bridge, Moray Estate		
Climate[1]	Very warm (W = 20°C) Subtemperate (M = 55) Humid/perhumid (S = 34.6-36.6 inches)		
Physiognomy[2]	2 Tree Layers	A. Canopy (20-35 m, continuous) B. Subcanopy (5-10 m, interrupted)	
	Shrub Layer (0.5-2 m, interrupted) Ground Layer Lianas Epiphytes		
Dominant or Characteristic Flora[3]	Emergents	*Doona gardneri, Doona zeylanica*	
	Canopy	*Stemonoporus cordifolius, Stemonoporus latisepalum, Stemonoporus acuminatus, Cryptocarya wightiana, Syzygium aqueum, Myristica dactyloides*	
	Subcanopy	*Meliosma simplicifolia, Mappia ovata, Acronychia pedunculata, Hortonia floribunda, Wormia triquetra*	
	Shrubs	*Memecylon gardneri, Euonymus walkeri*	
	Herbs	*Chloranthus glaber,Chassalia ambigua, Lindsaea* sp.	
Plant Communities[4]	(i) *Doona-Syzygium/Calophyllum* (ii) *Doona-Cullenia/Calophyllum* (iii) *Doona gardneri-Cryptocarya wightii* (iv) *Doona gardneri/Stemonoporus* spp. (proposed)		

Table 5. Lower montane notophyllous evergreen mixed rain forest. [1]W = effective temperature, M = equability, S = effective precipitation, Bailey (1958, 1960); [2]Perera (1975), Holmes (1958); [3]Koelmeyer (1958a, 1985b); [4]De Rosayro (1950), Holmes (1958), Nisbet (1961), Greller *et al.* (1987), Gunatilleke and Gunatilleke (1980).

Characteristic	Description	
Sri Lanka Forest Type (Walter 1985 equivalent)	Notophyllous Evergreen Mixed (OB I/2-2)	
Location	Widespread at elevations between 900-1370 m, e.g. Diyatalawa, Passara, Talawakelle	
Climate[1]	Very warm (W = 17.9-19.0°C) Very temperate/temperate (M = 55-67) Perhumid (S = 13.0-17.5 inches)	
Physiognomy[2]	2 Tree Layers	A. Canopy (15-30 m, continuous) B. Subcanopy (5-10 m, interrupted)
	Shrub Layer Ground Layer Lianas Epiphytes	
Dominant or Characteristic Flora[3]	Canopy	*Eleaeocarpus glandulifer, Myristica dactyloides, Semecarpus nigro-viridis, Cryptocarya wightiana, Palaquium hinmolpedde, Aglaia congylos, Calophyllum acidus, Fahrenheitia, Pygeum zeylanicum, Bhesa montana, Gordonia ceylanica*
	Subcanopy	*Nothopegia beddomei, Hortonia floribunda*
	Lianas and Climbers	*Elaeagnus latiolia, Asparagus falcatus, Freycinetia walkeri, Fagraea ceilanica, Pothos remotiflorus*
	Shrubs	*Rauvolfia densiflora, Agrostichachys coriacea, Strobilanthes* spp. *Hedyotis* spp.
	Herbs	*Scutellaria, Pogostemon, Impatiens* spp.
Plant Communities[4]	(i) *Syzygium-Ficus-Fahrenheitia* (ii) *Myristica dactyloides-Aglaia congylos-Syzygium-Bhesa* (iii) *Elaeocarpus glandulifer-Pygeum-Syzygium gardneri*	

Table 6. Upper montane microphyllous evergreen dipterocarp rain forest. [1]W = effective temperature, M = equability, S = effective precipitation, Bailey (1958, 1960); [2]Perera (1975), Holmes (1958); [3]Koelmeyer (1958a, 1985b); [4]De Rosayro (1950), Holmes (1958), Nisbet (1961), Greller *et al.* (1987), Gunatilleke and Gunatilleke (1980).

Characteristic	Description
Sri Lanka Forest Type (Walter 1985 equivalent)	Microphyllous Evergreen Dipterocarp (0B I/1-2)
Location	Southern escarpment of the Peak Wilderness above 1525 m, e.g. Carney Estate (1525 m), Hapugastenne Estate (1525 m)
Climate[1]	Warm (W = 17.5°C) Very temperate (M = 69) Perhumid (S = 40.7-44.0 inches)
Physiognomy[2]	1 Tree Layer Canopy (12-15 m, closed to relatively open) Shrub Layer (2-3 m tall) Ground Layer (1-2 m tall) Epiphytes (common)

Dominant or Characteristic Flora[3]	Canopy	*Stemonoporus rigidus, Stemonoporus cordifolius, Stemonoporus gardneri, Garcinia echinocarpa, Alphonsea coriacea, Gordonia* spp. *Palaquium rubiginosum, Syzygium* spp. *Mastixia* sp. *Cinnamomum ovalifolium, Semecarpus* spp.
	Shrubs	*Agrostistachys coriacea, Strobilanthes* spp. *Indocalamus, Hedyotis, Psychotria, Lasianthus*
	Root climbers	*Leucocodon reticulatum, Kendrickia walkeri*
	Herbs	*Impatiens* spp. *Sonerila* spp.
	Epiphytes	Hymenophyllaceae, Orchidaceae, Byrophyta and Hepatophyta

Plant Communities[4]	(i) *Stemonoporus rigidus-Garcinia echinocarpa* (II) *Stemonoporus rigidus-Alphonsea coriacea* (iii) *Stemonoporus cordifolius-Cinnamomum ovalifolium* (iv) *Stemonoporus gardneri-Palaquium rubiginosum*

Table 7. Upper montane microphyllous evergreen mixed rain forest. [1]W = effective temperature, M = equability, S = effective precipitation, Bailey (1958, 1960); [2]Perera (1975), Holmes (1958); [3]Koelmeyer (1958a, 1985b); [4]De Rosayro (1950), Holmes (1958), Nisbet (1961), Greller *et al.* (1987), Gunatilleke and Gunatilleke (1980).

Characteristic	Description	
Sri Lanka Forest Type (Walter 1985 equivalent)	Microphyllous Evergreen Mixed (OB I/2-2)	
Location	Widespread in elevations above 1370 m, e.g. Nuwara Eliya	
Climate[1]	Mild (W = 15.0°C) Constant (M = 84) Perhumid (S = 19.4 inches)	
Physiognomy[2]	2 Tree Layers	A. Canopy (12-24 m tall, continuous to nearly scattered, flat-topped crowns, gnarled branches and twisted boles; leaves small and hard) B. Subcanopy (6-12 m tall, interrupted)
	Herb Layer Epiphytes	
Dominant or Characteristic Flora[3]	Emergents	*Calophyllum walkeri, Palaquium rubiginosum*
	Canopy	*Calophyllum trapezifolium, Cinnamomum ovalifolium, Garcinia echinocarpa, Neolitsea fuscata, Michelia anilagirica, Syzygium rotundifolium, Gordonia speciosa, Gordonia ceylanica*
	Subcanopy	*Actinodaphne speciosa, Symplocos* spp. *Glochidion montanum, Microtropis ramiflora, Eugenia cyclophyllum*
	Shrubs	*Actinodaphne speciosa, Symplocos* spp. *Glochidion montanum, Microtropis ramiflora, Eugenia cyclophyllum*
	Herbs	*Disporum leschenaultianum, Exacum walkeri*
	Epiphytes	*Lichenes, Hepatophyta, Bryophyta, Orchidaceae*
Plant Communities[4]	(i) *Calophyllum trapezifolium-Garcinia echinocarpa* (ii) *Calophyllum walkeri-Syzygium rotundifolium* (iii) *Calophyllum walkeri-Syzygium rotundifolium-Neolitsea fuscata-Cinnamomum ovalifolium-Michelia nilagirica-Elaeocarpus* spp.	

Table 8. Description of lowland semi-deciduous forest. [1]W = effective temperature, M = equability, S = effective precipitation, Bailey (1958, 1960); [2]Perera (1975), Holmes (1958); [3]Koelmeyer (1958a, 1985b); [4]De Rosayro (1950), Holmes (1958), Nisbet (1961), Greller *et al.* (1987), Gunatilleke and Gunatilleke (1980).

Characteristic	Description	
Sri Lanka Forest Type (Walter 1985 equivalent)	Semi-deciduous Forest (ZB II/1)	
Location	Lowlands of the dry zone, e.g. Amparai, Anuradhapura, Batticaloa, Trincomalee	
Climate[1]	Hot (W = 22.7-23.0°C) Subtemperate (M = 40-41) Humid/subhumid (S = 8.0-10.2 inches)	
Physiognomy[2]	Varies from dense, closed forest 20-24m tall, to lower less dense forest 18 m tall, with large spreading crowns; emergents are deciduous and evergreen; main canopy is mostly evergreen	
Dominantor Characteristic Flora[3]	Emergents	Deciduous: *Chloroxylon swietenia, Vitex pinnata, Grewia polygama, Berrya cordifolia* Evergreens: *Manilkara hexandra, Alseodaphne semecarpifolia, Diospyros ebenum*
	Main Canopy	Evergreen: *Drypetes sepiaria, Lepisanthes tetraphylla, Eugenia breteata, Garcinia spicata, Walsura piscidia* Deciduous or semi-evergreen: *Diospyros ovalifolia, Cassia fistula, Mitragyna parvifolia*
	Subcanopy	*Dimorphocalyx glabellus*
	Lianas and climbers	*Ventilago maderaspatana, Derris scandens*
	Shrubs	*Glycosmis pentaphylla, Phyllanthus polyphyllus, Croton laccifer, Polyalthia korinthii, Stenosiphonium cordifolium*
	Herbs	*Barleria mysorense*
Plant Communities[4]	(i) *Manilkara-Chloroxylon-Eugenia-Vitex/Drypetes* (ii) *Manilkara/Drypetes* (iii) *Alseodaphne-Berrya-Diospyros*	

Table 9. Lowland semi-deciduous woodland/thornshrub. [1]W = effective temperature, M = equability, S = effective precipitation, Bailey (1958, 1960); [2]Perera (1975), Holmes (1958); [3]Koelmeyer (1958a, 1985b); [4]De Rosayro (1950), Holmes (1958), Nisbet (1961), Greller *et al.* (1987), Gunatilleke and Gunatilleke (1980).

Characteristic	Description	
Sri Lanka Forest Type (Walter 1985 equivalent)	Semi-deciduous Woodland/Thornshrub (ZB II/2)	
Location	Lowlands of the arid zone, e.g. Jaffna, Kankesanturai, Mannar, Puttalam	
Climate[1]	Torrid/hot (W = 23.0-24.7°C) Subtemperate (M = 39-42) Subhumid (S = 5.2-7.3 inches)	
Physiognomy[2]	Low woodland, 9 m tall; trees scattered, with broad crowns; understory of thorny shrubs; lianas well developed	
Dominant or Characteristic Flora[3]	Canopy	*Manilkara hexandra* (evergreen dominant), *Sapium insigne* (deciduous); *Sapindus emarginatus, Strychnos potatorum*
	Treelets and Shrubs	*Diospyros ferrea, Randia dumetorum, Dichrostachys cinerea, Flueggia leucopyrus, Carissa spinarum, Gymnosporia emarginata, Azima tetracantha, Memecylon umbellatum, Cassia auriculata*
	Lianas and climbers	*Cissus quadrangularis, Abrus praecatorius, Hugonia mystax*
	Herbs	*Sansevieria zeylanica, Aloe barbadensis, Vicoa indica, Eragrostis viscosa, Dactylotsenium aegyptium*
Plant Communities[4]	(i) *Manilkara/Randia*	

Table 10. Some climate statistics of zonal forests in Sri Lanka. [1]Sri Lanka Department of Meteorology (1971) (all stations 1931-1960, except Bandirippuwa Est. 1960-1980); [2]WM = average temperature, warmest month, CM = average temperature, coldest month, A = annual range of average monthly temperatures, T = average annual temperature; [3,4]W = effective temperature, M = equability, Bailey (1960); [5]S = effective precipitation, Bailey (1958); [6]Temperatures estimated from Ratnapura; [7]Precipitation at Carney Estate, elev. 305 m; Precipitation at Hapugastenne Estate, 595 m elev.

ZONOBIOME	STATION[1] (elevation in m)	WM (°C)	CM (°C)	A	T	W[3] (°C)	M[4]	Ppt. S[5] (mm)	(in.)
Mesophyllous evergreen dipterocarp (ZB I/1)	Colombo (7.3)	27.9	26.1	1.8	26.9	24.7	42	2395	13.0
	Galle (8.5)	27.5	25.8	1.7	26.6	24.2	42	2513	13.8
	Ratnapura (34.4)	28.1	26.4	1.7	27.2	25.0	42	3888	20.6
Mesophyllous evergreen mixed (ZB I/2)	Badulla (670)	24.4	21.2	3.2	23.1	20.5	50	1791	11.8
	Bandirippuwa Est. (n.a.)	28.3	26.4	1.9	27.4	24.8	41	1935	10.3
	Kandy (477)	26.0	23.1	2.9	24.1	21.5	48	2022	12.4
	Kurunegala (116)	28.2	25.6	2.6	27.0	23.8	42	2075	11.2
Notophyllous evergreen dipterocarp (OB I/1-1)	Dolosbage (954)	22.4	20.4	2.0	21.4	20.0	55	5007	34.6
	Norton Bridge (transitional, 893)	22.8	20.8	2.0	21.8	20.2	55	5394	36.6
Notophyllous evergreen mixed (OB I/2-1)	Diyatalawa (1247)	21.4	18.2	3.2	20.2	18.3	59	1731	13.0
	Passara (1006)	22.7	19.2	3.5	21.3	19.0	55	2274	16.0
	Talawakelle (n.a.)	19.8	18.2	1.6	18.7	17.9	67	2212	17.5
Microphyllous evergreen dipterocarp (OB I/1-2)	Carney Est.[6,7] (1525)	18.9	17.5	1.4	18.2	17.5	69	5535	44.0
	Hapugastenne Est.[6,7] (1525)	18.9	17.5	1.4	18.2	17.5	69	5123	40.7
Microphyllous evergreen mixed (OB I/2-2)	Nuwara Eliya (1847)	16.7	14.3	2.4	15.4	15.0	84	2163	19.4
Semi-deciduous forest (ZB II/1)	Amparai (27)	29.3	25.2	4.1	27.6	23.0	40	1879	10.2
	Anuradhapura (93)	28.7	24.6	4.1	27.3	22.8	41	1447	8.0
	Batticaloa (3)	29.5	25.3	4.2	27.4	22.1	41	1705	9.5
	Trincomalee (3)	29.9	25.5	4.4	27.9	23.0	40	1727	9.4
Semi-deciduous woodland/ thornshrub (ZB II/2)	Hambantota (15)	21.9	26.0	1.9	27.1	24.7	42	1075	5.8
	Jaffna (4)	29.4	25.3	4.1	27.6	23.0	40	1329	7.3
	Kankesanturai (15)	30.2	26.1	4.1	28.2	23.4	39	1252	6.8
	Mannar (4)	29.5	26.0	3.5	27.8	23.1	40	967	5.2
	Puttalam (2)	28.7	25.5	3.2	27.3	23.4	42	1110	6.0

Figure 1. Nomograph (Bailey, 1960) of warmth (W), growing period in days (t_d) and equability (M) of weather stations representing three forest zones (subzones). The stations are listed in Table 10. Numbers 1-4 represent ZB I/2 (mesophyllous evergreen mixed); 5-7 represent OB I/2-1 (notophyllous evergreen mixed);, 8 (Nuwara Eliya) represents OB I/2-2 (microphyllous evergreen mixed). Code: A, annual range of average monthly temperatures (°C); T = average annual temperature (°C); W (°C) = (8T+14A)/8+A, M = 109-30 log $[(14-T)^2 + (1.46+0.366A)^2]$; M is a rating of temperateness from 0-100 (supertemperate or constant) (Greller and Balasubramaniam, 1988).

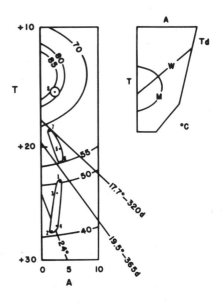

Figure 2. Moisture provinces and effective precipitation (Bailey 1958) of weather stations for 6 subzonal forests of Sri Lanka. Dashed lines (- - -) are boundaries of moisture provinces. Bailey calculated moisture provinces in inches, so that 4.7-8.7 inches (11.9-22.1 cm) delimit the subhumid province, 8.7-16.2 inches (22.1-41.1 cm) delimit the humid province and > 16.2 inches (> 41.1 cm) is the lower limit of the perhumid province. MT (*Manilkara-Thornshrub*) is referred to in the present study as semi-deciduous woodland/ thornshrub (ZB II/2).

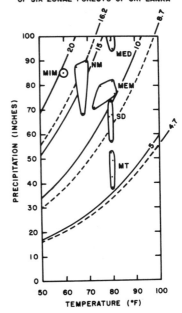

MOISTURE PROVINCES AND EFFECTIVE PRECIPITATION
OF SIX ZONAL FORESTS OF SRI LANKA

MEM = MESOPHYLLOUS EVERGREEN MIXED
NM = NOTOPHYLLOUS EVERGREEN MIXED
MIM = MICROPHYLLOUS EVERGREEN MIXED
MED = MESOPHYLLOUS EVERGREEN DIPTEROCARP
SD = SEMI-DECIDUOUS
MT = MANILKARA-THORNSHRUB

71

Figure 3. Mixed dipterocarp stand, including *Doona affinis, Doona trapezifolia, Mesua nagassarium* var. *pulchella*, as well as *Anisophyllea, Syzygium, Palaquium,* and other species of *Doona.* Elevation 305 m; Sinharaja Forest Reserve, Kalutara District; early December 1984. (ZB I/1).

Figure 4. *Artocarpus nobilis*-dominated stand; trunks are covered with *Drynaria*, a fern; other large trees recorded nearby are: *Filicium, Elaeocarpus, Caryota, Nephelium, Ficus.* In the understory are *Rejouia* and *Angiopteris evecta.* Elevation 476 m; Udawattekele Sanctuary, Kandy District; 29 December 1984. (ZB I/2).

Figure 5. *Doona gardneri* emergents over *Stemnoporus oblongifolius*-dominated canopy. Other trees are: *Gordonia speciosa, Mastixia, Syzygium, Calophyllum, Elaeocarpus, Bhesa, Ternstroemia.* Shrub layer includes: *Gaertnera, Agrostistachys, Indocalamus, Smilax, Strychnos.* Elevation 1326 m; Fishing Hut, Moray Estate, Maskeliya, Nuwara Eliya District; 19 August 1984. (OB I/1-1).

Figure 6. Interior view downhill of *Doona garneri*-dominated stand. Trees are approximately 20 m tall; small trees in the area include: *Euodia, Gyrinops, Litsea, Cinnamomum, Stemonoporus, Wormia triquetra. Agrostistachys* is a common shrub in the area.*Lindsaea lancea* is the dominant herbaceous plant; *Leucobryum* is the common moss. Elevation 1280 m; SW side of Aberfoyle Ridge on road from Bulutota Circuit Bungalow to Kadamuduna Peak, Deniyaya Range, Ratnapura District; 29 August 1984. (OB I/1-1).

Figure 7. Notophyllous evergreen mixed stand with *Nephelium longan* (human figure) and *Fahrenheitia zeylanica*; other trees nearby are: *Meliosma, Myristica dactyloides, Ficus microcarpa, Cryptocarya wightiana, Nothopegia beddomei*. Elevation 1295 m; Kabaragala Elamulla Estate, near Padiyapellala, Nuwara Eliya District; August 1984. (OB I/1-1).

Figure 8. *Doona gardneri* forms emergent stratum over a canopy of mixed taxa, including: *Gordonia, Acronychia, Calophyllum, Palaquium rubiginosum, Actinodaphne speciosa, Timonius, Syzygium, Cinnamomum ovalifolium*. Understory plants include: *Agrostistachys, Coffea*. Elevation 1600 m; saddle below Meriocotta Peak, Fairlawn Estate, Upcot, Nuwara Eliya District; 16 August 1984. (transitional OB I/1-2).

Figure 9. *Stemonoporus gardneri-*
dominated stand, with *Palaquium*
rubiginosum. Strobilanthes is
dominant in the understory with
Coleus and a bamboo. Elevation is
1554 m; near Adam's Peak, above
Carney Estate, Ratnapura District,
near Seethagangula;
28 February 1985. (OB I/1-2).

Figure 10. Low forest (ca. 7 m tall) of *Calophyllum walkeri* and a mixture of dominants including
Cinnamomum ovalifolium, Actinodaphne, and *Litsea;* understory includes *Cyathea,* a tree fern.
Elevation is 1890 m; above Poojagoda Division, Frotoft Group, Weddemulle Estate, Ramboda, Nuwara
Eliya District; 12 August 1984. (OB I/2-2).

Figure 11. Semi-deciduous forest. Emergent trees include *Schleichera, Chloroxylon, Diospyros ebenum*, above a canopy of *Drypetes*. Elevation is ca. 90 m; near Vatadage in Polonnaruwa, Polonnaruwa District; 24 December 1980. (ZB II/1).

Figure 12. Semi-deciduous woodland/thornshrub stand; trees are 15 m tall and occupy 60% of canopy space. Dominant is *Manilkara hexandra*. Other trees are *Sapium insigne, Sapindus emarginatus, Lepisanthus tetraphylla, Bauhinia racemosa, Ixora arborea* and *Diospyros ferrea*. Understory treelets and shrubs include: *Salvadora, Randia, Flueggia, Dichrostachys, Scutia, Gmelina, Acalypha; Opilia* is a common liane. Elevation is ca. 15 m; 3 km N of Illuppaikkadarai, on the road to Poonarkary, Mannar District; 25 March 1981. (ZB II/2).

Figure 13. *Manilkara hexandra* trunk and lower branches, in an island of semi-deciduous woodland/thornshrub, surrounded by villu grassland. Elevation is ca. 15 m; at Yala National Park, Yala, Hambantota District; August 1981. (ZB II/2).

Proceedings of the International and Interdisciplinary Symposium
ECOLOGY AND LANDSCAPE MANAGEMENT IN SRI LANKA
W. Erdelen, C. Preu, N. Ishwaran, C.M. Madduma Bandara (eds.)
Colombo, Sri Lanka, 12-26 March 1990
© 1993
Margraf Scientific Books, D-97985 Weikersheim
ISBN 3-8236-1182-8

Phytosociological Studies of Mid-Elevational (Lower Montane) Evergreen Forests in Sri Lanka

A.H.M. JAYASURIYA, A.M. GRELLER, S. BALASUBRAMANIAM,

C.V.S. GUNATILLEKE, I.A.U.N. GUNATILLEKE AND M.D. DASSANAYAKE

Abstract

Mid-elevational evergreen mixed forests (MEM) occur within the 900-1400 m elevation belt in the three main mountain massifs of Sri Lanka. The floristic composition of this forest type was quantitatively investigated and the important constituent species were determined. A total of 120 species of flowering plants in 80 genera and 40 families were recorded. Of these, 49 species (41%) were endemic to Sri Lanka. MEM forests were heterogeneous in their floristic composition, and they mainly comprised taxa common in the lowland wet zone. Species from the montane evergreen forests were found to a markedly lesser degree. The occurrence of *Doona* spp. at certain sites represented a variation of the MEM forests, apparently influenced by specific environmental factors. Areas under MEM forests have been widely used for the cultivation of cardamom (*Elettaria cardamomum*), which has seriously disturbed a forest type that is rich in endemics. Numerous understory taxa and perhaps some canopy taxa were absent from many sampled stands.

Introduction

In Southeast Asia, striking differences in the composition of evergreen angiosperm forests at different elevations have been documented (Brown, 1919). Robbins (1968) suggested that the upper elevational limit of lowland rain forest in tropical latitudes be recognized at the 1000 m (3280 ft) contour. Grubb (1971) correlated the boundary between the lowland tropical rain forest and lower montane rain forest (warm temperate, oak-laurel forest) with the 20-22°C isotherm of mean annual temperature. Webb (1959) proposed the term "notophyll" (2025-4500 mm^2) to describe the small mesophyll leaves that are characteristic of "subtropical rain forest" in

Australia. Greller and Balasubramaniam (1988) showed that notophyllous leaf size is also characteristic of lower montane forests in Sri Lanka.

In Southern India, Champion and Seth (1968) noted that the change in composition from lowland tropical evergreen to "montane temperate [evergreen] forests" is subtle. Their montane subtropical forest appears to reflect only a "falling off in the luxuriance of the [lowland] forest," and not the presence of a "characteristic subtropical flora," as it is presented in Southeast Asia. Chandrasekharan (1962a, 1962b, 1962c) listed the following genera as characteristic of lower montane forests at 1220-1525 m (4000-5000 ft) in Kerala State in southwestern India: *Beilschmiedia, Diospyros, Elaeocarpus, Myristica, Dimocarpus, Palaquium, Cinnamomum, Cullenia* and *Mesua*.

For Sri Lanka, Gaussen *et al.* (1968) summarized information on lower montane forests (900-1500 m). They described the forests as of "lower size" without the "emergents" of the lowland forests, and as having upper elevation species and "in particular the family Lauraceae" being present in large numbers. Werner (1984) characterized forests in this elevational zone as reaching 20-35 m with small mesophyll leaves and covered by lianas and root-climbers. Gaussen *et al.* (1968) listed the following genera as characteristic of the best-developed in these forests: *Doona, Palaquium, Homalium, Calophyllum, Syzygium, [Bhesa], Cullenia, Mastixia, Myristica, Cryptocarya, Neolitsea* and *Celtis* in the canopy, and *Carallia, [Dillenia], Semecarpus, Acronychia, Cinnamomum, Litsea* and *Meliosma* in the subcanopy layer.

Greller and Balasubramaniam (1980) recognized two subzones of mid-elevational (lower montane) forests in Sri Lanka. They gave floristic lists for both types (Balasubramaniam and Greller, 1981). One type, i.e. the mid-elevational evergreen mixed (MEM), was dominated by a mixture of families (*Myristicaceae, Lauraceae, Euphorbiaceae, Anacardiaceae, Myrtaceae,* etc). The other, namely the mid-elevational evergreen dipterocarp type, was dominated by *Doona* (*Dipterocarpaceae*), with fewer subdominant families. Werner (1984) distinguished a *Myristica*-forest from a *Doona*-forest as two of four subdivisions of rain forests.

In this study, we present quantitative data on the arborescent composition of 10 stands of mid-elevational forests that are dominated by a mixture of families. Pure stands of *Doona gardneri* were excluded from our samples, although stands that contain *Doona* as a major dominant were included. These are the first quantitative data for lower montane forests in Sri Lanka.

Study Area

Study areas were located in the three general mountain massifs of the island, namely, the central highlands, the Knuckles Range and the Rakwana Range. Sample areas at Loolkandura (Kandy District) and Kabaragala (Nuwara Eliya District) represented the central highlands. Brae and Midcar (Matale District), Corbet's Gap, Rangala and Woodside (Kandy District) represented the Knuckles Range. Hayes (Ratnapura District) represented the Rakwana Range (Fig. 1).

All sites (Tab. 1, annexed) were underlain by metamorphic rocks of the Highland Series, that date back to the Middle Pre-Cambrian Age (Cooray, 1984). Soils on the sites were reddish brown latosols (Moorman and Panabokke 1961, Whitmore 1984). The sites were located on gentle to moderately steep slopes at 1000-1350 m altitude. Climatic data (Tab. 2), obtained from some stations close to the study areas, were compiled from Mueller-Dombois (1968). Greller and Balasubramaniam (1988) analyzed the climates of three stations they consider representative of their notophyllus evergreen mixed forest, i.e. Diyatalawa (1247 m), Passara (1006 m) and Talawakelle (1220 m). They characterized the climate at mid-elevations in Sri Lanka as very warm, temperate to very temperate and perhumid.

The sampled forests measured between 15 m and 20 m in height with occasional emergents reaching 30 m. Canopy was closed and a subcanopy layer was evident. In the Loolkandura and Hayes areas where *Doona* species were present (Figs. 2-4, annexed), the characteristic cauliflower- or mushroom-like crowns could be recognized from a distance.

The MEM forests apparently were the choice land for cardamon (*Elettaria cardamomum*) cultivation. The main conditions favoring cardamom cultivation in this mid-elevational belt are temperatures lower than in lowlands, moisture and shade. In accessible areas in the mid-elevational belt between 900 m and 1500 m undisturbed forests were scarce. All areas which were investigated were cultivated with cardamom; natural undergrowth was largely absent. However, moderately dense undergrowth was observed in adjacent patchy forests, especially on steep slopes. A number of rare shrubs and herbs were encountered in this understory vegetation. It is likely that all of our stands were "second-growth" types, with trees of much smaller diameter than are present in "old growth" stands in the Western Ghats of South India (K. Balasubramanyan, pers. comm.).

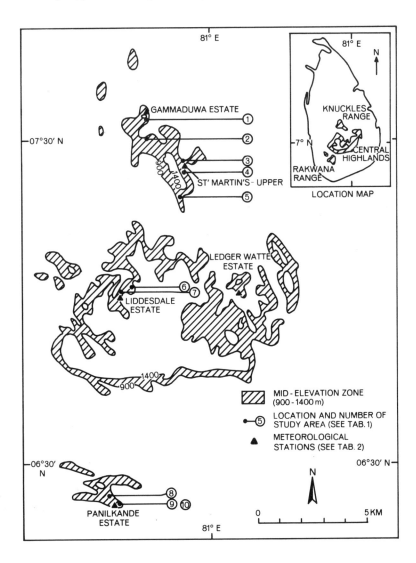

Figure 1. Potential MEM Zone (approximate elevation 900-1400 m) showing the location of study areas in the three mountain massifs of Sri Lanka. Inset is an outline map of Sri Lanka showing major geographical coordinates and mountain ranges (shaded).

Table 2. Climate data obtained from some stations close to the study areas (Mueller-Dombois, 1968). Stations 1, 3 and 5 are extraterritorial to MEM Zone.

Station	Location	Altitude (m)	Mean Annual Temperature (°C)	Mean Rainfall (mm)
1. Gammaduwa Estate	Knuckles Range 80°42'E 7°34'N	290	25.7	2480
2. St. Martin's Upper	Knuckles Range 80°50'E 7°24'N	1091	20.1	4024
3. Liddesdale Estate	Central Highlands 80°51'E 7°02'N	1560	17.3	2287
4. Ledger Watte Estate	Central Highlands 81°00'E 7°01'N	1030	20.9	2610
5. Panilkande Estate	Rakwana Range 80°37'E 6°22'N	545	24.5	3362

Methods

Each site was sampled by at least one belt transect of 100 m x 5 m, located more or less parallel to the contour of the land. Individuals over 10 cm diameter at breast height (dbh) within each belt transect were measured. If a given transect did not contain at least 100 individuals, the investigation was extended beyond 100 m until sufficient numbers of individuals were recorded. Representative specimens of all species encountered were collected for identification in the herbarium. Duplicate specimens were deposited at the National Herbarium, at the University of Peradeniya in Peradeniya, at Queens College of the City University of New York, at the Arnold Arboretum of the Harvard University in Massachusetts, and at the Missouri Botanical Garden in St. Louis.

Results

The arborescent components over 10 cm dbh in all sites which were investigated are listed in Table 3 (annexed). 120 species belonging to 80 genera and 40 families were recorded. Of these, 49 (41%) were endemic to Sri Lanka. Table 4 (annexed) summarizes data for the 10 stands by ranking the most important species in order of decreasing importance value index (IVI) where IVI = (% basal area + % density)/2. A prominent species, *Myristica dactyloides*, was ranked first in two stands and second in one other sample. Often highly ranked, though rarely ranked first, were the following species: *Fahrenheitia zeylanica* (ranked second three times), *Nothopegia beddomei, Calophyllum acidus, Syzygium* spp. *Elaeocarpus glandulifer* and *Semecarpus nigro-viridis. Doona* spp. *(D. gardneri* and *D. zeylanica)* were also ranked first in two samples and second in another. *Myristica* played a smaller role in those stands. *Cryptocarya wightiana* reached its highest values in two of the *Doona*-dominated samples. *Acronychia pedunculata* (2), *Hortonia floribunda* (2), *Dillenia triquetra, Aporosa fusiformis, Cinnamomum litseaefolium, Stemonurus tetrandrus, Evodia lunu-ankenda,* and *Tricalysia erythrosperma* appeared to be important only in the *Doona*-dominated samples. Observations in certain parts of the MEM forests that were devoid of *Doona*, indicated that *Achronychia, Hortonia, Dillenia, Cinnamomum, Stemonurus* and *Euodia* occurred irregularly there.

Perhaps the most distinctive of the sample sites that did not have either *Myristica* or *Doona* as important taxa was site number 4. In that site only two of the aforementioned important species were found (*Elaeocarpus* and *Syzygium*). Genera that were important in site 4 were not important in other sites: *Prunus, Gordonia, Rapanea* and *Fagraea*. Similarly in site number 2, *Schefflera racemosa* was a major dominant species (Tab. 4, annexed), although only a few individuals occurred. *Ficus* species were important in stands 1 and 5 but were restricted to a few large individuals. Stands 9 and 10 are similar at the 53.2% level (Fig. 5). They were adjacent stands on slightly different upland habitats. Stands 7 and 8 showed 34.7% similarity; both occurred on overly well-drained sites. Stands 1 and 3 had 32% similarity and represented steep sites on deep soils. In the dendrogram, stands 4 and 6 were the most distinctive from each other, as well as from the other stands. Stand 4 was floristically distinct, and it was the most dry and rocky site that was sampled. Stand 6 was the only one dominated by *Doona gardneri*, a major dominant in locations where precipitation was highest in Sri Lanka. Stands 5 and 2, as already noted, were nearly as distinctive as 4 and 6.

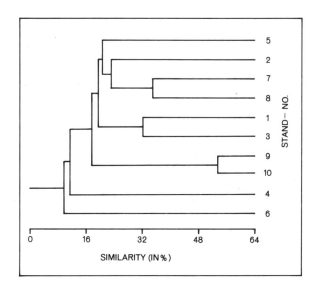

Figure 5. Dendrogram generated by the UPGMA method (SAS 1985) relating the 10 sampled stands by percentage similarity, using the Sørensen formula.

As stands were selected for convenience of access, and the range of variation was unknown, it was not possible to fully characterize the contribution of individual species to the MEM forest. Table 5 is a preliminary assessment of the relative contributions of the sampled species to the composition of this forest type. Dominance was ranked by species frequency, maximum basal area and average basal area (when present in a sample). Despite the rather wide diversity among samples in species ranked first in IVI, 11 species might be considered major dominants ($\geq$ 5% basal area) that occur in at least 5 stands. These species were *Elaeocarpus glandulifer, Myristica dactyloides, Fahrenheitia zeylanica, Nothopegia beddomei, Acronychia pedunculata, Semecarpus nigro-viridis, Cryptocarya wightiana, Hortonia floribunda, Palaquium hinmolpedde, Aglaia congylos* and *Litsea gardneri*. One, *Elaeocarpus glandulifer*, occurred in all 10 stands (although it was ranked first in only one). When the dominant species were ranked in this manner, *Doona gardneri* and *Doona zeylanica* cannot be included in the list of dominants characterizing MEM forests. They were restricted to only three stands and, although usually first or second dominants in these stands (Tab. 4, annexed), they were completely absent from the others. Assessment of species dominance in Table 5 supported the recognition of the *Doona* spp. as marginal to the mid-elevational forests which comprise dominants from several families.

Table 5. Dominant species in MEM quadrats ranked by number of stands, maximum basal area, and average basal area (≥ 5% basal area in at least one stand).

	Species	Family	No. Stands	Max. % basal area	Ave. % b.a. where present
1.	*Elaeocarpus glandulifer*	Elaeocarpaceae	10	21.9	6.5
2.	*Myristica dactyloides*	Myristicaceae	9	35.9	8.7
3.	*Fahrenheitia zeylanica*	Euphorbiaceae	9	12.7	5.9
4.	*Nothopegia beddomei*	Anacardiaceae	9	5.6	2.5
5.	*Acronychia pedunculata*	Rutaceae	8	12.2	2.5
6.	*Semecarpus nigro-viridis*	Anacardiaceae	8	9.1	2.6
7.	*Cryptocarya wightiana*	Lauraceae	7	19.4	6.0
8.	*Hortonia floribunda*	Monimiaceae	6	5.2	2.1
9.	*Palaquium hinmolpedde*	Sapotaceae	5	19.3	4.9
10.	*Aglaia congylos*	Meliaceae	5	9.8	3.1
11.	*Litsea gardneri*	Lauraceae	5	7.8	3.3
12.	*Prunus ceylanica*	Rosaceae	4	16.4	4.7
13.	*Bhesa montana*	Celastraceae	4	15.9	5.1
14.	*Calophyllum acidus*	Clusiaceae	4	12.6	7.2
15.	*Gordonia ceylanica*	Theaceae	4	8.2	4.2
16.	*Canthium coromandelicum*	Rubiaceae	4	5.3	1.9
17.	*Flacourtia inermis*	Flacourtiaceae	4	5.0	2.4

Discussion

When the dominant species were analyzed by frequency and percentage basal area (Tab. 5), it was clear that a number of families contributed to arborescent composition: Elaeocarpaceae, Myristicaceae, Euphorbiaceae, Anacardiaceae, Rutaceae, Lauraceae, Monimiaceae, Sapotaceae, Meliaceae, Rosaceae, Celastraceae, Clusiaceae, Theaceae, Rubiaceae, and Flacourtiaceae. Anacardiaceae and Lauraceae were represented by 2 species, both listed in the first 11. Myrtaceae (represented by many species of *Syzygium*) and Moraceae (represented by a few species of *Ficus*) probably should also be included in the list of dominant families. These data supported the categorization, mid-elevational evergreen mixed [families] forest (MEM), proposed by Greller and Balasubramaniam (1980). Differences among the 10 samples appeared not to be related to geographical area, viz. the Knuckles Range, central highlands and Rakwana Range. Rather, they were probably related to edaphic (soil depth) and climatic (rainfall) factors. We consider MEM the major forest type of the elevational belt between 900 m and 1400 m. It represents optimum vegetation on well-drained uplands lacking extremes of soil types under regional climatic conditions that are less moist than in dipterocarp forests. MEM forests usually occur between lowland evergreen mixed forest and the montane evergreen mixed forest belts.

Species that were either common or relatively rare in our samples but were largely restricted to MEM stands should be designated, tentatively, as "indicator species": *Aglaia congylos, Cinnamomum litseaefolium, Elaeocarpus glandulifer, Palaquium hinmolpedde* (all endemic to Sri Lanka). Other species that were dominants in our MEM samples were wide ranging in evergreen forests of Sri Lanka, although nowhere as important as they were in MEM stands: *Myristica dactyloides* and *Fahrenheitia zeylanica* (also in lowland forests), *Acronychia pedunculata* (sea level to 1600 m), and *Semecarpus nigro-viridis* (lowland evergreen and, locally, semi-evergreen forests).

In comparison with the previous characterization of the MEM forest type (Balasubramaniam and Greller, 1981), the role of species such as *Acronychia pedunculata, Elaeocarpus glandulifer, Nothopegia beddomei, Palaquium hinmolpedde* and *Semecarpus nigro-viridis* was firmly supported by the present study. On the other hand species such as *Actinodaphne* spp. *Cullenia rosayroana, Eurya japonica, Helicia zeylanica, Litsea gardneri, Neolitsea fuscata* and *Turpinia malabarica* were shown to be of lesser importance.

The other subzone of the mid-elevational belt was represented mainly by *Doona gardneri* stands. The distinctiveness of this type was supported by observations of Ashton (1980) and Werner (1984) which showed that *Doona gardneri* was often the sole upper canopy species. Werner (1984) mapped the present distribution of *Doona gardneri* forests as continuous in the Peak Wilderness, and as widely scattered in the western part of the central highlands and local in the Rakwana Range between 900 m and 1525 m. Where *Doona* spp. *(D. gardneri, D. zeylanica, D. oblonga)* occurred in our samples, they were usually major dominants and appeared to be co-dominated by a few taxa that were less important *(Cryptocarya, Calophyllum)* or absent *(Stemonurus, Aporosa)* in the other samples. Many species, although they occurred in small numbers, were encountered only in samples dominated by *Doona* spp. e.g. *Aporosa* spp. *Gaertnera walkeri, Hydnocarpus octandra, Memecylon* spp. *Microtropis wallichiana, Stemonurus tetrandrus* and *Syzygium lissophyllum*. Apparently, these samples represented a variation of the MEM forests. From an ecological perspective, the very local occurrence of *Doona* species in our samples might be explained by the presence of deep soils (Ashton, 1980), which would provide the wet environment usually associated with large populations of Dipterocarpaceae.

The stands that were exposed to drier parts of the MEM climatic range showed some affinities to the semi-evergreen forest (Balasubramaniam and Greller, 1981) of the "dry" (subhumid) zone, or to transitional forests of the "intermediate" (drier part of the humid) zone. The occurrence of *Dimocarpus longan, Filicium decipiens, Glycosmis angustifolia, Mallotus philippensis, M. rhamnifolius, Mangifera zeylanica* and *Pterospermum canescens*, common in northeastern regions of the Knuckles Range, indicated subnormal precipitation and/or excessive desiccation, compared to the general climatic factors of the region. None of these species occurred on sites in the Rakwana Range which indicated that the standard moisture regime prevailed there. Werner (1989) listed the following taxa as characteristic of "dry facies of lower montane rain forests" that occurred in two patches, one southwest of Wellimada, the other northeast of Badulla, in the eastern part of the central highlands: Lauraceae, especially *Cinnamomum verum, Myristica dactyloides* and *Calophyllum tomentosum* as well as *Filicium decipiens* and *Dimocarpus longan*. Recently, diameters of tree species were recorded in a forest near Maduga in the Knuckles Range, that showed some floristic affinities to drier types of lowland mixed evergreen forests. The following species showed the largest percentages of total basal area of the sample: *Syzygium spathulatum* (34%), *Semecarpus nigro-viridis* (17%), *Isonandra lanceolata* (9%), *Neolitsea cassia* (8%), *Plecosperum spinosum* (7%), *Vitex altissima* (7%), *Ficus virens* (6%), and *Eurya acuminata* (5%). Most of these genera and some of the species were recorded in our ten stands (Tabs. 3, 4, annexed). *Semecarpus nigro-viridis*, *Syzygium* spp. and *Ficus* spp. as noted earlier in this section, were dominants of our lower montane mixed forests (Tab. 4, annexed). Therefore, we consider this sample to be representative of the dry phase of the lower montane notophyllous evergreen mixed [families] type.

The widespread disturbance observed in the areas we investigated clearly encouraged the appearance of many adventive woody species. The disturbance was mainly due to the removal of undergrowth which is a prerequisite for cardamom cultivation. Wherever canopy openings were formed due to the removal of trees or their death, species such as *Callicarpa tomentosa, Macaranga peltata, Maesa perrotetiana, Mallotus tetracoccus,* and *Symplocos cochinchinensis* were seen. Several of these species occurred in the Knuckles Range, suggesting a relatively higher proportion of disturbance. Many of them are soft-wooded and fast-growing and hence are capable of establishing themselves as soon as canopy openings occur. When canopies are subsequently closed by the growth of resident trees, the weedy species disappear. *Macaranga peltata* is evidently the most common secondary species appearing in disturbed forests. Species such as *Cedrela toona, Erythrina subumbrans, Michelia champaca,* and *Toona sinensis* are escapes from cultivation. *Cedrela* and *Michelia* are popular timber trees of the region.

The floristic data (Tab. 3, annexed) suggest that MEM forests have become enriched with species migrating from the lowland "wet zone." Species such as *Carallia brachiata, Cullenia zeylanica, Hydnocarpus octandra* and *Myristica dactyloides* clearly indicate the direction of migration. On the other hand, migration from the montane evergreen forests to the MEM forests is apparently impeded by factors related to high temperatures. Rare occurrences of *Actinodaphne* spp. *Adinandra lasiopetala, Agrostistachys coriacea, Eurya nitida, Gaertnera walkeri, Gordonia zeylanica, Ilex denticulata, Isonandra montana, Michelia nilagirica, Neolitsea fuscata, Prunus ceylanica, Rapanea robusta,* and *Saprosma foetans* illustrate the feeble species richness from montane evergreen forest.

Furthermore, the species composition of MEM forests suggests Gondwanan affinities. Important families such as Myristicaceae, Sapotaceae, Euphorbiaceae, Elaeocarpaceae, Anacardiaceae, Meliaceae and Rutaceae have been shown to have had major presence in West Gondwanaland (Raven and Axelrod, 1974). Those families constitute the bulk of the present MEM woody flora, and further indicate that this is an archaic formation dating back to the Cretaceous, when the ancestors of the present groups would have migrated to this region. However, rare occurrences of genera such as *Cinnamomum, Litsea (Lauraceae), Michelia (Magnolicaceae), Symplocos (Symplocaceae)* and *Celtis (Ulmaceae)* suggest remote Laurasian relationships. This is in accordance with the widely accepted view that the Sri Lanka flora had been enriched during the Tertiary by floristic elements from Laurasian land masses in what is now the Malaysian region.

Acknowledgments

This project was funded by a Fulbright Senior Lectureship and a US National Science Foundation (NSF) grant, INT-8317600, awarded to Andrew M. Greller, who feels especially thankful to Osman Shinaishin, NSF grants officer, for excellent direction of procedures. The authors gratefully acknowledge the assistance of Janalal Rodrigo, President, Kabaragalla Estate Ltd, Elamulla, J.A.P.A. Atapattu, M.C.I.P. Manager of the Hayes State Plantation, Deniyaya, and Nihal C.I. de Silva M.C.I.P., Manager, "Hope" Tea Plantation, Hewaheta, for graciously hosting us and facilitating our study of forests under their supervision. Our thanks also go to P.S. Wijesooriya of the Land Use Division, Department of Agriculture, Peradeniya, for preparation of Figure 1 and to the following Queens College personnel: Leslie Marcus, Professor of Biology, for assistance in computer-generation of Figure 5; to Odile Garcia, Teacher of Biology, Townsend Harris High School at Queens College, for assistance in compilation of data; and to Nancy Bareis, Photographer, Multi-Media Services, for preparation of Figures 2, 3 and 4.

Literature Cited

Ashton, P.S. 1980. Dipterocarpaceae. *In* M.D. Dassanayake and F.R.Fosberg, eds. *A Revised Handbook to the Flora of Ceylon 1*, pp. 364-423. Amerind, New Delhi.

Balasubramaniam, S. and A.M. Greller. 1981. Floristic analysis of the eight zonal forest types of Sri Lanka. *Phyta (Univ.of Peradeniya, Sri Lanka)* 2: 13-20.

Brown, W.H. 1919. *Vegetation of the Philippine Mountains*. Publ. 13. Department of Agriculture Philippines and Natural Resources, Manila.

Champion, H.G. and S.K. Seth. 1968. *A Revised Survey of the Forest Types of India*. Manager of Publications, Delhi.

Chandrasekharan, C. 1962a. Forest types of Kerala State. *The Indian Forester* 88: 660-674.

Chandrasekharan, C. 1962b. Forest types of Kerala State. *The Indian Forester* 88: 731-747.

Chandrasekharan, C. 1962c. Forest types of Kerala State. *The Indian Forester* 88: 837-847.

Cooray, P.G. 1984. Geology, with special reference to the Precambrian. *In* C.H. Fernando, ed. *Ecology and Biogeography in Sri Lanka*, pp. 1-34. Junk Publ, The Hague.

Gaussen, H., P. Legris, M. Viart and L. Labroue. 1968. *Explanatory Notes on the Vegetation Map of Ceylon*. Govt. Press, Colombo.

Greller, A.M. and S. Balasubramaniam. 1980. A preliminary floristic-climatic classification of the forests of Sri Lanka. *The Sri Lanka Forester* 14: 163-170.

Grubb, P.J. 1971. Interpretation of the 'Massenerhebung' effect on tropical mountains. *Nature* 229: 44-46.

Moorman, F.R. and C.R. Panabokke. 1961. Soils of Ceylon. *Trop. Agricult. (Ceyl.)* 117: 4-65.

Mueller-Dombois, D. 1968. Ecogeographic analysis of a climate map of Ceylon with particular reference to vegetation. *The Ceylon Forester* 8: 39-58.

Raven, P.H. and D.I. Axelrod. 1974. Angiosperm biogeography and past continental movements. *Ann. Missouri Bot. Gard.* 61: 539-673.

Robbins, R.G. 1968. The biogeography of tropical rain forest in Southeast Asia. *Proc. Symp. Recent Advances Trop. Ecol., Varanasi* 2: 521-535.

SAS Institute, Inc. 1985. *User's Guide: Statistics*. 5th Edition. SAS Circle, Cary, North Carolina.

Webb, L.J. 1959. A physiognomic classification of Australian rain forests. *J. Ecol.* 47: 551-570.

Werner, W.L. 1984. Die Höhen- und Nebelwälder auf der Insel Ceylon (Sri Lanka). *Tropische und subtropische Pflanzenwelt 46*. Steiner, Wiesbaden.

Werner, W.L. 1989. Die Wälder des östlichen Hochlandes von Ceylon. *In* U. Schweinfurth, ed. *Landschaftsökologische Forschungen auf der Insel Ceylon*, pp. 43-72. Steiner, Wiesbaden.

Whitmore, T.C. 1984. *Tropical Rain Forests of the Far East*. 2nd Edition. Oxford University Press, Oxford.

Table 1. Descriptions of sampled forests.

Location	Coordinates	Altitude (m)	Site Description	Sampling Date	No. Trees	Total Basal Area (m²)	Diversity (Shannon H')
MATALE DISTRICT							
Rattota-Midlands Rd. Bambaragala Forest near Midcar Estate	80°40'E 07°31'N	1130	Steep, W-facing slope, moderately deep soil	29 March 1981	94	16.4	4.44
Brae Group, Laggala Estate	80°45'E 07°29'N	1005	N-facing slope deep soil	19 January 1981	107	9.5	4.48
KANDY DISTRICT							
Corbet's Gap, Ferndale Rd.	80°50'E 07°21'N	1215	Steep S-facing slope, deep soil	15 January 1982	99	2.9	3.75
Rangala Estate, Burnside, Division Field No. 2	80°49'E 07°20'N	1220	Hilltop, rocky eroded	20 March 1981	74	7.5	3.96
Meda-Mahanuara, Woodside Group	80°50'E 07°16'N	930	Moderately sloping to flat streamside, adjacent to steep N-facing hill	20 March 1981	64	9.1	4.53
Loolkandura Group, Kondagala Division, Field No. 4	80°42'E 07°07'N	1320	W-facing slope deep soil	25 October 1984	101	3.6	4.65
Ela-mulla, Kabaragala Estate	80°45'E 07°03'N	1350	Steep, SE-facing slope deep soil	30 October 1984	101	10.1	4.14
RATNAPURA DISTRICT							
Hayes Estate, Longford Division, Field No. 14	80°38'E 06°22'N	1035	Gentle S-facing slope	14 March 1985	99	6.9	4.54
Hayes Estate, Longford Division Field No. 4A	80°39'E 06°22'N	1050	S-facing convex slope (16°) to edge of ravine	28 August 1984	132	10.7	4.50
Hayes Estate, Longford Division Field no. 4A	80°39'E 06°22'N	1050	S-facing ravine (V-shaped valley)	29 August 1984	91	9.6	4.13

Table 3. List of species (120) recorded within belt transects at ten sites of the MEM forests in Sri Lanka.

Species	Family	Endemicity in Sri Lanka
Acronychia pedunculata (L.) Miq.	RUTACEAE	
Actinodaphne ambigua (Meissner) Hook.f	LAURACEAE	*
A. elegans Thw.	"	*
A. speciosa Nees	"	*
Adinandra lasiopetala (Wight) Choisy	THEACEAE	*
Aglaia congylos Kosterm.	MELIACEAE	*
Agrostistachys coriacea Alston	EUPHORBIACEAE	*
Allophylus varians (Thw.) Radlk.	SAPINDACEAE	*
Alphonsea zeylanica Hook.f. & Thomson	ANNONACEAE	*
Alseodaphne semecarpifolia Nees	ANACARDIACEAE	
Antidesma pyrifolium Muell. Arg.	EUPHORBIACEAE	*
A. walkeri (Tul.) Pax & Hoffm.	"	*
Aporosa acuminata Thw.	"	
A. fusiformis Thw.	"	
Bhesa ceylanica (Arn.) Ding Hou	CELASTRACEAE	*
B. montana Kosterm.	"	*
Breynia vitis-idaea (Burm.f.) C.E.C. Ficher	EUPHORBIACEAE	
Callicarpa tomentosa (L.) Murr. in L.	VERBENACEAE	
Calophyllum acidus Kosterm.	CLUSIACEAE	*
C. tomentosum Wight	"	*
C. trapezifolium Thw.	"	*
Canthium coromandelicum (Burm. f.) Alston	RUBIACEAE	
C. dicoccum (Gaertner) Merr.	"	*
Carallia brachiata (Lour.) Merr.	RHIZOPHORACEAE	
Caryota urens L.	ARECACEAE	
Casearia zeylanica (Gaertner) Thw.	FLACOURTIACEAE	
Celtis cinnamomea Lindl. ex Planch.	ULMACEAE	
Cinnamomum capparu-coronde Bl.	LAURACEAE	*
C. litsaeaefolium Thw.	"	*
C. verum Presl	"	
Cleistocalyx operculatus (Roxb.) Merr. & Perry	MYRTACEAE	
Cryptocarya wightiana Thw.	LAURACEAE	
Cullenia ceylanica (Gardn.) Schumann	BOMBACACEAE	*
C. rosayroana Kosterm.	"	*
Dillenia triquetra (Rottb.) Gilg.	DILLENIACEAE	*
Dimocarpus longan (Lour.) Leenh.	SAPINDACEAE	
Diospyros insignis Thw.	EBENACEAE	
D. racemosa Roxb.	"	
Doona gardneri Thw.	DIPTEROCARPACEAE	*
D. oblonga Thw.	"	*
D. zeylanica Thw.	"	*
Elaeocarpus glandulifer (Hook.f. ex Wight) Masters	ELAEOCARPACEAE	*
Erythrina subumbrans (Hassk.) Merr.	FABACEAE	
Euodia lunu-ankenda (Gaertner) Merr.	RUTACEAE	
Eurya acuminata DC.	THEACEAE	
E. ceylanica Wight	"	
E. nitida Korth.	"	
Fagraea obovata Wall.	LONGANIACEAE	
Fahrenheitia zeylanica (Thw.) Airy Shaw	EUPHORBIACEAE	

Species	Family	Endemicity in Sri Lanka
Ficus callosa Willd.	MORACEAE	
F. exasperata Vahl	"	
F. fergusoni King	"	
F. microcarpa L.f.	"	
F. nervosa Heyne ex Roth in Roehmer et Schultz	"	
Filicium decipiens (Wight & Arn.) Thw.	SAPINDACEAE	
Flacourtia inermis Roxb.	FLACOURTIACEAE	
Gaertnera walkeri (Arn.) Bl.	RUBIACEAE	*
Garcinia echinocarpa Thw.	CLUSIACEAE	*
G. morella (Gaertner) Desr.	"	
Gironniera scabrida (Thw.) Alston	ULMACEAE	
Glochidion pycnocarpum (Muell. Arg.) Bedd.	EUPHORBIACEAE	*
G. zeylanicum (Gaertner) A. Juss.	"	
Glycosmis angustifolia Lindl.	RUTACEAE	
Goniothalamus thwaitesii Hook.f. & Thomson	ANNONACEAE	
Gordonia ceylanica Wight	THEACEAE	*
Gyrinops walla Gaertner	THYMELAEACEAE	
Homalium zeylancium (Gardner) Benth.	FLACOURTIACEAE	
Hortonia floribunda Wight & Arn.	MONIMIACEAE	*
Hydnocarpus octandra Thw.	FLACOURTIACEAE	*
Ilex denticulata Wall. ex Wight	AQUIFOLIACEAE	
Isonandra montana (Thw.) Gamble	SAPOTACEAE	
I. zeylanica Jeuken	"	
Litsea gardneri (Thw.) Meissner	LAURACEAE	*
L. walkeri Meissner	"	*
Macaranga peltata (Roxb.) Muell. Arg.	EUPHORBIACEAE	
Maesa perrottetiana A.DC.	MYRSINACEAE	
Mallotus philippensis (Lam.) Muell. Arg.	EUPHORBIACEAE	
M. rhamnifolius (Willd.) Muell. Arg.	"	
M. tetracoccus Kurz	"	
Mangifera zeylanica (Blume) Hook.f.	ANACARDIACEAE	*
Meliosma simplicifolia (Roxb.) Walp.	SABIACEAE	
Memecylon parvifolium Thw.	MELASTOMATACEAE	*
M. sylvaticum Thw.	"	*
Michelia champaca	MAGNOLIACEAE	
M. nilagirica Zenker var. *walkeri* Hook. f. & Thomson	"	*
Microtropis wallichiana Wight ex Thw.	CELASTRACEAE	
Myristica dactyloides Gaertner	MYRISTICACEAE	
Neolitsea cassia (L.) Kosterm.	LAURACEAE	*
N. fuscata (Thw.) Alston	"	*
Nothopegia beddomei Gamble	ANACARDIACEAE	
Palaquium hinmolpedde P. Royen	SAPOTACEAE	*
P. petiolare (Thw.) Engl.	"	*
Persea macrantha (Nees) Kosterm.	LAURACEAE	
Prunus ceylanica (Wight.) Miq. var. *ceylanica* Tirvengadum	ROSACEAE	
Pseudocarapa championii (Thw.) Hemsley	MELIACEAE	*
Psychotria nigra (Gaertner) Alston var. *nigra* Sohmer	RUBIACEAE	
Pterospermum canescens Roxb.	STERCULIACEAE	
Rapanea robusta Mez	MYRSINACEAE	
Saprosma foetens (Wight) Schumann	RUBIACEAE	
Schefflera racemosa (Wight) Harms	ARALIACEAE	
Scolopia crassipes Clos	FLACOURTIACEAE	*

Species	Family	Endemicity in Sri Lanka
Semecarpus gardneri Thw.	ANACARDIACEAE	*
S. nigro-viridis Thw.	"	*
Stemonorus tetrandus (Wall.) Alston	ICACINACEAE	
Symplocos cochinchinensis (Lour.) S. Moore	SYMPLOCACEAE	
S. obtusa (Wall.) D. Don var. obtusa Nooteb.	"	
S. macrophylla (Wall.) ex DC.	"	
Syzygium amphoraecarpus Kosterm	MYRTACEAE	*
S. batadamba Kosterm.	"	*
S. caryophyllatum (L.) Alston	"	
S. gardneri Thw.	"	
S. hemisphericum (Wight) Alston	"	
S. lissophyllum Thw.	"	
S. micranthum Thw.	"	*
S. umbrosum Thw.	"	*
Toona sinensis (A. Juss.) M.J. Roemer	MELIACEAE	
Tricalysia erythrospora (Thw.) Alston	RUBIACEAE	*
Turpinia malabarica Gamble	STAPHYLEACEAE	
Vitex altissima L.f.	VERBENACEAE	
Wendlandia bicuspidata Wight & Arn.	RUBIACEAE	

Table 4. Important species (≥ 5% basal area/ ≥ 5% density by stand).

Species

Stand 1
1. *Aglaia congylos* (9.8/11.7)
2. *Myristica dactyloides* (10.3/6.4)
3. *Cullania zeylanica* (9.9/6.4)
4. *Syzygium gardneri* (7.9/7.7)
5. *Pseudocarapa championii* (7.6/7.5)
6. *Ficus callosa* (7.4/2.1)
7. *Syzygium amphoraecarpus* (7.2/2.1)
8. *Fahrenheitia zeylanica* (3.8/5.3)   4.
9. *Mallotus tetracoccus* (2.1/6.4)
10. *Cryptocarya wightiana* (2.3/5.3)

Stand 2
1. *Schefflea racemosa* (20.6/3.7)
2. *Fahrenheitia zeylanica* (8.7/12.1)
3. *Persea macarantha* (15.2/3.7)
4. *Nothopegia beddomei* (3.4/8.4)
5. *Dimocarpus longans* (4.8/6.5)
6. *Macaranga peltata* (2.1/6.5)
7. *Canthium coromandelicum* (5.3/2.8)
8. *Mallotus rhamnifolius* (0.5/1.9)
9. *Flacourtia inermis* (5.0/1.9)
10. *Symplocos cochinchensis* (0.5/5.6)

Stand 3
1. *Myristica dactyloides* (35.9/27.3)
2. *Bhesa montana* (15.9/13.1)
3. *Syzygium* sp. (10.4/7.1)
4. *Elaeocarpus glandulifer* (5.3/8.1)
5. *Neolitsea fuscata* (4.9/5.1)

Stand 4
1. *Elaeocarpus glandulifer* (21.9/13.5)
2. *Prunus ceylanica* (16.4/16.2)
3. *Gordonia ceylanica* (8.2/9.5)
4. *Syzygium gardneri* (10.9/5.4)
5. *Rapanea* sp. (8.9/6.8)
6. *Semecarpus obscura* (5.9/5.4)
7. *Fagraea ceylanica* (5.8/5.49
8. *Cinnamomum* sp. (5.9/4.1)
9. *Symplocos cochinchensis* (1.4/5.4)

Stand 5
1. *Ficus fergusonii* (22.6/3.1)
2. *Fahrenheitia zeylanica* (9.4/10.9)
3. *Syzygium amphoraecarpus* (12.0/7.8)
4. *Garcinia morella* (6.1/9.4)

Stand 6
1. *Doona gardneri* (28.0/9.9)
2. *Acronychia pedunculata* (12.2/14.8)
3. *Aporosa fusiformis* (12.2/8.9)
4. *Semecarpus nigro-viridis* (3.9/7.9)
5. *Cinnamomum litsaeaefolium* (5.6/5.0)
6. *Stemonurus tetrandrus* (6.6/4.0)
7. *Euodia lunu-ankenda* (2.1/5.9)

Stand 7
1. *Palaquium hinmolpedde* (17.8/19.3)
2. *Nothopegia beddomei* (13.9/5.6)
3. *Semecarpus nigro-viridis* (9.9/9.1)
4. *Elaeocarpus glandulifer* (4.9/12.9)
5. *Fahrenheitia zeylanica* (4.0/10.1)
6. *Litsea gardneri* (4.9/7.8)
7. *Syzygium batadamba* (4.9/5.4)
8. *Cryptocarya wightiana* (5.9/4.2)

Stand 8
1. *Myristica dactyloides* (21.1/8.1)
2. *Fahrenheitia zeylanica* (12.7/12.1)
3. *Nothopegia beddomei* (5.6/11.1)
4. *Calophyllum acidus* (4.9/6.1)
5. *Casearia zeylanica* (3.1/7.1)
6. *Scolopia crassipes* (6.2/3.0)

Stand 9
1. *Cryptocarya wightiana* (19.4/18.39
2. *Doona zeylanica* (19.6/6.9)
3. *Calophyllum acidus* (9.8/7.6)
4. *Hortonia floribunda* (2.5/8.4)
5. *Myristica dactyloides* (5.3/5.3)
6. *Dillenia triquetra* (6.2/3.0)
7. *Tricalysia erythrosperma* (2.6/5.3)
8. *Fahrenheitia zeylanica* (3.2/5.3)

Stand 10
1. *Doona zeylanica* (35.7/15.4)
2. *Cryptocarya wightiana* (8.4/13.2)
3. *Calophyllum acidus* (12.4/5.5)
4. *Hortonia floribunda* (5.2/12.1)
5. *Elaeocarpus glandulifer* (8.5/2.2)
6. *Acronychia pedunculata* (2.1/6.6)
7. *Myristica dactyloides* (2.0/5.5)

Figure 2. Forest at 1050 m elevation at Field No. 4, Longford Division, Hayes Estate, at the eastern end of the Deniyaya Range. The view is toward the east. Tea plantations occupy areas cleared of forests. Stands 9 and 10 are located in the forest at center left.

Figure 3. Profile of stand 9. Note tall specimens of *Doona zeylanica* at the left.

Figure 4. View of the interior of stand 9. Note cardamom in understory.

Proceedings of the International and Interdisciplinary Symposium
ECOLOGY AND LANDSCAPE MANAGEMENT IN SRI LANKA
W. Erdelen, C. Preu, N. Ishwaran, C.M. Madduma Bandara (eds.)
Colombo, Sri Lanka, 12-26 March 1990
© 1993
Margraf Scientific Books, D-97985 Weikersheim
ISBN 3-8236-1182-8

The Montane Forests of the Horton Plains Nature Reserve

S. BALASUBRAMANIAM, S. RATNAYEKE AND R. WHITE

Abstract

Using 5 m x 25 m plots, woody taxa of the montane forests of Horton Plains Reserve were sampled. Within plots, all individuals over 5 cm diameter at breast height were identified, measured and numbered with aluminium tags. In all, 1252 individuals were tagged. Using density, frequency and basal area, importance value indices were calculated. Floristic analysis shows that Lauraceae was the dominant family while Symplocaceae, Myrtaceae, Rubiaceae, Ericaceae and Guttiferae were other leading families. At the species level, the first five dominant taxa were *Cinnamomum ovalifolium*, *Syzygium revolutum*, *Neolitsea fuscata*, *Symplocos elegans* and *Calophyllum walkeri*. About fifty percent of the woody species enumerated were endemic to Sri Lanka. Sixty-two percent of the individuals sampled were below 15 cm in diameter and the mean density for the forests at Horton Plains was 2861 individuals per hectare.

Introduction

Tropical mountains above 1500 m and below 2500 m support evergreen forest formations called cloud forests or upper montane rain forests (Whitmore, 1984) especially in areas of high rainfall. According to Werner (1982, 1984, 1988), upper montane rain forests cover an area of approximately 400 km² in the central mountains of Sri Lanka. In 1873, an administrative order was issued by the colonial government prohibiting the clearing and felling of forests above 5000 feet (1524 m). This measure was adopted to protect the natural vegetation cover of the upper montane zone that formed the water catchment of major rivers, and also to minimize soil erosion from steep slopes above tea plantations. Botanical collections and faunal surveys of montane habitats have recorded a large number of endemic species. At present, the following areas have been designated as conservation areas in the montane zone. They are (1) the Hakgala Strict Natural Reserve (1142 ha, established in 1938), (2) the Horton Plains Nature Reserve (3162 ha, established in 1969), and (3) the Adam's Peak Wilderness Sanctuary (22,400 ha, established in 1940). Steps have been taken by the Ministry of Lands and Land Development to declare the Knuckles Area for rehabilitation, reforestation and conservation with assistance from agencies like the International Union for Conservation of Nature and Natural Resources (IUCN) and the Overseas Development Administration (ODA) of the United Kingdom. Other areas demarcated for the preservation of natural montane ecosystems and habitats are Pidurutalagala (6853 ha), Kikiliyamana (4883 ha), Pattipola (1498 ha), Seetha Eliya and Kandapola. These areas are referred to as proposed forest reserves but they do not have the status of nature reserves, and some of the sites have been partially degraded and encroached upon along their boundaries. Galways Land in Nuwara Eliya and Thangamalai near Haputale are small areas designated as sanctuaries in the montane zone. These nature reserves, sanctuaries and proposed forest reserves are shown in Figure 1.

Botanical studies of Horton Plains are largely collections and taxonomic descriptions of plants (Thwaites 1858-1864, Trimen 1893-1900, Dassanayake and Fosberg 1980-1987). Very few ecological studies have been undertaken on the montane vegetation types of Sri Lanka. Mueller-Dombois and Perera (1971) sampled the wet grasslands of Horton Plains in a study covering the different montane grasslands or patanas of Ceylon. Wijesundra *et al.* (1984) studied the montane forests of the Hakgala Natural Reserve and published an abstract of their findings. Greller *et al.* (1987) presented some quantitative data on the *Stemonoporus*-dominated forest stands of the Peak Wilderness Sanctuary and showed that these forests were floristically different from the other montane forests of Sri Lanka. Werner (1982, 1984) has published general accounts of the upper montane rain forests and also summarized human impact on the natural montane forests and the landscape of the central highlands of Sri Lanka.

Although Horton Plains has been well known among naturalists and biologists for a relatively long period of time, there has been no quantitative study of the forest formations of this high plateau. In this paper, we present quantitative data of the structure and floristic composition of relatively undisturbed stands of montane forests of this nature reserve. During field work observations were also made on some forest patches showing dieback. These field observations were matched with recent aerial photographs of the study sites. Based on these preliminary data, we present our views of the possible causes of canopy dieback in the montane forests of the Horton Plains Nature Reserve.

Physical Features, Climate and Vegetation of Horton Plains

The Horton Plains Nature Reserve lies south of Nuwara Eliya (6°47'-6°50'N; 80°46'-80°51'E) in the central montainous part of Sri Lanka. The plains occupy a plateau at the southern edge of the main ridge of the anchor shaped central highlands (Figs 1, 2). It forms the highest tableland in Sri Lanka, and the altitude of the reserve ranges from 2100 m to 2300 m. Kirigalpota (2395 m) and Totapolakanda (2359 m) are two peaks within this reserve. The plains were named in honor of Sir Robert Horton, a former British Governor of Ceylon. The nature reserve occupies an area of approximately 3160 ha, and it is contiguous with the eastern part of the Peak Wilderness Sanctuary (Fig. 1). Tributaries of the Mahaweli Ganga and the Walawe Ganga originate within the Horton Plains Reserve. Belihul Oya drains southwards and joins the Walawe Ganga. The north-flowing streams join to form the Uma Oya. The Bogawantalawa Oya and other westerly flowing streams feed the Castlereigh Reservoir and also drain into the tributaries of the Kelani Ganga and the Mahaweli Ganga. The Walawe Ganga, the Mahaweli Ganga and the Kelani Ganga have been harnessed for major irrigation and hydroelectric power generation projects, and the Horton Plains Nature Reserve Area and the Peak Wilderness Sanctuary serve as important water catchments for these river systems.

No long-term climatic records are available for the Horton Plains. Nuwara Eliya (1895 m), which is situated at a slightly lower elevation has a mean annual rainfall of 2153 mm. The rainfall is fairly well distributed, but dry weather prevails during the months of January and February. During these two months the day temperatures at Nuwara Eliya and the Horton Plains can be as high as 27°C while the night temperatures drop to 5°C. Mueller-Dombois and Perera (1971) give 12°C as the mean February temperature for Horton Plains. Nocturnal

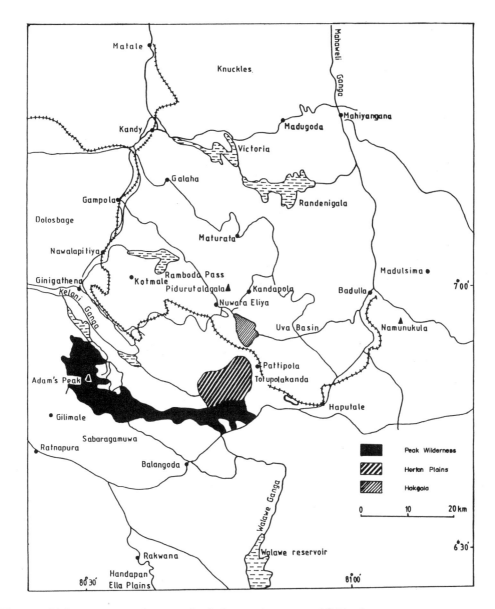

Figure 1. Major reserves and sanctuaries in the montane zone of Sri Lanka.

ground frosts normally occur in February at the Horton Plains, but these are more frequent on open grasslands. The mean annual temperature recorded for the humid lowlands of Sri Lanka is 27°C, while the mean annual temperature for Nuwara Eliya is 15.4°C. Fog occurs frequently during the early afternoons and it may persist throughout the whole day during the wet season at the Horton Plains. Strong winds are common during the southwest monsoon period. On sharp ridge crests the strong winds reach gale force and bring about a stunting of the forests.

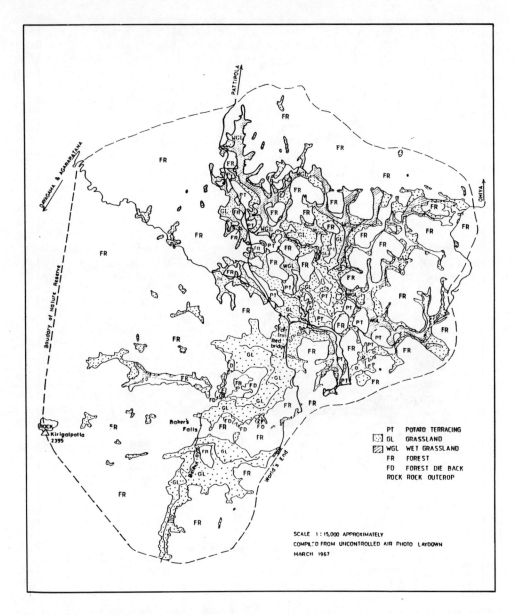

Figure 2. The Horton Plains National Park.

In 1961 a potato seed station was established at the Horton Plains, but this scheme was abandoned in 1969 due to protests from environmentalists and conservationists. The aftereffects of ploughing and terracing are still evident within the reserve. In 1969, this area was declared a nature reserve, and at present it has the status of a national park. The major vegetation cover types of the plains are vast expanses of undulating montane grasslands, also called wet black patanas and low stature evergreen cloud forests. The elevational differences between knolls and depressions are not very great. The low-lying areas and depressions are occupied by wet or water-logged swamp communities and slow-flowing streams. The ploughed up grasslands have been colonized by successional grass and forb species. The disturbed forest margins and some other sites are colonized by indigenous and exotic shrubs and climbers. Man-made fires are not uncommon during the dry months of February and early March. Extensive burning of the grasslands occurred in 1980 and 1989. The severe fires in 1980 spread to some forest patches killing many woody species and these burnt forest patches can be identified in the recent areial photographs of the Horton Plains. The burnt grasslands quickly recover with the onset of rains in late March or April.

In the slow-flowing streams of the Horton Plains, aquatic macrophytes like *Aponogeton jacobsenii*, the sedge *Isolepis fluitans* and a bladderwort *Utricularia* sp. are to be found. Along stream banks the bamboo *Arundinaria densifolia* forms dense thickets. In water-logged depressions and swampy areas, the rush *Juncus primatocarpus*, the grass *Garnotia mutica*, the ferns *Dennstaedtia scabra*, *Eriocaulon* spp. and *Exacum macranthum* are common species. The vast expanse of rolling grasslands of the Horton Plains are dominated by the grass species *Arundinella villosa* and *Chrysopogon zeylanicum*. Other species growing in association with the two dominant grass species are *Cyanotis pilosa*, *Osbeckia parvifolia*, *Anaphalis brevifolia*, *Wahlenbergia marginata*, *Emilia speeseae* (*E. scabra*) and the bracken fern *Pteridium aquilinum*. Grasslands ploughed up for potato cultivation and abandoned about twenty years ago have been colonized by many Gramineae and Compositae. Also naturalized herbs like *Rumex acetosella*, *Hydrochoeris radicata*, *Aristea ecklonii* and *Polygonum* spp. are common in successional grassland communities and along roadside clearings, trails and other disturbed sites. Periodically burnt grassland patches and the margin of some forests have scattered clumps of *Rhododendron arboreum* forming a savanna-like community. *Gaultheria fragrantissima*, *Hypericum mysorense* and *Rhodomyrtus tomentosa* are woody species found along forest margins and the savanna. Sun-loving shrubs and scramblers that are common along forest margins and clearings are *Berberis aristata* (*B. tinctoria*), *Elaeagnus latifolia*, *Osbeckia* spp. and *Rubus* spp. Many of the disturbed sites and clearings have been invaded by naturalized herbs and shrubs such as *Aristea ecklonii*, *Eupatorium riparium*, *Cestrum elegans*, *Tibouchina urvilleana* and *Ulex europaeus*. Some garden escapes like *Passiflora mollissima* and *Fuchsia* sp. are found along forest margins and scrubs at the Horton Plains. The floristic composition of the upper montane rain forests forms the main topic of study of this paper and it will be described and discussed separately.

Recent aerial photographs of the Horton Plains show the extent and distribution of grasslands and forests very clearly. The grasslands can be further distinguished into wet black patanas and the successional phase of grasslands on areas that were ploughed and terraced for potato cultivation. The photographs also show the patches of dying forests having a different appearance from the closed, healthy forests. Streams, roads and many other landmarks of the Horton Plains are very clearly discernible in the recent aerial photographs.

Vegetation Sampling, Selection of Sites, Plot Size, Parameters Measured and Data Analysis

Healthy forests with closed canopies were selected for sampling. These were located along the roads leading from Farr Inn to Pattipola, Ohiya, Agrapatana and along trails to Bogawantalawa, Kirigalpota and World's End (Fig. 2). In all, 35 plots were demarcated. Each plot was 5 m x 25 m and the corners were marked with red and yellow paint. The boundaries of the plots were marked by nylon and coir ropes, and the main plot was subdivided into 5 subplots. All woody plants over 5 cm diameter at breast height (dbh) were measured and numbered with aluminium tags. Voucher specimens of all individuals measured were collected and treated with formalin or methylated spirit pressed and dried for the preparation of herbarium specimens. Some were tentatively identified in the field, but all samples were further identified and checked at the National Herbarium at Peradeniya and also with the help of Trimen's Handbook to the Flora of Ceylon (1893-1900) and the revised flora edited by Dassanayake and

Fosberg (1980-1987). Shrubs in the study plots were sampled along a 25 m transect running across the plot. Herbarium samples of the vascular plants of the Horton Plains Reserve were collected for the preparation of an annotated checklist but this information has not been included in this paper. Soil samples were collected from plots but the analyses of these soil samples have not been completed and they will be presented in a separate paper. Profile diagrams of some forest sites were drawn and Figure 3 is one such representative diagram. From the raw data, relative density, relative basal area, relative frequency and importance value indices (Curtis and MacIntosh 1950, Curtis 1959) were calculated. Importance value of different taxonomic categories such as family and species level dominance were also analyzed.

Results and Field Observations

In all, 1252 woody plants were sampled in the study plots, and they represent 57 species, 44 genera and 31 families of vascular plants. Except for the tree fern *Cyathea crinita*, all other woody trees and shrubs measured belong to dicotyledonous families. Cane-like bamboos of the genus *Arundinaria* (= *Indocalamus*) and a Zingiberaceae (*Alpinia abundiflora*) were large monocotyledons present in the sublayer. Of the 57 species recorded within the plots at the Horton Plains, 29 are species endemic to Sri Lanka (50.87%) and 18 are species confined to the montane forests of Sri Lanka and South India (31.58%). Only 10 species (17.54%) have a distribution beyond Sri Lanka and South India. Of these, many are found in the flora of the Malayan archipelago and some also in South China. The family Lauraceae was represented by 4 genera and 7 species while the family Myrtaceae was represented by 3 genera and 5 species. A list of the families, genera and species and their geographic distribution are given in Table 1.

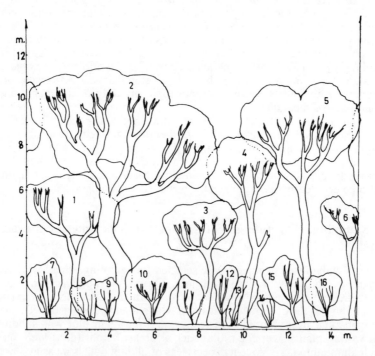

Figure 3. The vertical arrangement of the montane forests of Horton Plains National Park; 1,6 = *Neolitsea fuscata*; 2,5 = *Calophyllum walkeri*; 3 = *Actinodaphne ambigua*, 4 = Vaccinium symplocifolium 7,11 = *Psychotria bisucata*; 8,9,14 = *Strobilanthes sexennis*; 10,16 = *Syzygium rotundifolium*; 12 = *Symplocos cochinchinensis*; 13 = *Toddalia asiatica*; 15 = *Cinnamomum ovalifolium*.

Table 1. List of trees and shrubs in the study plots at the Horton Plains and their geographic distribution; E = endemic; SL & SI = Sri Lanka and South India; WS = widespread.

	Family	Species	Distribution
1.	Acanthaceae	*Strobilanthes* sp.	E
2.	Aquifoliaceae	*Ilex walkeri*	SL & SI
3.	Araliaceae	*Schefflera racemosa*	SL & SI
4.	Buxacea	*Sarcococca zeylanica*	E
5.	Caprifoliaceae	*Viburnum erubesens*	SL & SI
6.	Celastraceae	*Euonymus revolutus*	E
		Microtropis ramiflora	SL & SI
7.	Cornaceae	*Mastixia montana*	E
		M. tetrandra	E
8.	Cyatheaceae	*Cythea crinata*	SL &SI
9.	Elaeocarpaceae	*Elaeocarpus glandulifer*	E
		E. montanus	E
		E. obovata	E
10.	Ericaceae	*Rhododendron arboreum*	SL & SI
		Vaccinium symplocifolium	SL & SI
11.	Euphorbiaceae	*Glochidion coriaceum*	E
12.	Flacourtiaceae	*Casearia coriacea*	E
13.	Guttiferae (Clusiaceae)	*Calophyllum walkeri*	E
14.	Icacinaceae	*Nothapodytes foetida*	WS
15.	Lauraceae	*Actinodaphne ambigua*	E
		A. molochina	
		A. speciosa	E
		A. stenophylla	E
		Cinnamomum ovalifolium	E
		Litsea ovalifolia	E
		Neolitsea fuscata	E
16.	Magnoliaceae	*Michelia nilagirica*	SL & SI
17.	Melastomaceae	*Osbeckia* spp.	E
18.	Myrsinaceae	*Maesa perrottitiana*	WS
		Rapanea robusta	SL & SI
19.	Myrtaceae	*Eugenia mabaeoides*	E
		Syzygium revolutum	SL & SI
		S. rotundifolium	E
		S. sclerophyllum	E
		Rhodomyrtus tomentosa	WS
20.	Oleaceae	*Olea paniculata (O. glandulifer)*	WS
		O. polyama	SL & SI
21.	Pittosporaceae	*Pittosporum tetraspermum*	SL & SI
22.	Rhamnaceae	*Rhamnus arnottianus*	E
23.	Rosaceae	*Photinia notoniana*	SL & SI
24.	Rubiaceae	*Hedyotis lawsoniae*	E
		H. lessertiana	SL & SI
		Lasianthus varians	E
		Psychotria zeylanica	E
		Tarenna flava (= Tasiatica)	WS
25.	Rutaceae	*Euodia lunuankenda*	WS
26.	Sabiaceae	*Meliosma wightii*	SL & SI
27.	Sapotaceae	*Isonandra montana*	E
28.	Staphyleaceae	*Turpinia malabarica*	WS
29.	Symplocaceae	*Symplocos cochinchinensis*	SL & SI
		S. elegans	E
		S. fuscata	SL & SI
		S. obtusa	SL & SI
30.	Theaceae	*Adinandra lasiopetala*	E
		Eurya japonica	WS
		Ternstroemia japonica	WS
31.	Ulmaceae	*Celtis cinnamomea*	WS

Besides these 57 species shown in Table 1, many other woody plants were recorded along the margins of forests and grasslands and also on disturbed sites and road embankments. *Berberis tinctoria* (= *B. aristata*), *Hypericum mysorense*, *Osbeckia lanata*, *O. rubicunda*, *Elaeagnus latifolia*, *Polygala arillata*, *Rubus fairholmianus* and other *Rubus* spp. were some of woody plants and straglers found along the margins of the forests. *Aristea ecklonii*, *Eupatorium riparium* and the fern *Pteridium aquilinum* are some invasive plants found along roadside clearings, trails and disturbed sites. Some of the naturalized species that are now common at the Horton Plains are *Cestrum elegans*, *C. aurantium*, *Tibochina urvilleana* and *Ulex europaeus*. None of these species were found within the relatively undisturbed upper montane rain forests.

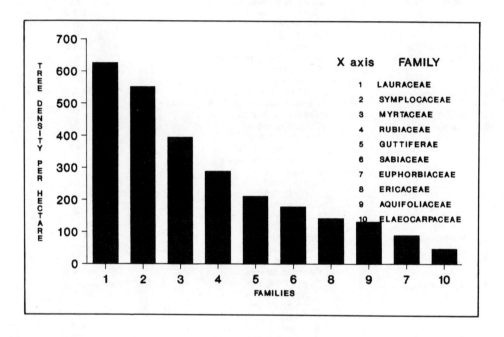

Figure 4. Density of the ten most frequently occurring families of trees in the study area (area sampled 4375 m²).

The family Lauraceae had a mean density of 614 individuals per hectare, while Symplocaceae and Myrtaceae had a mean density of 544 individuals per hectare and 379 individuals per hectare respectively (Fig. 4). The family Rubiaceae (278 individuals per hectare) was mostly represented by woody shrubs within the forests at the Horton Plains. Species of Rubiaceae do not form typical canopy species, but they constitute the shrub species of natural forest stands. A mean density of 2861 individuals per hectare was calculated for the forests at the Horton Plains. Based on density, Lauraceae, Symplocaceae, Myrtaceae, Rubiaceae, Guttiferae (Clusiaceae), Sabiaceae, Euphorbiaceae, Ericaceae, Aquifoliaceae and Elaeocarpaceae are found to be well represented in the forest vegetation of this nature reserve.

The importance value index (IVI) of Curtis (1959) uses relative density, relative frequency, and relative basal area in assessing the contribution of component species that determine the structure of a community. Based on IVI values the first five species are (Fig. 5): *Cinnamomum ovalifolium* (24.15), *Syzygium revolutum* (2.61), *Neolitsea fuscata* (20.74), *Symplocos elegans* (20.42) and *Calophyllum walkeri* (18.04). They can be regarded as the dominant tree species of the upper montane rain forests at the Horton Plains.

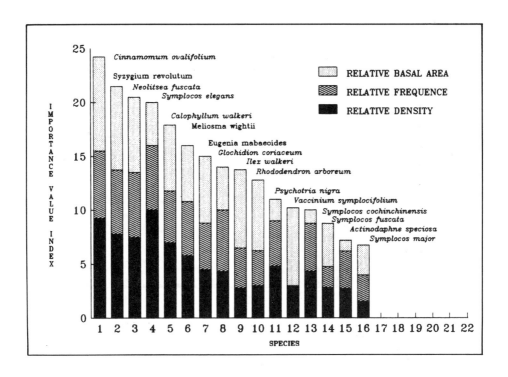

Figure 5. The importance value index (IVI) of sixteen woody species found in the study plots.

Of these five tree species, *Calophyllum walkeri* tends to stand slightly above the other canopy tree species forming umbrella-like crowns. Overall it gives a very characteristic appearance to the landscape at the Horton Plains, Ambawela, Pidurutalagala and in the Knuckles Area. The profile diagram (Fig. 3) shows that *Calophyllum walkeri* and other canopy trees reach heights above 12 meters at Horton Plains. It is rather difficult to distinguish two layers in the canopy. *Actinodaphne speciosa* (IVI = 7.46) rarely reaches the canopy, and it is usually a subcanopy species. Lianas are not very common in the upper montane forests. *Toddalia aculeata* (with stout spines) and *Rubia cordifolia* (slender climber) were encountered in some plots. Most tree species of the montane zone have a low branching habit, and the branches are twisted and gnarled. The trees do not have buttresses. Leaves are usually small (notophylls to microphylls), leathery and evergreen. The high humidity, cloud cover and mist billowing through the forests favor the growth of a great diversity of epiphytic lichens (*Usnea barbata*), bryophytes, ferns (*Asplenium* spp. *Crypsinus montanus, Coniogramme serra, Loxogramme* sp. *Elaphoglossum* spp. and *Vittaria* spp.) and orchids (*Eria baccata, E. bicolor, Robiquetia brevifolia,* etc.) In the undisturbed forests or forests with closed canopies, shrubs are represented by genera belonging to the family Rubiaceae (*Hedyotis, Lasianthus, Psychotria, Saprosma, Urophyllum,* etc.). Along steep slopes and forests with not very dense canopies clumps of *Arundinaria wightiana* and *A. walkeriana* were observed. Common herbs covering the ground layer of the forests were an iridiscent species of *Selaginella, Elastostemma* sp. *Hydrocotyle javanica, Pogostemon heyneanus, Disporum leschenaultianum, Asplenium* spp. and *Pteris* spp.

Most of the stems measured belong to the first three diameter classes of 5-9 cm, 10-14 cm, and 15-19 cm (Fig. 6). 62% of the stems sampled were under 15 cm in diameter. The general

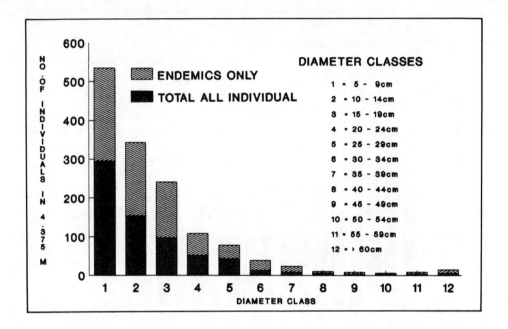

Figure 6. Distribution of individuals of different stem diameter classes in the study area (area sampled 4375 m^2).

pattern of distribution is characteristic of relatively undisturbed natural forests. *Calophyllum walkeri*, *Cinnamomum ovalifolium*, *Ilex walkeri*, *Elaeocarpus glandulifer*, *E. montana*, *Vaccinium syplocifolium* and *Syzygium revolutum* were some of the large diameter trees recorded in this study.

Discussion

Floristically the upper montane rain forests of the Horton Plains are less diverse than the lowland forests of Sri Lanka. 57 species of woody plants belonging to 43 genera and 30 families were identified in the study plots at the Horton Plains. Gunatilleke and Gunatilleke (1985) identified 211 species of woody plants belonging to 119 genera and 43 families within the Sinharaja lowland rainforest reserve. The montane rain forests of the Horton Plains are dominated by evergreen dicotyledonous families. Based on importance value index, Lauraceae was the most dominant family while Symplocaceae, Myrtaceae, Ericaceae and Guttiferae were other leading families at the Horton Plains. At the species level, the five dominant taxa were *Cinnamomum ovalifolium*, *Syzygium revolutum*, *Neolitsea fuscata*, *Symplocos elegans* and *Calophyllum walkeri*. As regards woody moncotyledons, cane-like bamboos were present in some habitats, but palms were absent in the montane forests of the Horton Plains. In the lowland rainforests of Sinharaja, the two most dominant families were Clusiaceae and Dipterocarpaceae (Gunatilleke and Gunatilleke, 1985). The floristic composition of the Hakgala mountane forests studied by Wijesundera *et al.* (1984) was similar to the Horton Plains forest. Both the Hakgala and Horton Plains are situated on the central ridge of the main mountain massif. The western ridge of the main mountain massif however supports floristically different montane forests. Greller *et al.* (1987) found that *Stemonoporus gardneri* and *Palaquium rubiginosum* were the dominants in two of the stands sampled by them on the western ridge. These two dominant species belong to the family Dipterocarpaceae and Sapotaceae, respectively. *Stemonoporus*-dominated montane forests are found in the Peak Wilderness Sanctuary on the western ridge of the central highlands. The slightly lower elevation (Carney, 1570 m; Rajamalay, 1680 m) and the higher mean annual rainfall probably accounts for the floristic differences in the canopy species of the forests of the Peak Wilderness and the forests of the Horton Plains. The montane forests of Namunukula on the eastern ridge of the main mountain massif have been examined by Werner (1982). Large areas of the montane forest on the eastern ridge have been cleared for tea cultivation. Some common tree species found in the remnant patches of montane forests at Namunukula are *Syzygium revolutum, Calophyllum walkeri, Garcinia echinocarpa* and *Actinodaphne speciosa*. Distinct differences in floristic composition also exist between the montane forests of the isolated Knuckles range of mountains and the central highlands (Werner 1982, Jayasuriya *et al.* this volume).

The floristic composition and other features of the upper montane forests of Kodaikanal on the Palni range and the Nilgiri Mountains of South India have close affinities to the mountain forests of the Horton Plains, Hakgala and Pidurutalagala. The upper montane rain forests of south India are locally referred to as shola forests. There are a large number of species of woody and herbaceous plants that are common to the montane forests and grasslands of Sri Lanka and South India. *Berberis tinctoria, Cyathea crinata, Gaultheria fragrantissima, Hypericum mysorense, Meliosma wightii, Michelia nilagirica, Microtropis ramiflora, Photinia notoniana, Pittosporum itetraspermum, Rhamnus wightii, Rhododendron arboreum, Schefflera racemosa* and *Viburnum erubescens* are some of the woody taxa confined to the mountains of Sri Lanka and South India. Genera such as *Actinodaphne, Elaeocarpus, Lasianthus* and *Symplocos* and the families Acanthaceae, Balsaminaceae, Lauraceae, Symplocaceae and Rubiaceae are well represented in the montane floras of Sri Lanka and South India (Trimen, 1893-1900). Though there are close floristic and other affinities between the sholas of the Nilgiris and the upper montane forests of the Horton Plains, it must be emphasized that climatic as well as floristic compostition impart certain unique features to the montane forests of the central highlands of Sri Lanka. About fifty percent of the woody species identified at the Horton Plains are endemic to Sri Lanka.

Conifers (*Dacrydium* spp.), oaks (*Castanopsis* sp. and *Lithocarpus* spp.) and southern beeches (*Nothofagus* spp.) are found in the upper montane rain forests of the Far East (Whitmore, 1984) and in the warm temperate and subtropical forests of South China and Southern Japan. These conifers and Fagaceae are not found in the natural montane forests of Sri Lanka. Tree families represented in the lowland rain forests of Sri Lanka and the Far East but not found in the upper montane rain forests of the Horton Plains are Anacardiaceae (except *Semecarpus coriacea*), Bombacaceae, Dilleniaceae, Dipterocarpaceae and Myristicaceae. Woody families that are better represented in the montane zone are Ericaceae, Lauraceae, Symplocaceae and Theaceae. Many temperate woody and herbaceous genera are found in the montane vegetation of Sri Lanka and South India. Of the herbaceous genera, the following are well known to botanists: *Galium* (1 sp.), *Ranunculus* (2 spp.), *Valeriana* (1 sp.), *Veronica* (4 spp.) and *Viola* (3 spp.).

The mean density of stems over 5 cm in diameter enumerated at the Horton Plains was 2861 individuals per hectare. More than sixty two percent of the individuals sampled were below 15 cm in diameter. Average heights of canopy tree ranged from 12-15 metres. In wind swept areas, the trees were stunted forming the so-called elfin woodlands or pygmy forests, but they were not sampled in this study. The canopy trees have umbrella-shaped crowns and rather small leathery leaves. The branches of the canopy trees are twisted and gnarled and support a large number of epiphytes. As mentioned before, lianas are not very common within the forests, but climbing plants and straglers are seen along the forest margins. The physiogiomic features of the upper montane forests of the Horton Plains are very similar to those of other tropical cloud forests (Whitmore, 1984).

Preliminary investigations of the forest dieback at the Horton Plains based on field observations and aerial photo interpretations indicated that dieback was confined to areas exposed to desiccating westerly winds and probably shallow soil. Some patches have been affected by recent fires. While the canopy showed dieback, the root systems remained healthy. Opening of the canopy led to luxuriant growth of shrub species of the genus *Strobilanthes*. The major cause of forest dieback appeared to be the cumulative effect of the climatic stress experienced by vegetation in these regions over the past ten years.

The quantitative studies of the montane forest formations by Greller *et al.* (1980, 1987), Wijesundera *et al* (1984), and the data presented in this paper, provide floristic and phytosociological information showing the distinctive features of the upper montane rain forests of Sri Lanka. The relatively wet upper montane forests of the Peak Wilderness Sanctuary are dominated mainly by *Stemonoporus* species and *Palaquium rubiginosum,* while the somewhat drier and cooler cloud forests of the Hakgala and Horton Plains are dominated by *Cinnamomum ovalifolium, Syzygium revolutum, Neolitsea fuscata, Symplocos elegans* and *Calophyllum walkeri.* The Knuckles Range of mountains separated from the central highlands by the Mahaweli Ganga Valley has some peaks that reach heights of 1863 metres (Knuckles) and 1904 metres (Gombaniya). Field studies carried out by Werner (1982) and by Greller and Balasubramaniam (1980) at Midcar, Niloomalay and Rangala in the Knuckles area record *Calophyllum trapezifolium, Garcinia echinocarpa, Aglaia congylos* and *Syzygium* species as the dominant trees of the montane forests of the Knuckles. Some remarkable differences in the floristic composition of the montane forests of the Knuckles Range and the central highlands were recorded by Werner (1982). Floristically, the montane forests of the Knuckles, the Horton Plains and Peak Wilderness are different and they need to be conserved to maintain the biological diversity of these areas. The Hakgala and Horton Plains have the status of nature reserves while the Peak Wilderness is a sanctuary. At present an area of approximately 18,290 ha has been demarcated for rehabilitation, reforestation and conservation in the Knuckles Area. Reforestation for soil conservation and watershed management will be carried out with technical and financial assistance from the Overseas Development Administration (ODA) of the United Kingdom. Rehabilitation of degraded lands, marginal tea estates and proposed changes in land use in the Knuckles Area will be assisted by Germany (GTZ). In 1987, the Government of Sri Lanka requested assistance from the IUCN to develop and implement sustainable management programs for Sinharaja (Lowland Rain Forest Reserve) and the Knuckles. An inventory of the endemic biota and ecological survey of the major natural forest formations of the Knuckles have already been initiated. The montane forests, the montane grasslands (patanas) and other habitats of the central ridge, the western ridge, the eastern ridge (Thangamalai, Namunukula), the Knuckles massif and the Rakwana or Sabaragamuwa Range support a large number of endemic species of flowering plants (Trimen, 1893-1900), ferns (Abeywickrama 1964, Sledge 1982) and vertebrate animals (Crusz, 1986). Not much information is available on the non-vascular plants and the invertebrate animals of these montane areas. Their study and documentation must be encouraged and supported by appropriate agencies.

During the past ten years the construction of major dams and the impounding of water in the Upper Mahaweli Catchment as part of the Accelerated Mahaweli Development Programme has brought about major shifts of population to the new downstream irrigated areas and the upstream hydroelectric projects of Kotmale and Victoria Reservoirs. Inappropriate land use, increased pressure on forest resources, poor management of tea on steep terrain, frequent fires during dry periods and intensive vegetable cultivation in the central highlands have resulted in large-scale degradation of land and excessive soil erosion. Soil erosion will lead to silting and reduce the effective life of these expensive dams and their power generating capacity. The Government of Sri Lanka with assistance from ODA, GTZ and IUCN is planning to identify areas for catchment protection, reafforestation and other land uses such as agroforestry or silvicultural forestry. The proposed projects will study the social and economic implications of land use in the Knuckles and the upper Mahaweli Catchment in order to find out if the changes are acceptable to the local people living in these development and conservation areas. One of the many benefits of this integrated land use plan will be the identification of biologically diverse and ecologically critical or sensitive areas for conservation.

Literature Cited

Abeywickrama, B.A. 1964. Pteridophytes of the Knuckles. *Ceyl. J. Sci. (Bio. Sci.)* 5: 18-29.

Crusz, H. 1986. The vertebrates of Sri Lanka: endemism and other aspects. *Rep. Soc. Res. Native Lifestock (Japan)* 11: 380-384.

Curtis, J.T. and R.P. McIntosh. 1951. An upland forest continuum in the prairie-forest region of Wisconsin. *Ecology* 32: 476-496.

Curtis, J.T. and R.P. McIntosh. 1951. The interelations of certain analytical and synthetic phytosociological characters. *Ecology* 32: 434-455.

Curtis, J.T. 1959. *The Vegetation of Wisconsin: an Ordination of Plant Communities*. Wisconsin University Press, Madison.

Dassanayake, M.D. and F.R. Rosberg. 1980. *A Revised Handbook to the Flora of Ceylon, Vol. 1-6*. Oxford and IBH Publishing Co. London.

Greller A.M. and S. Balasubramaniam. 1980. A preliminary floristics - classification of the forests of Sri Lanka. *The Sri Lanka Forester* 14: 163-170.

Greller, A.M., I.A.U.N. Gunatilleke, A.H.M. Jayasuriaya, C.V.S. Gunatilleke, S. Balasubramaniam and M.D. Dassanayake. 1987. *Stemonoporus (Dipterocarpaceae)*-dominated montane forest in the Adam's Peak Wilderness, Sri Lanka. *J. Trop. Ecol* 3: 243-253.

Gunatilleke, C.V.S. and I.A.U.N. Gunatilleke. 1985. Phytosociology of Sinharaja - a contribution to rain forest conservation in Sri Lanka. *Biol. Conserv.* 31: 21-40.

Jayasuriaya, A.H.M., A.M. Greller, S. Balasubramaniam, I.A.U.N. Gunatilleke, C.V.S. Gunatilleke, and M.D. Dassanayake. This volume. Phytosociological Studies of Mid-Elevational (Lower Montane) Evergreen Mixed Forest in Sri Lanka.

Mueller-Dombois, D. and M. Perera. 1971. Ecological differentiation and soil fungal distribution in the montane grassland of Ceylon. *J. Sci.* 9: 1-41.

Sledge, W.A. 1982. An annotated check-list of the Pteridophyte of Ceylon. *Bot. J. Linn. Soc. London* 84: 1-30.

Thwaites, G.K. 1858-1864. *Enumerantio Platarun Zeylaniae*. Dulau and Co. London.

Trimen, H. 1893-1900. *The Handbook to the Flora of Ceylon*. Dulau and Co. London.

Werner, W.L. 1982. The upper montane forest of Sri Lanka. *The Sri Lanka Forester* 15: 119-135.

Werner, W.L. 1984. *Die Hohen- und Nebelwalder auf Insel Ceylon (Sri Lanka)*. Steiner Verlag, Wiesbaden.

Werner, W.L. 1988. Canopy dieback in the upper montane rain forests. *Geojournal* 17: 245-248.

Wijesundra, D.S.A., C.V.S. Gunatilleke and I.U.C.N. Gunatilleke. 1984. Woody vegetation of Hakgala Strict Natural Reserve. *Proc. Sri Lanka Association for the Advancement of Science (SLAAS)*.

Whitmore, T.C. 1984. *Tropical Rain Forests of the Far East*. Clarendon Press, Oxford.

Proceedings of the International and Interdisciplinary Symposium
ECOLOGY AND LANDSCAPE MANAGEMENT IN SRI LANKA
W. Erdelen, C. Preu, N. Ishwaran, C.M. Madduma Bandara (eds.)
Colombo, Sri Lanka, 12-26 March 1990
© 1993
Margraf Scientific Books, D-97985 Weikersheim
ISBN 3-8236-1182-8

Vegetation Studies as a Base for Park Planning: Wasgomuwa National Park, Sri Lanka

T. JAYASINGAM

Abstract

An "ecological area" is often characterized by its vegetation, primarily owing to the immobility and thus "stability" of the plants. However, it follows that the animals in that site are often dependent on the vegetation and all changes be they small, large, seasonal or otherwise on the vegetation tend to have important effects on animals as well. Vegetation studies therefore play a key role in planning and management of 'ecological areas', such as national parks. In this study, conducted under the Mahaweli Environment Project, the following results were obtained. 1. The vegetation in the park might predominantly be divided into grasslands, abandoned lands, high forest and riverine forest. 2. The vegetation within these divisions showed significantly different subunits. Uniformity was lacking and a mosaic pattern was prominent within each vegetation type. 3. Soil analyses revealed that the soil was heterogenous and might be associated with different types of vegetation. 4. Periodic fires influenced certain vegetation types to a greater extent than others. 5. The influence of people on the surrounding areas was important, even many years after the establishment of the park. The use of these data for the planning and management of the national park are highlighted and more detailed future studies are suggested.

Introduction

Chamber's dictionary defines "landscape" as the "esthetic appearance or the eye-catching arrangement of land". "Landscape management" is the way in which we attain that. A national park may be considered as a complex landscape where not only the esthetic appearance matters but also the ecological characteristics of the landscape to provide a shelter, home for the multitude of organisms in that environment. Thus, it is a special type of an "ecological landscape" and care is needed in planning and maintaining more compared with other landscapes.

In this paper, I would like to brief about the nature of a national park, explain the importance of study of vegetation, discuss its relevance incorporating the data we have on the Wasgomuwa National Park and finally emphasize the need for more scientific information not only on Wasgomuwa National Park but on Sri Lanka as a whole.

What is a national park? It is a sanctuary, it is a reserve, it is a park. It is the sanctuary for wildlife where there is protection for nature and recreation for man. It is a defined space with or without corridors where animal communities live within a mosaic of landscape patches. Landscapes are often denoted by physiographical features as hills, valleys, lakes, etc. Biomes of the world are classified on the basis of vegetation into tundra, taiga, etc. A variety of reasons may be attributed to this:

1. Immobility: Sites may be identified by their plant communities.
2. Lifespan: Most plants, especially trees, will outlive most animals and hence using these as markers is more suitable.
3. Plasticity: Most plants respond to environmental impacts with plasticity in their behavior. They are unable to escape unlike animals and often respond by compensated growth and development, and thus represent the site history in their structure.
4. Primary producers: As primary producers plants are able to tolerate extremes of environments and also support a range of consumers. They are able to form the base of a large community.
5. Habit: Plants produce a mosaic of habitats by their habit and structure where other organisms shelter and survive.

The static nature and the long lifespan especially make vegetation a key tool in describing the landscape and a potential base for management plans as a stationary phase where the animals become the mobile phase.

Methods and Study Area

Fieldwork was carried out in the Wasgomuwa National Park from September 1987 to December 1989. The vegetation survey was a part of the research program whose counterpart was the faunal survey and these together were a part of the Mahaweli Environment Project, funded by the Government of Sri Lanka and USAID.

The Wasgomuwa National Park is situated in the north central part of the island bordered by Amban Ganga and Kalu Ganga in the north and west and Mahaweli Ganga in the east. Dunuwila Oya marks the boundary in the south (Fig. 1). Wasgomuwa was declared a strict natural reserve in 1938 and was given the status of a national park in 1984. The present area of the park is about 33,791 ha or 140 square miles. Sudukande range of hills which are linked to the Knuckles Range runs north south at the west end of the park. The ridge is about 500 m high and divides the streams draining into the Amban Ganga and the Mahaweli Ganga. There were human settlements at Angamedilla in the north and Kadurupitiya in the south until about 1982. Remnants of these settlements, abandoned chena and paddy fields can still be seen within the park.

All woody vegetation with girth greater than 10 cm was recorded in randomly selected 10 m x 10 m plots throughout the forest covering all different types of vegetation. Relative density, relative frequency, relative basal area and importance value index (IVI) was calculated for each species in different types of vegetation, i.e. primary forest, disturbed or secondary forest, riverine vegetation, etc. 10 plots each were sampled in riverine vegetation bordering four waterways, viz. Mahaweli Ganga; a large river, Wasgomuwa Oya and Ellewela Oya, both seasonal medium rivers, and Karapanagala Ela, a seasonal stream. Some physical and chemical properties of soil were measured at random within a given type of vegetation throughout the park.

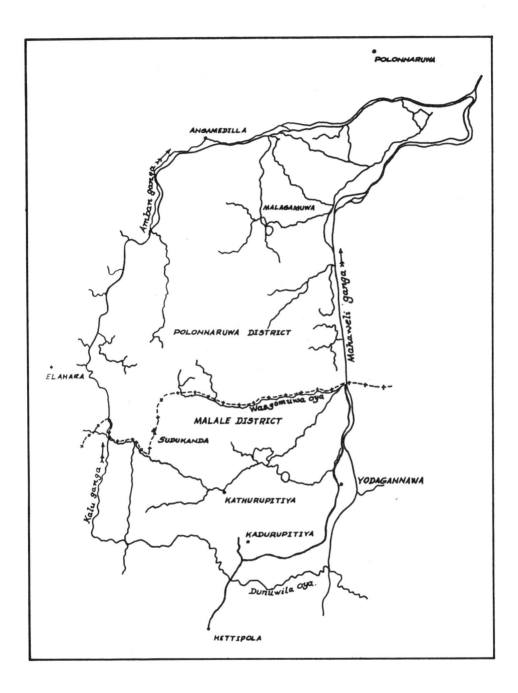

Figure 1. Map of the Wasgomuwa National Park, Sri Lanka.

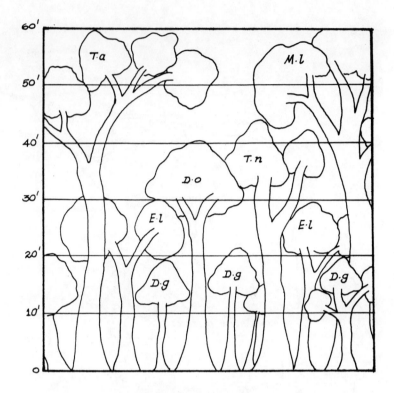

Figure 2. Profile diagram of riverine vegetation at the Mahaweli Ganga site, Wasgomuwa National Park: T.a. = *Terminalia arjuna*, M.l. = *Maduca longifolia*, D.o. = *Diospyros ovalifolia*, T.n. = *Trewia nudiflora*, E.l. = *Euphoria longana*, D.g. = *Dimorphocalyx glabellus*.

Results

Anything ranging from the preparation of simple species lists to complicated transition matrices may be considered under vegetation study. Series of soil studies too may be included. We shall look at a few of them which are basic and essential. Broadly these include two types of study; description and dynamics. The results from our study at Wasgomuwa is given wherever possible to emphasize the statements.

The species list of the woody vegetation was prepared for the Wasgomuwa National Park. A few herbs and very prominent herbs which were of special interest were also included. The vegetation comprised of 155 species belonging to 130 genera and to 45 families. Euphorbiaceae had the maximum number of species (17), followed by the Rubiaceae (13) and Leguminosae (16). 16 families were represented by one species. 102 tree species, 13 lianas, 3 climbers and 35 shrubs were found. The structure of the forest is shown in Figure 2.

Based on site characters and physiognomic features of the vegetation and species composition, the vegetation of the Wasgomuwa National Park may be divided into (1) forests, in particular riverine forests, semi-evergreen forests, hill forests, monsoon forests, degraded secondary forests and seral scrubland, (2) grasslands, such as iluk (*Imperata cylindrica*) grasslands as well as other grasslands, and (3) abandoned cultivated lands comparing highland chena land and low-lying paddy fields (Fig. 3).

112

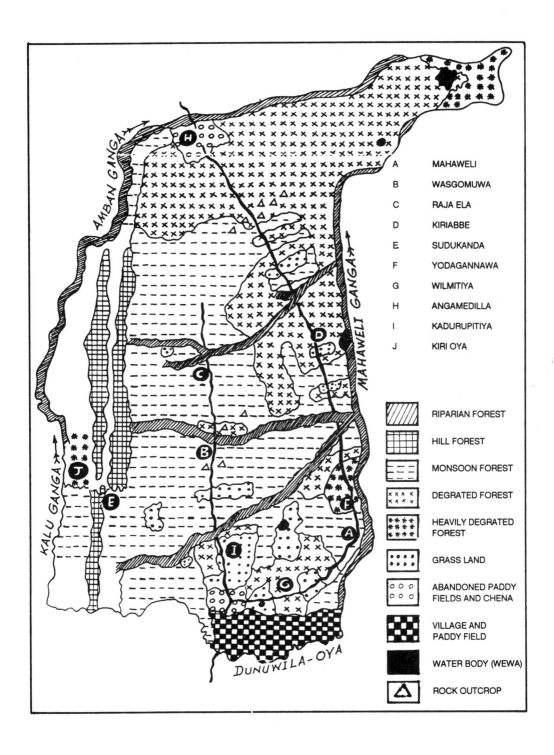

Figure 3. Vegetation map of the Wasgomuwa National Park.

A   MAHAWELI
B   WASGOMUWA
C   RAJA ELA
D   KIRIABBE
E   SUDUKANDA
F   YODAGANNAWA
G   WILMITIYA
H   ANGAMEDILLA
I   KADURUPITIYA
J   KIRI OYA

RIPARIAN FOREST
HILL FOREST
MONSOON FOREST
DEGRATED FOREST
HEAVILY DEGRATED FOREST
GRASS LAND
ABANDONED PADDY FIELDS AND CHENA
VILLAGE AND PADDY FIELD
WATER BODY (WEWA)
ROCK OUTCROP

Table 1. Relative importance value indices (IVI) of woody species at the Wasgomuwa Oya site in the Wasgomuwa National Park.

Species	IVI
Dimorphocalyx galbellus	39.162
Pityranthe verrucosa	38.093
Drypetes sepiaria	28.091
Diospyros ovalifolia	22.379
Polyylthia korintii	21.261
Mallotus rhamnifolius	20.916
Glycosmis pentaphylla	17.828
Chloroxylon swietenia	13.927
Memecylon umbellatum	13.583
Pterospermum canescense	13.150
Phyllanthus polyphyllus	10.673
Lepisanthus tetraphylla	7.395
Diospyros malabaricum	6.419
Randia dumetoram	5.921
Manilkara hexanddra	5.891
Zizyphus napeca	5.284
Eleaodendron glaucam	4.560
Derris scandans	4.466
Diospyros queasita	4.327
Cassia fistula	3.740
KIRIWAL (local name)	3.459
Diospyros ebenum	1.789
Pleiospermum alatum	1.012
Ochna squarrosa	1.734
Sapindus emarginatus	1.424
Ventilago maderaspatana	1.385
Hugonia mystax	1.109
Premna tomentosa	1.021
Carrissa spinarum	0.995
Randia sp.	0.593
Sapium insigne	0.558
Grewia polygama	0.490
Premna tomentosa	0.487
Croton laccifer	0.000
Carmona macrophylla	0.000

In terms of importance values *Dimorphocalyx glabellus* is the most important species in the forest at the Wasgomuwa Oya site (Tab. 1). There is no pronounced dominance of any species in the vegetation. The maximum theoretical value of a monoculture would be 300 and the maximum obtained by *D. glabellus* scores only 39 which is far less.

The result of the site classification of riverine vegetation indicates that the Mahaweli vegetation is very distinct from the rest of the vegetation (Fig. 4). Figure 5 gives the ordination map of the riverine vegetation, where groups of species are spread on an axis. Many tree species tend to remain for long periods as "saplings" with stunted growth which is referred to as sapling bank. They grow very fast filling available space when they finally receive their requirements of light. Figure 6 shows the composition of saplings in different types of vegetation whithin the monsoon forest in Wasgomuwa. It is interesting to note that species found in the canopy or tree layer are rare in the sapling bank. It is an indication that the species composition may change in the years to come, an indication of the succession, and an indication

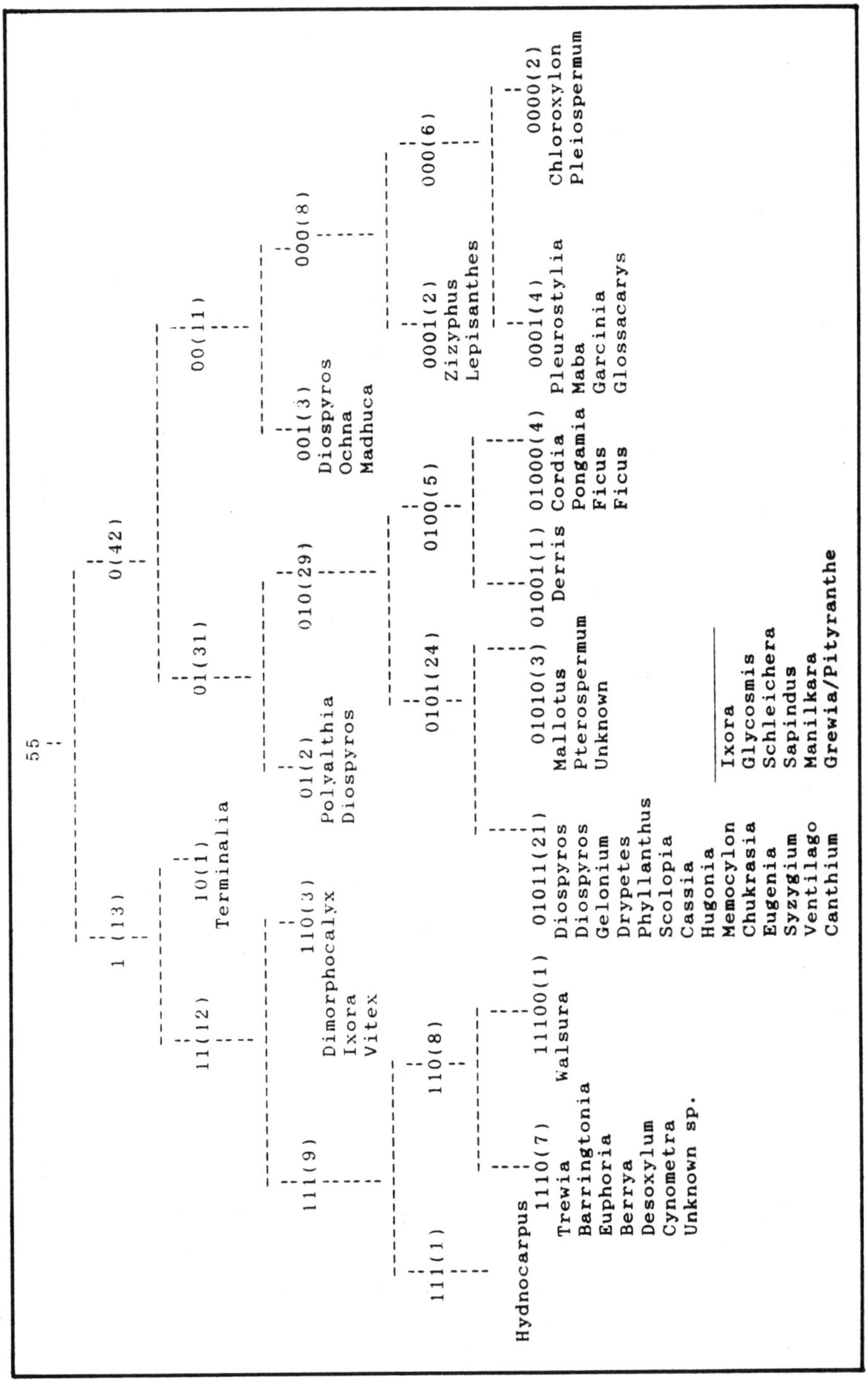

Figure 4. Dendogram of species association in the Riparian vegetation of Wasgomuwa National Park.

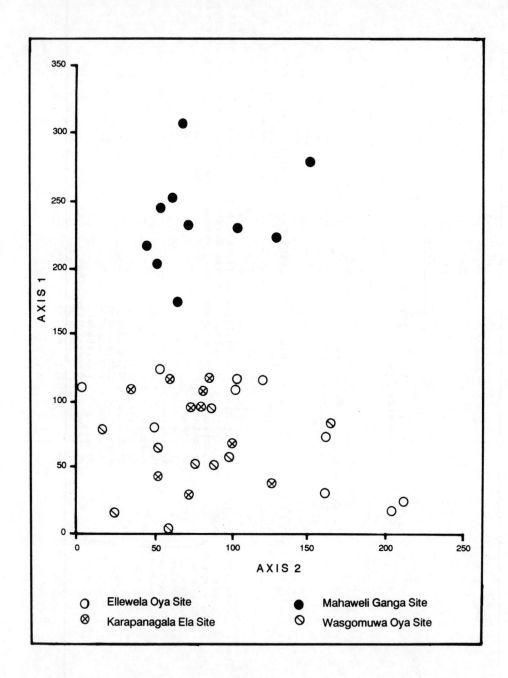

Figure 5. Ordination map of riverine vegetation.

116

Table 2. Distribution of pH of soil in the Wasgomuwa National Park: SD = Standard deviation.

Sites		Mean	SD	Range	pH<7
Forest	Mahaweli	6.75	0.44	6.0-8.5	78%
	Wasgomuwa	6.79	0.43	6.0-8.5	66%
	Raja Ela	6.70	0.40	6.1-7.5	68%
	Kiriabbe	6.73	0.42	6.3-8.1	77%
	Sudukanda	6.70	0.18	6.4-7.5	80%
Grassland	Yoddagannawa	6.37	9.36	5.5-7.5	94%
	Wilimitiya	6.31	0.37	5.4-7.0	98%
Chena	Angamedilla	6.95	0.49	6.0-8.5	54%
	Kathurupitiya	6.43	0.37	5.8-7.0	91%
Degraded	Kiri Oya	6.75	0.15	6.5-7.0	93%

that the forest is not in a "climax" state yet, but is changing. The seed bank, sapling bank, treelets and the number of trees altogether provide information on the transition of species composition from one state to another and indicate the possibilities of the next generation's composition.

The physical and chemical properties of soils under different types of vegetation is an important factor. It may be the factor determining the vegetation at some sites and in others it the soil factors may be the result of the vegetation at that site. The grassland soils were found to be more acidic than the forest soils (Tab. 2), however the distribution of various parameters was very patchy. It was noted that *Eragrostis*-dominated grasslands were found to have grey soils indicating poor nutrient status (Tab. 3).

Fire was found to be frequent in the grasslands in the Wasgomuwa National Park, often accidental spreading from neighboring villages. However, this tends to have a control over the regrowth of the vegetation in the grasslands, to prevent survival of tree saplings. Even the trees found in these "mini-savannas" are fire resistant with thick corky barks e.g. *Bauhinia racemosa*. Regeneration in these areas was often found to be from germination in ant/termite hills. They establish an island and a shrubby vegetation develops around it, often bordered by fire resistant and thorny shrubs at the periphery, which help the other species grow within.

Management

Management is like machinery, it is important to understand its parts to understand the mechanism of its function, yet we need to know all parts to make the machinery work. Vegetation is one part, animals another, man a third. It is only when we have information on all these sectors that we can scientifically manage the park. This is not to state that we remain dormant during the "day" but that we should be more critical. We have information through history, experience, and studies at other sites. We could formulate tentative plans and move forward cautiously but unless we are willing to propagate our own data and plans based on them, management of any of our resources will always pose problems. In this context I would like to point out a often mismatched statement in the scientific community with reference to reconnaissance studies and surveys. Often faced with the question, IS THIS RESEARCH? If the question is whether the work is novel, the answer is NO. But that is a vital start which

Table 3. Distribution of soil color in the Wasgomuwa National Park.

Vegetation	Site	Color	Modal frequency
Forest	Mahaweli	Reddish brown Dark brown	40% 14%
	Wasgomuwa	Reddish brown Dark red grey	46% 14%
	Raja Ela	Reddish brown Brown	42% 22%
	Kiri abbe	Reddish brown Dark red grey	32% 19%
	Sudukanda	Yellowish red Reddish brown	32% 32%
Grassland	Yoddagannawa	Grey brown Very dark grey	20% 18%
	Wilmitita	Dark grey brown Dark red grey	56% 16%
Chena	Angamedilla	Dark grey brown Dark grey brown	40% 24%
	Kathurupitiya	Red brown Dark brown	28% 24%
Disturbed forest	Kiri Oya	Yellowish red Red brown	44% 15%

forms the base for the rest. In the scientific method the sequence is observation, data collection, inference, hypothesis, experiment. Reconnaissance surveys cover the first two aspects, and it is the base for the rest especially referring to natural resources.

Short-term studies like ours can only produce very basic information on the natural system and cannot shed light on the dynamics. Systematic long-term studies in permanent plots is the only way by which we could gather reliable and effective data on any ecosystem. It is not necessary for one individual or a group to perform this. It is important that these data are available and are collected over an extended period of time. Many countries have a record of all the permanent plots and recordings are taken periodically. A bulletin named "Permanent Plotter" is also available highlighting various permanent recordings throughout the world. A machinery, i.e. a coordinating national body embracing a range of disciplines is urgently needed which must be in a position to indicate, question, analyze, advise, advertise, discuss, promote and pursue environmental issues within the constraints of the national development.

It is only by understanding the system that we can scientifically manage the system and only from scientific data we can understand the system and data can only be obtained through organized programed work. It is possible to manage a system by trial and error. This may even be successful, but the unfortunate fact is that we will never know the reason for the success or failure. We must be Lamarckian in this aspect and not Darwinian, passing the information from generation to generation.

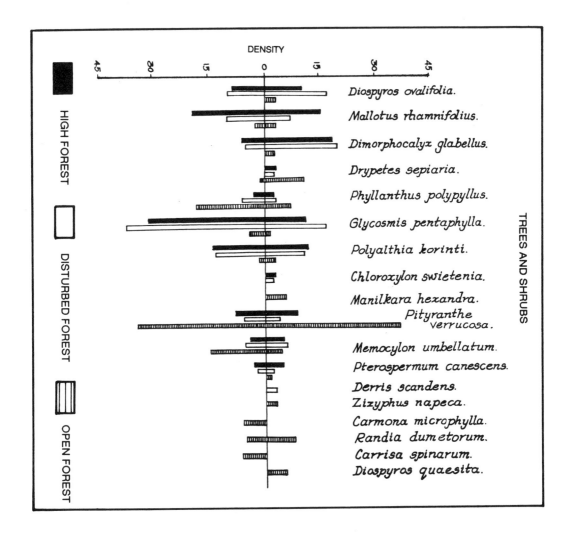

Figure 6. Abundance of trees and shrubs in the surface vegetation and sapling vegetation in the Wasgomuwa Forest in the Wasgomuwa National Park: 1. High forest: semi-evergreen forest, perturbation unknown; 2. Disturbed forest: semi-evergreen forest, perturbation noted; 3. Open forest: open canopy savanna type forest.

Literature Cited

Anon. 1986. *Masterplan of Wasgomuwa National Park*. Mahaweli Environment Project, Dept. of Wildlife Conservation, Ministry of State, Sri Lanka.

Curtis, J.T. and R.P. McIntosh. 1950. The interrelations of certain analytic and synthetic phytosociological characters. *Ecology* 31. 434-455.

Jayasingam, T. 1991. *Preliminary survey of the vegetation of the Wasgomuwa National Park.* Mahaweli Environment Project MEP/142/1A Report. Dept. of Wildlife Conservation,/ USaid, Sri Lanka.

Proceedings of the International and Interdisciplinary Symposium
ECOLOGY AND LANDSCAPE MANAGEMENT IN SRI LANKA
W. Erdelen, C. Preu, N. Ishwaran, C.M. Madduma Bandara (eds.)
Colombo, Sri Lanka, 12-26 March 1990
© 1993
Margraf Scientific Books, D-97985 Weikersheim
ISBN 3-8236-1182-8

The Mountain Stream Fauna of Sri Lanka with Special Reference to Molluscs

A Summarizing Review

F. STARMÜHLNER

Abstract

This review summarizes our information on the freshwater fauna (macro- and mesofauna) of the mountain streams of the tropical continental island of Sri Lanka. The longitudinal distribution of the species from the headwaters down to the river mouths and their occurrence with regard to current velocities is discussed, with special reference to freshwater molluscs.

Introduction

Systematic studies of the aquatic fauna of the running waters of the central mountain ranges of Sri Lanka were carried out for the first time by the Fisheries Research Station of the Department of Fisheries in Colombo after World War II. Further information on the mesofauna of mountain streams was compiled by Mendis and Fernando (1962), Fernando (1963, 1964, 1969a, 1969b, 1974, 1980). Special studies were carried out by Schmid (1958), Silas (1955) further by Fernando and Indrasena (1969), Costa (1974), Costa and Fernando (1967) and Geisler (1967). Moreover, animals of mountain streams were studied in the context of the Swedish mission of the University of Lund to Sri Lanka in 1962 (e.g. Brinck et al. 1971, Bott 1970, Encke 1970, Déléve 1973a, Kuiper 1979). In 1970, the Hydrobiological Mission of the Institute of Zoology of the University of Vienna (Austria), in cooperation with the Department of Zoology of the University of Sri Lanka, Vidyalankara Campus Kelaniya, took place. In these two missions the aquatic meso- and macrofauna of the running waters in the mountains of southwestern Sri Lanka were studied. Results of this latter mission were mainly published in the Bulletin of the Fisheries Research Station of Sri Lanka, Colombo (Costa and Starmühlner

121

1972, Weninger 1972, Viets 1972, Van den Elzen 1972, Costa 1972, St.Quentin 1972, Délève 1973b, Reichholf 1973, Wewalka 1973, De Beauchamp 1973, Bertrand 1973, St. Quentin 1973, Kaltenbach 1973, Pretzmann 1973, Malicky 1973, Starmühlner 1974, Hadl 1974, Polhemus 1979, Müller-Liebenau 1982a, 1982b, 1982c, Jäch 1984). In addition, results were published elsewhere by Kuiper (1979) and Zwick (1980). Contributions to the fauna of mountain streams were also published in Fernando (1984), amongst them a checklist of the meso- and macrofauna (Starmühlner, 1984b).

General Situation

The interior of Sri Lanka is occupied by the central highlands reaching an elevation of 1400-1800 m in the central parts and to 2524 m at the highest peak (Pidurutalagala). Geologically, Sri Lanka is a detached part of the Deccan Plate of ancient crystalline rocks (Sawicky 1925, Cooray 1967, Sievers 1967, Cooray 1984). Only the peninsula of Jaffna and the northwest coast are covered by Miocene limestones. Along the other coasts and the outflows of the large streams alluvial soils, containing mainly sand, clay and silt, cover large areas. In the southeast non-calcic soils developed a deficiency of ferromagnesium materials in the acidic gneisses (Brinck et al. 1971). In the Uva Province, in the southeast, the slopes of the hills are intercalated by limestone-marble zones, enriched with silicates, calcite, diopside and biotite (Brinck et al. 1971).

Climate, Vegetation, Physical and Chemical Conditions of the Running Waters

Sri Lanka is a tropical island situated within the equatorial belt of calms and the intensity and narrow amplitude of insolation are important factors affecting climate. In the wet zone of the mountains there is only slight seasonal variation in temperature, air humidity, and day length. The ascending of the main winds, the SW monsoon (May to August) and the NE monsoon (November to February) on the flanks in the central massifs of the montane areas leads to well-differentiated rainfall patterns. In the so-called wet zone in southwestern Sri Lanka precipitation is very high with annual averages between 2000 mm and 7000 mm. Mean annual climatic measurements are given in Figure 1, Figure 2 and in Table 1.

Up to an altitude of 500-800 m the wet zone lowlands are covered with evergreen tropical lowland rain forest. In the valleys of the bigger rivers the forests are mainly replanted by tropical plantations. About 250 species of trees are found in this region, mainly belonging to the

Table 1. Temperature and humidity conditions in Sri Lanka (Brink et al. 1971 and Starmühlner 1984b).

Area	Mean annual temperature (°C)	Maximum variation (°C)	Humidity (%)	
			Day	Night
Lowlands (Colombo)	27.2	1.8	68-79	87-93
Uplands (Kandy)	24.2	2.7	60-70	87-94
Highlands (Nuwara Eliya)	15.4	2.4	60-84	88-93

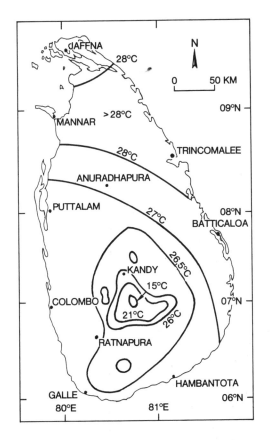

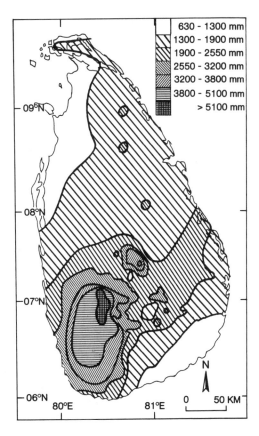

Figure 1. Average annual air temperature in Sri Lanka (Brink *et al.* 1971 and Starmühlner 1984b).

Figure 2. Annual average distribution of rainfall in Sri Lanka (Brink *et al.* 1971 and Starmühlner 1984b).

genera *Dipterocarpus, Doona, Artocarpus, Cinnamomum,* or *Ficus.* In the uplands, at altitudes between 800 m and 1500 m the wet warm mountain area follows, covered by tropical mountain rain forest. A decrease in the luxuriance of plant growth is observed. In the wet, cool highland between 1500 m and 2500 m, natural vegetation is upper montane rain forest. The genus *Calophyllum* is also characteristic for the montane forests. Most of the running waters in the mountain areas of the south and southwest drain regions of crystalline rocks (Fig. 3). In the southwestern uplands, some rivers traverse crystalline chalk layers such as Wetakei Ela (Fig. 19) or Kuda Oya (Fig. 20).

Because of their relatively short courses, compared to continental streams, most running waters in the mountains of Sri Lanka have steep gradients (Figs. 4, 5, 9). Average gradients are between 15% and 20%. In the region of the headwaters and upper courses gradients rise up to 50%-100% in waterfalls. Frequently cascades descend for several hundred meters, in some instances, in steep gradients, like cataracts (Costa and Starmühlner, 1972). The remarkable falls cause very high to high flow velocities in the regions of the headwaters and upper courses, partly in the transition zone to the middle courses. The average flow velocity on the surface of the mountain streams reaches up to 75-100 cm/sec, in the rapids, cascades and waterfalls the

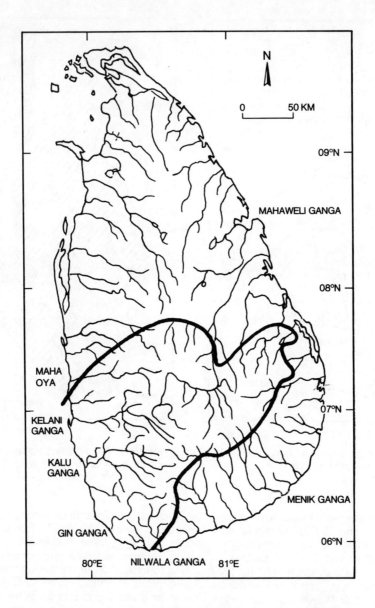

Figure 3. Drainage pattern and location of the mountain streams (bold line) in the southwestern and central parts of Sri Lanka (Brink *et al.* 1971 and Starmühlner 1984b).

current becomes turbulently rapid and soars to more than 200-300 cm/sec. Between the cascades frequently groove-like pools and lentic regions occur, where surface currents range between 0 cm/sec to 20-30 cm/sec (Fig. 19).

Similar velocities may also be found at the river banks (Fig. 21). These pools are often relatively deep (from 50 cm to 1 m and more). Typical stillwater fauna and many fish populations may dwell there, however, these microhabitats are flooded from time to time, after heavy showers, especially in the season of the SW monsoon. During this period they show characteristics of zones with strong currents (Costa and Starmühlner, 1972).

Flow velocity and bottom structure are very important factors for the occurrence of aquatic life (Hora 1928, 1930, 1936, Costa and Starmühlner 1972). In waterfalls (Fig. 9) and cascades (Figs. 10, 17) with extremely strong to strong currents (1-2 m/sec to 3 m/sec) the bottom is formed by standing, smooth granitic pyroxen rock with an average water-depth of only 5 mm and a maximum of 5 cm. Large granitic boulders with 1 to several m² surface and up to 1 m or 2 m in diameter are typical for torrents and rapids with strong currents of 1-2 m/sec (Figs. 3, 8, 13, 14, 15, 16, 18). The depth reaches up to 10 cm. In areas with smaller cascades and scale-like lotic areas, interrupted by pools, medium-sized granitic boulders of 30-80 cm in diameter dominate, mixed with gravel of 5-10 cm in diameter (Fig. 7). Lotic areas with a current speed between 50 cm/sec and 75 cm/sec have a bottom of gravel and pebbles (Figs. 11, 12). The depth reaches up to 50 cm. In lotic areas with slow current between 20 cm/sec and 30 cm/sec sand where sporadic stones dominates the depths are between 20 cm and 50 cm or even more. In very slow current or stagnant water of the lentic areas in pools, on river banks and reservoirs, the bottom is composed of very fine sand, gradually mixed with mud covered by a stratum with dense layers of plant debris. Depth in these regions reaches sometimes more than 50 cm (Figs. 6, 21, 22, 23). Data are summarized in Table 2 and Figure 34.

Table 2. Characteristics of the mountain streams of Sri Lanka.

Flow velocity	Stream section	Bottom type	Water depth
1.5-3 m/sec	waterfall	standing, smooth granite, pyroxen rocks	0.5 - 5 cm
1 - 1.5 m/sec	cascades	large, granite boulders 1-2 m in diameter	5 - 10 cm
75 - 100 cm/sec	small cascades interrupted by pools	medium granite boulders, gravel	10 - 30 cm
50 - 75 cm/sec	lotic section	gravel, pebbles	10 - 50 cm
10 - 30 cm/sec	lotic section	sand, sporadic stones stones	20 - 50 cm
0 - 10/20 cm /sec	lentic section: pools between cascades and bays	fine sand, mud, silt debris	50 cm and more

Over a distance of 100 to 150 km from the headwaters at about 2000 m altitude down to the lower courses, the water temperature of the mountain streams of Sri Lanka on the average increases from 15°C to 28°C, i.e. the difference is about 13°C (Fig. 46). The average increase of the water temperature per 100 m altitude is between 0.75°C and 1.5°C, depending on the exposition (free or overshadowed). According to Costa and Starmühlner (1972), day-night differences in water temperature are higher in shady forests (4-5°C) compared to open hill regions (tea estates, 3-4°C) or open valleys (rice fields, 2-3°C).

The physiography, geology, geochemistry and climate, to a large extent, determine the hydrochemistry of the mountain streams of Sri Lanka (Geisler 1967, Weninger 1972, Starmühlner 1984a, 1984b). In the wet zone of the crystalline series the extreme poverty in

Table 3. Chemical conditions in crystalline zones of the mountain streams. Based on Weninger (1972).

Parameter	Headwater (1500-2000 m)	Upper course (500-1500 m)	Middle course (50-500 m)	Lower course (5-50 m)	Mouth (0-5 m)
El_{20} (μS)	18.27	26.65	41.56	44.4	288
pH	5.8 - 6.1	5.9 - 6.5	6.3 - 6.8	6 - 6.47	7
Total Hardness (10 mg/l CaO)	0.322	0.81	0.98	0.75	1.4
$KMnO_4$-Consumption	22.9	13.5	16.3	25.2	13.3
Humic Acids (ppm)	0.703	0.158	0.306	0.019	0.1
CaO (ppm)	1.8	2.7	5.9	4.4	1.6
MgO (ppm)	1.06	1.8	2.79	3.25	9.68
Ca^{++} (ppm)	1.3	1.98	4.35	3.3	1.15
Mg^{++} (ppm)	0.64	0.99	1.67	1.95	5.81
Na^+ (ppm)	1.42	1.76	2.84	3.4	1
K^+ (ppm)	0.42	0.73	0.97	2.97	3.5
$Fe^{++}+Fe^{+++}$ (ppm) 0.004	0.126	0.0085	0.008	0.022	
Al^{+++} (ppm)	0.68	0.064	0.058	0.035	0.09
NH_4^+ (ppm)	0.186	0.1	0.072	0.0125	0.04
NO_2 (ppm)	0	0.003	0.01	0	0
NO_3^- (ppm)	0.235	0.198	0.089	0.1425	0.21
Cl^- (ppm)	0.1985	2.41	2.72	5.11	85.2
P_2O_5 (ppm)	0.03	0.11	0.128	0.03	0.08
SiO_2 (ppm)	4.97	8.58	11.16	3.25	6.95
Alc (HCO_3) (mval)	0.08	0.3	0.4	0.22	0.44
Free CO_2 (ppm)	52.25	30.1	50.6	0	0
Aggr. CO_2 (ppm)	5.3	3.6	3.9	0	0

dissolved mineral salts and the slightly acidic nature of the mountain streams are typical. Sodium (Na^+) predominates calcium (Ca^{++}) sometimes, while calcium (Ca^{++}) predominates magnesium (Mg^{++}) depending on the composition of the underlying crystalline rocks (Tab. 3). Concentrations of dissolved minerals decrease with increasing altitude. Weninger (1972) measured an extremely low electric conductivity (El_{20}) with only 8.8 µS in the headwaters from the upper montane forest region, with high contents of humic substances and ammonium. The content of free CO_2 (Tab. 3) seems responsible for the aggressivity against calcareous shells of aquatic molluscs which do not occur in such montane headwaters.

Electric conductivity (El_{20}), total hardness (also Fig. 46), of Ca^{++}, Mg, and alcalinity increase nearly linearly with the decreasing altitude. Trends are similar for Al^{+++} and SiO_2 with maximum amounts in tributaries running through plantations, as well as for the humic acids. Chloride and sodium are slightly increasing. Only ammonium concentrations are higher upstream, while nitrate concentrations are stable (Weninger 1972). The linear increase in conductivity is occasionally shaped by a noticeable increase in electrolytes as, for instance, in the affluents of the Kelani Ganga near Kitulgala. This effect may be due to the influence of crystalline limestones on the hydrochemistry of some tributaries. Characteristic rivers in the wet rain forest areas such as the affluents and tributaries of the Gin Ganga are acidic and have a higher content of ammonium and humic acids compared to the mountain rivers in the tea estate areas. "Rain forest rivers" contain very little dissolved calcium, but a relatively high concentration of magnesium, sodium, potassium and silicate. This may be due to more active soil filtration and the vegetation cover (Weninger 1972). In the big waterfalls and cascades conductivity and total hardness (more Ca^{++}) as well as pH and Cl^- increase slightly. Free carbon dioxide content appears not to be influenced but free CO_2 decreases as well as Mg^{++}, Na^+, Al^{+++}, NO_3^- and SiO_2. According to Weninger (1972), this may be a direct result of rainwater drained by the rock. Remarkable are also the high amounts of humic acids and ammonium. Headwaters and upper courses of streams from the mountaineous tea-estate regions such as in the area of Maskeliya-Hatton (Fig. 15) have a higher conductivity and total hardness than the headwaters from the areas under montane forests (Fig. 8). Acidity is similar

Table 4. Chemical conditions of the mountain streams in the limestone-marble zone of the Uva Province (middle courses with an altitudinal range of 50-200 m). Based on Weninger (1972).

Parameter	Value	Parameter	Value
El_{20}(µS)	327.5	$Fe^{++}+Fe^{+++}$ (ppm)	0.0085
pH	7.4 - 8	Al^{+++} (ppm)	0.02
$KMnO_4$ consumption	15.5	NH_4^+ (ppm)	0.05
Humic Acids (ppm)	0.265	NO_2^- (ppm)	0.0025
Total Hardness (10mg/l CaO)	10.4	NO_3^- (ppm)	0.1045
CaO (ppm)	55.68	Cl^- (ppm)	4.285
MgO (ppm)	34.81	P_2O_5 (ppm)	0.095
Ca^{++} (ppm)	40.3	SiO_2(ppm)	41.8
Mg^{++} (ppm)	20.39	Alc (HCO_3) (ppm)	4.125
Na^+ (ppm)	22.65	Free CO_2 (ppm)	154
K^+ (ppm)	2.8	Aggr. CO_2 (ppm)	0.25

to that of the reddish soil (pH 5.5-6.0) which is supposed to be ideal for tea cultivation. The amount of aggressive CO_2 of 5.8-6.4 ppm is extremely high for surface waters and explains, as indicated above, the absence of water snails in these headwaters.

The northeastern slopes of the hills with their crystalline rocks are interspersed by limestone-marble zones, enriched in silicates, calcite, diopside and biotite. The mountain streams of these areas flow through dense, typical dry forest of the *Chloroxylon*-ecosystem (Brinck *et al.* 1971). Particularly the content of dissolved silicate is notable, but also the occurrence of calcareous sinter (Fig. 19). The amount of free CO_2 seems to be very high, possible as as result of the presenece of extensive humus layers in the rather brown soil. The high contents of SiO_2 originate presumably from the gneisses while the crystalline limestones are at most locally important (Weninger, 1972). The chemical conditions of the mountain streams in the limestone-marble areas of the Uva Province (Buttala-Wellawaya) have been studied in detail (Tab. 4).

Remarks on the Freshwater Fauna of the Mountain Streams of Sri Lanka

Average densities of the mesofauna in mountain streams are very high in sections with strong currents (Tab. 5). However, species diversity is low and species occur in high numbers and show special adaptions to strong currents such as in the larvae of Simuliidae, Blephariciridae and Chironomidae. Table 6 (annexed) summarizes mesofauna species of the headwaters communities at elevations between 1500 m and 2000 m. Table 7 (annexed) summarizes the meso- and macrofauna of the upper course communities at elevations between 500 and 1500 m (Fig. 34 for a schematic cross sectional diagram).

Table 5. Densities (in 100 individuals/m^2) of the mesofauna in different sections of the mountain streams of Sri Lanka.

Flow velocity	Headwater (1500-2000 m)	Upper course (500-1500 m)	Lower course (30-500 m)
0-30 cm/sec	3.2-4.8	4.8	1.6
30-75 cm/sec	8.0-32.0	8.0-32.0	3.2-11.2
75-300 cm/sec	320-480	320-480	80-120

Some Remarks on the Mollusc Fauna of the Mountain Streams

Starmühlner (1974, 1977, 1979) described 31 species of fresh (and brackish) water gastropods from Sri Lanka. Hadl (1974) has listed 4 species of freshwater mussels from the running waters and Kuiper (1979) reported 3 species of pea-shell cockles, genus *Pisidium,* from the borders of mountain streams.

Archaegastropoda-Neritidae

This group is represented by 2 species: *Neritina (Neripteron) auriculata* which settles only in the lower reaches of streams below stones near the borders with flow velocities between 20cm/sec and 50 cm/sec. This snail species tolerates slightly brackish water (recurrent flow during high tide). The other species is *Septaria lineata* (Fig. 35), found in the lower courses in pure freshwater, settling on the surface of stones and floating vegetation in moderate currents.

Mesogastropoda

The biggest group of prosobranch-gastropods are the Mesogastropoda. Of them the Viviparidae are represented by *Bellamya dissimilis* var. *ceylanica* inhabiting stagnant waters and the margins of slow running streams in the lowland. The Ampullariidae are represented by *Pila globosa* (Fig. 37), occurring in stagnant waters of both uplands and lowlands. The Sri Lankan Hydrobiidae also have only one representative, *Tricula montana*, found only in small upland mountain streams. 4 species were recorded from the Stenothyridae: *Gangetia burmanica* occurs exclusively in brackish water near the northern coast of Sri Lanka. *Bithynia inconspica* (Fig. 36) and *B. stenothyroides*, but also the rare *Mysorella costigera* are typically inhabitants of swamps, pools, ponds, reservoirs and the margin of slow running lowland and upland streams with muddy bottoms and are rich in debris or dense vegetation. The Synceridae with 2 recorded species (*Syncera* (=*Assiminea*) cf. *hidalgoi* and *S.* (=*A.*) cf. *woodmasoniana*) occur sympathetically with *Gangetia burmanica* (reported above), in brackish rivers, crossing salt meadows, near the northern coast of Sri Lanka. The Thiaridae (=Melaniidae) is, with 14 species, the biggest family of the Mesogastropoda in Sri Lanka. *Faunus ater* and *Melanoides (Stenomelania) torulosas* are found only in coastal areas with slightly brackish water. Like the marine species of prosobranchs, both species have free-living veliger larvae. *Melanoides (M.) tuberculata*, pantropically distributed, is viviparous with parthogenetic development of the eggs in broodpouches. Mostly only females were found. This species is eurytopic and is found in stagnant waters near the coasts as well as in the lowlands and uplands in stagnant waters, but also along the margins of slow and moderately flowing streams with current velocities up to 30 cm/sec. Rich in species and typical for Sri Lanka is the genus *Paludomus*, which contains some endemic species. *Paludomus (Paludomus) chilinoides* (Figs. 38-40) is very frequent in slow to fairly fast running streams in the lowlands and uplands. This species prefers streams outside the crystalline series with an average conductivity of 300-600 µS and a total hardness of 9-13°dH. *P. (P.) inflatus* is found in rivers with sandy bottoms. *P. (P.) palustris* is endemic to the Northern Central Province, mostly occurring along the grassy margins of tanks. *P. (P.) tanschauricus tanschauricus* inhabits the margins of slow flowing streams and canals in northern Sri Lanka. *P. (P.) tanschauricus nasutus* (Fig. 41) is an endemic subspecies living near the margins of streams in the uplands of the central and eastern parts of the mountains in southern Sri Lanka. *P. (Philopotamis) bicinctus*, endemic to Sri Lanka, occurs in mountain streams with cascades, between 250 m and 1100 m altitude. *P. (Ph.) decussatus*, a rare species in fast running mountain streams, is endemic to the uplands of the Uva Province. *P. (Ph.) nigricans* occurs exclusively in cool brooks and torrents of the central highland with water temperatures of about 15°C, slightly acidic and very soft waters (El_{20}: 26 µS, Total Hardness: 0.65°dH, CaO: 2.6 ppm). *P. (Ph.) regalis* (Fig. 42) is a rare endemic species in fast running, stony streams of the upland and occurs, like *P. (Ph.) sulcatus*, in the uplands of southwestern Sri Lanka.

P. (Tanalia) loricatus, endemic to the highlands of the central mountains, shows high variability in shell morphology (Figs. 44-45). It is a typical inhabitant of fast running mountain streams with current velocities between 30 cm and 100 cm/sec and prefers stones and rocks. This species prefers the main tributaries of the mountain stream system, contrary to *P. (T.) neritoides*, the second-most frequent species of the subgenus *Tanalia*, which is found in smaller streams. The distribution of these two endemic species overlaps. The shell of *P. (T.) neritoides* (Figs. 43, 45) is also highly variable in size and shape. Both species dwell mostly under the surface of the water and sometimes move out of the water around waterfalls. *P. (T.) solidus* is the only representative of the subgenus *Tanalia* in the calcareous streams of the limestone areas of the hilly regions of the Uva Province (near Buttala and Wellawaya). The waters in that area are alkaline and moderately hard (El_{20}: 350 µS; Total Hardness: 11.6 ; CaO: 59.4 ppm; SiO_2: 54.8 ppm). *Thiara (Plotia) scabra*, like *M. (M.) tuberculata* widely distributed in the Indopacific coastal areas, occurs in the stagnant waters of both lowlands and uplands, but also in slow running streams or in pools between cascades of mountain streams.

Pulmonata-Basommatophora

The pond-snails, Lymnaeidae, are represented in Sri Lanka by one species, *Lymnaea (Cerasina) luteola var. pinguis*, occurring in stagnant waters (pools, paddy fields, swamps, ponds and tanks), sometimes also in slow running streams with muddy bottoms and dense vegetation in lowlands and uplands. *Indoplanorbis exustus* (Bulinidae) was recorded from slightly brackish water near the coast and from stagnant waters up to 1200 m. This species is very frequent in the Oriental region between India and Thailand. The same wide distribution is shown by *Gyraulus (G.) convexiusculus* (Planorbidae). It is very frequent in all types of stagnant waters, sometimes also at the margins of slow running streams with dense vegetation.

Bivalvia

The Bivalvia are represented in the inland waters of Sri Lanka by the families Unionidae with *Lamellidens lamellatus, L. testudinarius* and *Parreysia corrugata,* the Corbiculidae with *Polymesoda ceylonica (= bengalensis),* only in slightly brackish water near the coast, and the Sphaeriidae with *Pisidium (Afropisidium) javanum, P. (Odhnerpisium) annandalei* (endemic) and *P. (O.) prasongi.* Only the Sphaeriidae are represented in the mountain streams of the upland near Kandy. The Unionidae inhabit the slow flowing streams with sandy bottoms in the lowland. Figure 46 shows the longitudinal distribution of the most important and frequent species of molluscs in the mountain streams of Sri Lanka between the headwaters and the lower courses and its relation to the water temperature, total hardness and conductivity.

Acknowledgments

The author thanks Prof. M. Mizzaro for the drawings of Figure 34, Prof. F. Dorner for the drawings of Figures 45 and 46, Mr. A. Bellingrath for the drawings of Figures 1, 2 and 3 (Brink *et al.* 1971 and Starmühlner, 1984a). The photographs of the freshwater animals and shells were taken by Prof. M. Mizzaro.

Literature Cited

Beauchamp, P. de. 1973. Results of the Austrian-Ceylonese Hydrobiological Mission 1970: Part X: Freshwater Triclads (Turbellaria, Tricladida) from Ceylon. *Bull. Fish. Res. Stn. Sri Lanka (Ceylon)* 24: 98-93.

Bertrand, H.P.I. 1973. Results of the Austrian-Ceylonese Hydrobiological Mission 1970: Part XI: Larvae and pupae of water beetles collected in the island of Ceylon. *Bull. Fish. Res. Stn. Sri Lanka (Ceylon)* 24: 95-112.

Bott, R. 1970. Die Süßwasser-Krabben von Ceylon (Crustacea, Decapoda). *Ark. Zool.* 22: 627-640.

Brinck, P., H. Andersson and L. Cederholm. 1971. Report No 1 from the Lund University Ceylon Expedtion in 1962: Introduction. *Ent. scand. Suppl. 1*: i-xxxiv.

Cooray, P.J. 1967. An Introduction to the Geology of Ceylon. *Spol. Zeylan.* 31: 1-324.

Cooray, P.J. 1984. Geology with special reference to the Precambrian. *In* C.H. Fernando, ed. *Ecology and Biogeography in Sri Lanka,* pp. 1-64. Junk Publ. The Hague.

Costa, H.H. 1972. Results of the Austrian-Ceylonese Hydrobiological Mission 1970: Part V: Decapoda, Caridea. *Bull. Fish. Res. Stn., Sri Lanka (Ceylon)* 23: 127-135.

Costa, H.H. 1974. Limnology and Fishery Biology of the Streams at Horton Plains, Sri Lanka (Ceylon). *Bull. Fish. Res. Stn. Sri Lanka (Ceylon)* 25: 15-26.

Costa, H.H. and E.C.M. Fernando. 1967. The food and feeding relationships of the the common meso- and macrofauna in the Maha Oya, a small mountainous stream near Peradeniya (Ceylon). *Ceyl. J. Sci. (Biol. Sci.)* 7: 74-90.

Costa, H.H. and F. Starmühlner. 1972. Results of the Austrian-Ceylonese Hydrobiological Mission 1970, Part I: Preliminary Report. Introduction and Description of the Stations. *Bull. Fish. Res. Stn. Sri Lanka (Ceylon)* 23: 43-76.

Delève, J. 1973a. Report No 25 from the Lund University Ceylon Expedition in 1962: Coleoptera: Dryopidae and Elminthidae of Ceylon. *Ent. scand. Suppl.* 4: 5-23.

Delève, J. 1973b. Results of the Austrian-Ceylonese Hydrobiological Mission 1970, Part VII: Dryopidae and Elminthidae of Ceylon. *Bull. Fish. Res. Stn. Sri Lanka (Ceylon)* 24: 69-74.

Elzen, P.M.M. van den. 1972. Results of the Austrian-Ceylonese Hydrobiological Mission 1970, Part IV: List of Reptilia and Amphibia collected in the mountains of SW Ceylon, with notes on finding localities. *Bull. Fish. Res. Stn., Sri Lanka (Ceylon)* 23: 113-125.

Enckell, P.H. 1970. Parastenocarididae (Copepoda, Harpacticoidea) from Ceylon. *Ark. Zool.* 22: 545-556.

Fernando, C.H. 1963. A guide to the freshwater fauna of Ceylon. Suppl. 1. *Bull. Fish. Res. Stn., Ceylon* 16: 29-38.

Fernando, C.H. 1964. A guide to the freshwater fauna of Ceylon. Suppl. 2. *Bull. Fish. Res. Stn., Ceylon* 17: 177-211.

Fernando, C.H. 1969a. A guide to the freshwater fauna of Ceylon. Suppl. 3. *Bull. Fish. Res. Stn., Ceylon* 20: 18-25.

Fernando, C.H. 1969b. Some freshwater molluscs from Ceylon with notes on their distribution and biology. *Bull. Fish. Res. Stn., Ceylon* 20: 135-140.

Fernando, C.H. 1974. A guide to the freshwater fauna of Sri Lanka. Suppl. 4. *Bull. Fish. Res. Stn., Sri Lanka (Ceylon)* 25: 27-81.

Fernando, C.H. 1980. The freshwater invertebrate fauna of Sri Lanka. *Centenary Volume, Colombo Museum, Sri Lanka* 35: 15-42.

Fernando, C.H. 1984. Freshwater invertebrates: some comments. *In* C.H. Fernando, ed. *Ecology and Biogeography in Sri Lanka*, pp.145-148. Junk Publ. The Hague.

Fernando, C.H. and H.H.A. Indrasena. 1969. The freshwater fisheries of Ceylon. *Bull. Fish. Res. Stn. Ceylon* 20: 101-134.

Geisler, R. 1967. Limnologisch-ichthyologische Beobachtungen in SW Ceylon. *Int. Rev. ges. Hydrobiol.*: 559-572.

Hadl, G. 1974. Results of the Austrian-Ceylonese Hydrobiological Mission 1970, Part XVIII: Freshwater mussels (Bivalvia). *Bull. Fish. Res. Stn., Sri Lanka (Ceylon)* 25: 183-189.

Hora, S.L. 1928. Animal life in torrential streams. *J. Bombay Nat. Hist. Soc.* 32: 111-126.

Hora, S.L. 1930. Ecology, bionomics and evolution of torrential fauna with special reference to the organs of attachment. *Phil. Trans. Roy. Soc.* 218: 171-292.

Hora, S.L. 1936. Nature of substratum as an important factor in the ecology of torrential fauna. *Proc. Nat. Inst. Sci., India* 2. 45-47.

Jäch, M. 1984. Die Koleopterenfauna der Bergbäche von Südwest-Ceylon (unter besonderer Berücksichtigung der Taxonomie, Ökologie sowie der allgemeinen geographischen Verbreitung der nachgewiesenen Taxa). *Arch. Hydrobiol./Suppl.* 69: 228-332.

Kaltenbach, A. 1973. Results of the Austrian-Ceylonese Hydrobiological Mission 1970, Part XIII: Some remarkable ripicol insects of the Ceylonese fauna. *Bull. Fish. Res. Stn. Sri Lanka (Ceylon)* 24: 125-128.

Kuiper, J.G.J. 1979. Report No 47 from the Lund University Ceylon Expedition in 1962: Mollusca, Lamellibranchiata, Sphaeriidae: Pisidium from Sri Lanka (Ceylon)(seen as manuscript).

Malicky, H. 1973. Results of the Austrian-Ceyloneses Hydrobiological Mission 1970, Part XVI: The Ceylonese Trichoptera. *Bull. Fish. Res. Stn. Sri Lanka (Ceylon)* 24: 153-177.

Mendis, A.S. and C.H. Fernando. 1962. A guide to the freshwater fauna of Ceylon. *Bull. Fish. Res. Stn. Ceylon* 12: 1-160.

Müller-Liebenau, I. 1982a. *Indobaetis*: A new genus of Baetidae from Sri Lanka (Insecta, Ephemeroptera) with two new species. *Gewäss. Abwäss.* 68/69: 26-34.

Müller-Liebenau, I. 1982b. Five new species of *Pseudocleon*, Klapalek, 1905. (Fam: Baetidae) from the oriental region (Insecta, Ephemeroptera) with some general remarks on *Pseudocleon. Arch. Hydrobiol.* 95: 283-298.

Müller-Liebenau, I. 1982c. A new genus and species of Baetidae from Sri Lanka (Ceylon): *Indocleon primium* (Insecta, Ephemeroptera). *Aquatic Insects* 4: 125-129.

Polhemus, J.J. 1979. Aquatic and semiaquatic Hemiptera of Sri Lanka from the Austrian Indo-Pacific Expedition 1970. *Bull. Fish. Res. Stn. Sri Lanka (Ceylon)* 29: 89-113.

Pretzmann, G. 1973. Results of the Austrian-Ceylonese Hydrobiological Mission 1970, Part XIV: The freshwater crabs of the Ceylonese mountain rivers. *Bull. Fish. Res. Stn. Sri Lanka (Ceylon)* 24: 113-124.

Quentin, D.G. St. 1972. Results of the Austrian-Ceylonese Hydrobiological Mission 1970, Part VI: A new *Drepanosticta* from Ceylon (Order: Odonata, Insecta). *Bull. Fish. Res. Stn. Sri Lanka (Ceylon)* 23: 137-139.

Quentin, D.G. St. 1973. Results of the Austrian-Ceylonese Hydrobiological Mission 1970, Part XII: Contribution to the ecology of the larvae of some Odonata from Ceylon. *Bull. Fish. Res. Stn. Sri Lanka (Ceylon)* 24: 113-124.

Radda, A.C. 1973. Results of the Austrian-Ceylonese Hydrobiological Mission 1970, Part XV: Collection on Fishes (Osteichthyes). *Bull. Fish. Res. Stn. Sri Lanka (Ceylon)* 24: 135-151.

Reichholf, J. 1973. Results of the Austrian-Ceylonese Hydrobiological Mission 1970, Part VIII: Larval stages of water moths (Lepidoptera, Pyralidae, Nymphulinae) from torrents of Ceylon and some South Pacific Islands. *Bull. Res. Stn. Sri Lanka (Ceylon)* 24: 75-81.

Sawicky, L. 1925. *On the Geomorphology of Central Ceylon.* Trav. de l'Inst. Geogr. de l'Univ. Cracovie (Krakau), Poland.

Sievers, A. 1964. *Ceylon. Gesellschaft und Lebensraum in den orientalischen Tropen.* Bibl. Geogr. Handbücher. Steiner Verlag, Wiesbaden.

Schmid, F. 1958. Trichoptères de Ceylan. *Arch. Hydrobiol.* 54: 1-173.

Starmühlner, F. 1974. Results of the Austrian-Ceylonese Hydrobiological Mission 1970, Part XVII: The freshwater Gastropods of Ceylon. *Bull. Res. Stn. Sri Lanka (Ceylon)* 25: 97-181.

Starmühlner, F. 1977. The Genus *Paludomus* in Ceylon. *Proc. 5th Malac. Congr. Malacologia* 16: 261-264.

Starmühlner, F. 1979. Distribution of freshwater molluscs in mountain streams of tropical Indo-Pacific islands (Madagascar, Ceylon, New Caledonia). *Proc. 6th Malac. Congr. Malacologia* 18: 245-255.

Starmühlner, F. 1984a. Checklist and longitudinal distribution of the meso- and macrofauna of mountain streams of Sri Lanka. *Arch. Hydrobiol.* 101: 303-325.

Starmühlner, F. 1984b. Mountain stream fauna with special reference to Mollusca. *In* C.H. Fernando, ed. *Ecology and Biogeography in Sri Lanka,* pp. 215-255. Junk Publ. The Hague.

Viets, K.O. 1972. Results of the Austrian-Ceylonese Hydrobiological Mission 1970, Part III: Über einige Wassermilben aus Ceylon (Hydrachnellae, Acari). *Bull. Fish. Res. Stn. Sri Lanka (Ceylon)* 23: 101-111.

Weninger, G. 1972. Results of the Austrian-Ceylonese Hydrobiological Mission 1970, Part II: Hydrochemical studies on mountain streams in Ceylon. *Bull. Fish. Res. Stn. Sri Lanka (Ceylon)* 23: 77-100.

Wewalka, G. 1973. Results of the Austrian-Ceylonese Hydrobiological Mission 1970, Part IX: Dytiscidae (Coleoptera). *Bull. Fish. Res. Stn. Sri Lanka (Ceylon)* 24: 83-87.

Zwick, P. 1980. The genus *Neoperla* (Plecoptera: Perlidae) from Sri Lanka. *Oriental Insects* 14: 263-269.

Table 6. Species composition of the headwater community (1500-2000 m).

Taxonomic Group	Flow velocity			
	0-30 cm/sec	30-75 cm/sec	75-100 cm/sec	>100 cm/sec
Annelida Oligochaeta	*Tubifex tubifex* *Limnodrilus hoffmeisteri* *Lumbricus variegatus*			
Turbellaria	*Dugesia nannophallus*	*Dugesia nannophallus*		
Crustacea Brachyura	*Paratelphusa rugosa*			
Insecta Odonata	*Lestes* sp. Anisoptera gen. sp.	*Euphaea spendens*		
Coleoptera	*Lacconectes simoni* *Hydaticus luzonicus* *Pelthydrus* sp. *Aulonogyrus obliquus* *Orectochilus* sp.	*Ilamelmis foveicollis* *Podelmis 4-plagiata* *P. ovalis* *P. humeralis* *P. cruzei* *P. ater* *Ohyia carinata* *Zeitzeviaria zeylanica* *Eubrianax* sp. Lampyridae cf. *Luciola*		
Heteroptera	*Sigara nilgirica* *Enithares simplex* *Metrocoris stali* *Strongylovelia formosa* *Pseudovelia gnoma*			
Ephemeroptera	*Indocloeon primum*	*Indocloeon primum* *Indobaetis costai* Leptophlebiidae gen. spp.	*Indobaetis costai* *Pseudocloeon orientale* *P. klapaleki*	
Diptera Nematocera	*Chironomus* (cf. *plumosa*)			*Simulium* spp. *Gomphostilbia (S.)* sp. Blephariciridae gen. sp.
Plecoptera		*Neoperla angulata* *Phanoperla* sp.		

Taxonomic Group	Flow velocity			
	0-30 cm/sec	30-75 cm/sec	75-100 cm/sec	>100 cm/sec
Trichoptera		*Apsilochroma diffinis*	*Chimarra* sp.	
		Synagapetus sp.	*Pseudolep- tonema* sp.	
		Hydroptilidae gen. spp.	Hydropsychiidae gen. spp.	
		Polycentropidae gen. spp.	*H. katugahakanda*	
		Economus sp.	*H. annulata*	
		Psychomyidae gen. sp.	*Diplectona* sp.	
		Marilia cf. *ceylanica*	*Diplectonella aprobanes*	
		Molanna taprobane	*Ceylanopsyche* spp.	
		Oecetis sumansara		
		Goerodes sp.		
		Helicopsyche amarawathi		
		H. ruprawathi		
Mollusca Gastropoda	*Paludomus (Philopotamis) nigrescens*	*P. (Ph.) nigrescens*		
Vertebrata Amphibia	tadpoles of *Rhacophorus cruciger eques* *Rana temporalis*			

Table 7. Species composition of the upper course community (500-1500 m).

Taxonomic Group	Flow velocity			
	0-30 cm/sec	30-75 cm/sec	75-100 cm/sec	>100 cm/sec
Turbellaria	*Dugesia nannophallus*	*D. nannophallus*		
Crustacea Caridea	*Atya spinipes* *Caridina fernandoi* *C. nilotica simoni* *C. pristis*	*Macrobrachium australe* *M. latimanus* *M. scrabiculum*		
Brachyura	*Paratelphusa rugosa*			
Acari		*Arrenurus maderaszi* *Torrenticola pusta* *T. oxyostoma hamata* *T. ceylonensis* *Atractides schwoerbeli*		
Insecta Ephemeroptera	Leptophlebiidae gen. spp. *Ephemera* sp. *Indocloeon primum* *Pseudocloeon difficilum*	Leptophlebiidae gen. spp. Ecdyonuridae gen. spp. *Indocloenon primum* *Pseudocloeon difficilum* *Indobaetis costai* *Proso- pistoma* sp.	*Pseudocloeon orientale* *P. difficilum* *Indobaetis costai*	
Plecoptera		*Neoperla angulata* *N. triangulata* *Phanoperla* sp.		
Odonata	*Libellago greeni* *L. finalis* *Vestalis apicalis nigrescens* *Neurobasis chinensis* *Lestes elata* *Drepanosticta* sp. *Ellatoneurix tenax* *Prodasineura sita* *Heliogomphus* sp. *Megalogomphus ceylonicus* *Paragomphus henryi*	*Euphaea splendens* *Zygonyx iris ceylanica*		

Taxonomic Group	Flow velocity			
	0-30 cm/sec	30-75 cm/sec	75-100 cm/sec	>100 cm/sec
	Anax immaculifrons *Macromia zeylanica* *Trithemis festiva*			
Orthoptera	*Rhabdoblatta* sp. - larva *Paranemobius pictus* *Euscelimena gavialis*			
Trichoptera		*Apsilochroma affinis* *Synagapetus hanumata* *S.* cf. *rudis* *Hydroptila kurukepitiya* *Oxyethira* sp. *Pseudo- neuroclepsis starmühlneri* Polycentropidae gen. spp. *Diplectrona* sp. *Paduniella mahanawana* *P. subhakara* Psychomyidae gen. spp. *Marilia ceylanica* *Trichosetodes meghawanabaya* *Adicella* sp. *Oecetis belihuloya* *O. hamata* *O. malighawa* *O. sumanasara* *Setodinella punctatissima* Leptoceridae gen. spp. *Goera katugalganda* *G. paragoda* *Goerodes fuscata* *G. puncta* *Helicopsyche amarawathi* *H. rupawathi*	*Chimarra* sp. *Gunungiella madakumbara* *Oestropsyche vitrina* *Macronema* sp. *Pseudplep- tonema* sp. *Hydrosyche katugahakanda* *H. flinti* *Synaptopsyche nikalandugola* *Diplectronella taprobanes* *Ceylanopsyche* gen. sp.	

137

Taxonomic Group	Flow velocity			
	0-30 cm/sec	30-75 cm/sec	75-100 cm/sec	>100 cm/sec
Coleoptera	*Lacconectes simonis*	*Helichus naviculus*		
	Hydaticus luczonicus	*Ceradryops punctatus*		
	Neptosternus sp.	*Potamophilinus impressicollis*		
	Pelthydrus sp.	*Ordobrevia fletcheri*		
	Aulonogyrus obliquus	*llamelmis brunnescens*		
	Canthydrus luctuosus	*I. foveicollis*		
	Laccophilus chinensis	*I. crassa*		
	innefficiens	*Cephalolimnius ater*		
	Berosus indicus	*Podelmis quadriplagiata*		
	Hydrophilidae gen. spp.	*P. aenea*		
		Illamelmis starmuehlneri		
		Zaitzeviaria bicolor		
		Hydrocyphon atratus		
		H. striatus		
		Eubrianax ceylonicus		
		Lampyridae cf. *Luciola* sp.		
		Aulonogyrus obliquus		
		Orectochilus sp.		
Heteroptera	*Micronecta memonidesi*			
	M. wrobleskii			
	M. quadristrigata			
	Aphelocheirus clivicolus			
	Heleocoris breviceps			
	Cercotmetus strangulatus			
	Enithares simplex			
	Ochterus marginatus			
	Limnogonus nitidus			
	Limnometra anadyomene			
	Metrocoris stali			
	Ptilomera ingalensis			
	Rheumatogonus custodiensis			

Taxonomic Group	Flow velocity			
	0-30 cm/sec	30-75 cm/sec	75-100 cm/sec	>100 cm/sec
Diptera Nematocera	*Ventidius henryi* *Timasius splendens* *Hydrometra greeni* *Microvelia longicornis* *M. pererai* *Rhagovelia ceylanica* *Rh. kaunaratnei* *Tetraripis asymmetricus* *Aedes (Finlaya) lineatus* Dixidae gen. sp. *Odontomyia* sp. Psilopinae gen. sp. *Limonia* sp.	Orthocladiinae gen. spp. *Rheotany-. tarsus* sp	Orthocladiinae gen. spp. *Rheotany- tarsus* sp	*Simulium 5- striatum Gomphostilbia (Simulium)* sp. Blephariciridae gen. spp. *Aulacodes* sp.
Lepidoptera Mollusca Gastropoda	*Paludomus (P.) tanschauricus nasutus* *P. (Philopotamis) bicinctus* *P. (Tanalia) loricatus* *P. (Tanalia) neritoides* *Melanoides tuberculata* *Thiara scabra*	*Paludomus (P.) tanschauricus nasutus* *P. (Philopotamis) bicinctus* *P. (Tanalia) loricatus* *P. (Tanalia) neritoides*	*P.(Tanalia) loricatus* *P. (Tanalia) neritoides*	
Bivalvia	*Pisidium (Odhnerpisidium) annandalei* *P. (O.) prasongi* *P. (Afropisidium) javanum*			
Vertebrata Reptilia	*Natrix piscator asperrimus* *Boiga ceylonensis*			
Amphibia	tadpoles of *Racophorus cruciger* *Rana temporalis* *R. cyanaophlictis* *R. limnocharis*			

Taxonomic Group	Flow velocity			
	0-30 cm/sec	30-75 cm/sec	75-100 cm/sec	>100 cm/sec
Pisces	*Danio malabaricus*	*Danio malabaricus*		
	Rasbora vaterifloris	*Rasbora vaterifloris*		
	R. daniconius	*R. daniconius*		
	Chela laubuca	*Chela laubuca*		
	Barbus (Puntius) bimaculatus	*Barbus (Puntius) bimaculatus*		
	B. (P.) dorsalis	*B. (P.) dorsalis*		
	B. (P.) filamentosus	*B. (P.) filamentosus*		
	B.(P.) nigrofasciatus	*B.(P.) nigrofasciatus*		
	B. (P.) sarana	*B. (P.) sarana*		
	Cyprinus carpio	*Garra lamta*	*Garra lamta*	*Garra lamta*
	INoemachilus notostigma	*Noemachilus notostigma*		
	Lepidocephalus thermalis	*Lepidocephalus thermalis*		
	Xenotodon cancila	*Xenotodon cancila*		
	Anguilla bicolor	*Anguilla bicolor*		
	A. nebulosa	*A. nebulosa*		
	Aplocheilus dayi	*Aplocheilus dayi*		
	Poecilia reticulata	*Poecilia reticulata*		
	Xiphophorus helleri	*Xiphophorus helleri*		
	Channa orientalis	*Channa orientalis*		
	Ophiocephalus gachua	*Ophiocephalus gachua*	*Ophiocephalus gachua*	
		Glossogobius giuris	*Glossogobius giuris*	*Glossogobius giuris*
	Belontia signata			
	Macrognathus aculeatus	*Macrognathus aculeatus*	*Macrognathus aculeatus*	

Table 8. Composition of the middle course community (50-500 m elevation).

Taxonomic Group	Flow velocity			
	0-30 cm/sec	30-75 cm/sec	75-100 cm/sec	>100 cm/sec
Turbellaria	*Dugesia nannophallus*	*Dugesia nannophallus*		
Crustacea Caridea	*Atya spinipes* *Caridina fernandoi*	*Macrobrachium australe*		
	C. nilotica simoni	*M. idella* *M. latimanus*		
	C. n. zeylanica			
Brachyura	*Paratelphusa (C.) rugosa* *P.(O.) senex*			
Acari		Hydrachnellae gen. spp.		
	Leptophlebiidae gen. spp.	Leptophlebiidae gen. spp.		
Insecta Ephemeroptera	*Pseudocloeon difficilum*	*Pseudocloeon difficilum* *Indobaetis starmuehlneri* Ecdyonuridae gen. spp.	*Pseudocloeon ambiguum*	
Plecoptera		*Neoperla angulata* *N. triangulata* *Phanoperla* sp.		
Odonata	*Libellago greeni* *Vestalis apicalis nigrescens* *Neurobasis chin. chinensis* *Copera marginipes* *Drepanosticta* sp. *Elattoneura centralis* *Microgomphus wiya* *Heliogomphus* sp. *Megalogomphus ceylonicus* *Macromia zeylania* *Trithemis aurora* *T. festiva*	*Euphaea splendens* *Zygonyx iris ceylanica*		
Orthoptera	larva of *Rhabdoblatta* sp.			
Coleoptera	*Guinotus flammulatus* *Neptosternus taprobanicus*	*Helichus naviculus* *Potamophilinus impressicollis*		

Taxonomic Group	Flow velocity			
	0-30 cm/sec	30-75 cm/sec	75-100 cm/sec	>100 cm/sec
	N. starmuehlneri	*P. costatus*		
	Pelthydrus sp.	*Stenelmis*		
	St. andersoni	*brinckii*		
	Aulonogyrus	*Ordobrevia*		
	obliquus	*fletcheri*		
	Orectochilus sp.	*flavolineata*		
		Leptotelmis		
		ceylonica		
		Graphelmis		
		ceylonica		
		Ilamelmis		
		foveicollis		
		P. virideanea		
		P. similis		
		Taprobanelmis		
		carinata		
		Zaitzeviaria		
		bicolor		
		Z. zeylanica		
		Unguiseta		
		rubrica		
		Hydrocyphon		
		atratus		
		Eubrianax	*Eubrianax*	
		lioneli	*lioneli*	
		Lampyridae		
		cf. *Luciola* sp.		
		Aulonogyrus		
		Orectochilus sp.		
Heteroptera	*Diplonychus*			
	rusticus			
	Cylindro stethus			
	productus			
	Onychotrechus			
	sakuntala			
	Ptilomera			
	cingalensis			
	Rheumatogonus			
	custodiensis			
	Ventidius			
	henryi			
	Hydrometra			
	greeni			
	Microvelia			
	douglasi			
	M. (Kirkaldya)			
	longicornus			
	Rhagovelia			
	ceylonica			
	Strongovelia			
	formosa			

Taxonomic Group	Flow velocity			
	0-30 cm/sec	30-75 cm/sec	75-100 cm/sec	>100 cm/sec
	Tetraripis asymmetricus *Xiphovelia iota* *Micronecta anatolica* *M. 4-strigata* *M. sanctae-catharinae* *M. desertana* *M. alterna* *M. punctinotum* *Hydrotrephes kirkaldyi* *Triphotrephas indicus* *Aphelocheirus clivicolus* *Heliocoris breviceps* *Cercotmetus strangulatus*			
Diptera	*Chlorichaeta tuberculata*	Orthocladiinae gen. spp. *Tanytarsus* sp. *Rheotanytarsus* sp. cf. *Lithotanytarus* sp.	Orthocladiinae gen. spp. *Tanytarsus* sp. *Rheotanytarsus* sp. cf. *Lithotanytarus* sp.	Orthocladiinae gen. spp. *Simuium 5-striatum* *S.* spp. *Gomphostilbia (S.)* spp. Blephariciridae gen. spp.
Trichoptera		*Synagapetus* cf. *hanumata* and spp. *Plethus cursitans* and sp. *Oxyethira* sp. *Nyctiphylax* sp. *Pseudoneureclipsis thuparama* Polycentropidae gen. spp. *Ecnomus* sp. Psychomyidae gen. spp. *Anisocentropus* sp. *Marilia* cf. *ceylanica*	*Chimarra* sp. *Oestropsyche vitrina* *Macronema* sp. cf. *Pseudoeptonema* sp. *Hydropsyche katugahakanda* *H. flinti* and *H.* spp. *Diplectrona* sp. div. Hydropsychidae gen. spp.	*Chimarra* sp. *Oestropsyche vitrina* *Macronema* sp.

Taxonomic Group	Flow velocity			
	0-30 cm/sec	30-75 cm/sec	75-100 cm/sec	>100 cm/sec
		Trichosetodes argentolineata cf. *T. megha-wanabaya* *Adicella biramosa* *Oecitis belihuloya* Leptoceridae gen. spp. *Goerodes* sp. *Helicopsyche amarawathi*		
Lepidoptera		Pyralidae gen. spp.	*Aulacodes* sp.	
Mollusca Gastropoda	*Paludomus (P.) tanschauricus nasutus* *P. (P.)chilinoides* *Melanoides tuberculata* *Thiara scabra* *Bithynia inconspicua* *B. stenothyroides* *Indoplanorbis exustus*	*P. (P.) bicinctus* *P. (P.) decussatus* *P. (T.) loricatus* *P. (T.) neritoides* *P. (T.) solidus*	*P. (T.) loricatus* *P. (T.) neritoides* *P. (T.) solidus*	
Bivalvia	*Lamellidens lamellatus*			
Vertebrata Amphibia	tadpoles of *Rana cyanophiictis* *R. temporalis* *R. tigrina crassa*			
Pisces	*Danio malabaricus* *Rasbora daniconius* *Esomus danrica* *Chela laubuca* *Barbus (Puntius) bimaculatus* *B. (P.) cummingi* *B.(P.) dorsalis* *B.(P.) filamentosus*	*Danio malabaricus* *Rasbora daniconius* *Esomus danrica* *Chela laubuca* *Barbus (Puntius) bimaculatus* *B. (P.) cummingi* *B. (P.) dorsalis* *B. (P.) filamentosus*	*Garra lamta*	*Garra lamta*

Taxonomic Group	Flow velocity			
	0-30 cm/sec	30-75 cm/sec	75-100 cm/sec	>100 cm/sec
	B. (P.) nigrofasciatus	*B. (P.) nigroasciatus*		
	B. (P.)sarana	*B. (P.) sarana*		
	B. (P.) titteya	*B. (P.) titteya*		
	B. (P.) vittatus	*B.(P.)vittatus*		
		Tor khudree longispinus		
	Noemachilus botia	*Noemachilus botia*		
	N. notostigma	*N. notostigma*		
	Lepidocephalus thermalis	*Lepidocephalus thermalis*		
	Macrones (=Mystus) keletius	*Macrones (=Mystus) keletius*		
	Clarias dussumieri			
	Cl. teysmanii brachysoma			
	Anguilla nebulosa	*Anguilla nebulosa*		
	Aplocheilus dayi	*Aplocheilus dayi*		
	Channa orientalis	*Channa orientalis*		
	Ophiocephalus gachua	*Ophiocephalus gachua*		
	Anabas testudineus	*Glossogobius giuris*	*Glossogobius giuris*	*Glossogobius giuris*
	Belontia signata	*Sicydium halei*	*Sicydium halei*	*Sicydium halei*
	Mastocembalus armatus	*Mastocembalus armatus*	*Mastocembalus armatus*	
	Macrognathus aculeatus	*Macrognathus aculeatus*	*Macrognathus aculeatus*	

145

Table 9. Species composition of the lower course community (approx. 20 m elevation).

Taxonomic Group	Flow velocity			
	0-30 cm/sec	30-75 cm/sec	75-100 cm/sec	>100 cm/sec
Crustacea	*Caridina nilotica*	*Macrobrachium*		
Caridea	*simoni*	*australe*		
	M. idella			
Insecta		*Ilamelmis* sp.		
Coleoptera	*Rasbora*	*Rasbora*		
Vertebrata	*daniconius*	*daniconius*		
Pisces	*Barbus*	*Barbus*		
	(Puntius)	*(Puntius)*		
	chola	*chola*		

146

Table 10. Altitudinal distribution of the meso- and macrofauna species of the mountain streams. x = found only in polluted river sections around Nuwara Eliya; xx = found only in river sections crossing the limestone zone near Wellawaya; ? = not found by the Austrian-Sri Lankan Hydrobiological Mission 1970, but probably occurring.

Species	Headwater (1500-2000 m)	Upper course (500-1500 m)	Middle course (30-500 m)	Lower course (0-30 m)
Dugesia nannophallus	<-->			?
Tubifex tubifex	x <-------------->	?	?	?
Limnodrilus hoffmeisteri	x <-------------->	?	?	?
Lumbriculus variegatus	x <-------------->	?	?	?
Atya spinipes		<---------------------------------->		
Caridina fernandoi		<---------------------------------->		
C. pristis		<-------------->		
C. nilotica simoni		<-->		
C.n.zeylanica			<-------------->	?
Macrobrachium australe		<-->		
M. idella			<-->	
M. latimanus		<---------------------------------->		
M. scrabiculum		<-------------->		
Paratelphusa (C.) rugosa	<-->			?

Species	Headwater (1500-2000 m)	Upper course (500-1500 m)	Middle course (30-500 m)	Lower course (0-30 m)
P. (C.) sorror	<-->			
P. (O.) senex			<-------------->	?
Arrenurus (M.) madraszi		<-->		
Torrenticola (M.) pusta		<-->		
T. (M.) oxystoma hamata		<-->		
T. (M.) ceylonensis		<-->		
Atractides schwoerbeli		<-->		
Leptophlebiidae gen. spp.	<-->			?
Ecdyonuridae gen. spp.	<-->			
Indobaetis costai	<-->			
Indobaetis starmuehlneri			<-------------->	?
Indocloeon primum	<-->			
Pseudocloeon klapaleki	<------------->			
P. orientale		<-------------->		
P. difficile		<-->		?
P. ambiguum			<-------------->	?

Species	Headwater (1500-2000 m)	Upper course (500-1500 m)	Middle course (30-500 m)	Lower course (0-30 m)
Prosopistoma sp.	<-->			
Povilla (L.) taprobanes			<------------------>	?
Ephemera sp.		<------------------>		
Neoperla angulata (Fig. 24)	<-->			
N. triangulata		<-->		
Phanoperla sp.	<-->			
Rhabdoblatta sp. juv.		<-->		
Paranemobius pictus	on border: in sprayed water <-->			
Euscelimena gavialis		on border: in sprayed water <-->		
Euphaea splendens (Fig. 25, 26)		<-->		
Libellago finalis		<------------------>		
L. greeni		<-->		
Vestalis apicalis nigrescens		<-->		
Neurobasis chinensis ch.		<-->		
Lestes elata	<-->			
Copera marginipes			<------------------>	

Species	Headwater (1500-2000 m)	Upper course (500-1500 m)	Middle course (30-500 m)	Lower course (0-30 m)
Drepanosticta starmühlneri		<---------------------------------->		
Elattoneura centralis		<--->		
E. tenax		<---------------->		
Prodasineura sita		<---------------->		
Microgomphus wijaya			<---------------->	
Megalogomphus ceylonicus		<-->		
Heliogomphus sp.		<-->		
Paragomphus henryi			<---------------->	
Anax immaculifrons			<---------------->	
Macromia zeylanica		<-->		
Trithemis aurora			<---------------->	
T. festiva		<-->		
Zygonyx iris ceylanica		<-->		
Apsilochorema diffinis	<-->			
Synagapetus hanumata		<-->		
S. rudis		<---------------->		
S. sp.	<---------------->			

Species	Headwater (1500-2000 m)	Upper course (500-1500 m)	Middle course (30-500 m)	Lower course (0-30 m)
Plethus cursitans			<------------------->	
Hydroptila kurukepitya			<------------------->	
Oxyethira sp.		<--->		
Hydroptilidae gen. spp.	<-->			
Chimarra sp.	<-->			
Gunungiella madakumbura		<------------------>		
Nyctiophylax sp.			<----------------->	
Pseudoneuroclepsis starmuehlneri		<--->		
P. thuparama			<----------------->	
Polycentropidae gen. spp.	<--->			
Ecnomus sp.	<-->			
Paduniella mahanawana		<------------------>		
P. subhakara		<------------------>		
Psychomyidae gen. spp	<--->			
Oestropsyche vitrina		<--->		
Macronema sp. larva A		<--->		

Species	Headwater (1500-2000 m)	Upper course (500-1500 m)	Middle course (30-500 m)	Lower course (0-30 m)
M. sp. larva B		<---------------->		
Pseudoleptonema sp. larva A	<--->			
Pseudoleptonema sp. larva B		<---------------->		
Hydropsyche annulata	<---------------->			
H. katuhakanda	<--->			
H. flinti		<--->		
H. sp. larva A	<--->			
H. sp. larva B		<--->		
H. sp. larva C			<---------------->	
H. sp. larva D		<---------------->		
Synaptopsyche nikalandugola		<---------------->		
Diplectrona sp. larva A		<--->		
D. sp. larva B	<-->			
Diplectronella taprobanes	<-->			
Anisocentropus sp.			<---------------->	
Marilia ceylanica	<--->			
Molanna taprobane	<---------------->			

Species	Headwater (1500-2000 m)	Upper course (500-1500 m)	Middle course (30-500 m)	Lower course (0-30 m)
Trichosetodes argentolineata		<-->		
T. meghawanabaya			<------------------->	
Adicella biramosa		<-->		
Oecetis belihuloya		<-->		
O. hamata		<------------------->		
O. malighawa		<------------------->		
O. sumanasara	<------------------->			
Setodinella punctatissima		<------------------->		
Goera katugalkanda		<------------------->		
G. paragoda		<------------------->		
Goerodes fuscata		<------------------->		
G. punda		<------------------->		
Ceylanopsyche asaka	<------------------->			
C. sp. case A-type	<------------------->			
C. sp. case B-type	<------------------->			
Helicopsyche amarawathi (Fig. 33)	<-->			
H. ruprawathi	<-->			

Species	Headwater (1500-2000 m)	Upper course (500-1500 m)	Middle course (30-500 m)	Lower course (0-30 m)
H. srilanka		<--------------->		
H. ceylanica	<--------------->	?		
H. sp. case type E	<--------------->			
H. sp. case type F	<--------------->			
Aulacodes sp. "cupula"- larva type (Fig. 30)		<--->		
Au. sp. "dispersed"- larva type			<--------------->	
Guignotus flammulatus			<--------------->	
Canthydrus luctuosus		<--------------->		
Laccophilus ceylonicus		<--------------->		
L. chinensis inefficiens		<--------------->		
Neptosternus horai ceylonicus			<--------------->	
N. starmuehlneri			<--------------->	
N. taprobanicus			<--------------->	
N. sp.	<--------------->			
Lacconectus simoni	<-->			
Hydaticus luzonicus	<-->			
Berosus indicus		<--------------->		

Species	Headwater (1500-2000 m)	Upper course (500-1500 m)	Middle course (30-500 m)	Lower course (0-30 m)
Oocytus latus	<--------	hygropetric	-------->	
Helochares sp.			hygropetric <-------->	
Paracymus sp.	hygropetric <-------->			
Pelthydrus sp. 1		<-------->		
P. sp. 2		?	<-------->	
Aulonogyrus obliquus	<--------		-------->	?
Orectochilus ceylonicus		<--------	-------->	?
O. sp.	<--------		-------->	?
Hydroscapha granulum	<--------	hygropetric	-------->	
Hydraena tubuliphallis	hygropetric <-------->			
Hydrocyphon atratus	<--------		-------->	
H. striatus		<-------->		
Eubrianax sp.1 Fig. 27	<--------	-------->		
E. sp. 2	<-------->			
E. sp. 3	<--------		-------->	
E. sp. 4			<-------->	

155

Species	Headwater (1500-2000 m)	Upper course (500-1500 m)	Middle course (30-500 m)	Lower course (0-30 m)
E. sp. 5		<--------------------->		
Ceradryops punctatus		hygropetric <--->		
Elmomorphus naviculus		on floating waterplants <--->		
Potamophilinus torrenticola		<--------------------->		
P. impressicollis	<--------------------->			
P. costatus			<--------------------->	
P. tuberculatus		?		
Stenelmis brincki		<-->		
St. anderssoni			<--------------------->	
Ordobrevia fletcheri		<--------------------->		
O. flavolineata			<--------------------->	
Leptelmis cederholmi			<-->	
Graphelmis ceylonica			<--------------------->	
Unguisaeta rubrica			<--------------------->	
Ilamelmis brunnescens		<-->		
I. foveicollis-	<--->			? (larva) - - - - - - - - - - - ->
I. crassa		<--------------------->		

Species	Headwater (1500-2000 m)	Upper course (500-1500 m)	Middle course (30-500 m) ·	Lower course (0-30 m)
I. starmuehlneri			<--------------------->	
I. sp. 5			<----------->	?
Cephalolimnius ater		<-->		
Podelmis ater	<--------------------->			
P. aena			<--------------------->	
P. cruzei	<--------------------->			
P. graphica			<--------------------->	?
P. humeralis		<--------------------->		
P. metallica		<-->		
P. ovalis	<-------------------->			
P. quadriplagiata	up to 2200 m <--->			
P. similis			<--------------------->	
P. viridiaena			<--------------------->	
Ohiya carinata	<--------------------->			
Aesobia pygmaea		<--->		
Taprobanelmis ceylanica		<--->		
Zaitzeviaria ceylanica	<-->			

Species	Headwater (1500-2000 m)	Upper course (500-1500 m)	Middle course (30-500 m)	Lower course (0-30 m)
Z. elongata		<------------	------------>	
Limnichus sp.			<---------->	
Luciola sp. (Fig. 28, 29)	<-----------	-------------	------------>	
Cylindrosththus productus			<---------->	
Limnogonus nitidus		<---------->		
Limnometra anadyomene		<---------->		
Metocoris stali	<------------	------------>		
Onychotrechus sakuntala	<-----------	-------------	---->	
Ptilamera cingalenis		<-----------	------------>	
Rheumatogonus custodiensis		<-----------	------------>	
Tenagogonus ceylonensis			<---------->	
Ventidius henryi		<-----------	------------>	
Tinasius splendens	<---------->			
Hydrometra greeni	<------------	------------>		
Mesovelia horvathi			<---------->	
Microvelia douglasi			<---------->	
M. (Kirkaldya) longicornis	<------------	------------>		

Species	Headwater (1500-2000 m)	Upper course (500-1500 m)	Middle course (30-500 m)	Lower course (0-30 m)
M. pererai	<---------------->			
Pseudovelia gnoma	<---------------->			
Rhagovelia ceylanica	<-->		
Rh. karunaratnei	<---------------->			
Strongyvelia formosa	<----------------> - - - - - - - - - ? - - - - - - - - - <---------------->		
Tetraripis asymmetrica		<-->	
Xiphovelia iota			<---------------->	
Diplonychus rusticus			<---------------->	
Micronecta alternata			<---------------->	
M. anatolica			<---------------->	
M. desertana			<---------------->	
M. memonides		<---------------->		
M. punctinotum			<---------------->	
M. quadristrigata		<-->	
M. sancta catharinae			<---------------->	
M. wroblewski	<---------------->			
Sigara nilgirica	<---------------->			

Species	Headwater (1500-2000 m)	Upper course (500-1500 m)	Middle course (30-500 m)	Lower course (0-30 m)
Hydrotrephes kirkaldyi			<------------------>	
Tiphotrephes indicus			<------------------>	
Aphelocheirus clivicolus		<--->		
Heliocoris breviceps		<--->		
Cercotmetus strangulatus		<------------------>		
Enitares simplex		<------------------>		
Ochterus marginatus		<------------------>		
Simulium (S.) sp. larva -"b" (Fig. 32)	<-->			?
S. (S.) sp. larva -"d"		<--->		?
S. (S.) sp. larva - "g"	<--->			
Gomphostilbia (=S.) sp larva I	<-->			?
G. (=S.) sp. larva III		<--->		?
Blephariciridae gen. spp. (Fig. 31)	<-->			
Odontomyia sp.		<------------------>		
Dixidae gen. sp.		<------------------>		
Psilopinae gen. sp.		<------------------>		
Aedes (Finlaya) chrysolineatus		<------------------>	?	?

Species	Headwater (1500-2000 m)	Upper course (500-1500 m)	Middle course (30-500 m)	Lower course (0-30 m)
cf. *Tanytarsus* sp.			<------------------->	?
cf. *Rheotanytarsus* sp.	<-->			
cf. *Lithotanytarsus* sp.			xx <------------------->	?
Orthocladiinae gen. spp.	<-->			?
Chironomus sp.	x <------------------->	?	?	?
Chlorichaeta tuberculata			<------------------->	
Paludomus (Tanalia) loricatus (Figs. 44, 45)		<-->		
P. (T.) neritoides (Figs. 43, 45)		<-->		
P. (T.) solidus			xx <------------------->	
P. (Philopotamis) nigricans	<------------------->			
P. (Ph.) regalis (Fig. 42)			<------------------->	
P. (Ph.) sulcatus		<------------------->		
P. (Paludomus) tanschauricus nasutus (Fig. 41)		<-->		?
P.(P.) chilinoides (Figs. 38, 39, 40)			<-->	
P. (P.) bicinctus			<------------------->	?

Species	Headwater (1500-2000 m)	Upper course (500-1500 m)	Middle course (30-500 m)	Lower course (0-30 m)
P. (P.) decussatus			<---------------------->	?
P. (P.) inflatus			<--->	
Melanoides tuberculata		<-->		
Thiara scabra		<-->		
Tricula montana		<---------------------->		
Bithynia inconspicua			<--->	
B. stenothyroides (Fig. 36)			<--->	
Septaria lineata reticulata (Fig. 35)				<---------------------->
Pila globosa carinata (Fig. 37)				<---------------------->
Indoplanorbis exustus			<--->	
Lamellidens lamellatus			<--->	
Pisidium (Afropisidium) javanum		<---------------------->		
P. (Odhnerpisidium) annandali		<---------------------->		
P. (O.) prasongi		<---------------------->		
Danio malabaricus		<-->		
Esomus danrica			<--->	

Species	Headwater (1500-2000 m)	Upper course (500-1500 m)	Middle course (30-500 m)	Lower course (0-30 m)
Rasbora daniconius		<-->		
R. vaterifloris		<-------------------->	?	?
Chela laubuca		<-->		
Barbus (=Puntius) bimaculatus		<-->		
B. (=P.) chola				<-------------------->
B. (=P.) cumingi			<-------------------->	?
B. (=P.) dorsalis		<-->		
B. (=P.) filamentosus		<-->		
B. (=P.) nigrofasciatus		<-->		?
B. (=P.) sarrana		<-->		
B. (=P.) titteya			<-------------------->	?
B. (=P.) vittatus			<-->	
Cyprinus carpio		introduced <-->		
Tor khudre longispinus			<-->	
Garra lamta	?	<-->		
Noemachilus botia			<-->	
N. notostigma		<-->		
Lepidocephalus thermalis		<-->		

Species	Headwater (1500-2000 m)	Upper course (500-1500 m)	Middle course (30-500 m)	Lower course (0-30 m)
Macrones (=Mystus) keletius			<-->	
Clarias dussumeri			<-->	
C. teysmanni brachysoma			<-->	
Xenentodon cancila			<-------------------->	
Aplocheilus dayi (=Panchax lineatus dayi)		<--->		
Poecilia (=Lebistes) reticulata		<---> introduced		
Xiphophorus helleri		<--->		
Channa orientalis		<--->		
Ophiocephalus gachua	?	<-->		
Glossogobius giuris	?	<-->	?	
Sicydium halei			<-------------------->	
Anabas testudineus			<--->	
Belontia signata		<--->		
Mastacembalus armatus			<--->	
Macrognathus aculeatus	?	<-->		
Anguilla nebulosa		<--->		
A. bicolor		<--->		

Species	Headwater (1500-2000 m)	Upper course (500-1500 m)	Middle course (30-500 m)	Lower course (0-30 m)
Rhacophorus cruciger eques	tadpoles <-------------------->			
Rh. cr. cruciger		tadpoles <-------------------->		
Rana (Hylarana) temporalis	<----------------------------------	--------------- tadpoles ---------------	---------------------------------->	
R. cyanophlictis cyanophlictis		<---------------- tadpoles ---------------->		
R. limnocharis limnocharis		tadpoles <-------------------->		
R. tigrina crassa			tadpoles <-------------------->	
Boiga ceylonensis ceylonensis		<-------------------->	?	?
Natrix piscator asperrimus		<-------------------->	?	?

Figure 4. View to the headwaters and upper courses (waterfalls) of the two branches of the Gartmore Estate Dola; in the foreground the reservoir of Maskeliya.

Figure 5. Headwater of the Gartmore Estate Dola just before the waterfall (see background of Fig. 4).

Figure 6. View from the region of the headwaters of the Gartmore Estate Dola to the reservoir of Maskeliya.

Figure 7. Outflow of the Gartmore Estate Dola behind the dam of the Maskeliya Reservoir.

167

Figure 8. Thanipita Dola, headwater brook in the Deniyaya forest.

Figure 9. Waterfall of the upper course of the Bodathpitiya Ela near Ratnapura.

Figure 10. Upper course of the Pasumela Dola, near Deniyaya, flowing over granitic, smooth rocks, bordered by mountain grassland.

Figure 11. Upper course of the Deniyaya Dola, bordered by plantations.

Figure 12. Upper course of the Campden Hill Dola, near Deniyaya, bordered by tea estates.

Figure 13. Granitic boulders (low water) in the upper course of the Campden Hill Dola, near Deniyaya.

Figure 14. Granitic boulders (low water) in the upper course of the Hoza Doza, near Deniyaya.

Figure 15. Upper course of the Mocha Dola, near Maskeliya, bordered by tea estates.

Figure 16. Transition between the upper to the middle course of a typical mountain river near Belihuloya, bordered by scrub and plantations.

Figure 17. Middle course of the We Ganga, near Belihuloya, flowing over smooth, granitic rocks, bordered by scrub and secondary forest.

Figure 18. Middle course of the Bibili Oya near Kitulgala, bordered by scrub and secondary forest.

Figure 19. Transition between the upper to the middle course of the Wetakei Ela, near Wellawaya in the limestone-marble zone in SE Sri Lanka; bordered by secondary forest of the *Chloroxylon*-ecosystem.

Figure 20. Middle course of the Kuda Oya, near Buttala in the limestone-marble zone in SE Sri Lanka, bordered by the secondary forest of the *Chloroxylon*-ecosystem.

Figure 21. Creek (with very low current) on the border of the middle course of the We Ganga near Belihuloya.

174

Figure 22. Transition between the middle to the lower course of the Kelani Ganga, near Kitulgala, bordered by secondary forest and coconut plantations.

Figure 23. Lower course of the Kelani Ganga, near Helwala with sand banks, bordered by coconut plantations.

Figure 24. Dorsal side of the nymph of *Neoperla angulata*, an endemic species of stoneflies (Plecoptera), typical for the upper courses of mountain streams.

Figure 25. Dorsal side of the nymph of the damselfly *Euphaea splendens*, living in the upper and middle course.

Figure 26. Ventral side of the nymph of the damselfly *Euphaea plendens*, with filiform and 3 sucker-like gills.

Figure 27. Ventral side of the larva of a beetle of the genus *Eubrianax* sp. (Psephenidae). The larva is protected by dorsal plates with peripheral bristles which fit the surface of the underground (stones, rock); brush-like abdominal gills; upper and middle courses.

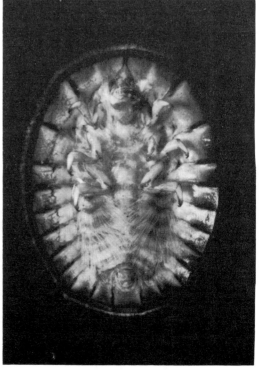

Figure 28. Lateral view of the larva (glowworm) of the beetle family Lampyridae, genus *Luciola* ; feeding on watersnails, such as species of *Paludomus*; upper courses.

Figure 29. Ventral side of the larva (glowworm) of the beetle family Lampyridae, genus *Luciola*.

Figure 30. Ventral side of the "underwater-caterpillar" of the watermoth (Pyralidae) genus *Aulacodes* sp. living, protected by flat shields of silk, on glossy rocks in the upper and middle courses; pairs of lateral gills.

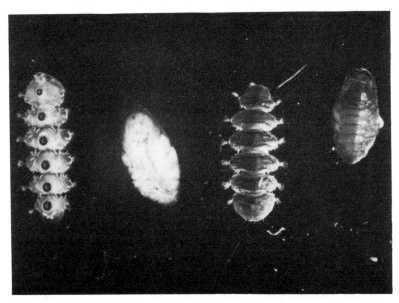

Figure 31. Dorsal and ventral sides of the pupa and larva of a species of Blephariciridae. Larva with central suckers, useful in the strong currents of the cascades and waterfalls in the torrents of the upper courses.

Figure 32. Pupa and 2 larva of the black-flies, genus *Simuliidae* gen. sp.; they are fixed on stones and rocks, floating waterplants in the strong current; the larva are carrying a large folding fan to catch drifting particles; upper and middle courses.

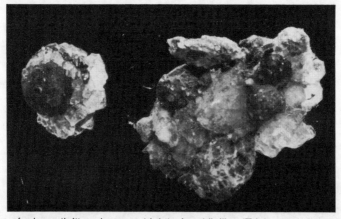

Figure 33. Cases of a larva (left) and a pupa (right) of caddisflies (Trichoptera) living on sandy bottom of the upper and middle courses. The left snail-shell like case from a species of the genus *Heliopsyche*. The cases are composed of fine splinters of sand (from the bottom), partly of splinters of precious and half-precious stones.

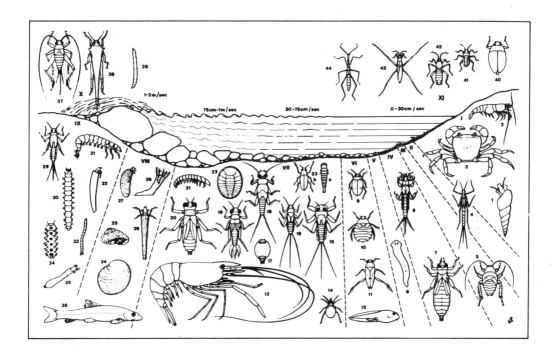

Figure 34. Microhabitat distribution of the benthos fauna in the upper course of a typical mountain stream of Sri Lanka (schematic cross section). Microhabitats and species:

I. Mud and sand surfaces, banks and pools between cascades: 1 *Melanoides tuberculata,* 2 *Caridina* sp. (Atyidae), 3 *Paratelphusa rugosa*

II. Sand surfaces, banks and pools between cascades: 4 *Neurobasis chinensis*

III. Under stones near banks: 5 larva of *Rhabdoblatta*

IV. In sand, banks and pools between cascades: 6 *Ephemera* sp. 7 nymph of Gomphinae

V. Stone surfaces, near banks and in medium current: 8 *Dugesia nannophallus*

VI. Swimmers in lentic areas in low current: 9 *Lacconectes simoni,* 10 *Aphelocheirus clivicolus,* 11 *Enithares simplex,* tadpole of *Rana temporalis*

VII. Gravel in medium current: 13 *Macrobrachium*-species, 14 Hydrachnellae-species, 15 Ecdyonuridae-species, 16 Leptophlebiidae-species, 17 *Prosopistoma* sp. 18 *Neoperla*-species, 19 *Euphaea splendens,* 20 *Zygonyx iris ceylanica,* 21 *Luciola* sp. 22 *Eubrianax ceylonicus,* 23 Elmintidae-species (12 genera, 31 spp)

VIII. Among boulders and gravel in medium to strong current: 24 *Paludomus (T.) neritoides,* 25 *Helicopsyche* sp. 26 Leptoceridae-species, 27 Hydroptilidae-species, 28 *Rheotanytarsus* sp.

IX. On boulders and rocks in rapids and cascades: 29 Baetidae-species, 30 *Aulacodes* sp. 31 Hydropsychidae-species, 32 Sericostomatidae-species, 33 Orthocladiinae-species, 34 Blepharicridae-species, 35 Simuliidae-species, 36 *Garra lamta*

X. On sprayed rocks: 37 *Paranemobius pictus,* 38 *Euscelimena gavialis,* 39 *Limonia* sp.

XI. Surface dwellers: 40 *Aulonogyrus* and *Orectochilus*-species, 41 *Microvelia*-species, 42 different species of water crickets (some genera and species), 43 different species of pond skaters (some genera and species), 44 *Hydrometra greeni.* (Starmühlner, 1984).

Figure 35. Dorsal and ventral view of the neritid snail *Septaria lineata reticulata,* with a narrow sucker-like foot, fastened floating stalks near the borders of the lower courses (Ambalangoda).

Figure 36. The endemic *Bithynia inconspicua* on muddy ground of slow running lowland rivers.

Figure 37. The apple snail *Pila globosa carinata* occurs on muddy-sandy ground, rich in dense growth of waterplants on the borders of slow running lowland rivers.

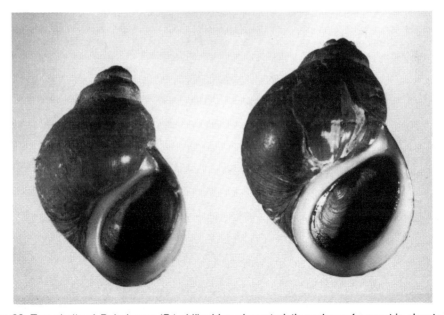

Figure 38. Two shells of *Paludomus (P.) chilinoides*, characteristic and very frequent in slow to fairly fast running streams.

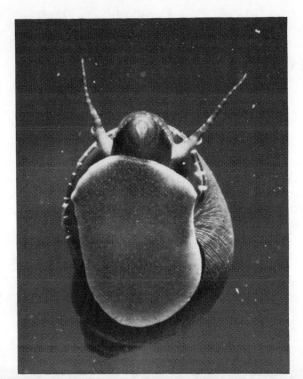

Figure 39. Underside of the foot, head and tentacles of *Paludomus (P.) chilinoides*.

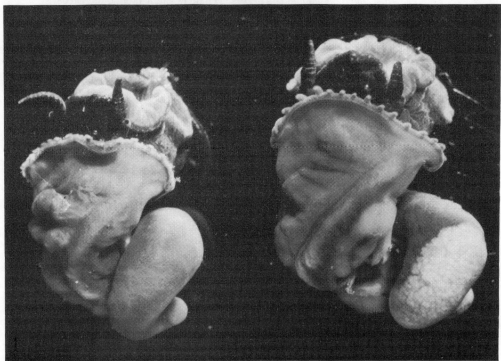

Figure 40. Male and female of *Paludomus (P.) chilinoides*. Typical for the family of Thiaridae is the fringed border of the mantle.

Figure 41. The high-turred shell of *Paludomus (P.) tanschauricus nasutus* inhabiting slow flowing streams.

Figure 42. *Paludomus (Philopotamis) regalis*, a rare endemic species in fast running, stony streams.

Figure 43. Five shells of the endemic, highly variable *Paludomus (Tanalia) loricatus*, frequent in smaller mountain streams, torrents and brooks.

Figure 44. Five shells of the endemic, highly variable *Paludomus (Tanalia) loricatus*, characteristic species of the main branches of the mountain streams.

Figure 45. Variations, with transitions, of the shells of *Paludomus (T.) neritoides* (upper row, see also Fig. 43) and *P. (T.) loricatus* (lower row, see also Fig. 44, Starmühlner, 1974).

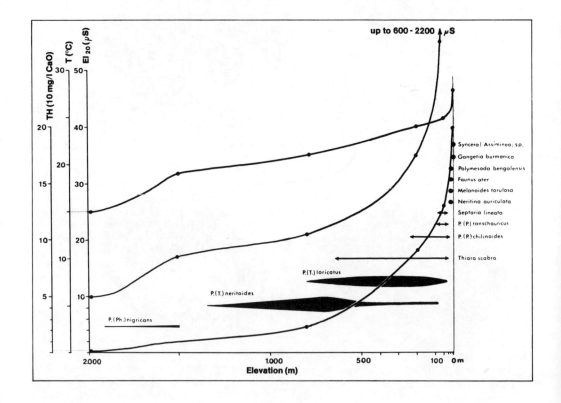

Figure 46. Altitudinal distribution of gastropods and bivalves in running waters of Sri Lanka and of major water parameter (Starmühlner, 1984).

188

Proceedings of the International and Interdisciplinary Symposium
ECOLOGY AND LANDSCAPE MANAGEMENT IN SRI LANKA
W. Erdelen, C. Preu, N. Ishwaran, C.M. Madduma Bandara (eds.)
Colombo, Sri Lanka, 12-26 March 1990
© 1993
Margraf Scientific Books, D-97985 Weikersheim
ISBN 3-8236-1182-8

Fossorial Amphibians and Reptiles: Their Distributions as Environmental Indicators

C. GANS

Abstract

Increasing demand of farmers for land and of others for its products inevitably generates pressures on those responsible for conservation. Particularly critical are land use practices that will conserve diversity. Accurate description of the distributions of individual species over space and time enabling an understanding of biogeographic patterns and indices of diversity, are urgently needed to meet this objective. Environmental changes due to human activity have complicated efforts to document such distributional patterns. Large organisms have been hunted for a long time and their current ranges may only be remnants of former, more extensive areas. Some smaller organisms are migratory or show the characteristics of weeds. Data from electrophoretic and immunological studies show that the ranges of various burrowing amphibians and reptiles seem to have been relatively constant. Hence, they represent good indicators of the distribution of biogeographic zones over relatively long periods of time. This information may be useful in evaluating the relative merits or protecting portions of particular biotopes. These concepts are illustrated on the basis of a series of studies on caecilians, scincid lizards and uropeltid and colubrid snakes of Sri Lanka.

Introduction

The environment of tropical countries has been changing rapidly and drastically. The original vegetation has often been destroyed, particularly the forests, and have been replaced with wide zones of monoculture, tea and coffee, cardamom and coconut. Even where forests "remain", their species composition has often changed drastically with many of the trees of some of the regions representing introduced, rather than indigenous, species comprising eucalyptus, pine and teak, rather than the original vegetation.

Periodically there has been discussion as to whether some patches of vegetation are worth saving, whether they represent part of the original fauna and flora. This is one part of the broader question about the original biota of the region and about the minor and major biotic

189

provinces that may have characterized the prehuman environment. Such issues become important if one chooses to decide whether it is better to flood a valley for hydroelectric development, or to preserve it as representing a relict of the primordial association.

What cues can be used for making decisions about the former divisions? The distribution of large- and medium-sized mammals transcends the limits of former components. Birds are often associated with tree types and their species composition is likely to have been affected by the major changes of the biota. Similar problems concern the distribution of the larger lizards and snakes. The present account documents that the subterranean reptiles and amphibians show a remarkable site-specificity, even after the environment has been drastically modified. They consequently indicate the areas they used to occupy prior to the advent of man, and accordingly, provide information about former biogeographic provinces. For this reason, this paper provides information about the ways that the data set here for Sri Lanka was generated, its strengths and weaknesses and the ways it could be supplemented.

The Sources of the Data

The work presented here is a function of serendipity. (As the term serendipity relates to a former name of this island, its use here seems curiously appropriate). It is a byproduct of my interest in the global adaptations of uropeltine snakes (Gans 1966, 1973, 1976, 1978, 1979). These are a unique family occurring only in India and Sri Lanka. Our electrophoretic and immunological study (Cadle *et al.* 1991) suggests that the snakes, formerly placed in the family Uropeltidae represent a sister group to those of the genus *Cylindrophis*, one species of which occurs in Sri Lanka. Hence, I refer to them as Uropeltinae and reserve Uropeltidae for the entire assemblage. I became involved in the study of uropeltine burrowing and tunnel movement (Gans *et al.* 1978), and later I became interested in their defenses against predators encountered on the surface and in tunnels (Gans 1987, Gans and Baic 1977). As part of this study, it was also necessary to deal with the reasons for their diversity. Why are there so many species in a relatively restricted space? Why is there such gerrymandering of geographic ranges?

To study the natural history of uropeltines, I came to Sri Lanka in 1972 and began a biogeographic analysis that lasted until about 1978. This involved the study of obvious and of more complex cryptic adaptations. What was the significance of altitude, temperature, and moisture to the distributions of the animals? Altitude seemed to lead to sharp divisions, a point that was important for regions in which the hillsides often had slopes of more than 45 degrees. Rainfall seemed to be critical not just in terms of range inhabited, but also in terms of the time at which the animals could be collected in particular sites. Also important proved to be the soil types and factors such as amount of sand, shade and drainage. The systematic analyses began with morphological data and the schemes were then tested by biochemical and immunological approaches. Most important for the repeatability of the results was the documentation of specimens and collecting localities, their coordinates and actual elevations.

Most collections we and our collaborators made were obtained in "disturbed" areas. We lacked access to the national parks and forest reserves, and intended to sample these at a later time, perhaps for use as a test of hypotheses regarding the more nearly original distributions. Hence, we sampled plantation areas involving the production of tea, coffee, cardamon and coconut. The species we sampled did not match the ranges of current agricultural production. The non-matching of patterns might have been due to changes in the local ecology. If so, the current distribution would represent residuals of the original ecological patterns.

The search for burrowing snakes also led to the discovery of other burrowing amphibians and reptiles. Examples are the caecilians of the genus *Ichthyophis,* and perhaps *Caudocaecilia,* although we never located any specimens in the field (Nussbaum and Gans, 1981), the limbless burrowing skinks of the genus *Nessia* (Greer and Gans, pers. comm.), the ant and termite associated burrowing snakes of the genus *Typhlops* were taken from the lowland to the highland sites, but their systematics are only now being worked on, the constricting *Cylindrophis maculatus,* a predator on small squamates and found over much of the lowland regions of Sri Lanka (Bachman, 1985), and the genus of colubrid earthworm-eating snakes

Aspidura, with some species often common in tea estates (Gans and Fetcho, 1982). These species are supposed to be rare, and the number of specimens in museums supports this. However, the scarcity seems to be only a lack of concentration on burrowers, as most of these species proved to be extremely common once we learned how to collect them, in short once we learned where to dig.

This suggests that the aggregate distribution map of such burrowing animals might provide indicators of soil and vegetation types. These indicators should be less affected by changes during historical time, i.e. during the period in which *Homo sapiens* has modified their environment by the large-scale shift to agriculture than surface dwelling forms.

The comments offered here and the biogeographical patterns shown are most limited. My collections emphasized regions where I knew we would find diverse species of uropeltines, or where I expected to find new ones. This means that the sampling is uneven, first concentrating on the central mountains, and next on the coastal belts between Colombo and Mannar. Other regions were still being sampled when it became impossible to continue. The collecting efforts changed our concepts of the actual ranges of these forms and of their systematics. The world's museums contain many specimens with inappropriate locality records (Bachman 1985, Gans 1989). For the squamate forms so far reviewed, approximately 20% of the species, characterized on the basis of our collections, obviously represent new species.

Results

Patterns of Distribution

The geographical distribution patterns for the diverse burrowers may be similar but tend not to be congruent. Thus the borders defining the ranges of the burrowers belonging to different genera are rarely coincident, or are coincident only in broad terms. In contrast, we found that congeneric species often replaced each other (Figs. 1-2). This may reflect the fact that the category "burrower" includes occupation of several quite distinct biotopes, and there is little reason to assume that their borders will be parallel. Our field observations furnished some general characteristics of species and these provided clues for the bases underlying some of the distributions. With this they provide some indications of reasons for the lack of congruence.

Caecilians were always found in moist zones. They were routinely collected on the edges of streams and rivulets, even temporary ones. In flooded marshes, they could be taken under the mat of plant roots. These are the sites where the Sarasin brothers described their egg batches more than a century ago (Sarasin and Sarasin, 1887). Whereas the larval stages are aquatic and have long external gills (Breckenridge *et al.* 1987), the adults are terrestrial and move effectively in moist soils, forming chambers in which they coil and apparently estivate during the dry season.

The difficulty caecilians have in traversing dry soils and their inability to dig in these soils as documented by tests in experimental chambers, suggests that they may estivate during the dry season and move only during the rainy season. Consideration of the places where *Ichthyophis* were taken suggests that they always move parallel to streams and do not seem to cross the dry zones between these. However, they definitely forage away from streams for at least 10 meters. They may follow odor cues as we commonly found them in small tips of organic refuse, in particular those accumulating beneath sheds for cows often sheltered along the edges of paths in the steep hill sides of the tea country. They may be seen to forage on the surface of such tips during the night. The caecilians range relatively widely, and the distribution of the most common form suggests an expansion of range. However, the two other species range relatively across the mid-level southern hills and across the highest regions of the mountains. Nothing is known about the actual range, or even the occurrence, of the genus *Caudocaecilia* in Sri Lanka.

The limb-reduced skinks of the genus *Nessia* occupy relatively shallow sites within soils. One commonly encounters them under small rocks and logs, including those exposed to some insolation during the day. In some regions, they occur in sandy soils down to about 60 cm.

They do not excavate tunnels effectively, and one commonly encounters them trapped at the bottom of roadside ditches. There are no observations about possible estivation. The genus includes seven well-characterized species, and these show fairly restricted ranges with no overlap observed (Taylor 1958, Deraniyagala 1968). Three species occupy areas of the eastern coastal plains, sandy ridges and foothills, one the lowland north, two the southern plains and mountains, and the remainder some of the peak regions of the south central mountains. There is no indication that the montane and coastal populations have modified their ranges.

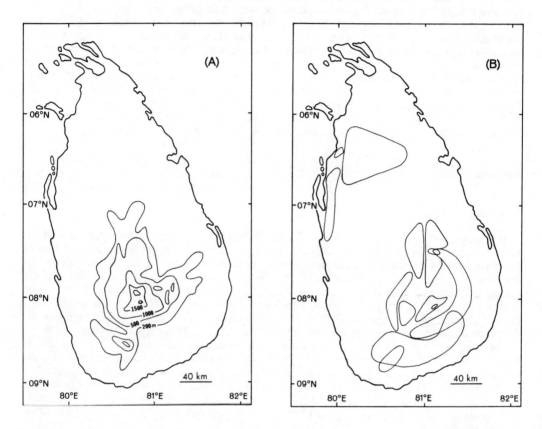

Figure 1. (A) Sketch map of the island of Sri Lanka indicating the pattern of mountains. (B) The distribution of species of the genus *Rhinophis* (including *Pseudotyphlops* and *Uropeltis*). Based only on data obtained from the present field effort.

The snakes of the genera *Typhlops* and *Rhamphotyphlops* are found on dry surfaces, within dry decaying pieces of wood and beneath rocks. They are commonly associated with ants and termites and can be taken from termitaria. At least one species occupies the sandy zones of the midwest coast. Taylor (1950) described a number of new and seemingly sympatric species from the vicinity of China Bay opposite Trincomalee. The sizeable samples taken from this field work are only now being analyzed, so it will be some time before distribution maps will be available.

The snakes of the genus *Cylindrophis* are surface litter foragers, which also enter tunnels and may feed on skinks and uropeltids found inside. They are constrictors and feed on various animals on and near the surface. Their coiling threat displays represent a response to a surface

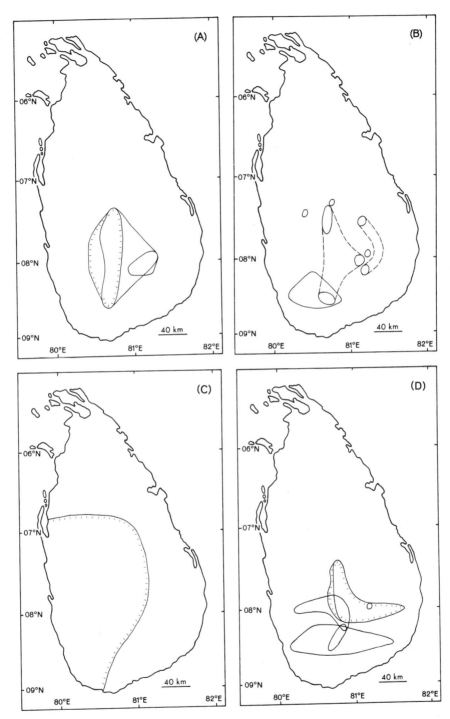

Figure 2. Sketch maps for the four genera of burrowing amphibians and reptiles to show the ranges for which distributions could be documented based on present collections. (A) *Ichthyophis.* (B) *Nessia.* (C) *Cylindrophis.* (D) *Aspidura.*

193

dwelling visual predator. This has often been described and illustrated (Greene, 1987), but its efficacy has never been tested against actual enemies.

The perhaps 13 species of shield-tailed or uropeltine snakes, of the genera *Uropeltis, Rhinophis* and *Pseudotyphlops* are true burrowers and predators on invertebrates. Moreover, the same study (Cadle *et al.* 1990) suggests that the snakes of the family Uropeltinae represent the results of a single invasion of Sri Lanka. The Indian uropeltine, closest to the Sri Lankan radiation is *Rhinophis travancoricus.* This implies that the generic names of all Sri Lankan forms may have to change, a nomenclatorial decision which is being reserved for a monograph of the group, which is now in process. The main conclusion, that is now readily based on the immunology, is that the genus *Uropeltis* as defined (Smith 1943, Gans 1966) is parapatric. Thus the assembly of Sri Lankan forms may temporarily be placed into *Rhinophis.* Uropeltine snakes have developed a two stroke digging pattern, alternately extending and widening their tunnels. The mechanism works best in soft soils and in some sands, and not at all in very hard soils, which poses problems in penetration of the surfaces of drying lateritic soils. Particularly, the large *Pseudotyphlops philippinus* cannot re-enter the soil if it emerges during nocturnal rains and becomes trapped in the hardened walls of an irrigation ditch or on the drying surface of the soil. This digging pattern, which generates meandering tunnels, suggests that this group of snakes may have originally been adapted to rain forest associations living among their root stocks.

The uropeltines of Sri Lanka may be subdivided into at least 13 species, two of which remain to be named. Two species occupy the west north-central coastal sands. Another species ranges over the northern dense and deep blackish soils; this species only approaches the surface during the rainy season. A large species occupies the southeastern lowlands, up to 400 m. One or two species occupy the southern forest regions. Four species occur in a mid-level belt between 700 m and 1400 m. One of these is apparently restricted to a single locality in the vicinity of the mid-central region, the other three species occupy fairly extensive ranges, two of them through the center of the mid-level mountains and the third in a belt fringing the eastern and southern portions of the mountains. Finally, there are four species occupying discrete ranges in the very high mountains between 1500 m and 1950 m in the southeast-central range; two of these (neither described thus far) occupy relatively small ranges, however, the other two range over a relatively wide zone.

The endemic colubrid snakes of the genus *Aspidura* are mainly excavators of the deeper layers of the surface litter of present or former forested areas (Gans and Fetcho, 1982). Here they predate local earthworms. Some species have become commensal to agricultural practices in high elevation areas. Both litter piles and tea plantations and those in kitchen gardens often have high densities of specimens. Two of the five species occur on very high mountains, two others at more medial elevations and the smallest species occupy the lowland forest of the southern ranges, including the Sinharaja. The montane species were found sympatric with a local *Rhinophis* in the litter windrows of carrot beds. It was interesting that the two forms had distinct parasitic worms (Baker and Crusz 1980, Crusz and Ching 1975).

Patterns of Invasion

The most obvious question for all of these animals may be their origin. How did they reach Sri Lanka? What is the relation of their origin to the putative pattern of distribution? We have limited and curiously conflicting information about these issues. Caecilians of the genus *Ichthyophis* occur in continental India, but the closest relatives of the Sri Lankan forms are Malaysian (Nussbaum and Gans, 1981). Also, the Sri Lankan pipe snake must have invaded from southeastern Asia as the genus only reaches the extreme eastern portions of continental India as *Cylindrophis rufus* (Smith, 1943). The limb-reduced skinks endemic to Sri Lanka are quite distinct from *Barkudia insularis,* the single, limbless species of India. Quite clearly the radiation is reasonably old, judging from the speciation pattern. However, this component of the fauna deserves further analysis. For the Typhlopidae, we again lack adequate revision that might permit assignment and demonstration of affinities. However, the occurrence of

194

Rhamphotyphlops braminus seems to represent an invasion by human agency, as this parthenogenetic species is known to have been widely transported with plant materials.

The snakes of the genus *Aspidura* and uropeltines appear to be closest to South Indian forms. For the former, we have only morphological data. These suggest affinity to the forest snakes of the genus *Xylophis,* with which they share many morphological, color pattern, body proportion and habitat characteristics (Smith, 1943). One lowland Indian species of *Xylophis* is very similar to the Sri Lankan *A. guentheri* the Indian form occurs in moist forest at the base of the southernmost area of the Western Ghats. The river draining the area is now westward entering the Arabian sea. However, the region is relatively flat and past drainage might easily have been eastward.

The distribution of the uropeltines has long been of concern to me as the patterns seen on the Indian mainland differ profoundly from those on Sri Lanka. On the mainland, the animals tend to be restricted to the Western Ghats and their outliers. The eastern plains are intermittently dry and now seem to lack any uropeltines. Other coastal regions are formed of estuarine silts and also lack uropeltids. In contrast, species endemic to Sri Lanka occur in coastal sands. This provides no evidence for direct crossing of the intermediate channel.

From this viewpoint, it is of interest that the analysis based on electrophoresis and immunology suggests that *Rhinophis travancoricus* represents the sister group for all Sri Lankan uropeltines. This species now is sympatric with *Xylophis,* and it may be that the initial invasion of these areas may have occurred by parallel rafting. In short, one may postulate invasion of the uropeltines via a stage in the moist lowlands of extreme southern India. This suggests rafting, rather than the land bridge, often adduced for the Mannar Island chain. Should there be geological evidence suggesting a South India-Sri Lanka connection, this hypothesis would have to be modified. Another kind of modification of the pattern might be forced once more if Indian species were subjected to analysis.

The combined immunological-electrophoretic analysis also provided some interesting information about the affinities of the uropeltine species and the ranges they presently occupy. What was most interesting is that the phylogenetically earliest radiation occupies the lowest elevations of the island. From this there are two distinct radiations; the first mainly to the mid-level mountains and the second to the high mountains. The several distinct tests differ in the patterns they disclose. In one, the largest species is closest to the high mountain sample, in another to the low group of species (where it fits geographically). At least two lowland and one southern form need to be sampled.

These conclusions are based on serum samples from approximately eighty per cent of the species with multiple populational samples for some of them. One might say that this is inadequate sampling, only sufficient for the statement just made and not capable of resolving some of the further internal uncertainties. The addition of another dozen samples would markedly decrease the intrinsic uncertainty, both regarding phylogenetic pattern and its biogeographic derivatives.

Patterns of Recent Change

It becomes clear that the preceding analyses lead to two major questions; (1) are the currently observed ranges original? and (2) to what extent do these ranges document past shrinkage or expansion? The comparison is not relative to a far-off historical state, but rather to the condition before the occurrence of recent large-scale environmental modification.

Shrinkage of the overall range of a species could occur due to the reduced ability of that species to tolerate changes, generated as an intrinsic part or coincidentally with the environmental modification. Examples are the applications of fertilizers and insecticides. Repeatedly, agricultural workers commented that the frequency of uropeltines encountered during hoeing dropped markedly after chemical sprays were introduced. Also, the change in the texture of the surface provided different access to old predators, as well as exposing the burrowers to new ones.

The determination of tunnel temperatures indicated that the burrowing animals occupy microhabitats drastically different from those prevailing on the surface. For instance, the uropeltids never occurred at soil temperatures above 26°C and at low moisture conditions. However, even the montane species of forested regions could be seen in deep tunnels, two meters or below, during the dry seasons. This opens the possibility of the second kind of range shrinkage, namely involving restriction to part of the former biotope, rather than to total loss of the species from the environment. Repeatedly, we encountered concentrations of uropeltines in patches of the environment, such as small forests amidst tea plantations; assemblies of original shade trees in coffee or cardamom plantations, and moist vegetable patches are obvious examples. In several cases, we found that such small remnant populations seem to retain their initial genetic state even when long separated from each other by past agricultural practice. For instance, the central valley north of Matale now seems to be bereft of uropeltine habitat. However, samples taken from the hills to the east and west showed minimal genetic differences. Similar constancy was seen in samples taken along a long ridge in the southern high mountains. Relatively few genetic substitutions were seen.

The second confounding factor for using these maps as biogeographic indicators is expansion. Expansion occurs if particular species can tolerate the modified environment and can spread from this into the adjacent not previously occupied ranges that are produced by destruction of the original limiting situation. Sometimes environmental change unlocks spectacular potential for future invasion and spread of the species no longer limited. The organisms we refer to as weeds belong in this category.

These are theoretical possibilities for evaluating the patterns disclosed by the mapping process. Decision among them allows different potential answers. It also establishes the demand for making the results more robust. Collections obviously need to be made in the gaps of the present ranges, and in the large areas to which I paid but cursory attention for various reasons. Then, there is the real need for sampling reserve forests and national parks. Such areas are often "strictly protected" against collectors with the result that we know less about their fauna than about that of the bordering regions. This is unfortunate, as the kinds of collecting proposed here will essentially have no effect on the local populations and the census data will provide baselines that permit monitoring trends about future changes in the environment. Beyond the consideration that inclusion of more amphibians and reptiles of the kinds considered here would help, I should like to note that there is a series of invertebrates for the taxonomy of which we know little or nothing, although it is clear that they have major economic importance in soil formation. These are the earthworm and other kinds of annelids. A sample sent to an Australian specialist, the only member of a tiny and exclusive coterie willing and perhaps able to help, resulted in the response that nearly 50 per cent of the material received was unknown on the "generic" level!

Documentation

The identification and mapping of animal species is a human activity, and hence, it incorporates the potential of error. Science, as an activity that requires generation of accurate, repeatable data, has to incorporate and publish methods that facilitate continuous present and future check of its results. In the present case, this is not easy as we are looking into systems that incorporate past and current change on multiple levels.

The first kind of documentation demanded concerns the sites from which the specimens derive. Roads, estates and villages may be ephemeral and so their names, hopefully written in more than one language and checked against post office and administrative records, should also be supplemented with reference to map grids and global coordinates. Elevation is essential, but it should be noted that altimeters are subject to error with climatic changes in barometric pressure. Often, it is useful to indicate the compass heading of the slope along which the animals are taken.

Once specimens are observed, it cannot be stressed too strongly that series thereof must be properly preserved, tagged and deposited at a reference site. The burrowing animals discussed here tend to live at very substantial densities. I have never encountered situations in which any effort at documentation could have had a significant effect on the status of the population. However, the initial sample must be large enough to assure that variability is encompassed. A randomly selected sample of half a dozen to ten specimens may be sufficient to include both males and females, but it must be larger if it is to include growth stages. If the population is polytypic, containing color pattern or other variants, the sample size must be adjusted to the frequency of the least common variant. Such collections must be made on a grid pattern, sampling the populations, for instance, on major topographical features, patches of vegetation, hills, and areas of obviously different soil type. It is important that sanctuary areas and national parks be included. Without intermittent surveys it will be impossible to determine whether the efforts at protection are achieving their aim.

The preserved specimens should be deposited in the permanent reference collection of a recognized natural history museum or public university. A recognized museum is one in which the materials are kept in long-term storage, being guarded and yet available for consultation by interested specialists. One assumes that taxonomic decisions will be governed by the International Code for Zoological Nomenclature.

Conclusions

The basic conclusion of the present report would seem to be that maps of the distribution of the small burrowing amphibians and reptiles would seem to indicate the ranges of former biotic and larger associations. Most cases suggest that the ranges seem little changed, although often perhaps restricted within the overall environment. Neither the burrowing herpetofauna of Sri Lanka nor that of India shows obvious loss of species. Is this real, or a sign of our ignorance? What is perhaps important is that the tests demanded by an expansion of the program remain possible, and that the cost could be spectacularly low. In contrast, the potential benefit of the results that can be generated remain substantial.

Acknowledgments

I remain indebted to Dr. P.H.D.H. de Silva for cautions regarding the multiple seemingly homonymous place names. The studies on which these comments are based were supported by collaboration with the field project of Dr. Karl Krombein of the National Museum of Natural History. Prasanna Fernando, Lalith Jayawickrama and S.A.M. Farook helped with the field work as did literally dozens of local people, only some of whom can be listed, namely Newton Amarasingha, J.D.J. Appuhami, M.P. Appuhami, M.J. Ariyadasa, I.G.D. Bodipala, Gilbert Babasingho, R.M. Danapala, Ratnayaka Darmadasa, R.A. Darmasena, T.P.T. Darmapala, Priyanka De Alwis, J.B. Ekanayaka, H.A. Edwin, W. John Fernando, W.M. Fernando, U.L.A. Hassan, M.A. Hemapala, S.H. Jothepala, K.A.D. Jayasena, K.D.S. Jayawardama, J.S. Karunasena, Walter Lowe, M.H. Mahatun, H.M. Mahindadasa, J.W. Marasinha, V. Nimal Muhndiram, K.G. Munidasa, M. Mustapha, P. Muttu, Nimal Perera, Nimalsiri Perera, P. Vigesena Perera, D.M. Premadasa, W.A. Premasiri, Lal B.V. Premaratna, A.M. Punchibanda, A. Rathnasinha, R.A. Ratnapala, Daniel Rayappu, A. Rajendran, M.V. Rajendran, H.W. Romel, Kithsiri Rupasinha, S. Selviah, Robeson Silva, M.P. Sirisena, W. Sirisena, Sarath Srilal, Ranil Sunanayaka, Kumarasiri Thennakoon, V. Velu, Upali Weerakoon, D.W.D. Weerasinha, Sarath Wijesinha, T.S. Wikramaratna, D. Yasananda. Mr. Anslem de Silva also helped by providing some independent collections. I thank Allen Greer for aid with the identification of the skinks. The parallel field work in India is proceeding in collaboration with the National Museum of Natural History, New Delhi, Dr. S.M. Nair, director, a project that involves support from the Foreign Currency Program of the Smithsonian Institution. Material collected on the various field trips has generally been deposited at the Carnegie Museum, Pittsburgh, Pennsylvania and the National Museum of Natural History, Washington DC and their curators helped with occasional payments for transport and field assistants. Some of the systematic work in the US proceeded with support of grants from the US National Science Foundation and the Leo Leeser Foundation. I thank G.P.B. Karunaratna for comments on the manuscript.

Literature Cited

Bachman, E.S. 1985. Distribution and variability of the Sri Lankan pipe snake (*Cylindrophis maculatus*). *J. Bombay Nat. Hist. Soc.* 8: 322-327.

Baker, M.R. and H. Crusz. 1980. *Cosmocercella uropeltdarum* (Crusz and Ching, 1975) n. comb. (Nematoda, Cosmocercidae), parasite de serpents (Uropeltidae) d'Asie. *Bull. Mus. Nat. Hist. Mus. Paris (Zool. Biol. Ecol. Anim.)* 2: 719-722.

Breckenridge, W.R., S. Nathanael and L. Pereira. 1987. Aspects of the biology and development of *Ichthyophis glutinosus* (Amphibia: Gymnophiona). *J. Zool. London* 211: 437-449.

Cadle, J.E., H.C. Dessauer, C. Gans, and D.F. Gartside. 1990. Phylogenetic relationships and molecular evolution in uropeltid snakes (Serpentes: Uropeltidae): allozymes and albumin immunology. *Biol. J. Linn. Soc. London* 40: 293-320.

Crusz, H. and C.C. Ching. 1975. Parasites of the relict fauna of Sri Lanka. V. New species of nematodes from uropeltid snakes. *Annls. Parasit. (Paris)* 50: 339-349.

Deraniyagala, P.E.P. 1955. *A Colored Atlas of Some Vertebrates of Ceylon. Vol. 3. Serpentoid Reptilia.* Govt. Press, Colombo.

De Silva, P.H.D.H. 1980. Snake fauna of Sri Lanka. with special reference to skull, dentition and venom in snakes. *Spol. Zeylan.* 34: 1-472.

Gans, C. 1966. Uropeltidae. *Liste der rezenten Amphibien und Reptilien. Das Tierreich, (Berlin)* 84: 1-29.

Gans, C. 1973. Uropeltid snakes - survivors in a changing world. *Endeavour* 32: 60-65.

Gans, C. 1975. *Reptiles of the World. Bantam Nature Guide (Knowledge Through Color).* Bantam Books Inc, New York.

Gans, C. 1976. Aspects of the biology of uropeltid snakes. *In* A. d'A. Bellairs and C.B. Cox, eds. *Morphology and Biology of Reptiles. Linn. Soc. London, Symp.* 3:191-204.

Gans, C. 1978. All animals are interesting! Presidential Address. *Amer. Zool.* 18: 3-9.

Gans, C. 1979. A subterranean snake with a funny tail. *Natural Hist.* 88: 70-75.

Gans, C. 1986. Evolution of limbless squamates: functional aspects. *In* Z. Rocek, ed. *Studies in Herpetology. Proc. 3rd Ordinary Gen. Meet. Societas Europaea Herpetologica (August 19-23).* pp. 71-74. Charles University, Prague.

Gans, C. 1987. Automimicry and batesian mimicry in uropeltid snakes: pigment pattern, proportions and behavior. *J. Bombay Nat. Hist. Soc. (Centenary Supplement)*83: 52-158.

Gans, C. 1989. *Aspidura* in the Maldives. *Herpet. J.* 1: 421-421.

Gans, C. and D. Baic. 1977. Regional specialization of reptilian scale surfaces: relation of texture and biologic role. *Science* 195: 1348-1350.

Gans, C. and J.R. Fetcho. 1982. The Sri Lankan genus *Aspidura* (Serpentes: Reptilia: Colubridae). *Ann. Carnegie Mus.* 51: 271-316.

Gans, C., H.C. Dessauer and D. Baic. 1978. Axial differences in the musculature of the uropeltid snakes: the freight-train approach to burrowing. *Science* 199: 189-192.

Greene, H.W. 1987. Defense behavior. *In* C. Gans and R.B. Huey, eds. *Biology of the Reptilia, Vol. 16, Ecology and Behavior B.* pp. 1-152. Alan Liss Inc. New York.

Nussbaum, R.A. and C. Gans. 1981. On the *Ichthyophis* (Amphibia: Gymnophiona) of Sri Lanka. *Spol. Zeylan.* 35: 137-154.

Rajendran, M. V. 1985. *Studies in Uropeltid Snakes*. Madurai Karamaj University, Publ. 80.

Sarasin, P. and F. Sarasin. 1887. *Ergebnisse Naturwissenschaftlicher Forschungen auf Ceylon in den Jahren 1884-1886*. Kreidel, Wiesbaden.

Smith, M.A. 1943. *The Fauna of British India, Ceylon and Burma including the whole of the Indo-Chinese Subregion. Reptilia and Amphibia. Vol. 3. Serpentes*. Taylor and Francis, London.

Taylor, E.H. 1947. Comments on Ceylonese Snakes of the genus *Typhlops* with descriptions of new species. *Univ. Kansas Sci. Bull.* 31: 283-298.

Proceedings of the International and Interdisciplinary Symposium
ECOLOGY AND LANDSCAPE MANAGEMENT IN SRI LANKA
W. Erdelen, C. Preu, N. Ishwaran, C.M. Madduma Bandara (eds.)
Colombo, Sri Lanka, 12-26 March 1990
© 1993
Margraf Scientific Books, D-97985 Weikersheim
ISBN 3-8236-1182-8

The Evolution of the Major Landscape Categories in Sri Lanka and Distribution Patterns of Some Selected Taxa: Ecological Implications

F. R. SENANAYAKE

Abstract

The island of Sri Lanka has evolved a biota whose distribution patterns provide keys to the nature and frequency of past climates. Many species can serve as indicators of both natural and human impacted landscape categories. In modern Sri Lanka, man-modified ecosystems in urban, industrial and agricultural areas have increased in percentage cover while natural ecosystems have decreased. In many regions, the original vegetation has been reduced to refugial patches with receding boundaries. Conservation action is urgently needed, but the data bases available for managing natural as well as man modified systems are poor and scattered. A system to catalog information and set up data bases to assist in rational land use and conservation is proposed.

Introduction - Geological History

The island of Sri Lanka has been a part of a Pre-Cambrian landmass that maintained some integrity through the upper and lower Paleozoic, as documented by the rocks of the highland series, Vijayan and Southwestern groups (Cooray 1967; Fig. 1). The other rocks of the island were formed during the Jurassic and Miocene. They provide the earliest fossil evidence from which biogeographical hypotheses can be made. The Jurassic rocks occur in two faulted basins within the Vijayan series and lie in almost a straight line to similar faulted basins near Madras in Southern India. These rocks are well-bedded and represent a series of sandstones, arkose, siltstones and mudstones. The mudstones are of biogeographical interest in that they are fossiliferous with clear imprints of plants. A study of the sedimentary features of these rocks (Money and Cooray, 1966) suggests that they were originally brackish or freshwater sediments laid down in shallow deltas. Money and Cooray hypothesized a semi-arid climate in the area due to an absence of coal bearing or even carbonaceous beds and noted that the plants represented in the rocks may have been carried down from cooler, wetter mountain systems. Nearly 18 species of plants have been described from these rocks (Jacob 1938, Sitholey 1944, Pascoe 1959). Of these the fern *Cladophlebis reversa* (Feist.), the cycads *Taeniopteris spatulata* (McCelland), *Nilssonia fissa* (Feist.) and the genus *Ptilophyllum* have also been recorded from the Jurassic Beds of India (Krishnan, 1960). These species are characteristic of the upper Gondwana formations and suggest that Sri Lanka and India shared a Gondwana derived biota. The Indian Shield was subject to fault movements that were widespread during the Jurassic and Cretaceous periods. These movements may have been responsible for the block uplift of the mountain masses of Sri Lanka and Southern India (Wadia, 1942). At the close of the Jurassic, the breakup of Gondwanaland caused the Indian Shield to separate from Africa and begin its northerly movement into the Tethys Sea (Flores, 1970).

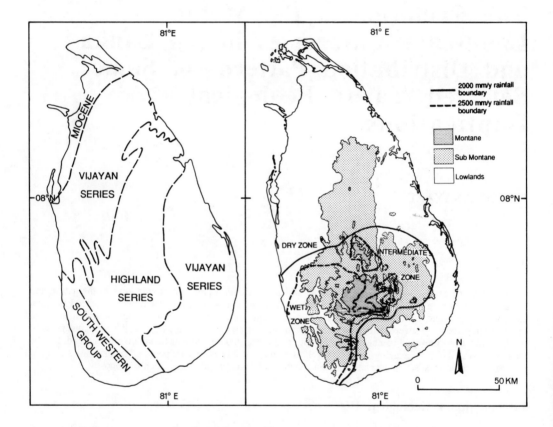

Figure 1. The main petrographic (left) and hygroclimatic (right) zones of Sri Lanka.

The landmass that was to become the island of Sri Lanka remained above sea level from this time until the Miocene, as there is no evidence of any marine deposits being recorded within its boundaries. During this period the peneplanation of the hills of Sri Lanka and Southern India took place (Cooray, 1967).

The Miocene was marked by an arm of the Tethys Sea that encroached the land surface between India and Sri Lanka (Fig. 2) turning Sri Lanka into an island for the first time. By the

Middle Miocene global sea levels attained much the same levels as today (Maxwell, 1973, Lloyd, 1973) and the island retained its general outline and remained above sea level for the period following the Miocene. However, there seems to have been repeated, protracted connections with the mainland. Biogeographically, these connections are significant. The similarity of the Pleistocene fossils of Sri Lanka with the Shivalik fauna of India has been known for a long time. According to Deraniyagala (1958), the Pleistocene climate consisted of three distinct phases termed the Ratnapura Phase, Palagaha Turai Phase and the Colombo Phase (Early Holocene).

The Ratnapura Phase was characterized by wet and cool climatic conditions. The fossil beds from this stage contain lake dwelling animals like the hippopotamus *Hexaprotodon* and aquatic vegetation suggesting large lakes and swamps. The Palagaha Turai Phase is represented by highly oxidized red earth and wind blown sands that suggest a dry and arid period, overlying

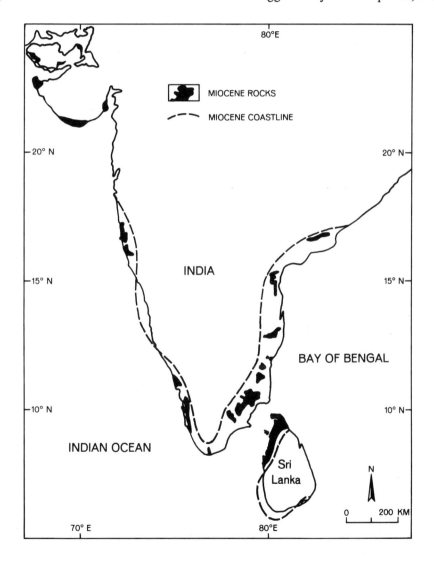

Figure 2. Miocene encroachment of the Tethys Sea.

the beds of the Ratnapura Phase. The Colombo Phase is essentially of the Early Holocene Age, during which conditions became wetter and stabilized themselves in the climatic conditions experienced today.

Regardless of the number of connections with the mainland, the immigration of species adapted to cool and moist conditions would have been possible only in the early part of the Pleistocene as later connections coincided with the Palagaha Turai Phase and the Colombo Phase. This trend is also suggested in the work of De Terra and Patterson (1939), who noted that the climate of central India had changed from wet-tropical to dry-tropical by Middle Pleistocene times.

Although the Pleistocene has been identified as the period of radiation and speciation of Sri Lankan biota, Holocene events also played a part in creating the present biogeographic patterns. The global phenomenon termed the Holocene transgression saw sea levels in 35,000 B.P. approximately the same level as today. But between these times, the sea level fell by about 130 m and rose again to present levels (Emory and Milliman, 1968). The form of the Holocene transgression has been computed using a range of indicators from around the world. Although the possibility of lag exists in sheltered or otherwise modified areas as shown by some temporal anomalies, the amplitude has been reasonably constant. The Holocene transgression trends for the Indian Ocean are assumed to have been similar to the trends measured for the Great Barrier Reef and South China Sea (Emory and Milliman 1968, Davies and Kinsey 1977, Hopley and Kinsey 1988) and its influence on the Sri Lanka is outlined in Figure 3.

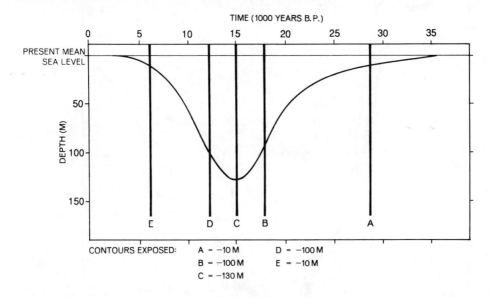

Figure 3. Holocene transgression and its impact on Sri Lanka.

The Holocene transgression began at about 35,000-34,000 B.P. at which time the island had very much the same outline as present. From this time on, the sea began to recede until about 28,000 B.P. when a large landmass was formed to the north extending the Jaffna Peninsula in size and extending Mannar island into a peninsula that connected Sri Lanka with the mainland. Two other significant geographical features were evident at this time, a new riverine floodplain south of the Mannar Peninsula and the complex of islands that emerged in the south (Fig. 4).

The riverine floodplain in the north was created by two large rivers, the old courses of which were described by Deraniyagala (1958). While it is probable that these two rivers joined at

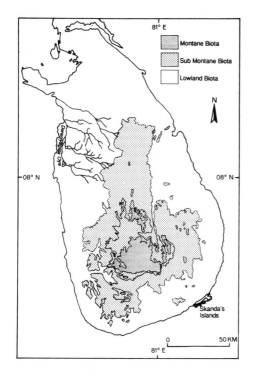

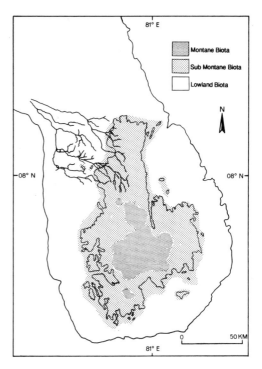

Figure 4. Early and Late Holocene transgression features.

Figure 5. Middle Holocene transgression features.

around the Middle Holocene, they have remained distinct during the early and later phases of the Holocene. One river was an extension of the Aravi Aru of today, the other drained the watersheds of the Kal Aru, Modaragam Oya, Kala Oya and Mi Oya. This large river created a series of riverine flats that existed for about 22,000 years. It is proposed that this river be named the "Deraniyagala Oya" after its discoverer.

The seven islands that emerged opposite the drainage basin of the Manik Ganga is another interesting feature that emerged at this time. These islands named "Skanda's Islands" also existed for about 22,000 years as prominent landscape features. They became hills during further oceanic retreat towards the Middle Holocene transgression. The Middle Holocene transgression saw a further fall in sea level until levels of about -100 m were reached. During this period the northern riverine flats became higher in elevation but still retained the character of the lowland dry zone. This period also saw the creation of flatlands to the south (Fig. 5) that would have allowed the rain forests to extend their range. These lands existed for about 4000 years and were resubmerged because of a rise in sea level that began at about 15,000 B.P. and culminated at the ten-meter level about 6000-7000 years ago (Fig. 4). The Late Holocene transgression seems to have happened rapidly as the present coastline is known to have stabilized at about 6000 B.P. (Hopley, 1983). The recent and rapid drowning of these lands in relatively recent (5500-6000 B.P.) times is also suggested by the presence of "drowned forests" along the old riverplain of the Deraniyagala Oya off the western coast (Fig. 4).

Biogeography

In a broad biogeographical sense Sri Lanka can be regarded as part of the Indian region. Blanford (1901) regarded the island as a part of his "Malabar tract" of India. Subsequent works have all accepted this perspective (Darlington 1957, Mani 1974). However, the internal dynamics and biogeographical patterns within the island are still imperfectly calculated. The distribution patterns of biota of the island were first addressed by ornithologists such as Legge (1880) and Wait (1931). They pointed out that the central mountains contained the largest number of endemic species. Ripley (1949) presented a hypothesis of how these distribution patterns may have come about by referring to serial immigration during the Pleistocene connections. Works on mammals demonstrated that distribution patterns similar to those of birds also existed for mammals (Phillips, 1942). Moore (1960) working on the origin and distribution of tree squirrel species developed a model for wet, cool, pluvial phases to support his hypothesis of repeated invasions. In some taxa, i.e. amphibians and reptiles, man has been identified as the agent responsible for extending the range of some mainland species to the island (Kirthisinghe 1954, Erdelen 1984).

Few botanists provided hypotheses on the patterns of movement (Abeywickrama, 1959). Most began classifying the island into different botanical zones. Their work presently identifies seven vegetational zones delineated by a combination of physical and climatic parameters (Gaussen *et al.* 1964, Mueller-Dombois and Sirisena 1967, Fernando 1968, Mueller-Dombois 1968). Zoologists using the same physical criteria have identified three to four zones (Henry 1955, Phillips 1942) but all these works deal with a single taxon. A synthesis of the distribution patterns has been attempted recently (Senanayake *et al.* 1977, Crusz and Nugaliyadde 1978), suggesting four zones based on a combination of altitude and rainfall. The distribution patterns of the fish fauna differ significantly from these models (Senanayake and Moyle, 1981).

The ichthyofauna is the most conservative element of a vertebrate fauna in terms of geographic radiation as fishes are strongly limited by the continuity of aquatic habitats. Therefore they can serve well as indicators of climate and thereby habitat change. While the fossil record of fishes is poor in Sri Lanka, a consideration of the fossil record of India is valid, especially as both countries shared a common biota until the Miocene. The Eocene fossils of India, the Inter-Trappan Beds of the Deccan Series yield a "variety of *Macropodus*" (Silas, 1952). The genus *Macropodus* of the family Anabantidae is still present on the island as well as on the mainland. The antiquity of this family on the island is suggested by the endemic genus *Malpulutta*, while its range at that period is suggested by another anabantid genus, *Belontia,* that is shared with Malaya and not with mainland India. The extinction of this genus on the mainland during the Deccan trap eruptions of the Late Miocene is not improbable. It has been suggested that the lava flows of these eruptions led to the extinction of many groups of plants and animals in India (Silas 1955, Menon 1973).

Another similarity with the Malayan region has been pointed out by Deraniyagala (1956). Some of the Sri Lankan Cyprinidae show a tendency to suppress the perforated lateral line, a feature common in the Malayan element of the Cyprinidae but absent in the Indian element. The endemic cyprinid genus *Horadandia,* for example, displays a complete suppression of the perforated lateral line and may represent another element of the Miocene fauna.

The fourth genus to be considered as a part of this fauna is the ophiocephalid genus *Channa,* known from tertiary fossil beds in India but presently absent on the mainland. Today it is confined to Sri Lanka and the Malayan region. *Channa* has been recorded from the Early Pleistocene in the Shivalik fauna of India by Silas (1955). The only other record (Lydekker, 1886) of freshwater fish is from the Pliocene horizons of the Shivalik. It shows all siluroid genera present on the island during this period. The evidence from other taxa is similar. For instance, the mammalian fossils of the Ratnapura Beds are essentially the same as the mainland Shivalik fauna (Deraniyagala, 1958), suggesting a large element of shared fauna until the close of the Ratnapura Phase of the Pleistocene.

An examination of the autochthonous genera of fishes on mainland India demonstrates that these fishes are mostly restricted to Southern India. None of these genera occur in Sri Lanka.

Further, a majority of these fishes are inhabitants of cool, or swiftly flowing streams and are confined to the southwestern mountain ranges of India (Jayaram, 1974). The fauna of the southwestern mountains of India has generally been held to be common with the mountains of Sri Lanka, so much so that zoogeographers have grouped both areas together as the "Malabar Tract" (Day 1889, Blanford 1901). Ripley (1945) working on the avifauna, Phillips (1935) and Moore (1960) working on mammals demonstrate the close relationship between the two areas. This suggests the nature of the last Pleistocene and Holocene connections to have been conducive to the interchange of larger or more vagile forms while being restrictive for less vagile forms like fishes.

Further evidence of the restrictive nature of the last Pleistocene and Holocene connections comes from the examination of the montane fish fauna of Sri Lanka. The mountains of the island contain no species specialized for life in hill streams. The fish fauna is depauperate and consists of immigrants from the lowlands (Senanayake, 1980). This suggests a loss of the autochthonous element, perhaps with Pleistocene uplift, the arid climates of the Palagaha Tuari Phase and an inability of the Indian autochthonous montane species to emigrate during subsequent connections. Such patterns of distribution amongst Sri Lankan fauna can now be looked at with a view to hypothesizing the biogeographical history of these taxa.

The earliest endemic elements of the ichtyofauna of Sri Lanka are the endemic genera *Malpulutta* and *Horadandia, Macropodus,* a genus shared with India, and the genera shared with the Malayan region, *Belontia* and *Channa.* Of these, only *Macropodus* has representatives on the mainland. The closest relatives of the other genera are found in the Malayan region (Deraniyagala, 1956). Fossil evidence confirms that this element of the fauna was once a part of an Eocene shared biota and can be identified as part of an distinct track (Croziat 1964, Croziat *et al.* 1974). This notion is strengthened by evidence from the reptile genera *Cophotis* and *Cylindrophis* which have similar distribution patterns (Deraniyagala 1952, 1955, Senanayake *et al.* 1976) as do the bird genera *Phoenicophaeus, Megalaima, Zoothera, Myiophoneus* and *Bradypterus* (Ripley, 1949). Some taxa may demonstrate even earlier tracks, such as the subfamily Acontianinae, a group of subfossorial lizards confined to Sri Lanka, Madagascar and South Africa (Deraniyagala, 1953).

The period following the Eocene was marked by extinctions and upheavals of the mainland (Menon, 1973). Although the island remained relatively stable (Cooray, 1967), it too experienced block uplift in the central hills (Wadia, 1945). The positioning of the sedimentary beds suggests uplift in both the Pliocene and Pleistocene (Deraniyagala, 1958). Botanists suggest that rain forests were widespread across the region by the Middle Miocene (Meijer, 1982). In terms of fauna, the Late Pliocene and Early Pleistocene period was well recorded in the fossils of the Shivalik System and the Ratnapura Beds. It was a period of faunal exchange between the two areas. The "Indian" element of the endemic fauna entered at this time. Movement of species from the mainland to the island was stronger as the direction of movement would have been from the area with the largest number of potential immigrants (Horton, 1974). However, some movement the other way has also been recorded in the earthworm genera *Notoscolex* and *Megascolex* (Deraniyagala, 1953). The prevailing climatological conditions would have allowed the spread of rain forest conditions to the mainland. Such a mechanism is required for the entry of rain forest or high rainfall adapted species. This period also saw an extension of the montane habitat. A fall in sea level to about -100 meters gave the island a new coastal lowland and effectively transformed much of the second peneplain into habitat for the montane biota by increasing its effective height above sea level. The biota of the montane zone expanded its range similarly (Fig. 5). With the close of the Ratnapura period two major changes were experienced. One was the drying up of many montane streams and the upward retreat of the montane forests, the other was the southward retreat of the lowland rain forests. The presence of an endemic species of fish in rain forest habitat in a refugial valley on the dry eastern side of the mountains (Senanayake, 1982) strengthens this hypothesis.

Any Pleistocene land connections after this period would have occurred during the dry Palagaha Turai Phase. In such a climate the interchange of forms adapted to rain forest or high rainfall habitats would not have been possible. For the ichthyofauna this means that there should be no species common to and restricted to rain forests in both Southern India and Sri Lanka. The distribution of the inland fishes confirms such a pattern (Senanayake, 1980).

There are two other geologic events that may have had an impact on the biota of the island. One is the Pleistocene oscillation, the other the Holocene transgression. On the basis of high gravel terraces and raised beaches Wadia (1941b) and Cooray (1967) suggested that 'minor' oscillations of the relative levels of sea and land occurred during the Pleistocene. The amplitude of the oscillations varied from +15 m to +30 m (Cooray 1967, Deraniyagala 1958). These events would not effect much of the terrestrial biota but might have had profound effects on aquatic systems. In the rain forest area of Sri Lanka, for example, all the deep slow rivers would have been submerged (Fig. 6). Above this elevation lie the folded hills of the mid-hill zone that has no major deep rivers. Thus any element of the riverine biota that was restricted to this zone would have been eliminated. An examination of the endemic fishes shows a marked absence of any primary freshwater, endemic riverine fishes in the rain forest rich Southwestern Province (Senanayake, 1980).

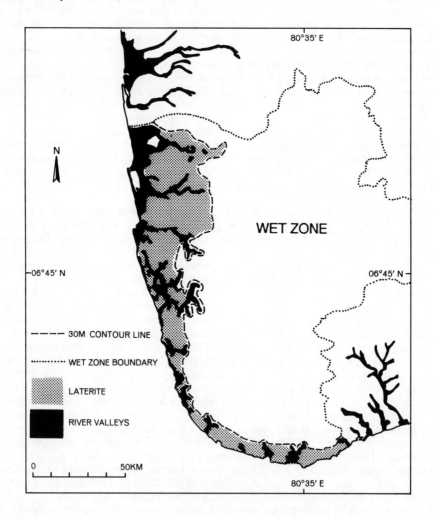

Figure 6. The 100 ft contour on the western coast, approximated by the laterite band.

The Holocene transgression occurred at about 35,000 B.P. and, as discussed above, exhibited a fall in global sea levels that reached a maxima of around -130 m at about 14,000 B.P. This event would have seen the emergence of a massive highly fertile lowland area with a dry exposed peninsula that served as a bridge to the mainland, but the habitats available on these lowlands or on the peninsula would not have allowed the passage of cold-adapted or wet-adapted species. Erdelen (1984), studying the distribution patterns of the reptile genus *Calotes*, suggests a post-Pleistocene date for the arrival of the most modern element of the mainland fauna and suggests a very recent man-influnced route. However, it is more likely that the Holocene transgression would have been the time of entry for a group of mainland biota represented by the lizard species *Calotes versicolor* and *Calotes calotes* or the frog species *Rana limnocharis, Microhyla ornata* and *Polypedates leucomystax maculatus*. These species are closely related to the mainland forms and they are adapted better to the lowland dry zone, which has a climate very similar to that of the southern end of India and, on the basis of geological evidence, a climate that prevailed during the Holocene transgression. The Middle H olocene transgression also saw an expansion of the montane habitats due to the increase in altitude above sea level. However, the short duration of this particular phenomenon (Fig. 3) lasting about 4000 years, may have been long enough for the exchange of only the more vagile species between mountain blocks.

The distribution patterns of the lizard genus *Ceratophora* and the amphibian genus *Polypedates* are interesting in this context. *Ceratophora* is confined to the upper montains and rain forests while *Polypedates* is distributed throughout the island. The genus *Ceratophora* is represented by four species: *C. stodartii,* confined to the central mountains, *C. tennenti,* confined to the Knuckles Range or northern mountains, *C.* sp. nov. confined to the Sabaragamuwa or northern mountains and *C. aspera*, confined to the southwestern lowland rain forests (Fig. 7). Each disjunct mountain massif has a distinct but related species confined

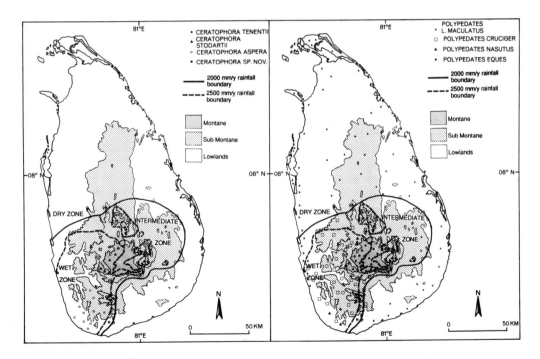

Figure 7. Distribution patterns of the lizard genus *Ceratophora.*

Figure 8. Distribution patterns of the amphibian genus *Polypedates* .

to the higher (above 2000 m) elevations, suggesting isolation by barriers effective even during its potential relaxation during the Holocene transgression. The lowland species is confined to southern and western rain forests. However, it would have been much more widely distributed during the Holocene transgression when the rain forest habitats would have had a large southerly expansion. In fact, *C. aspera* the rain forest species, displays a remarkable degree of polymorphism and deserves closer study.

The genus *Polypedates* is also represented by four species: *P. leucomystax maculatus* is found on the mainland and distributed through the lowland dry zone, *P. cruciger*, its closest congener, is a lowland form confined to the wet and intermediate zones, *P. nasutus* is distributed through the lowland rain forests and mid hills to 2000 m, *P. eques* is a montane form more or less confined to the upper montane areas (Fig. 8). *P. eques* is found on all three mountain blocks, in a similar distribution pattern to the montane species of *Ceratophora*. Unlike *Ceratophora* there is no distinct speciation between the three populations. Although the three populations demonstrate a slight morphological variation, they belong to the same species, suggesting gene flow across the populations until recently. In this species, the relaxation of barriers during the last (Holocene) period have proved sufficient for gene flow.

As a consequence of these geological and climatic events, the biota of Sri Lanka have achieved their individual distribution patterns. The less the relative vagility of a taxon is, the more conservative is its distribution pattern. The most universal patterns are those generated by a combination of rainfall and altitude. This yields seven distinct areas (Tab. 1) each with its own complement of unique ecosystems (e.g. coastal, riverine, woodland).

Table 1. Biogeographical areas in Sri Lanka.

Zone	Altitude (ft)	Rainfall (mm)
1. Montane zone	over 4000	
2. Sub-montane zone	1000-4000	over 2000
3. Sub-montane zone	1000-4000	under 1750
4. Lowland wet zone		over 2500
5. Lowland intermediate zone		under 2500 and over 1750
6. Lowland dry zone		under 1750
7. Lowland dry zone		under 1000

Determining Landscapes

Landscapes have been defined as heterogenous land areas composed of a cluster of interacting ecosystems that is repeated in similar form throughout. Further landscape development or formation has seen to be a result of three mechanisms operating on a landscape boundary; specific geomorphological processes taking place over a long time, colonization patterns of organisms and local diturbances of individual ecosystems over a shorter time (Foreman and Godron, 1986). When considering the conservation of ecosystems in Sri Lanka, two other definitions are of use. One is a "plesioclimatic landscape" containing ecosystems that have matured without the influence of man. The second is "anthropomorphic landscapes" containing ecosystems that have been modified or formed by the influence of man. This allows the address of the landscape as a distinct measurable unit defined by its recognizable and spatially repetitive clusters of interacting ecosystems. The characteristics of the landscapes are as follows:

1. The structure or the spatial relationships among the distinctive ecosystems or "element" of a landscape, e.g. the distribution of energy, materials and species in relation to the sizes, shapes, numbers, kinds and configurations of these ecosystems.
2. The function or the interaction between these spatial elements, e.g. the flow of energy, materials or species among the components of the landscape.
3. The change or the alteration in the ecological mosaic over time in relation to structure and function.

In terms of ecosystems or species conservation, it is human impact that has affected the viability of many indigenous systems. It will therefore be of use to consider the landscapes of Sri Lanka in a historical context.

Characteristics of Precolonial Landscapes

Precolonial landscapes are diverse and are dictated by the ecosystem, anthropomorphic elements(a) closely interwoven with plesioclimatic elements(p), the rapid movement of the anthropomorphic elements in space and time and a large ratio of p:a. Man has been recorded in Sri Lanka since 125,000 B.P. starting with small-flake industries and evolving to microlithic stone tool (Mesolithic) industries by about 30,000 B.P. (Deraniyagala, this volume). Globally, the period between 8000 B.P. and 10,000 B.P. is significant in that this period saw the domestication of plants such as wheat, barley and rice (Harrison *et al.* 1969) and the evolution of agriculture. In Sri Lanka, the period between the Mesolithic and settled agriculture would have seen the formation of large land masses to the north and south. During the transgression, emerging marine deposits produced some of the richest flatlands in the region, the social consequences of which may have been the development of a settled lifestyle. Many old river systems can still be traced over the now submerged landscape (Figs.4, 5), but no conclusions about this land can be drawn with current knowledge. Thus, the landscapes of today represent the upper part of a landmass that was existant in the Holocene. Man's impact on these landscapes can be traced fairly clearly from the Middle Holocene onwards, due to the existence of recorded history. However, it must be noted that, while empirical evidence such as for Giants Tank near Mannar suggests sophisticated agriculture long before the advent of the Sinhalese (Brohier, 1934), the oldest historical chronicle of the island, the Mahavamsa, places the time of agricultural development at about 543 B.C. (Geiger, 1934). No major landscape changes can be detected in this record until the arrival of Buddhism in 307 B.C. Buddhism with its philosophy of reverence to life changed the eating habits of the people. Meat and fish were excluded from the diet of the people (Tennent, 1856). Thus by 200 B.C. there were many references to the growing of leguminous crops, grain, fruit trees, nut trees and floriculture.

Precolonial history also records a consistent growth of agricultural landscapes in certain parts of the country. The forest ecosystems that are represented in the dry zone were the main regions of human landscape modification. The number of "tanks" (reservoirs) constructed in this area alone exceeds 10,000 (Fernando, 1965). During the 11th and 12th centuries, agricultural surplus supported cities, schools, libraries and a large monastic population (Ellawela, 1969). This agricultural system and social order was sustained until about the 14th century, when a series of invasions and their ecological consequences destroyed its viability (Senanayake, 1977). The anthropomorphic landscapes reverted back into secondary and finally climax dry zone forests. While there are still no clear ways to reconstruct the early anthropomorphic landscapes, their ability to coexist with the natural ecosystems is illustrated by the fact that when these areas were examined 400-500 years later, a full complement of expected dry zone biota was evident.

During the precolonial period, the wet zone and the montane zone became populated towards the 15th and 16th centuries, but even then the only anthropomorphic landscapes were in the floodplains and river valleys which were turned into rice fields (Gorrie, 1954). However, these landscape elements were closely interlinked with the natural systems, the elements of one contributing to the stability of the other (Senanayake, 1983). In a biogeographical context, only one ecosystem was severely affected during this period, that being the swamp and riverine floodplain ecosystems of these zones.

Another attribute of the precolonial landscape was the fact that man as an agriculturist moved his field regularly. Thus, at low levels of land use the consequence of man's activity was absorbed by the natural system. Further, the practice of ahimsa or the non-taking of life within the village community encouraged a non-exploitative relationship between man and wildlife (Moyle and Senanayake, 1983).

Characteristics of Colonial Landscapes

Colonial landscapes are reliant on exotic species, have low biodiversity and are relatively independent of the native ecosystem, The anthropomorphic elements are sharply separated from plesioclimatic elements and there is a slower movement of anthropomorphic elements in space and time. The ratio of p:a decreases rapidly.

The colonial landscape emerged in the 18th centurieswhen forests were felled for timber export and plantation industry was in its infancy with small monocultures or cinnamom for the East India trade. The large-scale felling of forests began after 1820 when all land without title was deemed "crown land" and sold to commercial interests. The "coffee boom" of 1835 was a rush for land that was only equalled by the gold rush in the U.S. (Tennent 1856). The intensity of this activity is reflected in the government land sale figures which show that over 290,000 acres of montane forest were sold for coffee growing in less than 10 years (Tab. 2).

Table 2. The sales of crown lands between 1837 and 1845.

1837	3,661 acres
1838	10,401 acres
1839	9,750 acres
1840	42,841 acres
1841	78,685 acres
1842	48,533 acres
1843	58,336 acres
1844	20,415 acres
1845	19,062 acres

The early colonial landscapes saw the creation of new ecosystems, "agroecosystems" that usually had exotic organisms as the dominant species. They contained large areas of monoculture, first coffee, then tea, rubber and coconut. These ecosystems replaced the more diverse indigenous land use systems. Coffee and tea replaced montane forests, rubber replaced lowland rain forest and coconut replaced lowland rain forest and evergreen forest. A further problem with these crops was the fact that large quantities of firewood were required in processing for export. The source of firewood was natural forest ecosystems. Thus, this period saw a reduction of indigenous landscapes not only as a consequence of forest clearing but also as a consequence of timber and firewood extraction. Much of the original agricultural endeavor at this time did not pay any heed to good management practices. Thus, large areas began to lose topsoil, became impoverished and were abandoned to become fire maintained grasslands.

Indigenous landscapes were transformed, the new landscape containing much less natural forest.

The late colonial period saw landscapes that were managed to sustain some element of ecological stability. The lessons of land degradation were learnt. Early and sound land management practices were embarked on. Shade trees, windbreaks, contour planting, terracing and draining began to emerge as management characters. Even at this time the loss of indigenous species and ecosystems continued, eliciting comment on the rapid loss of species (Kelaart 1852, Tennent 1856). The landscape of the village began to take a different character. The wealth of exotic tree crop species allowed the replacement of low utility indigenous species with high utility exotic species.

Characteristics of Postcolonial Landscapes

Postcolonial landscapes are less diverse and are relatively independent of indigenous ecosystems. They are the result of an influx of biocides and environmental toxins. The anthropocentric elements are antagonistic to pleisoclimatic elements. The landscapes are permanent settlements and have a very small ratio of p:a.

Postcolonial activity has radically altered many landscape elements. During this period, the greatest ecosystem modifications took place in the dry zone. Habitat loss slowed in the wet zone as a consequence of both a lack of forest for clearing and an increasing desire on the part of the estate owners to protect their investment. In fact, some of the more visionary attempts at forestry by the Forest Department were also implemented at this time; the highly diverse species-rich reforestation block at Bataleeya near Kurunegala being a good example. There was an increase in the awareness of wildlife conservation as an institution.

The last quarter century of postcolonial activity has seen a great erosion in both anthropomorphic and plesioclimatic elements of landscapes. Biologically, this period has seen a tremendous increase in the input of biocides. The rate of human deaths from biocides had reached 6083 during the period 1975-1980, hospital admissions for poisoning by biocides reached 79,961 during this period (Jeyaratnam *et al.* 1983). The effect on the environment has also been catastrophic. Studies on the ichthyofauna confirm the loss of species due to theapplication of biocides (Senanayake and Moyle, 1981). Data from the Zoological Survey of Sri Lanka (ZSSL) suggest similar trends in the amphibian fauna (Senanayake and Lokuge, in prep.).

The loss of habitat accelerated during this period. International development projects involving the modification of large areas of indigenous ecosystems were promoted as the national need. However, an examination of environmental impact reports indicates that reporting of specialized habitats has been poor (Alexis, 1984). This has resulted in many specialized habitats being destroyed or having no legal status. Another landscape feature that is gaining prominence are monocultures of *Pinus* and *Eucalyptus* which do not serve the same ecological function as the indigenous forest or the village (Senanayake, 1987). These landscape elements have also been seen to affect site conditions negatively.

Future Needs

In the future, there will be a need for the cataloging and conservation of endangered ecosystems, a rational landscape design and an increase in the ratio of p:a. Forest patches in many of the Sri Lankan landscapes usually represent the only habitat for rare or endangered indigenous species. But most remnant forest patches will go unrecognized because they are not part of any scheduled or protected area. The ability of the area presently scheduled or under protection to provide habitat to all the species represented in Sri Lanka is poor. This is due to the fact that protected areas do not cover all the different ecosystems of the island. These ecosystems still exist in small patches of refugial forest and are scattered over the landscape.

These remnant forest patches have to be cataloged and addressed, if any potential for future ecosystem rehabilitation work is to be retained.

One technique to address this problem is the Tropical Forest Register (TFR) whose format has been accepted by a large group of non-government agencies (NGOs) working on tropical forest loss (Senananyake, 1988). The registering of tropical forests in Sri Lanka has been initiated by the Neo-Synthesis Research Centre (NSRC). Their data demonstrate the utility of this system to the tropical ecosystem conservation effort. On a mapping scale of 1:10,000, the resolution allows forests of 2.5 acres (1 hectare) or over to be clearly notated. Interrogation of the TFR data base provides output at many user levels. Level 1 information presents a physiognomic description of the vegetation following Kuchler's (1966) classification and is discussed more fully in Senanayake (1988).

Another feature that needs address is the ecological function of the anthropomorphic element of the landscape. Present land use patterns as agriculture or forestry produce ecosystems which do not provide habitat to most elements of the indigenous biota. The concept of analog forestry may provide a land use technique with greater positive impact (Senanayake, 1987). Tropical

Table 3. Interrogation of the Tropical Forest Register data base to levels 1 and 2. Data from Ferguson (1857).

Tropical Forest Register   ID no. 01,0001,00001.

Level 1: B6c, S5i, C, X, 3i; H2i; w.l.;

Level 2:

A.   Descriptors

2.1	Country	Sri Lanka
2.2	Elevation	1112 m
2.3	Landform	Steep, hilly, < 20% slope
2.4	Coordinates	80°56'-57' (long), 6°30'-32' (lat)
2.5	Local classification	Tropical montane evergreen rain forest
2.6	Dominant tree species	*Michelia champac, Listea ovalifolia, Sizygium operculatum, Meliosma simplifolia, Turpina malabarica*
2.7	Status	Refugial forest, endangered
2.8	Area under forest	995 m^2
2.9	Area scheduled	none
2.10	Responsible authority	Govt. Agent, Katcheri, Badulla
2.11	Neighborhood communities	Mirahawatte village, Malpotha village
2.12	Closest town or city	Bandarawela
2.13	Map availability	yes
2.14	NGO involvement	yes - NSRC, Mirahawatte

B.   Special Features

2.15	Geological	The forest is located in the Uva Basin, a montane plateau surrounded by a wall of higher mountains, mean annual temperature 20°C, mean annual rainfall 1743 mm, wet season (> 100 mm/month) II-IV and X-XII, dry season (< 100 mm/month) V-X
2.16	Scenic	
2.17	Tree	Tree species have been extensively surveyed, files in level 3.
2.18	Plant	Introduction of native orchids begun by NSRC
2.19	Animal	Lady Torrington's Wood Pigeon breeding area
2.20	Human	

forests tend to possess an architectural form that creates a modified environment. This form, consisting of a closed, multilayered diverse canopy allowed many species to become specialized in this environment. Analog forestry recognizes these relationships and seeks to create a similar physical structure to the natural forest of any area. It also seeks to reestablish the ecological functions of the original system through the design of analogous structures. This modified environment will allow many species presently restricted to remnant forests to extend their ranges and create a system of land use that is environmentally more benign than the current models.

Response to the urgent national need for rational planning can only be generated when there is the political will to implement the concept of sustainability. Meanwhile, a technique needs to be developed so that some of the emerging environmental problems can be identified. This process will also develop models that will prove valuable for a better informed future than today. In addressing landscape management, the most fundamental units, in which a landscape can be envisaged, are as plesioclimax and anthropomorphic elements. The nature, proportion and juxtapostion of these elements in any landscape will vary with respect to its geographical location and economic or ecological history, but they can be used to design landscapes that will meet with the needs of sustainable development. The science of managing these two elements has a long history. It has emerged as conservation biology (May 1984, Soulé and Wilcox 1980) for the plesioclimax element and as forestry or agriculture (Odum, 1971) for the anthropomorphic element. The postulates of these disciplines will allow the generation of design criteria for each element. For instance, Soulé (1985) postulates that:

1. Many of the species that constitute natural communities are the products of coevolutionary processes.
2. Many, if not all, ecological processes have thresholds below and above which they become discontinuous, chaotic or suspended.
3. Genetic and demographic processes have thresholds below which non-adaptive, random forces begin to prevail over adaptive, deterministic forces within populations.
4. Nature reserves are inherently disequilibrial for large, rare organisms.

Postulates for the anthropomorphic element may follow those of Altieri (1983) who argues that stability in an agroecosystem can be gained by a system which (a) reduces energy and resource over use. (b) facilitates the operation of production methods that restores homeostatic mechanisms conducive to community stability, optimizes the rate of turnover and recycling of matter and nutrients, maximizes the multiple use capacity of the landscape and ensures an efficient energy flow, (c) encourages local production of items adapted to the natural and socioeconomic setting, and (d) reduces costs and increases the efficiency and economic viability of smaller and medium-sized farms, thereby promoting a more diverse and potentially more resilient agricultural system.

The challenge of the present is to use the knowledge of the two fundamental elements to generate sustainable models and to interdigitate them in design so that both the functional and esthetic goals of a sustainable landscape are attained. In Sri Lanka, a knowledge of the evolution of the various categories will assist in reaching these goals.

Acknowledgments

The assistence given by Ms Val Lyon of the Department of Geography, Australian National University, in the preparation of the maps is gratefully acknowledged.

Literature Cited

Abeywickrama, B.A. 1959. The evolution of the flora of Ceylon. *Proc. 14th Sess. Ceyl. Assoc. Adv. Sci.* : 217-229.

Alexis, L. 1984. Sri Lanka's Mahaweli Project: The damnation of paradise. *In* E. Goldsmith and N. Hilyard , eds. *Social and Environmental Effects of Large Dams*. The Wadebridge Ecological Centre, Cameleford, Cornwall, UK.

Altieri, M. 1983. *Agroecology*. University of California, Berkeley, California.

Blanford, W.T. 1901. The distribution of vertebrate animals in India, Ceylon and Burma. *Phil. Trans. Roy. Soc.* CXCIV: 334-436.

Brohier, R.L. 1934. *Ancient irrigation works in Ceylon*. Colombo. Govt. Publ. Bureau.

Brohier, R.L. 1974. *Discovering Ceylon*. Lake House Investments Ltd, Colombo.

Cooray, P.G. 1967. An Introduction to the Geology of Ceylon. *Spol. Zeylan.* 31: 1-324.

Croziat, L. 1964. *Space, time and form: Biological synthesis*. Publ. by the author, Caracas.

Croziat, L., G. Nelson and D.E. Rosen. 1974. Centers of origin and related concepts. *Syst. Zool.* 23: 265-287.

Crusz, H. and L. Nugaliyadde. 1978. Parasites of the relict fauna of Ceylon VII, *C.R. Soc. Biogeogr.* 477: 85-106.

Darlington, P.J. 1957. *Zoogeography: The geographical distribution of animals*. Wiley, New York.

Day, F. 1878. *The fishes of India*. Text and atlas in four parts. London.

Davies, P.J. and D.W. Kinsey. 1977. Holocene reef growth - One tree island, Great Barrier Reef. *Marine Geology* 24: M1-M11.

Deraniyagala, P.E.P. 1953. *Tetrapod reptiles of Ceylon*. Govt. Press, Colombo.

Deraniyagala, P.E.P. 1953. *A coloured atlas of some vertebrates of Ceylon. Vol. 2. Tetrapod reptiles*. Govt. Press, Colombo.

Deraniyagala, P.E.P. 1955. *A coloured atlas of some vertebrates of Ceylon. Vol. 3. Serpentoid reptiles*. Govt. Press, Colombo.

Deraniyagala, P.E.P. 1956. *A coloured atlas of some vertebrates of Ceylon. Vol. 1. Fishes* Govt. Press, Colombo.

Deraniyagala, P.E.P. 1958. *The Pleistocene of Ceylon*. Govt. Press, Colombo.

Deraniyagala, S.U. This volume. *Pleistocene Human Ecology in Sri Lanka* (this issue).

De Terra, H. and T.T. Patterson. 1939. Studies on the Ice Age in India and associated human cultures. *Carnegie Inst. Publ.* 293.

Ellawela, H. 1969. *The Social History of Early Ceylon*. Colombo.

Erdelen, W. 1984. The genus *Calotes* (*Sauria, Agamidae*) in Sri Lanka: Distribution patterns. *J. Biogeogr.* 11: 515-525.

Ferguson, M. 1857. The statistics of Ceylon coffee plantations. *Ceylon Observer*, July 1857, Colombo.

Fernando, C.H. 1965. Development of Ceylon's fisheries. XI. The role of inland waters in relation to the development of Ceylon's fisheries and a note on the pearl oyster fishery. *Bull. Fish. Res. Stn. Ceylon* 17: 291-297.

Flores, G. 1970. Suggested origin of the Mosambique Channel. *Trans. Geol. Soc. South Africa* 73: 1-16.

Foreman, R.T. and M. Godron. 1986. *Landscape Ecology.* John Wiley & Sons, New York.

Gaussen, H., M. Viart, P. Legris and I. Labroue. 1968. *Explanatory notes on the vegetation map of Ceylon.* Govt. Press, Colombo.

Gorrie, R.M. 1954. *Report of Kotmale landslides and adjoining river catchments.* Sessional paper XVII. Govt. Press Ceylon.

Geiger, W. 1934. *The Mahawamsa.* Pali Text Soc. London.

Harrison, B.G., G.B. Mansfield and M. Wallis 1969. *The Oxford Book of Food Plants.* Oxford University Press, Oxford.

Henry, G.M. 1955. *Birds of Ceylon.* Oxford University Press, Oxford.

Hopley, D. 1983. Australian sea levels during the last 15,000 years. *James Cook Univ. of Nth. Qld. Dept. of Geogr. Monogr. Series, Occ. Pap.* 3: 1-104.

Hopley, D. and D.W. Kinsey. 1988. The effects of a rapid short term sea level rise on the Great Barrier Reef. *In* G.I. Pearman, ed. *Greenhouse - Planning for climate change,* pp.189-201. CSIRO, Melbourne.

Horton, D.R. 1974. Species movement in zoogeography. *J. Biogeogr.* 1: 155-158.

Jacob, K. 1938. Jurassic plants from Tabbowa, W. Ceylon. *Proc. 25th Ind. Sci. Congr. Sec.: Paleobotany*: 1-162.

Jeyratnam, J., R.S. De Alwis and C.F. Coppleston. 1983. Pesticide poisoning in Sri Lanka. *Econ. Rev.* 8: 14-19.

Kelaart, E. 1852. *Prodromus Faunae Zeylanicae.* Observer Press, Colombo.

Kirthisinghe, P. 1854. *The Amphibia of Ceylon.* Publ. by the author, Colombo.

Krishnan, M.S. 1960. *The Geology of India and Burma.* Madras, India.

Legge, W. 1880. *A history of the Birds of Ceylon.* London.

Lydekker, R. 1886. India tertiary and post-tertiary vertebrata. *Palaeont. Indica* 3: 241-264.

Mani, M.S. 1974. (ed.) *Ecology and Biogeography in India.* Junk Publ. The Hague.

May, R.M. 1984. An overview: real and apparent patterns in community structure. *In* D.R.Jr. Strong, D.S. Simberloff, L.G. Abele and A.B. Thistle, eds. *Ecological communities,* pp. 25-58. Princeton University Press, Princeton, New Jersey.

Meijer, W. 1982. Plant refuges in the Indo-Malesian Region. *In* G.T. Prance, ed. *Biological diversification in the tropics.* pp. 553-584. Columbia University Press, New York.

Menon, A.G.K. 1973. The origin of the freshwater fish of India. *Curr. Sci.* 42: 553-584.

Money, N.J. and P.G. Cooray. 1966. Sedimentation in the Tabbowa Beds of Ceylon. *Spol. Zeylan.* 9: 134-141.

Moore, J.C. 1960. Squirrel geography of the Indian subregion. *Syst. Zool.* 9: 1-19.

Moyle, P.B. and F.R. Senanayake. 1983. Wildlife conservation in Sri Lanka - A buddhist dilemma. *Tigerpaper* 9: 1-4.

Mueller-Dombois, D. and V.A. Sirisena. 1967. *Climate map of Ceylon.* Surv. Dept., Colombo.

Mueller-Dobois, D. 1968. Ecogeographic analysis of a climate map of Ceylon with particular reference to vegetation. *The Ceylon Forester* 8: 39-58.

Odum, H.T. 1971. *Environment, power and society.* Wiley-Interscience. New York.

Pascoe, E.H. 1959. *A manual of the geology of India and Burma.* 3rd Edition. New Delhi, India.

Phillips, W.W.A. 1942. Distribution of the mammals of Ceylon, with special reference to the need of wildlife sanctuaries. *Loris* 3: 4-9.

Ripley, D.S. 1949. Avian relicts and double invasions in peninsular India and Ceylon. *Evolution* 3: 150-159.

Senanayake, F.R. 1977. *An ecological perspective of Malaria resurgence in Sri Lanka.* Unpubl. M.Sc. dissertation. University of California, Davis.

Senanayake, F.R. 1980. *The biogeography and ecology of the inland fishes of Sri Lanka.* Unpubl. Ph.D. dissertation. University of California, Davis.

Senanayake, F.R. 1982. Barbus srilankensis, a new cyprinid fish from Sri Lanka. *Ceyl. J. Sci.* 15: 396-402.

Senanayake, F.R. 1983. The ecology, energetic and agronomic systems of ancient and modern Sri Lanka. *In* G.K. Douglas, ed. *Agricultural sustainability in a changing world order.* pp. 227-237. Westview Press, Boulder, Colorado.

Senanayake, F.R. 1989. The tropical forest register. *In* N.D. Jayal, ed. *Drought, deforestation and desertification,* pp. 134-140. INTACH, New Delhi, India.

Senanayake, F.R. and A. Lokuge. (in prep.). Distribution patterns of some amphibians in Sri Lanka.

Senanayake, F.R. and P.B. Moyle. 1981. Conservation of freshwater fishes in Sri Lanka. *Biol. Conserv.* 22: 191-195.

Senanayake, F.R., M. Soulé and J.W. Senner. 1977. Habitat values and endemicity in the vanishing rain forests of Sri Lanka. *Nature* 265: 351-354.

Silas, E.G. 1952. Further studies regarding Hora's Satpura Hypothesis, taxonomic assessment and levels of evolutionary divergency of fishes with the so-called Malayan affinities in peninsular India. *Proc. Nat. Inst. Sci. India* 18: 423-448.

Silas, E.G. 1955. Speciation among freshwater fishes of Ceylon. *Bull. Nat. Inst. Sci. India* 7: 248-259.

Sitholey, R.V. 1944. Jurassic plants from the Tabbowa Series in Ceylon. *Spol. Zeylan.* 24: 3-27.

Soulé, M.E. and B.A. Wilcox. 1980.(eds.) *Conservation Biology: An ecological perspective.* Sinauer Associates. Sunderland, Massachusetts.

Soulé, M.E. 1985. What is conservation biology? *Bio Science* 35: 727-734.

Tennent, E. 1856. *Ceylon. An account of the island, physical, historical and topographical.* Vols. 1-2. Longmans, London.

Wadia, D.N. 1941a. The geology of Colombo and its environs. *Spol. Zeylan.* 23: 76-82.

Wadia, D.N. 1941b. The role of waterfalls in central Ceylon and its bearing on the geological structure of earth movements. *Spol. Zeylan.* 23: 19-20.

Wadia, D.N. 1942. The making of India. *Proc. 20th Ind. Sci. Congr.* General Presidential Address: 1-15.

Wait, W.E. 1931. *Manual of the birds of Ceylon.* 2nd Edition. Govt. Press, Colombo.

Proceedings of the International and Interdisciplinary Symposium
ECOLOGY AND LANDSCAPE MANAGEMENT IN SRI LANKA
W. Erdelen, C. Preu, N. Ishwaran, C.M. Madduma Bandara (eds.)
Colombo, Sri Lanka, 12-26 March 1990
© 1993
Margraf Scientific Books, D-97985 Weikersheim
ISBN 3-8236-1182-8

The Relevance of Scale and Hierarchy Concepts for Landscape Management

A Sri Lankan Perspective

W. ERDELEN

Abstract

Landscape management encompasses natural and man-made environments. Subsets of hierarchically organized systems are selected for analyzing specific questions or problems. These subsets vary in scale and may range from conservation of endemic species to management at the landscape level. Global scale phenomena, such as climate change, could also have implications for management at the regional level. Apart from spatial scales, temporal and taxonomic scales are of relevance for studies on the landscape level. Natural disturbance processes or patch dynamics may cover temporal scales between 1 year and 1000 years and spatial scales between 0.0001 m² and 1 million m², respectively, and extend over a wide range of plant and animal taxa. At times, even approaches to include different scale levels are necessary if, for instance, dynamics between hierarchical aspects of landscape management are to be considered. Independent of scale, a variety of ecological concepts are applied within the framework of landscape management. This paper gives an outline of the landscape mosaic in Sri Lanka and discusses the problem of scale with regard to conservation of the island's indigenous flora and fauna.

Introduction

Hierarchy theory has proven a powerful tool in the study of complex systems (Allen and Starr 1982, Pattee 1973, Salthe 1985). It has evolved along with general systems theory, and quite recently has been applied and developed further for research at the ecosystem level (O'Neill *et al.* 1986). Moreover, hierarchy theory and scale concepts are useful in the analysis of questions on the next higher spatial level, the landscape (Urban *et al.* 1987). Hierarchical approaches are useful deductive means of analyzing or conceptualizing landscape management issues and problems. Based on knowledge of the characteristic spatial scale and patch dynamics of a given landscape, they can, in particular, substantially contribute to the development of resource management strategies (Urban *et al.* 1987). Hierarchy considerations presently evolve along four major lines, viz. empirical approaches, evolutionary approaches, network theories, and a fourth line that links theory and testing (O'Neill, 1989).

In a recent paper that relates the state of contemporary ecology to global ecological issues, the importance of considerations of scale was pointed out (Brown and Roughgarden, 1990). This underscores the relevance of hierarchy theory which is considered a comprehensive theory of ecological scale (O'Neill *et al.* 1991). With regard to the environmental situation in Sri Lanka, three aspects as discussed in this paper are of special relevance, the scaled nature of ecological systems, the interdependence of ecological subdisciplines, and the increasing need for collaboration among disciplines. Therefore, attempts to find solutions to ecological problems should not only be restricted to analyses of structural and functional characteristics of complex ecological systems but should also include socioeconomic and political considerations. Consequently, approaches based on hierarchy theory need not be limited to levels within ecological systems but could, depending on the questions to be analyzed, even be extended to a systems analysis which covers all levels, from ecological studies on individual organisms to analyses of factors that govern decision-making processes. In this paper an outline of the landscape mosaic of Sri Lanka is given and the problem of scale with regard to the conservation of indigenous plant and animal species is discussed within the framework of the importance of the regional landscape level for conservation and management, particularly for maintaining viable populations of large and wide-ranging animals (e.g. Noss, 1992).

The Study Unit Sri Lanka

Sri Lanka is a tropical island, located southeast of the Indian peninsula, with an area of some 65,610 km². The island comprises three peneplains with average altitudes of 30 m, 500 m and 1500-1800 m, respectively (Adams 1929, Domrös 1976). The central highlands in the southern part of the island are formed by the second and third peneplain (Fig. 1). They consist of three different geographic units, the Knuckles mountains in the northeast (highest peak: Gombaniya, 1906 m), the central massif (Pidurutalagala, 2524 m), and the Sabaragamuwa ridges in the southwest (Beralagala, 1386 m).

The dominating climatic factors are the southwest monsoon, from May to September, and the northeast trade wind, from November to February. The southwest monsoon causes most of the precipitation in the southwestern parts of Sri Lanka. During the northeast trade wind, the northern and eastern regions receive their maximum precipitation. Convectional rains prevail during the intermonsoon periods. Based on seasonal and spatial differences in rainfall Sri Lanka is subdivided into two major hygroclimatic zones, the wet zone with a mean annual rainfall above 1904 mm and the dry zone with a mean annual rainfall below 1904 mm (Domrös, 1974; Fig. 1). The definition of these zones applies for Sri Lanka only; they do not represent general climatic classification units (Domrös, 1976).

Temperature, relative humidity and day length show little seasonal variation. However, average annual temperatures which are about 27°C at sea level, decrease about 0.50-0.65°C per 100 m altitudinal difference. Monthly temperature means vary only little, but daily maxima and minima differ between 5°C and 10°C. Relative humidity is high throughout the year, annual means are between 77% (Trincomalee) and 85% (N'Eliya) and vary on a regional and, more markedly, daily scale (for details see Domrös 1974, 1976).

The natural vegetation of the island has been subdivided into various units as summarized, for instance, by Greller and Balasubramaniam in this volume. In the "National Atlas of Sri Lanka" (Somasekaram, 1988) 11 major formations are distinguished, including seral stages such as tropical savanna forest and grasslands which in most cases represent secondary vegetation (Pemadasa, 1984), as well as edaphically controlled formations such as mangroves. For this overview a subdivision of the island into 7 zones with 6 major types of natural vegetation seems sufficient. These include tropical thorn forest (or monsoon scrub jungle) in the driest parts of the island (northwest and southeast), semi-evergreen forests, mainly in the northeastern, eastern and southern parts, an intermediate type between semi-evergreen forest and rain forest in the so-called intermediate zone of the island, and the rain forest in the southwestern part (Fig. 1). The latter may be subdivided into lowland forest (sea level to about 900 m), submontane forest (900-1500 m), and montane forest (above 1500 m). Floristic and physiognomic characteristics of these formations are discussed in Gaussen *et al.* (1968), Werner (1984) and Gunatilleke and Ashton (1987).

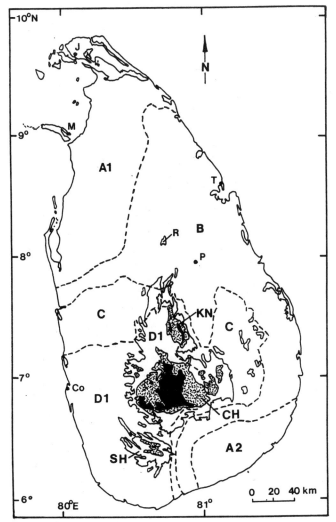

Figure 1. Relief and major vegetation types of Sri Lanka (after Erdelen, 1989). CH = Central hills, KN = Knuckles mountains, R = Ritigala, SH = Sabaragamuwa hills. A1, A2 = Tropical thorn forest, B = semi-evergreen forest, C = intermediate forest, D1 = rain forest below 900 m, D2 (stippled) = submontane rain forest (900-1500 m), D3 (black) = montane rain forest (above 1500 m). Towns: Co = Colombo, J = Jaffna, M = Mannar, P = Polonnaruwa, T = Trincomalee.

The Landscape Mosaic of Sri Lanka

Sri Lanka has a complex landscape mosaic which is characterized by natural landscapes comprising elements such as forests of the different hygroclimatological regions (Fig. 1), coral reefs and mangroves. Large tracts of formerly natural landscapes, in particular in the wet zone (Fig. 2), have been replaced by managed, cultivated, or suburban and urban landscapes

223

(terminology *sensu* Forman and Godron, 1986). In a very simplified way such mosaics are normally shown on land use maps depicting natural vegetation and land use types (Fig. 2). Major crops are paddy, tea, rubber and coconut (details in Somasekaram, 1988). According to the ecological requirements of these crops, land use varies regionally within the island. For instance, rubber is planted in areas with high annual precipitation (over 2000 mm) and altitudes below 600 m. These conditions which allow formation of sufficiently large quantities of latex are essentially met in the wet zone lowlands. Tea, though also grown in the same zone, is mostly planted in the montane areas. Another crop typical for the more humid regions is cardamom (*Elettaria cardamomum*), grown under natural forest cover in submontane and montane rain forests.

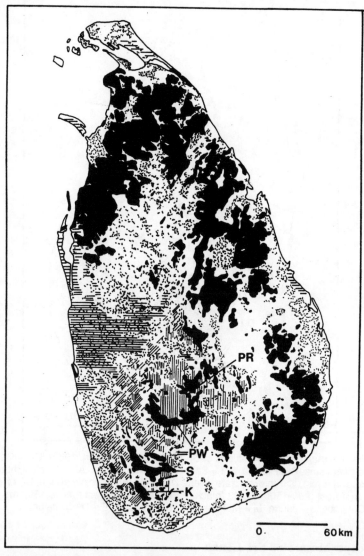

Figure 2. Forest cover and major land use categories in Sri Lanka (Erdelen, 1988). Black = dense natural forest, dots = land under rice cultivation, hatched = rubber, vertical lines = tea, horizontal lines = coconut. Major remaining forest tracts in the wet zone: K = Kanneliya Forest, PR = Pidurutalagala Ridge, PW = Peak Wilderness, S = Sinharaja Forest.

For an environmental analysis on the landscape level the following issues are of special relevance in the Sri Lankan context. First, geomorphological features, such as steepness of terrain, govern specific processes as, for instance, soil erosion. Second, the type of land use in a given area has ecological implications depending on the crops grown, the planting schemes and their temporal variation. For instance, the uprooting of old tea fields may be associated with a high probability of soil erosion. Third, the distribution of patch elements, i.e. the spatial configuration of cultivated land and natural vegetation, has important implications for management strategies. Fourth, depending on the spatial configuration, system-interlinking processes such as the transfer of matter and energy flow vary. For example, the terrestrial and aquatic flora and fauna of forests adjacent to tea fields may be directly affected by pesticide wash off. Similar processes may occur on a long-distance scale. For instance, alterations in sediment discharge patterns in upstream areas due to accelerated soil erosion may increase sediment transport and lead to the siltation of river mouths or coastal accretion in Sri Lanka (Preu, 1991). Naturally, this list is not complete, but it underlines the necessity for an integrated approach which takes into account the mosaic nature of landscapes and considers both structural elements and the relevant functional interrelationships. To date the use of such an approach is far from having materialized in Sri Lanka.

Scale Levels and Conservation

Conceptual Considerations

Though hierarchy theory implies that higher levels of organization incorporate and constrain the behavior of lower levels (Allen and Starr 1982, O'Neill et al. 1986), the lower levels in the "classical" biological hierarchy contain important details for conservation as, for example, population characteristics of endangered or rare species. Therefore, one of the central points in conservation, the preservation of biodiversity (e.g. WCMC, 1992), should be analyzed and monitored at multiple levels of organization and at multiple spatial and temporal scales (Noss, 1990). As already indicated by Allen and Hoekstra (1992) levels of biological organization as conventionally defined (Fig. 3, left) do not correspond to scale levels. Following the classical scheme of biological organization, it is difficult to allow for facts that, for instance, certain ecosystems like pockets of water in pitcher plants, in epiphytes or potholes may be smaller than large organisms. Consequently, to represent both ecological criteria and scale, biological systems need to be arranged in a way that differs fundamentally from the classical scheme (Fig. 3, right). The layers shown are not ordered according to size but by "strictly scale-defined criteria based on the principle of constraint, using grain and extent to define the scale of observation" (Allen and Hoekstra, 1992). Each type of biological system occurs on every layer. Comparisons are thus possible not only between the same systems at different scales, i.e. along one of the cones shown in Figure 3, but also between different system types at different scales, i.e. diagonal comparisons between upper and lower levels. An approach which considers scale criteria has important implications for conservation and management. As already indicated by Brown and Roughgarden (1990), ecological systems are open systems determined both by within-system processes and also by processes operating in the larger system of which they form a part. For instance, population resilience, the time a population requires to return to its former state after it has been perturbated and displaced from this state (Begon et al. 1986), depends not only on the characteristics of the species itself but also on its interactions between other species in the community (Pimm, 1991). As a consequence, treating species as isolated units to be preserved only on the basis of their autecological features may not be sufficient in many situations. Instead, conservation must be pluralistic (Noss, 1992) considering factors such as genetics, disease, predator-prey relationships, patchiness and connectivity of the relevant landscape elements as well as habitat changes or disturbance patterns, both natural and man-made.

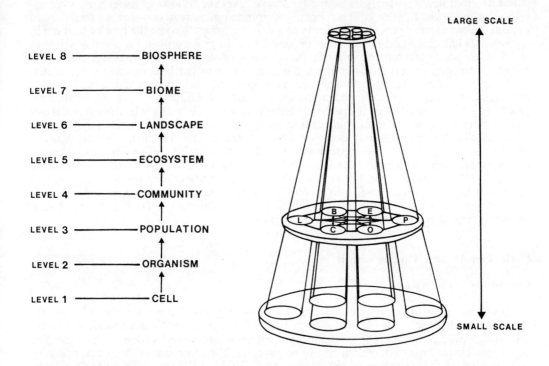

Figure 3. "Classical" levels of biological organization (left) and a conceptual frame that considers scale criteria (right, modified after Allen and Hoekstra, 1992). B = biome, C = community, E = ecosystem, L = landscape, O = organism, P = population. See text for explanations.

Conservation Issues in Sri Lanka - Some Examples

As already indicated above, management programs developed to meet specific conservation objectives are always scale-dependent. For instance, programs to preserve a locally endemic plant or animal species may target at preservation of small habitat patches whereas programs aiming at preserving biodiversity of a given region may focus on the landscape mosaic. Ecological variability of target organisms requires use of different scales of investigation for conservation programs (Wiens, 1989). For example, mobile organisms like the elephants in Sri Lanka need to be studied from a landscape rather than a habitat perspective, particularly with regard to their migratory behavior and habitat utilization. The habitat scale, however, may suffice if our focus is on sedentary organisms. Besides mobility, the size and shape of activity ranges of the organisms to be protected are of prime importance. In general, factors such as home range size or population density are correlated with body size or biomass (Fig. 4; see Calder 1984, Peters 1986 and LaBarbera 1989, for detailed discussion). This relationship between population density and biomass also applies for plants (Bonner, 1988). In addition, it is particularly important for the conservation of rare species that they may differ in their dispersal and scaling functions compared to common species (Wiens, 1989).

As most of the indigenous floral and faunal elements of Sri Lanka are restricted to natural landscapes, preservation of the remaining natural forests, mangroves, coral reefs, etc. should have maximum priority in conservation planning and management. In this context the highest ranking unit is the vegetation zone (Fig. 1). The focus of our analysis may be the dry zone

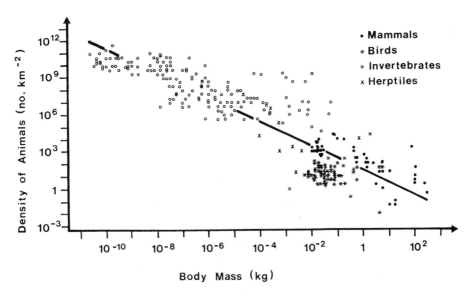

Figure 4. Relationship between body size and population density in animals (modified from Peters, 1986).

forests, the lowland rain forests, the montane forests, etc. These systems are naturally dynamic, they are patchily distributed and - due to human interference - have been reduced to more or less isolated fragments (Fig. 2). One of the best known examples in this context is the Sinharaja forest, with an extent of about 90 km² the largest of the remaining lowland rain forests in the southwestern part of the island. Problems associated with the conservation of this remnant forest which contains a high proportion of Sri Lanka's flora and fauna, particularly of endemics (Collins *et al.* 1991), have recently been analyzed (Ishwaran and Erdelen, 1990). Sinharaja itself shows not only gradual changes in forest community composition with increasing altitude, but is, already in its pristine condition, a heterogeneous assemblage of communities (Fig. 5). The most distinctive differences are those between gallery forests or forests along ridges and the surrounding forest. Detailed studies have shown that even forests on more or less isolated hills may have a rather "individualistic" character in species composition. Examples are Hinidumkande (668 m) in the southwestern part of the wet zone (Gunatilleke and Gunatilleke, 1984) and Ritigala (766 m) in the northern part of the dry zone (Jayasuriya, 1984; see Fig. 1 for location). In general, studies of woody species in the lowland wet zone have shown that most of them have a very localized geographic distribution as well as small population sizes (Gunatilleke, 1985). Both are features which make species susceptible to extinction. To what extent such small-scale heterogeneity in plant species composition, and also in physiognomy, "shapes" the respective animal communities is only poorly understood. A better understanding of the interrelationships between plant and animal communities would be required for a systems approach that could ensure successful conservation in the longer term.

For long-term successful conservation spatial variability and dynamics within such heterogeneous assemblages should be adequately considered. This implies the search for answers to questions such as (1) whether all this variability can be preserved as a whole or in parts only and, if the latter applies, (2) which criteria should be used for identifying and selecting the most "precious" of them. Moreover, it is important to ensure that (3) a protected area system meets the need for long-term stability and/or maintenance. In other words, the system's inherent stabilizing mechanisms or metastability (*sensu* Forman and Godron, 1986) should be adequately considered.

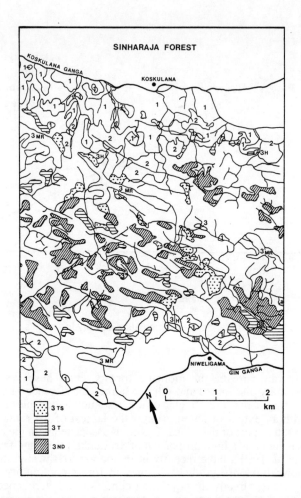

Figure 5. Part of the Sinharaja forest mosaic (based on Merritt and Ranatunga, 1959). 1 = non-forested areas, 2 = secondary forest, 3H = high ridge forest, 3MR = medium ridge forest, 3T = Thiniya (*Doona congestifolia*) forest, 3TS = Thiniya and softwood forest, 3ND = Na-Dun (*Mesua-Doona*) forest. Open areas (between Koskulana and Gin Ganga): *Mesua-Doona-Shorea* forest.

The successful extension of a protected area system needs to optimize its spatial configuration, i.e. the design of nature reserves. The development of design criteria has been a matter of debate for many years (overview in Simberloff 1988, Shafer 1990). Disagreement among conservation biologists may be due to insufficient consideration of scaling differences between organisms (Wiens, 1989). However, in most, if not all, situations we do not have "free" design options but have to improve on already existing protected area systems. In Sri Lanka, protected area coverage is much higher in the dry than in the wet zone (Fig. 6). The dry zone, however, is generally poorer in plant and animal species, particularly in endemics, compared to the more humid zones of the island (e.g. Erdelen, 1989).

Looking at conservation from a landscape perspective, features such as patch size distribution, heterogeneity, perimeter-area ratio, and connectivity are generally important with regard to species composition, abundance, and population viability (Noss 1990, Noss and Harris 1986). To date the protected area system of Sri Lanka has not been analyzed within such a framework. A first step into this direction are studies which have been launched in Sinharaja (e.g. Dayanandan *et al.* 1990, De Zoysa *et al.* 1991).

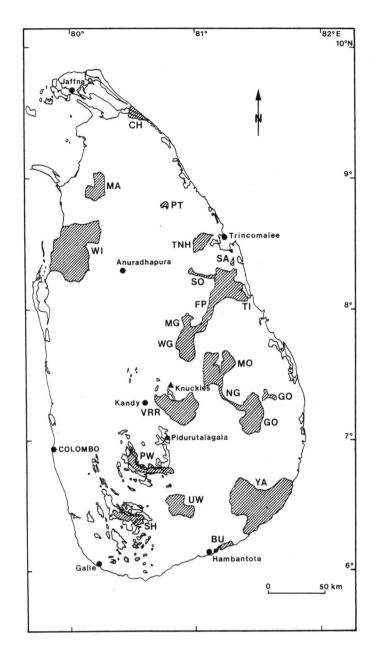

Figure 6. Protected area system of Sri Lanka. Simplified after Collins *et al.* 1991. Only wet zone forests shown. Sanctuaries: BU = Bundala, CH = Chundikulam, MA = Madhu Road, PT = Padaviya Tank, PW = Peak Wilderness, SA = Seruvila-Allai, TNH = Trincomalee Naval Headworks, VRR = Victoria-Randenigala-Rantambe. Jungle Corridor: NG = Nilgala. Nature Reserves: MG = Minneriya-Giritale, TI = Tirikonamadu. National Parks: FP = Flood PLains, GO = Gal Oya, MO = Maduru Oya, SO = Somawathiya Chaitiya, UW = Uda Walawe, WG = Wasgomuwa, WI = Wilpattu, YA = Yala. World Heritage Sites: SH = Sinharaja.

224e

Conclusions

The major ecological problems in Sri Lanka have been outlined in many publications (overviews e.g. in CEA 1988, Gelbert 1988, Fernando and Samarasinghe 1989, Baldwin 1991; see also papers in this volume). The question as to how to solve the most pressing of them is not only a matter of extending our knowledge of species distribution and ecology as well as structure and function of the systems, but, more importantly, of focusing on system interlinkages, considering the landscape mosaic as the study unit, and developing a new organizational framework that links all relevant institutions and authorities, brings together the expertise and efficiently contributes to the decision making process. Therefore, emphasis with regard to future conservation activities should be laid on the implications of analyzing different levels within the systems hierarchy and on using the differently "scaled" information in a synthetic way to contribute to a better overall analysis of the environmental situation in Sri Lanka.

Acknowledgments

I am grateful to Ralf Peveling, Nigel Stork and Sonya Hetherington for critical comments on an earlier draft of the manuscript. I thank Elke Huschens for preparation of the figures.

Literature Cited

Adams, F.D. 1929. The geology of Ceylon. *Canad. J. Res.* 1: 425-511.

Allen, T.F.H. and T.W. Hoekstra. 1992. *Toward a Unified Ecology.* Columbia University Press, New York.

Allen, T.F.H. and T.B. Starr. 1982. *Hierarchy. Perspectives for Ecological Complexity.* University of Chicago Press, Chicago.

Baldwin, M.F., ed. 1991. *Natural Resources of Sri Lanka.* Keells Business Systems Ltd, Colombo.

Begon, M., J.L. Harper and C.R. Townsend. 1986. *Ecology. Individuals, Populations and Communities.* Blackwell Scientific Publications, Oxford.

Bonner, J.T. 1988. *The Evolution of Complexity by Means of Natural Selection.* Princeton University Press, Princeton.

Brown, J.H. and J. Roughgarden. 1990. Ecology for a Changing Earth. *Bull. Ecol. Soc. America* 71: 173-188.

Calder, W. A. 1984. *Size, function, and life history.* Harvard Univ. Press, Cambridge, Mass.

CEA (Central Environmental Authority). 1988. *Sri Lanka National Conservation Strategy.* Central Environmental Authority, Colombo.

Collins, N.M., J. Sayer and T.C. Whitmore, eds. 1991. *The conservation atlas of tropical forests. Asia and the Pacific.* Macmillan Press, London.

Dayanandan, S., D.N.C. Attygalla, A.W.W.L. Abeygunasekera, I.A.U.N. Gunatilleke, and C.V.S. Gunatilleke. 1990. Phenology and Floral Morphology in Relation to Pollination of

Some Sri Lankan Dipterocarps. *In* K.S. Bawa and M. Hadley, eds. *Reproductive Ecology of Tropical Forest Plants*, pp. 103-133. UNESCO, Paris.

De Zoysa, N.D., C.V.S. Gunatilleke and I.A.U.N. Gunatilleke. 1991. Comparative Phytosociology of Natural and Modified Rain Forest Sites in Sinharaja MAB Reserve in Sri Lanka. *In* A. Gómez-Pompa, T.C. Whitmore and M. Hadley, eds. *Rain Forest Regeneration and Management*, pp. 223-233. UNESCO, Paris.

Domrös, M. 1974. *The Agroclimate of Ceylon. A Contribution towards the Ecology of Tropical Crops*. Geoecological Research 2. Steiner Verlag, Wiesbaden.

Domrös, M. 1976. *Sri Lanka. Die Tropeninsel Ceylon*. Wiss. Länderkunden 12. Wiss. Buchgesellschaft, Darmstadt.

Erdelen, W. 1988. Forest Ecosystems and Nature Conservation in Sri Lanka. *Biol. Conserv.* 43: 115-135.

Erdelen, W. 1989. Aspects of the Biogeography of Sri Lanka. *In* U. Schweinfurth, ed. *Forschungen auf Ceylon III*, pp. 73-100. Steiner Verlag, Wiesbaden.

Fernando, R. and S.W.R. de A.Samarasinghe, eds. 1989. *Forest Conservation and the Forestry Master Plan for Sri Lanka. A Review*. Wildlife and Nature Protection Society, Colombo.

Forman, R.T.T. and M. Godron 1986. *Landscape Ecology*. John Wiley & Sons Inc. New York.

Gaussen, H.P., P. Legris, M. Viart and L. Labroue. 1968. *Explanatory notes on the vegetation map of Ceylon*. Govt. Press, Colombo.

Gelbert, M. 1988. *Chena (shifting) cultivation and land transformation in the dry zone of Sri Lanka*. Dept. of Geography, University of Zürich.

Greller, A.M. and S. Balasubramaniam. This volume. Physiognomic, Floristic and Bioclimatological Characterization of the Major Forest Types of Sri Lanka.

Gunatilleke, I.A.U.N. 1985. Floristics of the Lowland Wet Zone Forests of Sri Lanka. *The Sri Lanka Forester* 17: 12-20.

Gunatilleke, C.V.S. and P.S. Ashton. 1987. New light on the plant geography of Ceylon II. The ecological biogeography of the lowland endemic tree flora. *J. Biogeogr.* 14: 295-327.

Gunatilleke, I.A.U.N. and C.V.S. Gunatilleke. 1984. Distribution of endemics in the tree flora of a lowland hill forest in Sri Lanka. *Biol. Conserv.* 28: 275-285.

Ishwaran, N. and W. Erdelen. 1990. Conserving Sinharaja - An Experiment in Sustainable Development in Sri Lanka. *Ambio* 19: 237-244.

Jayasuriya, A.H.M. 1984. Flora of Ritigala Natural Reserve. *The Sri Lanka Forester* 16: 61-156.

LaBarbera, M. 1989. Analyzing Body Size as a Factor in Ecology and Evolution. *Ann. Rev. Ecol. Syst.* 20: 97-117.

Merritt, V.G. and M.S. Ranatunga. 1959. Aerial photographic survey of Sinharaja forest. *The Ceylon Forester (New Series)* 4: 103-156.

Noss, R.F. 1990. Indicators for Monitoring Biodiversity: A Hierarchical Approach. *Conserv. Biol.* 4: 355-364.

Noss, R.F. 1992. Issues of Scale in Conservation Biology. *In* P.L. Fiedler and S.K. Jain, eds. *Conservation Biology. The Theory and Practice of Nature Conservation, Preservation, and Management,* pp. 240-250. Chapman and Hall, New York.

Noss, R.F. and L.D. Harris 1986. Nodes, networks and MUMs: preserving diversity at all scales. *Environm. Managem.* 10: 299-309.

O'Neill, R.V. 1989. Perspectives in Hierarchy and Scale. *In* J. Roughgarden, R.M. May and S.A. Levin, eds. *Perspectives in Ecological Theory,* pp. 140-156. Princeton University Press, Princeton.

O'Neill, R.V., D.L. DeAngelis, J.B. Waide and T.F.H. Allen. 1986. *A Hierarchical Concept of Ecosystems.* Monogr. Pop. Biol. 23. Princeton University Press, Princeton.

O'Neill, R.V., S.J. Turner, V.I. Cullinan, D.P. Coffin, T. Cook, W. Conley, J. Brunt, J.M. Thomas, M.R. Conley and J. Gosz. 1991. Multiple landscape scales: An intersite comparison. *Landscape Ecol.* 5: 137-144.

Pattee, H.H. 1973. *Hierarchy Theory. The Challenge of Complex Systems.* George Braziller, New York.

Pemadasa, M.A. 1984. Grasslands. *In* C.H. Fernando, ed. *Ecology and Biogeography in Sri Lanka,* pp. 453-492. Junk Publ, The Hague.

Peters, R.H. 1986. *The ecological implications of body size.* Cambridge Univ. Press, Cambridge.

Pimm, S.L. 1991. *The Balance of Nature? Ecological Issues in the Conservation of Species and Communities.* University of Chicago Press, Chicago.

Preu, C. 1991. Human impact on the morphodynamics of coasts: A case study of the SW coast of Sri Lanka. *In* W. Erdelen, N. Ishwaran and P. Müller, eds. *Tropical Ecosystems. Systems Characteristics, Utilization Patterns, and Conservation Issues.* pp. 121-138. Verlag Margraf, Weikersheim.

Salthe, S.N. 1985. *Evolving Hierarchical Systems.* Columbia Univ. Press, New York.

Shafer, C.L. 1990. *Nature Reserves - Island Theory and Conservation Practice.* Smithsonian Institution Press, Washington DC.

Simberloff, D. 1988. The Contribution of Population and Community Biology to Conservation Science. *Ann. Rev. Ecol. Syst.* 19: 473-511.

Somasekaram, T., ed. 1988. *The National Atlas of Sri Lanka.* Survey Dept. Colombo.

Urban, D.L., R.V. O'Neill and H.H. Shugart Jr. 1987. Landscape Ecology. A hierarchical perspective can help scientists understand spatial patterns. *BioScience* 37: 119-127.

Werner, W.L. 1984. *Die Höhen- und Nebelwälder auf der Insel Ceylon (Sri Lanka)*. Trop. subtrop. Pflanzenwelt 46. Steiner Verlag, Wiesbaden.

Wiens, J.A. 1989. Spatial scaling in ecology. *Funct. Ecol.* 3: 385-397.

WCMC (World Conservation Monitoring Centre) 1992. *Global Biodiversity: Status of the Earth's living resources*. Chapman & Hall, London.

Proceedings of the International and Interdisciplinary Symposium
ECOLOGY AND LANDSCAPE MANAGEMENT IN SRI LANKA
W. Erdelen, C. Preu, N. Ishwaran, C.M. Madduma Bandara (eds.)
Colombo, Sri Lanka, 12-26 March 1990
© 1993
Margraf Scientific Books, D-97985 Weikersheim
ISBN 3-8236-1182-8

Settlement of Oyster Spat *Crassostrea madrasensis* (Preston) on Four Selected Types of Substrates in the Kala Oya Estuary of Puttalam Lagoon, Sri Lanka

(Poster)

W.M.T.B. WANNINAYAKE, A.A.D. SARATH KUMARA AND W.V.F. UDAYA

The edible oyster, *Crassostrea madrasensis*, is naturally found in the Kala Oya Estuary of Puttalam Lagoon. Settlement pattern of its spat on different types of substrates were studied for a period of one year in an attempt to identify the potential substrates which can be used for collection of spat for aquacultural purposes. Strings of coconut shells, windowpane oyster shells (*Placuna placenta*), oyster shells (*Crassostrea madrasensis*) and asbestos plates (10 cm x 10 cm) were used as collecting substrates at three selected sites in the estuary. Hydrobiological parameters such as salinity, temperature, Secchi disc transparency and abundance of plankton at the experimental sites were also monitored throughout the study period. Sampling was carried out twice a month at fortnightly intervals. On each sampling day old strings of collectors were replaced by new ones and the number of spat that had settled on the older ones were counted. Although spat were present throughout the year the abundance was observed to be high from November to March. Mean abundance of spat that had settled on coconut shells and windowpane oyster shells was 6 individuals/cm^2. 2 and 3 individuals/cm^2 were found on oyster shells and asbestos sheets respectively. Therefore it appears that coconut shells and windowpane oyster shells are more suitable as collecting substrates than asbestos sheets and oyster shells. Higher numbers of spat were found to be settled on the under surface of the collectors. It was also noted that they prefer smooth surfaces for attachment rather than rough ones. Results further indicate that sufficient amounts of spat could be collected from the Kala Oya Estuary during the northeast monsoon period for transplanting purposes. Financial support from IDRC-Canada is gratefully acknowledged.

Proceedings of the International and Interdisciplinary Symposium
ECOLOGY AND LANDSCAPE MANAGEMENT IN SRI LANKA
W. Erdelen, C. Preu, N. Ishwaran, C.M. Madduma Bandara (eds.)
Colombo, Sri Lanka, 12-26 March 1990
© 1993
Margraf Scientific Books, D-97985 Weikersheim
ISBN

Experimental Studies on Raft Culture of Oyster *Crassostrea madrasensis* (Preston) in Sri Lanka

(Poster)

W.M.T.B. WANNINAYAKE, A.A.D. SARATH KUMARA AND W.V.F. UDAYA

Studies on raft culture of oyster, *Crassostrea madasensis,* were carried out in Puttalam Lagoon, on the northwest coast of Sri Lanka using strings of coconut shells, windowpane oyster shells and asbestos plates (10 cm x 10 cm) in an attempt to determine growth and survival rates and the most suitable culture substrates. Rafts were constructed using bamboo poles. Styrofoam blocks were used as floats. Spats were collected from wild populations occurring naturally in Kala Oya Estuary of Puttalam Lagoon, 8 km away from the culture sites. During the culture period of 12 months, large spat having an initial length of 20 mm and above showed a mortality rate of 7.5%. The mortality rate of smaller individuals was observed to be 19%. The growth rate of spat was found to be relatively rapid during the first 3 months, registering an average increase of 13.9 mm in total length per month. Mean size of the spat after the growing period of one year was found to be 88 mm in all three culture substrates. These growth rates were found to be significantly greater than those observed for wild populations. Crabs (*Scylla serrata* and *Neptunus sp.*) and gastropods (*Cymatium sp.*) were found to be potentially harmful predators, while barnacles, sponges and filamentous algae were identified as fouling organisms. Results of the present study indicate that raft culture of oyster, *Crassostrea madrasensis* could successfully be carried out in the Puttalam Lagoon. Financial support from IDRC-Canada is gratefully acknowledged.

PAPER PRESENTATIONS

II. IMPACT STUDIES
AND
CONSERVATION ASPECTS

Proceedings of the International and Interdisciplinary Symposium
ECOLOGY AND LANDSCAPE MANAGEMENT IN SRI LANKA
W. Erdelen, C. Preu, N. Ishwaran, C.M. Madduma Bandara (eds.)
Colombo, Sri Lanka, 12-26 March 1990
© 1993
Margraf Scientific Books, D-97985 Weikersheim
ISBN 3-8236-1182-8

Destruction of Natural Resources and Conservation Efforts

S.H.C. DE SILVA

Abstract

Sri Lanka's demographic expansion (6.6 millions in 1946 rising to 17 millions in 1989) and economic stagnation have led to increasing exploitation of its natural resources. Such exploitation is promoted both by the "haves" and by the "have nots". Multinational agencies operating in the country fit the first category and subsistence farmers represent the second. No country could effectively conserve its resources without adequately mitigating these pressures. Soil erosion may be considered the most critical ecological problem that affects management of catchment areas. Development activities such as reservoir construction, hydroelectric projects, settlement schemes, and industries have direct impacts on the environment. Intensive agricultural practices, urban sewage, pesticides and weedicides pollute waterways and affect water quality in rivers and streams. Some of the subsistence activities of the poor also contribute to the degradation of natural resources. Conservation efforts to preserve resources, though they propagate an awareness in the public mind, sometimes create distrust and dismay in the younger generation which fails to come to terms with differences between principle and practice.

Introduction

Natural resources have been exploited by man and animal for their sustenance. But in the struggle for survival animals fell victim to man and plant and animal species continue to become endangered. On a global scale, about four species become extinct every hour. Overexploitation of nature's resources results in their destruction and environmental management has become a high priority issue in negotiations in the international arena. Scientists and nature lovers have spearheaded the drive towards enhancing environmental awareness. Rachel Carson was perhaps the creator of this Renaissance since her seminal work, "Silent Spring", published in 1964. The gradual and almost imperceptible growth of the environmentalist's cry has compelled reluctant industrialists, manufacturers, consumers and governments to increasingly heed the call to stop the reckless exploitation of natural resources. In today's context wanton destruction of natural resources is no longer considered a fair price to pay for industrial growth. But in a

231

country like Sri Lanka where subsistence farming is still widespread, over half the population is dependent on food stamps and unemployment is rising, commitment to environmental protection and efforts in conservation generally end up in slogans and shibboleths or as seminar topics.

Causes leading to the destruction of natural resources in Sri Lanka can be enumerated, in order of their priority as follows: soil erosion, water resource projects and accompanying settlements in downstream development, intensive and shifting agriculture, human waste disposal, human energy needs and ground water withdrawal and water level management. Sound management for sustainable development is the required "Modus operandi" to alleviate the disruption ensuing from these causes contributing to environmental disruption. This is easily said. But can it be implemented? Is conflict inevitable between development and conservation? The way out has to depend on compromise. What steps should one embark on if the environment is to be managed without seriously affecting development potentials? The priority goals for conservation efforts are the use of safe and clean technology, organic fertilizer avoiding chemicals as far as possible; wherever possible multi-cropping systems should be given preference over monocultures, thirdly the reforestation of fragile zones denuded of forest cover and landscape management and fourthly a national scheme to alleviate unemployment or under-employment by the judicious use of human resources which are available in abundance. These goals are to be achieved in the development sectors of industry, agriculture, soil erosion and planning respectively.

Industries

Gem and Coral Mining

Coral mining is a means of livelihood in the southwest and eastern sectors of Sri Lanka. Submarine coral mining off the coral reefs in the foreshore and sea has become a source of lime, a building material investment which can be quite profitable. When extracted from foreshore and the coastal zone, the land is rendered useless by pits, 10 meters in depth. During the mining process pumping of sea water promotes salinity intrusion and the surrounding lands are rendered saline. In Madampe, a coastal town in the south, about 1000 acres of paddy land have been abandoned due to saltwater intrusion. In the foreshore its removal has opened the coast to sea erosion, resulting in the loss of several thousand square meters of land along the coastline.

After representations were made by the Wildlife and Nature Protection Society, the government, by gazette notification of April 19th, 1973, banned removal of coral, sand, and stone from an area extending 25 miles northwards from the coast of Pannaikuday Bay. Despite this proclamation, the removal of the coral seems to continue. When burning coral an almost equal volume of firewood is consumed. The firewood is generally obtained from mangroves or from coconut palms. The destruction of mangroves in Sri Lanka is hence related to coral mining activities along coastal areas.

State fiscal policy has permitted auction of potential reservoir beds for exploitation by the State Gem Corporation. On a deposit of Rs. 1000 a person could bid and obtain gemming rights not only in proposed reservoir beds but also in cultivated areas as in Ridiyagama, Elahera and Rattota. Used pits are left opened leaving the responsibilty of filling them again to the state. While the exploiters forego the deposit, the pits remain to collect water and provide breeding grounds for larvae of the malaria mosquito.

Sand, Clay and Stone

Removal of river sand for the building industry has drawn the saline wedge upstream so much that drinking water intakes on Gin Ganga, Kelani Ganga and Nilwala Ganga become seriously affected during periods of low river flow.

Excavation of clay along the high water beds of rivers like the Kelani River and Gin Ganga have left large waterholes that cannot be drained. These provide habitats for the vectors of malaria and filariosis. Clay is a prerequisite in the building industry for bricks and in pottery and forms the raw material that generates a livelihood for the people living along riverine settlements.

Material for road building and manufacture of concrete is extracted from rock quarries leaving water-logged holes in disused quarries.

Coconut Fibre, Textiles and Batik

Effluent from textile mills are released into streams and rivers causing pollution. Dyes from batik industry, which is a popular cottage industry, add their quota of chemicals to the surface or subterranean water resources of the area. The state-owned Thulhiriya mill is located along the banks of the Maha Oya and has an effluent discharge of 2.2 cusecs. This water course is not perennial and is named an "Oya" and not "Ganga". In spite of these drawbacks intake for the Negombo water supply was located downstream and commissioned in 1986.

Production of white and brown fibre from coconut husks has been an industry that has grown steadily since independence. Once a cottage industry, it is now developed to the extent of producing 91,000 tons of brown fibre per year in 1000 mills located in the Western Province. White fibre production is estimated at 7000 tons annually and is carried out along the coast from Kosgoda to Dikwella. Travellers could locate these by the hydrogen sulfide smell that emanates during the rotting of fibre which may take several months.

Paper Factories, Tanneries and the Cement Industry

Paper factories at Valachenai and Embilipitiya continue to pollute the rivers. Walawe River and Maduru Oya are badly affected during drought periods. Residents in Ambalantota get their drinking water by bowser as the Walawe waters are toxic during periods of low river flow. Effluent release form Valachenai paper factory probably contributed towards the collapse of the prawn fisheries in Valaichenai lagoon and the loss of income and employment opportunities for many fishermen.

Several tanneries close to Colombo on the Kelani Valley dispose of their chromium and other toxic residues into the Kelani River, which is used by hundreds of people for bathing and other daily purposes.

Dust pollution has rendered several residents to abandon their homes in Kankesanturai where the first cement factory was built in 1950. The distinct ash color covers the vegetation giving an unpleasant sight to the greenery. The second factory at Puttalam is said to emit 120 tons dust per day which has been tracked by satellite photos.

Urban Sewage and City Refuse

In Sri Lanka, only the city of Colombo is provided with a sewage network, even though it does not service all of the city's dwellings. About 50% of the population of Colombo live in slums and disposal facilities for human wastes are not possible. The number of houses with septic tanks is numerous and often poorly located, i.e. at elevations above wells from which people collect drinking water. Nitrate content of such well water has reached 100 ppm. compared to the World Health Organization's permissible maximum of 45 ppm. Proliferation of septic tanks especially in low-cost housing schemes will ensure introduction of salts and nutrients to the ground water acquifers. None of these can be stopped in the name of development but the health authorities should at least provide funds to monitor the pollution so that a scientific base is available to plan necessary regulatory measures in the cause of an outbreak of an epidemic.

There is no plan for city refuse. Some landfills are used but the Colombo municipality uses the high flood level bed of the Kelani River as a reclamation site for city refuse, against persistent opposition from the Irrigation Department. City refuse as landfill continues to be a source of air and aesthetic pollution in several sites.

Deforestation and Soil Erosion

The opening up of the hill country for coffee, followed by tea and rubber during colonial times, was the starting point for increasing rates of deforestation which had continued till recent times. Sir Joseph Hooker in 1873 decreed that no lands above 5000 ft be cleared of forests. Nevertheless this land order has been increasingly ignored. However, tea and rubber estates did contribute to soil conservation programs, by terracing as well as by the paving of gullies. With the opening up of the hill country for potato and horticulture all ecological constraints were ignored resulting in the bleeding of hill sides as muddy torrents which replaced the sparkling mountain streams of a yonder age. The government's preparedness for issuing licenses for furniture exports to bring foreign exchange needs to be urgently reviewed. The entire outlook on furniture, making use of timber, needs rethinking. Recent trends on use of steel and aluminium for furniture is a good development as wooden furniture is a luxury even in the west. Tropical forest is fast disappearing in Sri Lanka. Estimates of true forest cover vary from 10% to 25%. The state television tower was erected on the highest peak Pidurutalagala, 8182 ft above sea level, and presently a motorable road up to the tower is under construction, mindless of the ecological damage these operations cause. This project has also destroyed 600 acres of the remaining grasslands from very vulnerable and fragile mountain slopes. Depending on wood burning for fuel is common in 78% of the homes in Sri Lanka. Timber to used for fuel wood is the latest source for deforestation. Teak and pinus plantations are often victim of those promoting the transport of fuelwood.

The extent of soil erosion that had been incurred over a century of tea and rubber plantations and two decades of potato cultivation is difficult to quantify. The wind swept Horton Plains and the barren mountain tops stand testimony to the environmental degradation that has prevailed. Flash floods and land slides are now more regular than the monsoons in the country's hinterland.

Conclusion

Of all the natural resources, water should be deemed the highest priority. This should cover both surface and ground water. A national policy is imperative to prevent its eutrophication, salinization and disappearance through the drying up or loss to other acquifers. Such policy should also prevent it being a channel for dispersion of environmental pollutants. Various disciplines will be involved if one is to follow the axioms above. Environmental research is the answer at least to provide a data bank to monitor the degradation of the environment. Once the degree of ecosystem decay has been quantified, conservation measures can be embarked on, through an "integrated multidisciplinary approach", a term frequently used by expatriates and others in developing countries.

Literature Cited

Carson, R. 1970. *Silent Spring*. Houghton Muffin & Co. Boston.

Central Environmental Authority (CEA). *Tolerance limits for Aqua Culture waste water discharge into Irrigation Water*. Appendix 3. Handbook on Environmental Impact Assessment 1987. CEA, Colombo.

de Silva, S.H.C. 1975. Water Resources Ecology. *Proc. 2nd World Congr. IWRA, New Delhi* 5: 361-372.

de Silva, S.H.C. 1975. Environmental Control of Irrigation Drainage and Flood Control Projects. *Proc. 9th Congress ICID, Moscow.* International Commission on Irrigation and Drainage, Central Office, New Delhi.

de Silva, S.H.C. 1988. Paper presented at Seminar on Engineering and Environment. Federation of Engineering Institutions of South and Central Asia (FIESCA) Colombo 22.10.88.

Ministry Plan Implementation 1986. *Environmental Sector Report.* Sessional Paper No. 5. Govt. Press, Colombo.

Proceedings of the International and Interdisciplinary Symposium
ECOLOGY AND LANDSCAPE MANAGEMENT IN SRI LANKA
W. Erdelen, C. Preu, N. Ishwaran, C.M. Madduma Bandara (eds.)
Colombo, Sri Lanka, 12-26 March 1990
© 1993
Margraf Scientific Books, D-97985 Weikersheim
ISBN 3-8236-1182-8

Impacts on the Knuckles Range of Forests in Sri Lanka

K.P. SRI BHARATHIE

Abstract

The hills of the Knuckles Range to the northeast of the city of Kandy are part of the catchment of the Mahaweli River. The flora and fauna of the Knuckles are unique. Damage, due to present uncoordinated and improperly planned land use practices, could lead to the extinction of flora and fauna if current trends continue. It is recommended that in areas prone to natural hazards, particularly at high altitudes, cardamom cultivation be stopped and proper soil conservation measures be undertaken. Moreover, management should also aim at regaining the ecological balance of the forest ecosystem of the Knuckles Range.

Introduction - Physiography and Climate

The Knuckles Range is located in the Central Province of Sri Lanka, in the Matale and Kandy Districts (Fig. 1). This is a rugged hill mass rising to 900 m from the Kandy Plateau, 600 m above average sea level, on its northeastern side. It drops even more precipitiously in a series of scarps to the plains of the dry zone in the east. The area is about 155 km². The core of the region is a long mountain range running northwest to southeast with an undulated crest at an average height of 1500 m punctuated at intervals by spectacular peaks. The main peaks are Gombaniya (1875 m), Knuckles (1837 m), Kehelpothdoruwe Gala (1805 m), Kirigalpotta (1621 m), Dumbanagala (1615 m), Kalupahana (1602 m), Dotalugala (1549 m), Wamarapugala (1533 m), Telambugala (1310 m) and Lakegala (13,023 m). Two of the most prominent extensions are Kalupahana-Lakegala and the Dumbanagalea-Kehelpathdoruwegala Ridge. These lie at right angles to the main divide. They serve to separate the drainage systems of the Kalu Ganga, the Heen Ganga and the Hasalaka Oya. Corbert's Gap lies where the Dumbanagala Ridge joins the main range and provides the southern entrance into the Heen Ganga Valley which is overlooked on the western side by the Knuckles and Kalupahana Ridge.

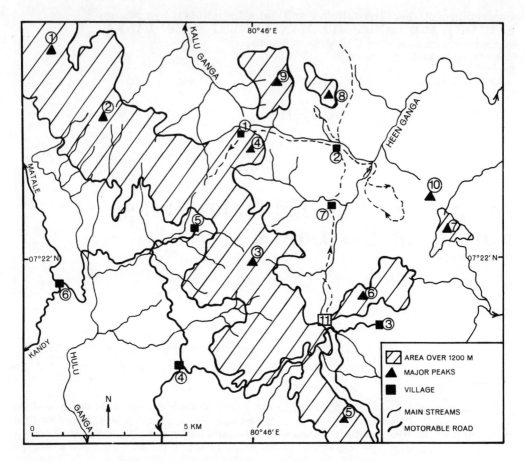

Figure 1. Map of the Knuckles Range. Major peaks: 1 = Kirigalpotta (1621 m), 2 = Gombaniya (1875 m), 3 = Knuckles (1837 m), 4 = Kalupahana (1602 m), 5 = Dotalugala (1549 m), 6 = Dumbanagala (1615 m), 7 = Kehelpothdoruwe Gala (1805 m), 8 = Lakegala (13,023 m), 9 = Wamarapugala (1533 m), 10 = Telambugala (1310 m). Villages: 1 = Kalupahana Camp, 2 = Mimure, 3 = Dehigolla, 4 = Rangala, 5 = Bambrella, 6 = Madulkele, 7 = Kaikawala.

The narrow Kaluphahana-Lakegala Saddle is an excellent point of observation as it commands an excellent view of the Kalu Ganga Valley and the extension of the Knuckles Range to the north of the peaks of Gombaniya and Yakungegala with their tremendous escarpments on the west side and the Heen Ganga Valley in the southeast which is overlooked by the impressive Dambanagala-Telambeyala Ridge. A characteristic feature of the area is the presence of numerous east-facing scarps backed by gentle westerly-dipping dip slopes, e.g. Wamarapugala. Short mountain torrents like the Mimure Oya and the Kaikawala stream cut into the scarps deeply while erosion is controlled chiefly by the prominent joint system, both horizontal and vertical.

The Kalupahana Saddle forms a narrow watershed between the headwaters of the Mimure Oya and the Kalu Ganga which are separated by a distance of about 500 yards. The steeper gradient and the greater exposure of the Mimure Oya to the torrential rains of the NE monsoon make it the more active stream, and rapid headward erosion caused by it enables it to capture the headwaters of the Kalu Ganga. The headwaters of the Kalu Ganga are a classic example of a tropical mountain torrent system.

The Knuckles Range acts as an effective barrier to both monsoonal winds. Between May and August, the western slope receives the full force of the SW monsoon with very heavy rainfall, while the eastern slopes remain a rain shadow receiving much less rainfall. During the NE monsoon from October to January the whole area receives very heavy rainfall accompanied by strong winds. This strongly seasonal rainfall also explains the low humidity at Mimure and high humidity at Kalupahana during August. More easterly regions like Lakegala lie in the dry zone which can be identified by the vegetation type. Temperatures in the region range between 15°C and 35°C.

Vegetation

The vegetation of the area comprises formations of the tropical dry evergreen forest and the wet evergreen montane rain forest. This combination of forest types results from the extreme climatic and altitudinal variations. Four major forest formations within the Knuckles Region are recognized based on phytosociological studies. They are lowland dry semi-evergreen forests, mid-elevational wet evergreen forests, mid-elevational dry evergreen forests and montane wet evergreen on cloud forests.

Lowland Dry Semi-Evergreen Forests

These forests occur on the foothills and are typical intermediate zone forest types. They receive rainfall mainly during the latter part of the year (November-February). The height of the canopy reaches over 30 m and the subcanopy. Four major forest formations within the Knuckles Region can be recognized too. Several species of woody climbers, epiphytic ferns and orchids have been recorded. Characteristic tree species are *Filicium decipiens, Melia dubia, Semecarpus obscura, Dimocarpus longan, Vitex altissima, Mangifera zeylanica, Calophyllum tomentosum* and *Nothopegia beddomei*. Characteristic shrub species of the understory are *Memeclon umbellalum, Glycosmis mauritana, Ardisia missionis* and *Saraca indica*.

Mid-Elevational Wet Evergreen Forests

This is a two-storied forest type not very rich in epiphytes. There are many locations in the Knuckles area where this type of forest is well developed. The height of the tree canopy is about 20-25 m. The dominant tree species of this forest community are *Crytocarya wightiana, Myristica dactyloides, Aglaia congylos, Elaeocarpus glandulifer, Litsea gardneri* and *Cullenia rosayroana*. A common understory species is *Hortonia floribunda*. Much of this forest type has been cleared for cardamom cultivation.

Mid-Elevational Dry Evergreen Forests

These forests have a distinctive floristic composition. They are found at an altitude between 450 m and about 1000 m in the Knuckles Range and occur in the Heen Ganga Basin. Tree species found in this formation are *Vitex altissima, Calophyllum lankaensis, Mangifera zeylanica, Myristica dactyloides, Nothopegia beddomei, Syzygium zeylanicum, Pittosporum zeylanicum* and *Actinodaphne stenophylla*. Some of the shrub species observed are *Eunymus* spp. and *Gnidia eriocephala*.

Montane Wet Evergreen Forests

This type of forest is found at elevations above 1300 m in the Kalupahana and Knuckles Regions. The upper reaches are described as cloud forests where the vegetation is rich in epiphytic orchids, ferns, mosses and liverworts. Filmy ferns are common on barks of trees and moist rocks. The canopy of this forest is single storied with an undergrowth of *Strobilanthes* spp. *Bambuos, Impatiens* spp. *Hedyotis* spp. and *Gaertneria* spp. The canopy reaches a height of about 15 m on sheltered sites. Crowns are spreading. Dominant species are *Calophyllum walkeri, Calophyllum trapezifolium* and *Garcinia echinocarpa*. At an altitude of about 1650 m in the Selvakanda Plateau, a dwarfed vegetation type described as "pigmy forest" occurs. The dwarfed nature of trees is due to continuous exposure to winds. *Syzygium* spp. and *Calophyllum* spp. of 1-1.5 m in height are found in these formations. Most of the herbs found in the Knuckles Region are of medicinal value.

Montane Grasslands

Throughout the Knuckles Region patches of grasslands are observed above 1000 m. Several patches of the grassland, however, are edaphic climax types. Other grasslands are fire climaxes or formations due to soil degradation.

Impact of Wildlife

Only a few species of animals have been recorded in the region. The introduction of cardamom has thinned out the animal population. The destruction of animals in defence of cardamom crops and their destruction by predators has exceeded the annual reproduction. Sambar, wild pig, purple-faced leaf monkey, large Ceylon grey flying squirrel and the yellow giant squirrel are still to be found in the Knuckles Region. One species of *Ceratophora* lizards occurs in the Knuckles as well as viper, cobra and many rare snakes too. Some endemic birds such as jungle fowl, spur fowl, Ceylon blue magpie, Leyards parakeet, Ceylon grackle and Ceylon lorikeet have been seen in these areas.

Status of the Forests in Sri Lanka

The four following forest types have been identified for the purposes of classification according to intended use categories: (1) reserved forests (FR), (2) proposed forest reserves (PR), (3) village forests (VF), and (4) other state forests (OSF). The forests of the Knuckles belong to categories 1, 2 and 4. The area of the Knuckles Region above the 1000 m contour is 18,290 ha. Located within this area is the proposed forest reserve of Dotalugala (Blocks 1-7) (1350 ha). It is situated on the northern boundary between Matale and Kandy Districts, with its northern and southern halves being within the Kandy District. This is the larger block of an aggregate of 7 blocks. Dotalugala is identified as a Man and Biosphere Reserve.

Also located within this area is Camble's Lane Forest Reserve, which has an area of 290 ha and lies on the northwestern boundary of the Matale and Kandy Districts. Cardamom cultivation in this area dates back over 100 years. Then it was carried out on a small scale. In the 1960s there was a rush for cardamom cultivation in the Knuckles area. The Forest Department was directed to lease out land for cardamom cultivation in Dotalugala, Camble's Lane and other forests in the Kalupahana area. The area which was leased was 620 ha and the period of lease was 20 years. In addition to these regular cardamom growers, 298 encroachers have been reported as cultivating an area of 700 ha, 160 ha of which are about 100 years old. About 620 ha are around 50 years of age and the balance is between 50 years and 100 years. Permits for cardamom cultivation have been issued for areas within the Kandy District. No permits are issued for areas within the Matale District by the Forest Department. 170 ha has been leased out by the LRC Matale for cardamom cultivation in some of the estates (e.g. Lebanon and Knuckles). 90 ha under the control of the District Forest Officer of Matale have been encroached by cardamom cultivators. The following encroachments were reported by the AGAA in these areas: (1) Laggala - 271 encroachers and estimated area of 142 ha, (2) Udadumbara - 250 encroachers and estimated area of about extent about 121 ha, (3) Ukuwala - 60 ha encroached in the Camble's Lane Forest by cardamom cultivators. The Land Commissioner has issued leases for cardamom cultivation of the Knuckles area on 32 ha over a period of 30 years from 1984. Another 40 ha leased out in 1967 on a special lease. There are also private lands along the 1000 m contour (e.g. Bray Estate).

As the conservation values of the Knuckles Range have become increasingly known in recent years, scientists have pointed out that all land areas over 1000 m contour should be kept free of cardamom or any form of cultivation and be allowed to revert to a natural ecosystem. Where the natural process is slow the Forest Department might have to carry out reforestation with appropriate tree species. In the lower areas (below the 1000 m contour) the cultivation of cardamom will be strictly controlled.

The above-described canopy density for cardamom cultivation is 75%. However, fuelwood requirements for curing cardamom forces a slow removal of the trees. Arrangements have to be made to provide for fuelwood supplies or to prohibit curing within the plantations. Curing of cardamom within the Knuckles area has resulted in heavy depletion of the montane forest. Therefore the best alternative seems to be an immediate closure of the barns within the Knuckles areas, thus requiring the producers to process the harvested cardamom below Rangala or Hunnasgiriya. Demand for fuel from natural forests for cardamom processing adds to the existing large demand from the tobacco industry and is difficult to regulate. Hence it might have to be prohibited.

Along the Corbet's Gap, Rangala and Duckwari areas heavy illicit felling of the forest is observed. Some blocks are supposedly private lands. Though the cardamom cultivators swear that only dead trees have been collected, fresh felled material has been observed near barn sites at Rangala, Kabaragala and Kalupahana.

The cardamom planted areas within the Kandy District are under the control of the Range Forest Officer, Hunnasgiriya. Hunnasgiriya Forest Office was opened in 1987 for the protection of the Ududumbara Forest Lands. A nursery has already been opened at Tangappuwa by the Divisional Forest Office, Kandy. Large extents of abandoned tea lands and patana lands belonging to the Land Reform Commission and the Sri Lanka State Plantation Corporation are found in the area. Immediate steps should be taken to reforest these abandoned areas. The road from Corbet's Gap to Mimure will be motorable beyond Kaikawala once the Heen Ganga Bridge is constructed. Then more efficient patrolling of the areas will be possible. It is recommended that one forest guard be employed to overlook about 1600 ha of forest lands in the Knuckles area.

There are valuable habitats both for flora and fauna in the Knuckles Region that need protection and management for the purpose of sustaining species and genetic diversity. The area is also an important watershed for the Mahaweli System. A proposal has been made to declare the forests of the Knuckles Range a National Heritage Wilderness Area under the National Heritage Wilderness Areas Act of 1988. This act provides for the declaration of state lands as National Heritage Wilderness Areas by the Hon. Minister, when such areas contain unique ecosystems, genetic or any other outstanding natural features.

Proceedings of the International and Interdisciplinary Symposium
ECOLOGY AND LANDSCAPE MANAGEMENT IN SRI LANKA
W. Erdelen, C. Preu, N. Ishwaran, C.M. Madduma Bandara (eds.)
Colombo, Sri Lanka, 12-26 March 1990
© 1993
Margraf Scientific Books, D-97985 Weikersheim
ISBN 3-8236-1182-8

Forest Conservation and Forestry Development in Sri Lanka

Conflicts and Compromise

I.A.U.N. GUNATILLEKE AND C.V.S. GUNATILLEKE

Abstract

One quarter of the angiosperm flora of Sri Lanka is endemic and concentrated in the perhumid southwest of the island where nine out of the fifteen floristic regions, some with exceptional floristic richness in the whole of South Asia, are located. Although 27% of the land area of the island is under natural high forest, undergraded primary lowland and montane forests of Deccan-Gondwana ancestry now comprise less than 1% and 3% of their respective original land areas. The protected areas that cover 40% of all natural vegetation remaining in the country do not represent the best assemblage of its biological diversity as many of them are located outside the floristically rich regions. An integrated Forestry Master Plan drawn up to meet future wood demands proposes major policy changes in forestry sector development from the present "protection-oriented" forest policy to a consumer-oriented and profit-driven policy to meet short-term wood demand by attracting foreign investments. The proposed intensive management of floristically diverse and at the same time timber-rich lowland rain forests for "maximum" human benefit will inevitably lead to biological impoverishment of this resource in which over 90% of endemic woody species are already listed as threatened by the IUCN Red Data Book. A more realistic forestry development program balancing the seemingly conflicting issues of conservation of biological and ecological diversity with meeting the long-term socioeconomic needs of the people based on available scientific knowledge is urgently needed.

Introduction

In Sri Lanka, the floral and faunal richness is overwhelmingly concentrated in the perhumid zone known as "wet zone" which includes both montane and lowland regions (Ashton and Gunatilleke 1987, Gunatilleke and Ashton 1987, Erdelen 1989). Even within the wet zone, the distribution of indigenous floristic elements shows remarkable localization. Based on recorded floristic distribution, primarily of angiosperms, 15 floristic regions have been recognized for

Sri Lanka and nine of them are located within the wet zone. Amongst these are some of the floristically richest areas of South Asia (Broun 1900, Ashton and Gunatilleke 1987). Among Sri Lanka's endemic flora and fauna, three fourths of the angiosperms and over a third of all terrestrial vertebrates are to be found in the wet zone (Gunatilleke and Ashton 1987, Erdelen 1989).

Historical Biogeography

The rain forests of Sri Lanka, both lowland and montane, are of primeval origin whose ancestry dates back to that of the Deccan Plate (Ashton and Gunatilleke, 1987). The Deccan Plate having been separated from the rest of the Gondwana fragments in early Cretaceous, rafted northwards in isolation from neighboring continents during the Paleogene period. Evolution of a high percentage of endemic species common to both Sri Lanka and peninsular India has been attributed to this isolated movement of the Deccan Plate in subtropical and tropical climates until it collided with the southern shores of Laurasia in mid-Eocene (Lakhanpal 1970, Axelrod 1974, McKenzie and Sclater 1973, Ashton and Gunatilleke 1987). This evolution, mostly at specific and infraspecific level continued particularly in the southwestern perhumid zone of Sri Lanka in the Neogene after the landbridges between Sri Lanka and India were severed in the Miocene (Cooray 1967, Erdelen 1989).

Human Impact

This floristically rich wet zone is also the most heavily populated region at present. The gradual clearance of forests for settlement, particularly along river basins in periods between 200 B.C. and 1250 A.D. was somewhat intensified after the irrigated agricultural systems of the dry zone were abandoned (Siriweera, 1983). During the occupation of the island by the Portuguese and Dutch in the 16th and 17th centuries, valuable timber was extracted from the rain forests which perhaps encouraged the opening up of coastal and hinterland areas for village expansion. However, the most severe impact on this rich flora of the wet zone occurred when montane, submontane and lowland rain forests were opened up for plantation agriculture of coffee, cinchona, tea and rubber during British occupation since the early 18th century (Karunaratne, 1987). The post-independence era (1948-today) saw the opening up of the secondary climax forests in the dry zone of the island through large- and medium-scale irrigated agriculture and hydropower development schemes such as Gal Oya, Padaviya, Uda Walawe, Mahaweli and Muthukandiya.

Present Status of Natural Forests

As a result of this historical sequence of population expansion at the expense of natural forests, the total natural forest area which was estimated to be around 89% in 1889 (Nanayakkara, 1987), was reduced to 46.5% in 1956 and 27% in 1981-1983. The average annual clearing rate of natural forests in the dry zone had been 42,000 ha during the last 25 years (Anon. 1986). With the opening up of land for the Accelerated Mahaweli Development Project in the 1980s, the remaining forest cover has decreased further and much of the remaining natural vegetation is now restricted to the protected areas of the island which cover 13% of the total land area of the island and 33% of the total extent of forest and scrub. However, the quality of the forests in these protected areas, particularly those in the dry zone, where most of the wildlife parks and reserves are located, is poor. The distribution of forests based on the 1981-1983 survey (FAO, 1986) indicate that the total area of high forest in the floristically rich wet zone is only 278,000 ha.

Table 1. Protected and production forest areas of Sri Lanka by forest type and climatic zone based on FAO Forest Inventory in 1982-85. (Anon. 1986): * = Percentage of the total land area of the island which is 6.5 million ha; DWLC = Department of Wildlife and Nature Conservation; FD = Forest Department.

	Protected Forest Land			Production	Total
	DWLC	FD	Total		
Natural high forest					
- wet zone and upcountry	63,000	96,000	159,000	119,000	278,000
- dry zone	478,000	39,500	17,500	954,000	1,471,500
Total high forest	541,000	135,500	676,500	1,073,000	1,749,500 (27%)*
Shrub forest and scrubland					
- wet zone and upcountry	2,200	22,100	24,300	49,000	73,300
- dry zone	106,000	-	106,000	484,500	590,500
Total shrub and scrubland	108,200	22,100	130,300	533,500	663,800 (10%)*
Mangrove forest	1,200	6,700	7,900	-	7,900 (0.1%)*
Forest plantations	6,000	348	6,348	97,673	104,000 (1.6%)*
Total	656,400	164,648	821,048	1,704,173	2,525,200 (39%)*
	(26%)	(6.5%)	(32.5%)	(67.5%)	(100%)

Even the patches of these so-called "high forests", particularly those in the lowland wet zone, have been selectively logged either in part or in their entirety for timber production. The growing stock has reached such a low level that sustained yield will only be realized through enrichment planting to rehabilitate overcut and degraded forest areas (World Bank, 1989). They may need long periods of resting before they can be logged again (Anon. 1989). As a result, the total area of ecologically undergraded forests in the lowland wet zone and in the montane zone could be estimated at about 1% and 3%, respectively (Gunatilleke et al. 1987). Most of these forests are fragmented and interspersed as small islands between human habitations. In addition to the impact on biodiversity from the surrounding human settlements, the threat of accelerated species extinction through stochastic processes such as genetic drift is also high, even in protected areas.

Unfortunately, there exists a disproportionate representation of protected areas in the floristically poor dry zone (623,500 ha) as compared with that of the floristically rich wet zone (183,300 ha; Tab. 1). A detailed phytosociological survey of five lowland wet zone forests distributed in three of the floristically rich regions of the island revealed that over 90% of endemic woody species encountered belong to either endangered (E), vulnerable (V), rare (R) or insufficiently known (K) categories of the IUCN Red Data Book (Tab. 2). Furthermore, studies on regeneration of these threatened endemics have shown that even after seven to eight

Table 2. Number of species of woody endemics in different study sites and their distribution according to the IUCN Red Data Book categories; E = endangered; V = vulnerable; R = rare; K = insufficiently known; O = out of danger (Gunatilleke and Gunatilleke, 1991).

Study Sites	Total area sampled (ha)	E	V	R	K	O	Total
Kottawa	4	11	27	40	1	1	80
Hinidumkanda	5	15	28	55	4	2	104
Kanneliya	5	16	26	50	1	1	94
Sinharaja	25	15	48	64	6	2	135
Gilimale	5	9	32	44	1	1	87
All sites	44	42	62	68	10	2	184

years establishment of threatened plants in selectively logged patches was poor (de Zoysa *et al.* 1990; Tab. 3). Similarly, studies on lichens (Hale, 1981) and small mammals (de Zoysa and Raheem, 1990) have revealed comparable trends.

Forestry Development Programs for the Future

A Forestry Sector Master Plan (FMP) for Sri Lanka has been formulated for scientific management of forest resources in Sri Lanka in order to meet the rapidly growing wood demands of the country while at the same time conserving adequate forest areas for environmental protection and maintenance of biological richness (Anon. 1986). The specific objectives of the preparation of the Forestry Master Plan (Anon. 1986) are to (i) compile and analyze the present state and the development of the forest resources of Sri Lanka, (ii) elaborate

Table 3. Distribution of woody plant species (< 30 cm GBH) encountered in natural unmodified (UF) and modified (SL = selectively logged, ST = skid or logging trail, SC = cultivated and abandoned) forest sites in Sinharaja MAB Reserve, according to the IUCN Red Data Book categories and in different habitat categories.

Habitat categories according to the density distribution of woody plants (< 30 cm GBH)	Number of species in each RDB category					
	E	V	R	K	O	Total
1. Higher population density in UF than in modified sites (SL, ST and SC).	09	09	12	01	62	31
2. Similar or higher densities in SL and UF but not in ST or SC.	04	15	27	05	–	51
3. Higher density in any one or more modified forest sites than in UF.	–	01	02	--	01	04
4. Higher density in all four sites.	–	07	10	–	03	20
Total number of species	13	32	51	06	04	106

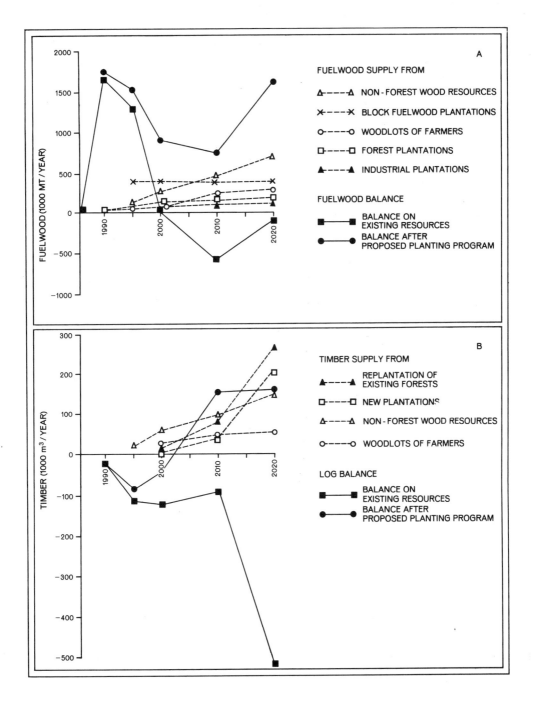

Figure 1. A. Estimates of fuelwood supply from natural and plantation forests and the projected fuelwood balance for Sri Lanka (Data from Anon. 1986). B. Estimates of timber supply from natural and plantation forests and the projected timber balance for Sri Lanka (Data from Anon. 1986).

sound management principles and develop a scientific forest management system for forest plantations and natural forests, (iii) evaluate the present and future wood supply potential under the suggested forest management system to provide a basis for future planting programs and for industrial planning, (iv) assess the resources required to implement the proposed plan and thus assure the realization of the wood supply potential, and (v) make recommendations for the implementation of the proposed forest management system.

Based on this plan, a detailed five year investment program consisting of training, institutional development and environmental management has been initiated with foreign funding in the form of loans and grants amounting to Rs. 1.5 billion (US $ 45 million, World Bank 1989, Anon. 1988). Analyzing the past and present trends of the usage of wood resources, the FMP forecasts an acute shortage of fuelwood and industrial wood which it claims would greatly reduce the development of the whole economy of the country as the forestry sector plays a pivotal role in Sri Lankan society. In 1988 the forestry sector contributed about Rs. 4.7 billion to the country's economy (4.2% of GNP). Industrial processing of timber and paper products contributed an additional Rs. 1.4 billion. Forestry employs about 170,000 people and forestry products are the country's major source of energy, accounting for about 71% of total energy consumption and 94% of the energy used in households (Anon. 1986).

The Rationale of the Forestry Development Program

In order to meet the almost exponentially growing wood demand of a population having a growth rate of 1.7%, the Forestry Master Plan recommends that the only rational alternative is to manage the existing and new forests to obtain maximum benefits from them and at the same time to achieve the required production of soil and environment (Anon. 1988). The alternatives to continuing the present protection-oriented forest policy would be a heavy burden on the balance of payments of the country and it might be difficult to find external assistance for the projects showing low profitability. The main rationale of the Forestry Master Plan for intensive logging of timber-rich wet zone natural forests and overmature forest plantations during the next 25-30 years is to provide the maximum (not optimum) benefits to consumers by supplying the market with adequate timber and fuelwood, thus keeping the wood prices down which in turn the planners hope, would make illegal cutting less profitable. In the meantime, it envisages that the new and existing plantations will be managed effectively to meet the demands beyond the year 2010. The estimated log and fuelwood output from the proposed intensive logging of the natural forests and forest plantations are given (based on Anon. 1988; Fig. 2). Intensive logging has been recommended primarily because of its high profitability in the short term which could attract external funding. The five year investment program for the forestry sector has an estimated economic rate of return of 28% (World Bank, 1989).

Conflicts and Compromise in Forestry Development

This major policy change with respect to forest management from a conservation-oriented one to a more consumer-oriented one, at a time when there is a greater concern for preservation of dwindling biological richness in Sri Lanka, alarmed the conservation-conscious public of Sri Lanka who obviously have conflicting opinions and interests on the issue. When the Forestry Master Plan (a main report and 10 annextures) was published by the consultants, Jakko Poyry Oy of Helsinki in September 1986 (Anon. 1986), serious concerns over the environmental impact assessment of the plan were made and moreover, an opportunity was given to environment-conscious public of this country to present their view points on the subject.

In response to the repeated public agitation on the issue of the Forestry Master Plan, two public seminars were held (Fernando and Samarasinghe, 1988). As a consequence of this strong public concern, the World Bank requested the World Conservation Union (IUCN) to review the Forestry Master Plan with respect to its environmental and biological consequences.

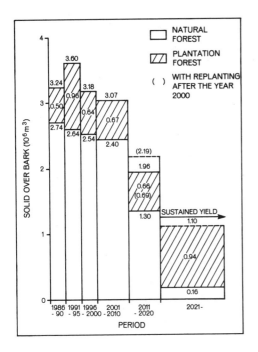
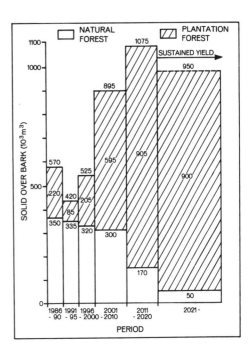

Figure 2. Projected average annual fuelwood supply from natural forest, existing and future plantations (million m³ solid over bark; left) and projected average annual log supply from natural forests, existing and future plantations (1000 m³ solid over bark/annum; right).

The terms of reference for the IUCN review team was (i) to assess the impact of proposed forestry operations on the environment, (ii) to devise a monitoring system for assessing change in biodiversity, (iii) to develop a conservation strategy for forest reserves, (iv) to draw up a research program to seek answers to the most important problems of forest management in relation to environmental issues.

Having sought views from a number of governmental and non-governmental organizations and individuals concerned with forestry and environment, the IUCN review report was published (FSDP-EMC, 1989). This IUCN report, having accepted views expressed by the environmentalists, recommended an immediate moratorium on further selective logging in natural forests or conversion to any other land use until the forests are evaluated and classified according to their conservation value in maintaining biological diversity and environmental stability. Those forests which are identified to have significant conservation value, are to be given protected area status and the report recommended that no further logging should be permitted in them. The IUCN report expressed serious apprehensions on the proposed selective cutting of trees over 60 cm DBH at 30 year intervals which was based on "very scanty data" available at the time. It recommended to test this hypothesis by maintaining and monitoring research plots over a long period. It was also suggested that the projected estimates of annual wood supply potentials from selective harvesting after 30 years and intermediate cutting after 15 years, which were heavily criticized by the environmentalists, be re-examined after assessing the damage which might be caused to the vegetation.

Yet another area of conflict in forestry development and conservation is the raising of fast growing monocultures of exotic species such as *Pinus* and *Eucalyptus* in watershed areas and their logging by clear-felling in 20-30 year cycles. While the FMP recommended this dual activity of conflicting interests, viz. environmental conservation and commercial timber production in the montane zone, the IUCN report endorsed the views expressed by the environmentalists. It recommended that in the case of protection of a water catchment, exploitation of timber must take second place to the protective function of the forest. It went on further to say that it may be necessary to limit or forbid commercial exploitation, and where the amount of water yield was of paramount importance, it might be necessary to avoid planting species that have high water demands. It recommended a review of land use policy, particularly in the montane zone, in order to identify most appropriate land use for each area. One of the key questions asked by some hydrologists in this regard is whether the reforestation of *Pathana* grasslands could seriously reduce the water yield in the downstream reservoirs of the Mahaweli Project. As both these ecosystems are subjected to fires at present, ensuing soil erosion problems will be similarly high under both vegetation covers.

The IUCN report has made several important recommendations with a view to reach a compromise between conservation of fast depleting, biologically valuable natural forests and the ever increasing wood demand of the growing human population of the country. It recommended the conducting of a conservation review of all remaining areas of natural forest and grasslands with respect to their relative ecological, biological and protective status. This will enable to develop a conservation strategy for natural vegetation types and determine the purposes for which they must be maintained. This will facilitate decision making on future management options. The report also recommended the establishment of a forest conservation unit primarily to advise on forest conservation issues and practices, establish conservation monitoring procedures, produce environmental guidelines on forestry activities, maintain and manage environmental data bases and coordinate conservation activities in relation to forestry with other organisations, both national and international ones. The third major recommendation of the IUCN report was the establishment of a research and monitoring program to ensure the sustainability of management practices and to monitor the development of both protective and productive natural forests and plantations. The final recommendation was to review the agroforestry policies and practices in order to find out what forestry inputs were needed in the development of agroforestry programs. This is rather important as over 50% of the timber requirements are met from private lands most of which are under some form of agroforestry systems.

Together with the staff appraisal report of the World Bank (1989) and the IUCN report on environmental management, the investment program for the forestry sector was submitted to the World Bank for voting by its Board of Executive Director in mid-June 1989. A conditional approval was granted subject to fulfilling the undertakings recommended in the IUCN report. Another conflicting issue in the forestry development programs and conservation which had not been adequately addressed by the IUCN report is the impact of the current silvicultural policies and their implementation on conservation of biodiversity. If the present silvicultural management of both natural forests and plantations is not geared to meet the acute shortage of the future wood demand, the legal or illegal encroachment into remaining natural forest, be they protected reserves or others, would be difficult to resist. The indiscriminate planting of monocultures of *Pinus caribaea* which is intended primarily for supplying long trachied paper pulp and for its ability to check soil erosion in the steep mountain slopes (Bandaratilake 1989, Gunawardana 1989) is not geared to meet the wood demands of the people. Since 1968, *P. caribaea* has been planted as the single major reforestation species by the Forest Department in the lowland and montane wet zone. The indigenous species planting carried out by the Forest Department has not been successful probably due to lack of proper understanding of the ecological requirements of the species planted. For its timber value, *P. caribaea* is known to be a low-density species and along with other properties such as low hardness, low impact bending, and high shrinkage along radial and tangential directions render its timber unsuitable for structural work or even furniture (Jayasekera, 1989). The recommended uses of *P. caribaea* at present are for sheltering, temporary applications and packaging.

Therefore, the raising of soft-wooded monoculture plantations of *P. caribaea* whose growth is severely affected by recurring anthropogenic fires (Perera, 1989) has not been geared to meet the projected demands of timber and fuelwood. Instead of ameliorating site conditions, they appear to affect the sites retrogressively by promoting forest fires (A.H.Perera, pers. comm.).

As a result, the pressure on the remaining natural forests even the protected ones will be greater in the future (Gunatilleke, 1988). Having forecasted that there will be an acute shortage of timber in the late 1990s and beyond, and that the major plantation species is inappropriate for this purpose due to its poor timber quality and fire-damage to the plantations, it is ironical that the FMP suggested that the intensive selectively logging of lowland rain forests rich in biological wealth was only a temporary measure until the man-made forests were ready to take over the function of supplying wood demands of the nation. The forestry development in the more recent past as well as that proposed for the future by the FMP had failed to recommend a long-term strategy to meet the timber and fuelwood needs of the country. What it had done was to provide a cosmetic solution by proposing an intensive timber extraction program from the remaining lowland rain forests which were already fragmented and some of them had been logged at least once in the past.

The FMP or its five-year investment program has not addressed the key issue of finding a more appropriate mixed species plantation system by researching on successional plantation systems that simulate the development processes of the respective natural forests in order to provide solutions to both fuelwood and timber needs in the major climatic zones of the island. There is tremendous potential for improvement of forestry practice through silvicultural research along ecological guidelines and indeed there are a number of promising indigenous species suitable for silviculture awaiting closer scrutiny (Ashton 1990, Ashton *et al.* 1990, Ashton and de Zoysa 1989, de Zoysa *et al.* 1990). In the light of silvicultural evidence for *Shorea* section *Doona*, the "polycyclic" selection regeneration system practised in lowland wet zone of Sri Lanka seemed to be detrimental to their establishment in logged forests (Ashton *et al.* 1990).

The mere fact that *P. caribaea* is capable of establishing itself in denuded, degraded, and retrograde lands and its ability to grow fast are no criteria for its indiscriminate planting on every conceivable landscape. A serious re-examination of forestry development is needed at this juncture in order to address the following questions:

1. To what extent and at what cost are the already planted *P. caribaea* plantations of nearly 30,000 ha capable of meeting the timber, fuelwood and paper pulp needs of the country?
2. If these plantations are unable to meet the future needs of the people, would it be advisable to manage the natural forests to obtain *maximum* benefits rather than to obtain *optimal* benefits considering the uncertainties of realizing the expectations of the wood-hungry nation from the plantations?
3. To what extent would the proposed silvicultural management of lowland rain forests affect their biodiversity?
4. Even at this late stage would it not be better to reactivate research and extension programs on mixed species planting according to ecological guidelines?

The proposed forestry development program envisages a wide range of activities in the forestry sector with massive infusion of assistance from international donor agencies. These include scientific management of natural plantation forests, building up of non-forest wood resources, establishment of forest plantations, forest protection, development of wood harvesting and forest industries, research, extension, education, and institutional strengthening. Of these activities, the production-oriented activity of immediate significance is the intensive management of 119,000 ha of lowland rain forests which are located in the biologically richest areas of the country. All the 33 forest reserves earmarked for logging and for which management plans have already been prepared are located in floristic regions 5, 6, 7, 9 and 11 in which except for the Sinharaja National Wilderness Area, no other forest has been protected (Tab. 4).

Table 4. Distribution of different categories of forests in each floristic region of Sri Lanka.

	Floristic region												
	Coastal and dry zone	Intermediate zone					Lowland wet zone			Montane zone			Total
	1 and 2	3	4	5	6	7	9	11	12	13	14	15	
National parks	10	-	-	-	-	-	-	-	-	-	-	1	11
Strict nature reserves	2	-	-	-	-	-	-	-	-	1	-	-	3
Nature reserves	2	-	-	-	-	-	-	-	-	-	-	-	2
Jungle corridors	1	-	-	-	-	-	-	-	-	-	-	-	1
Sanctuaries	30	1	3	3	-	-	-	1	-	1	1	-	45
MAB reserves	10	4	1	-	2	7	1	-	-	3	-	2	3
World Heritage sites	-	-	-	-	1	-	-	-	-	-	-	-	1
Reserves proposed for selective logging	?	?	?	-	10	18	5	-	?	?	?	?	33+
Floristic regions that need to be represented among the protected areas		*	*	*	*	*	*	*		*			

In the light of our own personal experience and also of the cautionary remarks of the FSDP-EMC report (1989), it might seem to be difficult to realize the wood balance forecasted in the FMP and at the same time conserve the biodiversity and the environment. This problem will perhaps be compounded by the inadequacy of supply of fuelwood and timber from the forest plantations. Unless there is a major policy change accompanied by a serious research initiative from raising monoculture plantations whose timber is more suitable for 'shuttering, temporary applications and packaging' to those which could meet the actual construction and fuelwood needs of the country, the threats to the protected natural forests will continue to exist for substantially long periods of time.

Having recognized the highly localized distribution of the biological richness of Sri Lanka and the impending threats to its maintenance (Gunatilleke and Gunatilleke 1990, 1991), the need to conserve at least one representative forest reserve encompassing the natural ecosystem diversity of each floristic region seems urgent and pertinent.

Literature Cited

Anon. 1986. *Forestry Master Plan for Sri Lanka.* Jakko Poyry International, Helsinki.

Anon. 1988. *Five Year Investment Programme for the Forestry Sector - Sri Lanka 1988-1992.* Forestry Resources Development Project, Ministry of Lands and Land Development, Colombo.

Anon. 1989. *Sri Lanka Forest Sector Development Project - Environmental Management Component.* IUCN Document. World Conservation Union, Gland.

Ashton, P.M.S. 1990. *Seedling Response of Shorea Species across Moisture and Light Regimes in a Sri Lankan Rain Forest.* Ph.D Thesis. Yale University, New Haven.

Ashton, P.M.S. and N.D. de Zoysa. 1989. Performance of *Shorea trapezifolia* (Thwaites) Ashton seedlings growing in different light regimes. *J. Tropical Forest Science* 1: 356-364.

Ashton, P.M.S., C.V.S. Gunatilleke and I.A.U.N.Gunatilleke. 1990. A shelterwood method of regeneration of self-sustained timber production in *Mesua-Shorea* forest of southwest Sri Lanka. This volume.

Ashton, P.S. and C.V.S. Gunatilleke. 1987. New light on the plant geography of Ceylon. I. Historical plant geography. *J. Biogeogr.* 14: 249-285.

Axelrod, D.I. 1974. Plate tectonics in relation to the history of angiosperm vegetation in India. *Birbal Sahni Institute of Paleobotany. Special Publication* 1: 5-18.

Bandaratilake, H.M. 1989. Development of pine plantation in Sri Lanka. *In* H.P.M. Gunasena, C.V.S. Gunatilleke and A.H.Perera, eds. *Reforestation with Pinus in Sri Lanka,* pp. 10-18. University of Peradeniya, Peradeniya.

Broun, A.F. 1900. On the forests and waste lands of Ceylon. *In* H. Trimen, ed. *Handbook to the Flora of Ceylon* 5: 355-363.

Cooray, P.G. 1967. An Introduction to the Geology of Ceylon. *Spol. Zeylan.* 31: 1-324.

de Zoysa, N.D., C.V.S. Gunatilleke and I.A.U.N. Gunatilleke. 1990. Comparative phytosociology of modified and undisturbed forest sites in Sinharaja MAB Reserve in Sri Lanka. *In* A. Gomez-Pompa, T.C. Whitmore and M. Hadley, eds. *Rain Forest Regeneration and Management,* pp. 154-168. Man and The Biosphere Series Vol. 7. UNESCO. Paris.

de Zoysa, N.D. and R. Rahean. 1990. *Sinharaja. A Rain Forest in Sri Lanka.* March for Conservation, Colombo.

Erdelen, W. 1989. Aspects of biogeography of Sri Lanka. *In* U. Schweinfurth, ed. *Forschungen auf Ceylon,* pp. 73-100. Franz Steiner Verlag, Stuttgart.

FAO 1986. *A National Forest Inventory of Sri Lanka 1982- 1985.* Forest Department, Colombo.

Fernando, R. and S.W.R. de A. Samarasinghe. 1988. *Forest Conservation and the Forestry Master Plan for Sri Lanka - A Review.* Wildlife and Nature Protection Society of Sri Lanka, Colombo.

FSDP-EMC 1989. *Forest Sector Development Project Environmental Management Component.* The World Conservation Union, Gland.

Gunatilleke, C.V.S. and P. S. Ashton. 1987. New light on the plant geography of Ceylon. II. The ecological biogeography of the lowland endemic tree flora. *J. Biogeogr.* 14: 295-327.

Gunatilleke, C.V.S., I.U.A.N. Gunatilleke and B. Sumitraarchchi. 1987. Woody endemic species of the wet lowlands of Sri Lanka and their conservation in botanic gardens. *In* D.

Bramwell, O. Hammann, V. Heywood and H. Synge, eds. *Botanic Gardens and the World Conservation Strategy*, pp. 183-196. Academic Press, London.

Gunatilleke, N. 1988. Forestry Master Plan - A Critique. *In* R. Fernando and S.W.R. Samarasinghe, eds. *Forest Conservation and the Forest Master Plan for Sri Lanka - A Review*. Wildlife and Nature Protection Society of Sri Lanka, Colombo.

Gunatilleke, I.A.U.N. and C.V.S. Gunatilleke. 1990. Distribution of floristic richness and its conservation in Sri Lanka. *Biol. Conserv.* 55: 17-36.

Gunatilleke, I.A.U.N. and C.V.S.Gunatilleke. 1991. Threatened woody endemics of the wet lowlands of Sri Lanka and their conservation. *Conservation Biology* 4: 21-31.

Gunawardana, E.R.N. 1989. Hydrological and soil erosion studies on *Pinus* in Sri Lanka. *In* H.P.M. Gunasena, C.V.S. Gunatilleke and A.H. Perera, eds. *Reforestation with Pinus in Sri Lanka,* pp. 46-55. University of Peradeniya, Peradeniya.

Hale, M.E. Jr. 1981. A revision of the lichen family Thelotremataceae in Sri Lanka. *Bull. Br. Mus. Nat. Hist. (Bot.)* 8: 227-332.

Jayasekera, K.P. 1989. Utilisation of *Pinus* in Sri Lanka. *In* H.P.M. Gunasena, C.V.S. Gunatilleke and A.H. Perera, eds. *Reforestation with Pinus in Sri Lanka*, pp. 61-70. University of Peradeniya, Peradeniya.

Karunaratne, N. 1987. *Forest Conservation in Sri Lanka from British Colonial Times (1818-1982)*. Trunpet Publishers, Sri Lanka.

Lakhanpal, R.N. 1970. Tertiary floras of India and their bearing on the historical geology of the region. *Taxon.* 19: 675-694.

McKenzie, D. and J.G. Sclater. 1973. The evolution of the Indian Ocean. *Sci. Amer.* 228: 63-72.

Nanayakkara, V.R. 1987. Forest history of Sri Lanka. *In* K. Vivekanandan, ed. *1887-1987. 100 Years of Forest Conservation*. Forest Department, Colombo.

Perera, A.H. 1989. Ecological issues on pines in Sri Lanka. *In* H.P.M. Gunasena, C.V.S Gunatilleke and A.H. Perera, eds. *Reforestation with Pinus in Sri Lanka,* pp. 46-50. University of Peradeniya, Peradeniya.

Siriweera, W.I. 1983. Settlement patterns and climatic fluctuations in Sri Lanka from the earliest times up to the beginning of the sixteenth century. *In* M.M. Yoshine, I. Kayana and C.M. Madduma Bandara, eds. *Climate, Water and Agriculture in Sri Lanka*, pp. 51-60.

World Bank. 1989. *Staff Appraisal Report.* Sri Lanka Forest Sector Development Project. Report No. 7699-CE.

Proceedings of the International and Interdisciplinary Symposium
ECOLOGY AND LANDSCAPE MANAGEMENT IN SRI LANKA
W. Erdelen, C. Preu, N. Ishwaran, C.M. Madduma Bandara (eds.)
Colombo, Sri Lanka, 12-26 March 1990
© 1993
Margraf Scientific Books, D-97985 Weikersheim
ISBN 3-8236-1182-8

A Shelterwood Method of Regeneration for Sustained Timber Production in *Mesua-Shorea* Forest of Southwest Sri Lanka

P.M.S. ASHTON, C.V.S. GUNATILLEKE AND I.A.U.N. GUNATILLEKE

Abstract

There is debate on the applicability of silvicultural management for the sustained production of timber and minor goods and services in lowland rain forest of Sri Lanka. Currently, the *Mesua-Shorea* forest community is managed for timber production using a "polycyclic" selection regeneration system. In light of the silvical evidence for the dominant timber species, this regeneration method appears detrimental to their establishment in new forests. Important timber species of the genera *Dipterocarpus, Mesua* and *Shorea* require the establishment of advanced regeneration for their development in future stands. For this to occur, seedlings of these trees need specific light regimes. Furthermore, most of these species produce irregular but large mast seed crops that are dependent on gravity for their dispersal, therefore requiring a nearby parent-tree source of seed. Also, their species distribution patterns are site-specific, with each species growing best on a different soil type within the forest. Based on these findings this paper proposes ideas on the development of a shelterwood regeneration method suited to their sustained management for timber production in the lowland rain forests of Sri Lanka. Quantitative silvical guidelines are given for the dominant mast tree species within the *Mesua-Shorea* forest community. Enrichment planting guidelines are provided for timber trees that are non-mast species as well as for suitable minor crops that at present are solely exploited from the forest by villagers.

Introduction

Sri Lanka's forests were first differentiated by Trimen (1893-1900) using distribution of mean annual rainfall to classify different climatic zones. These zones were further modified and refined by De Rosayro (1942), Chapman (1947) and Holmes (1956). The lowland wet zone of southwest Sri Lanka is classified as wet evergreen rain forest. De Rosayro (1942) identified four forest communities in this region that he considered late successional high forest in dynamic equilibrium.

The *Dipterocarpus* forest community is described as occupying the coastal plains, valleys and lower slopes of the lowland hills. It is considered to occur rarely above 750 m in elevation. The *Mesua-Shorea (Doona)* forest community is described as occupying the smaller valleys and the skeletal soils of the steeper slopes and ridgetops of the lowland hills. De Rosayro (1942) identified two other forest communities (*Vitex-Dillenia-Chaetocarpus-Anisophylla* community, *Campnosperma* and other species community), which have been classified by Gunatilleke and Ashton (1987) as secondary in origin and are now considered early successional stages of the *Dipterocarpus* and *Mesua-Shorea* forest communities. Accepting this view, *Dipterocarpus* and *Mesua-Shorea* forests comprise the two main forest community types of Sri Lanka's lowland wet zone. For many years, the feasibility of sustained timber production from tropical rain forest has been debated. Sri Lanka has a microcosm of this discussion that has been recently accentuated by the proposed management plan for the island's remaining natural forests.

In this paper, we do not attempt to discuss the economic, social, biological or moral rationales of conserving or preserving natural forests. We understand a balance must be obtained between the use of natural forest for yielding more direct and tangible goods and services and that of preserving it as a refugia for gene pools of future and as yet undiscovered products and values and as an ethical and cultural obligation for the benefit of future generations. Instead, we choose to concentrate specifically at the technical level on the silviculture of quality timbers and minor crops that occur within the forest. This paper is based on silvicultural studies done in the *Mesua-Shorea* forest community. It describes the current silvicultural method for the regeneration of timber species in the lowland wet zone and discusses its flaws. It provides a case for the development of sustainable timber production using the shelterwood method of regeneration and suggests specific treatments for particular forest associations identified within the *Mesua-Shorea* forest community.

Silviculture of the Lowland Wet Zone

Selection Regeneration Methods

Selection regeneration methods have been developed for forests that are uneven-aged. With these methods, one assumes that by removing mature single trees or groups of trees frequently the nature of the age and structure of the forest can be maintained in perpetuity while, at the same time, a sustainable production of timber is achieved.

Today's lowland wet zone forests are harvested for timber using the polycyclic felling system. Like its counterparts in similar forest regions of aseasonal Indonesia (Indonesian Selection System) and Malaysia (Selective Management System), it is a variant of the single tree selection method of obtaining regeneration (Smith, 1986). Single tree selection removes individual trees from throughout the stand. The whole stand is regenerated by requiring many light cuttings whose intensity and frequency is based on the turnover rate of the natural forest. Its application is most suited to forest types whose dominant tree species are shade-tolerant, requiring only small gap or understory light conditions for seedling germination, establishment and growth.

For Sri Lanka's lowland wet zone forests, continued entry and treatment of stands is costly and the protection of young trees on the ground from logging is a problem. Maintaining such a frequent cutting cycle is therefore economically and logistically infeasible. To partially avoid this situation, Sri Lanka's polycyclic system has a less frequent cutting interval of approximately a 30-year period. The name polycyclic has been given to the system to suggest that, at the time of cutting, a subcanopy stratum of pole and early saw timber exists that can be released as the next future crop. The method infers that this stratum contains the same important timber species as that of the canopy, and that it is present at every cutting. The cycle can then be repeated over time periods of between 20 years and 40 years, allowing for the sustained production of timber. Cuttings are relatively heavy to compensate for the lighter harvests that should have been made more frequently at shorter intervals of time. Each cutting is based on a diameter limit, where trees greater than a certain diameter at breast height (dbh) are removed. Diameter limits are based on the reverse J-shaped curve, a theoretical diameter distribution for a stand (Fig. 1). In diameter-limit cuttings, trees of the largest diameter size classes are removed and are assumed to be replaced by ingrowth from smaller size classes. Cutting coupes cover relatively large areas of forest irrespective of cover-type, stand or site.

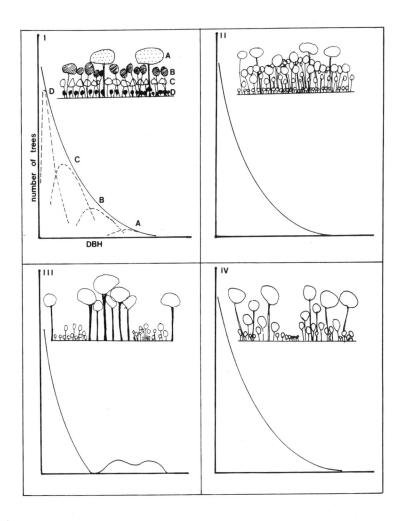

Figure 1. Some hypothetical reverse J-shaped diameter distributions of uneven-aged and even-aged stands. I. A mixed-species even-aged stand with a reverse J-shaped diameter distribution. Different species occupy different parts of the distribution in relation to their size class and the stratum they occupy. II. A single-species even-aged stand with a reverse J-shaped diameter distribution attributed to self-thinning processes. III. An uneven-aged stand with a maladjusted diameter distribution related to past historical events. IV. An uneven-aged single-species stand in which size is related to age.

Selection Methods and their Associated Flaws

Selection methods are widely improperly used throughout both temperate and tropical moist forests. Canopy trees of many forest stands classified as uneven-aged are actually aggregates of numerous "little" even-aged stands (Smith, 1986). Openings created by the death of one or two mature trees are replaced by an even-aged group of many smaller individuals. With time and from self-thinning, these even-aged cohorts will eventually sort to only several. Forests with these stands are dominated by canopy timber species that are relatively light-demanding. Their regeneration requires partial shade protection for establishment and gaps for their release.

Forests with stands that are truly uneven-aged lack groups of similarly aged individuals that are clumped in a spatial mosaic within a forest. Rather, they often rely on canopy species that are shade-enduring, with individuals that are able to establish and grow up within the canopy in competition with others that are of different species composition and age. Differentiation between even-aged and uneven-aged stands is often blurred on scales where forest disturbances are small. The nature of light tolerance and growth strategy of canopy tree species is important in determining the conceptual difference between them.

A stratified mixed-species stand contains many tree species in mixture, with different species tending to occupy particular canopy strata (emergent, canopy, subcanopy, understory; Richards, 1952). When stratified mixed-species stands that are composed of even-aged aggregates are managed as uneven-aged using selection systems, forest regeneration and structure can become degraded. Small openings created by the removal of single trees often closed by crown expansion of the residual overstory or subcanopy. The forest stature declines as canopy species are removed and subcanopy species close to form a new canopy inhibiting the establishment and release of regeneration of the relatively more light-demanding canopy species.

Further, there are many misconceptions about reverse J-shaped diameter distributions, methods of maintaining them through diameter-limit cutting and their association with uneven-aged stands (Fig. 1). Forests that have even-aged stands often have reverse J-shaped curves. Though trees within these stands are of the same age, individuals can have a gradient of sizes and conditions, from dominant to suppressed, solely through the process of self-thinning and competition. Based on past historical events, uneven-aged stands can frequently have diameter distributions that are irregular and in no way resemble a reverse J-shaped curve. Lastly, to assume that stands that are composed of stratified mixtures of species and that have reverse J-shaped curves can be harvested sustainably for timber by cutting above a certain diameter-limit is fundamentally flawed. In these cases, diameter distribution and frequency is more strongly correlated with species growth habit and their vertical position in space. Species with small diameters tend to occupy the understory; those with larger diameters occupy higher strata. Usually there are fewer individuals within each stratum climbing the profile from understory to canopy. Also, as a single diameter-limit in the polycyclic felling system is applied to a cutting coupe irrespective of cover-type, a wide variation of cutting intensities can be created because individual stands can have different size classes. This ignores the specific silvicultural need of each stand.

Stand Dynamics of the *Mesua-Shorea* Forest Community and their Relevance to Other Forest Types

Based on work carried out by Holmes (1956, 1957, 1958) and the authors (Peeris 1975, Gunatilleke and Gunatilleke 1981, 1983, De Zoysa *et al.* 1991, Ashton 1989, 1990, in prep.), stands in *Mesua-Shorea* forest are largely composed of relatively even-aged aggregates of stratified species. These stands are often dominated in the canopy stratum by relatively light-demanding species of the genus *Dipterocarpus* and *Shorea* in the family Dipterocarpaceae and the genus *Mesua* of the family Clusiaceae.

It is our belief that management of Sri Lanka's *Mesua-Shorea* forest using the polycyclic felling system is incompatible with its known silvical properties. We also suspect this to be true of Sri Lanka's other wet zone forest community (*Dipterocarpus*) and its similar associates in other parts of everwet tropical Asia. This is because these forest regions have canopies that are dominated by timber trees that are taxonomically related to the timber trees of the *Mesua-Shorea* forest type. They therefore share many silvical properties (Tab. 1).

Table 1. Important timber families and their genera from everwet mixed dipterocarp forest of South and Southeast Asia and their common silvical properties.

Family	Genus	Silvical Characteristics
Clusiaceae	*Mesua*	* Heavy fruit or seed dispersed by gravity (sometimes aided by wind or animals)
Dipterocarpaceae	*Anisoptera*	
	Dipterocarpus	* Mast fruiting, seed or fruit that is dispersed together in abundance over a short period of time, fruiting times can be at regular intervals but are often irregular and supra-annual
	Dryobalanops	
	Hopea	
	Neobalanocarpus	
	Parashorea	* Propagation and requirement of partial shade protection for germination and early establishment with a further increase in light for continued growth
	Shorea	
	Vateria	
	Vatica	
Leguminosae	*Dialium*	* Species are site-specific, usually occurring in part of the topography that has particular biotic, climatic and edaphic characteristics best suited to their growth
	Intsia	
	Parkia	
		* Large canopy or emergent trees that attain canopy dominance as aggregates within a forest
		* Attain dominance of the stand during mid to late successional stages of forest development

We suggest that the development of shelterwood methods for *Mesua-Shorea* forest are more appropriate in establishing a sustainable timber supply. These ideas are not new. Original work was started in everwet mixed-species forest types of tropical Asia at the turn of the last century. These include parts of southwestern India (Kadambi 1954a, 1954b) the Andaman Islands (Chengappa, 1944), western Malaysia (Wyatt-Smith, 1963) and Sri Lanka (Holmes 1957, 1958). Though much of this work was never completed, regeneration systems that showed preliminary promise were all shelterwoods. Perhaps the best known was the Malayan Uniform System that was adopted for lowland mixed-dipterocarp forests of Malaya.

Shelterwood Regeneration Methods

The purpose of the shelterwood method is to establish a new even-aged crop of trees before the old one is completely removed. It involves the manipulation of the old stand removing it in a series of cuttings that extend over a fraction of the total rotation. Its method is to retain mast trees of the canopy timber species for the establishment of advanced growth. As the term shelterwood denotes, the mast tree density and spacing can be adjusted to meet the environmental requirements of the seedlings established beneath. The desired environment can be created for seedlings of almost all species.

Usually those individuals chosen to remain till the last cutting are trees that are not only capable of providing seed and shelter for new stand establishment but also have the capacity to increase in value. Trees that are left therefore make good biological as well as economic sense. They are those that are of greatest vigor and quality and grow most rapidly in monetary value.

Procedures for shelterwood contain two or three treatments. These are listed as preparatory cutting, establishment cutting and removal cutting. Preparatory cuttings are initial treatments that prepare the stand for regeneration establishment. They can comprise cleaning, weeding or improvements to the stand. They are often not necessary or can be done synchronously with establishment cutting. The second treatment is a cutting that creates openings within the stand upon which new regeneration can become established. Those trees chosen to remain provide the mast and shelter. Depending on the light tolerance of the species, a time will come when the shelter will stop the regeneration process. It is then necessary to remove the remaining overstory. This whole process is usually accomplished over a 5-10 year period, but in forest types with more unpredictable masting years or of slower growth and longer rotations, the

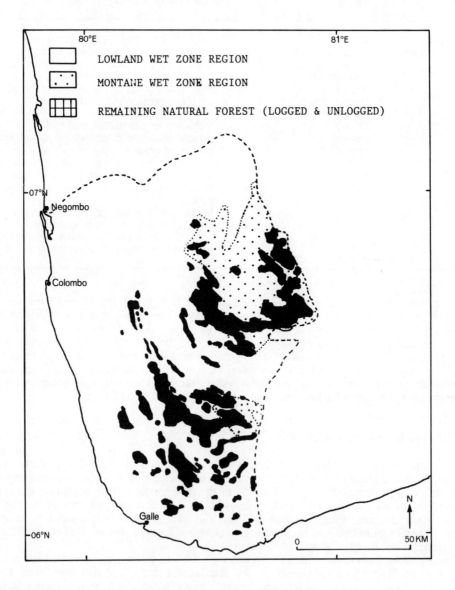

Figure 2. Remaining wet zone forests in the southwest of Sri Lanka.

duration may sometimes range up to twenty years. Apart from being more compatible with the natural processes of canopy timber species regeneration that is relatively light-demanding, shelterwoods are more cost-effective when compared to selection systems. Entries into the stand to extract commercial timbers are done over a relatively short period at the end of the rotation. This causes little damage to the growth and development of the new residual stand and costs are less for the administration and set-up of harvesting systems.

Ideas toward the Development of a Shelterwood Regeneration Method for the *Mesua-Shorea* Forest Community

Description of the *Mesua-Shorea* Forest Region

The *Mesua-Shorea* forest community described by De Rosayro (1942) is located mostly in the hill region of Sri Lanka's lowland wet zone (Fig. 2). The topography is one of a series of parallel ridges and valleys that lie along an east-west axis. The rock types are largely khondalites or charnokites of metamorphic origin (Cooray, 1967). Soils vary with gradients in topography. Using the USDA (1975) soil classification, thin to bedrock ridges and steep slopes are entisols or inceptisols, midslope and valley bottom soils comprise mostly ultisols, except those directly affected by seasonal flooding of rivers which are again entisols. The mean annual rainfall of the region is between 3750 mm and 5000 mm. Most rain falls during the SW (May-August) and NE (October-January) monsoons. Mean annual temperatures range between 18°C and 27°C. Average elevations of the *Mesua-Shorea* forest community are between 300 m and 900 m.

The floristic composition of the forest community has been well described by De Rosayro (1942) and Gunatilleke and Gunatilleke (1981, 1985). Its dominant species have been listed by canopy stratum (Tab. 2). Within the community, three forest associations exist that are governed by the topographical gradient. Each has been categorized by the authors from distribution patterns of certain dominant timber species.

Current studies show that some dominant canopy timber species (*Shorea, Dipterocarpus*) separate out across the topography based on differences due to light and soil moisture status (Ashton, in prep.). Natural forest disturbances are larger and more frequent on the lower slopes and valleys as compared to the ridges and upper slopes. This affects quality, intensity and sunfleck duration of forest light regimes, favoring more light-demanding canopy timber species

Table 2. Dominant tree species by stratum for the *Mesua-Shorea* forest community (modified after Gunatilleke and Gunatilleke, 1981).

Stratum	Species
Canopy	*Anisophyllea cinnamomoides, Cullenia rosayroana, Dipterocarpus hispidus, Mesua ferrea, Mesua nagassarium, Myristica dactyloides, Palaqium petiolare, Shorea affinus, Shorea congestiflora, Shorea disticha, Shorea megistophylla, Shorea trapezifolia, Shorea worthingtoni, Syzygium rubicundum*
Subcanopy	*Chaetocarpus castanocarpus, Garcinia hermonii, Syzygium neesianum, Xylopia championi*
Understory serrata,	*Aporusa lanceolata, Dillenia triquetra, Humboldtia laurifolia, Ouratea Timonius jambosella, Xylopia championi*
Shrub	*Agrostistachis hookeri, Gaertnera vaginans*

Table 3. Timber species suitable for enrichment planting in *Mesua-Shorea* forest. Their silvics and suggested planting guidelines are described. Most information on the silvics of these species has been adapted from Holmes (1957).

Species		Characteristics
Artocarpus nobilis	Fruit/Crop	A large compound fruit that contains many seeds. It is both dispersed and eaten by monkeys. Fruit is borne regularly, a few at a time.
	Regeneration	Germination requires partial shade (< 50% of full sun). Seedlings and saplings can endure shade but grow better in full sun.
	Post Establishment Growth Dynamics	In open conditions, it is liable to excessive branching unless side shade is maintained.
	Pathogens	Under shade, shoots susceptible to borers Coffeae (Cossidae). Leaves and shoots also susceptible to browsing by deer and cattle.
	Enrichment Planting Guideline	Attaining best growth in full sun conditions, seedlings should be planted within a training matrix of more light-demanding regeneration to reduce branching. Conditions requiring full sun are best provided after an establishment treatment within the *S. megistophylla-M. ferrea* forest association.
Bhesa zeylanica	Fruit/Crop	Capsules with many seeds dispersed by gravity and aided by animals.
	Regeneration	Susceptible to drought. Requires light shade for satisfactory development.
	Post Establishment Growth Dynamics	Fast-growing and relatively light-demanding, it does best in light shade conditions (50%-75% of full sun).
	Enrichment Planting Guideline	Most suitable for planting on midslopes (*S. trapezifolia-S. disticha*) where soils are deep and establishment treatments provide both partial shade and short duration of full sun.
Canarium zeylanicum	Fruit/Crop	The fruit and seed is large and is dispersed and eaten by bats and rodents.
	Regeneration	Germination requires some shade (50% of full sun). After the seedling stage, it is light-demanding (> 75% of full sun) and cannot endure understory shade.
	Post Establishment Growth Dynamics	Grows well under gap conditions, but does not recover readily from suppression. Best growth occurs on deep, moist loams.
	Pathogens	In understory shade, subject to soot fungus and susceptible to dieback.
	Enrichment Planting Guideline	Requires the same planting guidelines as *Artocarpus nobilis*. As it is a light-demanding species, it will not compete well with timber species that grow as fast but that are more shade tolerant.
Diospyros quaesita	Fruit/Crop	The fruit is dispersed and eaten by monkeys, rodents and large fruit-eating birds.
	Regeneration	Best germination requires understory shade (5%-10% of full sun). Seedlings are drought susceptible and require some partial shade (20%-30% of full sun) for best growth and are are also shade endurant.
	Post Establishment Growth Dynamics	Best training and growth is attained from saplings growing in small gaps created by death of single trees.
	Enrichment Planting Guideline	Plantings should be in the establishment treatments of the midslope or ridgetop forest associations where canopy gaps are relatively smaller and where, if desired, standards can be left that provide partial shade protection. As a slow growing, shade-enduring species it should be planted within relatively faster growing more light-demanding timber species regeneration.

Horsfieldia iryaghedi and *Myristica dactyloides*	Fruit/Crop	Large, edible and dispersed by large fruit-eating birds and and rodents.
	Regeneration	For best germination understory light conditions (5%-10% of full sun) are required. Seedlings are shade-tolerant requiring partial shade (20%-30% of full sun) for best development.
	Post Establishment Growth Dynamics	Best growth of saplings continue to require partial shade.
	Pathogens	In exposed "open" conditions attacked by soot fungus and are susceptible to drought and dieback.
	Enrichment Planting Guideline	The same suggestions as those for *Diospyros quaesita* are required.
Mangifera zeylanica	Fruit/Crop	Fruits edible and dispersed by animals.
	Regeneration	Moderately shade tolerant, but does best in full sun after germination.
	Post Establishment Growth Dynamic	Grows best in full sun but requires a surrounding training matrix to promote growth upwards.
	Pathogens	Browsed by deer.
	Enrichment Planting Guideline	The same planting suggestions as *Artocarpus nobilis* are required.
Pericopsis mooniana	Fruit/Crop	Fruits are eaten and seeds are dispersed by animals
	Regeneration	Seedlings require partial shade and are susceptible to drought. Growth is best when established regeneration is exposed to full sun for a short period each day.
	Post Establishment Growth Dynamics	Trees grow best on alluvial soils.
	Enrichment Planting Guideline	The same planting suggestions as *Artocarpus nobilis* are required
Vitex altissima	Fruit/Crop	Fruit is small, edible and dispersed by birds.
	Regeneration	Requires light shade (50%-75% of full sun) for best germination and early growth. Light-demanding.
	Post Establishment Growth Dynamics	Requires a heavy opening up of the overstory for best growth. To obtain best form, saplings need a tight surrounding training matrix.
	Enrichment Planting Guideline	The same planting suggestions as *Artocarpus nobilis* are required.

in the low-lying areas and more shade-enduring canopy timber species on its uplands. The second effect that sorts these timber species across the gradient is the susceptibility of some to drought. Species that are susceptible tend to be restricted to low-lying areas of the topography or to midslopes with deep soils. It would also seem apparent that changes in soil nutrient status in relation to the topographical gradient play an important role, but this has yet to be investigated.

Description of the Forest Associations

On the lower slopes and valleys of the topography, small rivers and perennial streams, the *Shorea megistophylla-Mesua ferrea* association is found; on the deep-soil midslopes and gentle ridges the *Shorea trapezifolia-Shorea disticha* association; on thin-soil steep slopes and rocky ridges the *Shorea worthingtoni-Mesua nagassarium* association. There is a considerable degree of overlap between associations. Patterns in species distribution and composition across the topography are diffuse and complicated. These categories are therefore simplifications intended for the purpose of understanding changes in species composition and in creating management units for their silviculture that can reflect the biology of the forest more accurately.

Principal Guidelines of the Shelterwood Regeneration Method

For the forest associations within *Mesua-Shorea* forest, we propose that the shelterwood regeneration method is most appropriate for obtaining a sustainable supply of timber. In particular, the treatments developed for each association should focus on providing for the regeneration establishment of the dominant timber species. These are the mast species after which the associations have been named. These trees can predictably provide the regeneration matrix and stocking for the next rotation's timber.

A second group of species that can be predicted to regenerate within newly created disturbance are fast growing, light-demanding tree species that establish from wind-blown or buried seed. *Macaranga peltata* and *Trema orientalis* are such tree species that can act as a nurse medium, and *Alstonia scholaris* and *Schumacheria castanaefolia* are species that can act as a training medium for the timber species. Though these species do not produce wood products of any value, they do serve as an important nurse and training matrix for regeneration of canopy timber species. Control of these trees is usually not necessary as they are short-lived and their removal would probably cause worse problems because of increased growth from climbers and shrubs.

A third group are those timber species that are not mast-fruiting but usually produce only a little fruit each year. Their natural patterns of distribution within forest stands are less predictable, sparser and more irregularly spaced. If desired, these species can be enrichment-planted at a more regular spacing within the regeneration matrix of mast-fruiting timber species. Timber species suited toward development of enrichment planting techniques in these forest associations have been listed in Table 3 along with their known silvics.

After establishment of the regeneration matrix and removal of the remaining mast trees, a long, relatively undisturbed interval of time can occur until the end of the rotation. This time interval can allow the natural establishment or artificial incorporation of a range of minor crops that can occupy various strata beneath the canopy of the forest. These species constitute the fourth and last group. They are relatively more shade-demanding than the canopy trees and, under natural conditions, most of their recruitment occurs over extended periods of time after establishment and canopy closure of the overstory.

Through planting they have the potential of being cultivated semi-naturally for products other than timber. There is little silvicultural information about most of these species. A select few have been well investigated (Attygalle *et al.* 1988, Bandulla *et al.* 1988, Ratnayake *et al.* 1988). Minor crop species suited for cultivation in subcanopy light environments have been listed in Table 4 along with their known silvics.

The Silvics of the Dominant Mast Timber Species in the *Mesua-Shorea* Forest Community

In the following sections, the known silvics of seedling regeneration of the dominant timber trees are described by their forest association. Unless otherwise cited information on their silvics is from studies by Holmes (1957) and Ashton (in prep.).

The *Shorea megistophylla-Mesua ferrea* Association

Mast crops are large and irregular (every 2-3 years) for *Dipterocarpus hispidus* and *S. megistophylla* (Dayanandan *et al.* 1988). *Dipterocarpus hispidus* seed is large, heavy and entirely reliant on gravity for dispersal. *Shorea megistophylla* seeds are the largest of section *Doona*. It is gravity dispersed, sometimes aided a little by strong gusts of wind. The seed is edible, desired both by people and rodents. *Shorea megistophylla* and *D. hispidus* are light demanding. Both require partial shade (40%-50% of full sun) for best germination, but after initial establishment require gap conditions that can have more than three hours of direct daily sunshine for release and best growth. These light conditions occur at the centers of gaps larger than 400 m². Observations also suggest that *S. megistophylla* and *D. hispidus* benefit from a certain amount of side shade.

Table 4. Important indigenous minor crop species that have potential for cultivation in *Mesua-Shorea* Forest. Most of the silvical information is based on the personal observations of the authors.

Stratum	Species	Growth and Uses
Understory	*Elettaria cardamomum* (Zingiberaceae)	Germinating in small gaps and light understory conditions from buried seed. Clumped distributions. Fruit used as a spice.
	Many species in the Labianthaceae and Marantaceae	Very shade tolerant herbs that can grow in deep shade understory conditions. Clumped distributions, frequently capable of spreading vegetatively through runners. Ornamental for house plant and commercial displays.
Subcanopy	*Garcinia quaesita* (Clusiaceae)	Seedlings shade demanding. Fruit is used as a spice for curry.
Climbers and Lianas	*Calamus* spp. (Palmae)	Best germination and establishment obtained in light shade. Shade tolerant and can endure understory conditions for some time. Requires exposure to periods of full sun for release and further growth. Needs support of surrounding tree regeneration. Stem is used for cane furniture and basketry.
	Coscinium fenestratum (Menispermaceae)	Seeds need to be passed through the gut of a pole cat and exposed to full sun for best germination. Seedlings require light shade for establishment but full sun for release. Tends to grow over the crowns of young trees "suffocating" them and so therefore needs to be judiciously planted. Stem is used as a medicine for colds, fevers and as an antiseptic. Can also be used for cordage.

Transpiration under full sun for *S. megistophylla* (and probably *D. hispidus*) is high. As a consequence seedlings of both species develop large tap roots. Nevertheless seedlings require deep ever moist soils with large water storage capacities for optimum growth.

Mesua ferrea fruits regularly each year but heavy mast crops are irregular (Kostermans, 1980). Fruits are dispersed by gravity and by animals. Seeds require deep shade (< 5% of full sun) for best germination (Holmes, 1957). Seedlings are delicate and drought susceptible but are not browsed. Saplings in the open are branchy and grow best in partial shade (50% of full sun) within a close training matrix. *Mesua ferrea* is slower growing and later successional and, provided there are no disturbances, will gradually replace the two more light-demanding timber species in the canopy.

The *Shorea trapezifolia-Shorea disticha* Association

Shorea trapezifolia flowers and fruits regularly and in abundance several times a year (Dayanandan *et al.* 1991). *Shorea congestiflora* flowers and fruits regularly once a year (Dayanandan *et al.* 1991). *Shorea disticha* flowers and fruits in abundance irregularly (once every 2-3 years; Dayanandan *et al.* 1991). *Shorea disticha* seed is edible, eaten by people and rodents. *Shorea trapezifolia* and *S. congestiflora* seed is not edible. Seed for all species is gravity dispersed but aided by wind. All three of these species require partial to relatively deep shade for best germination (10%-40% of full sun). For establishment and best growth, seedlings of *S. trapezifolia* and *S. disticha* require approximately 2-3 hours of direct daily sunshine. These light conditions occur at the centers of gaps that are between 300 m^2 and 400 m^2 in area.

Seedlings and saplings of *S. trapezifolia* are susceptible to drought, especially in understory environments of low light (< 2% of full sun) because of a poor ability to develop an adequate root system. *Shorea disticha* seedlings have a wider light tolerance spectrum than *S. trapezifolia* being able to endure both more shade and sun. *Shorea disticha* seedlings are also more drought tolerant.

Shorea trapezifolia seedlings are often present in abundance on the forest floor before the initiation of any regeneration treatment. Occurrence of saplings under closed canopy conditions are rare for *S. trapezifolia,* but for *S. disticha* they are more common. Though each of these species tends to occupy topographically similar sites, they appear to be somewhat mutually exclusive. It is suspected that *S. disticha* dominates the canopies of stands that are of later successional age than either *S. trapezifolia* or *S. congestiflora.* It is more shade enduring and is able to grow in light conditions beneath the canopy.

The *Shorea worthingtonii-Mesua nagassarium* Association

Mast crops of *S. worthingtonii* are irregular and do not produce abundant seed (personal observation). *Shorea worthingtonii* seed is small, eaten by rodents and dispersed by gravity that can be partially aided by wind. The mast crops of *M. nagassarium* are irregular with fruit that is dispersed by gravity and aided by animals. Successful germination requires understory light conditions (5% of full sun). Establishment and best growth of *S. worthingtonii* requires relatively intense but diffuse below canopy light conditions (20%-35% of full sun) or durations of full sun that do not last more than one and a half hours a day. These conditions can occur in centers of gaps that are approximately 200 m^2 in area. *M. nagassarium* seedlings appear to establish and grow best at lower light levels than *S. worthingtonii.*

Canopy timber trees of both species are relatively more shade tolerant than those timber species of the other associations. Advanced regeneration of seedling, sapling and pole size classes usually exist in strata beneath the canopy. It is suspected that *M. nagassarium* is slower growing and later successional than *S. worthingtonii.*

Treatments of the Shelterwood Regeneration Method for the Forest Associations

Treatments for the associations have been described by using the three shelterwood stages. In general, regeneration establishment of the mast timber species of the valley association require the heaviest treatment cuttings of the forest canopy because they are the most light-demanding. Treatment cuttings are progressively lighter for establishing the more shade-demanding regeneration of the midslope and ridgetop associations.

Preparatory Cutting

In most circumstances, preparatory cutting can be carried out simultaneously with treatments for regeneration establishment. In some cases, it might be favorable to perform understory cleaning and weeding before the establishment treatment to initially prepare the site for seed germination and to eliminate existing understory vegetation (e.g. *Ochlandra stridula*) that would otherwise respond favorably to increased light conditions through vegetative suckering. Most understory herbs and shrubs do not respond well to light increases and therefore their removal is inconsequential. In some instances, climber cutting might also lessen canopy damage to the residual overstory from felled trees.

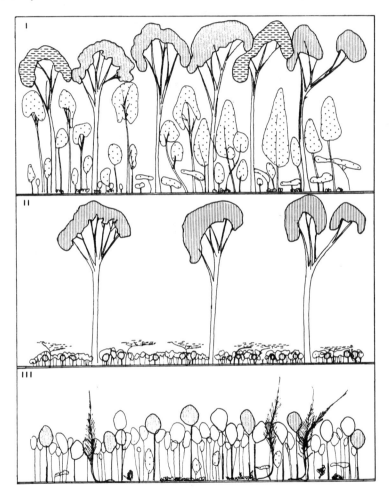

Figure 3. A schematic diagram illustrating the different treatment stages for the shelterwood method in the *Shorea megistophylla-Mesua ferrea* association. I. A representation of forest structure before treatments. II. To establish regeneration of the more light-demanding timber trees subcanopy and understory strata are removed along with canopy trees that have not been selected to provide some side-shade and mast. Note the spacing of the canopy trees are far apart to allow adequate amounts of direct sun to reach the ground. III. A new stand exists after the removal of the mast trees.

Establishment Cutting

Cutting of the understory and the subcanopy is required to initially germinate and establish matrix regeneration of the mast timber tree species for all the associations. For the more light-demanding regeneration of the valley and midslope associations, it is also necessary to partially remove the canopy allowing suitable mast trees to be left. After the establishment treatment, parent trees should be uniformly spaced for adequate seed dispersal. Their crowns should also project enough partial shade protection for their seed germination and enough full sun for their establishment.

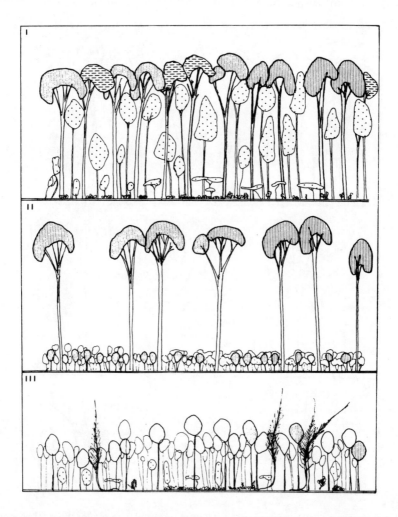

Figure 4. A schematic diagram illustrating the different treatment stages for the shelterwood method in the *Shorea trapezifolia-Shorea disticha* association. I. A representation of the forest structure before treatments. II. To establish the regeneration matrix of timber species, the subcanopy and understory strata are removed along with canopy trees that have not been selected to provide partial shade and mast. Note the spacing of the mast tree canopy is tighter than the spacing in the valley association, but still allows enough sun to penetrate the canopy for a short period of the day. III. A new stand exists after the removal of the mast trees.

In the valley association, parent tree spacing of *D. hispidus* and *S. megistophylla* should allow for relatively long durations of full sun to occur over the majority of the microsites and within the area demarcated for regeneration establishment (Fig. 3). Initial estimates indicate that removal of all subcanopy basal area and approximately two-thirds of the canopy basal area would achieve this. To encourage establishment of *M. ferrea* regeneration, a tighter overstory crown spacing can project more diffuse partial shade over a majority of the ground beneath. To obtain matrix regeneration of the *S. trapezifolia-S. disticha* association, crown spacing of parent trees should be at a closer spacing than that for *S. megistophylla* and *D. hispidus*. In this circumstance, gaps would be large enough to allow short periods of full sun (2-3 hours a day) to penetrate to the forest floor. Initial estimates indicate that removal of all subcanopy basal area and half of the canopy basal area would achieve this light regime (Fig. 4).

To establish regeneration of *S. worthingtonii* and *M. nagassarium*, subcanopy cutting is probably all that is required. Canopy crown closure should remain relatively intact allowing only short periods of direct sunlight through (< 1.5 hours a day) and increasing the intensity of diffuse light penetration. Under circumstances where canopy crown closure is uniformly closed, estimates suggest that the removal of one quarter of the canopy basal area would achieve this light regime (Fig. 5). The establishment phase of the shelterwood is the critical period when enrichment planting can be done within the regeneration matrix of the mast timbers. Species selected can be planted within the different establishment treatments of the associations according to their site and light requirements. Suitable species for enrichment planting at this stage are the non-mast timber species and light-demanding minor crops.

Removal Cutting

After satisfactory establishment of advanced regeneration, removal of the parent tree overstory can be carried out. There are many exceptions to canopy tree removal. For instance, to favor *M. ferrea* establishment and growth in the valley association, their mast trees could be left as standards after the removal treatment and harvested at the end of the next rotation. In the upper associations of the midslope and ridgetop, logging damage could harm a significant proportion of the established regeneration because of the nature of the topography. In these situations, some of the mast trees could remain as standards to minimize damage and to serve as a source of mast for more prolonged re-establishment of regeneration on sites damaged after removal cutting.

For the *S. worthingtonii-M. nagassarium* association, it is suspected that after the establishment cutting, because of their shade tolerance, regeneration can attain a pole size class beneath the overstory. This can perhaps be achieved before any release from removal cuttings of the overstory. Removal cuttings in this association should probably be done in stages as regeneration is likely to be susceptible to dieback if overexposed. At least one third of the remaining canopy trees could be chosen to remain as standards to minimize dieback of released pole size regeneration and to avoid its damage to logging. Using standards in this way can create a two-aged stand. This might also be economically advantagous by selecting relatively young mast trees that could potentially produce veneer quality logs. Standards would be the first trees to be removed in the establishment treatment of the shelterwood at the end of the next rotation.

In some instances, seedlings and saplings are present in abundance beneath the canopy before any treatments have been done. If this exists in the valley association, one cutting that combines both establishment and removal treatments is more appropriate. Advanced regeneration of both *Dipterocarpus* and *S. megistophylla* that has persisted in the shade of a closed canopy has the ability to respond to full sun exposure without dying back significantly (Holmes, 1958).

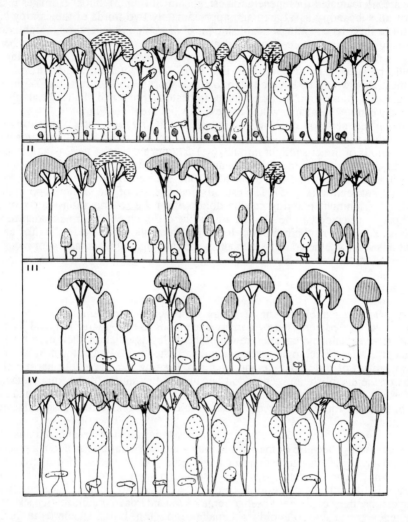

Figure 5. A schematic diagram illustrating the different treatment stages for the shelterwood method in the *Shorea worthingtonii-Mesua nagassarium* association. I. A representation of the forest structure before treatment. II. To establish regeneration the subcanopy and understory trees are removed. Note the canopy is relatively intact, but diffuse light penetration to the ground is higher. III. Removal cuttings of the overstory are done in a series of stages. Some can remain as standards until the end of the next rotation IV. A new stand exists with standards.

If there is a presence of sapling advanced regeneration on the midslope or ridgetop associations that has persisted in the shade of a closed canopy, it is unlikely to have the same capacity to respond to full sun exposure without dying back significantly. Mast timber species of these associations are more shade-demanding than those in the valley and have less ability to acclimatize. In these situations, treatments should proceed as if no regeneration exists.

Post-Removal Cuttings

Establishment cutting allows much light to reach the forest floor in treatments within the valley and midslope associations. Apart from favoring establishment of the regeneration matrix of the mast timber species, it also encourages weed vegetation (*Uncaria* spp. *Dalbergia pseudosisoo*) that must be controlled. Periodic liberation treatments are necessary to free crop trees from climber and shrub competition. After canopies have at least partially closed, many of the shade tolerant minor crops can be enrichment planted and subsequently cultivated beneath.

Conclusions

We provide a case for using a shelterwood regeneration method, based on research we have done in *Mesua-Shorea* forest over a 12-year period at the Sinharaja MAB Reserve and its adjacent forests. The method and treatments suggested for each association should be tested and compared to existing treatments using the polycyclic method of regeneration. If proven to work satisfactorily, particular quantitative guidelines for the suggested shelterwood method need to be evaluated, developed and refined. We also believe that with the incorporation of other non-mast timber tree species by enrichment planting and with the cultivation of minor crops, natural forest can be made more productive and cost efficient than it is currently. It is important to note that if a shelterwood method for obtaining regeneration in the *Mesua-Shorea* forest is adopted, much of the forest that is degraded or has been selectively logged would have to be correctly readjusted. This paper has not suggested or considered techniques for restoring an appropriate age, structure and species composition to degraded forests. Based on the known silvics of these tree species, techniques to restore degraded forest are urgently required.

Acknowledgments

We would like to thank the Forest Department of Sri Lanka for giving us permission and allowing us to use their facilities to carry out our studies in the Sinharaja forest region. We would like to thank NARESA, the Botany Department of the University of Peradeniya and the School of Forestry and Environmental Studies of Yale University for administering and supporting our work. We would also like to thank Prof. David Smith of Yale University for his helpful comments. Lastly, we would like to express thanks for grants received from USAID, IFS of Sweden, Monsanto Agricultural Company and the Tropical Resources Institute at the School of Forestry of Yale University.

Literature Cited

Ashton, P.S. 1980. Dipterocarpaceae. *In* M.D. Dassanayake and F.R. Fosberg, eds. *A Revised Handbook to the Flora of Ceylon Volume I*, pp. 364-423. Amerind Publ., New Delhi, India.

Ashton, P.M.S. 1989. A guide for the evaluation of *Shorea* (section *Doona*) advanced reproduction in the southwest of Sri Lanka. *In* G. Maury-Lechon, ed. *Proceedings of the Fourth Round Table on Dipterocarps*, pp. 87-112. Bogor, Indonesia, 12-15 December, 1989.

Ashton, P.M.S. 1990. A method for the evaluation of advanced reproduction in forest types of south and southeast Asia. *J. For. Ecol. Mgt.* 36: 163-175.

Ashton, P.M.S. (in prep.). *Establishment and Growth of Co-occuring Species within Shorea section Doona under Contrasting Moisture and Light Regimes.* Ph.D. Thesis, School of Forestry and Environmental Studies, Yale University, New Haven, Connectict.

Attygalle, D.N.C., C.V.S. Gunatilleke and I.A.U.N. Gunatilleke. 1988. *The Reproductive Biology of Elettaria Ensal in relation to its Conservation and Domestication.* An unpublished report for USAID, Washington DC.

Bandulla, S., C.V.S. Gunatilleke and I.A.U.N. Gunatilleke. 1988. *The Reproductive Biology of Coscinium fenestratum (Menispermaceae) in relation to its Conservation and Domestication.* An unpublished report for USAID, Washington DC.

Chapman, V.J. 1947. The application of aerial photography to ecology as exemplified by the natural vegetation of Ceylon. *The Indian Forester* 73: 287-314.

Chengappa, B.S. 1944. The Andaman forests and their regeneration. *The Indian Forester* 70: 450-611.

Cooray, P.G. 1967. An Introduction to the Geology of Ceylon. *Spol. Zeylan.* 31: 1-314.

Dayanandan, S., A.W.W.L. Abeygunasekera, D.N.C. Attygalle, I.A.U.N. Gunatilleke and C.V.S. Gunatilleke. 1991. Phenology and floral morphology in relation to pollination of some dipterocarps. *In* K.S. Bawa and M. Hadley, eds. *Reproductive Ecology of Tropical Forest Plants,* pp. 148-159. Man and the Biosphere Series 7. UNESCO, Paris.

Dayanandan, S., A.W.W.L. Abeygunasekera, D.N.C. Attygalle, I.A.U.N. Gunatilleke and C.V.S. Gunatilleke. 1988. *Reproductive Biology of some Dipterocarps in relation to their Conservation and Domestication.* An unpublished report for USAID, Washington DC.

De Rosayro, R.A. 1942. The soils and ecology of the wet evergreen forests of Ceylon. *Trop. Agricult.* 56: 108-121.

De Zoysa, N.D., C.V.S Gunatilleke and I.A.U.N. Gunatilleke.1991. Comparative phytosociology of natural and modified rain forest sites in Sinharaja MAB Reserve, Sri Lanka. *In* A. Gomez-Pompa, T.C. Whitmore and M. Hadley, eds. *Rain Forest Regeneration and Management*, pp. 154-168. Man and the Biosphere Sreies 7. UNESCO, Paris.

Gunatilleke, C.V.S. and P.S. Ashton. 1987. New light on the plant geography of Ceylon. II. The ecological biogeography of the lowland endemic tree flora. *J. Biogeogr.* 14: 295- 327.

Gunatilleke, C.V.S. and I.A.U.N. Gunatilleke. 1981. The floristic composition of Sinharaja - a rain forest in Sri Lanka with special reference to endemics and dipterocarps. *Malays. For.* 44: 386-396.

Gunatilleke, C.V.S. and I.A.U.N. Gunatilleke. 1985. Phytosociology of Sinharaja - a contribution to rain forest conservation in Sri Lanka. *Biol. Conserv.* 31: 21-40.

Holmes, C.H. 1956. The broad pattern of climatic vegetational distribution in Ceylon. *The Ceylon Forester* 2: 207-225.

Holmes, C.H. 1957. The natural regeneration of the wet and dry evergreen forests of Ceylon. *The Ceylon Forester* 3: 15-41.

Holmes, C.H. 1958. The natural regeneration of the wet and dry evergreen forests of Ceylon. *The Ceylon Forester* 3: 111-127.

Kadambi, K. 1954a. *Dipterocarpus indicus*, Bedd. (Syn. *D. turbinatus*, Gaertn. f.) - its silviculture and management. *The Indian Forester* 80: 368-391.

Kadambi, K. 1954b. *Hopea parviflora* Bedd., its silviculture and management. *The Indian Forester* 80: 610-622.

Kostermans, A.J.G.H. 1980. Clusiaceae. *In* M.D. Dassanayake and F.R. Fosberg, eds. *A Revised Handbook to the Flora of Ceylon Vol. 1*, pp-72-110. Amerind Publ., New Delhi, India.

Peeris, C.V.S. 1975. *The Ecology of the Endemic Tree Species of Sri Lanka in Relation to their Conservation.* Ph.D. thesis. Aberdeen University, Aberdeen, Scotland.

Ratnayake, P.K., C.V.S. Gunatilleke and I.A.U.N. Gunatilleke. 1988. *Reproductive Biology of Caryota urens in Relation to its Conservation and Domestication.* An unpublished report for USAID, Washington DC.

Richards, P.W. 1952. *The Tropical Rain Forest.* Cambridge Univ. Press, Cambridge.

Smith, D.M. 1986. *The Practice of Silviculture.* Wiley, New York.

Trimen, H. 1893-1900. *A Handbook to the Flora of Ceylon.* Vols. 1-5. Dulav Publ., London.

USDA Soil Conservation Survey. 1975. *USDA Soil Taxonomy A Basic System of Classification for Making and Interpreting Soil Surveys.* USDA Ag. Handbook 436. US Govt. Printing Office, Washington DC.

Wyatt-Smith, J. 1963. *Manual of Malayan silviculture for inland forests* (2 Vols.). Malays. For. Rec. 23.

Annex

Table 5. A glossary of technical terms used in the text.

Advanced regeneration. Regeneration which appears spontaneously or is induced under existing stands.

Forest association. Subdivisions of a forest community which are distinguished from each other by species composition alone.

Forest community. A general term used for any unit of vegetation regardless of rank or developmental stage but that have similar dominant species in common.

Cover-type. A forest type now occupying the ground with no implication being conveyed as to whether it is temporary or permanent.

Coupe. The area demarcated for a treatment or harvest.

Even-aged. Stands composed of trees having no or relatively small differences in age. The maximum differences admissible is generally twenty years, though where rotations are greater than 100 years, larger differences of up to 25% of the rotation period are accepted.

Improvement cutting. A cutting designed to free desired trees from those that are undesired (trees of poor form or undesired species).

Light-demanding. Plants (trees) that require sun for their growth and survival.

Production forest. A forest that is actively managed through manipulation for the purpose of providing direct and indirect goods and services.

Protection forest. A forest that is passively managed with no manipulation for indirect and intangible goods and services.

Over-topped. Trees with crowns entirely below the general level of the crown canopy receiving no direct light either from above or from the sides.

Rotation. A period of years required to establish and grow a crop (timber) to a specified condition of maturity.

Shade-enduring. Plants (trees) that are able to survive under deep shade.

Shade-demanding. Plants (trees) that require shade for their best growth.

Stands. A community of trees possessing sufficient uniformity as regards composition, constitution, age, spatial arrangement or conditions distinguishable from adjacent communities so forming a silvicultural or management identity.

Standards. Selected trees that are carried on a much longer rotation than most.

Tolerance. Ability of a tree species to become established and grow satisfactorily in the shade of and in competition with other trees. Tree species are classified according to their degree of tolerance.

Turnover. The average interval of time required for the natural cycle of forest succession to be completed within a forest.

Uneven-aged. Stands in which there are considerable differences in age of trees and in which trees of three or more age classes are represented.

Proceedings of the International and Interdisciplinary Symposium
ECOLOGY AND LANDSCAPE MANAGEMENT IN SRI LANKA
W. Erdelen, C. Preu, N. Ishwaran, C.M. Madduma Bandara (eds.)
Colombo, Sri Lanka, 12-26 March 1990
© 1993
Margraf Scientific Books, D-97985 Weikersheim
ISBN 3-8236-1182-8

A Case for the Evaluation and Development of Mixed-Species Even-Aged Plantations in Sri Lanka's Lowland Wet Zone

P.M.S. ASHTON, C.V.S. GUNATILLEKE AND I.A.U.N. GUNATILLEKE

Abstract

In the lowland wet zone of Sri Lanka most quality timber is produced from slow-growing tree species that are relatively shade-demanding, requiring protection from the environmental extremes of wind, sun and rain. Their establishment in plantations has thus far been poor. Production of quality timber is therefore dependent solely on natural forest resources. We suggest ideas on their incorporation into successional plantations that simulate the development processes in natural forests. Furthermore, minor crops have unrealized economic potential. Many of their products are presently solely exploited from natural forests. Experimental incorporation of such crops into these plantations also needs to be explored. Lastly, it is suggested that low value products, such as species that provide fuelwood and fodder, that have been traditionally planted as monocultures, can be made more socially acceptable by their incorporation together with other more desirable crops. The strength of our proposed plantation system is its adaptibility to a range of management intensities, depending on crop value and the resources available within a particular region. The growth categories for each plantation phase are described along with the silviecological characteristics of the plant species suited to them.

Introduction

Natural forests and their man-made analogs are going to play an increasing role in both temperate and tropical regions where site conditions mitigate against the development of forestland for non-tree uses. An example is Sri Lanka, an island nation of approximately 65,600 km^2 and a population of over 16 million people. Two hundred years ago the land was cloaked almost entirely by natural forests. These forests have been developed over a long period of time and managed in a sustained way that compared to other developing nations is largely in harmony with its people's desires. Today the island is still predominantly covered

275

with some kind of forest cover, either natural or man-made. Forest cover serves as a moderating and tempering effect to the extremes of the island's macroclimate. It protects the island's soil from the continual flux of rain and sun, and regulates the flow of water that allows cultivation of arable crops.

Cultural and historical knowledge of forest and tree cultivation on the island can make it a guide for sustainable land use for other temperate and tropical moist forest regions. In particular, its tree and shrub plantations (tea, rubber, coconut) produce the country's largest exports and employ the most labor. Its people's home gardens dominated by trees produce a variety of fruit, vegetables, spices and medicinal herbs and its natural forests provide an array of both tangible and intangible goods and services. If Sri Lanka is to continue this tradition of land use and at the same time develop its resources further, it must find new tree crops, refine silvicultural techniques for its existing home gardens, natural forests and plantations and explore and develop new and better cultivation systems. It must equally emphasize the creation and development of markets for these products both for export and home consumption.

For the wet zone of Sri Lanka its wealth of natural forest ecosystems can be exploited as an information source for potential new crops. Ecological principles derived from studies on these natural plant communities can be judiciously applied to the development of crop systems suited to the island's climate and soil (Hart, 1980). Examples of such studies done elsewhere, but applicable, are the classic experiments on competition between plant populations conducted by Harper (1961, 1964, 1977) and observations on patterns and processes of plant communities done by Watt (1919, 1947), Whittaker (1975) and Bormann and Likens (1979). The use of successional crop systems has been suggested for other moist forest regions (Holdridge 1959, Trenbath 1975), but only a few such systems have been well described (Hart, 1980).

Here we propose ideas for the successional development of mixed-species even-aged plantations particularly suited to the cultivation of quality timbers, minor crops and trees that produce low value products. Many of the species that yield these goods are currently solely exploited from Sri Lanka's lowland wet zone natural forests. The strength of the plantation system proposed is its adaptibility to a range of management and silvicultural practices depending on the value of the goods and services it can produce, the need to optimize yields and the resources available within the particular plantation area.

This paper briefly discusses first the socioeconomic rationale for mixed-species even-aged plantation silviculture. It then describes in more detail the silvicultural rationale and the ecological characteristics of each growth phase of the suggested plantation system.

The Social and Economic Rationale for the Development of Mixed-Species Even-Aged Plantations

Currently in many regions of the world, natural forests supply the world demand for quality hardwood timber for furniture, interior paneling, flooring, turnery, veneer and other special wood products. Though Sri Lanka is not a major exporter of quality hardwood timbers, the island's natural forests have some of the most valuable timbers in the world. In natural forests of the lowland wet zone a key problem is the establishment of advanced regeneration of these timber species necessary for their sustained production. In many instances, their mode of exploitation has led to a degraded forest that has declined forest production and value. Apart from the development and evaluation of better silvicultural methods for the management of these natural forests (Wyatt-Smith 1963, Champion and Seth 1968, Mergen and Vincent 1985), an alternative is the incorporation of these timber species into plantations.

Use of these timber species in conventional plantation systems has thus far been generally poor. This can perhaps be attributed to their inability to compete and establish with weedy vegetation in full sun, and if they do establish their tendency to compete between themselves for the same growing space, leading toward plantation stagnation and poor form. Most are also site-specific showing poor establishment after planting, if their preferred soil requirements are not met.

Minor crop species in Sri Lanka's lowland wet zone are often associated with these same forests. Minor crops are classified here as those species yielding products (sugar, latex, spice, medicine, fiber or fruit) that are obtained from wild populations of plants. They are usually harvested in small amounts and at irregular intervals for use within the local community. For many of these plants similar trends of exploitation and depletion have occurred. An example is rattan (*Calamus* spp.), a vine requiring support and therefore grown obligatorily in mixture with trees. A cottage industry has developed on cane furniture and basketry, but now that stocks have been mostly depleted from natural forests their future existence is in doubt.

Generally, there are few reliable data on potential production (yield), on channels for distribution or on the economic value for minor crop products which are not yet commercially exploited but have been a traditional source of living for the rural population (Ashton and Ashton, in press). Two important examples of this in Sri Lanka's wet zone are the yield of sugar or the distillation of arrack (a palm whiskey) from kitul palm (*Caryota urens*) and the many medicinal values of weni-wal-geta (*Coscinium fenestratum*). A frequently mentioned reason for the neglect of cultivating minor crops is that there are few if any established markets for them. Also, when expressed as a percentage of timber exports, their value is small. Nevertheless these products have been traditionally valuable to local communities within these forests and many have great economic potential. Most of these minor crop species are not conducive to monoculture plantation systems because of silvicultural establishment requirements similar to those of the valuable timber trees. These crop species also usually have below canopy growth habits that occupy particular strata within the forest.

Lastly, a social consideration concerning crop cultivation in Sri Lanka is that of the reliability of yield. The more reliable the plant crop, the less risk of crop failure, and hence the more desirable it is for cultivation by private landholders. These crops are of high value and/or produce at least once a year, most produce more frequently. In Sri Lanka's wet zone important examples are tea (*Camellina sinensis*), rubber (*Hevea brasiliensis*) and coconut (*Cocos nucifera*). Less reliable products are often the most scarce because of this preference. In the world today over 1.1 billion people are experiencing scarcities of fuelwood, a common source of household energy (NAS, 1980). Other examples can be poles and timber for housing and arboreal fodder for livestock. These plants are not producing constant yield or it may take many years to become productive. The monetary value of these products is low or none, in part because villagers have historically had the right to have relatively unrestricted access to these goods and services on what is now government land, but once belonged to the king. Their public ownership can allow for periodic losses to be shared and spread over time (Ashton and Ashton, in press). Currently though, these low value tree crops are usually exploited from community or state forest lands on which no effective techniques are applied for their sustained production. They are best produced in conventional plantation systems as most of these products come from fast growing light-demanding trees. In many instances though, their planting in monoculture is not socially acceptable to the local community which often has no vested interest in their protection.

Ways must be found to alleviate the pressure on remaining natural forests from exploitation by villagers and timber merchants of these three crop categories, viz. quality timbers, minor crops and low value tree crops. One avenue to explore is the development of these crops in mixed plantations. Their mixture reduces the risk of monetary loss if any one crop failed whilst also potentially providing a crop yield at least once a year. Government or private support and investment can create new economic markets for the most promising crops and help establish cottage industries within the local community. Values for the protection and the sustained management of these species mixtures would then be realized. Species in these categories can also be made more acceptable by including them with crops that provide reliable, early and directly tangible benefits, and that are at least initially of more importance to the local community.

Silvicultural Rationale for the Development of Mixed-Species Even-Aged Plantations

Understanding patterns of forest growth and development in Sri Lanka's wet zone is important for the cultivation of mixed-species plantations that incorporate important timber trees, minor crops and low value tree crops. We discuss here in particular detail (1) disturbance and regeneration, (2) site specialization, and (3) stand competition and stratification. These aspects lay the biological base for the case of developing mixed-species even-aged tree plantations. They are critical toward understanding how to create a growth environment suited to the establishment of the quality timber and minor crop species.

Disturbance and Regeneration

The nature of forest disturbance varies between and within regions. The three main attributes of disturbance can be categorized as frequency, type and size. The nature of disturbance frequency can be categorized into several kinds. Some forests have predictable cycles of disturbance that can occur between the passing of long periods of time. Others have disturbance that show significant seasonality. Disturbance can also be entirely stochastic at certain scales in nature with no seasonality or periodicity at all. Most commonly though, regions have disturbances that are stochastic on the scale of the forest mosaic but are caused by more predictable patterns in climate. Natural disturbance in lowland wet zone forests of Sri Lanka reflects those frequency patterns of the last category. This disturbance is usually associated with effects of the island's monsoon seasons.

Type of disturbance affects the nature of the forest understory. In the wet zone, disturbances are most often caused by flooding, wind, rain or lightning strikes or some combination of their interactions. Sri Lanka's lowland wet zone landscape is undulating and because of this, different parts of the topography are prone to different types of disturbance (Ashton, in prep.). Along valleys rain-soaked soils and winds can interact to create large blowdowns and windthrows. On ridges, where rooting is more secure, lightning strikes are a more important disturbance. Occasionally during severe dry periods, drought can cause death of emergent or canopy trees on the upper slopes and ridges.

Size of disturbance is also associated with the nature of topography, and therefore is also associated with disturbance type. Lightning strikes kill only one or two trees that can remain standing for many years. The disturbance created is small. Blowdowns can often only include one tree, but usually include several or many. This kind of disturbance can be small or large, depending on the number of trees involved.

All these disturbance patterns allow wet zone forests to have understory vegetation that can survive when a canopy opening is created (De Zoysa et al. 1991). Many important quality timber and minor crop species in these forest types are relatively shade-tolerant and are able to germinate and survive for a period in understory conditions. For their full establishment and growth these same species are more light-demanding, requiring the creation of canopy gaps for their release. The intensity of shading required is specific to the light tolerance of the species. This method of seed germination and establishment of a new group of trees is known as advanced regeneration.

A second group of tree species relies on seed recruitment, germination and establishment after the creation of a disturbance (De Zoysa et al. 1991). These species have seeds often distributed by wind or are present within the soil as a "buried seed bank". Regeneration establishment and growth is fast and light demanding. Preferring full sun conditions, their crown canopies often give the partial protection required for advanced regeneration of the other species group beneath. Many of these species are also low value tree crops.

Seedlings or saplings of most tree species, therefore, become established or are released when a disturbance creates space previously occupied by mature individuals. The newly created young stand is an even-aged cohort of individuals growing in mixture. This strongly suggests that mixed-species plantations in Sri Lanka's wet zone should emulate such processes of natural forest growth and development. Species mixtures should therefore be established together as even-aged aggregates.

Site Specialization

Maintenance of tree species richness of plant communities has been explained in terms of equilibrium and non-equilibrium hypotheses. The equilibrium theory states that after a natural disturbance a forest will revert back to its former structure and composition. This is supported by evidence for species differentiation due to soil moisture and nutrient status (Ashton 1964, 1969, Whitmore 1982, Baillie and Ashton 1983), by density dependence of host-specific seed predation (Janzen 1971, Becker *et al.* 1985) and by relatively predictable patterns of forest growth after disturbance (Clements 1916, Egler 1954, Drury and Nisbet 1973, Oliver 1981). The non-equilibrium strategy hypothesizes that forest composition and structure is influenced largely by stochastic processes. According to this theory, the pattern of succession following disturbance is mostly unpredictable and species distribution is largely unrelated to site (van Steenis 1958, 1969, Federov 1966, Hubbell 1979, Hubbell and Foster 1986).

Both equilibrium and non-equilibrium processes within a forest are influential and can play differing roles at different scales in time and space, but it is important to determine when and where each process dominates the other for a given forest region. It appears that with the undulating and complex topography of Sri Lanka's wet zone lowlands and with the effect of relatively predictable and small disturbance regimes, species distribution and growth would follow processes favoring a forest in dynamic equilibrium (Gunatilleke and Gunatilleke 1981, Ashton, in prep.). It therefore follows that seedlings of many species in Sri Lanka's lowland forest require site specialization for their establishment and growth. Knowledge of these site requirements must be acquired in order to evaluate their suitability to specific planting sites. This is particularly so when evaluating potential quality timber or minor crop species.

Alternatively, light-demanding species that have rapid growth rates but produce low value products are often less site-specific, can grow in a range of soils and often prefer open conditions. These patterns stress that the specific site and light requirements, mode of establishment of the timber, minor crop and low value tree crop species should be known before they are cultivated in plantations.

Stand Competition and Stratification

Much of the classic work on stand crown stratification within a forest was done by Davis and Richards (1933, 1934), Beard (1944), Black *et al.* (1950) and Ashton (1964). Their vertical profile diagrams illustrate the complexity of species stratification from the canopy down to the understory. This has been summarized well by Whitmore (1984). These studies have shown that different species occupy different parts of the vertical profile of an everwet rain forest. Using terminolgy initially developed for temperate forest (Watt, 1947) and now used in the paleotropics (Whitmore, 1984), stands have been grouped as belonging to gap, building or mature phases. This is an attempt to categorize species according to particular stages and kinds of development within a forest. Though seedlings and saplings of most species are present after initial formation of a canopy opening, those light-demanding species that are usually established from buried or wind-blown seed dominate the stratification process during both gap and building phases of young stand development. The slower-growing, more shade-enduring species dominate the canopy stratification process in later successional time during the stand's mature phase.

The direct cause of canopy stratification can perhaps be mainly traced to the water relations of the soil (Bruenig 1969, Janzen 1974, Whitmore 1984) and to the frequency of disturbance (Denslow, 1980). For instance, soils susceptible to continued water stress (both xeric and hydric conditions) mute the ability of the physiological and morphological processes that favor canopy stratification. Further, regions with more marked seasonal climates are prone to more frequent disturbances. This is because most disturbances are associated with the climatic fluctuations or extremes in climate. This results in a shortening of the turnover period of the forest within which crown stratification can develop.

Canopy stratification within the lowland wet zone forests of Sri Lanka is clearly apparent (Peeris, 1975). Compared to other moist forest regions, turnover periods are relatively long, disturbances are small and are not severe. The development of mixed-species even-aged plantations that can emulate the stratification process therefore appears appropriate for Sri Lanka's lowland wet zone.

Model for the Development of Mixed-Species Even-Aged Plantations

The model we propose is based largely on our observations of the dynamics of lowland wet zone forest (Peeris 1975, Gunatilleke and Gunatilleke 1981, Ashton, in prep.), as discussed broadly in the preceding section. We also incorporate information on the use of shade trees and ground covers in tea and rubber plantations. The model consists of three phases (Fig. 1). All start simultaneously at the initiation of the plantation, but each is most important at particular times through the plantation's development.

The Nurse Phase

The first is the nurse phase and consists of the introduction of pioneer "nurse" tree species and ground covers, chiefly for restoration and protection of soil structure and nutrient retention on the site. Ground covers imitate the roles and processes of herbaceous forb and grass vegetation that invade bare land (Safford and Filip 1974, Bormann and Likens 1979). They have added advantages of a regular low uniform growth habit and a loose root structure that does not form a compact mat. These attributes allow a vegetation cover that is not in direct physical competition with planted tree seedlings for above-or-below ground growing space. They can also serve as a live mulch that can avoid topsoil baking, inhibit soil particle erosion and enrich soil nitrogen through fixation.

Families of plants that appear suitable as ground covers for the lowland wet zone of Sri Lanka are Leguminosae (*Puerraria* spp. *Desmodium* spp.) and Rubiaceae (*Shistostigma* sp.). Ground covers are currently successfully used during initial phases of establishing a rubber plantation. Nurse trees are also part of this phase. Seeded or planted at a wide spacing, their main function is to provide, as cheaply and as rapidly as biologically possible, a protective canopy umbrella for the partial shade requirements of the minor crop and timber seedlings that are planted beneath. Within several years, nurse trees should have grown enough to have a spreading but thin monolayered crown, approximately 4-5 meters above the ground. Many pioneer species in Sri Lanka have these characteristics and would be classified as gap phase species (Watt 1947, Whitmore 1984). Suggested indigenous species are *Trema orientalis* and *Macaranga peltata*. Suitable exotic species are *Muntingia calabura* and *Gliricidia sepium*. Some of the shade trees used in tea cultivation also appear to be suitable candidates for nurse trees.

Most of the nurse tree species are short-lived and start dying back within 10-20 years (Whitmore, 1984). Many perhaps act as nutrient sinks trapping mineral ions that could otherwise be rapidly leached from the soil after disturbance. Over time, they gradually release the ions back, particularly during their dieback, making them available for uptake by the slower-growing quality timber trees and minor crop species (Budowski 1961, Stark 1970, Marks 1974).

Leaves of nurse tree species are also often more palatable than slower-growing species having fewer toxic compounds or protective characteristics such as having surface wax, hairs or being coriaceous (Ewel, 1980). Their fast growth and palatability make them suitable for supplementary arboreal fodder. Nurse tree species particularly suited to producing arboreal fodder are those with tendencies to coppice or pollard or those that can boost leaf protein through nitrogen fixation.

Figure 1. Profile diagrams depicting the phases for each growth stage during the development of a mixed-species even-aged plantation.

During the nurse phase, plant species that bring direct and early tangible benefits to the local community could also be included so long as their interplanting does not interfere with future stand development. A successful example of this is the Taungya System used in timber plantations of Burma and India in the late 1800s (Brandis 1897, Champion and Seth 1968). More recent examples can be found with the village forest systems used in Thailand (Boonkird *et al.* 1984) and until recently a similar system was used by the Sri Lanka Forest Department in the north and east. This encouraged the protection and care of tree crops that would otherwise be neglected or underappreciated by the local population.

Early successional light-demanding species are most suited as taungya crops as they grow rapidly, produce in only a short period and are the most socially desirable to the local community. Staple carbohydrate food crops (*Musa* spp. *Manihot esculenta, Dioscorea* spp. *Carica papaya*) that are short-lived are best. Many of these species, if grown as a commercial venture, have the added advantage of producing quick returns on income that could offset the initial costs of plantation establishment. Species that require tillage are not recommended for interplanting, as soils which require reforestation with tree plantations are generally infertile and susceptible to erosion.

The Training Phase

The second phase of plantation development is the rapid growth of training matrix species. Planted at close spacing at the initial time of plantation establishment, these tree species would fit the building phase of Watt's (1947) classification for forest successional development. Species suited as a training matrix are the fast-growing light-demanding trees with small columnar crowns and grow together in dense uniform stands. They belong to the group of species that produce abundant light seed regularly every year. Seed is usually dispersed by wind or sometimes by animals and their regeneration relies on post-disturbance recruitment from buried seed or seed rain for their establishment and growth. Their purpose in a mixed-species even-aged plantation is to provide a medium of support, training and protection for quality timber tree and minor crop species growing beneath or beside them. A suggested training matrix species indigenous to Sri Lanka is *Alstonia scholaris*. Introduced species that might be suitable candidates are *Gmelina arborea, Sesbanea grandiflora* and *Alstonia macrophylla*.

Most of these species have small leaves orientated in such ways as to present several compact layers, all of which may experience direct sunlight for prolonged periods. Their arrangement also allows sufficient diffuse light to penetrate below for growth of the more shade-tolerant quality timber and minor crop species. It follows then that they have high leaf area indices and therefore most likely have high carbon assimilation rates. This permits them to put on large diameter increments in bole growth using relatively small crowns. Compared to the slower-growing more shade-tolerant trees, they therefore have very favorable bole growth to crown volume ratios making them ideal as trees that can produce large bole volumes over short rotations. Many of these training matrix species are low value tree crops that can produce reasonable timbers, suitable for light construction in housing, for fuelwood or for pulp in paper manufacture.

The Tree Crop Phase

The tree crop phase of the plantation would be classified as the mature phase by Watt (1947). This phase takes precedence over the training phase when the slower-growing quality timber trees attain canopy dominance. These species are best planted on establishment of the plantation. Being more shade-tolerant, they are able to grow steadily but slowly through the training matrix, eventually overtopping their canopy to become emergents. During this process of overtopping, their crown morphology changes from that of a monopodial and columnar shape to one that is broadly branched and expansive. At this stage, height increment decreases and more growth is allocated to the bole.

Most of these shade-tolerant species do not perform well in competition with each other, but require a shade-intolerant training matrix to surround them. This serves as a medium for allowing their crowns to expand at the expense of the matrix. In natural forests these species are slow-growing and site-specific. Their advanced regeneration requires particular micro-environments for superior growth and establishment. At the end of the plantation rotation, the quality timber species can be harvested to produce furniture, interior paneling, flooring, ornamentation and turnery.

After the occurrence of initial canopy closure by the training matrix, minor crops (Tab. 1) can be interplanted beneath, replacing taungya crop species that require more sun. Growth habits of each minor crop species (subcanopy trees, lianas, shrubs, ground herbs) can be manipulated to optimize the growing space of the different strata that exist within the plantation. With the exception of lianas, below canopy conditions favor cultivation of species that are relatively slow-growing and shade-tolerant.

Table 1. An abbreviated list of minor crop species suggested as suitable candidates for cultivation in mixed-species even-aged plantations. They are listed by the canopy stratum they best occupy along with their common names and use and country of origin.

Stratum	Species	Common Name	Uses	Origin
Understory	*Curcuma domestica*	turmeric	spice	Java
	Eletttaria cardamomum	cardamon	spice	native
	Zingiber spp.	ginger	spice	native
	Anthurium andreanum	anthuriums	cut flowers	Colombia
	Impatiens balsamina	impatiens	seed for cultivation as ornamental annual in temperate regions	native
	Begonia spp. and species in the Orchidaceae, Bromeliaceae and Gesneriaceae families		suitable as house plants, cut-flowers and as perennial commercial displays	
Subcanopy	*Caryota urens*	kitul palm	sugar beverage	native
	Garcinia mangostena	mangosteen	fruit	Malaysia
	Garcinia quaesita	goraka	spice	native
	Myristica fragrans	nutmeg	spice	India
	Nephelium longana	rambuttan	fruit	Malaysia
	Syzygium aromaticum	cloves	spice	Mollucas Islands
Lianas and climbers	*Calamus* spp.	cane	furniture basketry	native
	Coscinium fenestratum	weni-wal-geta	medicine cordage	native

These species allocate more of their energy budget toward "harvesting" more light at the sacrifice of fixing less carbon for growth. Their leaves are usually broad and often variegated and are arranged as layers that can form either deep or flat and spreading crowns. Many are also important producers of secondary chemicals that are retained within their tissues for their protection from herbivory. Because of these attributes, the crops they produce are often richly flavored fruits, syrups, latexes, condiments, spices and medicines. Others with ornamental foliage or flowers are desired as house plants or for commercial displays. Most of the lianas are relatively more light-demanding. Planted along with the training matrix they can be "carried up" with the canopy. These species provide cordage or canes and a few have medicinal values. Care must be taken to avoid suppression of other crops because of their growth habit.

The rotation lengths of these mixed-species even-aged plantations are subject to the growth of the quality timber trees. Depending on species choice this may be anywhere between 40 and 150 years (Tab. 2). At the end of the rotation the nature of these plantations can allow for their artificial reestablishment or by careful manipulation, they can be encouraged through the establishment of natural regeneration to revert back to secondary forest.

Table 2. An abbreviated list of important quality timber species suggested as suitable candidates for incorporation as final crop trees in mixed-species even-aged plantations.

Native		Introduced
Artocarpus nobilis	Mesua ferrea	Dryobalanops aromatica
Bhesa zeylanica	Myristica dactyloides	Khaya ivorensis
Canarium zeylanicum	Pericopsis mooniana	Michelia champaca
Dipterocarpus hispidus	Shorea congestiflora	Swietenia macrophylla
Dipterocarpus zeylanicus	Shorea congestiflora	Tabebuia rosea
Diospyros quaesita	Shorea stipularis	
Horsfieldia iryaghedi	Shorea trapzifolia	
Mangifera zeylanica	Vitex altissima	

Conclusions

In this paper we have provided a general framework for the social, economic and silvicultural rationale of developing mixed-species even-aged plantations. These plantations are a successional crop system suited to the cultivation of slow-growing quality timbers, minor crops and trees that yield low value products. Currently, most of these products are solely exploited from species that grow in natural forest. The development of mixed-species even-aged plantations could provide avenues toward their sustainable cultivation, the potential expansion of their existing markets and the creation of new ones.

Based on the knowledge of the processes of lowland wet zone natural forest, establishment of these plantations is most applicable to sites within this region where costs of maintaining increased agricultural production is high. Mixed-species even-aged plantations, because they emulate the natural patterns of succession, should allow for lower costs in maintenance through more efficient biological methods of disease control, weeding, pruning and fertilization. To test and evaluate our ideas, a proper experimental procedure needs to be designed and implemented.

Acknowledgments

Studies that have allowed us to formulate these ideas were conducted in forest reserves in the lowland wet zone of Sri Lanka. We gratefully thank the Forest Department for allowing us to carry out these studies and for providing much of the infrastructure necessary for their implementation. We also thank the Botany Department of University of Peradeniya and the Tropical Resources Institute of the Yale School of Forestry and Environmental Studies. Financial support came from the United States Aid for International Development and from the International Foundation for Science of Sweden.

Literature Cited

Ashton, P.S. 1964. *Ecological Studies in the Mixed Dipterocarp Forests of Brunei State.* Oxford Forest Memoirs.

Ashton, P.S. 1969. Speciation among tropical trees: some deductions in the light of recent evidence. *Biol. J. Linn. Soc. London* 1: 155-196.

Ashton, P.M.S. (in prep.) *Establishment and Growth of Co-occuring Species within Shorea Section Doona under Contrasting Moisture and Light Regimes.* Ph.D. thesis. School of Forestry and Environmental Studies, Yale University.

Ashton, P.M.S. and P.S. Ashton. (in press). Plant resources for agroforestry systems in the Asian tropics. *In* P.K. Khosla and W.D. Bentley, eds. *Agroforestry Systems for South Asia.* Oxford University Press, New Delhi, India.

Baillie, I.C. and P.S. Ashton. 1983. Some soil aspects of the nutrient cycle in mixed dipterocarp forests in Sarawak. *In* S.L. Sutton, T.C. Whitmore and C. Chadwick, eds. *Tropical Rain Forest: Ecology and Management*, pp. 347-356. Blackwell Scientific Publ. Oxford.

Beard, J.S. 1944. Climax vegetation in tropical America. *Ecol.* 25: 127-158.

Becker, P., L.W. Lee, E.D. Rothman and W.D. Hamilton. 1985. Seed predation and co-existence of tree species: Hubbell's models revisited. *Oikos* 44: 382-390.

Black, G.A., T. Dobzhansky and C. Pavan. 1950. Some attempts to estimate species diversity and population density of trees in Amazonian forests. *Bot. Gaz.* 111: 413-425.

Boonkird, S.A., E.C.M. Fernandes and P.K.R. Nair. 1984. Forest villages: an agroforestry approach to rehabilitating forest land degraded by shifting cultivation in Thailand. *Agroforestry Systems* 2: 87-102.

Bormann, F.H. and G.E. Likens. 1979. *Pattern and Process in a Forested Ecosystem.* Springer Verlag, New York.

Bourdeau, P.F. 1954. Oak seedling ecology determining segregation of species in Piedmont oak hickory forests. *Ecol. Monogr.* 24: 297-320.

Brandis, Sir D. 1897. *Forestry in India.* Empire Press, London.

Brunig, E.F. 1969. Forestry on tropical podozols and related soils. *Trop. Ecol.* 10: 45-58.

Budowski, G. 1961. *Studies on Forest Succession in Costa Rica and Panama*. Unpubl. Ph.D. thesis. School of Forestry and Environmental Studies, Yale University.

Champion, Sir H.G. and S.K. Seth. 1968. *General Silviculture of India*. Govt. of India Press, Delhi.

Clements, F.E. 1916. *Plant Succession: an Analysis of Development of Vegetation*. Carnegie Institute, Washington DC.

Davis, T.A.W. and P.W. Richards. 1933. The vegetation of Moraballi Creek, British Guyana: an ecological study of a limited area of tropical rain forest. Part I. *J. Ecol.* 21: 350-384.

Davis, T.A.W. and P.W. Richards. 1934. The vegetation of Moraballi Creek, British Guyana: an ecological study of a limited area of tropical rain forest. Part II. *J. Ecol.* 22: 106-155.

Denslow, J.S. 1980. Gap partitioning among tropical trees. *Biotropica* 12: 47-55.

De Rosayro, R.A. 1954. A reconnaissance of Sinharaja Rain Forest. *The Ceylon Forester* 1: 68-74.

De Zoysa, N.D., C.V.S. Gunatilleke and I.A.U.N. Gunatilleke. 1988. Comparative phytosociology of natural and modified rain forest sites in Sinharaja MAB Reserve, Sri Lanka. *In* A. Gomez-Pompa, T.C. Whitmore and M. Hadley, eds. *Rain Forest Regeneration and Management.*, pp. 154-168. Man and the Biosphere Series 7. UNESCO, Paris.

Drury, W.H. and I.C.T. Nisbet. 1973. Succession. *J. Arnold Arbor* 54: 331-368.

Egler, F.E. 1954. Vegetation science concepts. Initial floristic composition - factor in old field vegetation development. *Vegetatio* 4: 412-417.

Ewel, J.J. 1980. Tropical succession: manifold routes to maturity. *Biotropica* 12: 2-7.

Federov, A.A. 1966. The structure of tropical rain forest and speciation in the humid tropics. *J. Ecol.* 54: 1-11.

Gunatilleke, C.V.S. and Gunatilleke, I.A.U.N. 1981. The floristic composition of Sinharaja Rain Forest - A rain forest in Sri Lanka with special reference to endemics and dipterocarps. *Malays. For.* 44: 386-396.

Harper, J.L. 1961. Approach to the study of plant competition. *Symp. Soc. Exp. Biol.* 15: 1-39.

Harper, J.L. 1964. The nature and consequence of interference amongst plants. *Proc. XI Int. Congr. Genet. 1963* 2: 465-482.

Harper, J.L. 1977. *The Population Biology of Plants*. Academic Press, London.

Hart, R.D. 1980. A natural ecosystem analog approach to the design. *Biotropica* 12: 73-82.

Holdridge, L.R. 1959. Ecological indications of the need for a new approach to tropical land use. *Econ. Bot.* 13: 271-280.

Hubbell, S.P. 1979. Tree dispersion, abundance and diversity in a tropical dry forest. *Science* 203: 1299-1309.

Hubbell, S.P. and R.B. Foster. 1986. Biology, chance and history and the structure of tropical rain forest tree communities. *In* J. Diamond and T.J. Case, eds. *Community Ecology,* pp. 314-324. Harper & Row, New York.

Janzen, D.H. 1971. Seed predation by animals. *Ann. Rev. Ecol. Syst.* 2: 465-492.

Janzen, D.H. 1974. Tropical blackwater rivers, animals and mast fruiting by the Dipterocarpaceae. *Biotropica* 6: 69-103.

Marks, P.L. 1974. The role of pin cherry (*Prunus pensylvanica* L.) in the maintenance of stability in northern hardwood ecosystems. *Ecol. Monogr.* 44: 73-88.

Mergen, F. and J.R. Vincent. 1987. *Natural Management of Tropical Moist Forests: Silvicultural and Management Prospects of Sustained Utilization.* School of Forestry and Environmental Studies, Yale University.

NAS (National Academy of Sciences). 1980. *Fuelwood Crops: Shrub and Tree Species for Energy Production.* NAS, Washington DC.

Oliver, C.D. 1981. Forest development in North America following major disturbances. *J. For. Ecol. Mgt.* 3: 169-182.

Peeris, C.V.S. 1975. *The Ecology of the Endemic Tree Species of Sri Lanka in Relation to their Conservation.* Ph.D. Thesis. University of Aberdeen, Scotland.

Safford, L.O. and S.M. Filip. 1974. Biomass and nutrient content of a 4-year old fertilized and unfertilized northern hardwood stand. *Can. J. For. Res.* 4: 549-554.

Stark, N., 1970. The nutrient content of plants and soils from Brazil and Surinam. *Biotropica* 2: 51-60.

Trenbath, R.B. 1975. Diversity or be damned? *Ecologist* 5: 76-83.

USDA Soil Conservation Survey. 1975. *USDA Soil Taxonomy: A Basic System of Soil Classification for Making and Interpreting Soil Surveys.* USDA Ag. Handbook 436. US Govt. Printing Office, Washington DC.

van Steenis, C.G.G.J. 1958. Rejuvenation as a factor for judging the status of vegetation types: the biological nomad theory. *Proc. Symp. Humid Tropics Vegetation, Kandy:* 121-218.

van Steenis, C.G.G.J. 1969. Plant speciation in Malesia with special reference to the theory of non-adaptive saltatory evolution in speciation in tropical environments. *Biol. J. Linn. Soc. London* 1: 97-138.

Watt, A.S. 1919. On the causes of failure of natural regeneration in British oakwoods. *J. Ecol.* 7: 173-203.

Watt, A.S. 1947. Pattern and process in the plant community. *J. Ecol.* 35: 1-22.

Whittaker, R.H. 1975. *Communities and Ecosystems.* MacMillan Press, New York.

Whitmore, T.C. 1982. On pattern and process in forests. *In* E. I. Newman, ed. *The Plant Community as a Working Mechanism,* pp. 45-60. Blackwell Scientific Publ. Oxford.

Whitmore, T.C. 1984. *Tropical Rain Forests of the Far East*. Clarendon Press, Oxford.

Wyatt-Smith, J. 1963. *Manual of Malayan Silviculture for Inland Forests*. (2 Vols.) Malay Forest Records 23.

Proceedings of the International and Interdisciplinary Symposium
ECOLOGY AND LANDSCAPE MANAGEMENT IN SRI LANKA
W. Erdelen, C. Preu, N. Ishwaran, C.M. Madduma Bandara (eds.)
Colombo, Sri Lanka, 12-26 March 1990
© 1993
Margraf Scientific Books, D-97985 Weikersheim
ISBN 3-8236-1182-8

Planning Constraints in Development and Management of Ecologically Sustainable Land Use and Conservation Farming in the Hill Country of Sri Lanka

J.S. GUNASEKERA

Abstract

Ecologically sustainable land use and conservation systems that have been developed to arrest the degradation of Sri Lanka's landscape are illustrated. The main constraint, however, is not lack of know-how, but constraints on the implementation of effective landscape management programs. The constraints are institutional and non-technical in nature. Institutional aspects primarily include the lack of a firm and coherent state policy with strong government support and the lack of an agency which could plan and coordinate activities utilizing existing financial and technical resources and collaborating with non-governmental organizations and local people. The non-technical aspects have historical, economic, social and political dimensions. Historically, they result from events connected with the establishment of large-scale plantation and the expropriation of peasant lands. Economically, the peasant farmer is unable to meet the cost of conservation. Socially, scarcity of land to meet the demands of an increasing population is a major constraint. From a political point of view, we should develop and implement a long-term policy of more appropriate land use and adopt conservation measures.

Introduction

In spite of its relatively small size, Sri Lanka is characterized by a number of drainage basins, natural regions, landforms and landscape features. 103 river basins or watersheds have been identified in the island. They radiate in all directions from the central highlands. Most of these have their upper catchments and headwaters in the hill country. The largest of these is the Mahaweli River, both in terms of its catchment area and its length.

Physiography

Several landscape features are found in the Mahaweli Catchment Area.

Natural Regions

Several natural regions have been identified in the hill country; Central Mahaweli Valley and Knuckles Range in the north, the upland platform in the east, the central highlands in the south and the wet zone uplands in the west. Several subunits of these have also been identified, e.g. the Uva Basin and Lunugala Ridges in the east, the highland core in the south, the Dolosbage Ridges, Kandy Plateau and Matale uplands in the west. These natural regions comprise varied, complex and heterogenous landscapes.

Landforms

The hill country landscapes encompass a number of landforms, identified as mountains, escarpments, hills and ridges, ridges and valleys, and ridge and valley bottoms. The more important of these have been categorized as extremely steep mountain ridges, steep to very steep mountain ridges, foothills, and foothill slopes of mountain, undulating to rolling valleys and plains with low rounded hills, valleys with flat to gently undulating colluvio-alluvial bottoms, steeply dissected plateaus or benches with rounded hills, hilly plateaus or benches with low rounded hills or undulating to rolling topography and escarpments with precipitous slopes and cliffs.

Soils

Seventeen main soil groups have been identified and mapped in Sri Lanka. Of these, four main soil groups with seven associate soil groups have been identified and mapped for a section of the Upper Mahaweli Catchment. Soils have also been mapped for the following areas; the Kotmale subcatchment, Mahaweli (Upper Catchment), Hapuwela-Naran Ela small watershed, the Leanwella small watershed, Belihul Oya subwatershed, and the peripheral area of the Victoria Reservoir. Soils identified are the red yellow pod zolics, immature brown loams, the reddish brown latosolics, reddish brown earths, wet mountain regosols, shallow lothosols, humic glei, half bog and bog and alluvials.

Topography

The land rises in the hill country from an elevation of 150 m to over 2500 m in the Piduruthalagala Ridge which includes the highest peak at over 2524 meters. Other high ridges predominant in the hill country include the highland core subregion, the Knuckles Range and the Lunugala Ridges subregion. The slopes are mostly steep to very steep generally ranging from 30% to 60% and with slopes of over 100% in some locations. Gentle slopes of less than 20% are relatively few in number. Five slope classes have been identified and mapped (1: 63,360) for some watersheds which are representative of the hill country. They are the Kotmale watershed, Upper Mahaweli watershed, Belihul Oya subwatershed and Hapuwela-Naran Ela small watershed. A slope map (scale 1: 10,000) indicating the five slope classes is being prepared for the Victoria Catchment under the Victoria Land Use and Conservation Project by the ODA (Overseas Development Authority of the UK).

Climate

Climate variation has a significant influence on the settlement, utilization, development of farming systems and management of hill country landscapes. Rainfall patterns are influenced primarily by two factors, namely the monsoonal winds and physiography. There are two monsoonal and two intermonsoonal seasons. During the SW monsoon (May to September) heavy rainfall occurs over the hill country. The intermonsoon from October to November is also referred to as the autumnal interim monsoon. The NE monsoon (December to February) is a period of heavy and maximum precipitation in the central Mahaweli Valley and slopes of the Knuckles Range. The second intermonsoon (March to April) where the rainfall is convectional has also been referred to as a vernal intermonsoon.

The hill country receives the highest rainfall particularly along the southwestern edge due to its exposure to the full force of the monsoon. It contains the high rainfall area where the mean annual rainfall is 5080 mm. The Knuckles Range of the hill country also receives a rainfall of over 4570 mm. However, some sections of the hill country are largely influenced by the NE monsoon and some locations within these sections have less than 140 mm of rain. They are subject to a dry spell which has profound effects on vegetation and farming systems. Rainfall in these drier locations is unevenly distributed and variable. High intensity storms frequently cause erosion hazards.

Seasonal changes in temperature are small and not marked, thus having little effect on landscape management and cultivation. However, variations in temperatures are marked with increasing elevation, e.g. mean temperatures range between 23°C and 26°C in Kandy at 500 m and drop to between 18°C and 22°C at Diyathalawa at 1300 m falling even lower to between 14°C and 17°C at Nuwara Eliya at 2000 m.

Drainage

The hill country area is drained by some of the principle rivers of the island whose upper catchments are located therein. They are the Mahaweli Ganga, Kirindi Oya, Walawe Ganga, Kalu Ganga and Maha Oya. The Mahaweli encompasses the largest extents in terms of length, area and number of watersheds and subwatersheds. The discharge into the Mahaweli in the hill country has been estimated at 76,000 cfs with a maximum of 129,000 cfs and a minimum of 49,000 cfs and an annual average yield of 4,591,593 ac ft over 27 years. The annual average yield of other major rivers in the region are 3,351,421 ac ft (Kelani Ganga), 2,797,564 ac ft (Walawe Ganga) and 597,035 ac ft (Maha Oya). Thus an estimated annual average yield of over 8 million ac ft characterizes the region, even if only some of the major rivers are taken into account. This indicates the importance and significance of these sections of hill country in respect to the yield and supply of water resources.

Natural Vegetation

The natural vegetation in the area is primarily forest and grassland. Much of this natural vegetation, particularly forests, have been substituted by plantation agriculture and to some extent by peasant agriculture. However, there are relatively large extents of forest reserves or proposed reserves and other forest areas.

Forest cover extends to an area of 55,920 ha in the wet zone sections of the hill country in the Mahaweli Catchment Area. This comprises approximately 19% of the total area. Forest cover in the intermediate zone sections of this catchment extends to an area of 46,765 ha or approximately 10% of the total area and comprises the central hill country including the Knuckles Massif, Kandy Plateau and the lower Uva Basin. An extent of approximately 36,423 ha is reserved in 39 reserves in the wet zone and another 2962 ha are found in 8 reserves in the intermediate zone.

There are also extensive areas of grassland in the hill country. Open grasslands in the hill country have been referred to as wet patana grasslands and dry patana grasslands. The former are located in the high plains and the latter in the Uva Basin, Knuckles Range and parts of the Central Mahaweli Valley and the Kandy Plateau. The wet patana grasslands are confined to the Horton, Moon and Elk Plains and in areas near Pattipola, Ambewela and Agrabopats. Soils of these grasslands form a thick humic layer and are located in less steeply sloping areas rather than in dry patana grasslands. The wet patana grasslands have a distinct floristic composition. The only tree encountered in the formation is the *Rhododendrom arboreum*, var. *nilagirica* often covered with the lichen *Usnea barbaa*. The dry patana grasslands, too, have a distinct floristic composition characterized by a lack of trees.

Land Use Types

The main land use types in the hill country landscapes are plantation and village agriculture. Tea plantations are generally well managed and are under the authority of state agencies and private owners. Although many tea lands are relatively well managed, there are several stretches where management is poor. There are also considerable extents of small tea holdings which are low in productivity and are subject to erosion. Village lands primarily consist of paddy tracts, associated homesteads and mixed gardens, comprising tree crops, some areas for arable cropping and gardens for marketable crops. In addition to plantation and village agricultural lands, there are also settlement and urban areas, bazars and recreation sites. Some of these lands in village areas have been brought under plantation crops. Although traditionally other crops were planted. Land settlement has also taken place under village expansion schemes implemented under the Land Development Ordinance.

Some of the land use categories are suitable and ecologically sustainable, e.g. mixed gardens, tree crops and paddy tracts. The same might be argued for the better managed tea estates. However, the poorly-managed estates in their present condition are uneconomical and ecologically non-sustainable. This also applies to steep lands which consist of small tea holdings and seasonally cultivated tracts. It is therefore necessary to bring about changes towards a more appropriate use of lands which are eroded, marginal or uneconomic. It is also necessary to improve the productivity of lands which could remain in their present use but are poorly managed. This particularly applies to both large and small tea holdings and to land under seasonal crops.

A large area of tea land is solely under the cultivation of tea as the only plantation crop and is under systematic management. Tea cultivation is therefore one of the most organized forms of agriculture practised in Sri Lanka. There are, however, large extents of tea lands under small holdings which are in a relatively poorly-managed state. But plantation lands comprise mostly of tea estates that are under state or private ownership. The tea lands form a homogenous cover in the elevations and upper sections of the catchments in the main Upper Mahaweli, Kotmale and Hulu Ganga. The terrain is rugged with steep to very steep slopes in the range of 30%-85% and with complex landforms in elevations ranging from 350 m to 2000 m. Any loss of tea land, due to changes in land use resulting from relocation and rehabilitation of peasant farmers, could be easily compensated by replanting and rehabilitating a third of the extent of other lands or estates elsewhere with high-yielding VP tea.

In spite of the special attention that has been given to this land use category small tea holdings remain in a poor state of management and are vulnerable to erosion. Many of these lands have been degraded to a marginal or submarginal condition. It is therefore necessary that these areas be improved by a change in land use to other crops or by reforestation. Eroded land might have to be surveyed and categorized according to the following types before better management systems may be introduced: (1) land that could remain under tea cultivation if improved with soil conservation measures including the introduction of infilling, shade and other management practices (this could be referred to the STHA (Small Tea Holdings Association) for inclusion under their subsidy program and priority treatment given), (2) land that should be diverted to tree crops, and (3) land that should be reforested (this could be referred to the Forest Department for inclusion under its Social and Community Forestry Programme.

In contrast to plantation lands located in the upper sections of the catchments, village lands are located mainly in the lower sections and valley bottoms. They are generally found along basal and mid-slopes, except in a few cases where they are situated on the upper slopes and crests of ridges. The village landscape is comprised of traditional mixed and homestead gardens, tree crops, highland seasonal crop areas, land under tea cultivation and the associated paddy lands which extend along the bottom and sides of the valleys.

Mixed gardens are of approximately the same composition as homestead gardens, but the trees are less densely planted and several tree species remain. They are considered commercial holdings, being considerably larger (0.25-2.0 ha or more) than homestead gardens. Mixed gardens are mostly confined to lower parts of the catchments and are closely associated with the villages. They are also present in other areas, especially in sheltered valleys and lands adjacent to paddy fields. The main crops are coconut, coffee, nutmeg and cloves. Fruit trees like jak, breadfruit, orange, durian, atha (*Annona* sp.) are mainly grown for domestic consumption but also for commercial purposes. Homestead gardens usually consist of coconut, jak, kitul, arecanut, mango, breadfruit and other trees including timber trees. A lower storey of coffee, spices, lime and bananas can also be found. From a conservation perspective, mixed and homestead gardens are favorable land use practices. The multiple land use, the three-tier vegetation, floristic composition and other aspects provide a sustainable and productive land use system which is ideally suited to the climatic and terrain conditions.

Highlands that are used for growing non-irrigated crops (dry cropping) year after year and may include crops which are found in chenas (shifting cultivation) as well as some others. These crops grow on the slopes of hills and are often marked with permanent borders. These lands have primarily been cultivated since ancient times for the growing of finger millet (Kurakkan), maize and other dry crops. These areas are seasonally cultivated with tobacco, vegetables and annual upland crops during the Maha season.

There are also rainfed and irrigated paddy fields. In irrigated lands, water is usually delivered by winding irrigation canals that take off from anicuts constructed across streams and then cross the land irrigating paddies below. Paddy cultivation is primarily a peasant activity, and land used for this purpose is almost invariably found in valley bottoms and basal slopes which are close to home gardens.

Market gardens are used for growing irrigated crops throughout the year and in close vicinity of towns often within the limits of an urban area itself. Vegetable crops are grown in rotation. They include exotics like carrots, beats, leeks, etc, but also local varieties. In recent years methods for growing market garden crops have changed. More and more market gardens ranging form 200 m^2 to one hectare in area have appeared on sloping lands formed into graded or bench terraces. Some market gardens are situated on valley bottoms.

Many forest plantations have been established to meet specific management purposes, e.g. extraction of timber, fuelwood, protection of water sources and reforestation of degraded land. The main species belong to the genera *Eukalyptus*, *Pinus* and *Albizia* species. Several other species are currently being tested.

A large extent of land is under cities, towns and bazars including residential, commercial and industrial areas. This type of land use is not only important as centers of habitat, work places and administration but also in relation to its influence on erosion, pollution and drainage. Land set aside for recreational purposes such as botanical gardens, parks, playgrounds, sports grounds and sanctuaries also form an important part of this land use. It is considered an essential component and should therefore be managed and maintained in the interest of the community and quality of life.

Water bodies such as lakes, reservoirs and tanks form an essential and integral part of the landscape and thus constitute an important land use, which is utilized for the purpose of domestic water supply, irrigation, power and recreation. It is therefore important that these be protected and maintained and that measures are taken against their sedimentation and pollution. Riparian lands adjoining streams and rivers have to be considered as an important land use influencing siltation, pollution and stream flow. Therefore, these areas should also be maintained and protected. Legislation necessary to ensure their protection by prescribing the width of strips of riparian land needing such protection has already been proposed.

Landscape Degradation

One of the salient features that could be linked to landscape degradation is erosion resulting from deforestation and cultivation of steep and unstable slopes contrary to the use capability of those lands. Landscape degradation could therefore be considered separately under deforestation, erosion and deposition.

Deforestation

Extensive deforestation that has taken place in many locations has resulted in a treeless landscape, water scarcity and sediment-generating land. The terrestrial and aquatic environment has thus been degraded and polluted rendering it inhospitable and affecting quality of life. Where there is adequate forest cover and where land use has been planned with the incorporation of conservation practices, soil erosion is reduced to minimum, infiltration increased and runoff controlled. This prevents the adverse effects of flash floods, droughts and the sedimentation of reservoirs.

Forest cover is a key factor in watershed management and water yield and contributes to the retension of water in the soil subsequent to infiltration and hence the maintenance of dry weather flow. It is therefore imperative that the existing forest and tree cover be maintained, improved and enriched through the protection of existing forest areas, areas proposed for reforestation and all other degraded lands.

Erosion Hazards

Considering the prevalent physiographic and climatic conditions, i.e. to the steep and rugged terrain with heavy rainfall, the area is conducive to erosion. This is aggravated further by some land use patterns and practices prevalent in the area. Practically all forms of erosion; i.e. splash, sheet, rill, and gully erosion, are present in the area and sometimes climax in gravity erosion and mass movement. Additional forms of erosion such as stream bank erosion, road erosion and site erosion also contribute to a large extent to erosion hazards and soil loss.

Data quantifying soil loss is limited. However, it has been estimated that the average annual soil loss is at 100 MT/ha. It has been estimated that the sediment carried in suspension by the Mahaweli River above Peradeniya is 132,000-833,000 MT/ha. The annual sediment contribution has been estimated at 11.5 MT/ha. It has also been estimated that there is an annual soil loss of 250 MT/ha during the replanting phases of tea. The average soil loss in tea lands for one year has been estimated at 51.93 MT/ha. The estimated soil loss for red-yellow pod solic soils per year is 178 MT/ha for slopes with a gradient of 21%-40% and 415 MT/ha for slopes over 40%.

Sedimentation and Deposition

Deposition leading to sedimentation has taken place at several locations. The area around Polgolla could be treated as a case study. Sedimentation at Polgolla behind the barrage is considered acute and it is estimated that approximately 40% of its storage capacity has been lost over a 10-year period due to sediment build-up. Sources of sediment originate in lands under poor management and the main effect is a loss in storage capacity of the reservoir. If further sedimentation takes place and some of the soil particles escape into the turbines at the hydropower station, serious damage to the installation as a whole may result. Sedimentation also lowers the esthetic value of the area. Removal of sediment by dredging is only a temporary solution as the problem is likely to recur. The optimal solution lies in reducing sediment production at its source. The costs of reducing sediment release from catchment areas could be met from funds saved by foregoing dredging operations. The adoption of conservation measures in catchment areas to minimize erosion in specific locations of sediment origin, assessment of the causes of sediment production and the implementation of necessary mitigative measures are all urgently needed.

Landscape Management

Landscape management should take into account conservation needs, conservation planning and implementation of plans.

Conservation Needs

Conservation strategies should be designed giving due consideration to the factors influencing erosion. These factors include rainfall, resistance of soil to detachment and topography. Erosion is a natural phenemnon and its extent is determined primarily by rainfall and soil type. Therefore, the development and adoption of conservation strategies and measures that would buffer and control erosion is essential. This could be done by adopting strategies that would protect the ground cover of the soil, enhance the resistance of the soil to detachment and increase the soil's absorptive capacity. Agronomic conservation measures that provide for ground cover include the addition of organic matter including mulch and plant residue and the use of tillage practices which cause minimal disturbance to the soil. Topographic factors influencing erosion could be controlled through slope modifications with respect to both gradient and length by manicuring, bench terracing, placing obstructions such as drains and bunds at specific intervals.

Land management is a key area where one can exercise the greatest restraint and control over land use and conservation practices. The designing of farming systems and cropping practices that are compatible with the topography and the use capability of the land is a key objective in the management of the land and can be achieved in several ways.

Conservation Planning

Conservation needs, land use aspects, conservation farming systems and the conservation measures, referred to here, should be incorporated into a conservation plan for a given area. The formulation and development of such a plan is considered an essential feature of landscape management in the hill country. A conservation plan should portray the pertinent land and water information of the area it covers. This should include information on major soil characteristics such as depth and texture, and associated land features such as slope, erosion, stoniness and rockiness. It should also include information on land use potential, actual land use patterns, locations where changes in land use are necessary, conservation measures and when and where they should be applied together with an indication of their type and specification.

Implementation and Implementing Agencies

The implementation of conservation measures has to be undertaken within three categories of land use; plantation lands, peasant lands and non-agricultural lands, and reserves and recreation areas. Implementation poses the greatest problem in policy, plans and programs involved in landscape management. If these are to be effective they have to be implemented.

The principle agencies which administer, advise or are in some way connected with land use management are the State Plantation Cooperatives, Small Tea Holdings Development Association, the Agriculture Department and Agrarian Services Department, Minor Export

Crops Department, the Forest Department, the Road Development Authority, the Urban Development Authority and the Housing and Construction Department.

Constraints

The necessary expertise required to implement the proposed changes in land use does indeed exist, but there are nonetheless several constraints. They are both technical and non-technical in nature.

Technical Constraints

Technical constraints refer to the training of personnel, equipment and mobility. The scientific and technical management of landscapes requires trained personnel. These persons should be trained to carry out feasibility studies, use capability studies, investigation surveys, land use and conservation planning and demarcation, and the formulation and implementation of conservation measures. The inadequacy of technical equipment of all types, which is a necessary tool for the technician, is a severe constraint. Another serious handicap is mobility. Vehicles are expensive even if manufactured locally. A part of the solution would be local recruitment training and stationing personnel within areas of vulnerable landscape, thus reducing mobility to a minimum. However, some vehicles are needed. International donor agencies could help here.

Non-Technical Constraints

Non-technical constraints refer to the political, social and economic obstacles hindering conservation and landscape management. The introduction of plantation industry resulted in the acquisition of a large extent of hitherto peasant land. This created a landless peasantry through denying them their very lands. This was further aggravated by the establishment of resettlement for expatriate laborers on these lands, but also by the lack of employment opportunities for these peasants on plantation lands. I suggest relocation and rehabilitation of the landless peasantry on a section of some of these plantation lands which, in any case, belonged to them at sometime in the past.

High density of population with limited land resources and non-availability of suitable land results in the inevitable use and cultivation of steep and fragile landscapes. Much of the lands under state ownership, referred to as "crown land" and "reserved land", has been encroached upon leading to clearing, cultivation and mismanagement. This is generally overlooked.

Another factor is that of land ownership and land tenure. Everyone likes to have his own piece of land. This is ethical and traditional, also partly historical. It is also justifiable when there is no other alternative. However, often the cultivator does not own the land he farms; he is only a tenant farmer or share cropper. Therefore he does not see the value of protecting the land and of good management as he does not own it and may lose it. On the other hand, the right of land ownership has led to fragmentation and the surfacing of non-economic holdings where little or no attention is given to the management and productivity. A solution may be to consolidate lands, but examples are few and not altogether a success story. There is also a reluctance to move and reluctance to change.

Ethical, scientific and technical aspects of sound management of landscapes may mean little to a poor farmer eeking out an existence and struggling for survival. His needs are immediate and he is thus unable to take risks and invest in long-term objectives, however profitable they may be, and he cannot be expected to do so. This applies more than anything else to land utilization management and conservation. Dudal illustrates this; "... the first requirement for efficient soil conservation is that income from the farm is large enough to provide a sufficient proportion for maintenance of the soil capital." This naturally leads to the next question; who should invest and meet the cost of conservation? This has to be considered not only from the point of view of the farmer but also from the point of view of those downstream, who are affected by sedimentation and floods. An answer to this problem has been provided by Hudson "that in countries where farmers are generally poor the ability to contribute towards cost is less or non-existent. In this case the answer has to be that since it is in the long-term interest of the state, nation or community which requires that soil should be conserved, then it is the state who should pay".

There are also political constraints to the implementation of adequate land use practices and landscape management. Conservation and landscape management according to the dictates of ecology is not considered feasible, and it may take years before we can see the benefits. Although such disciplines are now accepted in principle, in practice, however little attention is paid and only little support is given. Thus current plans and programs can have very little effect.

There is still another constraint to adequate landscape management which is related to quality of life, in particular its esthetic and spiritual aspects. No monetary value can be given to the beauty, serenity, tranquillity and contentment of a particular landscape when it is protected and well-managed either in its natural state or under some other land use. Land use patterns have been maintained and cared for from generation to generation. However, only today's generation is guilty of permitting the degradation of landscapes as a result of mismanagement during the last decades of this century. It is therefore the duty of this generation to take cognizance of this fact and to ensure the protection of these lands so that a well-managed and protected landscape can be handed down to future generations.

Landscape Management Strategy

The present condition of many hill country landscapes is in conflict with the principles of scientific landscape management. Are we to accept this situation and remain complacent? The answer is obviously no, or we will be held liable for this misadventure and its consequences. A landscape management policy and program should be formulated, planned and meaningfully implemented before it is too late. A landscape management strategy could be briefly outlined as follows:

1. The non-technical constraints in relation to social and economic aspects have to be given as much consideration as the technical constraints. There must be an easing of pressure on land, security of tenure, relocation and rehabilitation of the landless and those in critical locations and available funds to meet the costs of conservation and changes in land use.
2. The technical constraints have to be eased in relation to the training of personnel and their mobility.
3. The formulation and promotion of a program of awareness in landscape management is required.
4. People's participation in all relevant aspects of landscape management must be mobilized and enlisted.
5. A land use and conservation program incorporating conservation farming systems under an overall landscape management policy and plan must be formulated and executed.
6. Landscape management programs involving a multidisciplinary and interdisciplinary approach must be coordinated through the establishment of a suitable institution or agency or standing committee for this purpose.

Proceedings of the International and Interdisciplinary Symposium
ECOLOGY AND LANDSCAPE MANAGEMENT IN SRI LANKA
W. Erdelen, C. Preu, N. Ishwaran, C.M. Madduma Bandara (eds.)
Colombo, Sri Lanka, 12-26 March 1990
© 1993
Margraf Scientific Books, D-97985 Weikersheim
ISBN 3-8236-1182-8

Decreasing Extent of Tea Plantations in Sri Lanka

Chance for Agricultural Diversification or Ecological Threat?

R. HUMBEL

Abstract

Since 1956, the extent of Sri Lanka's tea cultivation has been continuously reduced by an overall amount of 20%. Political, economical and agroecological reasons are responsible for this reduction which, however, has proved to be far from uniform in the different regions of the country. The Southern Galle and Matara Districts have experienced a significant increase of area cultivated with tea (mostly by smallholders). Other areas, especially those with tea cultivations in the midlands, are characterized by decreases ranging from 20% to 50% of the formerly cultivated area. Detailed investigations in the central core-area of midland and highland tea cultivation (Kandy and Nuwara Eliya Districts) revealed the extent and location of land use transformation in such areas. Physical, climatic and other ecological variables as well as economic and political factors are responsible for these transfomations. The changes from tea to rubber, minor export crops, forest plantations, rangeland, sparsely used cropland and natural forest since 1956 are investigated and adopted as six indicators for an evaluation of the success and extent of agricultural diversification programs and of ecological hazards. Small areas of former tea land were successfully redeveloped into multicrop systems (crops like vegetables, tobacco, coffee, cacao, spices), fuelwood plantations and settlements to provide housing and other facilities for a growing population. However, substantial amounts of tea land were just abandoned and left fallow. Such sparsely used areas, covered with grass, ferns and scrub, are susceptible to such ecological hazards as soil erosion and landslides, particularly if located on steep slopes. It is recommended that greater efforts be directed towards an ecologically stable and an economically profitable utilization of this land. Such projects could contribute to the conservation of the few remaining reserves of tropical rain forest by lessening the pressure on forested land for new development and by securing fuelwood and timber supplies from planted trees rather than from the destruction of natural forest.

Introduction

The ideas and findings presented in this paper are to a large extent part of a research study started in 1986 on the subject of "Changes of the Area under Tea Cultivation in Sri Lanka since 1956." This study has been carried out under the technical supervision of Prof. Dr. K.I. Itten, Department of Geography, University of Zurich, together with the Tea Research Institute of Sri Lanka, especially under its Deputy Director (Research), Dr. S. Kulasegaram, and the officers of the TRI Land Use Unit, Messrs. M.B.A. Perera and J.P. Fonseka. This study was completed in 1991 and published as a Ph.D. thesis.

A preliminary result of this study is a comprehensive Tea Map of Sri Lanka, which was printed by the Survey Department of Sri Lanka and published in late 1988. This map shows areas under tea cultivation in 1956 and in the 1980s as well as corresponding area increases and decreases. Therefore, the map provides an overview of the spatial distribution of the changes in area of land under tea cultivation in Sri Lanka since 1956. The map is accompanied by a list of figures showing the area of land under tea cultivation for the ten Sri Lankan administrative districts where tea is cultivated.

Map and statistics both reveal that there is undoubtedly an overall trend towards a decrease in the area of land under tea cultivation in Sri Lanka since 1956, amounting to a loss of about 20% of former tea land by the early 1980s. The distribution of these areas showing a decrease is, however, less than uniform in different tea-growing areas of the country. While the areas in the northern midlands, the central highlands, the Uva Basin as well as the Sabaragamuwa Province all confirm the general declining trend, we can observe remarkable increases in tea cultivation in the south. These increases reach 50% or more in the districts of Galle and Matara. They comprise typical smallholdings which have come increasingly under tea cultivation since the tea boom in the 1950s. Due to general population pressure and the increasing demand for land, employment and income, settlements as well as agricultural areas were considerably expanded in these formerly rather loosely populated areas. Whenever tea prices were high and the expected profits from tea were better than for other crops such as rubber and cinnamon, tea cultivation was extended partly at the expense of other agricultural commodities.

While the traditional high-quality and high-yielding tea areas in the districts of Nuwara Eliya, Badulla and Ratnapura experienced decreases in tea land close to the entire country's average of 20%, the oldest tea areas in the northern and western midlands of the Kandy, Matale and Kegalle Districts account greatly for the total reduction in tea land, showing up to 50% less tea acreage now (1980) than in 1956. They are often neglected and planted with old, sometimes degenerated and usually low-yielding seedling tea, and are therefore economically less attractive. Planted frequently on steep slopes without much consideration for soil conservation measures like contour planting, terracing, proper drainage and shade trees, extensive soil erosion has occurred in many places, which, in a vicious circle, again has had negative implications on the vigor of the tea plants, on the size and density of the bushes and on the quantity and quality of tea produced. Negligence of such tea plantations accelerated soil loss and diminished the possible profits to be gained from tea to such a degree that the planting, fertilizing, maintaining and finally the plucking of the tea fields were completely abandoned.

Materials and Methods

The compilation of an inventory of land use changes countrywide requires comprehensive and thematically consistent coverage of the data sources selected to perform such a study. In addition, to detect changes in the geographic distribution and extent of such a land use category, at least two sets of data based on different years are required. Sri Lanka is particularly lucky to possess two such complete data sets: the land use map series of 1956/61 and a similar series of 1979/90. Both land use map series are based on the interpretation of aerial photographs. The data source of the first series is an islandwide coverage of 1: 40,000 aerial photographs taken in 1956, which were assembled as semi-controlled photographic

Table 1. Area statistics on tea cultivation in Sri Lanka.

Administrative District	Present Tea Cultivation Reference Year	Area (ha)	Cultivation in 1956 Area (ha)	Changes since 1956
Kurunegala	1981	270	280	4%
Matale	1981	5,390	9,080	-41%
Gampaha	1981	10	30	-71%
Kegalle	1981	5,300	10,170	-48%
Kandy	1981	28,000	52,530	-47%
Nuwara Eliya	1979/81	60,620	73,240	-17%
Badulla	1982	35,620	4,596	-22%
Monaragala	1982	1,150	1,800	-36%
Colombo	1981	220	240	-10%
Kalutara	1981/84	3,800	4,020	-5%
Ratnapura	1983	20,970	26,410	-21%
Galle	1983	15,740	10,570	+49%
Matara	1983	19,910	12,470	+63%
Hambantota	1983	90	90	-
Total		197,090	246,890	-20%

mosaics and finally published in 1960/61 in 74 map sheets of 1: 63,360 (1 inch: 1 mile) scale. The new series uses aerial photographs of different scales. Landsat satellite images served as a geometric base for the compilation of the interpretation of these photographs. This series is published district by district at the scale of 1: 100,000. Maps of both series can be obtained from the Survey Department of Sri Lanka. Since the new land use maps are based on aerial photographs from different years, this inconsistency in time is also characteristic of the results (Tab. 1).

After the necessary scale adjustments, corresponding map sheets of these two series were superimposed one onto the other on a light table, and subsequently, the areas mapped as under tea cultivation were compared. Corresponding to this rather simple, visual and analog methodical approach, similar visual, practice-oriented methods were selected for correcting geometric incompatibilities between the map series and for solving various other problems. Increases and decreases in the area under tea cultivation were mapped separately, and so were all relevant land use classes which have either preceded or followed tea cultivation. All these different types of changes were divided among the administrative areas of which they were part and finally measured using an electronic area meter in order to compile a comprehensive table of area statistics.

Spatial Distribution of Changes in Tea Area

For various reasons it was decided to adopt the administrative districts and subdistricts or the official Assistant Government Agent Divisions (AGADs) as units for the statistics as well as for the cartographic representation of results. As an additional advantage, this corresponds also to the mapping and statistics approach by the Sri Lanka/Swiss Remote Sensing Project to its land use map series 1: 100,000. Figure 1 (annexed) shows the location, size and names of all 102 AGADs relevant for tea cultivation.

Similar to the Tea Map of Sri Lanka Figure 2 (annexed) shows the area, geographic distribution and importance of land currently under tea cultivation for the different AGADs, while Figure 3 (annexed) shows the corresponding area changes. Figure 2 (annexed) shows the importance of the central highlands, especially the Ambagamuwa Korale, Nuwara Eliya and

Kotmale AGADs of the Nuwara Eliya District. There are two other regions of fairly significant importance for tea cultivation, namely the northeast of the Matara District, or the Deniyaya area, and the Uva Basin in the Badulla District. We have to be aware, though, that the uneven size of the AGADs may distort to some extent the impression given by the figures, as the shades are usually in proportion to the absolute values encountered for the particular AGADs.

Figure 3 (annexed) confirms what has been mentioned earlier about the uneven distribution of changes in tea land area. The south, mainly the Morawak Korale and Hinidum Pattuwa AGADs in the Matara and Galle Districts form the core of increases in land under tea cultivation. Such an increase also occurs, but to a lesser extent, in the Southeastern Kalutara and the Central Ratnapura Districts. Due to the very small absolute areas cultivated with tea, the increases for two AGADs of Kurunegala District are considered insignificant. The decreases are concentrated in the midlands of the Kandy and northern Kegalle Districts.

Indicators of Agricultural Diversifiation

The basic question of this entire symposium "Conflict or Compromise?" is translated for this investigation into "Diversification or ecological threat?" In order to attempt to find a reply to this crucial question, indicators shall be used to test the significance of these hypotheses. The statistics do not only apply to the land use category of tea but also include information about other land use categories related to the changes in tea cultivation, i.e. the land use types prevalent before new tea cultivations were started are analyzed as well as new land uses established on former tea land. Some of these categories and their changes in relation to tea cultivation may serve as indicators for the success of diversification, or for the significance of possible ecological dangers.

Rubber

There is an overall decrease in rubber plantations and a corresponding increase in tea, but with various regional exceptions such as in the Kegalle and Kalutara Districts (Fig. 4, annexed). The Galle and Matara Districts in southern Sri Lanka comprise the most important former rubber areas now being converted into tea land. In addition, the Atakalan Korale and Ratnapura AGADs (Ratnapura District) and the Yatiyantota AGAD (Kegalle District) have experienced the same development but on a larger scale. We can assume that during the latter half of the 1950s, the so-called "rubber boom", rubber plantations were expanded considerably, not significantly at the expense of former tea land, but in rather marginal areas. In later years, with rising tea prices and falling rubber prices, such areas, as well as new virgin land, would have been converted into tea land.

Minor export crops

Minor export crops comprise spices, coffee, cacao and certain fruit crops. Propagating their cultivation is the declared target of various agricultural diversification schemes and subsidies. We can observe that such efforts have had significant success mainly in the Kandy District and to a lesser degree also in the eastern Kegalle District, southwestern Matale District, central Ratnapura District, northeastern Galle and northwestern Matara Districts (Fig. 5, annexed). The fact that subsidies for diversification are offered irrespective of the administrative or agroecological area possibly accounts for the rather equal distribution of such diversification between the different AGADs.

Forest Plantations

Besides minor export crops, the establishment of new forest plantations is the second most important indicator for the positive effects of agricultural diversification and reduction in tea land area. The major areas of newly established forest plantations lie in the upper catchment of the Mahaweli River and its tributaries, for example, the Kotmale Oya, the upper catchment of the Kelani and Kalu Ganga (Fig. 6, annexed). Projects to protect the environment of these catchment areas, specifically in connection with the Accelerated Mahaweli Programme, and strategies to encourage tea plantations to grow their own fuelwood plantations in order to become self-sufficient in regard to energy, are thought to be responsible for this. The second most important area of new forest plantations is in the Haldummulla AGAD in the southern Badulla District where tea is planted along the agroecological margins impeding profitable cultivation, thus presenting tea farmers with an additional incentive to convert unprofitable tea land into profitable timber plantations. On the other hand, various areas, shown in dark tones in Figure 6 (annexed) experienced new tea encroachments on previous forest plantations, although to a much lesser extent in terms of size and area.

Indicators of Ecological Threat

Rangeland

We now turn to some indicators pointing to ecologically more problematic and probably unplanned and undesired transformations of former tea land. The transformation of land formerly under tea cultivation to rangeland (grass and scrub areas) is considered to be one of these. Figure 7 (annexed) shows two distinct areas where there is such a decrease due to the founding of new tea plantations. The opposite effect is observed in a large area of the highland and in the center of the island. In the southern Nuwara Eliya District, Ambagamuwa Korale, Nuwara Eliya, Kotmale AGADs, in Kandy District, primarily Pasbage Korale, Panwila and Uda Dumbara AGADs, encompassing the Knuckles area, as well as in the Haldummulla AGAD and the Imbulpe AGAD of the Ratnapura District, we notice a significant increase in rangeland on abandoned tea cultivations, thus forming large areas of a kind of semi-artificial patanas. In contrast, the central Badulla District and, to a larger extent, in the Northern Galle and Matara Districts (Hinidum Pattuwa North and South, Morawak Korale West AGADs), a significant amount of new tea land replaces former grassland. In summary, tea decreases have led to an increase of 1600 ha in rangeland in Sri Lanka.

Sparsely-Used Cropland

This category, including chena land (shifting cultivation), sparsely used rainfed upland (permanent dry cropping), and neglected and recently abandoned cultivation of plantation crops including tea, proves to be the most important one in regard to the analysis of tea area changes in terms of area and also in regard to its potential for planning measures. In the south, where we find an overall increase in tea cultivation, the welcome effect of converting such sparsely used cropland into the more intensive, profitable and possibly ecologically stable tea cultivation is indicated (Fig. 8, annexed). The traditional tea-growing districts further north, most prominently the Uda Palata and Pata Hewaheta AGADs of the Kandy District all underwent developments in the opposite direction. It is exactly these areas which provoke anxieties regarding the possible negative ecological impacts of the estimated 20% decrease in tea cultivation in Sri Lanka.

Forest

In many areas in the south of Sri Lanka, especially in the areas showing a general increase in land under tea cultivation, new tea plantations were established on former forest land. This includes areas where, in general, a negative development of tea cultivation is observed (Fig. 9, annexed). This is indeed most alarming and every effort should be made to prevent this. To a lesser extent, there are the more marginal tea AGADs where the reduction of tea areas started early so that a certain amount of former tea land has developed into a new, semi-natural, secondary type of forest. Most prominent here are the Panwila and Meda Dumbara AGADs (Knuckles Area) and the Uda Dumbara AGAD of the Kandy District as well as the Kotmale and Uda Hewaheta AGADs of the Nuwara Eliya District. Table 2 gives a statistical overview of all six indicators discussed. For reasons of simplicity, the figures given here are cumulative for the entire area of the administrative districts. It must be noted that negative figures represent a reduction in the area of land formerly under tea cultivation in favor of the new land use types listed, while positive figures stand for a corresponding increase in land under tea cultivation.

Table 2. Area changes of tea versus some indicator land use categories (ha).

Adminstrative District	Rubber	Minor Export Crops	Forest Plantations	Rangeland	Sparsely Used Cropland	Natural Matale Forest
Matale	266	-349	-427	-48	-1,856	-365
Kurunegala	14	-	-	8	-23	3
Gampaha	-	-	-	-	-10	-
Colombo	-27	-	-	-	-	-
Kegalle	-519	-266	-28	11	-3,361	51
Kandy	282	-2,061	-305	-1,653	-11,474	-2131
Nuwara Eliya	-74	-79	-1,318	-2,471	-2,722	-402
Badulla	105	-119	-613	362	-4,440	-815
Monaragala	44	33	5	-80	-344	-129
Ratnapura	681	-203	-65	-143	-4,782	560
Kalutara	-730	-4	-15	-27	-107	934
Galle	1,302	-212	-5	2,312	1,259	1449
Matara	1,876	-175	-14	543	1,231	2509
Hambantota	-	-6	-	-	30	10
Total	3,220	-3,507	-2,785	-1,624	-26,599	1674

Conclusions and Recommendations

In an attempt to answer the original question "Diversification or Ecological Threat?" I feel tempted to say "Chance for agricultural diversification *and* ecological threat".

Undoubtedly, some former tea areas have been diversified into other crops, but compared to the general decrease in tea, this has been to a rather limited extent of less than 5%. At least another 5% may have been reafforested before 1982. More recent efforts to protect the Upper Mahaweli Catchment Area in the late 1980s possibly added somewhat more to this figure. Another significant proportion of former tea land was used for village expansion and other infrastructure and appears today as built-up or homestead land, roads, etc. Due to existing, although somewhat reduced population pressure, such a development seems unavoidable and, at least in the short term, tolerable. The majority of abandoned tea land, however, was just left as it was. It was gradually used as cropland or rangeland, utilized sparsely in an unplanned and uncoordinated manner. These areas are likely to pose an ecological threat, especially because the tea fields which have been abandoned are in many cases on steep slopes and are therefore the most difficult to maintain and pick. Soil erosion and degradation, silting of rivers and reservoirs, landslides and other natural hazards are the possible consequences arising from this development. All efforts should be taken by the planners and decision-makers of Sri Lanka to convert unprofitable tea land (as well as, of course, other abandoned land) to ecologically more stable and economically more profitable land use types.

Acknowledgments

I am most indebted to Prof. Dr. K.I. Itten for his continuous support of my study and for all his efforts through which it was possible for me to complete this paper, my thesis and to attend this symposium. Thanks also to Dr. A. Herzog and Mr. P. Schmid, Dept. of Geography, University of Zurich, for the programming and documentation of the cartographic software packet "PS Copam" used to produce Figures 2 to 9, and for their enormous patience and help to overcome all the problems and loopholes that seem unavoidably associated with computer-assisted processing and presentation of geographic data.

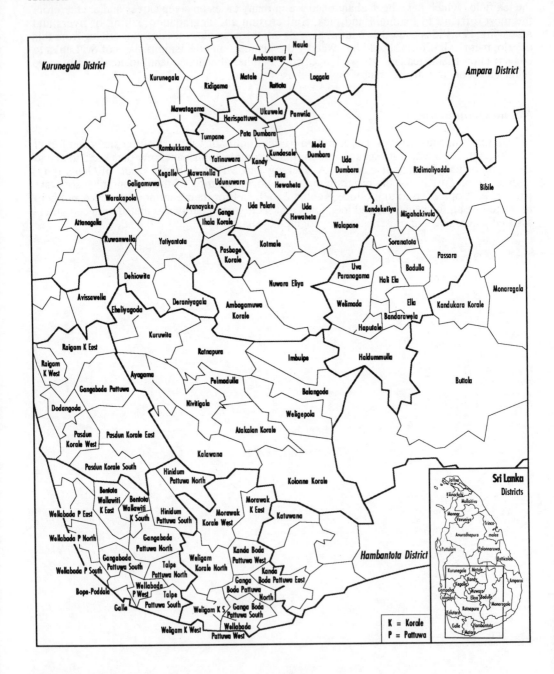

Figure 1. Districts and Assistant Agent Divisions (AGADs) with tea cultivation in central and southwestern Sri Lanka.

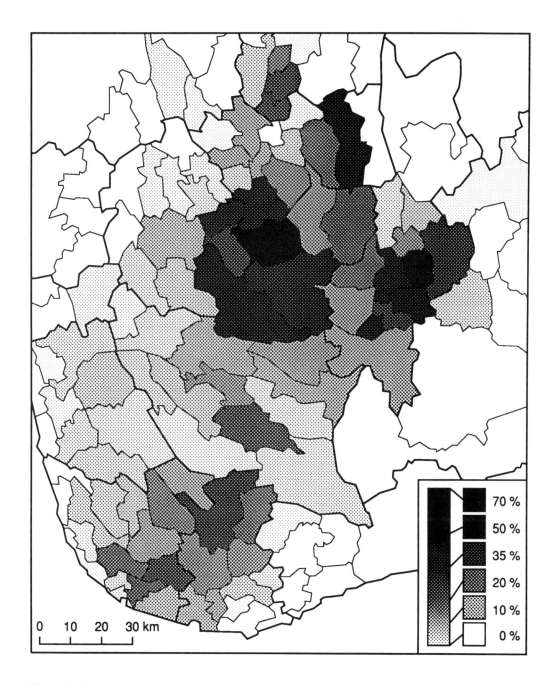

Figure 2. Tea cultivation in the 1980s (in % of the area of each AGAD).

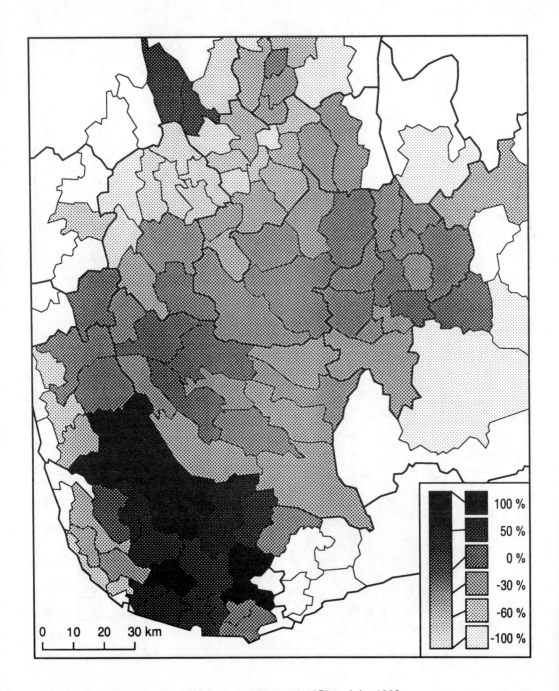

Figure 3. Tea area increases and decreases between 1956 and the 1980s.

The legend shows shading for 100 %, 50 %, 0 %, -30 %, -60 %, -100 %. The scale bar reads 0 10 20 30 km.

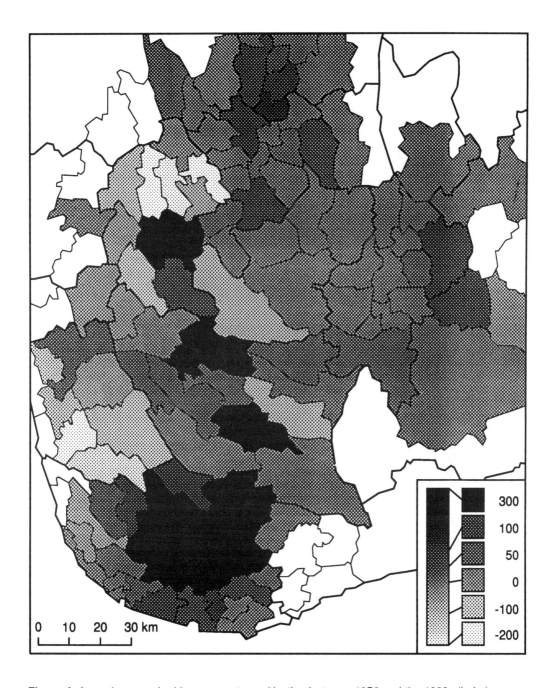

Figure 4. Area changes of rubber versus tea cultivation between 1956 and the 1980s (in ha).

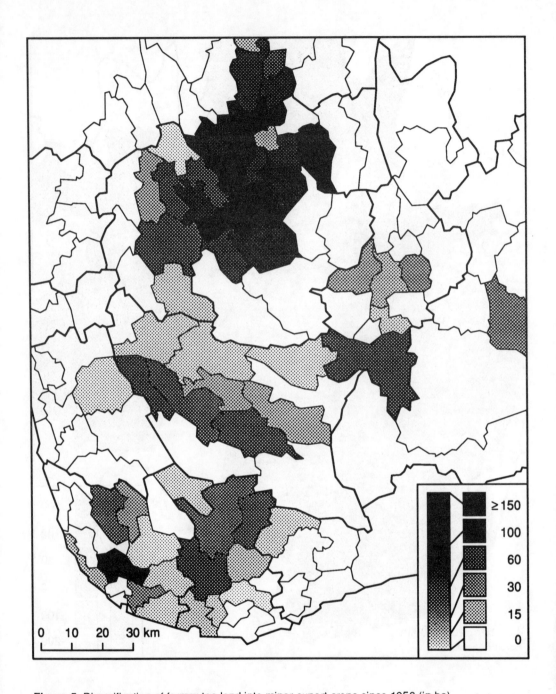

Figure 5. Diversification of former tea land into minor export crops since 1956 (in ha).

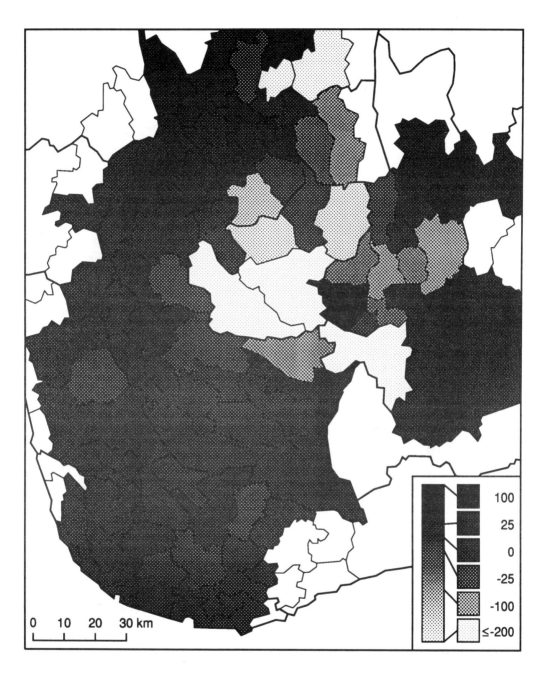

Figure 6. Area changes of forest plantations versus tea land from 1956 to the 1980s (in ha).

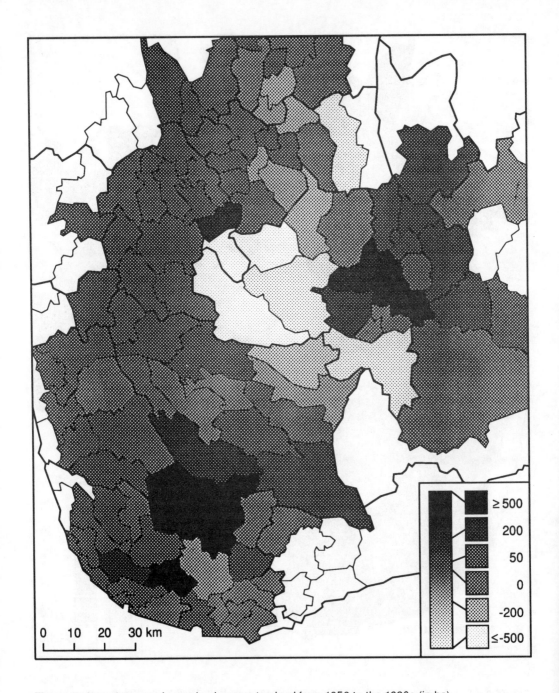

Figure 7. Area changes of rangeland versus tea land from 1956 to the 1980s (in ha).

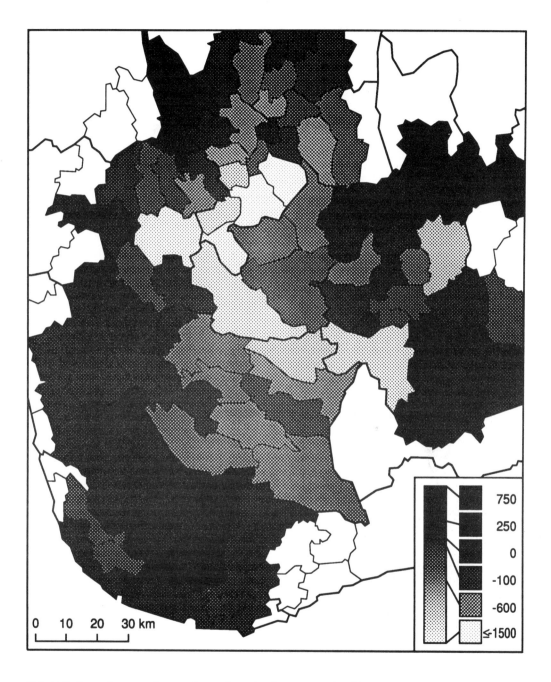

Figure 8. Area changes of sparsely used cropland versus tea land from 1956 to the 1980s (in ha).

313

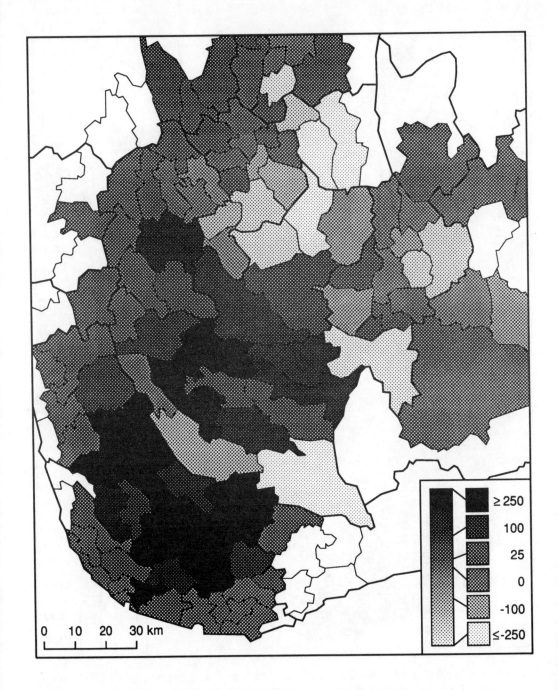

Figure 9. Area changes of natural forest versus tea land from 1956 to the 1980s (in ha).

Proceedings of the International and Interdisciplinary Symposium
ECOLOGY AND LANDSCAPE MANAGEMENT IN SRI LANKA
W. Erdelen, C. Preu, N. Ishwaran, C.M. Madduma Bandara (eds.)
Colombo, Sri Lanka, 12-26 March 1990
© 1993
Margraf Scientific Books, D-97985 Weikersheim
ISBN 3-8236-1182-8

Impact of Landslide Hazards in Sri Lanka

Preventive and Mitigating Measures

P.W. VITANAGE

Abstract

Landslides are generally not as spectacular as other natural hazards. However, landslides are more widespread and may cause more loss of property and life than other geological hazards. In many developing countries such as Sri Lanka, landslides may give rise to continuing and serious impacts on social and economic conditions which cannot be evaluated in monetary units alone. Disruption of lifestyles and resultant misery of individual lives as seen during the landslides of 1986 and more recently in 1989 cannot be compensated purely on a financial basis. In 1986, after the occurrence of a series of disastrous landslides in the hill country, multidisciplinary committees carried out field investigations and several high level seminars were held. Important practical proposals were submitted to the government. Although the official response to these proposals was rather limited, one central organization, i.e. the National Building Research Organization (NBRO), has been officially entrusted to carry out research and field surveys on landslides. A pilot project of systematic landslide hazard mapping had been carried out in 1987 and was followed in 1988 by a training program for the members of the district units monitoring landslides. But similar training at the grassroot level was delayed and might have contributed to the loss of several lives during the landslide of 1989. Results of the landslide hazard mapping project, case histories of landslides, preventive and mitigating measures recommended since 1985 and the difficulty of implementing these recommendations under the prevalent bureaucratic set up are discussed.

Introduction

Landslides are more widespread and may cause more loss of property and life than any other geological hazard. As the landslides in 1986 and the more recent ones in 1989 and early 1990 demonstrate, serious impacts on social and economic conditions with resulting continuing misery of individual lives have occured in Sri Lanka. Generally, landslides in Sri Lanka occur in the western, southwestern and central upland and in the highland areas of Kegalle, Kandy,

Nuwara Eliya, Badulla and Galle Districts. However, upland areas in Kalutara, Matara and Matale Districts have been subjected to major landslides (Fig. 1, Tab. 1) with heavy casualties to life and property (see Department of Social Services). Records to 1990 indicate that the incidence of major landslides in Kegalle District is the highest.

Figure 1. Map of Sri Lanka showing the districts.

Causes

Extensive investigations of landslides in different districts of Sri Lanka and the regional detailed landslide hazard mapping project in Uda Pussellawa (Nuwara Eliya District) have indicated that, in addition to the obvious factors causing the triggering of landslides, particularly

Table 1. Incidence of major landslides in various districts of Sri Lanka.

Year	District	No. of deaths	No. of houses damaged
1947	Kegalle	40	Not known
1957	Kegalle	05	15
1970	Nuwara Eliya	19	Not known
1973	Nuwara Eliya	13	Not known
1978	Kegalle	03	10
1979	Ratnapura	05	10
1981	Kegalle	02	20
1981	Kegalle	Not known	30
1981	Kegalle	02	03
1982	Ratnapura	08	15
1982	Matale	23	Not known
1984	Kalutara	04	Not known
1984	Ratnapura	02	05
1985	Nuwara Eliya	05	Not known
1985	Nuwara Eliya	-	40
1985	Kegalle	10	03
1985	Kandy	04	10
1985	Ratnapura	Not known	46
1989	Kegalle	296	Not known

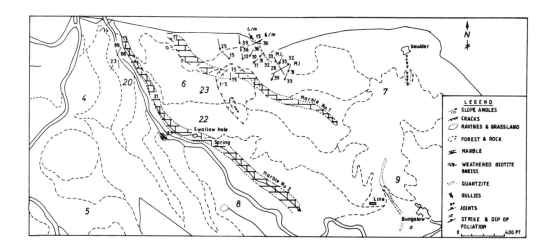

Figure 2. Landslide areas in Glen Devon Estate, Nuwara Eliya.

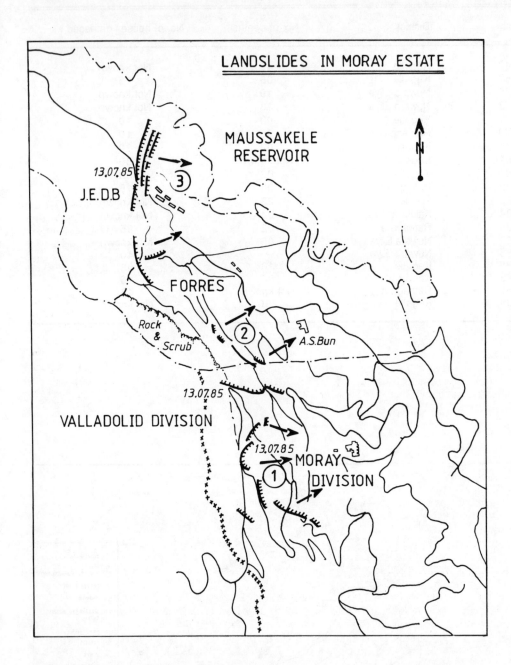

Figure 3. Landslides in Moray Estate, Nuwaraeliya.

excessive intensity and duration of daily rainfall, degree of slope and weathering, the contributing factors are mainly geological and tectonic in nature: (1) fracture density, (2) lithology and degree of weathering, (3) local and regional lineament tectonics, (4) local microtremors, and (5) possible influence of impounding and drawdown of the newly constructed water reservoirs such as Moussakelle, Kotmale, Victoria and Randenigala. The last three (3, 4, 5) factors have not been seriously considered in landslide investigations in Sri Lanka. Figure 2 shows the influence of marble on slope failure in Glen Devon Estate in Nuwara Eliya District and Figure 3 indicates the results of drawdown of a reservoir and possible subsurface seepage in Moray Estate also in Nuwara Eliya District. The common concentration of landslides along some of the major lineaments suggests possible neotectonic amd minor seismic activity.

Landslide Hazard Mapping

After the occurrence of a series of disastrous landslides in the central highlands, several multidisciplinary committees carried out field investigations and several high-level seminars were held in 1986. Moreover, important practical proposals for the prevention and mitigation of slope failures were submitted to the government. Although the official response was rather limited, the cabinet entrusted the National Building Research Organization (NBRO) to conduct research and field surveys on landslides. NBRO carried out systematic landslide hazard mapping in the Obada Oya Basin (Nuwara Eliya District) in 1987, which was followed in 1988 by a training program for the members of the district units monitoring landslides in 1988.

However, on account of the prevailing terrorist activities, similar training programs at grassroot level in the villages were delayed and might have contributed to the loss of several lives during the landslides in 1989. When the disastrous landslides occurred in Kegalle District which took toll of 296 persons, not a single member of the district monitoring unit was able to help and assist in any possible mitigating measures. As usual, dry rations and clothing were distributed to the people after hundreds were buried alive. To avoid another repetition of such an event, NBRO has planned to undertake a three-year (1990-1993) project in cooperation with technical assistance of UNDP/UNCHS to map the landslide hazard in Badulla and Nuwara Eliya Districts.

Landslide Investigations and Case Histories

After the occurrence of a series of disastrous landslides in the central highlands in 1986, several multidisciplinary committees and the author, requested by the Government, carried out field investigations in affected areas, especially in the state-owned tea and rubber estates (JEDB and SLSPC) in Badulla, Nuwara Eliya, Kandy, Kalutara and Galle Districts (Fig. 4). During the surveys, it was observed that the triggering agent of the slope failures was mainly the excessive daily rainfall (over 255 mm in 24 hours and 900-1000 mm in 3-4 days) for several successive days. The other causing factors included: (1) the degree of slope, (2) intensity of weathering, (3) fracture density, (4) lithological patterns, such as rock types, and (5) local and regional lineament tectonics and local microtremors.

Another possible factor is the influence of the effects of hydrological changes (water table and pore pressure) induced by the newly constructed water reservoirs such as Moussakelle, Kotmale, Victoria and Randenigala. The slumping and creep of 400 acres in the estates of Moray and Forres along the banks of the Moussakelle Reservoir in the Maskeliya area (Fig. 3), and the slow creep of 7 villages (Niyangandora, Wattaddara, Pusulpitiya, Nawangama, Kalapitiya, Gankewela and Maswela, 8 km^2) with 500 families towards the reservoir provide evidence for neotectonic movements resulting from impounding and drawdown of man-made reservoirs.

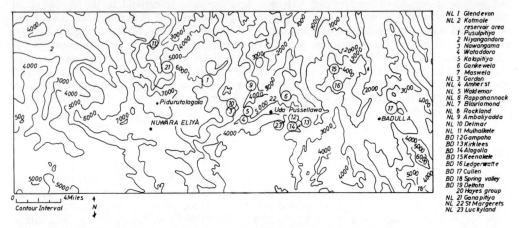

Figure 4. Landslide affected tea estates in Nuwaraeliya and Badulla Districts.

Remedial and Mitigating Measures

After detailed field investigations by different teams of scientists, the recommendations regarding the direct options of mitigating the landslide hazard included (1) permanent avoidance of unstable areas which is usually achieved by government land acquisition, (2) temporary avoidance of unstable areas, (3) restricted land use activities, (4) imposition of building design standards, e.g. vibration tolerance, (5) prevention of potential landslides by engineering or other treatment, (6) control of landslide activity, e.g. installation of rockfall chutes, debris runoff areas or tree planting to reduce movement rates, and (7) relief, compensation, repair and replacement by insurance or government grants.

Difficulties in Implementation

With the exceptions of a few estates, such as Kerkles, Leddgerwatte, and Gampaha in Badulla District, Gonapitiya and Glendevon in Nuwara Eliya District and the Hayes Group in Galle District, the recommendations were not fully implemented. Another example is the high risk area around the Kotmale Reservoir, where 8 km² with about 500 families (over 2000 persons) are creeping into the reservoir after impounding and drawdown of the reservoir in 1985. Around Kotmale, over 80 houses were damaged beyond repair and 30 percent of the buildings were in immediate danger of collapse. The poor deteriorating foundation conditions make rebuilding of new structures impossible. After intensive geological and geomorphological surveys in mid-1986, the writer recommended immediate evacuation of the villagers in order to avoid human casualties, and recommended monitoring and rehabilitation of the slopes around the reservoir in order to prevent large-scale sliding and creeping into the reservoir.

In spite of these warnings, there was a delay of nearly two years in resettling 500 families, who were facing immediate danger from heavy monsoonal rains. Fortunately, the SW monsoon failed for two years thus preventing a heavy toll on human life. After direct intervention by the President of Sri Lanka in 1987, these families were resettled in neighboring tea estates. However, the monitoring and rehabilitation of the slopes around the Kotmale Reservoir have not yet been started.

Similar problems of evacuation and resettlement of people as well as implementation of remedial measures exist in the area of Hanguranketa and other areas of the central highlands

320

where heavy landslide damage occurred in 1986. These difficulties and long delays in implementing the mitigating measures will continue in the future under the present bureaucratic system. Perhaps a special government organization under the President or Prime Minister and a special presidential fund reserved for landslide control may be able to implement the recommended remedial and mitigating measures without further delay. Committees of villagers and assistant government agents in the afflicted villages could help such organizations to take action in time.

Acknowledgments

The illustrations were prepared by Mr S.W. Amunugama and the typing of the manuscript was done by Mrs S.S. Weerasekera.

Proceedings of the International and Interdisciplinary Symposium
ECOLOGY AND LANDSCAPE MANAGEMENT IN SRI LANKA
W. Erdelen, C. Preu, N. Ishwaran, C.M. Madduma Bandara (eds.)
Colombo, Sri Lanka, 12-26 March 1990
© 1993
Margraf Scientific Books, D-97985 Weikersheim
ISBN 3-8236-1182-8

Short-Term Effects of Denudation of Mangroves on the Fish and Crustacean Communities of the Negombo Lagoon

L. PINTO AND N.N. PUNCHIHEWA

Abstract

While studying fish and crustacean communities of the Negombo Lagoon, destruction of mangroves near two experimental stations was observed. The immediate effect was an increase in the biomass and number of fish and crustaceans due to the accumulation of detritus. Preponderance of catfishes (*Tachysurus caelatus*) and some species of prawn (*Penaeus semisulcatus* and *Metapenaeus elegans*) was noted at these stations. The species diversity index of fish and crustacean communities also increased immediately following the destruction of mangroves. However, about four months after this destruction, the biomass, number of species and species diversity of the fish and crustacean communities dropped significantly.

Introduction

The Negombo Lagoon has been considered an important wetland of Sri Lanka with faunal and floral qualities as well as peculiarities in its genetic and ecological diversity, which makes it a representative wetland of the region (Scott, 1989). The lagoon covers an area of about 3500 ha with about 350 ha of mangroves on its shores and islands, and about 900 ha of submerged seagrasses. These two habitats provide food and a multitude of niches for the lagoon organisms which contribute to the ecological diversity of the lagoon. The main use of the mangroves in this lagoon is brush-pile fishery. The mangroves have been systematically thinned by fisherman in order to obtain a continuous supply of mangrove branches for the brush-piles. In recent years, extensive clearing of mangroves for housing, aquaculture and tourism have taken place. During a faunal survey of the mangroves, two stations in the north and south of the lagoon were denuded. This provided an opportunity to compare the impact of denudation on the fish and prawn communities with those of nearby intact mangroves.

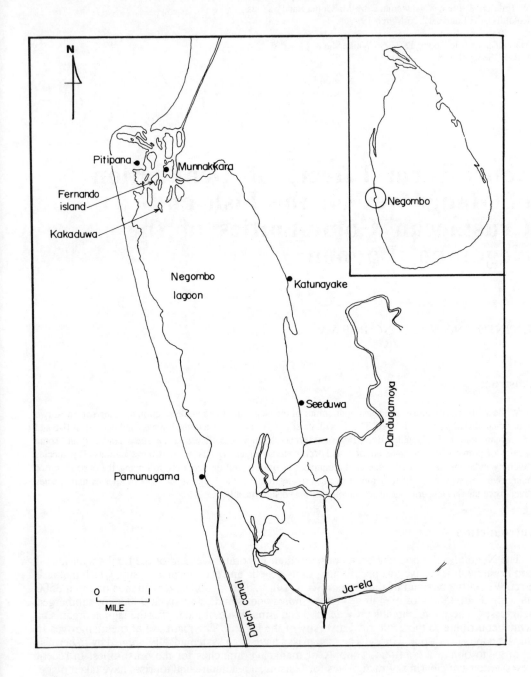

Figure 1. Study site in the Negombo Lagoon.

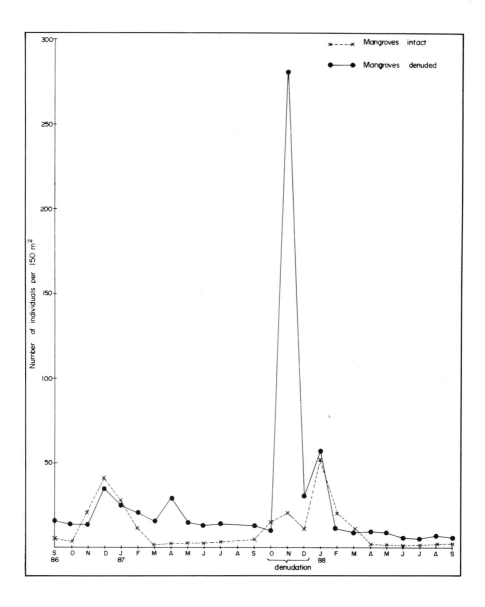

Figure 2. Seasonal variation in the number of individuals of fish in the denuded and intact mangroves in the southern lagoon.

Location

This study was conducted in the Negombo Lagoon at latitude 7°11'N and longitude 79°50'E on the west coast of Sri Lanka (Fig. 1). In the northern lagoon the two stations are located on the islets of Kakaduwa and Fernando about 500 m apart. *Rhizophora mucronata* forms a mangrove fringe around these two islets. The mangroves of Fernando Island were partially felled leaving the roots intact. In the southern lagoon, the two stations were located at

Katunayake and Seeduwa about 30 km apart on the east coast of the lagoon. At Katunayake, there were *Rhizophora mucronata*, *Excoecaria agallocha*, *Acanthus ilicifolius* and *Acrostichum aureum* on the shores. At Seeduwa, *Excoecaria agallocha* was the predominant species with *Acrostichum aureum* and *Acanthus ilicifolius*. The mangroves of Seeduwa were totally denuded during the course of this study.

Materials and Methods

A net with the mesh size of 0.9 cm, length 5.5 m and aperture of 1.5 m^2 was dragged along the side of the mangroves for 150 m at walking speed. Sampling was done once a month at high tides on spring tide days. The specimens were identified, measured and weighed in the laboratory. Diversity was determined using the Shannon Index, $H^1 = - (p_i \ln p_i)$.

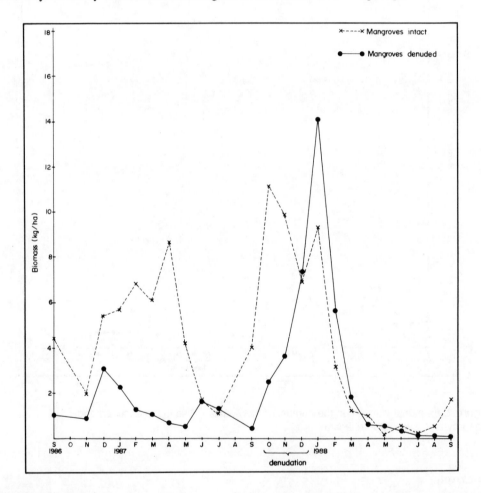

Figure 3. Seasonal variation in the biomass of fish in the denuded and intact mangroves in the southern lagoon.

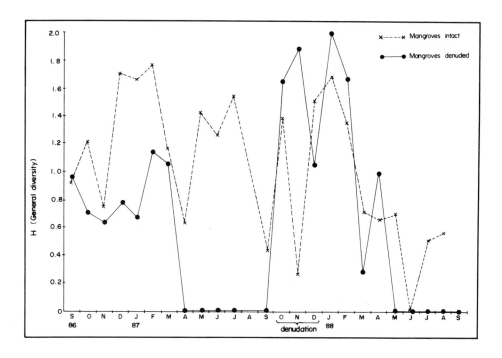

Figure 4. Seasonal changes in diversity (H^1) of fish in the denuded and intact mangroves in the southern lagoon.

Results

During this study which lasted for 2 years, 57 species of fish and at least 10 species of prawns were identified from the mangroves of the Negombo Lagoon. (Tab. 1, annexed). *Panchax melastigma* and *Ambasis dayi* were the most abundant fish species, *Penaeus indicus*, *P. semisulcatus* and *Metapenaeus dobsoni* were the most abundant prawn species associated with these mangroves.

Fish

After the denudation of mangroves the number of fish increased ten times, but after about 3 months the number dropped below the previously maintained steady level at Seeduwa and Katunayake in the southern lagoon (Fig. 2). Maximum biomass was reached about 3 months following denudation (Fig. 3). Thereafter the biomass decreased below the previously maintained level. Fish diversity reached a maximum following denudation, but thereafter it reached its lowest level (Fig. 4).

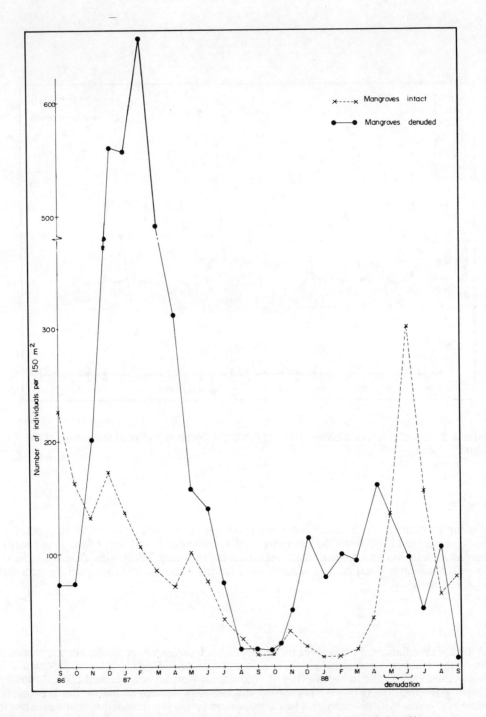

Figure 5. Seasonal variation in the number of individuals of fish in the denuded and intact mangroves in the northern lagoon.

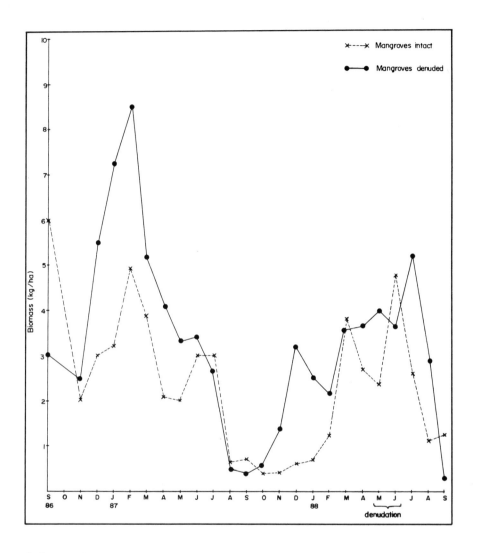

Figure 6. Seasonal variation in the fish biomass of the denuded and the intact mangroves in the northern lagoon.

For the mangroves of Kakaduwa and Fernando in the northern lagoon the numbers and biomass increased during January and February 1987 during the NE monsoon mainly due to the abundance of *Panchax melastigma* and *Ambasis dayi*. There was also an increase in the biomass of fish after denudation but not in the number of individuals (Figs. 5, 6). The diversity index did not increase along with denudation, instead decreased after denudation (Fig. 7).

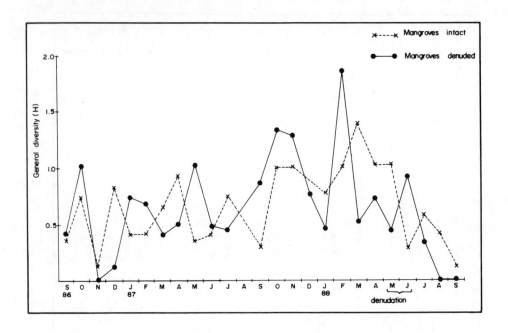

Figure 7. Seasonal variation in the diversity (H[1]) of fish in the denuded and intact mangroves in the northern lagoon.

Prawns

The number of prawns increased after the denudation of the mangroves in the southern lagoon (Fig. 8). The fluctuations in the biomass correspond to that of the numbers (Fig. 9). The diversity index increased, with the denudation but thereafter dropped to its previous level (Fig. 10).

In the northern lagoon highest densities and biomass were recorded in September 1986 during the SW monsoon (Figs. 11, 12). The partial denudation of mangroves had very little effect on the pattern of fluctuation except for the fact that the number of individuals and the biomass decreased following denudation. Seasonal variation in the diversity index did not show much sensitivity to partial denudation. This was however the case in the southern lagoon (Fig. 13).

Figure 14 shows the variation in salinity, dissolved oxygen (DO), temperature and rainfall for the Negombo Lagoon. The lagoon receives heavy rainfall during the intermonsoon period, which dilutes the lagoon water and influences the dissolved oxygen content. The water temperature is high during March and April and low during January and February in the lagoon.

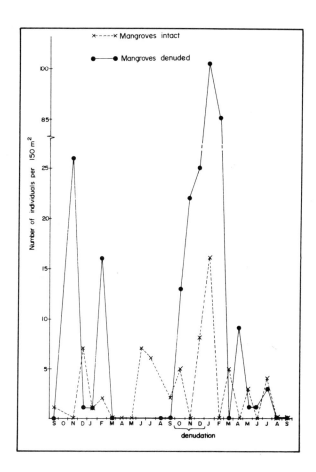

Figure 8. Seasonal variation in the number of individuals of prawns in the denuded and intact mangroves in the southern lagoon.

Discussion

Fish

There are about 136 brackish water fish species in Sri Lanka (De Silva and De Silva, 1984), out of which about 62 occur in the Negombo Lagoon (De Silva and Silva, 1979). In this study 57 species of fish were recorded from the mangroves. Since De Silva and Silva (1979) analyzed samples from brush-piles only, species and even family composition in their study differ from those of the current study. The number of fish species recorded in this study is higher than that in the mangroves of the West Indies (Louis and Lasserre, 1982) but lower than that in Florida (Thayer *et al.* 1987), Philippines (Pinto, 1987) and India (Jeyaseelan, 1981).

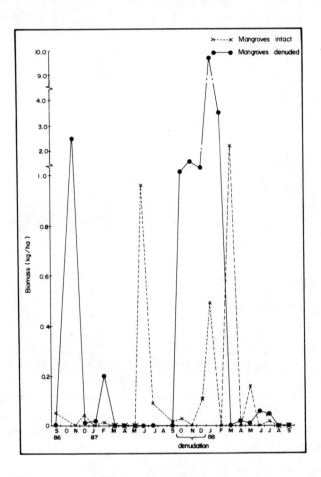

Figure 9. Seasonal variation in the biomass of prawns in the denuded and intact mangroves in the southern lagoon.

The current study shows that the fish density is higher in the northern lagoon mangroves than in the southern lagoon. But the biomass was higher in the southern lagoon indicating that the few fish in the southern lagoon were larger in size. The presence of a large number of *Panchax melastigma* considered to be estuarine (Munro, 1955) in the northern lagoon is a deviation from the normally abundant glassfish and slip mouths in the mangroves (Hermes *et al.* 1984). This study agrees with the conclusion of De Silva and Silva (1974) that the major peak in the number of fish species in the Negombo Lagoon occurs in February when salinity is high.

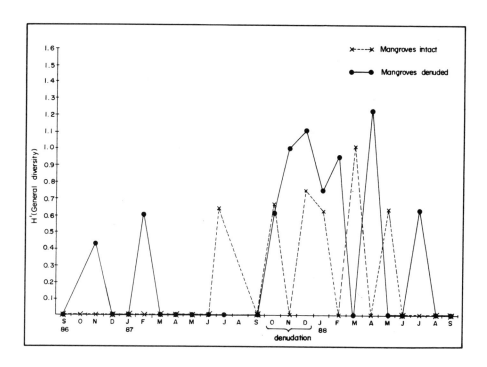

Figure 10. Seasonal variation in the diversity (H^1) of prawns in the denuded and intact mangroves in the southern lagoon.

In the southern lagoon, where denudation was complete, a large number of fish was aggregated due to the accumulation of detritus. As decomposition proceeded the number of fish decreased, but biomass increased and reached its peak four months later. The increase in biomass was due to the attraction of the catfishes, *Tachysurus caelatus* and *Pseudarius platystomus* to detritus and the organisms associated with detritus. Partial destruction of mangroves did not attract much fish as in the case of total destruction. In all cases a few months after the destruction, the number, biomass and the species diversity decreased considerably.

Prawns

Species of prawns are not as numerous as fish species. The 10 species of Penaeid prawns listed by De Bruin (1971) were all recorded in this study. In addition, members of families Alpheidae and Palaemonidae were also recorded for the mangroves. In an earlier study, Pinto

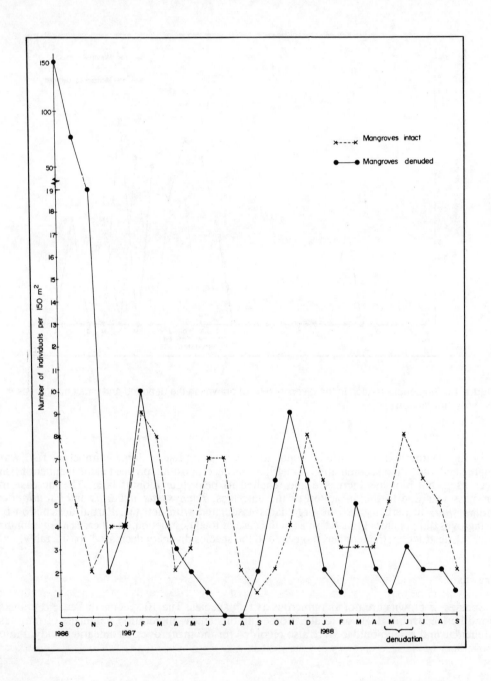

Figure 11. Seasonal variation in the number of individuals of prawns in the denuded and intact mangroves in the northern lagoon.

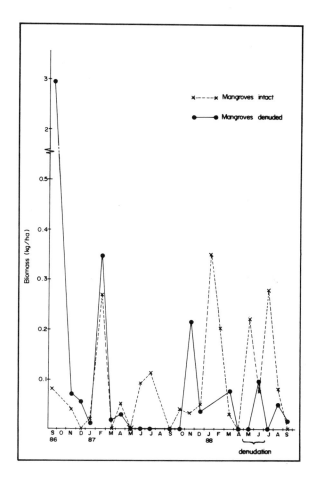

Figure 12. Seasonal variation in the biomass of prawns in the denuded and intact mangroves in the northern lagoon.

and Wignarajah (1980) noted the occurrence of the snapping shrimp *Alphaeus edwardsii* on oysters attached to mangrove roots. Densities and biomass of prawns in the lagoon were lower than those for fish in the mangroves. Like the fish community, the density and biomass of prawns in the northern lagoon was higher than those for the southern lagoon.

The current study also showed peaks in the occurrence of prawns during October and November in the second intermonsoon in accordance with observations made by Samarakoon and Raphael (1972). However, this pattern in the occurrence of prawns in the lagoon was disturbed due to the felling of the mangroves.

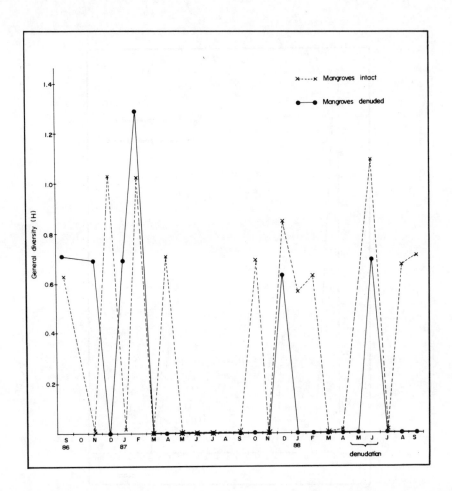

Figure 13. Seasonal variation in the diversity (H^1) of prawns in the denuded and intact mangroves in the northern lagoon.

Similar to the fish community, the number of individuals, their biomass and the diversity increased after the denudation of mangroves. *Penaeus semisulcatus* and *Metapenaeus elegans* were specially attracted to the detritus that accumulated. 3-8 months after the felling, the number of individuals, biomass and diversity decreased supporting the proposition of Martosubroto and Naamin (1977) that with the decrease in mangrove areas shrimp catches also drop. However, when mangroves are partially felled leaving stumps and roots, the fish and prawn communities were less affected than if a total denudation of the mangroves had occurred. This observation supports the conjecture that thinning mangroves for brush-pile fishery affects the fish and prawn communities less adversely than a total removal of mangroves for 'development projects'.

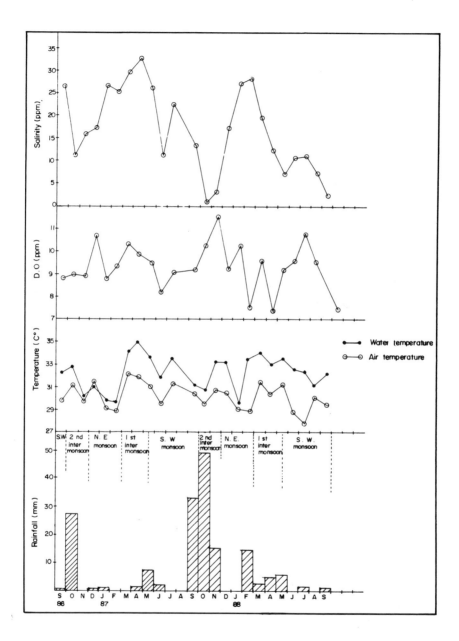

Figure 14. Seasonal variation in some physicochemical factors of the environment on the sampling dates.

Acknowledgments

This study was supported by NARESA grant RG/BS/86/10. We are thankful to Mrs Ramya Dissanayake for the illustrations and to Miss Preethi Kumari for typing the manuscript.

Literature Cited

De Bruin, G.H.P. 1971. Fluctuations in species composition of penaeid prawns in estuaries. *Bull. Fish. Res. Stn. Ceylon* 22: 47-51.

De Silva, S.S. and C. De Silva. 1984. Coastal lagoons. *In* C.H. Fernando, ed. *Ecology and Biography in Sri Lanka,* pp. 297-320. Junk Publ. The Hague.

De Silva, S.S. and E.I.L. Silva. 1979. Fish fauna of a coastal lagoon in Sri Lanka: distribution and seasonal variation. *Bull. Fish. Res. Stn. Sri Lanka* 29: 1-9.

Hermes, R., N. Navaluna and A.C. de Norte. 1984. A pushnet ichtyoplankton sampler attached to an outrigger boat. *Proc. Fish. Cult.* 46: 85-89.

Jeyaseelan, M.J. 1981. *Studies on ichthyofauna of the mangroves of Pichavaran (India)* Ph.D. dissertation. Annamalai University, India.

Louis M. and G. Lasserra. 1982. Etude du peuplement de poissons dans les legunes des mangroves de Guadeloupe (Antilles francaises) *Oceanologica Acta*, 1982: 333-338.

Martosubroto, P. and N. Naamin. 1977. Relationship between tidal forests (mangroves) and commercial shrimp production in Indonesia. *Mar. Res. Indonesia* 18: 81-88.

Munro, I.S.R. 1955. *The marine and freshwater fishes of Ceylon.* Dept. of External Affairs, Canberra.

Pinto, L. 1987. Environmental factors influencing the occurrence of juvenile fish in the mangroves of Pagbilao, Philippines. *Hydrobiol.* 150: 283-301.

Pinto, L. and S. Wignarajah. 1980. Some ecological aspects of the edible oyster *Crassostrea cucullata* (Born) occurring in association with mangroves in Negombo Lagoon, Sri Lanka. *Hydrobiol.* 69: 11-19.

Samarakoon, J.I. and Y.I. Raphael. 1972. On the availability of seed of culturable shrimps in the Negombo Lagoon. *In* T.V.R. Pillai, ed. *Coastal Aquaculture in the Indo-Pacific Region,* pp. 251-259. Fishing News Books, Surrey.

Scott, D.A. 1989. *A Directory of Asian Wetlands.* IUCN, Gland, Switzerland.

Thayer, G.W., D.R. Colby and W.F. Heltler. 1987. Utilization of the red mangrove prop root habitat by fishes in South Florida. *Mar. Ecol. Prog. Ser.* 35: 25-38.

Annex

Table 1. Fish and prawn species associated with the mangroves of Negombo Lagoon.

Family	Species
Fish	
Engraulidae	*Anchoviella indica* (Van Hasselt, 1823)
Chanidae	*Chanos chanos* (Forsskal, 1775)
Cyprinidae	*Puntius vitatus* (Day, 1865)
Plotosidae	*Plotosus canius* (Hamilton-Buchanan, 1822)
Tachysuridae	*Tachysurus caelatus* (Valenciennes, 1840)
	Pseudaris platystomus (Day, 1875)
Bagridae	*Macrones gulio* (Hamilton-Buchanan, 1822)
Muraenidae	*Thyrosoidea macrura* (Bleeker, 1834)
Ophichthyidae	*Ophichthys rhytidodermatoides* (Bleeker, 1832)
Belonidae	*Tylosurus strongylurus* (Van Hasselt, 1823)
Hemirhamphidae	*Zenarchopterus dispar* (Valenciennes, 1846)
	Hemirhamphus marginatus (Forsskal, 1775)
Syngnathidae	*Ichthyocampus carce* (Hamilton-Buchanan, 1853)
Cyprinodontidae	*Panchax melastigma* (McClellan, 1839)
Sphyraenidae	*Sphyraena jello* (Cuvier, 1829)
Mugilidae	*Liza oligolepsis* (Bleeker, 1859)
	Liza macrolepsis (Smith, 1849)
Atherinidae	*Pranesus duodecimalis* (Valenciennes, 1835)
Latidae	*Lates calcarifer* (Bloch, 1790)
Ambassidae	*Ambassis dayi* (Bleeker, 1874)
Serranidae	*Epinephelus tauvina* (Forsskal, 1775)
Theraponidae	*Pelates quadrilineatus* (Bloch, 1790)
	Austisthes puta (Cuvier, 1829)
	Therapon jarbua (Forsskal, 1775)
Apogonidae	*Apogon thermalis* (Cuvier, 1829)
Carangidae	*Caranx sexfaxiatus* (Kenoy and Gaimard, 1824)
Lutianidae	*Lutianus fulviflama* (Forsskal, 1775)
Gerridae	*Gerres oyena* (Forsskal, 1775)
Leiognathidae	*Leiognathus brevirostris* (Cur. & Val. 1835)
Sparidae	*Acantthapagrus catus* (Honttuyh, 1782)
Monodactylidae	*Monodactylus argenteus* (Linnacus, 1758)
Scadaphagidae	*Scatophagus argus* (Linnaeus, 1758)
Chaetodontidae	*Heriochus acuminatus* (Linnaeus, 1758)
Cichlidae	*Etroplus maculatus* (Bloch, 1785)
	Etroplus suratensis (Bloch, 1785)
Scaridae	*Callyodon fasciatus* (Valenciennes, 1839)
Siganidae	*Siganus oramin* (Bloch & Schneider, 1801)
	Siganus javus (Linnaeus, 1766)
	Siganus vermiculatus (Cuv. & Val. 1835)
	Siganus concentenata (Cuv. & Val. 1905)
Acanthuridae	*Acanthurus weberi* (Ahl. 1923)
Electridae	*Eleotris fusca* (Bloch & Schneider, 1801)
	Butis butis (Hamilton-Buchanan, 1822)

Family	Species
Gobidae	*Glossogobius biocellatus* (Cuv. & Val. 1837)
	Glossogobius celebius (Cuv. & Val. 1837)
	Bathygobius fuscus (Ruppell, 1828)
	Apparius acutipinnis (Cuv. & Val. 1801)
Soleidae	*Brachirus orientalis* (Bloch, 1801)
Cynoglossidae	*Cynaglossus bilineatus* (Lacepede, 1802)
Tricanthidae	*Tricanthus brevirostris* (Schlegel, 1842)
Tetradontidae	*Monotretus cutcutia* (Hamilton-Buchanan, 1822)
	Chalonodan patoca (Hamilton-Buchanan, 1822)
	Arothron immaculatus (Bloch & Schneider, 1801)
	Arothron hispidus (Lacepede, 1802)
	Arothron reticularis (Bloch & Schneider, 1801)

Prawns

Family	Species
Penaeidae	*Penaeus indicus* (Milne-Edwards, 1837)
	Penaeus latisulcatus (Kishinonye, 1896)
	Penaeus semisuleatus (de Hann, 1844)
	Penaeus monodon (Fabricius, 1798)
	Metapenaeus dobsoni (Miers, 1878)
	Metapenaeus elegans (de Man, 1907)
	Metapanaeus moyebi (Kishinonye, 1896)
	Metapenaeus affinis (Milne-Edwards, 1837)
Alphaedae	*Alpheus* sp.
Palaemonidae	*Macrobrachium* spp.
	Other *caridians*

Proceedings of the International and Interdisciplinary Symposium
ECOLOGY AND LANDSCAPE MANAGEMENT IN SRI LANKA
W. Erdelen, C. Preu, N. Ishwaran, C.M. Madduma Bandara (eds.)
Colombo, Sri Lanka, 12-26 March 1990
© 1993
Margraf Scientific Books, D-97985 Weikersheim
ISBN 3-8236-1182-8

Prawn Culture Development and Present Land Use Patterns in Coastal Areas of Sri Lanka

J.M.P.K. JAYASINGHE AND J.A. DE SILVA

Abstract

The recent rapid expansion of shrimp culture in Sri Lanka has resulted in considerable changes in land use patterns of the northwestern and western coastal areas of Sri Lanka. Much of the land use categories such as scrubland, grassland, mangroves and salt marshes have now been changed or earmarked for individual prawn ponds or clusters. Potential aquaculturable land, for shrimp farming, in these two areas amounts to 0.9% and 1.3% of total land area. Furthermore, land which falls into the categories such as scrubland, grassland, mangroves and salt marshes, accounts for more than 80% of the crown land in these areas. The changes in land use patterns have reduced the areas available for traditional animal husbandry and fishing practices. Village expansion activities in the agricultural and fishing communities in those areas have also been restricted and have resulted in conflicts between developers and local inhabitants in certain areas. The areas developed or earmarked for development are also abundant in wildlife and include unique ecological habitats such as mangroves and salt marshes which are rare or absent in other non- aquaculturable areas. Reduction in paddy growing areas due to saltwater intrusion, and the gradual decrease in fin fish and shellfish catches, due to the destruction of natural habitats for the early stages of life histories are some of the impacts of shrimp culture development on land use patterns. Conversion of some of the potential acid sulphate areas into prawn farms has also led to changes in the chemical environment in the immediate vicinity of such areas. A decrease in pH values and an increased level of aluminium, iron and manganese have been observed in water bodies adjoining the developed areas.

Introduction

The expansion of the prawn culture industry has contributed to the socioeconomic welfare of the coastal areas of Sri Lanka. However, this new activity has also resulted in changes in the land use patterns of these areas and has created new problems in its wake. Prawn culture in the western coastal belt between Kalpitiya and Negombo commenced in the mid-1980s. When first recorded prawn production amounted to 10 tons in 1984. Within 4 years the production of cultured shrimp rose to 669 tons in 1988 and is still increasing. The revenue from cultured shrimp in 1988 was approximately Rs 174 million and led to 222 new jobs in the Northwestern Province (Siriwardane *et al.* 1988). In terms of area, 160 ha of water area was under cultivation. The total area of land utilized for prawn farming is estimated to be in the range of 300-450 ha, and could rise to as much as 2000 ha in the next few years. At present the majority of farms which have come into operation are leased on state land.

Present government policy of Sri Lanka is based on the promotion of small-scale business through projects such as the 'Poverty Alleviation Programme' and the encouragement of small enterprises. These types of program have proved to be more socioeconomically feasible in developing countries. In recent times, there has also been a policy of limiting crown land to approximately 50 acres per entreprenuer, thus actively encouraging a greater number of small farms rather than a few large farms. At present aquaculture ventures, using state land, in the coastal belt have been approved by the Inter-Ministerial Scoping Committee which is a multidisciplinary body representing all government agencies involved in the management of these areas, to which applications for setting up aquaculture have to be sent. Farms of less than 1 ha are usually exempt from this procedure as well as those that are to be started on private land.

Materials and Methods

The information used for this paper is taken from land use maps and from the 1 inch to 1 mile map published by the Survey Department. Statistical information on livestock, population and operational as well as proposed farm sites is based on data collected at the Puttalam Kachcheri. Other information presented was collected by NARA through interviews and interpretation of historical records. This study focuses on the Puttalam and Gampaha Districts in general. The area between Palavi and Bangadeniya was considered in greater detail, because most of the projected farms and nearly all operational farms of the Puttalam District are in this area. The land use categories for farms, both operational and proposed, are based on the land use maps of the Survey Department and personal observations.

Table 1. Types of prawn farming.

	Extensive	Semi-intensive	Intensive
Stocking density (no/ha)	4000-5000	30,000	150,000
Average production (kg/ha/year)	200	1475	10,800
Extent of land (ha) required for 1 mt/yr	5.0	0.67	0.09

Results

Types of Prawn Farming

Prawn farming practices can be classified into three major categories, i.e. intensive, semi-intensive and extensive culture. These three types differ (1) in the manner in which they operate, (2) in land requirements, (3) in stocking densities, (4) in feeding requirements, and (5) in their complexity and capital. In Sri Lanka, the majority, if not all, of the operational farms practice either semi-intensive or intensive culture and culture *Penaeus monodon*. These two types of culture have a distinct advantage over extensive culture with respect to land requirements, needing less land to produce a ton of prawns (Tab. 1).

Land Use Patterns Prior to Culture

Potential areas for prawn culture are generally limited to areas such as scrubland, grassland, sparsely used cropland and mangroves, and depend on the particular soil characteristics of the area. Areas suitable for culture also border or are close to saline water sources. Potential and existing prawn culture ventures are situated in the vicinity of coastal lagoons and saline waterways such as the Hamilton Canal. Table 2 shows the land use distribution in the 6 divisions of the Puttalam and Chilaw Districts in 1985 before the culture activities started. It can be seen that homesteads, coconut plantations, paddy fields and sparsely used cropland are the predominant land use categories in this area. As mentioned before scrubland, grassland, mangroves and marshlands are most likely to be utilized for aquaculture. Scrubland dominates

Table 2. Land use categories of six divisions in the Puttalam and Gampaha Districts (ha). Data from land use map (Survey Dept. Colombo, 1985). Divisions (D): 1 = Kalpitiya, 2 = Pitigal Korale North, 3 = Pitigal Korale South, 4 = Puttalam Pattu, 5 = Wennapuwa, 6 = Arachchikattuwa.

	D1	D2	D3	D4	D5	D6
Built-up land	40	0	110	470	0	0
Associated non-agricultural land	0	0	20	600	0	50
Homesteads	7,420	2,000	2,190	2,740	150	4,890
Coconut plantations	3,640	90	8,840	7,780	0	6,370
Cashew	0	0	0	0	0	0
Mixed tree and perennial crops	30	0	0	30	10	0
Paddy fields	690	2,900	2,250	1,360	1,340	2,430
Sparsely used cropland	25,110	12,270	1,210	5,360	8,210	2,630
Other cropland	20	0	10	0	0	0
Dense forest	90	11,190	0	0	1,850	0
Open forest	600	7,590	10	220	870	0
Forest plantations	880	3,450	350	1,690	380	440
Scrubland	2,280	5,960	10	1,270	1,170	270
Grassland	1,640	930	10	550	250	10
Mangroves	70	70	50	200	0	880
Marsh	0	0	360	500	0	160
Barren land	70	450	120	1,240	70	410
Water area	3,170	2,060	200	910	920	1,920
Total area	50,750	48,960	15,840	24,920	16,220	20,460

the potential aquaculturable land in the administrative divisions 1, 2 and 4, while marshes dominate this category in division 3. Grassland is extensive in divisions 1, 2, 4 and 5. It may be noted that the extent of mangroves in these coastal areas is low. In terms of land area suitable for prawn culture, the administrative divisions 3, 4 and 6 are the most suitable (NARA, 1988).

Present Status of Land for Prawn Farming

After the scoping committee had officially approved 774 ha for prawn farming in September 1988, 428 ha were converted to prawn farms. However, this value is estimated to be slightly higher and may be around 465 ha, if small farms constructed on private land which have come into operation without being placed for approval to the committee are taken into account. Table 3 shows the distribution of land under prawn culture and that which has been earmarked by investors together with that which falls within the study area. It can be seen that approximately 49% of the land constructed or earmarked for prawn culture and 92% of operational or near operational land falls within the study area (Tab. 3).

Table 3. Present status of state land in hectares (ha) for prawn farming in Puttalam District.

Puttalam District	
Operational land or near operational	465
Land applications	1596
Total area	2061
Area between Palavi and Bangadeniya (study area)	
Operational or near operational	431.4
Land applications	574.8
Total area	1006.2

The Effects of Prawn Culture on Land Use Patterns

Farms have mainly been constructed or proposed on wetland; 34.7%, bareland; 29.3% and agricultural areas; 18.9% (Fig. 1, Tab. 4). Marshlands, coconut plantations, sparsely used cropland and paddy fields are the main subdivisions of the wetland and agricultural land. Table 5 summarizes these potential areas available in the study area for prawn culture by land use category. It should be noted, however, that all those areas indicated are not suitable, because limiting factors such as soil and water quality have not been taken into account.

Mangroves are an economically valuable resource both in terms of their direct uses and their contribution to coastal and estuarine fisheries (UNEP, 1984). The communities living in the coastal areas have many traditional uses for mangroves. They are used for firewood, construction materials, brush-park fishery, cattle feed and medicinal purposes (NARA, 1986). The mangroves are also important as they support many types of fishing. In addition, mangrove areas are important breeding grounds where many marine fish species live during their juvenile stages. Mangrove areas also offer a buffer zone between sea and land preventing erosion as their roots act as sediment binders (Odum and Johannes, 1975). 19 of the 21 species of true mangroves and all 16 associated species are found along the west coast. The mangrove area of the west coast amounted to 2820 ha in 1983 (based on land use map). These areas have been subjected to natural exploitation as a result of their traditional uses. With the increase in shrimp farming, the reduction and destruction of mangrove areas has increased mostly due to farms not keeping to the regulations.

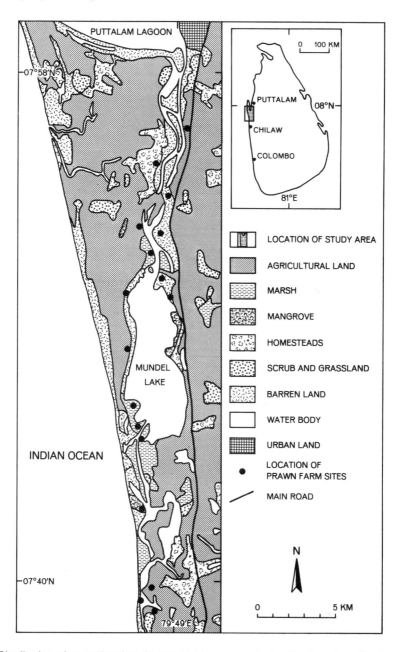

Figure 1. Distribution of operational and proposed farm areas in the Northwestern Province.

Table 4. Distribution of prawn farms (constructed or proposed) by land use patterns.

Type of Land	ha (%)		No. of farms (%)	
Bare land	294.54	(29.3)	13	(29.5)
Agricultural land				
Homestead	30.36	(3.0)	3	(6.8)
Coconut	97.16	(9.7)	5	(11.4)
Paddy	6.19	(1.6)	4	(9.1)
Sparsely used				
Cropland	53.80	(5.3)	4	(9.1)
	197.51	(18.9)	16	(36.4)
Wetland				
Marshlands	349.02	(34.7)	9	(20.5)
Mangroves				
Unclassified	159.17	(16.4)	6	(13.6)
Total	1006.24		44	

The coastal swamps (marshlands) of the west coast and the brackish water bodies are characterized by having a very rich fauna. 8 species of polychaetes, 17 species of molluscs, 22 species of decapods, 3 species of holorhurians, 75 species of fish, 7 species of frogs and toads, 14 species of reptiles, 50 species of birds and 15 species of mammals are known from these areas (de Silva and de Silva, 1982). Coastal areas are also important habitats for migratory and resident species of birds. These areas act as vital staging and feeding area for these birds. With the advent of shrimp farming, which has been primarily carried out in these areas or areas bordering them, the land available for nesting has been affected. Coastal swamps

Table 5. Potential area for prawn farming in study area.

Land Use Type	ha
Mangroves	150
Marsh	243
Scrubland	267
Grassland and Bareland	550
Total	1210

around Mundal Lake are of special importance for ducks, waders and other water birds, while swamps around Puttalam also offer shelter to seabirds not found in the Mundal Lake. Waders and water birds have been identified as important members of the swamp community around Negombo and Chilaw. According to the mid-winter fowl census of 1988 (Hoffman, 1988), approximately 70,000 birds inhabit the coastal swamps of the western coastal areas (Tab. 6).

Table 6. Summary of water bird census (Hoffman, 1988).

Group of birds	Number of species	Number recorded in coastal swamps	
		Puttalam/ Mundal	Chilaw/ Negombo
Grebes	1	90	12
Pelicans	1	1	0
Cormorants	4	907	122
Herons	12	1,563	632
Storks	5	29	20
Ibises	2	274	0
Ducks	4	15,217	212
Rails/coots	15	877	237
Waders	132	31,782	168
Gulls/terns	10	16,753	0
Total	77	67,493	1,403

Traditional paddy growing areas are located adjacent to the low lying areas of aquaculture development. Paddy fields are also found in the upper reaches of the small waterways which debouch into the lagoons and estuaries. The total land, cultivated with paddy in the 6 divisions, amounts to approximately 13,540 ha (Tab. 7). With the advent of prawn farming, the water has become more saline as a result of the large quantities of water discharged. The effects of this discharge on nearby paddy fields are apparent in terms of the number of complaints received from farmers. A survey in Uddappu (division 6) indicated that 11 of the 14 small-scale paddy farmers interviewed, noted that one of the major problems faced is saltwater intrusion from the nearby farms. In certain areas, it is also believed that drinking water wells have been affected, but this has so far not been substantiated. Therefore, regular testing is being carried out.

Table 7. Extent of paddy land in the Northwestern Province. Data from the land use map (Survey Dept. Colombo, 1985).

Administrative division	Area of paddy land (ha)
Puttalam Pattu	5690
Kalpitiya	2900
Arachikatuwa	2250
Pitigal Korale North	1360
Pitigal Korale South	1340

The communities living in the coastal areas are traditionally involved in animal husbandry. Cattle, buffalos and goats are the most common forms of livestock reared. Most of the open grazing land and scrubland is used for maintaining these stocks, but this land is also a potential area for prawn culture. Considering the projected demand for this class of land (based on applications and availability) it can be seen that the demand is about 53% of the available land for culture (Tabs. 4, 5). It was also noted that areas suitable for prawn culture and with a high number of farms also have large livestock populations, and as such the conflict between the need for grazing land and that for prawn culture is inevitable. Competition between village expansion and the development of prawn culture is one of the most important areas where conflict is likely to arise, and has already begun. It can be seen for the six divisions that urban land accounts for less than 1% of the total area while homesteads account for 11.5%.

Table 8. Population statistics for the Northwestern Province (based on 1981 census figures).

Area	Population	
	1981	1989
Puttalam	45,588	57,034
Kalpitiya	48,816	61,072
Arachchikatuwa	44,460	55,683
Chilaw	81,508	101,972
Wennappuwa	97,165	121,560

Table 8 shows that the population in these areas is increasing at a rate of approximately 3% per year. Consequently, the demand for residential land is increasing. The most common land source of prawn culture would be land types such as barren land, sparsely used cropland and grassland. Conflicts of interest would be difficult to predict, but the annual population increase of 10,000 persons per year in these areas will have a significant effect on land demand. In the Karukopone area, land allocated for prawn culture has been contested by villagers, who planned to use the area for village expansion. It is interesting to note that this area has been classified as unsuitable for human settlement. The displacement of small cultivators resulting from farms being already set up could also have an impact. Furthermore, it should be noted that any new land for village expansion activities is most likely to be taken from state land.

Table 9. Livestock statistics (Puttalam Kachcheri,1989).

Area	Cattle	Buffaloes	Goats	Sheep	Total
Wennapuwa	6,255	2,171	2,437	0	10,863
Natandiya	10,080	2,171	2,435	160	14,846
Chilaw	7,460	2,429	4,260	0	14,149
Arachikatuwa	23,790	2,280	5,055	225	31,350
Puttalam	12,875	1,169	4,715	260	19,019
Kalpitiya	9,593	165	10,676	55	20,489

A considerable proportion of land categorized under mangroves, marshland and grassland consists of acid sulphate or potential acid sulphate sediments. Acid sulphate soils in the western coastal areas amount to approximately 5000 ha. As such some of the farms in operation have been constructed in such areas. Jayasinghe (unpublished) observed high concentrations of manganese, iron and aluminium in flushed water after pond preparation from 3 farms which had been constructed in acid sulphate soils. The values recorded were higher than the standard levels set for industrial effluent discharge (ESCAP, 1985).

Table 10. Concentrations of selected heavy metals and pH values in flushed water during pond preparation at 3 farm sites (Jayasinghe, unpublished).

Iron (mg/l)	Aluminium (mg/l)	Manganese (mg/l)	pH
19.30	2.50	4.16	3.5
12.78	1.80	1.12	3.9
17.36	2.35	3.18	2.7

Discussion

The development of prawn culture in the Puttalam District is still in its initial stage but nevertheless rapidly expanding. Operational farms amount to approximately 465 ha and further 1600 ha of state land has been requested by prospective developers. Within the study area, land under prawn culture amounts to 431 ha, and a further 575 ha has been requested by prospective investors. Estimations of the actual land suitable for prawn culture in the Northwestern Province range between 1000 ha and 1400 ha. To date not all of the land suitable for prawn culture has not been brought under culture. However, based on the applications received for land and the increasing number of small-scale private farms in the area, it is expected that the maximum level will be reached very shortly. The majority of land already under prawn culture was owned by the government or its agencies. However, the use of private land for prawn culture has already begun, and it will contribute significantly to prawn production in the near future. Data analysis for the coastal area between Palavi and Bangedeniya shows that the land most likely to be exploited and already in production belongs to the land use categories marshland and bareland. Agricultural land is less significant, but this could be due to the fact that this study concentrates on state land. Most agricultural land is private and would not be under the purview of the GA's Office, and as such has not been taken into consideration. The contribution of private land to prawn culture is important, but at present it is believed that the majority of these lands come into operation without the necessary authorities being informed.

However, based on the findings presented, it can be seen that the two land classes most heavily in demand for culture are that of bareland (including scrubland) and wetlands. The implications of this on the current land use patterns are twofold. The demand on wetlands, which is mostly state land, is significant (based on present requests). This area potentially approximates to 89% of the wetland surrounding the water fringes. The potential effects of this on wildlife, particularly bird life, would be significant, if all of it were to be converted into prawn farms. As a rule of thumb, it is believed that for every 10% reduction in land area, the species number decreases by 50%. The direct loss of mangrove areas for prawn culture is not apparent. The bareland and scrubland class for the use of prawn culture has an important human aspect especially with respect to village expansion and the raising of livestock. The availability of land for expansion in the coastal communities bordering these areas is minimal, and as such most future expansion will compete with areas where prawns could be cultivated, even though some of these areas might not be suitable for human habitation.

Agricultural land is the category of least demand, and the classes of importance within this category are homesteads, coconut plantations and paddy land. However, it is the impact on the paddy land where conflict will arise in the future. At present, the paddy-growing areas that have been converted, or are to be converted, to prawn farming are small. However, it is envisaged that more paddy lands will be converted to prawn farms in the near future as the revenue from prawn farming is greater than that from paddy. Furthermore, paddy cultivation is seasonal and depends on the availability of freshwater which is a problem in these areas. There is a further impact on paddy growing areas in the vicinity and along the upper reaches of the waterways; salinity intrusion. The full effect of salinity intrusion has not yet been felt as the number of operational farms in these areas is still small. However, complaints on this matter have been recorded and are likely to increase with more farms being constructed on private land.

All state land granted passes by the governmental scoping committee, and as such areas deemed to be of value from a sociological and ecological aspect would be taken into consideration. The uncontrolled destruction of these land areas, which come under the purview of the state, would be unlikely. It would be important to include farms on private land into this system and to monitor their effects on the land use patterns in such areas. Other factors limiting prawn culture are very likely in the future.

Acknowledgments

We wish to thank the Chairman and Director General of the National Aquatic Resources Agency for the encouragement and help provided. We are also grateful are to the Government Agent, Puttalam for providing statistical information used in this paper.

Literature Cited

de Silva, K.H.G.M. and P.K. de Silva. 1982. An ecological study of mangrove fauna in the west coast of Sri Lanka.Ceylon. *J. Sci. (Bio. Sci.)* 9: 36-53.

ESCAP (Economic and Social Commission for Asia and the Pacific). 1985. *Marine environmental problems and issues in the ESCAP region.* ESCAP. Bangkok, Thailand.

Hoffman, T. 1988.The fifth water fowl census in Sri Lanka. *Loris* 18: 80-82.

NARA (National Aquatic Resources Agency). 1986. *Survey to identify suitable areas in the coastal belt of Sri Lanka for prawn culture,* Report 1. National Aquatic Resources Agency, Colombo.

NARA (National Aquatic Resources Agency). 1988. *Survey to identify suitable areas in the coastal belt of Sri Lanka for prawn culture,* Report 2. National Aquatic Resources Agency, Colombo.

Odum, W.E. and R.E. Johannes. 1975. The response of mangroves to man-induced environmental stress. *In* W.E.J. Furgeson and R.E. Johannes, eds. *Tropical Marine Pollution,* pp. 52-61. Elsevier Publishing Company, Amsterdam.

Siriwardene, P.P.G.S.N., A. de Alwis and K.U. Dias. 1988. Shrimp farming in Sri Lanka: Present status in Sri Lanka and future strategies. *J. Inland Fisheries* 4: 123-145.

UNEP (United Nations Environmental Program). 1984. *Handbook for Mangrove Area Management.* East West Center and Environment and Policy Institute, Honolulu.

Proceedings of the International and Interdisciplinary Symposium
ECOLOGY AND LANDSCAPE MANAGEMENT IN SRI LANKA
W. Erdelen, C. Preu, N. Ishwaran, C.M. Madduma Bandara (eds.)
Colombo, Sri Lanka, 12-26 March 1990
© 1993
Margraf Scientific Books, D-97985 Weikersheim
ISBN 3-8236-1182-8

Impact of Sri Lankan Reservoirs, their Fisheries, Management and Conservation

C.H. FERNANDO

Abstract

Sri Lanka, which has no natural lakes, is well served by reservoirs ranging from a few ha to 10,000 ha surface area. About 2% of the area of the country is covered by reservoirs, and this value will increase to about 4% relatively soon. The reservoirs extant today include ancient reservoirs dating from 400 B.C. recently constructed reservoirs and many ancient reservoirs that have been restored and enlarged. The ancient reservoir system was a highly sophisticated irrigation network of reservoirs, irrigation channels and other auxiliary constructions for irrigation. The impact of reservoirs on the physical, chemical and biological regimes in Sri Lanka is among the most profound human imprint comparable to anthropogenic changes caused by agriculture and human habitations. The landscape has been dramatically altered, but most of the reservoirs blend into the surroundings enhancing the natural beauty and high diversity of landscapes especially in the dry zone. Sri Lankan reservoirs are colonized by a diverse range of organisms. Bird life is rich and varied. Fish, although not very diverse in species, nevertheless support some of the most productive fisheries in reservoirs anywhere in the world. The introduction of African lacustrine fishes has made possible this high yield of fish. The invertebrate fauna drawn from rivers, marshes and temporary ponds is rich and varied, and plant life, both aquatic and in the vicinity of reservoirs, is rich and diverse. Management of reservoirs by conservation of the flora and fauna and orderly exploitation of the fisheries will greatly enhance the value of this ancient heritage as a major natural resource in Sri Lanka.

Introduction

Reservoir construction has become an intensive and extensive enterprise worldwide. There are a variety of reasons for this phenomenon. River systems can be readily dammed in many parts of the world. Reservoirs, considered as an energy resource, do not cause direct pollution, unlike thermal power generation, and there has been a rapidly growing demand for irrigation water. Reservoirs are more common in arid areas. Large areas of Spain, the northeastern part of Brazil and the dry zone of Sri Lanka are dotted with reservoirs. Many modern reservoirs are multipurpose and not restricted to arid areas by any means. During the past fifty years or so,

351

reservoir construction has been accelerating in many parts of the world. Reservoirs comprise the only large bodies of standing water in large areas of the world.

On a global scale, the landscape over wide areas has been dramatically altered by reservoirs. The impact of reservoir construction on the physical environment and living organisms is both profound and pervasive. The damming of rivers and streams causes the formation of large areas of standing water. Apart from changes of a physical and chemical nature, the biological components are radically altered. Rivers are old and most existing lakes are young. The riverine fauna and flora is not adapted very well for a lentic life. The living components of reservoirs are also drawn from temporary ponds and marshes. Lakes and reservoirs are young habitats, and therefore their living components do not represent well-adapted communities. There are a few old lakes, like Lake Baikal and Lake Tanganiyka, which are old and have diverse living components including many endemics. Fernando and Holcík (1989, 1991) have discussed the origin and role of riverine and lacustrine fish in reservoirs.

Reservoir builders often neglect the role of reservoirs as biologically rich environments. However, reservoirs have a real potential for the conservation and diversification of living organisms. The fisheries of reservoirs can also be very productive, as in Sri Lanka (De Silva, 1988). Oglesby (1985) put fisheries in reservoirs in perspective very succinctly when he said that reservoirs and lakes are more than sites for the storage of water, they are highly productive biological systems which, when viewed anthropocentrically, are seen as producers of fish and shellfish. Trefethen (1973) commenting on reservoirs as habitats for wildlife, states that even without deliberate planning and management of shorelines and watersheds of many man-made lakes, these sites develop food and cover as good as or better than those of the river complex. As reservoirs age, their ecology becomes more settled and the landscape looks more attractive. Although reservoirs are hailed as a cheap source of energy with no pollution and a boom to agriculture, they have negative impacts too. Flooding destroys habitats of animals and human habitations. Siltation is also a bane of reservoirs and can curtail their life dramatically.

In Sri Lanka, reservoir construction has a history dating back about 2500 years. The sophistication of reservoir construction reached a high level especially between 700 A.D. and 1200 A.D. when transbasin transfer of water was accomplished. This level of reservoir sophistication was superseded only in the era of modern engineering in the past fifty years or so. Thus, unlike many parts of the world, the extant reservoirs consist partly of ancient reservoirs that have been restored or expanded, and new (usually large) reservoirs.

Reservoirs have changed the landscape of Sri Lanka by creating a new and extensive set of habitats unrepresented naturally. Reservoirs have made possible extensive and intensive agriculture especially in the dry zone and have provided energy for industry and domestic use. They also represent some of the most biologically diverse habitats in the country. Reservoirs and associated waters can provide an ecologically rich component of the landscape, attractive for recreation, while fisheries can provide a substantial quantity of food. Research, both short-term and long-term are essential if their potential is to be realized.

My own studies on the aquatic fauna of Sri Lanka have indicated that reservoirs have diverse fauna (and presumably flora and microorganisms) just like natural lakes. Reservoirs are also highly productive biologically and give very high fish yields if lacustrine fish are present. In this presentation, I provide background information on the extent and nature of reservoirs in Sri Lanka. Using available data on the living organisms, I shall comment on the richness of the biological components. The fisheries of Sri Lankan reservoirs will be presented and the role of introduced fish will be discussed. Some strategies for the conservation of living organisms and the management of fisheries will be mentioned.

Global Perspectives on Reservoirs

With the acceleration of reservoir construction, scientific literature on various aspects of reservoirs and their ecology has grown exponentially during the past fifty years. There have been a series of international scientific meetings on reservoirs and their ecology beginning in

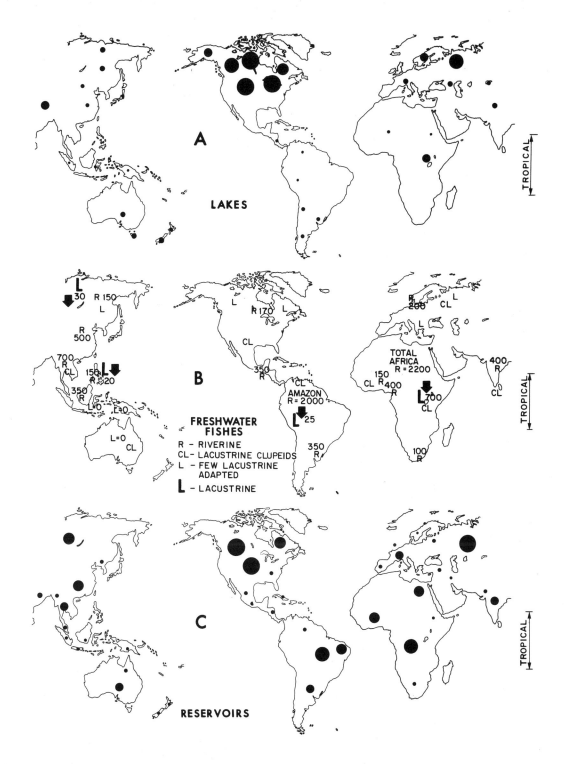

Figure 1. Global distribution of lakes, reservoirs and lacustrine and riverine fish. The circles indicate water areas and their relative distribution (modified from Fernando, 1980d).

353

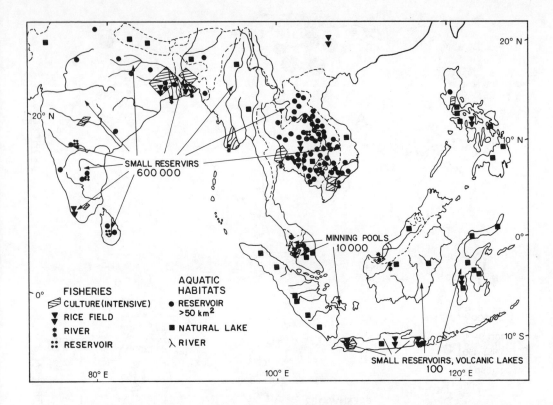

Figure 2. Reservoir distribution in Southeastern Asia and the location of fisheries and fishculture (updated from Fernando and Furtado, 1975).

1965 (Lowe-McConnell, 1966). Four subsequent meetings have been held in Ghana, Tennessee, USA, Quebec City, Canada, and most recently (1987, 1992) in Ceské Budêjovice, Czechoslovakia. A number of individual reservoirs have been studied in Asia, Africa, North America, South America, Europe and Australasia. Tundisi (1988) edited a series of studies on the management of reservoirs and Straskraba *et al.* (in press) have edited a volume on reservoir limnology, fisheries and water quality to be published in 1993. Reservoir engineering, hydrology, ecology, management, conservation and fisheries comprise fields of research activity where considerable work is being done at the present time.

It is not possible to obtain an accurate figure for the extent of reservoirs globally. However, I wish to make some remarks on the subject in order to convey a perspective of their extent. SCOPE (1972) gave estimates of large reservoirs (over 100 km^2) for each continental and sub-continental area. The former USSR and North America had the most extensive reservoir areas (over 5 million ha each), followed closely by Africa, while Asia, Europe and Australasia had considerably less. South America had a substantial reservoir area amounting to about half that of Africa. Frey (1966) commenting on reservoirs over 500 acres in the USA and USSR stated that the reservoir area in the USSR was increasing by 3.5% annually. He pointed out that in the 48 contiguous states of the USA, there was more reservoir area than the area of the 3000 or so larger lakes (excluding the Great Lakes). Figure 1 shows the distribution of lakes and reservoirs globally. Apart from large reservoirs, there are numerous small reservoirs. In southeastern Asia, Fernando and Furtado (1975) estimated 500,000 such reservoirs (Fig. 2). I have raised this to 60,000. Hawley (1973) states that there are over 2 million artificial ponds, pits, reservoirs and earthen tanks in the USA. In Sri Lanka, there are supposed to be over

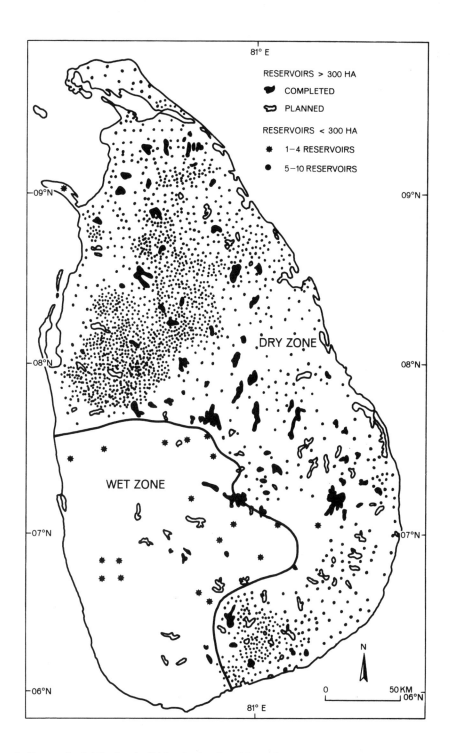

Figure 3. Reservoir distribution in Sri Lanka (updated from Fernando, 1971).

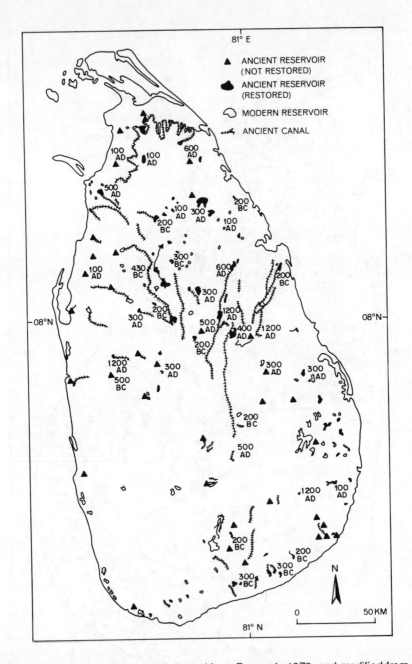

Figure 4. Ancient reservoirs in Sri Lanka (adapted from Fernando,1979, and modified from Fernando and De Silva, 1984).

10,000 small reservoirs in an area of 65,000 km² (Fig. 3). During a recent visit to northeastern Brazil, I was told that there are over 100,000 reservoirs in the "arid triangle" of that region. Similar heavy concentrations of reservoirs are found in other parts of the world such as Spain, Romania and Mexico.

356

History, Nature and Extent of Reservoirs in Sri Lanka

Sri Lanka has one of the longest histories of reservoir construction on an extensive scale in the world. This activity appears to have commenced around 600 B.C. although sophisticated reservoir systems with transbasin transfer of water was a later development around 700 A.D. (Perera, 1984). The extent of ancient reservoirs has been given by Fernando (1979). The earliest reservoir extant, the Abhayawewa (Basawakkulama), near Anuradhapura, was built around 430 B.C. (Fig. 4). Brohier (1934-1936) has given a detailed account of the layout of ancient reservoirs and their mode of construction.

The ancient reservoirs now extant, mainly due to restoration and expansion, have the appearance of natural lakes. The landscape has been stabilized with lush vegetation and there is a rich and diverse assortment of aquatic and semiaquatic organisms. Figures 5 and 6 (annexed) show some of these reservoirs. Minneriya and Parakrama Samudra (Fig. 5, annexed) are both ancient reservoirs, restored and expanded in recent years. Kandalama (Fig. 6, annexed), a recently constructed reservoir has the trees of the inundated forest still standing. The Moonplains Reservoir (Fig. 6, annexed) is a deep reservoir with negligible fish production, unlike the other reservoirs shown. The morphometry of some reservoirs is shown in Figure 7.

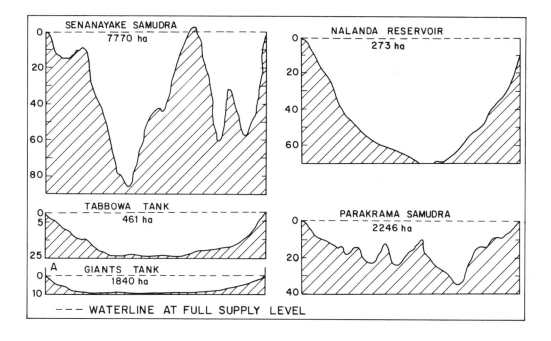

Figure 7. Morphometry of some representative Sri Lankan reservoirs (modified from Fernando and Indrasena, 1969).

Although Sri Lanka has a large number of rivers (103), some of them are not perennial (Fig. 8). Reservoirs in the dry zone however tap the water of the rivers during the rains. The largest river, the Mahaweli Ganga, flows through the dry zone but it is perennial and receives water from year round rainfall in the hills of the central highlands. This river is the basis for the largest irrigation and power scheme which stores water in a series of reservoirs (De Silva, 1985).

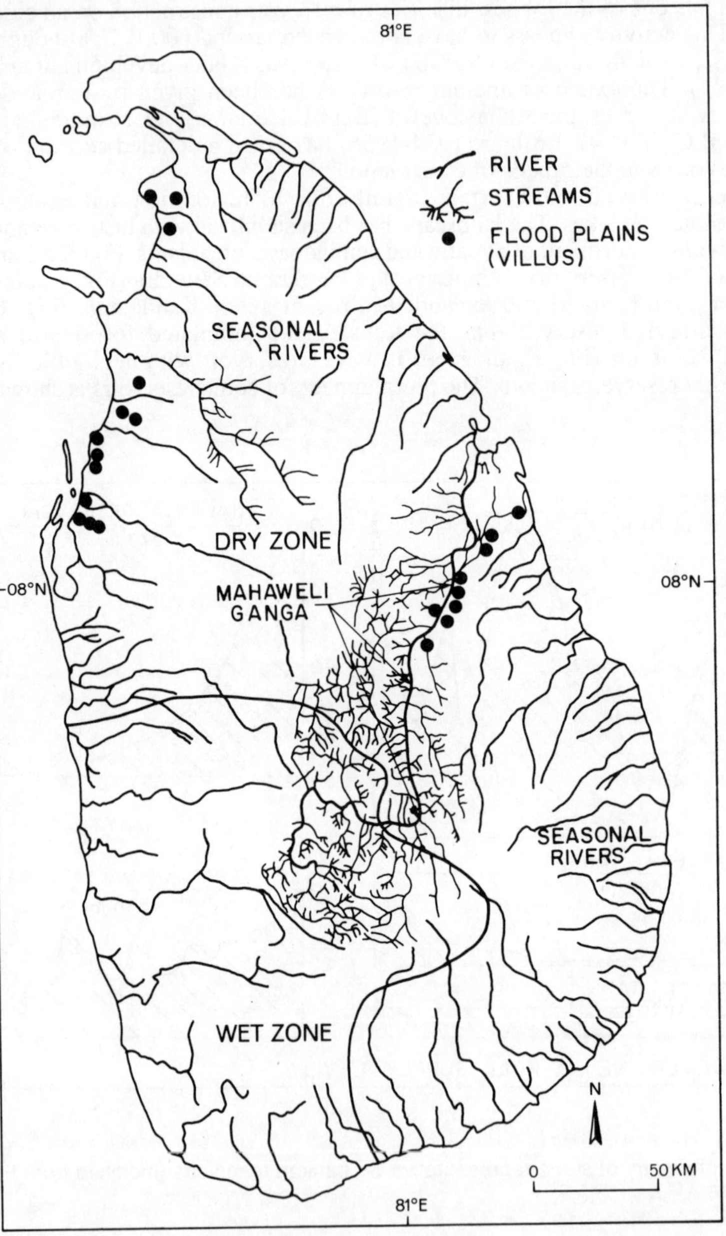

Figure 8. River systems in Sri Lanka with two rivers showing their streams and the distribution of flood plains/villus (modified from Fernando, 1971).

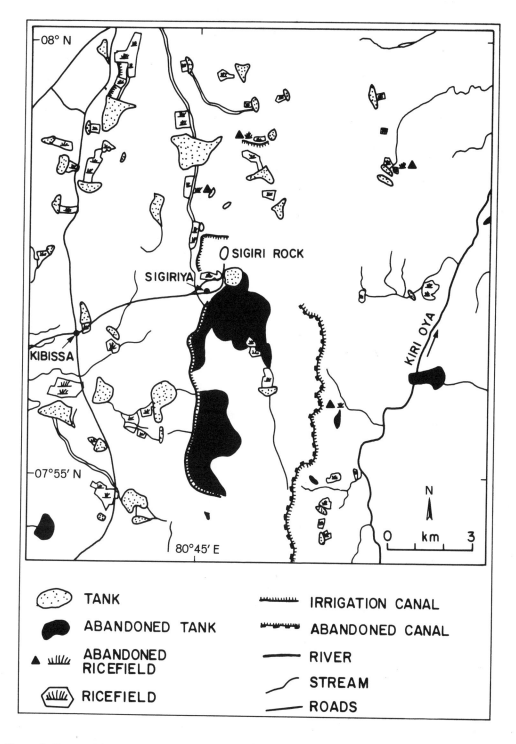

Figure 9. Reservoirs in a small area of the dry zone near Polonnaruwa drawn from a 1 inch/1 mile map (modified slightly from Fernando and De Silva, 1984).

Apart from the larger reservoirs, there are as many as 1 per km² of small (< 300 ha) reservoirs in some parts of the dry zone (Fig. 9). Brohier (1975) mentions that there are as many as 11,200 small reservoirs in the Northern Provinces and the Anuradhapura District alone. Fernando and De Silva (1984) give the number and area of reservoirs in each district. It is evident that the actual number of smaller reservoirs is not readily obtainable. This is due to the fact that many reservoirs of small size are now similar in appearance to natural ponds. Also anicuts (river diversions) are sometimes included in the list of small reservoirs.

Reservoirs in Sri Lanka are part of an extensive and highly sophisticated irrigation system originally designed to supply water to rice fields. In recent times, irrigation of other crops and power generation have also been served. In ancient times, the land was farmed by owner cultivators who had an extent of rice field and high ground for the cultivation of vegetables and dryland crops (Perera, 1984). The layout of the ancient reservoir system is detailed by Brohier (1934-1936). Figure 9 shows the distribution of ancient reservoirs and rice fields still in use in the Polonnaruwa District. The Gal Oya multipurpose scheme is a modern version of the ancient irrigation system with greater storage of water and hence a higher intensity of cultivation (Fig. 10). Hydroelectric power production is an added output from the system. The most recent and the largest and most ambitious project involves the Mahaweli Ganga (Fig. 8) and a series of channels and large reservoirs (De Silva, 1985). The total area of reservoirs in Sri Lanka at full supply level is about 150,000 ha (Fernando and De Silva, 1984). This figure will rise to over

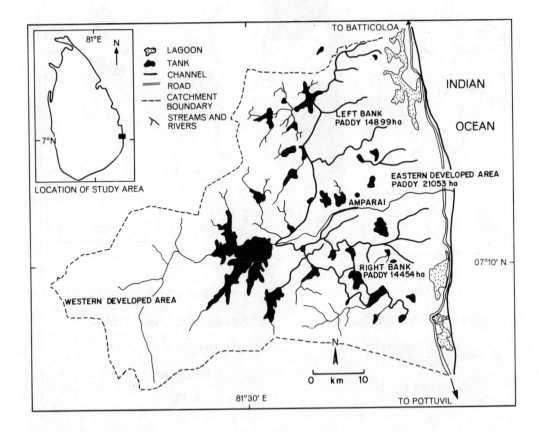

Figure 10. A modern multipurpose irrigation and power production scheme involving 32 reservoirs in the Gal Oya Valley (modified from Fernando, 1971).

250,000 ha when the enterprise of reservoir building is completed in all the river basins, giving 4 ha/km^2 of standing waters for the country as a whole. By comparison, Britain, a well-watered country, has only 1% (= 1 ha/km^2) of standing waters calculated for the whole country (Burgis and Morris, 1987). To the area of standing waters must be added the extensive system of irrigation channels (Figs. 9, 10), and the 103 river systems with their streams (Fig. 7). Almost all the aquatic habitats in Sri Lanka owe their present form to human intervention stretching back 2500 years. Reservoirs are well integrated into the landscape and the human factor has blended with this configuration. Figure 9 shows the physical relationship of Parakrama Samudra and the surrounding cultivated land, Polonnaruwa town and ancient ruins. This area is now a tourist attraction. As the town grows, the reservoir is likely to be heavily polluted unless careful planning is introduced at an early stage. Polonnaruwa is one of the most picturesque of the ancient capitals of Sri Lanka. Today it is a thriving agricultural community and an important transport center. Parakrama Samudra has a very productive fishery which has been exploited for over 30 years. The conflicting demands of the various uses must be resolved through careful planning.

Biological Diversity in Reservoirs

In Sri Lanka there are no natural lakes. The habitats most closely resembling lakes are the villus or floodplains of rivers (Fig. 8). They have an estimated area of 12,500 ha according to Fernando (1971). Ponds also resemble lakes but they often have a short life before drying up annually or seasonally. Organisms colonizing reservoirs are drawn from rivers and streams (lotic) and ponds and marshes (lentic). Organisms are usually adapted primarily for living either in running or standing waters. It is a truism that rivers are old and lakes are young. There are a few lakes though that are old, e.g. Baikal, Tanganiyka. Most lakes in temperate regions are glacial in origin and therefore around 10,000 years or less in age. Of course, reservoirs like lakes are juvenile and have not been in existence long enough for the evolution of lacustrine adapted organisms. The organisms colonizing reservoirs normally are thus eurytopic forms and occasionally, as in the case of clupeids, marine. Some old lakes, on the other hand, for example Baikal and some rift valley lake in Africa, have lacustrine fishes (Fig. 1). Lake Baikal has a large number of endemic crustaceans (Koshov, 1963) and the rift valley lakes in Africa have a very diverse lacustrine fish fauna (Beadle, 1981). It is generally believed that lacustrine invertebrates are derived from riverine faunas. However, Williams (1988) has drawn attention the fact that temporary habitats (ponds and marshes) are geologically old and have supplied recruits for the colonization of lakes. Backwaters of rivers have rich faunas as shown for the Paraná River by Paggi and Paggi (1990). Fernando (1980c) found that in tropical lakes and reservoirs there are no exclusively limnetic zooplankton species. In the temperate region, on the other hand, there are some exclusive species of zooplankton in the limnetic region. Also, this region has a greater diversity of zooplankton than the tropics. Invertebrate zooplankton predators are particularly low in diversity in tropical as compared to temperate lakes and reservoirs (Fernando et al. 1990). This disparity may well have important implications for fishery management in the tropics.

Lakes and reservoirs are inhabited by a wide range of organisms from microscopic size to large vertebrates. There is a high biotic diversity in reservoirs in spite of the negative impact of water drawdown. In Sri Lanka, 35 species of fish (5 of them introduced) were found in Parakrama Samudra (Fernando, 1984a). Sri Lanka has a relatively depauperate fish fauna for a tropical continental island with only 60 freshwater species. The number of fish species in reservoirs relative to the total number indicates a high diversity as compared to any habitat. Rice fields which have streams, shallow standing water and marsh-like conditions also have about 35 species of fish (Fernando, 1956). Admittedly, the freshwater fish fauna of Sri Lanka is not highly diverse as compared to that of neighboring countries like Malaysia and Thailand (Fernando, 1977). Ubolratana Reservoir in Thailand has a fish fauna of only 37 species (Bhukeswan, 1985), although the fish fauna of Thai freshwaters is very diverse numbering nearly 600 species (Fernando, 1977). This probably indicates the low diversity in the littoral of lakes when the fish involved are not lacustrine. Old African rift valley lakes have well over 300 species, many of them endemics. Bird life is very diverse and abundant in reservoirs. Winkler (1983) records 27 species of fish-eating birds during visits in 1979, 1980 and 1982 in Parakrama Samudra (Fig. 5, annexed). In this reservoir of 2262 ha, peak numbers of 102, 13,700 and 1850 individuals of 3 species of cormorants were recorded. He calculated that annually the birds eat 112-161 kg/ha of fish. The mean fish yield of this reservoir for the past 32 years was 227 kg/ha. These figures indicate a highly productive biological system which is not only exploited by humans, but which supports a wide range of other animals. The high production of fish is also evidence of a thriving plant and animal community in the reservoir.

When we consider the invertebrate, plant and microorganism composition of reservoirs in Sri Lanka, we have much less data compared to vertebrates. Fernando (1965) gives some data on the marginal fauna of some larger reservoirs, and Fernando and Ellepola (1969) gives a list of invertebrate and vertebrate inhabitants they identified in two small reservoirs. The zooplankton of reservoirs has been discussed in detail by Fernando (1980a). This data is indicative of a diverse fauna. We have however no single comprehensive catalog of the freshwater invertebrates in any reservoir comparable to the list of Cunnington (1920) for the large African rift valley lakes.

Sri Lanka has a rich and varied fauna in freshwater habitats, both lentic and lotic. There is extensive data on the faunal composition and their distribution. The freshwater invertebrate fauna has been reviewed by Fernando (1980b). Major contributions to the freshwater fauna and their identification include the early monograph of Daday (1898), keys, lists and illustrations of the fauna by Mendis and Fernando (1962), and Fernando (1963, 1964, 1969, 1974). Two expeditions, one from Lund University, Sweden 1962 (Brinck et al. 1972) and the University of Vienna (Costa and Starmühlner, 1972) dealt with much material from aquatic habitats. The ecology of Parakrama Samudra and some of the flora and fauna were dealt with in the monograph of Schiemer (1983). Freshwater fauna received major attention in the volume on ecology and biogeography of Sri Lanka (Fernando, 1984b). There are also numerous studies on individual families (e.g. Simuliidae) or groups (zooplankton) especially during the past forty years. I think it can be said that the freshwater fauna of Sri Lanka is better known taxonomically than that of any other tropical country.

We know less about the aquatic flora, although Abeywickrema (1980) states that reservoirs have a rich aquatic flora and some of these are floating plants. He also states that the marshy edges are colonized by amphibious plants. The phytoplankton of Sri Lankan reservoirs has been studied in some detail. A recent study of Parakrama Samudra (Rott, 1983) also reviews earlier literature. Little is known of the microorganisms although they are important as decomposers and food for organisms which feed on detritus. During the dry season, large areas of the reservoir are exposed (Fig. 5, annexed). However, since many reservoir organisms are drawn from ponds and marshes, they are well adapted to estivate and recolonize the reservoir.

The origin and composition of the reservoir fish fauna is of great interest because the presence of lacustrine fish species can mean very high fish yields. This subject has been discussed in detail by Fernando and Holcík (1982, 1989, 1991). Sri Lanka has a depauperate fish fauna and no lacustrine species. The reservoir fish fauna is therefore of riverine, pond and marsh origin. The success of introduced African cichlids which are better adapted to lacustrine conditions has provided one of the most productive fisheries in tropical reservoirs anywhere in the world.

Conservation of Diversity

Reservoirs are productive biological systems with diverse organisms from large to microscopic in size. The attractiveness of a habitat is strongly influenced by the diversity of its living components and the maintenance of such diversity must be considered an important enterprise for reservoir conservation. Also the high potential productivity of reservoirs in fish is a great asset. Fish stocks should be conserved and exploited in a sustainable manner. From the

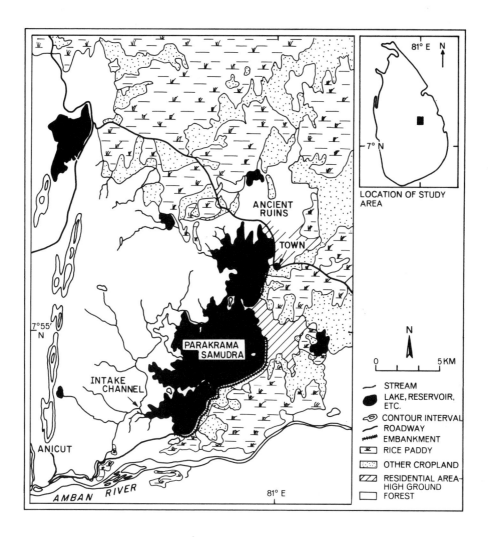

Figure 11. The catchment and surrounding area of the best studied reservoir in Sri Lanka, Parakrama Samudra (modified from Fernando, 1984).

educational aspect, reservoirs can be used as sites for both teaching students and training researchers. The ready accessibility of reservoirs throughout most of the country can serve to educate students and the general public on the rich heritage of living organisms in reservoirs and how they contribute to biological processes and food production. As human densities increase, reservoirs, like other habitats, will come more and more under the influence of pollution and other human-induced changes. Measures must be adopted to maintain water quality, the watersheds and the immediate surroundings of reservoirs in as good a condition as possible. Investment of funds in the orderly development of fisheries and in the maintenance of a pleasant landscape in the vicinity of reservoirs will give good returns in fish yields and tourism and enable the long-term use of reservoirs for a wide variety of purposes.

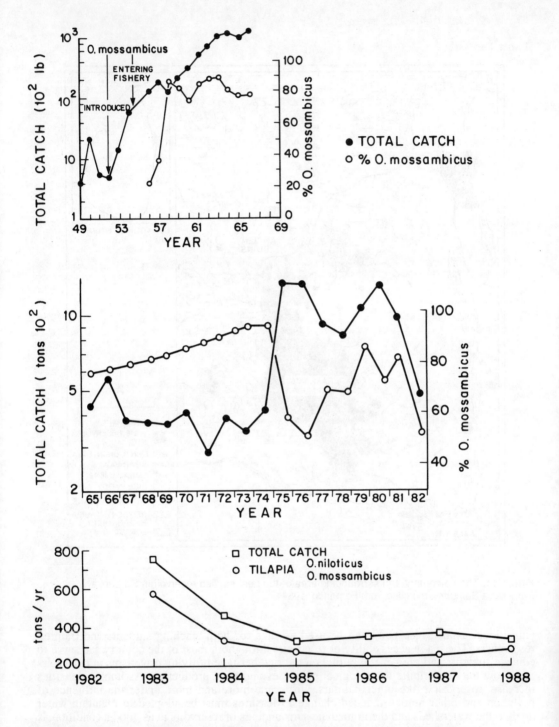

Figure 13. Fish yields from Parakrama Samudra from 1943-1988. Data for 1943-1965 from Fernando (1971), data from 1966-1982 from De Silva (1988), data for 1983-1988 supplied by Mr. A. Hettiarachchi, Sri Lanka. Percentage of tilapias from 1967-1972, fide Mendis (1977).

Fisheries and their Management

Large Reservoirs

Fisheries in large shallow reservoirs in Sri Lanka can be considered among the most productive in the world. There is a wealth of published material on these fisheries, the most comprehensive are those of Fernando and Indrasena (1969) and De Silva (1988). The dominant fish *Oreochromis mossambicus*, an African cichlid fish and the simple gear used by fishermen are shown in Figure 12 (annexed). Reservoir fisheries on a commercial scale is a relatively recent enterprise and has been possible due to the introduction of African cichlid fish beginning in 1952. The fish yields of Parakrama Samudra since 1943 are illustrated in Figure 13. The annual fish yield before the introduction of tilapias was around 1 kg/ha. Tilapias started entering fishery soon after their introduction in 1952 and by 1958 the percentage of tilapias had risen to 80% of the catch by weight and a viable commercial fishery had been established. The average annual yield for 32 years since tilapias dominated fishery is 227 kg/ha. The indigenous fish comprise a sizeable porportion of the catch and consist of herbivorous carps, carnivorous catfishes, snakeheads and an indigenous cichlid *Etroplus suratensis*. The percentage of tilapias has varied from 55 to 94 for the 32 years of commercial fishing.

De Silva and Sirisena (1988) have speculated that indigenous cyprinids could yield as high catches as the tilapias. This seems unlikely because no cyprinid fishery in the tropics has very high fish yields in reservoirs or lakes comparable to that given by tilapias. In Ubolratana reservoir, a large and relatively shallow body of water in Thailand, all the fish species, mainly cyprinids, are exploited. The annual fish yield from the reservoir is only 42 kg/ha (1967-1986) and includes 10% contributed by an indigenous clupeid *Clupeichthys aesarnensis* (Bhukeswan, 1985). A small-sized clupeid *Ehirava fluviatilis* was reported to colonize Parakrama Samudra and have a large biomass (Newrkla and Duncan, 1984). However, there is no record of this fish being exploited commercially nor is *Hyporamphus gaimardi*, another marine colonizer of reservoirs (De Silva, 1985) an important commercial fish. Clupeidae sometimes comprise an important component in reservoir and lake fisheries (Marshall 1984, Fernando and Holcík 1991).

Most large shallow reservoirs (> 300 ha) have fisheries of the same level of production as Parakrama Samudra. Deeper reservoirs like Senanayake Samudra (Fig. 7) have lower fish yields. Deep reservoirs without a littoral like Nalanda (Fig. 7) have negligible fish catches. Upcountry reservoirs (Fig. 6, annexed) which are deep and cool have low fish yields too. The total fish yield from the larger reservoirs is 27,000-30,000 tons annually which works out at over 300 kg/ha each year (De Silva, 1988).

In spite of the consistently high yields of tilapias and the fact that these fish are self-propagating unlike exotic carps, attempts have been made to use exotic carps by regular stocking since 1940. This effort has now been intensified (Sreeniwasan 1988, Jayasekera 1988). Claims have been made that these carps can add considerably to the production. However, these claims have still to be proved over a long-term period.

Management of large reservoirs as a fishery resource needs careful, objective and long-term study and analysis. Some data on which management can be based is already available. The high sustained fish yields consisting mainly of tilapias but including indigenous species have been obtained at low cost. Stocking with exotic carps bred and raised in hatcheries will involve considerable expense. Whether such expense is warranted will be shown in due course. A consistent policy of funding for research and development will go a long way to obtaining maximum sustainable fish yields.

Small Reservoirs

The number of small reservoirs (< 300 ha) can only be estimated very roughly at present. There are supposed to be over 10,000 such reservoirs varying in size from about 1 ha to 300 ha. The very high density of these reservoirs is illustrated in Figure 9. Brinck *et al.* (1972) illustrate the very high density of these reservoirs in the dry zone of the south, while Brohier

(1934-1936) shows the very high concentration of these reservoirs in specific parts of the country such as the Mannar region near Giants tank (Fig. 7).

A feature common to all small reservoirs is that they are dry for periods of 2-10 months of the year. These reservoirs can be used for fish culture with proper measures which take into account their short life. Fernando and Ellepola (1969) studied the limnology and fish production of two reservoirs in the Polonnaruwa area. *Oreochromis mossambicus* was introduced in 1963 and harvested in 1964. The annual fish yields were 89 and 62 kg/ha. The tilapias were collected from reservoirs in the vicinity. The fish catch was modest, but no large amount of funds was involved.

In more recent years, exotic carps have been used to stock small reservoirs. Thayaparan (1982) and De Silva (1988) also suggested the use of exotic carps although their data shows the dominance of tilapias in the catch from these reservoirs. Presumably the tilapias were of small size. There is however no long-term data on the fish yields from small reservoirs. There is also no analysis of the cost of stocking these reservoirs with exotic carps which have to be bred in hatcheries at considerable expense. Over the past 45 years, extensive fish culture (in reservoirs) and intensive fish culture (in ponds) have been an unmitigated failure in Sri Lanka.

In considering management strategies for fisheries in these small reservoirs, it is important to undertake a study of the types and seasonal availability of natural food. The use of tilapias (*O. mossambicus* and *O. niloticus*) must be re-examined in view of their low cost and potential for high yields. If small size of harvestable fish is a problem, then attempts should be made to counter this trend. The use of indigenous predators like *Ophiocephalus* to thin out tilapias should also be explored.

In spite of rather optimistic reports of fish culture in small reservoirs using exotic carps, there is no consistent record of high fish yields using these fish species. The fish culture enterprise set up by the Chinese in the early seventies in Udawalawe, using Chinese carps folded after their departure and the more recent enterprise using Indian carps and involving Indian experts, may suffer the same fate.

Small reservoirs are biologically diverse and potential producers of high fish yields. They must be studied in a consistent and long-term way, and the findings could then be used for management. Small reservoirs are also useful for enhancing the natural attractiveness of landscapes, and for this they should be maintained in good condition and their surroundings kept in an appropriate state.

Summary and Discussion

The extensive and varied reservoirs in Sri Lanka provide a major resource. They enhance the quality of the landscape and ameliorate the arid conditions in the dry zone, besides providing water for irrigation and hydroelectricity. Reservoirs have by their ubiquity altered the landscape to an extent comparable to agriculture and human habitations. At present, reservoirs occupy over 2% of the total area of Sri Lanka, and this figure will increase to 4%. Maximization of the value of reservoirs needs careful planning and investment in management and research on a long-term basis.

Reservoirs are biologically diverse habitats. They provide refuges for a wide variety of aquatic and semiaquatic organisms. The proper management and conservation of this biological resource must be placed high on the priorities for natural resource management in the country. Reservoirs enhance the attractiveness of the landscape almost everywhere in Sri Lanka. Water is a preferred site for recreation and reservoirs provide this in an attractive setting. To preserve the reservoirs as attractive habitats, they must be protected from the ill-effects of urbanization. Strict codes for land use in the vicinity and the watersheds of reservoirs must be enforced. Sewage and other forms of pollution must not be allowed into reservoir inflows.

Fisheries in the larger reservoirs in Sri Lanka rank among the most productive in the world. They are based on indigenous riverine, pond and marsh species as well as introduced African cichlids adapted to lacustrine conditions. Small reservoirs remain largely underexploited as a fishing resource. Management strategies must be devised for maintaining the high fish yields of large reservoirs and must also be directed towards the use of small reservoirs for productive fisheries. The pelagic of the larger lakes are fishless by and large, except for the occasional occurrence of the indigenous clupeid *Ehirava fluviatilis*. There is a potential for a pelagic fishery as has been shown in African and Thai reservoirs. Deep waters and cooler waters in the uplands are still not productive in fish. Eccles (1975) suggested introducing deepwater African fish into large and deep tropical reservoirs. This enterprise has not been undertaken so far.

Sri Lanka has been exploited agriculturally on an intensive scale for at least 2500 years. The reservoirs, although man-made, form an integral part of the agricultural enterprise and comprise an important well-integrated resource. Just like the physical landscape, the vegetation has been altered by human activities, and about 7.3% of the higher plants are exotic (Abeywickrama, 1955). This proportion of exotic plants does not seem high. In Canada, higher exotic plants comprise 27% of the flora (Scoggan, 1978).

The reservoirs have been colonized by aquatic plants, animals and microorganisms and the moist margins are home to semiaquatic and amphibious organisms. Some of these organisms are exotics. Burgis and Morris (1987) have pointed out that gravel pits in Britain, usually considered wastelands, are biologically more rich and interesting than the land they replace. Reservoirs in Sri Lanka although man-made like gravel pits, are nevertheless extremely rich in organisms and make the countryside more attractive. In England, hedgerows, a human created biological entity, are the most biologically diverse habitats left in the country (Muir and Muir, 1987). Charles Elton, a pioneer of the science of ecology, defined conservation as keeping or putting in the landscape the greatest possible ecological diversity, in the world, in every continent and island, and so far as practicable, in every district (Elton, 1958). He went on to state that provided the native species have their place, there is no reason why the reconstitution of communities to make them interesting and stable should not include a careful selection of exotic forms as many of these are in any case going to arrive in due course and occupy some niche.

Reservoirs in Sri Lanka comprise an ancient heritage which has been greatly expanded and remodelled in modern times for intensified agriculture and hydroelectric power production. Fisheries has been a bonus which was not part of the reservoir resources planned originally but it has now become viable thanks to introduced lacustrine adapted fishes from Africa. The proper management of reservoirs, besides maintenance and repair, must extend to the conservation of the living organisms, the maintenance of water quality and the beautification of the surroundings. Reservoirs and biologically rich environments which add an aquatic dimension to landscapes. They are both an ornament to an already varied landscape when properly managed, and one of the most valuable resources in the country.

Acknowledgments

I wish to thank Dr. S.R. Kottegoda, formerly Dean, Faculty of Medicine, Colombo University for sending me literature and photographs of reservoirs. Mr. A. Hettiarachchi supplied data on recent fish catches in Parakrama Samudra when he was in charge of the Fisheries Station, Polonnaruwa. Dr. M. Kottelat, Zoologische Staatssammlung, Munich, provided data on fish used in Figure 1. Dr. T. Petr, FAO, Rome unfailingly provided literature and answers to queries. Miss Renu Sirimongkongthawarn, my student working at Ubolratana Reservoir, provided assorted data on fish catches from that reservoir. Dr. S.S. De Silva, National University of Singapore, provided literature and some data for Figure 13. I am grateful for this assistance.

367

Literature Cited

Aberwickrama, B.A. 1955. Origin and affinities of the flora of Ceylon. *Proc. Ceyl. Ass. Adv. Sci. II Sess. (D).* 1-23.

Abeywickrama, B.A. 1980. The flora of Sri Lanka, *Spol. Zeylan.* 35: 1-8.

Beadle, L.C. 1981. *The Inland Waters of Tropical Africa.* Longman, London.

Bhukeswan, T. 1985. The Nam Pong Basin (Thailand). *In* T. Petr, ed. *Inland Fisheries in Multipurpose River Basin Planning and Development in Tropical Asian Countries: Three Case Studies*, pp. 55-99. FAO, Rome.

Brinck, P., H. Andersson and L. Cederholm. 1972. Report from the Lund University Ceylon Expedition in 1962. Introduction. *Ent. Scand. Suppl.* 1: 4-36.

Brohier, R.L. 1934-1936. *Ancient Irrigation Works in Ceylon. Part I-III.* Ceyl. Govt. Press, Colombo.

Brohier, R.L. 1975. *Food and the People.* Lake House, Colombo.

Burgis, M. and P. Morris. 1987. *The Natural History of Lakes.* Cambridge University Press, Cambridge.

Costa, H.H. and F. Starmühlner. 1973. Results of the Austrian-Ceylonese Hydrobiological Mission 1970 Part I: Preliminary Report. Introduction and description of stations. *Bull. Fish. Res. Stn. Sri Lanka (Ceylon)* 23: 43-76.

Cunnington, W.A. 1920. The fauna of the African lakes: A study in comparative limnology with special reference to Tanganiyka. *Proc. Zool. Soc. London* (1920): 507-623.

Daday, E. 1898. Microskopische Süsswassertiere aus Ceylon. *Termész. Füz. (Budapest)* 21: 1-123.

De Silva, S.S. 1985. The Mahaweli Basin (Sri Lanka). *In* T. Petr, ed. *Inland Fisheries in Mutltpurpose River Basin Development in Tropical Asian Countries: Three Case Studies*, pp. 91-160. FAO Tech. Pap. 265. FAO, Rome.

De Silva, S.S. 1988. Reservoirs in Sri Lanka and their fisheries. *FAO Tech. Pap.* 298: 1-128.

De Silva, S.S. and H.K.G. Sirisena. 1988. New fish resources of reservoirs in Sri Lanka 3: Results of commercial trials and yield estimates of a gill net fishery for minor cyprinids. *Fish. Res.* 7: 279-287.

Elton, C. 1958. *The Ecology of Invasions by Animals and Plants.* Methuen, London.

Fernando, A.D.N. 1979. Major ancient irrigation works of Sri Lanka. *J. Roy. Asiatic Soc. (Sri Lanka Branch) New Series* 22: 1-24.

Fernando, C.H. 1956. The fish fauna of paddy fields and small irrigation ditches in the western lowlands of Ceylon and a bibliography of references to fish in paddy fields. *Ceyl. J. Sci.* 7: 223-227.

Fernando, C.H. 1963. A guide to the freshwater fauna of Ceylon. Suppl. 1. *Bull. Fish. Res. Stn. Ceylon* 16: 177-227.

Fernando, C.H. 1964. A guide to the freshwater fauna of Ceylon. Suppl. 2. *Bull. Fish. Res. Stn. Ceylon* 17: 177-211.

Fernando, C.H. 1965. A preliminary survey of 21 Ceylon lakes. 3. Parasites and predators, food of fish and marginal fauna. *Bull. Fish, Res. Stn. Ceylon* 18: 17-27.

Fernando, C.H. 1969. A guide to the freshwater fauna of Ceylon. Suppl. 3. *Bull. Fish. Res. Stn. Ceylon* 20: 101-134.

Fernando, C.H. 1971. The role of introduced fish in fish production in Ceylon's fresh waters. *In* E. Duffey and A.S. Watt, eds. *The Scientific Management of Animal and Plant Communities for Conservation*, pp. 295-310. Blackwell, Oxford.

Fernando, C.H. 1974. A guide to the freshwater fauna of Sri Lanka (Ceylon). Suppl. 4. *Bull. Fish. Res. Stn. Sri Lanka (Ceylon)* 25: 27-81.

Fernando, C.H. 1977. Reservoir fisheries in Southeast Asia: past, present and future. *Proc. Indo-Pacif. Fish. Counc. 17 Sess. Sect. 3*: 475-489.

Fernando, C.H. 1980a. The freshwater zooplankton of Sri Lanka with a discussion of tropical freshwater zooplankton composition. *Int. Rev. ges. Hydrobiol.* 6: 85-125.

Fernando, C.H. 1980b. The freshwater invertebrate fauna of Sri Lanka. *Spol. Zeylan.* 35: 15-42.

Fernando, C.H. 1980c. The species and size composition of tropical freshwater zooplankton with special reference to the oriental region (Southeast Asia). *Int. Rev. ges. Hydrobiol.* 65: 411-426.

Fernando, C.H. 1980d. Tropical reservoir fisheries. A preliminary synthesis. *In* J.I. Furtado, ed. *Tropical Ecology and Development*, pp. 883-892, Kuala Lumpur, Malaysia.

Fernando, C.H. 1984a. Reservoirs and lakes of Southeast Asia (Oriental Region). *In* F.B. Taub, ed. *Ecosystems of the World: Lakes and Reservoirs*, pp. 411-446. Elsevier, The Netherlands.

Fernando, C.H. 1984b. ed. *Ecology and Biogeography of Sri Lanka*. Junk Publ. The Hague.

Fernando, C.H. and S.S. De Silva. 1984. Man-made lakes: Ancient heritage and modern biological resource. *In* C.H. Fernando, ed. *Ecology and Biogeography of Sri Lanka*, pp. 431-451. Junk Publ. The Hague.

Fernando, C.H. and W.B. Ellepola. 1969. A preliminary study of two village tanks in the Polonnaruwa area with biological notes on these reservoirs in Ceylon. *Bull. Fish. Res. Stn. Ceylon* 20: 3-13.

Fernando, C.H. and J.I. Furtado. 1975. Reservoir fishery resources of Southeast Asia. *Bull. Fish. Res. Stn. Sri Lanka* 26: 83-95.

Fernando, C.H. and J. Holcík. 1982. The nature of fish communities: a factor influencing the fishery potential and yields of tropical lakes and reservoirs. *Hydrobiol.* 97: 127-140.

Fernando, C.H. and J. Holcík. 1989. Origin, composition and fish yields in reservoirs. *Arch. Hydrobiol. Beih. Ergebn. Limnol.* 33: 637-641.

Fernando, C.H. and J. Holcík. 1991. Fish in reservoirs. *Int. Rev. ges. Hydrobiol.* 76: 149-167.

Fernando, C.H. and H.H.A. Indrasena. 1969. The freshwater fisheries of Ceylon. *Bull. Fish. Res. Stn. Ceylon* 20: 101-134.

Fernando, C.H., C. Tudorancea and S. Mengestou. 1990. Invertebrate zooplankton predator composition and diversity in tropical lentic waters. *Hydrobiol.* 198: 13-31.

Frey, D.G. 1967. Reservoir research - objectives and practices with an example from the Soviet Union. *Proc. Reservoir Fishery Resources Symposium Amer. Fish. Soc. Georgia,* pp. 26-36.

Hawley, A.J. 1973. Farm ponds in the United States: A new resource for farms. *In* W.C. Ackerman, G.F. White and E.B. Worthington, eds. *Man-Made Lakes: Their Problems and Environmental Effects,* pp. 746-749. American Geophysical Society, Washington DC.

Jayasekera, A.M. 1988. The use of common carp and Asian carps in the management of larger water bodies in Sri Lanka. *FAO Fish. Rep.* 405: 114-150.

Koshov, M. 1963. *Lake Baikal and its Life.* Junk Publ. The Hague.

Lowe-McConnell, R.H. ed. 1966. *Man-Made Lakes.* Academic Press, New York.

Marshall, B.E. 1984. Small pelagic fishes and fisheries in African inland waters. *CIFA Tech. Pap.* 14: 1-25.

Mendis, A.S. 1977. The role of man-made lakes in the development of freshwater fisheries in Sri Lanka. *Proc. Indo-Pacif. Fish. Counc. 17 Sess. Sect.* 3: 247-257.

Mendis, A.S. and C.H. Fernando. 1962. A guide to the freshwater fauna of Ceylon. *Bull. Fish. Res. Stn. Ceylon* 12: 1-162.

Muir, R. and N. Muir. 1987. *Hedgerows, their History and Wildlife.* Michael Joseph, London.

Newrkla, P. and A. Duncan. 1984. The biology and density of *Ehirava fluviatlis* (Clupeoid) in Parakrama Samudra, Sri Lanka. *Verh. Internat. Verein. Limnol.* 22: 1572-1578.

Olgesby, R.T. 1985. Management of lacustrine fisheries in the tropics. *Fisheries* 10: 16-19.

Paggi, J.C. and S.B. Paggi. 1990 Zooplankton of the lotic and lentic environments of the middle Paraná river. *Acta. Limnol. Brasil.* 3: 685-719.

Perera, N.P. 1984. Natural resources, settlements and land use. *In* C.H. Fernando, ed. *Ecology and Biogeography of Sri Lanka,* pp. 453-492. Junk Publ. The Hague.

Rott, E. 1983. A contribution to the phytoplankton species composition of Parakrama Samudra, an ancient man-made lake in Sri Lanka. *In* F. Schiemer, ed. *Limnology of Parakrama Samudra, Sri Lanka: A Case Study of an Ancient Man-Made Lake in the Tropics,* pp. 209-226. Junk Publ. The Hague.

Schiemer F. ed. 1983. *Limnology of Parakrama Samudra, Sri Lanka: A Case Study of an Ancient Man-Made Lake in the Tropics.* Junk Publ. The Hague.

Scoggan, H.J. 1978. *The Flora of Canada*. National Museums of Canada, Ottawa.

SCOPE. 1972. Man-made lakes as modified ecosystems. *SCOPE Report* 2: 1-76.

Sreenivasan, A. 1988. Fish stock enhancement in larger Indo-Pacific inland water bodies using carp and tilapia. *FAO Fish. Rep.* 405: 6-33.

Straskraba, M., J.G. Tundisi and A. Duncan. 1993. *Comparative Reservoir Limnology and Water Quality Management*. Kluwer, Netherlands.

Thayaparan, K. 1982. The role of seasonal tanks in the development of freshwater fisheries in Sri Lanka. *J. Inland Fish. Sri Lanka* 2: 133-167.

Trefethen, J.B. 1973. Man-made lakes and wildlife values. *In* W.C. Ackerman, G.F. White and E.B. Worthington, eds. *Man-Made Lakes: Their Problems and Environmental Effects*, pp. 750-754. American Geophysical Society, Washington DC.

Tundisi, J.G. ed. 1988. *Limnologia e manejo de repressas. Vol. I-II*. Monografias em Limnologia, Universidade de Sao Paulo, Sao Paulo.

Williams, W.D. 1988. Limnological imbalances: an antipodean viewpoint. *Freshw. Biol.* 20: 407-420.

Winkler, H. 1983. The ecology of cormorants (genus *Phalacrocorax*) *In* F. Schiemer, ed. *Limnology of Parakrama Samudra, Sri Lanka: a case study of an ancient man-made lake in the tropics,* pp. 193-199. Junk Publ. The Hague.

Figure 5. A. Minneriya tank, an ancient reservoir 6300 ha in area. Note exposed shoreline due to drawdown and the fishing boat at the waters edge. A beach scene is being operated by fishermen seen near the base of the tree. B. Parakrama Samudra, an ancient reservoir 2262 ha in area at low water level. Cattle grazing on grass near the edge add nutrients to the water. Note settled appearance of the landscape resembling a natural lake.

Figure 6. A. Kandalama tank, recently impounded with trees still standing in part of the reservoir. B. Moonplains Reservoir near Nuwara Eliya. These deep, cool reservoirs are not productive in fish at present.

Figure 12. A. *Oreochromus mossambicus* which accounts for about 70% (mean) of the 300 kg/ha annual fish yield of large reservoirs. The upper darker specimen as a male and the lower, lighter, usually smaller one, a female. B. Fishermen mending gill nets at Nachchaduwa tank near Anuradhapura. Simple and cheap gear is used to catch fish in reservoirs.

Proceedings of the International and Interdisciplinary Symposium
ECOLOGY AND LANDSCAPE MANAGEMENT IN SRI LANKA
W. Erdelen, C. Preu, N. Ishwaran, C.M. Madduma Bandara (eds.)
Colombo, Sri Lanka, 12-26 March 1990
© 1993
Margraf Scientific Books, D-97985 Weikersheim
ISBN 3-8236-1182-8

Sport Diving and Coral Reef Conservation in Sri Lanka

I.F.W. JAYEWARDENE

Abstract

The reefs around Sri Lanka cover about 5% of its 1700 km coastline. During the second half of the 20th century, tropical island communities began to appreciate the important role coral reefs play in their economies. As far back as 1953, Jonklaas suggested the setting up of a series of reef sanctuaries. The potential yield of fish, crustaceans and molluscs from reefs is estimated at 9 million tons a year, which is around 12% of the total world catch. Hence, the need to conserve or manage coral reefs optimally has grown in importance. In recent years the diver has been viewed as a culprit involved in the degradation of reef ecosystems. In this paper the author attempts to outline methods by which an organized sport diver club could help in the efforts to conserve reef communities. Management issues of reefs such as those found around Bambalapitiya, Kosgoda and Polhena, on which some members of the society have been diving for over a decade, are considered as case studies in this presentation. Also, possibilities such as the utilization of the diver in ground truthing applications for satellite data verification and sanctuary stocking are discussed.

Introduction - The Coral Reef Ecosystem

The relatively recent discoveries of the dynamic nature of reef ecosystems, their extreme biological diversity and the important role that relationships between species play brought into focus by the population explosions of starfish (*Acanthaster planci*) have repeatedly indicated to conservationists that physical disturbances such as wave action, predators, exposure and alterations in sediment load could count as any one of the many factors which adversely effect a healthy reef ecosystem.

The following are a few cases which can be cited as examples of Sri Lanka's reefs:

1. The sandstone Colombo Mount Lavinia Reef 1-10 m deep is a reef which could be utilized for the lobster fishing. The lobster catches at present are of a very small percentage. Compared to 10 years ago very few tropical fish collectors make use of this reef for molluscs and gorgonians.
2. The nearshore reef at Hikkaduwa. Even as far back as 1953 it was noted that this reef was in a degraded condition. Since then 110 acres of sea have been declared a reef sanctuary
3. Having dived on the unspoilt Polhena Reef 15 years ago, I have noted the rapid growth of algae on this reef due to pollutants from coconut husk retting. There are also reports of the existence of the seaweed (*Ulva lactuca*) 7 m in length, a seaweed which scientists generally consider as an indicator of pollution. It is interesting to note that 15 years ago this reef was unofficially "maintained" by a group of collectors who controlled the catch of others.
4. Further north of Colombo, bottomset netting has caused great damage to parts of the nearshore reef benthos in Negombo.
5. Pollution from a paper factory seems to have depleted a once thriving sandstone reef and associated fisheries in Vandaloos Bay on the east coast. It has been the author's personal experience to witness visibility given by Secchi dish readings which show a 50% drop during the tidal cycle when pollutants cover this reef.

Human-Induced Damage

Interest in sport diving has gradually increased over the last decade among the local populace. This is in contrast to the previous decade (1970-1980) when most of the Sri Lankans who dived were making a living from it. In comparison to the professional diver, the present-day sport diver tends to spend most of his time on the reefs close to Colombo. Some of us who have befriended and dived with these divers who make their living from the ocean have learnt to admire their knowledge of reef ecology and reef denizen behavior, but are, at the same time, disturbed by the tendency of some of these divers to ignore certain basic conservation measures. For instance, a technique called "moxieng" has been employed in the reefs, as noted by Dr Wood of the Marine Conservation Society of UK. This is a very destructive form of netting. The wanton killing of denizen such as octopii for the payment of less than US $ 1 per animal has also been recorded. Living organisms have been collected from the nearshore reefs to the extent that some of these reefs could not be utilized to "harvest" the reef for tropical fish on a cyclic basis.

Conservation Strategies

The 1981 Coast Conservation Act No. 57 emphasized the importance of reef ecosystems, in that it stipulates the preparation of an inventory of all coral reefs in the coastal zone which is defined as a zone 2 km seaward and 300 metres landward of a line on the seashore taken to be the highwater mark. This act also has brought into being a permit procedure which could be utilized to monitor and control development activity in the coastal zone. With the paucity of trained diving biologists in the country, user conflicts such as those experienced at Polhena Reef, where coconut retting is carried out on a 0.7 km stretch of beach, cannot be proscribed. Some sort of cost benefit analysis with respect to user conflicts such as tropical fish export and tourism on this reef cannot be worked out either. It is in this context that the experienced sport diver could prove useful. In 1984, five members including the author who belonged to a sport diving society carried out a reef inventory on a 400-metre stretch at Wellawatte Reef using transect quadract methodology. Although many technical shortcomings could not be avoided but could have been overcome with more sophisticated underwater recording systems and better knowledge of coral taxonomy, 160 hours were spent in the water and a fairly comprehensive inventory was carried out on a voluntary basis. Observations of reef associated organisms, fish species and coral cover, were made and indicate fish species which have been sighted and classified as common (16 species), uncommon (14 species) and cyclically common (14 species) over the last three years. The less mobile reef dwellers such as the echinoderms, holothurians nudibrachs, sponges and corals were also classified (Tabs. 1-2, annexed).

Faulty Management Strategies

In the past, mistakes made by well-meaning and yet hasty conservation methods have at times proved to be expensive and irreversible. For example, on Hawaiian reefs (where 30% of the world's identified reef and shore fish are endemic) the valueless mullet was unintentionally introduced by the state government in 1955 in an attempt to introduce sardines to the area. Now they have replaced the highly esteemed local mullet *Mugel cephalus*.

Successful Management Strategies

Fairly successful management strategies of reef and ecosystems are not unknown in Sri Lanka. The conservationist has to travel only 40 miles south from Colombo to Kosgoda to visit one of the most successful turtle hatchery projects that has been in existence for around eight years. This is backed by the Victor Hasselbad Turtle Trust Fund and managed by the Wildlife and Nature Protection Society of Sri Lanka. The author had the good fortune to dive on a few occasions on the reefs outside Kosgoda, where at least five species of turtle nest and many hundred thousand hatchlings have been released. Here too, it must be noted that, although the turtles are being studied on shore, no intensive work has been done offshore and proper funding of a sport diving society could lead to some systematic diver observations.

As I have mentioned earlier, regarding the fairly successful conservation strategy of a few local collectors in Polhena Reef, here too, it is the enthusiasm and influence of the local head fisherman, Similias, and his son, Chandre, that has brought to fruit successful strategies suggested by the Wildlife Society.

Although in the final analysis the considered opinion of professional biologists is in many instances warranted especially in the assessment of the "condition" of reef corals and growth rate measurement, here in Sri Lanka, a sport diving society which counts amongst its membership professional fish collectors and a group of around twenty divers trained over the past four years to the level of the British Sub Aqua Club 3rd Class Diver could very well be used in reef inventorying. Approximately 40 scuba diving outings have been carried out in the period between 1988 and 1990 on the south and west coasts of Sri Lanka from Galle to Negombo. Members also have been diving in the northwest reefs, Tangalle and in the Maldive Islands in a private and professional capacity. In fact, the specialized skill of the collectors in identification and collection proved very useful in the limited survey carried out in 1984. The action taken at Point Lobos in California where such measures as limiting divers to ten per designated area and supervision by shore observers helped successful management. How successfully these techniques could be applied to a Third World country has yet to be seen.

Cycles on a Reef

The cycles of the nillu seed is well known to the forester. The population explosions of starfish (*Acanthaster planci*) brought in to sharp focus the danger of uncontroled breeding on reef habitat. Pioneer collectors, Victor Athukorale and Eric Convey, recalled that in thirty years of diving on the Bambalapitiya Reef they had met up with only one polycheate proliferation, whereas in the past five years there have been at least three such population explosions. Whether this could be attributed to the stoppage of dye along the Wellawatte Canal has to be investigated. Likewise, collectors seem to recall outbreaks of porcupine fish (*Diodum histrix*) in

1974, and in more recent times there has been a larger increase in *Chaetodon collare* and octopii this year as there was of *Chaetodon auriga* last year. Likewise, the population of cleaner wrasse (*Labroides dimidiatus*) has reportedly decreased considerably in comparison with last year. In this context it does seem that the nearshore reef could serve as a laboratory.

The Reef as a Laboratory

The need for environmental awareness is often stressed as a necessary management strategy. In this context, a sport diving club such as the Sri Lanka Sub Aqua Club could very well help to mark out a small area as has been done by the Siam Diving Club on Phuket's Coral Reefs. If a sufficient area could be proclaimed as a reserve, as has been done in the Philippines with the support of the local urban council, it could serve as a replenishment zone for waters adjacent. The area envisaged by the author would be 40 metres in extent and cover the total breadth of the reef.

The Use of Remote Sensing Data

With the advent of new technology such as satellite data collection and the increased use of computer systems to process such data, it would be only natural for any management system which has to monitor over 100 km of reef to gear itself to utilize such technology. The drawback of utilizing satellite data on Sri Lankan reefs is the small size of reef unit in comparison to the minimum area coverage of satellite landsat data or, in other words, pixel size of 30 x 30 m^2. Hence the judicious use of ground survey data and color aerial photography of an adequately large scale is essential.

With the use of SPOT data, where the resolution is reduced to a pixel size of 10 x 10 square metres, it may prove possible to utilize satellite data for the study of Sri Lankan reefs. Although SPOT is not particularly suitable for water studies, preliminary investigations with SPOT data have proved successful in the Maldives. A method where landsat data having a much lower resolution and pixel size (30 m x 30 m) was utilized quite successfully on Heron Island Reef (which would be much larger than our reefs). However, the use of a trained sport diver team could very well be a useful resource in obtaining "training samples". A training sample is a pixel or a collection of pixels known to be spectrally similar. These techniques could be utilized on some of the larger reefs of the Northwest Sector.

Conclusions

It is evident that at particular periods within the last decade reef systems such as those in Polhena and Kosgoda have been conserved with varying degrees of success. It is only by working in very close liaison with those utilizing the resources of these reefs that effective management strategies could be worked out. There is also a belief among collectors that by and large the tropical fish stocks on nearshore reefs such as Bambalapitiya reef have dwindled over the last twenty years. Statistics of exports from these reefs could well be utilized as indicators of breeding cycles on these reefs. Also, these statistics could be utilized as a source to evaluate earnings obtained from a kilometre of sandstone reef. This value, in turn, could be used as the minimum earning from a coral reef, such as Polhena, when it is required to evaluate opportunity cost benefit strategies where decisions have to be made with regard to reef preservation versus coconut husk retting. Much, if not all, of this information could be acquired by the diving club in these areas. It is also evident that an organized sport diving society could assist a great deal in recording photographically and inventorying reef ecosystems, as indicated by the inventory undertaken at the nearshore Bambalapitiya Reef. The sport diver could also be utilized when promoting the use of more recent advances in technology such as remote sensing data analysis where large areas have to be surveyed in less detail.

Annex

Table 1. Some shells found on the reef in the last three years. Data from the reef inventory at Wellawatte Canal site.

Common Species	Uncommon Species
1. *Trochus* sp.	1. *Lambis lambis*
2. *Cypraea arabica*	2. *Cypraea erosa*
3. *Cypraea caputerpentis*	3. *Cypraea mappa*
4. *Cypraea caurica*	4. *Cypraea nivosa*
5. *Cypraea cribraria*	5. *Cypraea staphylaea*
6. *Cypraea felina*	6. *Conus arenatus*
7. *Cypraea gracilis*	7. *Conus auger*
8. *Cypraea hirundo*	8. *Conus aulicus*
9. *Cypraea isabella*	9. *Conus flavidus*
10. *Cypraea lynx*	10. *Conus lividus*
11. *Cypraea ocellata*	11. *Conus nicobaricus*
12. *Cypraea vitellus*	12. *Conus nigropunctatus*
13. *Murex adastus*	13. *Conus steecus muscarum*
14. *Drupa ricinus*	14. *Conus terebra*
15. *Phos senticosus*	
16. *Phos cordis*	
17. *Conus abbas*	
18. *Conus coronatus*	
19. *Conus ebraeus*	
20. *Conus miles*	
21. *Conus obscurus*	
22. *Conus* sp.	
23. *Spondylus*	

Table 2. Fish observed on reef and classified in last three years. Data from the reef inventory at Wellawatte canal site.

Common species	1.	Red Squirrelfish (*Holocentrus ruber*)
	2.	Blue-lined Coral-cod (*Cephalopholis boenack*)
	3.	Oriental Sweetlips (*Plectorhynchus orientalis*)
	4.	Painted Sweetlips (*Spilotichthys pictus*)
	5.	Vagabond Coralfish (*Chaetodon vagabundus*)
	6.	Blue Damsel (*Pomacentrus melanochir*)
	7.	Five-banded Sargeant Major (*Abudefduf saxatilis*)
	8.	Green Damsel (*Chromis caeruleus*)
	9.	Polkadot Wrasse (*Lepidapois* sp.)
	10.	Moon Wrasse (*Thalassoma lunare*)
	11.	Cleaner Wrasse (*Labroides dimidiatus*)
	12.	Convict Surgeon (*Acanthurus triostegus*)
	13.	Black-barred Surgeon (*Acanthurus nigricans*)
	14.	Short-snouted Unicorn (*Naso brevirostris*)
	15.	Black Damsel
	16.	Red-tailed Goby
Cyclically common species, most likely due to the ambient conditions on the reef	1.	Round Batfish (*Platax orbicularis*)
	2.	Threadfin Coralfish (*Chaetidon auriga*)
	3.	Collared Coralfish (*Chaetodon aurigo*)
	4.	Ringed Angelfish (*Pomacanthops semicirculatus*)
	5.	Blue Angelfish (*Pomacanthops semicirculatus*)
	6.	Coral-hopper (*Cirrhitichthys aprinus*)
	7.	Moorish idol (*Zanclus canescens*)
	8.	Blue Surgeon (*Acanthurus leucosternon*)
	9.	Blue-lined Surgeon (*Acanthurus lineatus*)
	10.	Winged Firefish (*Pterois volitans*)
	11.	Miles' Firefish (*Pterois miles*)
	12.	White-barred Triggerfish (*Rhinecanthus aculeatus*)
	13.	Wedgetailed Triggerfish (*Rhinecanthus echarpe*)
	14.	Spotted Porcupinefish (*Diodon hystrix*)
	15.	Rock Damsel
Unknown species	1.	Peacock Rock-cod (*Cephalopholis argus*)
	2.	Yellow-banded Sweetlips (*Plectorhynchus lineatus*)
	3.	Pennant Coralfish (*Heniochus acuminatus*)
	4.	Chevroned Coralfish (*Megaprotodon strigangulus*)
	5.	Coralfish (*Chaetodon trifasciatus*)
	6.	Pig-faced Coralfish (*Chaetodon falcula*)
	7.	Coralfish (*Chaetodon lunula*)
	8.	Citron Coralfish (*Chaetodon citrinellus*)
	9.	White-spot Humbug (*Dascyllus trimaculatus*)
	10.	Wrasse (*Halichoeres* sp.)
	11.	Green Unicorn (*Callicanthus lituratus*)
	12.	Blue-spotted Boxfish (*Ostracion lentiginosum*)
	13.	Black Boxfish (*Ostracion lentiginosum*)
	14.	Black-saddled Puffer (*Canthigaster cinctus*)

Proceedings of the International and Interdisciplinary Symposium
ECOLOGY AND LANDSCAPE MANAGEMENT IN SRI LANKA
W. Erdelen, C. Preu, N. Ishwaran, C.M. Madduma Bandara (eds.)
Colombo, Sri Lanka, 12-26 March 1990
© 1993
Margraf Scientific Books, D-95985 Weikersheim
ISBN 3-8236-1182-8

Limnological Aspects of Landscape Management in Sri Lanka

A. DUNCAN, A. GUNATILAKA AND F. SCHIEMER

Abstract

The impact of the Mahaweli River Scheme and increased needs for water upon the ecology of upland and lowland reservoirs were predicted on the basis of studies carried out during the last decade on Parakrama Samudra, an ancient lowland irrigation reservoir. Two effects, namely markedly enhanced flow-through rates and increased fluctuations in water levels, are likely to be of considerable importance, amongst others, for the functioning and biological structure of the lake ecosystems following changes in the management of its inflow rates and water storage capacities. The impact of these two effects on the biological structure and functional dynamics of reservoirs are considered in relation to the hydrochemistry, primary and secondary production and the fish fauna. The Dillon-Rigler (1980) Regression is used here to classify the reservoirs with regard to their respective trophic status, and consequences of eutrophication are examined. The role of reservoir sediments as a sink for nutrients as well as pollutants (pesticides, herbicides, heavy metals) is discussed. As the reservoirs form an interconnected closely knit network the contamination of reservoir sediments is unavoidable. Therefore attention is focused on heavy metal concentrations in Parakrama Samudra sediments which probably have their origins in the upcountry plantation industry. The use of an ecosystem approach in developing reservoir management strategies is recommended.

Introduction

Landscapes consist of a series of interacting ecosystems, with rivers often forming the main link between them. From a landscape management perspective, two aspects have to be considered with regard to the limnology of inland waters. Firstly, there is the question of man's impact on various kinds of aquatic systems such as rivers, wetlands, reservoirs and ground water. Some of these result from direct alterations made upon the water body such as river diversions, connecting of watersheds, damming of rivers which fragments their longitudinal integrity, and river regulations which break the lateral gradients or links between land and water. The indirect effects are caused by different patterns of land use in the catchment area, such as deforestation, plantation and settlement. Secondly, a country's water resources are subject to multiple demands. There is the need for domestic water of an acceptable quality, usually simultaneously with the requirement to exploit water resources for fisheries, irrigation, recreation, nature conservation as well as, more recently, for hydroelectric power. Obviously, these are all conflicting demands.

A fundamental insight into how aquatic ecosystems function is necessary in order to be able to control and solve future problems of eutrophication, pollution and waterborne diseases as well as to achieve a harmonious integration of the multiple use of Sri Lankan reservoirs. For this reason, the present paper is largely concerned with reservoirs as an important component of the country's landscape in the dry zone, with its significant present and past centers of human activities. We will use the experiences gathered during long-term multidisciplinary studies on the ecosystem of one of the lowland reservoirs, Parakrama Samudra, resulting from the collaboration of scientists from several Sri Lankan and European institutions (Duncan and Schiemer 1988, Gunatilaka and Senaratne 1981, Gunatilaka 1983, 1984, 1988, Schiemer 1983, Schiemer and Duncan 1988). These results are compared with the more recent information on the limnology of the new upland reservoirs (Piyasiri 1988, Silva 1991 and this volume). These experiences have been used here to explain how such reservoirs function limnologically in order to estimate their vulnerability to changes caused by different landscape

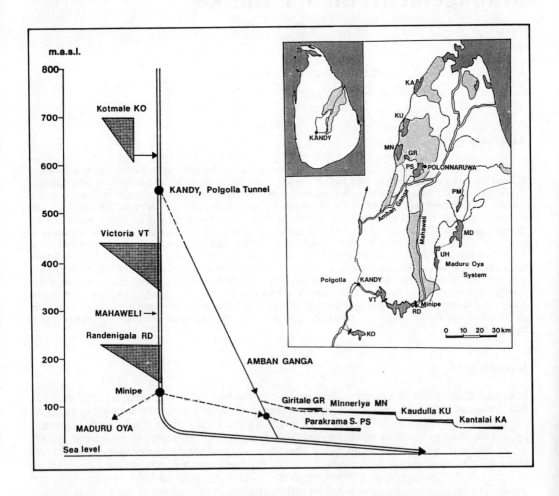

Figure 1. Location and hydrological characteristics of major reservoirs in the Mahaweli River Basin. Maduru Oya System: MD = Maduru Oya Reservoir, PM = Pimburettewa, UH = Ulhitioya.

management practices. Attention is drawn to some problems and dangers associated with the new Mahaweli scheme and recommendations on remedial measures as well as on future research requirements are discussed.

Through an ecosystem approach, it is possible to obtain a functional understanding of these interconnected riverine reservoir systems and their regulatory processes. There are two significant ecological concepts on the functioning of rivers which are helpful theoretically for understanding man's impact upon the various parts of the water network. One is the river continuum concept which describes the longitudinal integration of biological and limnological processes along the watercourse (Vannote *et al.* 1980). The ecotone concept is the other and is mainly concerned with the lateral land-water interactions (Hansen *et al.* 1988).

Large-Scale Geographical Aspects

All ancient lowland and new upland reservoirs are linked to an aquatic network under the control of the Mahaweli Development Board (Fig. 1). These water bodies fall into two distinct limnological groups: the new, deep and hydroelectric reservoirs sited in the upper montane course of the Mahaweli River and the older, shallow, multipurpose irrigation reservoirs lying in the lowlands of the dry zone.

Limnologically these reservoirs differ fundamentally in their basin and catchment morphology, depth, flow-through regime and nutrient status, underwater light regime and, consequently, in their biological productivity. The V-shaped mountain basins of the upland reservoirs have small areas of littoral zones and a greatly reduced extent of bottom sediments (Fig. 1). The low surface area to volume and sediment to volume ratios of the upland reservoirs imply reduced biological productivity. Moreover, what internal nutrient loading that does occur is lost downstream by the very high flow-through rates at which they are operated for their hydroelectric function.

Nevertheless, recent observations by Piyasiri (1988) have demonstrated thermal stratification and some degree of oxygen depletion in deeper layers (Fig. 2). This is related to the earlier flooding of fertile land, now permanently under water and subject to decomposition processes as well as to new organically rich runoffs entering the reservoirs from the recently disturbed catchments and new agricultural land. The results of Piyasiri (1988) suggest that these deep

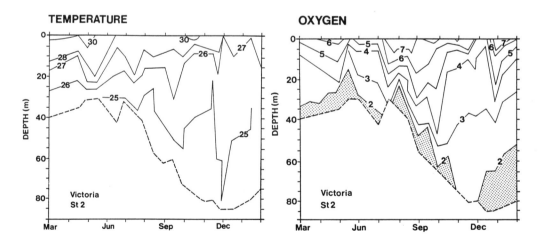

Figure 2. Temperature (°C) and dissolved oxygen (mg O_2/l) distributions between March 1987 and January 1988 in Victoria Reservoir (Piyasiri, 1988).

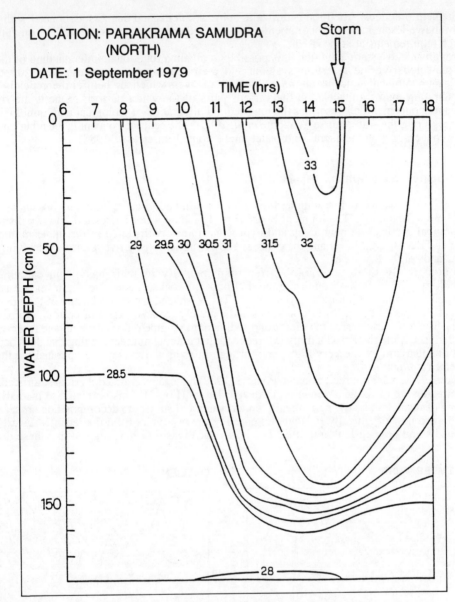

Figure 3. Diurnal pattern of thermal stratification in Parakrama Samudra (North).

reservoirs are very sensitive to eutrophication and pollution. Presently, although both external and internal nutrient loading is low compared to lowland reservoirs, these lakes are much more susceptible to eutrophication and pollution because of the water depth and long-term thermal stratification.

In contrast, the shallow irrigation reservoirs of the dry zone have very high surface area to volume ratio as well as very extensive littoral ecotones between land and water during the periods of low water (Fig. 1). These are very important for pasture, bird feeding and fish breeding. In this littoral ecotone significant exchanges of organic matter and nutrients in both directions occur which normally would be greatly reduced in the upland reservoirs with their small littoral regions. The sediment-water interface greatly contributes to the internal nutrient loading in the reservoir and the recycling of nutrients is enhanced by wind-induced stirring during windy periods or by diurnal convective currents during windless periods (Bauer, 1983). During such calm periods, diurnal thermal stratification (Fig. 3) acts as a thermal barrier for wind-induced erosion processes during the day and, due to cooling at night, result in convective currents which play an important role in resuspension of bottom sediments (Bauer, 1983).

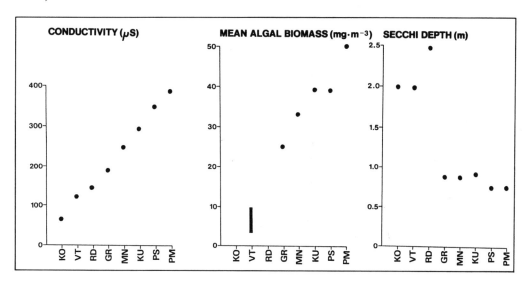

Figure 4. Conductivity, mean algal biomass, and Secchi depth in the reservoirs (Piyasiri 1988, Silva and Davis 1986, 1987). For names and locations of reservoirs see Figure 1.

Superimposed upon these limnologically contrasting types of reservoirs, there is a geographical dimension. Along the course of the Mahaweli River, the reservoirs show a marked increase in conductivity (Fig. 4). This is correlated with the trophic state of the water bodies. The oligotrophy of the three upland reservoirs illustrated contrasts strikingly with the eutrophic-hypertrophic condition of the lowland reservoirs. The trend observed implies some form of external nutrient loading taking place increasingly along the water path, mainly due to agricultural practices. As a consequence, it is no surprise to find that the mean annual algal biomass of the lowland reservoirs is very high (Silva and Davis 1986, 1987) compared with the low chlorophyll-a values recorded (Fig. 4) for one new hydroelectric reservoir (Piyasiri, 1988).

The high Secchi depths of the three upland water bodies (Fig. 4) reflect their low algal biomass due to nutrient-limited primary productivity. The low Secchi depths of the irrigation reservoirs are due to self-shading from high algal biomass. One might have expected even deeper light penetration in the upland reservoirs from the low chlorophyll-a levels, but the massive erosion in the catchment area contributes to high suspended solid load with fine clay particles in suspension which absorb light.

Seasonal Patterns, Management, Irrigation and Hydroelectric Reservoirs

Climatic factors such as the seasonal patterns of wind, monsoonal rains and the level of solar radiation affect the ecology of the reservoirs in Sri Lanka. Within these major constraints, both

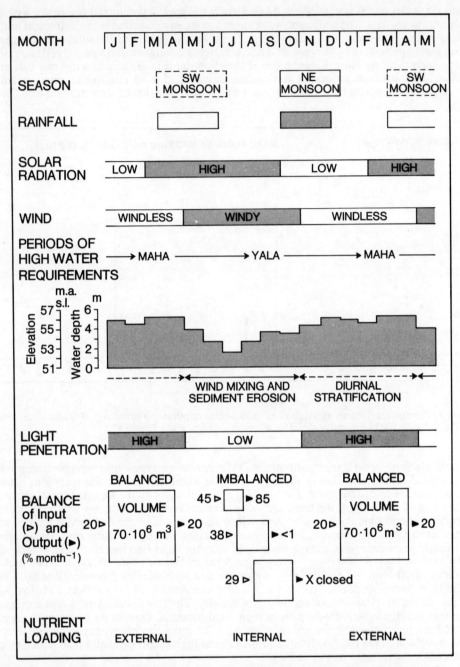

Figure 5. Combined influences of climate and water requirements for paddy cultivation on the limnological conditions in Parakrama Samudra.

kinds of reservoirs are managed for different purposes and management practices again affect their limnology. In the upland reservoirs management is geared to the generation of hydroelectric power which requires a continuous and high flow-through of water that is ten times the rate characteristic of the lowland reservoirs (1700% per year compared with 170% per year). The products of primary production, already low due to nutrient and light limitation, are not retained in the upland reservoirs but lost downstream by high flushing rates. The low concentrations of dissolved oxygen in the deeper water layers, reported by Piyasiri (1988), implies that it is the surface layers of water that are flushed through, and that the eroded products from soils in the catchment of these reservoirs accumulate in deeper water.

In contrast, in the dry zone reservoirs, management of the water resources permits the cultivation of the Yala rice crop despite the sparse rain from the SW monsoon (Fig. 5). Satisfying the high water requirements of the growing Yala crop greatly depletes the reservoir's stored volume and water depth due to an imbalance in the water input and output rates. In contrast to this, during the period of the Maha crop, both stored volume and water depths remain high because of balanced water inputs and outputs. Some representative values are given in Figure 5 as monthly flow rates in percentage of the reservoir volume. Thus, the combination of climate (rainfall patterns) and management imposes a seasonally regular variation in the three fundamental limnological parameters of volume, depth and flow-through rates (Fig. 5).

These two sets of distinctive limnological conditions for shallow flow-through reservoirs in the dry zone, like Parakrama Samudra, are illustrated in more detail in Figure 6. During the period between May and October, the characteristic features are low water, high wind and a strong water imbalance (Fig. 6). Erosion of bottom sediments and the release of nutrients stored there make this a limnological phase with high internal nutrient loading. Primary production is enhanced by this internal nutrient supply on the one hand, but is impaired by the reduced penetration of light due to the suspension of bottom detritus. The imbalance in the water flow-through rates results in a concentration of nutrients and algal biomasses, but these are subject to loss from the reservoir. The low water depth dramatically increases the

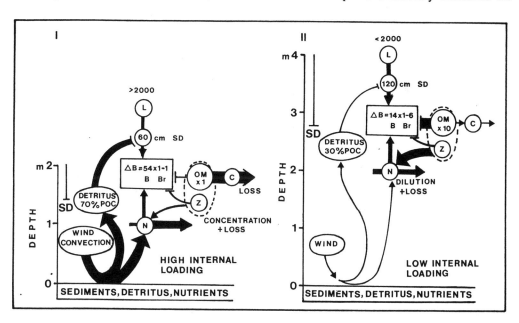

Figure 6. Ecosystem functions of Parakrama Samudra during two limnological phases: I. First intermonsoon period (May-October) and II. Second intermonsoon period (November-April); L = light (μE/m² sec), SD = Secchi depth (cm), B = algal biomass (chlorophyll-a in mg/m³), B = change in algal biomass, Br = daily turnover of algal biomass, OM = relative density of the herbivorous fish, *Oreochromis mossambicus*, Z = zooplankton grazers, C = cormorants and their relative level of fish predation, N = nutrients, POC = particulate organic carbon.

effectiveness of predation upon fish by cormorants and storks. This large-scale bird predation has several consequences. One is loss of nutrients by terrestrial defecation, but another is that cormorant aquatic defecation can speed up nutrient cycling in the reservoir. Here, there is also a top-down effect upon the algal biomass (which is enhanced) by the predator control of the population of herbivorous fish.

Another characteristic limnological phase takes place during the NE-W monsoon and the first intermonsoonal period from November to April, when the lowland irrigation reservoirs are maintained at high water levels and have high flow-through rates (Fig. 6). During this period, the distinctive features are high water levels, windlessness and a water balance with inputs equal to outputs (Fig. 6). As a result, external nutrient loadings become predominant. Sediment erosion is mediated by nightly convective forces, but the magnitude of the erosion is comparatively less. The deeper light penetration (with Secchi depths of more than 1 m) ensures higher turnover rates of algal biomass, but this is subject to both dilution and some loss through relatively high and balanced flushing rates. A second loss imposed upon the algal biomass is due to grazing by abundant small-sized *Oreochromis mossambicus*. Why such dense populations of *O. mossambicus* were found to exist at this period is not clear and needs more study. According to Amarasinghe and Upasena (1985), this may be due to successful breeding in an earlier season. However, during this period cormorant predation is less effective because their numbers are low and they are forced to fish in greater water depths.

Table 1. Rates of orthophosphate incorporation (k) and PO_4^{3-} turnover times (tt) in Parakrama Samudra (Sri Lanka) and African lakes; SRP = soluble reactive phosphate (data from Sri Lanka see Gunatilaka, 1984, for Africa see Peters and MacIntyre, 1976).

Date	Time (hrs)	Lake	k (min^{-1}/ tt)	SRP (µg/l)	tt (min)
Sri Lanka					
27.7.1982	13.00	Parakrama Samudra North - PSN	0.713	4	1.41
30.7.1982	13.00	Parakrama Samudra North - PSN	0.788	5	1.27
31.7.1982	13.00	Parakrama Samudra North - PSN	0.780	4	1.31
10.8.1982	13.00	Parakrama Samudra Middle- PSM	0.761	6	1.31
12.8.1982	07.00	Parakrama Samudra North - PSN	0.330	9	3.02
Africa					
28.6.1974		Elementeita	1.5000	<3	0.66
26.6.1974		Naivasha, main basin	1.0000	<3	1.00
27.6.1974		Naivasha, crater	0.2000	<3	5.00
24.6.1974		Nakuru	0.0029	23	345.00
25.6.1974		Nakuru	0.0014	714	
30.6.1974		Nakuru	0.0010	1000	
17.7.1984		Nakuru	0.0039	7	256.00
26.6.1974		Crescent Island Crater	0.0000	117	

Nutrients

Looking at the nutrient situation in Parakrama Samudra in detail, it is obvious that the orthophosphate levels in the lake water are very low, and the lake is phosphate limited (Gunatilaka and Senaratne 1981, Gunatilaka 1983). Despite the low concentration of dissolved orthophosphate the levels of primary production in the lake is high (Dokulil *et al.* 1983) and the turnover of nutrients is rapid (Gunatilaka 1984, 1988). It is also apparent that most of the nutrients in the system are locked in the algal biomass of which some are eventually recycled. The overall effect of this biological coupling in the system is demonstrated by the short turnover time of orthophosphate (Tab. 1). Similar situations are also reported for tropical African lakes (Peters and MacIntyre, 1976). High turnover rates are considered as an indication of nutrient limitation and tight nutrient cycles.

In the lake ecosystem of Parakrama Samudra, a tight biological coupling was observed between ambient orthophosphate concentrations and enzyme activity (phosphatase), between labile phosphate level in algae and enzyme activity, and also between nutrient deficiency and enzyme activity. The coupling between these different ecosystem components mediated through enzyme activity (Fig. 7) shows the delicately balanced nature of the nutrient cycles. Such situations are characteristic for stressed ecosystems for example, hypertrophic lakes and man-made perturbations which can have adverse effects on the delicate balance that exists.

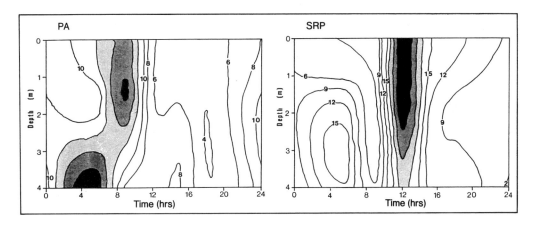

Figure 7. The diurnal pattern of coupling between the phosphatase enzyme activity (PA in mmols) and ambient orthophosphate concentrations (SRP in µg/l) in the lowland reservoir Parakrama Samudra (Gunatilaka, 1984).

Trophic Status and the Effect of Flushing and Grazing

The trophic state of a water body can be classified on the basis of the Dillon-Rigler Regression (1980) which relates mean algal biomass in terms of chlorophyll-a to nutrient concentration expressed as total phosphorus (Fig. 8). The relationship is derived from the data for temperate lakes and shows that the higher the nutrient level, the greater the mean algal biomass. Our studies on Parakrama Samudra between 1979 and 1982 indicate that this reservoir is eutrophic but may almost reach hypertrophic conditions.

Values for Parakrama Samudra were close to the Dillon-Rigler line during periods of no flushing in 1982, but were well below in 1979, due to high flushing out of algal biomass, and in 1980, due to loss of algal biomass through a combination of herbivorous fish grazing and flushing, even though the total phosphorus level had increased. This indicates a state of delicate balance in the lowland reservoirs during very low flushing that might topple into hypertrophy with disastrous consequences for the fish populations. Progressive eutrophication can lead to an algal collapse which happens when the chlorophyll concentrations reach over 200 µg/l. At the next stage the increase of dead organic matter shunts the microbial loop and bacteria take over the dominant role. As a result, decomposition processes dominate and lead to the depletion of dissolved oxygen and eventually to fish kills.

Sediments as a Sink for Pollutants

Sediments act not only as a sink for nutrients (C, P and N) but also for pollutants such as pesticides, herbicides and heavy metals. In temperate lakes undergoing eutrophication in Europe and North America, it was found that accumulation of heavy metals in the sediments is strongly correlated with inputs of phosphorus and nitrogen. Förstner et al. (1974) compared the accumulation of Zn and Pb with nitrogen and phosphorous content in Lake Constance sediment cores and found that their accumulation coincided with the development of both industry and agricultural development in the lake catchment. Similar observations were made for the metals Cu, Zn, Pb, Cd and Hg in Lake Ontario (Thomas, 1972), in Lake Geneva (Vernet, 1972), Lago Maggiore (Damiani and Thomas, 1974) and Greifensee (Stumm and Baccini, 1978).

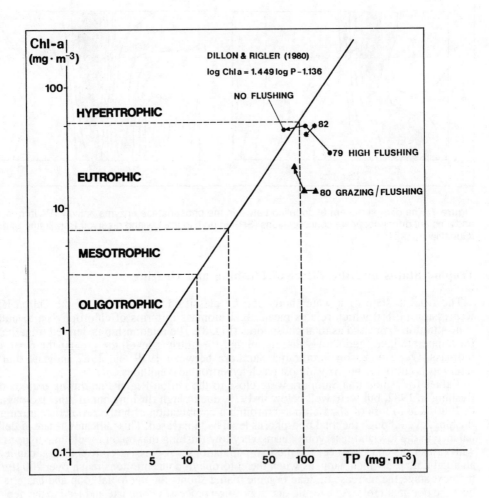

Figure 8. Effect of flushing and grazing upon the prediction of the trophic status of Parakrama Samudra based on the Dillon-Rigler Regression (1980): TP = total phosphorus, Chl-a = chlorophyll-a.

Through intensive agricultural practices in the catchment with emphasis on usage of artificial fertilizer, pesticides and herbicides, these metals are bound to find their way into most of the reservoir sediments in the lowlands via Mahaweli waters. Therefore, accumulation and their pathways into the food chain need special attention. We have measured heavy metal concentrations in Parakrama Samudra sediment cores, and they show very high levels of Zn, Cu and Cr compared to temperate lakes which are situated close to industrial centers (Tab. 2, Fig. 9) and also record elevated levels of phosphorous and nitrogen. The origin of this metallic contamination is not known but is probably of anthropogenic origin as it is also accompanied by high levels of P and N. Another fact that has to be taken into consideration is that fungicides containing Zn and Cu are widely used in the plantation industry in Sri Lanka, especially in tea plantations.

Table 2. Heavy metal concentrations (ppm) in surface sediments (0-10 cm) of Parakrama Samudra (Sri Lanka), Neusiedlersee (Austria) and Lake Constance (Germany). (1) Gunatilaka (in prep); (2) Gunatilaka (in print); (3) Salomons and Förstner (1984); (4) Wedepohl (1969).

Lake	Cd	Pb	Zn	Cu	Cr
Parakrama Samudra (1)					
Parakrama Samudra North, PSN3	0.38	29	440	141	110
Parakrama Samudra North, PSN8	0.27	21	191	92	61
Neusiedlersee (2) (shallow lake)	0.47	30	68	58	57
Lake Constance (3) (deep lake)	0.20	19	95	45	90
Mean sediment (4) (background)	0.17	19	95	33	72

Little is known about the presence of toxic agrochemicals in Sri Lankan waters, but a widespread dispersal is to be expected due to the practice of permitting both intensive agriculture in the catchments of the upland reservoirs and streams, and uncontrolled and unchecked application of artificial fertilizers, pesticides and herbicides there and along the irrigation water pathways. As a result, pesticide and herbicide residues are likely to accumulate in the sediments of the lowland reservoirs which act as the ultimate sink for the whole of the Mahaweli River Drainage basin.

This threat is exaggerated by the characteristic ecosystem properties of the shallow water bodies because sediments are not an isolated compartment but they are, in contrast, in an active dynamic equilibrium with the overlying water body. Due to rapid turnover rates of these toxic substances they are liable to be accumulated relatively fast in phytoplankton and subsequently in fish. Moreover, short food chains with a predominantly herbivorous fish fauna are characteristic of these reservoirs. As they are subjected to strong fishing pressure by man, and as human beings form the last link in the food chain, the presence of toxic substances in fish constitutes a potential threat to human health which should receive urgent scientific attention.

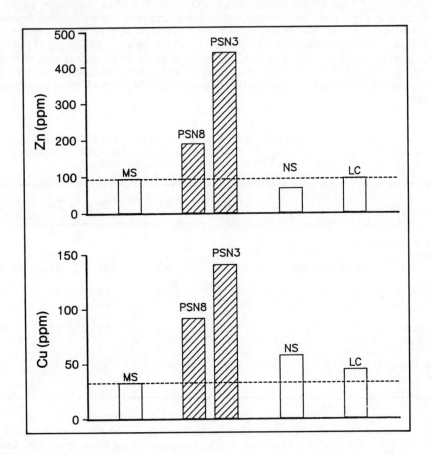

Figure 9. Concentrations of zinc (Zn) and copper (Cu) in the sediment of Parakrama Samudra (PSN3, PSN8) compared with a reference mean sediment (MS) (Wedepohl, 1968) and sediment concentrations from Neusiedlersee (NS) (Gunatilaka, in print) and Lake Constance (LC) (Solomons and Förstner, 1984).

Dangers and Remedial Measures

Listed below are some remedial measures for a set of clearly defined problems that have been identified:

Problem: Deoxygenation in the upland hydroelectric reservoirs.
Remedies: 1. Restrict agriculture and animal husbandry and human settlements in the vicinity of reservoirs.
2. Active maintenance of the land-water ecotone as a barrier/filter to erosion and/or nutrient leaching for example by planting bamboo, reeds or Kumbuk *Termialia arjuna*.

Problem:	Deoxygenation of lowland reservoirs following algal collapse due to combination of hypertrophy and low flushing rates.
Remedies:	1. Limnologists and hydrologists should be on the operational staff of lowland irrigation reservoirs.
	2. Local rather than central control of the reservoirs' flushing rates is advisable.

Problem:	Organic pollution and accumulation of toxic chemicals in the hydrological network.
Remedies:	1. Control excessive use of fertilizer and agrochemicals.
	2. Canalize sewage effluents and by-pass reservoirs.
	3. Instal simple village water treatment and sewage treatment facilities, exploiting the achievements of alternative technology.

Problem:	The danger of siltation of rivers arising from clogging of the sediment interstices with eroded fine clay particles thus disrupting the connectivity between the river's epirheal and hyporheal strata (surface and sub-surface water regimes).
Remedy:	Active maintenance of ecotone barrier.

Problem:	Lack of a database for management problems of aquatic components of the landscape.
Remedy:	Establish and strengthen existing regular monitoring of the hydrological network, with regard to plant nutrients, chlorophyll-a, suspended solids, toxic chemicals, Secchi depths and disease organisms.

Literature Cited

Amrasinghe, U.S., and T. Upasena. 1985. Morphology of a man-made lake in Sri Lanka: a factor influencing recruitment to cichlid fishery. *J. Nat. Aq. Res. Ag. Sri Lanka* 32: 121-129.

Bauer, K. 1983. Thermal stratification, mixis and advective currents in Parakrama Samudra Reservoir, Sri Lanka. *In* F. Schiemer, ed. Limnology of Parakrama Samudra: a case study of an ancient man-made lake in the tropics. *Dev. Hydrobiol.* 12: 27-34.

Dillon, P. and R.H. Rigler. 1980. A test of a simple nutrient model prediction the phosphorus concentration in lake water. *J. Fish. Res. Bd. Canada* 31: 1771-1778.

Damiani, V. and R.L. Thomas. 1974. Mercury in the sediments of the Palanza Basin. *Nature* 251: 696-697.

Dokulil, M., K. Bauer and I. Silva. 1983. An assessment of the phytoplankton biomass and primary production of Parakrama Samudra, a shallow man-made lake in Sri Lanka. *In* F. Schiemer, ed. Limnology of Parakrama Samudra: a case study of an ancient man-made lake in the tropics. *Dev. Hydrobiol.* 12: 4976.

Duncan, A. and F. Schiemer. 1988. Fish pressures on ecosystems: dynamic, holistic indices. *In* S.S. De Silva, ed. *Reservoir Fishery Management in Asia, Proc. Int. Workshop, Kathmandu, Nepal,* pp. 177-182. IDRC, Ottawa.

Förstner, U., G. Müller and G. Wagner. 1974. Schwermetalle in den Sedimenten des Bodensees. *Naturwissenschaften* 61: 270-272.

Gunatilaka, A. and C. Senaratna. 1981. Parakrama Samudra (Sri Lanka) Project - a study of a tropical lake ecosystem: II- Chemical environment with special reference to nutrients. *Verh. Internat. Verein. Limnol.* 21: 994-1000.

Gunatilaka, A. 1983. Phosphorus and phosphatase dynamics in Parakrama Samudra based on diurnal observations. *In* F. Schiemer, ed. Limnology of Parakrama Samudra: a case study of an ancient man-made lake in the tropics. *Dev. Hydrobiol.* 12: 35-47.

Gunatilaka, A. 1984. Observations on phosphorus dynamics and orthophosphate turnover in a tropical lake - Parakrama Samudra, Sri Lanka. *Verh. Internat. Verein. Limnol.* 22: 1567-1571.

Gunatilaka, A. 1988. Nutrient cycling in tropical reservoirs with special reference to Parakrama Samudra, Sri Lanka. *In* S.S. De Silva, ed. *Reservoir Fishery Management in Asia, Proc. Int. Workshop, Kathmandu, Nepal,* pp. 34-46. IDRC, Ottawa.

Hansen, A.J., F. di Castri and P.G. Risser. 1988. A new SCOPE project. Ecotones in a changing environment: the theory and management of landscape boundaries. *Biol. Internat.* 17: 137-163.

Peters, R.H. and S. MacIntyre. 1976. Orthophosphate turnover in East African lakes. *Oecologia* 25: 313-319.

Piyasiri, S. 1988. *Limnology Project at Mahaweli: a Study of Physical, Chemical and biological Parameters of Victoria, Kotmale and Randenigala Reservoirs.* Annual Report 1987/1988. Dept. Zool. Univ. Sri Jayawardenepura, Nugegoda, Sri Lanka.

Salomons, W. and U. Förstner. 1984. *Metals in the Hydrocycle.* Springer Verlag, Heidelberg.

Schiemer, F. 1981. Parakrama Samudra (Sri Lanka) Project, a study of a tropical lake ecosystem. I. An interim review. *Verh. Internat. Verein. Limnol.* 21: 993-999.

Schiemer, F. ed. 1983. The limnology of Parakrama Samudra, Sri Lanka: a case study of an ancient man-made lake in the tropics. *Dev. Hydrobiol.* 12: 236.

Schiemer, F. and A. Duncan. 1988. The significance of the ecosystem approach for reservoir management. *In* S.S. De Silva, ed. *Reservoir Fishery Management in Asia,* Proc. Int. Workshop, Kathmandu, Nepal, pp. 183-194. IDRC, Ottawa.

Silva, E.I.L. 1991. Limnology and fish yields of newly built standing water bodies in the Mahaweli Basin, Sri Lanka. *Verh. Internat Verein. Limnol.* 24: 1425-29

Silva, E.I.L. and R.W. Davies. 1986. Primary productivity and related parameters in three different types of inland waters. *Hydrobiol.* 137: 239-249.

Silva, E.I.L. and R.W. Davies. 1987. The seasonality of monsoonal primary productivity in Sri Lanka. *Hydrobiol.* 150: 165-175.

Stumm, W. and P. Baccini. 1978. Man-made chemical perturbations of lakes. *In* A. Lerman, ed. *Lakes - Chemistry, Geology, Physics,* pp. 91-123. Springer Verlag, Berlin.

Thomas, R.L. 1972. The distribution of mercury in the sediments of Lake Ontario. *Can. J. Earth Sci.* 9: 636-651.

Vannote, R.L., G.W. Minshall, K.W. Cummins, J.R. Sedell and C.E. Cushing. 1980. The river continuum concept. *Can. J. Fish. Aquat. Sci.* 37: 130-137.

Vernet, J.P. 1972. Levels of mercury in the sediment of some Swiss lakes including Lake Geneva and the Rhone River. *Ecologae Geol. Helv.* 65: 293.

Wedepohl, K.H. 1969. *Handbook of Geochemistry*. Springer Verlag, New York.

Proceedings of the International and Interdisciplinary Symposium
ECOLOGY AND LANDSCAPE MANAGEMENT IN SRI LANKA
W. Erdelen, C. Preu, N. Ishwaran, C.M. Madduma Bandara (eds.)
Colombo, Sri Lanka, 12-26 March 1990
© 1993
Margraf Scientific Books, D-97985 Weikersheim
ISBN 3-8236-1182-8

Discontinuum of the Mahaweli River and its Impact on the Distribution and Diversity of Indigenous Riverine Fish Fauna

E.I.L. SILVA

Abstract

The drainage basin of the Mahaweli River (349 km), which has the largest catchment area and the highest annual discharge of all rivers in Sri Lanka, has been subjected to significant modifications since the time of the ancient rulers. Recently, this river has been dammed for the creation of three major hydroelectric reservoirs and partially diverted to innundate two irrigational tanks in the lowland dry zone. The locations of irrigation works, water quality, and the distribution of indigenous riverine fish were determined from headwaters to downstream with a special emphasis on habitat alteration and potamodromus fish movements. The data indicate that the diversity of indigenous fishes significantly decreases with increasing altitude. A number of fish species occurs between 250 m and 750 m elevation where most of the irrigation works are located. Upstream movements of riverine fish were observed at weirs. Potamodromus riverine fish may be territorial. Modification of the Mahaweli River Basin shows a pronounced impact on the population size of several riverine species.

Introduction

Running water ecosystems are susceptible to two major natural perturbations, spates and desiccation. However, anthropogenic disturbances in stream ecosystems and their impact on mankind have been reported as far back as 4500 B.C. Intensive irrigated agriculture on the Tigris-Euphrates floodplain in Mesopotamia was so intense that it directly or indirectly changed the ancient civilization of Samaria (Whyte, 1961). The most pronounced man-made activities associated with river basins are irrigation, dryland-farming, deforestation, cultivation, urbanization, and industrialization. As a result of human activities, stream ecosystems may be subjected to secondary salination (Silva, 1987), sedimentation (Cooper, 1987), morphological changes in stream channels, eutrophication and deterioration in water quality. Eventually detrimental effects on the biotic components of the stream ecosystems may occur.

Recent developments in damming and diversion of natural river systems for hydropower generation are cosmopolitan. However, very little attention has been paid to the impact of damming or partial diversion on abiotic and biotic components of the river ecosystem, especially in developing countries. Discontinua of river ecosystems as a result of the construction of physical structures on the trunk stream or on tributaries may have profound effects in terms of structure and functioning of stream communities from headwaters to downstream. In Sri Lanka, it has been recognized that many fish species endemic to the island are being threatened with extinction in the near future due to several anthropogenic activities (Evans 1980, Senanayake and Moyle 1982). This paper attempts to highlight the ecological consequences of discontinua along the Mahaweli River, Sri Lanka, on the distribution and diversity of riverine ichthyofauna indigenous to the island.

Sri Lanka

The island of Sri Lanka (6°-10°N and 80°-82°E) is essentially an extension of the Indian peninsula which forms part of the Gondwana shield from geologically remote times. In surface configuration Sri Lanka comprises a highland massif situated in the south center which is surrounded by an intermediate zone of upland ridges and valleys at a lower elevation than the highland massif. The intermediate zone is in turn surrounded by an outer lower zone of lowlands. A coastal fringe consisting of peninsulas, sand bars, marshes, spits, dunes, lagoons and other associated features, skirts the island. Sri Lanka with an area of 65,610 km² has a maximum length of 432 km and maximum width of 224 km. The Precambrian Shield which covers about 90% of the surface area of the island consists predominantly of charnockite metasedimentary rocks. The rest of the geological forms are Jurassic deposits and limestone of Miocene forms developed in the northeast and northern peninsula, respectively.

There is a marked climatic variation in Sri Lanka, due to the central highlands being surrounded by an extensive lowland area. The regional difference in temperature in the lowlands (27°C annual mean with 6°C daily range) compared to the highlands (16°C annual mean with 10°C daily range) is mainly due to altitude. The island is influenced by two wind regimes, the SW monsoon (summer monsoon) from May to September and NE monsoon (winter monsoon) from December to February. The monsoonal rainfall is mainly orographic, and convectional rains are experienced between monsoons. The annual rainfall in the southwest is 2500 mm while in the northeast and southeast the annual average is less than 1250 mm. The island is rich in tropical flora and fauna, but the remaining natural forest cover today is less than 30%.

Mahaweli Basin

Sri Lanka has no natural lakes. The surface water occurs in rivers, streams and marshes in the wet zone. Several small perennial standing pools that occur in the highest plains (i.e. Horton Plains) may be considered as the only natural perennial standing water bodies in the country. Man-made lakes (irrigation "tanks") in the dry zone lowlands and hydropower reservoirs in the highland cover 2500 km². The perennial rivers of Sri Lanka radiate from the central highland and are less than 160 km in length, except for the Mahaweli Ganga (river) which is 349 km long. The Mahaweli River Basin, which covers about 16% (10,329 km²) of the island's land area carries the largest discharge amounting to a seventh of the island's runoff. It is an integrated drainage course consisting of several discharge courses of both highland and lowland drainage. It is also the only perennial river traversing the northeastern parts of the dry zone.

Watercourse

The uppermost tributaries of the trunk stream of the Mahaweli River, the Agra Oya (stream), the Dambagastalawa Oya and the Nanu Oya originate from the western slope of the highest region of the hill country at an elevation between 2000 m and 3000 m (Fig. 1). The Agra Oya and the Dambagastalawa Oya descend with steep gradients and join together at Caledonia state and flow westward to Talawakele where the stream turns sharply northward before its confluence with the Nanu Oya to form the Kotmale Oya, a major tributary of the Mahaweli in the central highlands. The second major tributary of the hill country, the Hatton Oya which originates farther west near the Hatton Plateau joins the Kotmale Oya at Pallegama, a few kilometres downstream from Nawalapitiya giving rise to the Mahaweli River proper. These streams and other small streams together drain an area of very heavy rainfall having its maximum during the SW monsoon period.

The Mahaweli proper then receives water from the Atabage Oya and the Nilambe Oya of the right bank and the Ping Oya of the left bank as important tributaries before Katugastota where the river turns sharply and flows in a southeasterly direction as far as Rantembe. Between Katugastota and Rantembe a number of major tributaries empty into the Mahaweli River from both right and left banks. Hulu Ganga, a major left bank tributary drains from the southern slopes of the Knuckles Range and confluences with the Mahaweli River at Teldeniya, 18 km from Kandy. The Huluganga drains a large area having a heavy rainfall during the intermonsoon and SW monsoon months. The other three major tributaries of the left bank, the Uma Oya, the Kehelella Ela (water course) and the Maha Oya drains the southeast slope of the Knuckles Range where the annual rainfall is relatively low but concentrated during the NE monsoon. The major right bank tributaries entering this reach of the Mahaweli River are the Maha Oya, the Belihul Oya, and the Kurundu Oya. Headwaters of these tributaries receive a pronounced rainfall during the NE monsoon and intermonsoon months. Their lower reaches flow through a drier intermediate zone which has a similar rainfall pattern of lesser magnitude.

Between Rantembe and the northward turn of the Mahaweli River near Minipe the main river receives water from the Uma Oya, the Badulu Oya, and the Loggal Oya. The Uma Oya which originates from the southern slope of the Uva Basin at an elevation between 3000 m and 5000 m intercepts densely cultivated lands before it reaches the drier areas in the intermediate zone. Headwaters of the Badulu Oya and the Loggal Oya rise from the southeastern part of the Uva Basin. These streams experience a heavy rainfall during intermonsoon and NE monsoon periods, but greater parts of their lower reaches flow through the drier intermediate zone having the same rainfall regime.

Near Minipe the Mahaweli River emerging from the Central Mahaweli Valley (Fig. 1) to the dry zone lowlands turns northward sharply. Between Minipe and the confluence with the Amban Ganga a number of tributaries empty into the main river from both the right and left banks. Although a majority of the tributaries have sizeable catchment areas, streams flow with relatively lower discharge due to low incident rainfall in the headwaters. Of the left bank tributaries the Hasalaka Oya and the Heen Ganga drain the northeast slope of the Knuckles Range and their headwaters rise in an area of fairly heavy rainfalll concentrated during the NE monsoon and intermonsoon periods.

The Hettipola Oya, the Dunuwila Oya, the Wasgomu Oya-Elleola Oya system and the Nawagaha Ela are minor left bank tributaries. The Hepola Oya, a right bank tributary which rises from the northern part of the Lunugala Ridge (Fig. 1), taps a fair amount of water during the NE monsoon. The Diyabana Oya, the Ulhiti Oya and the Hungamala Ela, the other right bank tributaries, drain a fairly large area, but tap only dry zone rainfall.

Amban Ganga, the largest tributary of the Mahaweli River, empties into the main river from its left bank, near Manampitiya, 95 river kilometers from the sea. The larger part of the courses of the three western tributaries, the Amban Ganga, the Kalu Ganga, the Sudu Ganga and the Nalanda Oya are in the wet zone part of the Matale valley (Fig. 1) where heavy rainfall is concentrated during the intermonsoon and SW monsoon periods. In addition, the Kalu

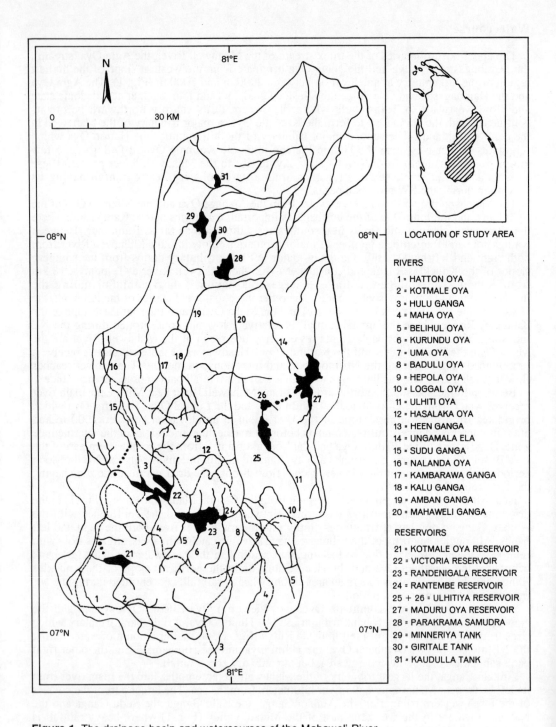

Figure 1. The drainage basin and watercourses of the Mahaweli River.

Inside the figure:

N

0   30 KM

81°E

08°N

08°N

07°N

07°N

81°E

LOCATION OF STUDY AREA

RIVERS

1 = HATTON OYA
2 = KOTMALE OYA
3 = HULU GANGA
4 = MAHA OYA
5 = BELIHUL OYA
6 = KURUNDU OYA
7 = UMA OYA
8 = BADULU OYA
9 = HEPOLA OYA
10 = LOGGAL OYA
11 = ULHITI OYA
12 = HASALAKA OYA
13 = HEEN GANGA
14 = UNGAMALA ELA
15 = SUDU GANGA
16 = NALANDA OYA
17 = KAMBARAWA GANGA
18 = KALU GANGA
19 = AMBAN GANGA
20 = MAHAWELI GANGA

RESERVOIRS

21 = KOTMALE OYA RESERVOIR
22 = VICTORIA RESERVOIR
23 = RANDENIGALA RESERVOIR
24 = RANTEMBE RESERVOIR
25 + 26 = ULHITIYA RESERVOIR
27 = MADURU OYA RESERVOIR
28 = PARAKRAMA SAMUDRA
29 = MINNERIYA TANK
30 = GIRITALE TANK
31 = KAUDULLA TANK

Ganga drains the northwestern slope of the Knuckles Range. The water of the three tributaries unite near Nalanda giving rise to the Amban Ganga proper. Between Nalanda and the confluence of the Amban Ganga with the Mahaweli Ganga, two major right bank tributaries (i.e. Kambarawa Ganga and second Kalu Ganga) drain the northeastern slopes of the Knuckles Range and empty into the Amban Ganga. Of the several minor left bank tributaries, only the Maha Oya, the Heerati Oya and the Radavige Oya are important.

After the confluence with the Amban Ganga, the Mahaweli breaks up into several braided perennial and seasonal tributary canals. The important seasonal left bank tributaries of this reach are the Gal Oya, the Kaudulla Oya and the Minneriya Oya which originate in the dry zone. The main stream of the Mahaweli Ganga bifurcates at 56 river kilometers from the Koddiyar Bay where the river empties into Indian Ocean. The Mahaweli proper continues northward to Koddiyar Bay, while the Verugal Aru flows eastward to the sea near Kathiraveli.

Water Quality

Principal physicochemical characteristics of running water ecosystems can be related to geomorphology and climate of a particular geographic region (Feth et al. 1964). Gibbs (1970) further elucidated three major aspects of the overall mechanism (viz. precipitation, rock dominance, and crystallization processes) which determine the quality of athalassic waters. Streams, especially those draining well-leached tropical basins, are rich in Na^+ and Cl^- which

Table 1. Some physicochemical parameters of the Mahaweli River from headwaters to downstream. Data compiled from Dissanayake and Weerasooriya (1986), TAMS (1980) and Silva (unpublished).

Site	Altitude (m)	River Distance (km)	pH	Cond µ °S	HCO_3^- (ppm)	TDS (ppm)
Horton Plains	2100	390	6.70	17	-	-
Talawakelle	1200	344	6.68	66	-	-
Ginigathena	700	325	6.80	32	57.0	111
			6.80	48		302
			7.22			
Gampola	629	304	6.45		73.0	210
						55
Gelioya	592	286	6.45		24.0	260
Kandy	555	268	6.93	55	34.3	267
			7.50			
Teldeniya	518	250	6.71	60	29.5	356
Hanguranketa	259	229	6.83		54.2	290
			7.25			
Minipe	140	197	6.37	90	24.7	157
			7.72	229		
			7.58			
Weragantota	111	167	6.38		93.0	146
Hemberawa	55	145	7.10		27.0	95
Yodagannawa	42	127	6.75		23.8	115
Manampitiya	38	95	6.00	95	43.5	110
			7.22	227		
			7.72			

are atmospheric fallouts evaporated from the ocean (Feth, 1971). The dominance of Ca^{++} or Mg^{++} with HCO$_3^-$ in temperate streams and rivers is an indication that the ionic composition is controlled by the geochemistry of the drainage basin as Ca^{++} and Mg^{++} dominant minerals are more susceptible to weathering and crystallization processes. Little information is available on physicochemical characteristics of the surface water in the Mahaweli River Basin. Temporal and seasonal variations of those principal water quality parameters of the Mahaweli River are not available. The available information on pH, specific conductivity, bicarbonate alkalinity and total dissolved salts (TDS) do not show a meaningful trend in their variation along the course of the river from headwaters to downstream (Tab. 1), perhaps due to inadequate or irregular sampling procedures. Low pH values and high TDS values have been recorded from Nawalapitiya to Manampitiya (Dissananyake and Weerasooriya, 1983) compared to TAMS (1980) and Silva (unpublished). Recent studies (Silva, unpublished) show a significant and gradual increase in pH, specific conductivity, bicarbonate alkalinity and TDs of the Mahweli River water from headwaters to downstream which is common for tropical rivers. A pronounced temporal distribution in major ions among the three prominent catchments, viz. central highlands, Uva Basin and Knuckles Range, of the Mahaweli River is also possible. Since the water course of the Mahaweli River intercepts highly urbanized and cultivated areas, patterns and concentration of major ionic components may deviate from the ones anticipated for tropical river systems.

Ancient Irrigation

Irrigation schemes for the storage or regulation of water have been in existence in the Mahaweli River Basin as attested both by history and the surveying artifacts. A publication of the United States Bureau of Reclamation when referring to the history of earth dams in the World states "one earth dam 11 miles long, 70 feet in height and containing about 17 million cubic yards of embankment was completed in Ceylon in the year 504 B.C." Some scholars contend that the origin of certain irrigation works had commenced even before the period of recorded history. The ancient Ceylonese chronicles, Mahawamsa and Culawamsa refer to the construction and restoration undertaken by the ancient kings. Two types of ancient irrigation systems known as storage reservoirs and diversion weirs are common in the Mahaweli Basin. Storage reservoirs which are commonly known as "tanks" serve a twofold purpose; that of impounding water for storage and detention of flood runoff. In perennial streams, diversion weirs which are commonly called anicuts have been constructed to convey the water to the field below or regulate the discharge of the river. In this case a masonry or concrete wall is built across the stream to keep back water which is diverted through a gate incorporated in the head wall itself or in a separate outlet structure built for this purpose. During the heavy river flow, the excess water is allowed to spill over the head wall of the anicut. A silt gate is provided in the head walls allowing accumulated silt to wash off with flow when necessary.

There were several major ancient irrigation schemes in the Mahaweli River Basin. One long channel trapped the Mahaweli Ganga near Minipe and led the waters to the north along the left bank of the river till it confluenced with Amban Ganga at Anganmedilla. The second major ancient irrigation system originated at Hattota on the Kalu Ganga and at Elahera on the Amban Ganga and it diverted water northward to Minneriya, Giritale, Kaudulla and Kantale tanks. There is also evidence that the ancient Sinhalese constructed many anicuts and irrigation canals in the Uva Basin and some of them are still in use. In 1962 the Hunting Survey Corporation Limited, in collaboration with the Survey General of Ceylon listed 391 existing irrigation works in the Mahaweli Ganga Basin of which 93 are anicuts. The majority of those anicuts are located at altitudes between 250 m and 750 m (Fig. 3). The lowest number of anicuts occur at the highest altitudes between 1250 m and 1500 m. The pattern of the distribution of irrigation weirs in the Mahaweli Ganga Basin indicates the areas of human settlement and thus demand for

402

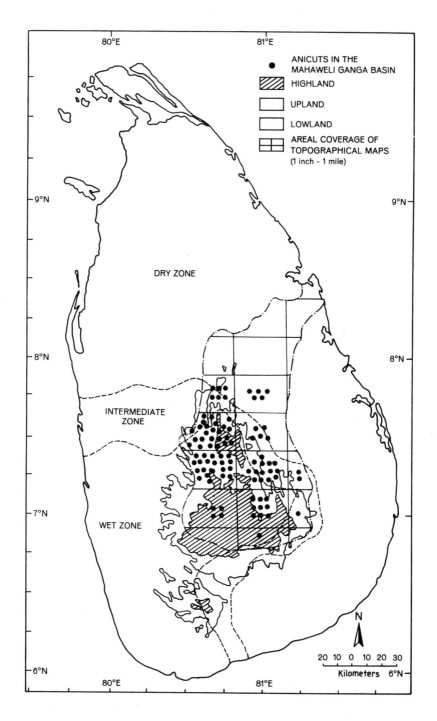

Figure 2. The distribution of the anicuts in different topographic sheets of the Mahaweli River Basin.

403

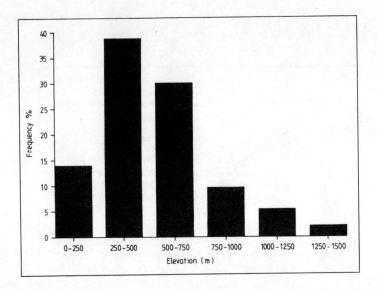

Figure 3. Percent frequency distribution of anicuts at different ranges of elevation.

water. It is not only the ancient irrigation works that were the biggest river development works of their age. The current development of the Mahaweli Basin is also one of the biggest river development projects to be undertaken in the recent past in developing countries.

The Accelerated Mahaweli Program (AMP)

The AMP is a farsighted economic development concept implemented recently by the Government of Sri Lanka. The major objectives of the AMP are to enhance irrigated agriculture, and to harness the hydropower generation to improve the quality of life of the nation. To achieve the goals of the AMP, the trunk stream of the Mahaweli River has been recently dammed to form four major hydroelectric reservoirs in the Central Mahaweli Valley, (Fig. 1) and partially diverted to innundate two major storage tanks in the lowland dry zone (Tab. 2). These newly built standing water bodies which have a total area of about 15,000 ha are considered to be multipurpose reservoirs, and it is also anticipated that they will be utilized as biological resources by increasing the fish yield (Silva, 1990).

Table 2. Some important physical features of the high dams constructed on the main stream under the Accelerated Mahaweli River Program.

Dam	Elevation (m)	Nature	Heigth (m)	Width (m)	Year of Selling
Kotmale	703	Rockfill	87.0	600	1985
Victoria	438	Concrete	118.0	553	1984
Randenigala	232	Rockfill	94.0	485	1986
Rantembe	220	Concrete	43.5	232	1990

404

The highest upstream reservoir at Kotmale has been constructed by blocking the Kotmale Oya by a rockfill dam (87 m high, 600 m long) at Kandedora village, about 6.6 km upstream of its confluence with the Mahaweli River. The trunk stream has subsequently been dammed by a double curvature arch, concrete structure (118 m high, 553 m long) close to Victoria falls, 58 km downstream of the Kotmale Reservoir, to give rise to the Victoria Reservoir. The Mahaweli water is conveyed to the Victoria Reservoir over the existing Polgolla barrage where water is diverted northward from the left bank of the river through a 6.5 km long transbasin tunnel to feed Bowatenna Reservoir. The Victoria Reservoir is also fed by the Hulu Ganga and the Maha Oya. The main stream of the river has been again blocked by a rockfill dam (94 km high, 485 m long), 19 km downstream of the Victoria dam creating the Randenigala Reservoir. The Randenigala Reservoir is also fed by the Belihul Oya, the Kurundu Oya and the Maha Oya on the right bank, and the Kehelella Ela and the Ma Oya on the left bank. The Mahaweli water is then conveyed into Rantembe Reservoir (43.5 m high, 410 m long) which is fed by the Uma Oya. The Mahaweli water is then partially diverted 500 m downstream of the ancient Minipe-Yoda Ela anicut to feed major storage tanks, the Ulhiti Oya, Ratkinda and the Maduru Oya Reservoirs. This right bank transbasin canal is essentially a conveyance canal from which the bulk supply is diverted to existing tanks enroute (viz. Mapakada, Dambarawa, and Horabora tanks) and finally empties itself into Ulhiti Oya and Ratkinda Reservoirs. The Ulhiti Oya Reservoir has been constructed by placing an earthfill dam on Ulhiti Oya. The surplus water of the Ulhiti Oya Reservoir is led through a transbasin link tunnel of 5.4 km into Maduru Oya Reservoir. The Maduru Oya Reservoir, the second largest standing water body in the country, has been built by arresting the Maduru Oya by an earthfill dam. This river which originates form the southern slopes of the Uva Hills does not lie within the Mahaweli River Basin.

The existence of ancient irrigation works, the construction of physical structures, and the creation of large standing water bodies by partial diversion of a river may result in tremendous changes in the natural processes of the river ecosystem. Such impacts can be categorized into different components of river ecology and be treated separately. Modification of river ecosystems and subsequent impact on riverine ichthyofauna have been well received as major ecological and evolutionary consequences. It is commonly hypothesized that replacement of riverine ecosystems with lacustrine ones may eliminate some species while benefitting others. As a result, the diversity and abundance of endemic or indigenous species may change significantly. On the other hand riverine fish which can survive in standing water bodies may invade newly built reservoirs, as their feeding or nursery grounds. To shed light on the impact of river modification of the Mahaweli River on indigenous fish fauna it is important to understand the present status of the ichthyofauna indigenous to the Mahaweli Basin.

Ichthyofauna

The number of freshwater fish species indigenous to Sri Lanka varied from 52 to 64 according to different authors (Munro 1955, Mendis and Fernando 1962, Fernando and Indrasena 1969, Fernando 1973, Evans 1980, Senanayake 1980, Schiemer and Hofer 1983, de Silva and Wansapura 1991). Apparently, there are 56 indigenous species completing their entire life cycle in freshwater (Tab. 3). Two catadromus eels present in freshwater habitat migrate to the sea for spawning. Of the 58 indigenous species, 18 are endemic to Sri Lanka. In addition, 18 exotic species have been introduced to Sri Lankan waters since 1882. Of the 18 exotics, three African cichlids (*Oreochromis mossambicus, Oreochromis niloticus* and *Tilapia rendalli*) and two species of ornamental fish commonly known as guppy (*Poecilia reticulata*) and sword-tail (*Xiphophorus helleri*), introduced for mosquito control (Radda, 1973), have successfully colonized inland waters. *Salmo gairdneri* and *Salmo trutta* were introduced into streams above an altitude of 2000 m in 1880-1890 and they spawn in natural habitats (Fowke, 1936). The giant goramy (*Osphronemus goramy*) and snake-skin goramy, (*Trichogaster pectoralis*) were introduced in 1939. Although they have established themselves in Sri Lankan waters their population sites are not very high. The common carp (*Cyprinus carpio*), Chinese carps

Table 3. A list of indigenous and endemic* species of Sri Lanka and their occurrence in the Mahaweli Basin according to different authors (cd = catadromus; tf = true freshwater; tp = transplanted; lt = lotic; 1 =TAMS (1980); 2 = Senanayake (1980); 3 = Schiemer and Hofer (1983); 4 = Amarasinghe and Pitcher (1986); 5 = Silva and Davies (1986); 6 = de Silva and Wansampura (1991); 7 = Silva (unpublished); 8 = de Silva (1991).

Family	Species	Type	Occurrence	Habitat	Status	Authors
Anabantidae	*Anabas testudineus*	tf	√	lt	rare	7
Anguillidae	*Anguilla bicolor*	cd	√	lt	rare	3
	Anguilla nebulosa	cd	√	lt,ln	common	3,4,6,7
Bagridae	*Mystus keletius*	tf	√	lt,ln	common	1,3,7
	Mystus vittatus	tf	√	lt,ln	common	3,6,7
Belonidae	*Xenentodon cancila*	tf	-	-	-	-
Belontiidae	*Belontia signata**	tf	√	lt	rare	6,7
	Macropodus cupanus	tf	-	-	-	-
	Malpulutta kretseri	tf	-	-	rare	6,7
Chanidae	*Channa gachua*	tf	√	lt	rare	6
	Channa marulus	tf	√	lt,ln	rare	1,6
	*Channa orientalis**	tf	√	lt	rare	6
	Channa punctatus	tf	√	lt	rare	6
	Channa striatus	tf	√	lt,ln	rare	1,3,7
Cichlidae	*Etroplus maculatus*	tf	√	lt,ln	rare	3,6,7
	Etroplus suratensis	tp	√	ln	common	3,4,6,7
Clariidae	*Clarias teysmanni*	tf	√	ln	rare	6
	Clarias nebulosa	tf	-	-	-	-
Clupeidae	*Ehirava fluviatilis*	tp	√	ln	common	3,7
Cobitiidae	*Lepidocephalus jonklaasi**	tf	√	lt	rare	7
	Lepidocephalus thermalis	tf	√	lt	rare	3,6,7
	Noemacheilus botia	tf	-	-	-	-
	*Noemacheilus notostigma**	tf	√	lt,ln	rare	6,7
Cyprinidae	*Chela laubuca*	tf	√	lt,ln	rare	3,6
	Barbus amphibius	tf	-	-	rare	-
	*Barbus bimaculatus**	tf	√	lt	rare	1,6
	Barbus chola	tf	√	lt,ln	common	3,5,6,7
	*Barbus cumingii**	tf	√	lt,ln	rare	6,7
	Barbus dorsalis	tf	√	lt,ln	common	3,5,6,7
	Barbus filamentosus	tf	√	lt,ln	common	1,3,5,6,7
	*Barbus pleurotaenia**	tf	-	-	-	-
	*Barbus nigrofasciatus**	tf	√	lt	common	6,7
	Barbus sarana	tf	√	lt,ln	common	1,3,5,6,7
	*Barbus srilankensis**	tf	√	lt	rare	1,6
	*Barbus titteya**	tf	√	lt	rare	7
	Barbus ticto	tf	√	lt	rare	1
	Barbus vittatus	tf	-	-	-	-
	Tor khudree	tf	√	lt,ln	common	4,5,6,7
	*Aplocheilus dayi**	tf	-	-	-	-
	*Garra ceylonensis**	tf	√	lt,ln	common	1,5,6,7
	Labeo dussumieri	tf	√	lt,ln	common	1,3,6,7
	*Labeo fisheri**	tf	√	lt,ln	rare	1,6,7,8
	*Labeo porcellus**	tf	-	-	-	-
	Amblypharyngodon melettinus	tf	√	lt,ln	common	1,3,6,7

406

	Danio aequipinnatus	tf	√	lt,ln	common	1,2,3,6,7
	Esomus danrica	tf	√	lt,ln	common	3,6,7
	*Horadandiya atukorali**	tf	-	-	-	-
	*Rasbora veterifloris**	tf	√	lt	rare	6,7
	Rasbora dandiconius	tf	√	lt,ln	common	1,3,6,7
Gobiidae	*Glossogobius giuris*	tf	√	lt,ln	common	1,3,6,7
	Gobius grammepomus	tf	-	-	-	-
	*Sicydium halei**	tf	-	-	-	-
Hemirham-phidae	*Hemirhamphus limbatus*	tp	√	ln	common	3,7
Heteropneus-tidae	*Heteropneustes fossilis*	tf	√	lt,ln	rare	3,7
Mastacem-belidae	*Mastacembelus aculatus*	tf	-	-	-	-
	Mastacembelus armatus	tf	√	lt,ln	common	2,6,7
Siluridae	*Ompok bimaculatus*	tf	√	lt,ln	common	2,6,7
	Wallago attu	tf	√	lt,ln	rare	5,7

(*Ctenopharyngodon idella, Hypothalmichthys molitrix* and *Aristichthys nobilis*) and Indian carps (*Catla catla, Labeo rohita,* and *Cirrhinus mrigala*) grow well in Sri Lankan freshwaters but except for the common carp others do not breed in the wild.

Of the 58 freshwater fish species indigenous to Sri Lanka, 26 belong to the family Cyprinidae. Dominants among the cyprinids are small carplets, (genus *Barbus*) of which *B. dorsalis* and *B. sarana* are important food fish. *Tor khudree* and *Labeo dussumieri* are among the other cyprinids which are important as a protein source. However, several carplets play an important role in aquarium trade as ornamental fishes. Eels and some of the snake-heads are also important as food fish. Two silurids (*Ompok bimaculatus* and *Wallago attu*) inhabiting both riverine and lacustrine habitats were among the major constituents in inland fish production prior to the introduction of exotics into Sri Lankan waters (Fernando, 1973). *Glossogobius giuris*, a widely distributed gobid, is also more important as a fish consumed by peasants, when compared to the other two species of gobies (*Gobius grammepomus* and *Sicydium halei*). The indigenous loaches are not commonly consumed as food. Of the four brackish water species transplanted in man-made lakes, *Etroplus suratensis* and *Hemiramphus limbatus* are more important in the reservoir fisheries of the dry zone than the other indigenous species (Amarasinghe and Pitcher 1986, Silva and Davies 1988a). Apparently there were about 12 species of freshwater fish consumed by peasants before the introduction of exotics but all of them are not significant for the present fish production of the island.

Zoogeography of the freshwater ichthyofauna of Sri Lanka is poorly understood. Faunistic lists have been prepared in several instances while conducting other surveys (de Silva and Wansapura, 1991). Mendis and Fernando (1962) have compiled a list of the freshwater fish found in Sri Lanka on the basis of the previous work by Deraniyagala (1952) and Munro (1955). Radda (1973) identified 31 freshwater species from five river basins (Kelani, Kalu, Nilwala, Menik and Walawe) from the samples collected during the Austrian-Ceylonese hydrobiological mission (Costa and Starmühlner, 1972). Senanayake (1980) studied the biogeography and ecology of inland fishes of Sri Lanka and identified three ichthyological provinces, viz. the southwestern province, the Mahaweli province, and the dry zone province. Each province has distinctive elements of fish fauna and is separated from the other provinces by geographical and ecological barriers (Senanayake and Moyle, 1982). Unfortunately, in this classification the author had not recognized the extension of the dry zone within the Mahaweli River Basin and did not separate the dry zone of the Mahaweli Basin from the dry zone ichthyological province itself. Senanayake (1980) identified 40 indigenous species from the Mahaweli River Basin of which 5 are endemic. However, there are 22 indigenous species in

Parakrama Samudra, a man-made lake (2650 ha) in the dry zone of the Mahaweli River Basin (Schiemer and Hofer, 1983). A recent faunistic study on freshwater fishes of the Central Mahaweli Valley (i.e. Kandy district) shows the presence of 34 indigenous species from both running and standing water bodies of which 9 species are endemic to Sri Lanka (de Silva and Wansapura, 1991). In addition, *Lepidocephalus jonklaasi,* endemic to Sri Lanka, occurs on the southern slopes of the Knuckles Range (Silva, unpublished; Tab. 4). Of the 18 endemic fish species recorded from Sri Lanka, *Aplocheilus dayi, Barbus pleurotaenea, Horadandiya atukorali, Clarias nebulosus, Mulpulutta kretseri* and *Sicydium halei* were not recorded from the Mahaweli River Basin. *H. atukorali* and *C. nebulosus* do not seem to have been reported in the island since their first description. However, *B. pleurotanea, A. dayi, M. kretseri* and *S. halei* have been reported from the southwestern part of the wet zone at several occasions (Radda 1973, Moyle and Senanayake 1984). There are another ten species found in other parts of Sri Lanka which do not occur in the Mahaweli River Basin (Tab. 3).

Table 4. The occurrence of indigenous and endemic fresh water fish in the Mahaweli River Basin according to different authors.

Site	Endemic	Indigenous	Total	Author
Parakrama Samudra	0	22	22	Schiemer and Hofer (1983)
Mahaweli Ichthyological Province	5	35	40	Senanayake (1980)
Central Mahaweli Valley	9	25	34	De Silva and Wansapura (1991)
Mahaweli River Basin	10	33	43	Silva (unpublished)

Habitat Alteration

True freshwater fish indigenous to Sri Lanka are riverine or marsh dwelling species. Schiemer and Hofer (1983) categorized the freshwater fish species in Sri Lanka into three groups, transplanted brackish water species, introduced exotic species, and indigenous true freshwater species. Nevertheless, a considerable number of indigenous riverine species have invaded man-made lakes. In addition to 22 indigenous species reported from Parakrama Samudra (Schiemer and Hofer, 1983), *Tor khudree, Wallago attu,* and *Labeo fisheri* have been occasionally recorded from the same water body (Amarasinghe and Pitcher 1986, Silva and Davies 1988a). However, it is apparent that there are 43 indigenous species of fish including 10 endemics in the Mahaweli River Basin (Tab. 4). Changes in species composition as a result of modification of the natural river ecosystems in Southeast Asia have been reported (Bhukswan and Pholprasith 1977, Natarajan 1977, Sreenivasan 1977, Srinivasan and Sreenivasan 1977). These studies document a significant increase in catfish and carp-like species in newly constructed standing water bodies with a noticeable disappearance of some true riverine species (*Tor khudree, Labeo* spp. etc.) which are potamodromus. Therefore a marked shift in fish community structure is anticipated with the modification of natural river ecosystems. The fish species which are likely to dominate new lentic habitats are those which presently occur in "villus" (flood lakes) and quiet water habitats of the downstream reaches of the river system. Accordingly, it has been anticipated that important food fish, namely *L. dussumieri, L. fisheri,*

B. dorsalis, B. sarana, Channa spp. *O. bimaculatus* and *W. attu* colonize downstream reservoirs of the Mahaweli River Basin (TAMS, 1980). A relatively higher abundance of *L. dussumieri, O. bimaculatus*, and *P. sarana* in gill net fishery of dry zone man-made lakes have been documented by earlier workers (Fernando 1965, 1971, 1973, 1977, Fernando and Indrasena 1969, de Silva and Chandrasoma 1980, de Silva and Fernando 1980). However, recent studies indicate a significant decline in *L. dussumieri* (Amarasinghe and Pitcher, 1986) and *O. bimaculatus* (Silva and Davies, 1987) and their contribution to commercial fishery is now negligible. Decline of *L. dussumeiri* and *O. bimaculatus* from downstream reservoirs may be attributed to habitat alteration as a consequence of new downstream development of the Mahaweli River Basin.

Fishes, like other aquatic organisms, are very sensitive to biotic or abiotic changes in their immediate environment. Modification of natural river systems in many cases will result in pronounced changes in flow velocity, channel morphology, bedload and suspended sediment loading. Regulated streams allow more suspended and bedload sediment to settle in the stream bottom altering the microhabitats of the bottom substrate. Recent studies on distribution and abundance of lotic benthos have focussed primarily on the above aspects. Silva (1987) found almost complete absence of macroinvertebrates in a temperate river affected by continuous input of bedload and suspended solid from a diverted irrigation canal. Similarly, decrease in standing crop of stream benthos in Bear Creek was primarily due to the sediment loading from an adjoining irrigated watershed (Cooper, 1987). Depletion in stream benthos can directly or indirectly affect the fish fauna of the river system as most of the stream fish are benthivorous. Senanayake and Moyle (1982) reported that reduced flow of the Mahaweli River may affect the natural habitats of *L. fisheri*, inhabiting the deeper pools below cascades and fast water streams. Reduction in flow through previously fast water pools below regulation weirs will quite probably cause a decline in population of such species.

Fish Movements

Riverine species, in most cases, are potamodromus but require a lotic habitat to complete their life cycle, especially for spawning. Spawning movements of indigenous species inhabiting lowland reservoirs in the dry zone have been observed (Silva and Davies, 1986). Nine riverine species were recorded attempting to jump over a small anicut at Diyabeduma when they were sexually mature (Tab. 5). There is no evidence for the breeding of riverine species in man-made lakes. It has also been observed that the spawning grounds of *Tor khudree* are confined to mountain streams (de Silva and Wansapura, 1991). Certainly, some species may spawn in the river systems in the vicinity of the man-made lake habitats. Chandrasoma (pers. comm.) has noticed fingerlings of *L. dussumieri* in the rivulets in the dry zone while Balasuriya (1983) collected fingerlings of the same species from a perennial tank in the same region. He also noticed two breeding cycles for *L. dussumieri* as evident from maturity of the adult fish. A single specimen of *O. bimaculatus* (20 mm) was collected from the littoral zone of Kaudulla lake, in the Polonnaruwa irrigation district (Silva and Davies, 1988b). This suggests that these reservoirs are not suitable spawning grounds for indigenous riverine fish even though the nursery grounds for most of the fish species are initially in the littoral zone before they move into deeper water with increasing size (Remane and Schlieper 1971, Silva and de Silva 1981). *Garra ceylonensis*, a typical riverine fish endemic to Sri Lanka, has morphological adaptions to inhabit rapids and occurs along the Mahaweli Basin from headwaters to downstream. This species is capable of creeping on solid objects mostly during late nights (Silva and Davis, 1986). Most of the indigenous riverine fish have invaded man-made lakes but are not yet physiologically adapted to complete their life cycle in lentic habitats and require to move into streams or irrigation canals to successfully reproduce. In addition to the nine riverine species attempting to jump over an irrigation weir at Diyabeduma (Silva and Davies, 1986), it was also observed that *L. fisheri* attempted to jump over the Minipe anicut while *Anguilla nebulosa* was swimming against the current at the same place (Tab. 5). The observations made by the author confirm that none of the species were successful in their attempt to jump over the Minipe anicut which is 270 m long and 5 m high.

Table 5. List of fish species attempting to cross over at Diyabeduma (Silva and Davies, 1986) and Minipe (Silva, unpublished) anicuts.

Species	Diyabeduma	Minipe
Garra ceylonensis	√	√
Labeo dussumeiri	√	√
Labeo fisheri	-	√
Barbus chola	√	√
Barbus dorsalis	√	√
Barbus filamentosus	√	√
Barbus sarana	√	√
Tor khudree	√	√
Ompok bimaculatus	√	√
Wallago attu	√	-
Anguilla nebulosa	-	√

Discussion

Today several freshwater fish species endemic to Sri Lanka are considered endangered, threatened or vulnerable due to anthropogenic activities such as deforestation, urbanization, gem mining, overexploitation of fish, streamflow regulation, application of agrochemicals and introduction of exotics (Evans 1980, Senanayake and Moyle 1982). Extensive deforestation has occurred since British occupation, as a result of the substitution of natural forest by tea, rubber plantations etc. Removal of riparian vegetation and subsequent reduction in input of allochthonous organic matter into streams may have detrimental effects on biotic communities (Vonnut *et al.* 1980). Removal of riparian vegetation may also affect stream flow, sedimentation processes as well as the temperature regime (Burns 1972, Moyle 1976). Although similar situations were noted in Sri Lanka, only little information is available on the impact of such factors on natural fish communities. Most of the aquatic habitats in densely populated areas of the island may be heavily polluted due to urbanization and industrialization. Excellent examples can be seen in the Mahaweli Basin where tributaries intercept small towns or cultivated land.

Lethal effects of herbicides on fish species have been well studied by experimental manipulation. However, use of herbicides in rubber plantations has caused severe depletion of fish populations in long stretches of a stream (Johnson, 1973). In Sri Lanka, Senanayake (1982) noticed a large kill of *Barbus cumingii,* following the application of herbicides to rice fields near the stream. Fish populations may also be depleted gradually over time due to environmental stress. Studies on Gambusa affinis (mosquito fish), a sexually dimorphic small proceiliid fish clearly demonstrated that environmental stress may determine life-history tactics (Stearns and Sage, 1982). Sri Lanka is an agricultural country in which an enormous amount of agrochemicals is used annually. Therefore, research on the effects of environmental stress on aquatic communities should be assigned a high priority. Overexploitation of stream fishes both for food and aquarium trade is a practice in Sri Lanka. The impact of such overexploitation is not known. Nevertheless, application of explosives and poison to catch fish may have detrimental effects on natural communities.

With respect to water diversion and stream flow regulations, the Mahaweli River in Sri Lanka has been discontinued at different levels. There are four major high dams and a barrage on the main stream of the river which have no devices installed to facilitate upstream movement of riverine fish. On the other hand, the Loggal Oya and the Ulhiti Oya have been blocked by physical structures with no natural connection to the Mahaweli River system. Compared to ancient anicuts at Minipe and Elahera, it is very unlikely that fish jump over high dams. But fish can swim through the Polgolla barrage when the sluice gates are opened. Movement of fish may also be arrested at the 93 small diversion weirs across the streams and tributaries which have no facilities for fish bypass. *Garra ceylonensis* may be considered as the most likely candidate to cross over small anicuts. However, several species of fish occur in between high dams and beyond the Kotmale Oya. This suggests that, although riverine species are potamodromus in nature, their movements which may be determined physiologically are restricted to a small stretch of the stream. Therefore, it is apparent that the discontinuum of the Mahaweli River may result in a gradual decrease in species number and population size due to habitat alteration, but a complete elimination of riverine species from the entire river basin is very unlikely in the near future. Even though it is possible to forward such speculations and predictions on the fate of the present fish fauna in the Mahaweli River, impacts of previous irrigation works on fish populations cannot be estimated due to lack of information on population census prior to initial damming and diversion of the river system. However, decline in several indigenous food fish such as *O. bimaculatus*, *W. attu*, *L. dussumeiri*, *L. fisheri* and *Channa* spp. since the introduction of exotics into Sri Lankan waters may be attributed to restoration of ancient irrigation works. A recent study on *O. bimaculatus* (Silva and Davies, 1987) showed that the growth and the potential fecundity of this species is similar to those recorded in Indian waters, but population size is very low.

Certainly some of the indigenous riverine fish species in Sri Lanka are endangered, threatened or vulnerable due to the magnitude of current degradation of their natural environment. Therefore, it is a prerequisite to preserve them because of ethical and ecological considerations. However, it is very important to identify species that need immediate protection through systematic surveys and biomonitoring programs. It is also necessary to implement positive steps to educate people on the value of protecting nature and the quality of the environment. Common methods of preserving endemic fish like captive breeding, watershed management, translocation, and fisheries regulation, have been discussed in detail by Senanayake and Moyle (1982). It is clear that stream flow regulations for both irrigation and hydropower generation play an important role with respect to natural elements and processes of stream ecosystems. Unfortunately, no attention has been paid to natural processes of river ecosystems in the majority of such modifications of running water ecosystems. The AMP is a classical example for a massive river modification project with little consideration on future impact on natural elements and processes. However, it is still not too late to implement conservation strategies to protect the ichthyofauna of the Mahaweli River Basin, a valuable natural resource of the island.

Acknowledgments

I am grateful to Professor Cyril Ponnamperuma, the Director of the Institute of Fundamental Studies for the facilities provided and his encouragement to complete this work. Sincere thanks are due to Uphul Lokumeegoda, Dias Withana, Shirani Nathanial and Manel Samarawickrema. Mr. D.G.A. Perera read the manuscript in draft. I am also thankful to Profs. C.M. Madduma Bandara and C.B. Dissanayake for their encouragement.

Literature Cited

Amarasinghe, U.S. and T.J. Pitcher. 1986. Assessment of fishing effort in Parakrama Samudra, an ancient man-made lake in Sri Lanka. *Fish. Res.* 4: 271-181.

Balasuriya, L.K.S.W. 1983. Preliminary trials on induced breeding of the local carp *Labeo dussumieri* in Sri Lanka. *J. Inland Fisheries, Sri Lanka* 1: 62-65.

Bhukswan, T. and S. Pholprasith. 1976. The fisheries of Ubolratana Reservoir during the first ten years of impoundment. *Proc. Indo. Pacif. Fish. Counc. 17th Sess. Sect. 2*: 195-201.

Burns, J.W. 1972. Some effects of logging and associated road construction on northern California Streams. *Trans. Am. Fish. Soc.* 101: 1-17.

Chandrasoma, J. and S.S. De Silva. 1981. Reproductive biology of *Puntius sarana*, an indigenous species and *Tilapia rendalli*, an exotic in an ancient man-made lake in Sri Lanka. *Fish. Mgt* 12: 7-28.

Cooper, C.M. 1987. Benthos in Bear Creek, Mississippi: Effects of habitat variation and agriculture sediments. *J. Freshw. Ecol.* 4: 101-113.

Costa, H.H. and P. Starmühlner. 1972. The Austrian-Ceylonese Hydrobiological Mission, 1970-1. Preliminary report: Introduction and description of the stations. *Bull. Fish. Res. Stn. Sri Lanka (Ceylon)* 23: 43-76.

De Silva, D.N. 1991. Preliminary observations and some aspects of biology of *Labeo fisheri* (Jordan and Starks, 1917) an endemic cyprinid in Sri Lanka. *In* E.I.L. Silva, ed. *Instream Ecology and Reservoir Production of the Mahaweli Basin: A Modified Ecosystem* (in press).

De Silva, K.H.G.M. and D.M. Wansapura. 1991. Distribution of fish species in the Mahweli River system in Kandy District. *In* E.I.L. Silva, ed. *Instream Ecology and Reservoir Production of the Mahaweli Basin: A Modified Ecosystem* (in press).

De Silva, S.S. and J. Chandrasoma. 1980. Reproductive biology of *Sarotherodon mossambicus* an introduced species in an ancient man-made lake in Sri Lanka. *Env. Biol. Fish.* 5: 253-259.

De Silva, S.S. and C.H. Fernando. 1980. Recent trends in the fishery of Parakrama Samudra, an anncient man-made lake in Sri Lanka. *In* J.I. Furtado, ed. *Tropical Ecology and Development. Proc. 5th Int. Symp. Trop. Ecol.* pp. 927-937. Kuala Lumpur, Malaysia.

Deraniyagala, P.E.P. 1952. *A Coloured Atlas of some Vertebrates from Ceylon. 1.* Pisces. Ceylon National Publication, Colombo.

Dissanayake, C.B. and S.V.R. Weereasooriya. 1986. The Environmental Chemistry of Mahaweli River, Sri Lanka. *Intern. J. Env. Stud.* 28: 207-223.

Evans, D. 1981. *Threatened Freshwater Fish of Sri Lanka.* IUCN Conservation Monitoring Centre, Cambridge.

Fernando, C.H. 1965. A preliminary survey of 21 Ceylon lakes. 3. Parasites and predators, food of fish and marginal fauna. *Bull. Fish. Stn. Ceylon* 18: 17-28.

Fernando, C.H. 1971. The role of introduced fish in fish production in Ceylon's fresh waters. *In* E. Duffey and A.S. Watt, eds. *The Scientific Management of Animal and Plant Communities for Conservation*. pp.295-310.

Fernando, C.H. 1973. Man-made lakes of Ceylon: a biological resource. *In* W.C. Ackermann, G.F. White and E.B. Worthington, eds. Man-made lakes: their problems and environmental effects. *Amer. Geophys. Monogr.* 17: 664-671.

Fernando, C.H. 1977. Reservoir fisheries in Southeast Asia: past, present and future. *Proc. Indo. Pacif. Fish. Counc. 17th Sess. Sect. 3*: 475-498.

Fernando, C.H. and Indrasena, H.H.A. 1969. The Freshwater Fisheries of Ceylon. *Bull. Fish. Res. Stn. Ceylon* 20: 101-134.

Feth, J.H. 1971. Mechanisms Controlling World Water Chemistry: Evaporation Cristallisation *Process. Science* 172: 870.

Feth, J.H., C.E. Roberson and W.L. Polzer. 1964. *Geological Survey Water Supply Papers, No. 1535,* Washington DC.

Fowke, P. 1936. Trout Culture in Ceylon, *Ceyl. J. Sci.* 6: 21.

Gibbs, R.J. 1970. Mechanisms Controlling World Water Chemistry. *Science* 170: 1088-1090.

Hunting Survey Corporation Report. 1962. *Report on a Survey of the Resources of the Mahaweli Ganga Basin, Ceylon*. Part 1. Govt. Press. Ceylon.

Johnson, D.S. 1973. Equatorial forest and the inland aquatic fauna of Sundania. *In* B.S. Colin and R.H. Groves, eds. *Nature Conservation in the Pacific*, pp. 111-116. Australian National Univ. Press, Canberra.

Mendis, A.S. and C.H. Fernando. 1962. A guide to the freshwater fauna of Ceylon. *Bull. Fish. Res. Stn. Ceylon.* 12: 111-125.

Moyle, P.B. 1976. *Inland Fishes of California*. Univ. of California Press, Berkeley.

Moyle, P.B. and F.R. Senanayake. 1984. Resource partitioning among the fishes of rain forest streams in Sri Lanka. *J. Zool. Lond.* 202: 195-223.

Munro, I.S.R. 1965. *The Marine and Freshwater Fishes of Ceylon*. Australian Department of External Affairs, Canberra.

Natarajan, A.V. 1977. Ecology and the State Fishery Development in Some Manmade Reservoirs in India. *Proc. Indo. Pacif. Fish. Counc. 17th Sess. Sect. 2*: 258-267.

Radda, A.C. 1973. Results of the Austrian-Ceylonese Hydrobiological Mission 1970: Collection of Fishes (Osteichthyes). *Bull. Fish. Res. Stn. Sri Lanka.* 24: 134-154.

Remane, A. and C. Schlieper. 1971. *Biology of Brackish Water*. (Die Binnengewässer, 2nd English Edn.). Stuttgart.

Schiemer, F. and R. Hofer. 1983. A contribution to the ecology of the fish fauna of the Parakrama Samudra. *Dev. Hydrobiol.* 12: 134-154.

Senanayake, F.R. 1980. *Biogeography and Ecology of the Inland Fishes of Sri Lanka.* Unpublished Ph.D. thesis. Univ. of California, Davis.

Senanayake, F.R. 1982. *Barbus srilankensis,* a new species of cyprinid fish from Sri Lanka. *Ceyl. J. Sci. (Biol. Sci.)* 15: 165-172.

Senanayake, F.R. and P.B. Moyle. 1982. Conservation of freshwater fishes of Sri Lanka. *Biol. Conserv.* 22: 181-195.

Silva, E.I.L. 1988. *The Effects of Irrigation on the Bioenergetics of Stream Ecosystems.* Unpublsihed Ph.D. thesis. Univ. of Calgary, Canada.

Silva, E.I.L. 1990. Limnology and fish yields of newly built standing water bodies in the Mahaweli River Basin, Sri Lanka. *Verh. Internat. Verein. Limnol.* 24: 1425-1429.

Silva, E.I.L. 1991. Discontinuum of the Mahaweli River and its impact on the structure and functioning of instream habitat: An overview. *In* E.I.L. Silva, ed. *Instream Ecology and Reservoir Production of the Mahaweli River Basin: A Modified Ecosystem.* In press.

Silva, E.I.L. and R.W. Davies. 1986. Movements of some indigenous riverine fishes in Sri Lanka. *Hydrobiol.* 137: 265-270.

Silva, E.I.L. and R.W. Davies. 1987. Aspects of the biology of *Ompok bimaculatus* (Bloch)(Family: *Siluridae*) in lake Parakrama Samudra, (Sri Lanka). *Trop. Ecol.* 31: 126-132.

Silva, E.I.L. and R.W.Davies. 1988a. The feeding of *Saratherodon mossambicus* (Family: *Cichlidae*) with comments on its colonization success in dry Zone man-made lakes in Sri Lanka. *Verh. Internat. Verein. Limnol.* 23: 1766-1769.

Silva, E.I.L. and R.W.Davies. 1988b. Notes on the biology of *Hemiramphus limbatus* (*Hemiramphidae: pisces*). *Trop. Freshw. Biol.* 1: 42-49.

Silva, E.I.L. and S.S. de Silva. 1981. Aspects of the biology of grey mullet, *Mugil cephalus* L. adult population of a coastal lagoon in Sri Lanka. *J. Fish. Biol.* 19: 1-10.

Stearns, S.C. and R.D. Sage. 1982. Maladaption in a marginal population of the mosquito fish *Gambusia affinis. Evolution* 34: 65-75.

Sreenivasan, A. 1976. Fisheries of Stanley Reservoir (Muttur Dam) and three other reservoirs of Tamil Nadu, India, a case history. *Proc. Indo. Pacif. Fish. Counc. 17th Sess. Sect. 2:* 292-302.

Srinivasan, R. and Sreenivasan, A. 1977. Fishery of the Cauvery River System, Tamil Nadu, India. *Proc. Indo. Pacif. Fish. Counc. 17th Sess. Sect. 2:* 167-172.

TAMS. 1980. Environmental Assessment. Accelerated Mahaweli Development Programme. Vol. 3. *Aquatic Environment* H: 2-8.

Vannote, R.L., G.W. Minshall, J.R. Sedell and C.E. Cushing. 1980. The river continuum concept. *Can. J. Fish. Aquat. Sci.* 37: 130 -137.

Whyte, R.O. 1961. Evolution of land use in southwestern Asia. *In* L.D. Stamp, ed. *Arid Zone Research - VII. History of Land Use in Arid Regions.* UNESCO, Paris.

Proceedings of the International and Interdisciplinary Symposium
ECOLOGY AND LANDSCAPE MANAGEMENT IN SRI LANKA
W. Erdelen, C. Preu, N. Ishwaran, C.M. Madduma Bandara (eds.)
Colombo, Sri Lanka, 12-26 March 1990
© 1993
Margraf Scientific Books, D-97985 Weikersheim
ISBN 3-8236-1182-8

Industrial Development and the Control of Pollution to Preserve the Natural Balance of Aquatic Resources

A.P. MATHES AND M.S. MOTHA

Abstract

A monitoring program was carried out to determine the type of pollutants being discharged by the industrial sector into the Kelani River and Bolgoda Lake, which are two of the major freshwater bodies receiving industrial effluents. The major pollutants were identified to be organic in nature, but toxic chemicals were also found to be present to a considerable extent. Effluents from most of the industries studied are neither controlled nor given any inhouse treatment before being discharged. The inherent difficulties in setting up treatment plants for individual industries were found to necessitate the creation of industrial zones or clusters of industries with provisions for common treatment plants, in order to achieve the objective of preserving the natural balance of aquatic resources. However, since the efficiency of the common treatment plants depends on the quality of the effluents, inhouse treatment seems essential for selected industries in the complex. The environmental damage caused by 10%-20% of the industries studied could be eliminated by simple pretreatment through effective oil trap systems. Since industries discharging toxic waste effluent, which comprise 50%-60% of those studied, find it extremely difficult to bear the cost of complete physicochemical treatment, it was concluded that primary treatment, as a first step, would be very helpful to reduce the present damage caused to the aquatic resources of Sri Lanka.

Introduction

The dynamics of an aquatic body results from the metabolism of its flora and fauna supported and the input and output of chemical substances to and from the surrounding environment causing minute daily variations in its quality. A natural balance is found in freshwater aquatic bodies which maintain the flora and fauna living in the water as well as on and in the bottom of the water body. These faunal and floral elements preserve the quality of the water and make the water suitable for aquaculture, recreation and sometimes for drinking purposes. However, changes in species diversity may occur from time to time, but the balance maintained ensures that the water body does not lose its character (Odum, 1971).

In contrast, any pollution of the water resulting from human activities causes changes in the quality of surface water streams, rivers, etc. The development of industrial plants is one of the major human related interferences with water quality. Additionally, population increase and the expansion of urbanization contribute to the problem of water pollution. The dimension of water pollution ranges from moderate to serious along the downstream parts of rivers and other surface water bodies. A further threat to the quality of water resources results from the waste being dumped into it. Although the effects of waste water discharge into water bodies are well known, very little consideration is given to that problem in industrial development programs in Sri Lanka. The two export promotion zones, located in Katunayake and Biyagama where waste water treatment was considered in order to maintain water quality are the only exceptions. Monitoring programs carried out by the Ceylon Institute of Scientific and Industrial Reseach (CISIR) attempted to determine the type of pollutants discharged into the three major freshwater bodies around Colombo, in particular the Kelani River, Bolgoda Lake and Lunawa Lagoon. The main objectives were the monitoring and assessment of the industrial-related water pollution levels in the downstream part of Kelani River and the water bodies between Moratuwa and Ratmalana; (1) to predict possible changes of the natural balance of aquatic bodies affected by the discharge of industrial pollutants, (2) to work out recommendations for effective control measures, and (3) to suggest suitable measures in future industrial planning and development.

Methods and Materials

In the Kelani River zone, 35 industries and installations were surveyed, which represent almost all the major industrial branches in that area. The nature and volume of the pollutants discharged were determined and the characteristics of the pollutants were analyzed. In the first stage of the program, 21 industrial plants were covered; the remaining 14 plants were surveyed during the second stage. A similar survey was carried out for 14 industrial plants in the area of Moratuwa and Ratmalana. In addition, results of extensive studies on pollutant effluents from particular industrial branches, such as the tannery and textile ones, were considered in order to estimate possible effects of these pollutants on the natural balance of aquatic systems. Finally, project-related data were collected also from other institutions which conducted similar investigations into the same or other aquatic bodies.

The abbreviations used in this paper are as follows: BOD = Biochemical Oxygen Demand, COD = Chemical Oxygen Demand, SS = Suspended Solids, TN = Total Nitrogen, TS = Total Solids, T°C = Temperature°, TCr = Total Chromium, O&G = Oil and Grease and NH_3-N = Ammonical Nitrogen, DO = Dissolved Oxygen.

Results and Discussion

The categorization system (Tab. 2, annexed) is used to indicate the number of industrial plants in each category for these areas (Tab. 1). Out of the 23 industrial plants studied in the Kelani River zone, 13 were found to be agrobased whereas 10 had not used raw materials of natural origin. However, only 2 plants were found to be agrobased in the Moratuwa-Ratmalana area. The majority of industries in this area was not based on natural raw materials and were mainly textile industries. Therefore, chemicals are the major contributors to the effluent discharged in this area (Tab. 3).

These results (Tab. 2, annexed, Tab. 3) were compared with the SLS standard for "Effluents discharged into Inland Surface Water" (SLS, 1984), so that each effluent could be categorized according to the degree of pollution caused by it, viz. high (H), medium (M) and low (L) degree (Tab. 4, annexed). The effluents of about 80%-90% of the industrial plants located in these 2 zones exceeded or did not comply with the limits of parameters such as pH, suspended solids, organic matter (COD and BOD), chemicals, nutrients and micronutrients.

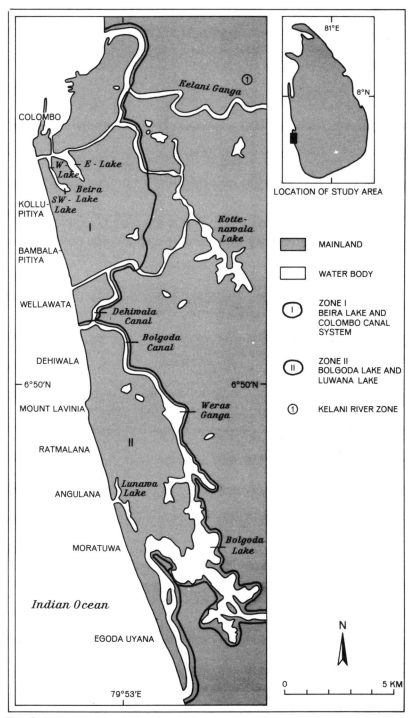

Figure 1. The Colombo water pollution survey.

417

Table 1. Nature of industries studied and pollution status; * = textile industries, ** = mainly textile industries.

Industries	Kelani River Zone	Moratuwa/ Ratmalana Zone
1. Industries/installations surveyed (Nos)	35	14
2. Industries/installations from which sampling was necessary (Nos)	27	11
3. Industries studied (Nos)	23	3*
4. Agro- or natural raw material based industries (Nos)	13	2
5. Non-agrobased industries (Nos)	10	9**
6. Miscellaneous industries (Nos) (pollution effect negligible)	4	-
7. Total volume of effluent discharged (mt/day)	4.5	2.2
8. Organic pollution load received by the water body (mt/day)	3.5-4.0	1.0-1.5
9. Ratio of agrobased industry to non-agrobased	1.30	0.22

The categorization (Tab. 4, annexed) considers the seasonal variation of some effluents. Due to this variation, however, it was not possible to determine the pollution load discharged into Kelani River. But average values and available volumetric flow rates for effluents obtained during the survey were used to indicate the approximate magnitude of the pollution load. The organic load discharged into the Kelani River is estimated at about 3.5-4.0 mt COD/day, the volumetric flow rate of the effluent at about 4.5-5.0 mt/day. Organic load discharged into the water bodies in the Moratuwa-Ratmalana zone is estimated at about 1.0-1.5 mt COD/day, and the volumetric flow rate of the effluent discharged here at about 2.2 mt/day.

Table 3. Analytical results obtained for textile industries as the major contributors to the total effluent that effect the aquatic bodies in the Moratuwa-Ratmalana zone. Data from CISIR technical reports.

	pH	BOD	COD	NH_3-N	O&G	SS
I	8.90	2500	4660	56	3700	89
II	6.91	120	6596	28	38	68
III	9.95	-	2500	-	175	1500
Average	8.59	1310	4585	42	1304	552

The results indicate that though these aquatic bodies are used for purposes such as aquaculture and drinking water, their quality does not conform to the standards required (Tab. 5, annexed). Negligence in maintaining water bodies at the required level could lead to further deterioration of their quality. Since the many effects resulting from the decrease of the water quality and their impacts on the environment are well known and the necessity to maintain a good chemical quality of water bodies is recognized in Sri Lanka, measures should be taken to improve the quality of the Sri Lankan water bodies and to consider for which purposes these water bodies may be used.

The pH value of a water body is an important factor for aquatic life. Variation in pH value may seriously affect invertebrate species sensitive to pH changes. In addition, the high quantity of organic matter in these water bodies creates an oxygen demand and consequently retards the natural self-purification of the water. Water bodies suitable for fishery and drinking water purposes should have a BOD of less than 5 mg/l, but values for the water bodies surveyed are beyond this level (Tab. 5, annexed). The effluents discharged into these water bodies contain a high amount of suspended solids including degradable organic matter. These components cause not only an oxygen deficit but also anaerobic conditions in the bottom sediment after they are deposited. Byproducts of this anaerobic activity will further affect the pH, hence, creating an environmental situation which exterminates most of the aerobic life forms. Accordingly species diversity is severely reduced and only a few species such as tubificids, chironomids, blue-green algae and fishes like catfish and snake head dominate the aquatic communities (Hynes, 1978). High amounts of suspended load cause high turbidity of the water body and disperses the light. There is also evidence that water bodies receiving pollutants face more constraints on species, e.g. molluscs, when they are discharged close to the river deltas (Zabel, 1989). Hence, their survival is presently threatened.

Average levels of water quality for the major aquatic bodies in Colombo, viz. Kelani River, Bolgoda Lake, Lunawa Lagoon, Beira Lake and Colombo Canal System determined by CISIR and other institutions is compared in Table 6. Based on the results of the water quality analysis conducted by the CISIR and other institutions for the major aquatic bodies in the area of Colombo, viz. Kelani River, Bolgoda Lake, Lunawa Lagoon, Beira Lake and Colombo Canal System, it is attempted to correlate the biological changes observed in these water bodies with the pollutants discharged into them.

Kelani River Zone

The Kelani River cannot be considered as a water body only marginally threatened by pollution because of its poor water quality (Tab. 5, annexed). The river receives discharges from industrial plants and other pollution-related sources, such as tanneries and the Colombo Canals which cause a localized water pollution due to the lack of complete water mixing. However, if the effluent plume is carried downstream without much mixing only about one tenth of the river width is affected, mainly along the river bank (BKH Consulting Engineers, 1986). Another example of a point-source-discharge is a tannery, from which chromium and hydrogen sulphide were released, and were found some 100 m downstrean from the discharge point. The amount of sludge built up is big enough to cause anaerobic conditions for the benthic organisms in particular sections of the river (CISIR, 1987).

Due to the high dilution, however, the spreading of these effects is limited to a great extent. As discussed above, the discharge of the effluents from the tannery leads not only to an increase in values of water parameters such as pH-value, saprobien system class and chemical oxygen demand, but also to an enrichment of chromium used as a tannic agent. The data recorded from a continuous monitoring program indicate that the effluents have a pH-value of about 9.5, that they cause a chemical oxygen demand of about 646 kg/day and biochemical oxygen demand of about 432 kg/day, and that they burden the water body with about 216 kg/day of suspended solids and about 134 kg/day of chromium. Effluent analysis of other tanneries show similar results (CISIR 1987, Indian Standards Institution 1977, ESCAP 1982).

Table 6. Average values obtained for selected parametres for different water bodies in and around Colombo. Data from CISIR (1987), Costa and de Silva (1978), NARA (1985), BKH Consulting Engineers (1986).

Parameter	Kelani River	Moratuwa/Ratmalana Zone	Beira Lake	Colombo Canal System
DO (mg/l)	4.0-6.0	<1.0-8.0	5.1-12.0	0-6.0
COD (mg/l)	20.0-40.0	185-833	10-438	-
BOD (mg/l)	-	-	15-57	15-320
pH	6.0-7.0	5.0-9.0	6.6-9.0	6.8-7.6
T°C	27	28	31	-
SS (mg/l)	9.0	15-318	-	60-200
O&G(mg/l)	<2	21-27	-	-
NH_3- N (mg/l)	1.0-3.0	2.0-5.0	0.8-2.0	0.5-7.0

An increase in the amount of organic pollutants may cause fish kills and fish diseases. The water body may lose its natural balance completely when additional polluted water is discharged from industrial plants where pollution control measures are not implemented. The loss of fish and other species within a short period of time may lead to an increase in the number of taxa and biomass at lower trophic levels and could lead to an increase in species diversity at these levels (Hynes, 1978).

Moratuwa Ratmalana Zone

It was shown that the major source of effluents discharged in the Moratuwa Ratmalana zone is the textile industry (Tab. 1). The organic load represented by the COD values (Tab. 3) is mainly of non-biodegradable nature and consists of textile chemicals including dyes, auxilliaries, dispersants, whiteners, emulsifiers, and solvents (Mathes 1989, Water Pollution Control Directorate 1982). Such pollutants discharged into surface waters increase the oxygen demand. In addition, the accumulation of sediments at the bottom causes greater constraints on aerobic benthic organisms due to the synthetic chemical dyes. Such a modified environment, in addition to the chemical effects, would reduce the amount of food available for fish. Similar studies conducted in various countries confirm the results presented here in Sri Lanka (Jorgensen, 1979).

Colombo Canal System

In addition to industrial pollutants, domestic effluents mainly from shanties, are discharged into the canal system of Colombo. Studies indicate that anaerobic conditions prevail throughout most parts of the bottom of the canal system (Tab. 6; BKH Consulting Engineers 1986). The report indicates that the water of the canal system is "dead" except in areas such as Kotte Ela and Kirillapone Canal where hardly any industrial effluents are discharged. Only hardy species of fish were observed thriving in large numbers in some places. The lack of flushing, the high input of wastes compared to the runoff and the tremendous amount of stagnant sediment are the major factors causing its environmental deterioration.

Table 7. Quality of water of Kelani River measured at discharge point of tannery effluent and at points up to 75 m away from the discharge point (CISIR, 1987).

	0 m	25 m	50 m	75 m	Average
pH	7.8	7.6	7.6	7.4	7.2
DO mg/l	5.5	4.7	4.7	4.7	5.5
Cond. mS/cm	7.2	7.1	6.9	6.7	6.4
Turb (NTU)	16.0	18.0	14.0	12.0	10.0

Beira Lake

Beira Lake, located in the heart of Colombo (Fig. 1), is the only large stagnant water body that receives domestic as well as industrial waste. However, the seasonal rainfall enables a certain dilution of the organic pollutants to a level which prevents the death of the entire water body. Ecologically, the lake is categorized as eutrophic. The results of analytical studies conducted by Costa and de Silva (1978) and by NARA (1985) demonstrated that the water body of Beira Lake experienced an overall increase in nutrient concentration within that period (Tab. 8, annexed). This increase indicates that the ecosystem is disturbed to such an extent that the nutrients cannot be absorbed. Frequent fish kills and degradation of large amounts of algae may also have contributed to the high nutrient content of the lake. Repeated fish kills in Beira Lake indicate that at least periodically, anaerobic conditions have prevailed causing a shift in dominance towards a few tolerant fish species. Moreover, the diversity of algal species has reduced significantly. The NARA study (1985) shows that blue-green algae, in particular *Microcystis*, contributed to 71%-98% of the algae species in 1985 whereas green algae dominated in 1972 (Costa and de Silva, 1978). In addition, the diversity of fish species has decreased in Beira Lake. While many fish species were recorded in 1964, the fish species *Tilapia* introduced in the early 1970s dominated in 1985 (NARA, 1985). But even the numbers of *Tilapia* have decreased due to the poor water quality. This is substantiated by *Tilapia* catches which decreased from about 450 kg/day in 1975 to about 200 kg/day in 1985 (NARA, 1985).

Control Technology

The CISIR has been a pioneering institute in the field of pollution treatment in Sri Lanka. The institute has always disseminated and published information on treatment technology but it has also experienced that the technology transfer is difficult because the industry is reluctant to introduce new technology. The main causes are limitations in available capital, lack of knowledge in environmental management, and lack of understanding about the benefits from protected aquatic bodies which are utilized by the industry. Moreover, it has also been experienced that industrial development has not been properly planned. Neither the environment of the surrounding area nor any precautionary measures mitigating pollution from their effluents were considered in the selection of the plant sites. These difficulties can be overcome by the creation of more industrial zones or clusters of industries with sewage plants where effluents can be collected and treated. The two zones already existing in Katunayake and Biyagama prove that success in mitigating pollution can be achieved by the implementation of such a procedure.

For further planning it would be desirable to select proper sites for future industrial zones. Different zones should be allocated for different types of industrial complexes varying from heavy, medium to small. Measures should be taken to mix domestic effluents with industrial effluents in order to lessen the complexity of required industrial technology and to achieve an effective treatment. The application of biological treatment methods is more economic for the majority of effluents compared to physicochemical and advanced treatment techniques. Suitable treatment methods already exist to treat effluents at least partially. Therefore, environmental damage caused by industries should be curtailed by the application of suitable methods within the means of the given industry. For instance, it is estimated that the direct and irreversible environmental damage, caused by 10%-20% of the Sri Lankan industry, could be eliminated by a simple pretreatment through effective oil trap systems. Hazardous waste discharging industries such as tanneries and the textile, chemical and metal industries which comprise 50%-60% of those studied require treatment systems which involve a series of unit operations and which involve a high capital operation and maintainance. Generally, attempts are made to encourage such industries to install an inital or physicochemical treatment system and to carry out the treatment of their effluents stage by stage. Even the plants in the industrial zones should be advised to have inhouse treatment because of the hazardous nature of their effluents.

Conclusions and Recommendations

This survey indicates that 80%-90% of the effluents discharged into aquatic bodies do not comply with the "Sri Lankan Standards for Effluents discharged into Inland Surface Waters" (SLS, 1984). Therefore, the industrialists should be encouraged to install treatment systems. The chemical assessment of the water bodies studied indicates that their water quality does not conform to the level required for the purposes of fishery, drinking water, bathing and washing. Therefore, suitable measures are recommended to permanently maintain the necessary quality. The adverse effects on the natural balance of Bolgoda Lake, Lunawa Lake and Beira Lake are greater than those in the Kelani River. This difference is caused by two major reasons, i.e. less dilution effects and higher accumulation of nutrients in the lakes than in the river and less biodegradable effluent discharged into the lakes than into the river. The controlled discharge of partially or completely treated effluents may assist to reduce the deterioration of the prevailing natural balance in these aquatic bodies. Regeneration of dead water bodies is possible but is extremely costly. The zoning of new industries with provisions for common effluent treatment plants and the allocation of land for such treatment plants in existing industrial clusters, whenever possible, is recommended. Management of aquatic ecosystems helps mankind to achieve a better living expectation from industrialization. However, industrial development will always be in conflict with the environment as long as no suitable measures for maintaining the ecological balance of the aquatic body are taken.

Acknowledgments

The staff of the Environmental Science and Technology Section of CISIR was involved in the work presented in this paper. We convey our gratitude to them. Gratitude is also expressed to CEA and BKH Consulting Engineers, Netherlands, who financed some of the studies.

Literature Cited

APHA (American Public Health Association)/AWWA (American Water Works Association) /WPCF (Water Pollution Control Federation). 1975. *Standard Methods for the Examination of Water and Waste Water*. 14th Ed. APHA, Washington DC.

BKH Consulting Engineers. 1986. *Water Pollution Survey with an Ultra-Light Aircraft - Colombo*. Final report to CEA. BKH Consulting Engineers, Netherlands.

CEA (Central Environment Authority). 1985. *Industrial Pollution in the Kelani River,* Preliminary survey and interim report. Vol. 2. CEA of Sri Lanka.

CEA (Central Environment Authority). in press. *Industrial Pollution in the Kelani River*. CEA of Sri Lanka.

CISIR (Ceylon Institute of Scientific and Industrial Research). 1987. *An analysis of tannery effluents*. A technical report to BKH Consulting Engineers. CISIR, Colombo.

Costa H.A. and S.S. de Silva. 1978. The Hydrobiology of Colombo (Beira Lake) II, *Spol. Zeylan*. 32: 19-34.

Costa H.A. and S.S. de Silva. 1978. The Hydrobiology of Colombo (Beira Lake) III, *Spol. Zeylan*. 32: 35-54.

Costa H.A. and S.S. de Silva. 1978. The Hydrobiology of Colombo (Beira Lake) VI, *Spol. Zeylan*. 32: 83-92.

Costa H.A. and S.S. de Silva. 1978. The Hydrobiology of Colombo (Beira Lake) VII *Spol. Zeylan*. 32: 93-110.

Costa H.A. and S.S. de Silva. 1978. The Hydrobiology of Colombo (Beira Lake) IX. *Spol. Zeylan*. 32: 129-140.

Environment Agency, Government of Japan 1987. *Quality of the Environment in Japan*. Printing Bureau, Min. of Finance, Japan.

ESCAP (Economic and Social Commission for Asia and the Pacific), Environment and Development Series 1982. *Industrial Pollution Control Guidelines*. VII, Tanning industry. UN. ESCAP, Bangkok.

Hammer, M.J. 1975. *Water and Waste Water Technology*. John Wiley & Sons Inc.

Hynes, H.B.N. 1978. *The Biology of Polluted Waters*. Liverpool University Press, Liverpool.

Indian Standards Institution 1977. *Guide for Treatment and Disposal of Effluents of Tanning Industry*. New Delhi.

Industrial Pollution Control of Japan. 1981. *Industrial Pollution Control* Vol. 1. IPCAJ, Tokyo, Japan.

Jorgensen, S.E. 1979. *Industrial Waste Water Management*. Elsevier Scientific, Amsterdam.

Mathes, J.A.P. 1989. Low waste technology applications in textile industry in Sri Lanka. *Proc. of Workshop on Selected Topics on "Clean Technology,"* AIT, Bangkok.

Mendis A.S. 1964. A contribution to the limnology of Colombo Lake. *Bull. Fish. Res. Stn. Ceylon* 17: 213-220.

NARA (National Aquatic Resources Agency). 1985. *Beira Lake, Report of a preliminary study*. NARA, Colombo.

Odum, E.P. 1971. *Fundamentals of Ecology*. Saunders Co, Philadelphia.

SLS (Sri Lanka Standards) 652. 1984. *Sri Lanka Standards for Effluents Discharged into Inland Surface Waters*. Sri Lanka Standards Institution, Colombo.

SLS (Sri Lanka Standards) 799. 1987. *Tolerance Limits for Inland Surface Waters for Fish Culture*. Sri Lanka Standards Institution, Colombo.

Water Pollution Control Directorate 1982. *Survey of Textile Wet Processing and Pollution Abatement Technology Report*. IEC International Environmental Consultants Ltd, Canada.

Zabel, T.F. 1989. Current standards and their relation to environmental behaviour and effects; the case of lead. *The Science of the Total Environment* 78: 187-204.

Annex

Table 2. Analytical results in mg/l (except pH results) for untreated effluents, unless otherwise indicated, studied under Kelani River area survey. Data from CEA (1985, in press). Analytical methods from APHA (1975).

Industry	pH	BOD	COD	SS	TN	NH₃-N	O&G	TCr	T°C	TS
Textile										
a. Untreated	5.0-11.0	300-400	830-1600	20-180	-	-	20-340	-	31-41	-
b. Treated	6.4-7.1	110	340-530	39	280	46	1	-	30	-
Bottling	7.0-12.0	160-430	125-2049	40	-	16	15-87	-	32	467-1840
Food Processing	-	180	4660	-	-	30	10	-	-	-
Power Plant (treated)	7.5	10	32	186	29	15	-	-	-	-
Oil Mills	7.0	120	194	55-587	-	-	-	-	44	-
Soap	7.0-10.5	162	243-2280	20	-	3	12	-	41	-
Water Works	6.6-7.3	-	50	-	-	-	-	-	-	75-187
Tannery	8.8-10.1	1500-2500	2400-3600	620-1320	200-250	-	-	-	-	8000-16,500
Chemical	6.3-7.3	-	198-380	50-74	4	-	-	350-1250	27	390-864
Tyre	6.6	-	2	19	-	-	4	-	30	-
Brewery	5.5	930	1132	34	16	13	-	-	28	514
Petroleum	6.1-9.8	5-120	92-607	10-214	11	9	3-81	-	30	965
Gas	7.3	-	400	50	-	-	-	-	27	400
Nylon	10.5	55	400	143	-	-	3-4	-	-	2300
Wood Processing	4.6-7.0	-	520-1025	11-52	-	-	-	-	-	-

Table 4. Degree of pollution by different types of industries in relation to SLS standards (in mg/l); VH = very high, H = high, N = neutral, L = low, VL = very low.

Industry	No	pH	BOD	COD	SS	TN/NH$_3$-N	O&G	TCr
Textile	4	H	L	H	L	-	-	-
Bottling	2	H	L	H	L	-	-	-
Food Processing	1	N	H	-	H	-	-	-
Power Plant	1	N	L	L	L	L	L	-
Oil Mills	1	N	L	-	VL	-	H	-
Soap	2	H	-	L	-	-	-	-
Water Works	3	N	L	H	VH	-	-	-
Tanneries	1	L	-	L	L	H	L	-
Chemicals	1	H	H	H	H	-	-	-
Tyre	1	N	-	L	L	L	-	-
Brewery	1	L	H	L	L	L	L	-
Petroleum	2	N	L	H	H	-	H	H
Gas	1	H	-	-	L	L	-	-
Nylon	1	N	-	L	L	L	H	-
Wood Processing	1	N	-	H	H	-	H	-
SLS Standards (1984)		6.0-8.5	30	250	50	50	10	0.1

Table 5. Average values for some parameters for the water bodies in the two areas studied in comparison with available standards for such bodies (* = data from CISIR).

Parameter	Kelani River*	Moratuwa-Ratmalana Zone*	Japanese Standards for Rivers-Fishery Class (1987)	Sri Lanka Standards (1984)	Sri Lanka Standards (1987)
DO (mg/l)	4.0-6.0	1-8.0	5.0 min	4.0 min	3.0 min
COD (mg/l)	20.0-40.0	60.0	10.0 max	-	-
BOD (mg/l)	-	-	5.0 max	5.0 max	5.0 max
pH T°C	6.01-7.0 27	5.0-9.0 28	6.5-8.5 -	6.0-9.0 -	6.0-9.0 -
SS (mg/l)	9.0	15.0-30.0	50.0 max	-	-
O&G (mg/l)	2.0	21-27	-	0.1 max	0.1 max
NH_3-N (mg/l)	1-3	2-5	-	-	1.2 max

Table 8. Comparison of values obtained for various parameters for Beira Lake (SW Lake) in 1972 and 1985. Data from Costa and de Silva (1978) and NARA (1985).

	pH	T°C	DO	OPO_4^{-3}	NH_3-N	NO_3^-	NO_2^-
1972	7.9-9.0	29-33	2-14	<0.05	0.01-0.11	0.01-0.05	absent
1985	7.7-9.2	29-34	8-18	0-88	0.8-2.0	0.1-1.2	31-456

Proceedings of the International and Interdisciplinary Symposium
ECOLOGY AND LANDSCAPE MANAGEMENT IN SRI LANKA
W. Erdelen, C. Preu, N. Ishwaran, C.M. Madduma Bandara (eds.)
Colombo, Sri Lanka, 12-26 March 1990
© 1993
Margraf Scientific Books, D-97985 Weikersheim
ISBN 3-8236-1182-8

Habitat Fragmentation and the Genetic Status of Leopards and Elephants in Sri Lanka

S. MIThTHAPALA, S.B.U. FERNANDO AND J. SEIDENSTICKER

Abstract

Using standard electrophoretic techniques, genetic variation was assessed in a sample of 22 leopards (*Panthera pardus kotiya*) and 31 Asian elephants (*Elephas maximus maximus*) from the collections of the National Zoological Gardens, Dehiwela, Sri Lanka. Two out of 50 loci were polymorphic in all the leopards and three out of 54 loci were polymorphic in all the elephants. Percentage polymorphism (P) and average heterozygosity (H) were calculated as 4% and 0.014 respectively for leopards. In the elephant sample, P = 5.56% and H = 0.04. Comparison was possible with a previous study which documented three additional polymorphic loci with P = 10% and H = 0.031 for mainland leopards. No other data are available for the comparison of elephants from Sri Lanka and other Asian elephant populations. The reduction in variation reported for the island leopards compared to mainland leopards parallels decreases reported between mainland and island populations across several taxa, as well as a reduction documented in an isolated population of mainland African lions (*Panthera leo leo*). The habitat/dispersal profile in leopards and elephants would be expected to facilitate the avoidance of inbreeding that has deleterious effects in captive leopard and elephant populations. Today, the insularization of suitable leopard and elephant habitats is fragmenting wild populations of the island's largest carnivore and herbivore. The extent of this disturbance regime and the long-term consequences of the fragmentation of leopard and elephant populations remain to be fully documented and explored.

Introduction

Sri Lanka has been isolated from continental India for about 10,000 years, since the end of the Pleistocene (Jacob, 1949). Islands are naturally fragmented habitats, and the consequences of island/mainland population fragmentation have long been the subject of biogeographical and evolutionary interest. Recently, conservation biologists have been investigating the consequences of habitat fragmentation on a smaller scale and its attendant effects (Soulé, 1986), especially the implications this has for the long-term preservation of biological diversity. We do not know the extent of habitat fragmentation the large mammals on Sri Lanka can tolerate.

During the last half century in Sri Lanka, the human population has increased to 16 million with a population doubling time of about 40 years (Library of Congress, 1978). The land area under development has increased while natural habitats have decreased in area. Once large, contiguous tracts of natural habitat are now fragmented into small patches, some of which are designated as reserves or national parks. Both natural and man-made habitat fragmentation have consequences for the behavior, demography, and genetic status of large, wide-ranging animals. Dispersal patterns may be disrupted and population structure may change as a result of fragmentation (Chepko-Sade and Halpin, 1987). One primary effect of population fragmentation is the reduction of genetic variation (Lande and Barrowclough, 1987). In small populations the effect of genetic drift, the effect due to random changes alone and not due to selection, becomes strong simply as a consequence of sampling (Hartl, 1988). In fragmented, isolated populations with no migration, the probability of inbreeding also increases. Both of these factors result in decreased genetic heterozygosity.

Most naturally fragmented island populations exhibit less genetic variation than their mainland counterparts and studies across genera have documented this (e.g. Selander and Johnson 1973, Nevo 1978). Mainland populations isolated as a result of habitat fragmentation also exhibit less genetic variation. For example, East African lions (*Panthera leo leo*) in Ngorongoro Crater, which is near to but isolated from the Serengeti, showed about 36% less genetic variation than free-ranging Serengeti lions (O'Brien *et al.* 1987). There appears to be a definite trend in the loss of genetic diversity: less variation from mainland to island and less variation from contiguous to isolated populations.

The loss of genetic variation is only detrimental if it is correlated with harmful effects (Templeton and Reed, 1983). However, during the last decade, several seminal studies of big cats have shown a correlation between decreased vulnerability to disease (O'Brien *et al.* 1983, 1985) and increased spermatozoal abnormalities (Wildt *et al.* 1987a, 1987b, Brown *et al.* 1989). Other studies have documented that increased inbreeding in zoo animals is correlated with increased infant mortality and decreased fecundity (Ralls and Ballou, 1983). Conversely, increased genetic variation has been associated with disease resistence and increased survival and growth rate (Allendorf and Leary, 1986). These studies demonstrate that a detailed knowledge of the genetic status of a species needs to be an integral part in the development of its conservation and management plan (Lacy, 1988). Genetic studies of captive populations are indispensable for providing information about the enormous problems facing small fragmented wild populations of mammals (Ballou and Seidensticker, 1987).

In this paper, we examine the consequences of habitat fragmentation in Sri Lanka as they relate to the genetic status of Sri Lanka's largest carnivore, the leopard (*Panthera pardus kotiya*), and the largest herbivore, the Asian elephant (*Elephas maximus maximus*). To do this, we sampled both species in the national living collections maintained by the National Zoological Gardens. Both of these species once ranged widely on the island, but are now largely restricted to national parks and contiguous areas - islands within the island. The leopard and the elephant are listed as endangered in the US Fish and Wildlife Service's "List of Endangered and Threatened Wildlife and Plants". In Sri Lanka they receive total protection.

Survey of Genetic Variation in Captive Leopards and Elephants

At the National Zoological Gardens, Dehiwela, Sri Lanka, seven wild-caught leopards from Sri Lanka and 15 captive-born leopards from the same subspecies were sampled (Miththapala *et al.* 1991). 31 elephants collected from all over the island and maintained at the Elephant Orphanage, Pinnawala, and the National Zoological Gardens, Dehiwala, Sri Lanka, were also sampled (Lawson *et al.* in prep.). Methods for blood collection and separation are described in Miththapala *et al.* (1991).

Electrophoretic methods and results are detailed for leopards in Miththapala *et al.* (1991) and for elephants in Lawson *et al.* (in prep.). Table 1 shows that both wild-caught and captive-born

Sri Lankan leopards had approximately 40% less variation than leopards from mainland founders housed in various zoos in the USA. 2 out of 50 were loci polymorphic (Miththapala *et al.* 1991, Newman *et al.* 1985). The elephant sample had 5.56% polymorphism and 0.04 average heterozygosity, with three out of 54 loci being polymorphic (Lawson *et al.* in prep.).

Table 1. Comparison of levels of genetic polymorphism in captive mainland and Sri Lankan leopards and the genetic status of Sri Lankan Asian elephants. Data from Miththapala *et al.* (1991) and Lawson *et al.* (in prep.).

Taxa (Sample Size)	% Polymorphism	Average Heterozygosity
Leopards		
Captive mainland (18)	10	0.031
Wild-caught Sri Lanka (7)	04	0.014
Captive-born Sri Lanka (15)	04	0.012
Asian elephants		
Pinnawala and Dehiwala Asian elephants (31)	5.56	0.04

Discussion

In leopards, population fragmentation through island isolation has had the effect of decreasing genetic variation as revealed by comparison of the Sri Lankan sample and mainland data (Tab. 1; Miththapala *et al.* 1991, Newman *et al.* 1985). The loss of variation observed is comparable, quantitatively, to the loss of variation observed between Serengeti and Ngorongoro Crater lions in Africa (Miththapala *et al.* 1991, O'Brien *et al.* 1987). At this time, the genetic data for elephants (Lawson *et al.* in prep.) are the only data available for an Asian elephant population. Thus, comparisons between mainland and island populations cannot be made. It should be noted, however, that the sample analyzed by Lawson *et al.* (prep.) was composed of elephants that were collected from all over the island and could, in fact, represent several subpopulations. When subpopulations are treated as a single population, a heterozygote deficiency known as the Wahlund Effect is created (Hartl, 1988). Therefore, the heterozygosity in each natural subpopulation could be higher than the value reported by Lawson *et al.* (in prep.). Studies have been carried out in zoos that demonstrate empirically that there is higher infant mortality with increased inbreeding in Asian elephants (Ralls and Ballou, 1983).

At this stage, we cannot draw conclusions about the effects of habitat fragmentation on the genetic status of leopards and elephants. We have no knowledge of dispersal patterns, or of effective population sizes in the wild, both of which are behavioral and demographic parameters that affect the genetic structure of a population (Chepko-Sade and Halpin, 1987). To examine this, samples are necessary from more free-ranging leopards and elephants from locations known to have been isolated for some time as well as from populations that have only recently been isolated. Chasing this elusive butterfly is a personal task that we are pursuing for leopards. More samples from elephant herds known to be isolated are also essential.

Highly structured captive breeding programs are essential components of conservation efforts throughout the world. The captive leopard and elephant populations at the Dehiwela Zoo and the Pinnawala Orphanage are invaluable collections. Both of these populations must be monitored carefully for the avoidance of inbreeding and to ensure adequate founder contribution to the captive populations. This requires rigorously planned breeding programs. What we know about the genetic status of leopard and elephant populations in Sri Lanka is much less than what we do not know. What we do know suggests that we cannot ignore the genetic status of these large mammals in landscape planning and management, if these wonderful animals are to survive in the long term.

Acknowledgments

Financial support for this project was provided by the Smithsonian International Exchange Program, Smithsonian Research Opportunities Fund, Smithsonian Special Foreign Currency Program, and Friends of the National Zoo. The cooperating institutions were: the National Zoological Park, National Zoological Gardens of Sri Lanka, Laboratory of Viral Carcinogenesis, National Cancer Institute, and School of Forest Resources and Conservation, University of Florida. Support for collecting the elephant blood samples was provided in part by the Detroit Zoological Park. We thank the above for assistance and loan of equipment. Our efforts have been supported by many people to whom we are grateful: J. Ballou, B. Beck, F. Berkowitz, J. Block, S. Boyle, M. Bush, J.C. Daniel, J. Eisenberg, L. Forman, K.G. Goodrowe, E. Gould, B. Kalashantha, K. Latinen, J. Lawson, S. Lumpkin, A.M.V.R. Manatunga, J.S. Martensen, M.M. Miyamoto, L.M.H. Molligoda and the animal keepers at the Dehiwela Zoo, S.J. O'Brien, L.G. Phillips, M. Robinson, R. Rudran, A. Shoemaker, M. Sunquist and C. Wemmer.

Literature Cited

Allendorfer, F.W. and R.F. Leary. 1986. Heterozygosity and fitness in natural populations of animals. *In* M.E. Soulé, ed. *Conservation Biology,* pp. 57-76. Sinauer Associates Inc. Sunderland, Massachusetts.

Ballou, J. and J. Seidensticker. 1987. The genetic and demographic characteristics of the 1983 captive population of Sumatran tigers *Panthera tigris sumatrae. In* R.L. Tilson and U.S. Seal, eds. *Tigers of the World*, pp. 329-347. Noyes Publications, Park Ridge, New Jersey.

Brown, J.L., D.E. Wildt, L.G. Phillips, J. Seidensticker, S.B.U. Fernando, S. Miththapala and K. Goodrowe. 1989. Adrenal-pituitary-gonadal relationships and ejuculate characteristics in captive leopards (*Panthera pardus kotiya*) isolated on the island of Sri Lanka. *J. Reprod. Fertil.* 85: 605-613.

Chepko-Sade, B.D. and Z.P. Halpin. 1987. *Mammalian Dispersal Patterns*. Univ. of Chicago Press, Chicago.

Hartl, D.L. 1988. *A Primer in Population Genetics*. Sinauer Associates Inc. Sunderland, Massachusetts.

Jacob, K. 1949. Land connections between Ceylon and Peninsular India. *Proc. Natl. Inst. Sci. India* 15: 341-343.

Lacy, R. 1988. A report on population genetics in conservation biology. *Conserv. Biol.* 2: 245-247.

Lande, R. and G.F. Barrowclough. 1987. Effective population size, genetic variation, and their use in population management. *In* M.E. Soulé, ed. *Viable Populations for Conservation,* pp. 87-123. Cambridge Univ. Press, Cambridge.

Lawson, R., J. Seidensticker, L. Phillips, S. Miththapala, K. Goodrowe and S.B.U. Fernando. (in prep.). Genetic survey of the Asian elephant (*Elephas maximus maximus*) in Sri Lanka.

Library of Congress, USA. 1978. *Draft Environmental Report on Sri Lanka.* Science and Technology Division, Library of Congress and US Man and Biosphere Secretariat, Department of State, Washington DC.

Miththapala, S., J. Seidensticker, L.G. Phillips, K.G. Goodrowe, S.B.U. Fernando, L. Forman and S.J. O'Brien. 1991. Genetic variation in Sri Lankan leopards. *Zoo Biol.* 10: 139-146.

Nevo, E. 1978. Genetic variations in natural populations. *Theor. Pop. Biol.* 13: 121-177.

Newman, A., M. Bush, E.E. Wildt, D. van Dam, M. Frankenhuis, L. Simmons, L. Phillips, and S.J. O'Brien. 1985. Biochemical genetic variation in eight endangered or threatened felid species. *J. Mammal.* 66: 256-267.

O'Brien, S.J., D.E. Wildt, D. Goldman, C.R. Merril and M. Bush. 1983. The cheetah is depauperate in genetic variation. *Science* 221: 459-462.

O'Brien, S.J., M.E. Roekle, L. Marker, A. Newman, C.W. Winkler, D. Meltzer, L. Colly, J. Everyman, M. Bush and D.E. Wildt. 1985. Genetic basis for species vulnerability in the cheetah. *Science* 227: 1428-1434.

O'Brien, S.J., J.S. Martenson, C. Packer, L. Herbst, V. deVos, P. Joslin, J. Ott-Joslin, D.E. Wildt and M. Bush. 1987. Biochemical genetic variation in geographic isolates of African and Asian lions. *Natl. Geogr. Res.* 3: 114-124.

Ralls, K. and J. Ballou. 1983. Extinction: lessons from zoos. *In* C.M. Schonewald-Cox, S.M. Chambers, B. MacBryde and L. Thomas, eds. *Genetics and Conservation,* pp. 164-184. Benjamin/Cumming Publishing Co. Inc. California.

Selander, R.K. and W.E. Johnson. 1973. Genetic variation among vertebrate species. *Ann. Rev. Ecol. Syst.* 4: 75-91.

Soulé, M.E., ed. 1986. *Conservation Biology.* Sinauer Associates Inc. Sunderland, Massachusetts.

Templeton, A.R. and B. Reed. 1983. The elimination of inbreeding depression in a captive herd of Speke's gazelle. *In* C.M. Schonewald-Cox, S.M. Chambers, B. MacBryde and L. Thomas, eds. *Genetics and Conservation,* pp. 241-261. Benjamin/Cumming Publishing Co. Inc. California.

Wildt, D.E., M. Bush, K.G. Goodrowe, C. Packer, A.E. Pusey, J.L. Brown, P. Joslin and S.J. O'Brien. 1987a. Reproductive and genetic consequences of founding isolated lion populations. *Nature* 329: 328-330.

Wildt, D.E., S.J. O'Brien, J.G. Howard, T.M. Caro, M.E. Roelke, J.L. Brown and M. Bush. 1987b. Similarity in ejaculate-endocrine characteristics in captive versus free-ranging cheetahs of two subspecies. *Biol. Reprod.* 36: 351-360.

Proceedings of the International and Interdisciplinary Symposium
ECOLOGY AND LANDSCAPE MANAGEMENT IN SRI LANKA
W. Erdelen, C. Preu, N. Ishwaran, C.M. Madduma Bandara (eds.)
Colombo, Sri Lanka, 12-26 March 1990
© 1993
Margraf Scientific Books, D-97985 Weikersheim
ISBN 3-8236-1182-8

Noise and its Management in the Sri Lankan Context

R.H. WICKRAMASINGHE

Abstract

The problem of noise is reaching significant levels in Sri Lanka. This is attributable to a number of factors including (a) population growth and increase in population density, (b) increase in the number of motor vehicles of all types, (c) increase in noise-generating institutions and establishments, (d) increase in the use of loudspeakers and radios, and (e) the appearance of record bars. Aircraft noise poses less of a problem as yet. In Colombo, fragmentation of large gardens and urbanization frequently leads to the loss of large trees and increased road construction. The gradual growth of the city over several centuries has resulted in many important thoroughfares, which are used by heavy vehicles passing through areas in which large numbers of residences are located. While some improvement may be effected by legislative means, other approaches, including provision of physical barriers to noise and attitudinal changes, are necessary.

Introduction

In 1505, when the Portuguese arrived in Sri Lanka, Colombo was an old-world trading center with only one street, which is today known as Bangasala Veediya or Bankshall Street (Brohier, 1984). Since that time, Colombo and its population has grown and may have reached a night-time population of around 660,000 and a floating population of about 400,000 in 1985. The island's population increased from 2.76 million and a density of 43 persons per km^2 in 1881 to 16.12 million with a density of 249 persons per km^2 in 1986 (Department of Census and Statistics, 1987).

The increase of total population and, hence, population density as well as factors, such as the growth of industries and the increase of motor traffic, have resulted in the gradual escalation of noise levels and noise nuisance in Sri Lanka. Although noise problems mainly prevail in urban areas, they also exist in rural areas. Recently, for instance, bees disturbed by loud music from portable radios and cassette recorders stung a group of 60 persons at the fortress of Sigiriya

(Anon. 1990). Although the existence of a noise problem and effects deriving from it is still under discussion in Sri Lanka, studies conducted in Australia indicate that the neglect of long-term noise strategies may contribute to noise escalation (Eddington and Eddington, 1988).

Few, if any, formal studies on environmental noise (not of occupational origin) have been conducted in Sri Lanka. A "Study Group on Noise Pollution" has commenced work on this problem but it has been hampered by the severe lack of background information. This paper attempts to give some scientific and technical background information about this problem and to call attention to the necessity of noise management as a scientific discipline in Sri Lanka.

General Overview on Effects of Noise

It may be helpful to give a general overview about some of the effects of noise under the categories used at the "Fifth International Congress on Noise as a Public Health Problem " in 1988 (Berglund et al. 1988, Berglund and Lindvall 1990).

Noise-Induced Hearing Loss

Damage to hearing may be caused by different mechanisms and may be temporary or permanent. In Sri Lanka, problems associated with occupation-related exposure to noise may come within the purview of the Division of Occupational Health, Department of Labour and/or the Ministry of Health. Workplace related noise is a field in which some experience is available in Sri Lanka. Textile mills and sawmills are two sources of such health complaints. It might be of interest to note that one of the earliest reports about noise-induced hearing loss (regarding blacksmiths and coppersmiths) was written by Carl Linnaeus in 1741.

Noise and Communications

This area comprises a variety of topics including warning signals for those people using hearing protectors, synthetic speech and reverberation systems. The widespread use of three languages in Sri Lanka should provide the opportunity to develop some interesting topics for research.

Non-Auditory Physiological Effects

A wide variety of non-auditory physiological effects can result from exposure to noise. An area in which research has been conducted is the possible influence of noise on development of heart disease. In Sri Lanka, much valuable information could be obtained from epidemiological studies in places where high noise levels are experienced in order to determine their health effects under local conditions.

Effects on Performance and Behavior

Noise can influence performance and behavior in a variety of ways ranging from performing tasks in factories or offices to children in a noisy environment at home. A noisy environment may, for instance, influence the capacity for aggressive behavior in individuals (Broadbent, 1990).

Effects on Sleep

A great deal of research has been accomplished and is being internationally performed on the effects of noise on sleep. Problems include the effect of noise during sleep on health problems of various types, the effect of noise at different times of the night and the effect of day-time noise on night-time sleep. Many of these studies are of immediate practical interest, such as for the administration of programs for traffic diversion, or for the regulation of traffic flow at night or on holidays and Sundays, or near hospitals, etc. These studies are also valuable to ensure the continued good health condition of shiftworkers.

Special studies should be performed in Sri Lanka on the health status of people who drive passenger vans and buses over long distances at night with the radio on at high volume. The cumulative effects on the health of this group combined with the inhalation of vehicle exhaust emissions and/or cigarette smoke (see below) may be serious, but they are unperceived and unrealized. The sensitivity of different individuals to noise-related problems are also not necessarily similar (Greifahn, 1990).

Combined Agents

There is some evidence that hearing loss and other physiological effects may be more severe when individuals are concurrently exposed to other agents, such as smoking, carbon monoxide, lead, mercury, sulphur dioxide and organic solvents. It is important to consider that the multiple types of pollution are encountered not only in certain industries but also at locations of traffic congestion, such as junctions. Epidemiological studies of individuals, such as traffic policemen, who have to spend long periods at such locations are recommend.

Effects of Noise on Animals

The information which is being gathered in this field (Myrberg Jr. 1990, Peterson 1990) is of much relevance to Sri Lanka. As animals differ from humans in becoming habituated to noise, the use of noise to protect crops from birds (Anon. 1989), elephants, fruit bats, etc. has to be carefully managed in order to be effective. This subject deserves attention particularly by agriculturists and wildlife conservationists. The sensitivity of whales to noise should be considered if the decision to establish an Ocean Thermal Energy Conversion (OTEC) plant near Trincomalee comes into action as the area is seasonally frequented by whales. For instance, it is known that the development of fishes and prawns kept in aquaculture systems is adversely affected by noise. Also domesticated (e.g. poultry) and wild animal species may be sensitive to unpredictable noises such as those of low-flying aircraft. The noise produced by striking a paddle on the water is used by fishermen to chase fish into a net. Myrberg (1990) has speculated that fish may congregate around offshore petroleum platforms due to hearing loss, but it is doubtful if this applies to Sri Lanka where brush-park or brush-pile fishing is practiced (e.g. Negombo Lagoon).

Noise Sources

The preceding gave a short overview of some general effects of noise as a public health problem. In the following the possible sources of noise in Sri Lanka are presented.

Noise from Road and Rail Transport

Noise from road transport is a problem all over the world. In tropical countries, however, the problem is aggravated because the warm climate necessitates open windows to ensure the circulation of air. But there is a great number of possibilities to reduce noise at its source. These measures include a diversity of approaches. First, better maintenance of the mechanical condition of vehicles can be required; second, special road surfaces can be used; third, the traffic flow can be controlled by using diversions, traffic lights, etc. fourth, the entry of traffic into a zone can be prohibited, either completely or during certain hours of the day and "silence zones" can be demarcated, in which the use of horns is prohibited. Other measures are possible as well. It has, for instance, been suggested that the Fort area of Colombo should be "off-limits" for private cars during the daytime and that the people who park their vehicles some distance from the Fort should reach their final destination by a bus shuttle service. It has also been mooted that long distance heavy vehicles are permitted to enter Colombo only at night and only on selected roads.

It should be noted that road traffic has increased in Sri Lanka in recent times. Between 1970 and 1986 new registration of vehicles amounted to 394,815 (Committee to Examine the Pollution caused by Vehicle Exhaust Emissions, 1988). As the motorized population increases, its management requires the development and introduction of adequate programs. It should be noted that the nuisance caused by traffic noise seems to depend, to some extent, on local conditions, the urban structure and the type of activities. For instance, the People's Republic of China considers any road with more than 100 vehicles per hour as a trunk road, whereas a number of 300 vehicles per hour is the criterion for attention to noise pollution in Hong Kong. It is also interesting to mention that, despite the relatively low number of motor vehicles for civil transport in the People's Republic of China (685,000 in 1973 and 2,250,000 in 1982), the people's consciousness of urban noise has been awakened by the installation of noise level display stands at street corners in some cities (Gao et al. 1987, Wang 1988). It is also of interest that Beijing has a road network of 233 km compared to 480 km in the Colombo municipality (Gao et al. 1987, Kwan 1987). In Singapore, where the roads can become congested at certain times, officials of the Registry of Vehicles and Traffic Police can take action against operators of noisy vehicles (Ho, 1987). The magnitude of the traffic-related noise problems in Japan cannot be estimated due to few complaints received (Suzuki, 1987).

Complaints about noise from railway operations have not been received in Sri Lanka.

Noise from Aircraft and in the Neighborhood of Airports

Noise from aircraft and in the neighborhood of airports is not yet an established source of complaint in Sri Lanka. In industrial countries, however, millions of people living near airports or along "boom carpets" are affected by jet aircraft noise and they could be exposed to several sonic booms a day. Their annoyance is increased if air transport movements take place also at night. Property values, for instance, have dropped near Gatwick and Heathrow airports in London (Commission on the London Airport 1971, Sharp and Jennings 1976). Noise has to be considered in environmental impact assessments (EIAs) when planning new airports in Sri Lanka. This could help to reduce costs for relocating public installations such as hospitals and schools, which may be adversely affected by noise. Studies available on airports in other countries may help to work out such EIAs.

Noise in and from Industrial Plants

Activities such as unauthorized garages, tinkering and sawing operations have led to general complaints about noise. Measures to protect workers can include better maintenance of machinery or the mounting of it on a rubber mat. This may reduce the noise level and vibration at the source, but measures, such as provision of sound insulation, are often effective. Some protection for the neighbors may be obtained from the construction of walls and the planting of trees. However, noise nuisance from industry is sometimes related to working late shifts or even at night, and to the location of the factories. An adequate buffer zone with well-designed noise barriers or sound insulation could decrease the noise level. Regarding noise reduction at source, the Wilson Report is recalled. There it is recognized that the reduction of noise to acceptable levels is presently not possible in some industrial processes, such as in drop forging and boiler making. In these cases, the Wilson Report recommends that a register of extraordinary noisy production processes should be compiled to protect both, the industry and the public, until a technique for reduction of noise is available.

Noise from Construction and Demolition

The construction and demolition industry causes some very noisy processes due to its equipment, such as pneumatic tools, pile drivers, concrete mixers, air compressors and diesel engines. The provision of hoardings and noise barriers are some of the measures which can reduce nuisance to the public. Developers as well as associations of architects and civil engineers should provide support and guidance to contractors in this topic. The preparation of construction material, particularly the sawing of timber and the blasting of granite also entails the generation of noise. In the United States of America, environmental impact assessments include certain construction activities and the noise generated by them (Eldred, 1990).

Noise within Buildings

In addition to noise within factories, noise can be encountered in places such as private residences, offices, schools, hospitals and restaurants. Noise experienced in buildings can be more annoying than outdoors. This applies to both, the noise originating within the building and noise intruding from external sources, such as traffic. In general, noise and its sources should be considered when buildings such as concert halls, luxury hotels, conference halls and cinemas are being designed, but developers often have not obtained sufficient professional advice in this field. In addition to the problem of open windows due to the climate (see above), the noise from the kitchen, bathroom or television set next to the living room of the adjoining residences may lead to a noise nuisance. An additional noise nuisance can derive from pets. Therefore, noise pollution is a field to which professional bodies should pay increased attention, because environmental noise may increase to such an extent that some buildings may be seriously affected well before the end of their projected lifespan (Committee on the Problem of Noise, 1963).

Noise from Loudspeakers

In Sri Lanka, many complaints are made about noise resulting from the (mis)use of loudspeakers. Loudspeakers are used, for example, at public meetings, rallies and carnivals, to sell goods on the roadside or from stationary vans, to clear the road for bicycle races, by all manner of religious and other institutions, and at festivals. It has often been remarked that the distance to which the noise is carried is further than a person would walk to purchase the goods advertized. The manner in which loudspeakers are used at certain weddings and other festivals diminishes the enjoyment of many guests. Complaints are also received about the use of loudspeakers in some schools, tutories and community centers. More use could be made of low-power baffle-type public address systems rather than horn-type speakers.

Entertainment

This source of noise pollution is not static in quality through time. In Japan, for instance, karaoke machines for music reproduction were very popular before 1987 and necessitated the restriction of their use at night (Suzuki, 1987). In Norway, the increased noise-induced hearing loss in young males between 1981 and 1987 has been ascribed to their increased exposure to loud music in discotheques and to the use of stereo and headsets (Borchgrevink, 1988). More transistor radios and juke boxes are presently used compared to previous years (Anon. 1990, Committee on the Problem of Noise 1963). In Sri Lanka, complaints are made about record bars, radios and television sets, cinemas, use of crackers and fireworks, domestic parties etc. These activities often go on into the night. Here again, policies emphasizing good neighborliness and consideration for others should be more effective than a regulatory approach.

Community Response to Noise

While an attempt to achieve a single dose-response relationship has not yet been realized, work and progress in studies on community response continues. One problem as regards legislation and administration of noise control in Sri Lanka is the lack of a general community response to noise. For instance, although complaints are frequently made regarding the use of loudspeakers by lottery ticket sellers, organizers of public events are not reluctant to use public address systems at unnecessarily high volume. Studies in this area in Sri Lanka will help to devise strategies to combat these problems effectively.

Some Legal Aspects and Other Control Measures

In addition to the National Environmental Act No. 47 of 1980 and the National Environmental (Amendment) Act No. 56 of 1988 over fifty items of legislation are of environmental relevance in Sri Lanka (Wickramasinghe, 1988). The National Environmental (Amendment) Act No. 56 (Sections 23 P to 23 R) provide for the control of noise pollution. A person convicted of an offence is liable to a fine of not less than 10,000 rupees and not more than 100,000 rupees, and to a fine of 500 rupees per day for each day on which the offence continues after conviction. Appropriate and enforceable standards are being developed. Because existing laws on noise pollution are sparse, inadequate and scattered, the problem of noise pollution has reached its present magnitude in Sri Lanka. If this development continues, this problem will reach levels seriously detrimental to human health. It is envisaged that local authorities will play a much more important role than in the past to control noise as is the practice elsewhere (Central Office of Information, 1988).

It should be stressed that, except in some cases, the control of noise pollution is not effectively achieved by resorting to the courts but by increased public awareness on the magnitude and nature of the problem. Legal back-up will be necessary, but much can be achieved by good neighborhood relations and consideration for others coupled with technical strategies including the provision of noise barriers, an increase in green belt zones, parks and other tree cover. In the United States, for instance, nearly forty different types of land use strategies are available to manage noise (Bragdon, 1990). "Pink noise" or noise cancellation technology will, also, probably play a part in noise management in Sri Lanka, in due course. Education from a young age on the problem of noise pollution is necessary as it appears likely to escalate if ignored much longer.

Acknowledgments

I am very grateful to Sir Alan H. Wilson, FRS, for a gift of a copy of "Noise: The Report of the Committee on the Problem of Noise".

Literature Cited

Anon. 1989. South Australian draft pamphlet on bird deterrence. *In* V.C. Goodwin, ed. *Government Officers' Conference on Community Noise.* Annex E. Department of Health, New Zealand.

Anon. 1990. Sixty raising hornets' nest get stung. Daily News 8 Feb. 1990, Colombo.

Berglund, B., U. Berglund, J. Karlsson and T. Lindvall, eds. 1988. *Noise as a Public Health Problem.* Vols. 1-3. Swedish Council for Building Research, Stockholm.

Berglund, B. and T. Lindvall, eds. 1990. *Noise as a Public Health Problem.* Vols 4-5. Swedish Council for Building Research, Stockholm.

Borchgrevink, H.M. 1988. One third of 18 year old male conscripts show noise induced hearing loss > 20 dB before start of military service - The incidence being doubled since 1961. Reflecting increased leisure noise? *In* B. Berglund, U. Berglund, J. Karlsson, and T. Lindvall, eds. *Noise as a Public Health Problem,* Vol. 2, pp. 27-32. Swedish Council for Building Research, Stockholm.

Bragdon, C.R. 1990. Noise as part of city planning. *In* B. Berglund and T. Lindvall, eds. *Noise as a Public Health Problem,* Vol. 5, pp. 347-354. Swedish Council for Building Research, Stockholm.

Broadbent, D.E. 1990. Summary of team 4: Influence of noise on performance and behaviour. *In* B. Berglund and T. Lindvall, eds. *Noise as a Public Health Problem,* Vol. 5, pp. 303-305. Swedish Council for Building Research, Stockholm.

Brohier, R.L. 1984. *Changing Face of Colombo.* Lake House Investments Ltd., Colombo.

Central Office of Information. 1988. *Control of Noise Pollution in Britain.* Foreign and Commonwealth Office, London.

Commission on the Third London Airport. 1971. *Report (The Roskill Report).* HMSO, London.

Committee on the Problem of Noise. 1963. *Noise (The Wilson Report).* HMSO, London.

Committee to Examine the Pollution Caused by Vehicle Exhaust Emissions. 1988. *Report.* Central Environmental Authority, Colombo.

Department of Census and Statistics. 1987. *Statistical Pocket Book of the Democratic Socialist Republic of Sri Lanka.* Government of Sri Lanka, Colombo.

Eddington, N. and I. Eddington. 1988. Environmental noise disamenity in an Australian provincial city. *In* B. Berglund, U. Berglund, J. Karlsson, and T. Lindvall, eds. *Noise as a Public Health Problem,* Vol. 3, pp. 181-186. Swedish Council for Building Research, Stockholm.

Eldred, K.Mck. 1990. Noise in the year 2000. *In* B. Berglund and T. Lindvall, eds. *Noise as a Public Health Problem,* Vol. 5, pp. 355-381. Swedish Council for Building Research, Stockholm.

Gao, G., Z. Wang and K. Liu. 1987. *Country Report: China.* WHO Regional Workshop on Noise Abatement and Control, Kuala Lumpur.

Greifahn, B. 1990. Summary of team 5: Effects of noise on sleep. *In* B. Berglund and T. Lindvall, eds. *Noise as a Public Health Problem,* Vol. 5, pp. 307-310. Swedish Council for Building Research, Stockholm.

Ho, R.C.P. 1987. *Country Report: Singapore.* WHO Regional Workshop on Noise Abatement and Control. Kuala Lumpur.

Kwan, R.K.Y. 1989. Environmental acceptable noise levels - A comparison between the models of China and Hong Kong. *In* V.C. Goodwin, ed. *Government Officers' Conference on Community Noise.* Annex B. Department of Health, New Zealand.

Myrberg Jr., A.A. 1990. Man-made noise and the behaviour of marine animals: A need for increased awareness. *In* B. Berglund and T. Lindvall, eds. *Noise as a Public Health Problem,* Vol. 5, pp. 189-200. Swedish Council for Building Research, Stockholm.

National Environmental (Amendment) Act. No. 56 of 1988. Govt. of Sri Lanka, Colombo.

Peterson, E.A. 1990. Summary of team 7: Noise and animals. *In* B. Berglund and T. Lindvall, eds. *Noise as a Public Health Problem,* Vol. 5, pp. 315-316. Swedish Council for Building Research, Stockholm.

Sharp, C. and T. Jennings. 1976. *Transport and the Environment.* Leicester University Press, Leicester.

Suzuki, S. 1987. *Country Report: Japan.* WHO Regional Workshop on Noise Abatement and Control. Kuala Lumpur.

Wang, J.-Q. 1988. Community noise and its control in China. *In* B. Berglund, U. Berglund, J. Karlsson and T. Lindvall, eds. *Noise as a Public Health Problem*, Vol. 1, pp. 159. Swedish Council for Building Research, Stockholm.

Wickramasinghe, R.H. 1988. *Contempory Environmental Challenges: A Sri Lankan Reader.* Institute for Tropical Environmental Studies, Colombo.

Proceedings of the International and Interdisciplinary Symposium
ECOLOGY AND LANDSCAPE MANAGEMENT IN SRI LANKA
W. Erdelen, C. Preu, N. Ishwaran, C.M. Madduma Bandara (eds.)
Colombo, Sri Lanka, 12-26 March 1990
© 1993
Margraf Scientific Books, D-97985 Weikersheim
ISBN 3-8236-1182-8

Changes in Land Use Pattern and the Role of Geoscientists in Developing Countries

S.D. LIMAYE

Abstract

In developing nations major changes in land use are mainly governed by socioeconomic and sociopolitical factors. Typical changes are deforestation and extension of agricultural land due to population pressure, reduction of agricultural land for expansion of industry and settlements, encroachment of cities and towns on all types of open lands in their vicinity, the unauthorized construction of huts in open lands in and around big cities, the submergence of fertile land and villages in the reservoir area of new major dams, rehabilitation of displaced population, the conversion of rainfed farmlands into irrigated farms and the opening of new mines in hilly and forested areas. Technical recommendations by geoscientists are not always considered in decision processes on changes in land use. These decisions involve big transactions of money and are influenced by vested interests, public opinions, both in favor and against, and political support to carry such changes out. It is left to the geoscientists to see that the environmental impacts of such decisions are not severely negative. This paper discusses the experience in India in projects for water resources management and also the role of geoscientists in helping the people affected by changes in land use.

Introduction

The complex scenario in developing countries that necessitates changes in land use patterns comprises the increasing demand for food for the growing population, the need to create irrigational facilities to increase agricultural production, promoting rural employment through irrigated agriculture and agroindustries, industrial growth around townships and at special industrial centers to boost the GNP, increased utilization of natural resources like forests, minerals and water for giving a broader and more stable base for industrial progress through the availability of indigenous raw materials, power and infrastructure; and the need to provide housing for the ever-growing influx of people from rural to urban areas. The changes in land use patterns are mainly governed by socioeconomic and sociopolitical forces, while technical factors do not play any decisive role. Such changes are associated with big transactions of money, influence of vested interests, public opinions both in favor and against, and are executed under political support. It is the role of geoscientists to ensure that the environmental impacts of the changes are not severely negative, whether or not they technically approve such changes. Exploitation of natural resources has been defined as an activity towards its optimum utilization for human welfare. Somewhere in this process the point of optimal utilization is passed and the resulting overexploitation of the resources undermines the sustainability of the economic benefits. In many developing countries, even before the state of overexploitation is reached, the mismanagement of development schemes threatens their ecomomic viability and also creates environmental problems which erode their benefits. Large-scale projects in river catchments often suffer from such mismanagement. A large-scale multipurpose project of dam construction on a major river is associated with substantial changes in ecology and land use patterns of the river basin. The planning office of the project in many cases is mainly concerned with the engineering and economical aspects. Efforts are, therefore, concentrated on obtaining meteorological, hydrogeological, and engineering geological data and not on the command area development, watershed protection or on the resources of the land to be submerged. The present agitation in India, against the multimillion dollar Narmada Project or Tehri Project, stems from the accumulated discontent over the performance of large river valley projects constructed during the past five decades. The Indian experience should therefore serve as a lesson to other developing countries.

The Indian Experience

Management of natural resources is crucial in India, because India has to support 15% of the world's population with only 6% of the world's water resources and 2.5% of the world's land area. From the total annual precipitation of about 400 million hectare metres (mha-m), the surface water availability is about 178 mha-m of which about 50% can be harnessed for beneficial use. In addition to this, there is a ground water recharge of about 42 mha-m per year. Large, medium and minor irrigation dams, some of them multipurpose in nature, received priority in the past five decades and were constructed with the assistance of government funds amounting to about US $ 15,000 million to create irrigation for about 20 million hectares of farmland. The government earns less than 1% return on this investment while the annual loss on the operation and maintenance of surface irrigation systems are about US $ 100 million. The transmission losses are about 40%, indicating collosal waste of valuable resources. Serious water-logging problems have been caused by these dams and their canals have rendered 7 mha of fertile land useless for agriculture; the very land that these dams were created to serve (Vora, 1975).

A river valley project for irrigation has four major components, viz. (1) dam construction, (2) construction of canals and distributories, (3) on-farm development in command area, and (4) reservoir watershed protection. The performance of the project may be seriously hampered due to lack of coordination amongst these components. There have been many examples from India and other developing countries where the dam and reservoir are completed but the canals are still under construction, or where the canals are ready but awaiting the completion of the dam, or where the absence of a drainage network in the command area has caused extensive water logging within the first few years or where the delay in watershed protection has resulted in heavy siltation of the reservoir within a couple of rainy seasons, thereby reducing the useful life of the reservoir. Proper coordination is essential to any project but even more so to large river basin projects where capital outlay is large; the components to be coordinated are numerous and the effects on ecology and landscape of the basin are far-reaching.

Public resistance to large river basin projects begins when political considerations overrule the negative technical factors evaluated in the feasibility study. It takes firm roots due to the neglect of sociological, cultural and environmental factors by the planners and executers of such projects. Problems associated with the submergence of villages and fertile land in the reservoir area, the rehabilitation of these villages in other parts of the basin, land acquisition for the project and for rehabilitation, the realignment of roads and railways in the reservoir area; training of farmers in command area for efficient use of canal water have not so far been satisfactorily solved. Even the directives of the World Bank regarding rehabilitation and environmental protection have not been strictly followed, thereby giving birth to a new group of people called "dam-affected people" (similar to flood-affected or earthquake-affected people). In geologically unstable or strategically vulnerable regions, a large dam with its huge reservoir is considered as a potential hazard by many. Against this background, do the interests of planners and those of environmentalists conflict with each other or is a compromise possible in the best interest of the national ecomomy? The answer to the question lies in what planners term as optimal utilization and the best deal they can sincerely work out and offer to "dam-affected people" and environmentalists. Implementation of major projects at most suitable locations may still be justified if the cost-benefit ratio has been realistically estimated, and also, if the construction and completion of the project is not viewed as an end in itself but as a means to deliver the benefits at the grassroot level, with equity and justice to "dam-affected people" and environmentalists.

Proposals for river valley projects at "not-so-ideal" sites therefore require re-evaluation. At the approval stage of such projects there is a tendency amongst the planners and technocrats to enhance the benefits and to curtail the costs. This is often done under political influence and pressure. The decisions regarding the selection of a dam-site, the alignment of canals, the awarding of contracts to local or international bidders, the schedule for the completion of the dam and commencement of irrigation, etc. are also taken under non-technical influence and interference. Such decisions often prove to be expensive and detrimental to the project. Only recently the "dam-affected people" in association with social organizations and environmentalists have started voicing their protests loudly and demanding re-evaluation of cost-benefit ratio of major projects.

As a compromise between ecological and economic targets, future emphasis has to be on smaller projects with components such as an integrated approach to surface and ground water utilization taking a basin or a subbasin as a unit, the conjunctive use of ground water and surface water so as to avoid the water logging of low lands, the infrastructural development in the command area, soil conservation and afforestation of the hill slopes in the reservoir watershed, the recognition of the rights of the "dam-affected people" as having an equitable share in the benefits of the project and sustainability of various interdependent ecosystems in the project area.

Geoscientists and Changes in Land Use

Other than river valley projects, there are various examples of land use changes over which geoscientists have no control but they are supposed to render technical services, especially to the people affected by these changes. Typical changes may be summarized as follows:

1. Deforestation for agricultural activity:
   This is mainly due to population pressure and the need for adequate food production. The aforest cover in many developing countries has declined drastically in the past four to five decades. Deforestation and incorrect agricultural practices on hill slopes have led to severe soil erosion, siltation of water reservoirs, slope instability and change in the runoff of streams. In low rainfall areas with deep rooted trees, deforestation increases ground water recharge and raises the water table. This may cause increased soil salinity in the effluent streams, as has been experienced in Australia. In medium to high rainfall areas, deforestation is more likely to increase runoff, reduce recharge and cause floods. The changes in the stream hydrographs depend on several factors such as the intensity and duration of rainfall, the nature of the soil, the climate and geomorphology of the basin and the type of vegetation. Although deforestation is not desirable, people practice it out of sheer necessity. But it is the geoscientist who has to ensure that the newly developed farmlands

have assured water supply for at least one or two crops per year from ground water resources which are locally available. In afforestation programs on barren hills the geoscientist can ensure successful plantations by exploring ground water resources for watering the young trees during the summer. Geoscientists can also monitor the stability of hill slopes.

2. Conversion of agricultural or forest land into industrial sites:

    In the industrial sector, chemical, paper and mining industries have greater impact on existing ecosystems especially on those connected with surface and ground water. It may seem rather ironical but some of the worst polluting industries are being run by government departments or semi-government corporations. They are fully aware of the pollution problems caused by these industries, but they are financially and politically in a strong position to get away with it or just to manage a false show of an effluent treatment plant. Geoscientists can play an important role in helping the local people to locate new sites for irrigation or drinking water wells, away from the polluted streams.

3. Encroachment of cities and towns on all types of open lands in their vicinity:

    In the planned expansion of cities and towns, master plans specify areas for the construction of houses which are occupied by middle and upper class residents. The urban poor occupy low grade, neglected land on hill slopes or stream banks that are not considered suitable for housing by the planners of the master plan. The hutments and shanty towns of the urban poor thrive illegally. Once they become voters for elections to local civic bodies, the hutments become a permanent and unavoidable feature of urban growth. The hutments and shanty towns are the result of the exodus of the rural population which seeks jobs in the cities because national planning has failed to provide employment in the rural sector. Geoscientists can hardly have control over these factors but at the same time they must realize that the urban poor are often using the worst polluted water for external use, if not for drinking. Polluted water is also used by residents of peri-urban areas where the water supply and drainage network of the town has not been extended. It is a great service to these residents when the geoscientists help them to find suitable sites for drilling deep bores and obtain good quality ground water.

Conclusion

Geoscientists have to play an increasingly important role. They can prepare surface and sub-surface geological maps, soil classification maps, land use maps, minerals and energy resources maps, hydrogeological maps, hydrogeochemistry maps, engineering geology maps, etc. depending on the needs of the planners of a particular project and hope that their comments and suggestions will be considered in the formulation of the project. However, they should also be prepared to do a "cleaning-up" job in many cases where their suggestions were not accepted, so as to safeguard the interests of the poor people adversely affected by the project. It is not in the hands of the geoscientists to control the non-technical influences and interferences in the project but is is certainly within their capacity to try to minimize the adversities suffered by the "project-affected people". In the river valley projects, increased attention will be given in future to integrated use of surface and ground water, soil and water conservation, afforestation, microlevel ecosystems in the project area and socioeconomic and cultural aspects of the rehabilitation of "dam-affected people". Geoscientists will be able to contribute their expertise to such projects by working in a team with other experts in fields like agronomy, civil engineering, forestry, sociology and economics.

Literature Cited

Vora, B.B. 1975. *Land and Water Management Problems in India*. Govt. of India, Cabinet Secretariat, New Delhi.

PAPER PRESENTATIONS

III. METHODOLOGICAL APPROACHES

Proceedings of the International and Interdisciplinary Symposium
ECOLOGY AND LANDSCAPE MANAGEMENT IN SRI LANKA
W. Erdelen, C. Preu, N. Ishwaran, C.M. Madduma Bandara (eds.)
Colombo, Sri Lanka, 12-26 March 1990
© 1993
Margraf Scientific Books, D-97985 Weikersheim
ISBN 3-8236-1182-8

Land Use Mapping in Sri Lanka

S. JAYATILAKA

Abstract

Planning and implementation of any type of land use management requires the identification of existing land use patterns. In 1956, the first land use map of Sri Lanka was produced and was followed in the 1980s by systematic land use mapping. The resulting map (scale 1: 100,000) was printed on a district basis and displayed estimates of area coverage of different land use types for each administrative unit. This paper illustrates the remote sensing techniques and methodology used in the production of this latest series of maps. Problems associated with their production are discussed. Maps covering 18 of the 24 districts have already been printed and the remaining areas are presently being mapped.

Introduction

For any type of land management data regarding existing features, land use and topography are a prerequisite. Land use maps, hence, play a very important part in land management or in development work. In Sri Lanka, land use maps were prepared for the first time between 1956 and 1961 by the Survey Department in collaboration with the Canadian Government in a scale of one inch to one mile, (1: 63,360) using air photographs of scale 1: 40,000. Due to development activities this map series became out of date. In early 1980s, the necessity arose to update this map series. In 1981, it was decided to produce a new land use map series as part of Sri Lanka/Swiss Remote Sensing Project. It was also decided that the scale of this map should be 1: 100,000 and that it should be produced on a district basis, as at this stage the government of Sri Lanka was moving towards a decentralized administrative structure. The map should also show area figures such as land use types and Assistant Government Agent (AGA) divisions.

In 1983, a preliminary map covering the Polonnaruwa District was printed in order to finalize the cartographic design and to consider comments from mapping specialists and potential users of this map series. This map was sent to a number of map users in Sri Lanka and abroad, and more than 50% responded with valuable comments. After a meeting had been held with the Sri Lankan map users, a decision was made to publish this new series of 1: 100,000 land use maps

449

on a district basis. Some of the major criteria finalized at this stage were: (1) the speed of achieving the final product, (2) accuracy in terms of the scale, (3) area figures of land use by AGA divisions, (4) classification system, (5) field verification, (6) cartographic representation, and (7) the scale of the map.

Land Use Classification

A three-level land use classification system was adopted for this series. There were very minor changes in the classification system adopted in 1956. A total of 24 types of categories were identified. This classification system closely corresponds with the land use classification of remote sensing data interpretations established in 1976 by the US Geological Survey. Table 1 illustrates this classification system.

Table 1. Three-level land use classification and associated categories.

Level I	Level II	Level III		Definition of the categories
URBAN LAND	Built-Up Land		1.	Residential (including hotels), industrial, commercial, institutional, administrative, transportation, power plants and urban open spaces
	Associated Non-Agricultural land		2.	Mining, quarries, salterns, parks and botanical gardens, cultural and archeological sites
AGRICULTURAL LAND	Homesteads		3.	Family residential units surrounded by home gardens and open space - cultivation includes fruit trees, spices vegetables, and small holdings of coconut, rubber, tea and other plantation crops
	Tree and Other Perennial Crops	Tea	4.	Land under tea cultivation, both seedling and vegetatively propagated tea, land under rehabilitation (Guatemala or Mana grass), partly interplanted with shade trees
		Rubber	5.	Systematic, continuous planting of rubber trees in plantations
		Coconut	6.	Systematic, continuous planting of coconut trees in plantations
		Cinnamon	7.	Cinnamon cultivation on elevated plots
		Cashew	8.	Systematic or unsystematic, scattered cultivation of cashew (cadju) plants, partly interrupted by shrubs and open land
		Palmyrah	9.	Systematic, continuous planting of palmyrah trees in plantations, similar in appearance to coconut, but slightly different crown shape
		Oilpalm	10.	Systematic, continuous planting of oilpalms in plantations, very dark in appearance and rough in texture
		Mixed Tree and other	11.	Continuous cultivation of mono-cultural or mixed coffee, cacao, jack,

450

		Perennial Crops		kitul, palmyrah, cinnamon, cashew, oil palm and other fruit trees or spices, partly intercropped with coconut, tea and rubber
	Cropland	Paddy	12.	Asweddumized paddy area, i.e. bunded and ridged land intended for cultivation of rainfed or irrigated wet rice
		Sparsely Used Cropland	13.	Chena (shifting cultivation), recently abandoned chena, sparsely used rainfed cropland (permanent dry cropping), neglected or abandoned tea, rubber and coconut lands and land under development
		Sugarcane	14.	Irrigated sugar cane cultivation in rows, with distinct system of irrigation channels
		Other Cropland	15.	Tabacco, vegetables, sugar cane, other cash crops and rainfed highland crops in continuous cultivation
FOREST LAND	Natural Forest	Dense forest	16.	Dense natural forest with a crown closure of more than approx. 75%
		Open forest	17.	Natural forest cover with a crown of approx. 45%-75%
	Forest Plantations		18.	Man-made monocultural forests of teak, eucalyptus and pines
RANGE LAND	Scrubland		19.	Low-growing vegetation with more than 50% area coverage, including trees with less than approx. 45% crown closure
	Grassland		22.	Open park country with less than 50% scrub coverage (damana and savannah), villus and other temporarily flooded land and patana (upcountry grassland)
WET LAND	Forested/ Mangroves		21.	Salt-tolerant and woody vegetation along sea coasts, lagoons and river mouths
	Non-Forested/ Marsh & Swamps		22.	Permanently wet and muddy, uncultivable and frequently inundated areas
WATER			23.	Sea, lagoons, tanks and reservoirs, and major rivers, all showing maximum water level
BARREN LAND			24.	Rock outcrops, sand dunes, beaches, earth slides and other unproductive land

Methodical Procedure

Data

The land use information shown on the 1: 100,000 map series was compiled from the interpretation of aerial photographs. However, in districts for which no recent aerial photographs were available, high resolution satellite images were used for the interpretation of

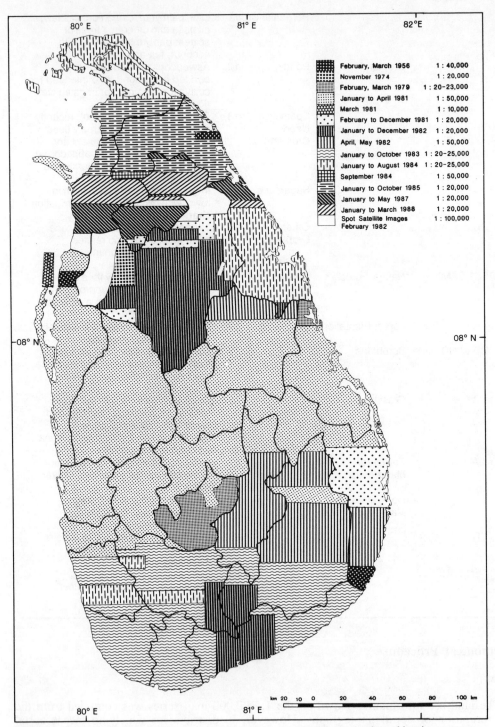

Figure 1. Spatial distribution of remote sensing data used in the production of land use maps (scale 1: 100,000).

The legend for the map contains the following entries:

Pattern	Period	Scale
	February, March 1956	1 : 40,000
	November 1974	1 : 20,000
	February, March 1979	1 : 20-23,000
	January to April 1981	1 : 50,000
	March 1981	1 : 10,000
	February to December 1981	1 : 20,000
	January to December 1982	1 : 20,000
	April, May 1982	1 : 50,000
	January to October 1983	1 : 20-25,000
	January to August 1984	1 : 20-25,000
	September 1984	1 : 50,000
	January to October 1985	1 : 20,000
	January to May 1987	1 : 20,000
	January to March 1988	1 : 20,000
	Spot Satellite Images February 1982	1 : 100,000

land use patterns. The geometrically corrected satellite images were used to support the base maps on which interpretations were compiled.

There had been a few drawbacks in the data collection. Firstly, the data were not consistent. As the mapping was done by districts, the aerial photographs were selected on the basis of the best quality available for the particular district. When the complete map series is considered, this method has led to two inconsistencies: (i) there were data on various scales viz. 1: 50,000, 1: 40,000, 1: 25,000, 1: 20,000 and 1: 10,000 and (ii) photographs from different years were used for the interpretations (Fig. 1). Since the mapping of each district was undertaken separately and in doing so the best available photographs at the time of mapping were selected, there were very few districts where no recent photographs which covered the entire district were available. In such cases, SPOT imagery was used for the interpretation and supplementation of other map information available from the Survey Department.

In most districts, ground verification was carried out in order to supplement the interpretation of the photographs. However, due to the prevailing security situation in Sri Lanka, most of the map sheets in the north, northwestern and northeastern areas were produced without field verification. This can also be considered a drawback in the inconsistency attributed to the accuracy standard of the entire map series. However, these drawbacks were known and in view of the fact that the completion of the map series was an urgent necessity, it was decided to proceed with the work.

Methodology

Figure 2 illustrates the basic concepts of the methodology adopted. Generally, the work in each district was assigned to one or two remote sensing technicians, who were responsible for the maps from the planning stage to the printing stage. During the planning stage the available data were investigated by flight diagrams and available satellite images. Date and scale of photography were the main selection criteria. Priority was given to the year of the photographs. The most desirable scale for the interpretation was 1: 20,000, but when this was not available, a 1: 50,000 photograph was used. Before interpretation, reconnaissance fieldwork was considered important in order to promote greater reliability and confidence in the remote sensing technicians and their work. Hence, the entire district was covered within one week by jeep in order to get an overview of the area. However, due to the prevailing situation in Sri Lanka this was not possible for the sheets from Anuradhapura northwards.

The next stage was the interpretation of the photographs using mirror stereoscopes. During the interpretation doubtful areas were located for further field verification. Steps were also undertaken to check whether the overlap of the photographs was consistent and the quality of the interpretation was maintained. Once the doubtful areas of interpretation were identified, a second field check, known as verification fieldwork, was undertaken. At this stage the updating of existing map features like roads, etc was also undertaken. However, again due to the situation in Sri Lanka in the districts of the Northern, Northeastern and Northwestern Province, no fieldwork could be done. Hence, here again, there is uncertainty about the uniform accuracy of the map series.

Once all interpretation was completed, the interpreted data were photographically reduced to the scale of 1: 100,000. These reductions were assembled over a geometrically rectified satelliteimage along with an overlay of the topographical sheet to compile the new 1: 100,000 land use map. Adjustments or corrections were done along the district boundary. Manual color checkings were done to control whether the interpretation had been carried out correctly.

Subsequently cartographic preparations were done in order to produce the map. This stage is as important as the compiling procedures, as it takes almost the same time. Scribing, peeling, checking, map legend, map text, area figures, printing simulation of proof copies, corrections and printing were undertaken during this process.

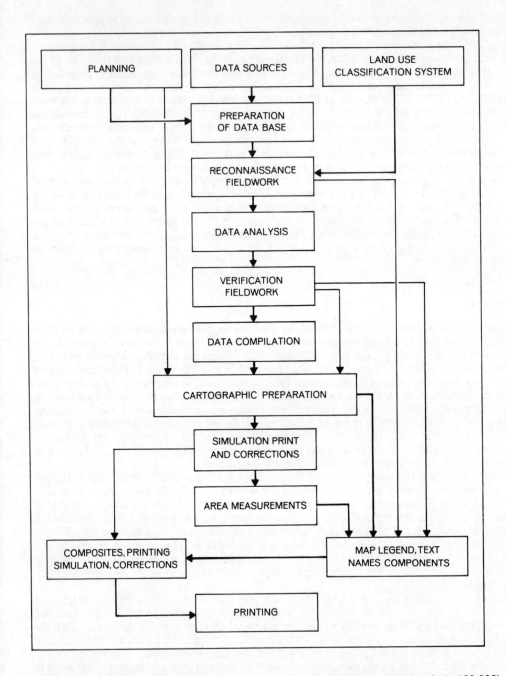

Figure 2. Methodological approach for the production of the land use maps (scale 1: 100,000).

Information Available for Map Users

The different types of information available from the land use map series are as follows:

1. Land use maps to a scale of 1: 100,000 for each district
2. Year in which the map sheet was printed
3. Data sources used for the map sheet
4. Year of data used for the production of the map
5. Publisher
6. Geographical coordinates
7. Map legend
8. Major and minor roads
9. Railroads with stations, airports
10. Major hill tops
11. Names of important places, locations
12. Reservoirs and reservoirs under construction
13. A guide showing Sri Lankan administrative boundaries
14. Explanation of the land use classification system
15. Percentage of each type of land use in the district
16. Area figures of each land use type on district level
17. AGA boundaries
18. AGA centers
19. Area figures of each land use type at AGA division level
20. Special remarks for each district
21. Feedback information reporting

Some Comments on the Series

Some map users suggested a scale of 1: 50,000 for this map series to be of more use than a scale of 1: 100,000. However, when the production of the map series started and decisions on the scale of the map series were taken, two important factors were considered, namely that a 1: 100,000 sheet would cover an entire district in one sheet for the majority of districts and that the time taken for the completion of the work would be too lenghty. The arguments brought forward to print the series in a scale of 1: 50,000 is that there are no maps in the 1: 100,000 series providing contour overlay, and hence it is difficult to overlay contours. Another factor which should be taken into account if a new series is to be considered is that the proposed land information system of the Ministry of Lands and Land Development will have an input map on a scale of 1: 50,000. Hence, a land use map in the scale of 1: 50,000 is required

Another factor which should be considered is that the method of data collection is uniform, so that we have homogenous data in the series. If a map series is to be published in the scale of 1: 50,000, it could be based on the 1: 50,000 topographical map - as a base map - and would have a high positional accuracy. The use of satellite images as a basis would not give enough cartographic accuracy for such a series. Although the map has an overall accuracy of land use categories between 82% and 91% and at a confidence level of 95% on the accuracy assessment using confusion matrix calculation method in test areas, it is recommended that more fieldwork should be done to check the map before printing. No fieldwork was done in seven districts. This should be avoided when the next series is being produced.

Another consideration should be to print these sheets in an uniform format rather than on a district basis. The normal practice adopted by the Survey Department in printing map sheets is that the sheets are designed by geographical coordinates and not by district boundaries.

The colors used in this map series are little more striking those used in the topographical series. It is true that the land use map is a thematic map, however, due consideration may be given to a uniform color scheme. One such example is paddy cultivation where this is showed in green in most topographical maps and in dark yellow in the land use maps.

It may also be worthwhile to consider having uniform legends in all types of map series produced for the island. It is not possible to have the same legend when one produces a land use map (which is a thematic map) and when the other produces a topographical map. However, steps should be taken to make them as close as possible and thus faciliating the map uses for comparison and overlay of information.

Proceedings of the International and Interdisciplinary Symposium
ECOLOGY AND LANDSCAPE MANAGEMENT IN SRI LANKA
W. Erdelen, C. Preu, N. Ishwaran, C.M. Madduma Bandara (eds.)
Colombo, Sri Lanka, 12-26 March 1990
© 1993
Margraf Scientific Books, D-97985 Weikersheim
ISBN 3-8236-1182-8

Establishing Data Bases for Land Use Planning: Experience from Sri Lanka

S. BERUGODA

Abstract

Ecology and landscape management have to consider important ongoing endeavors of overall land use planning to ensure a higher quality of life for all members of society. Such planning requires a variety of data pertaining to land use and socioeconomic characteristics. The government of Sri Lanka is presently introducing scientifically based land use planning programs covering both ecological and landscape management aspects. Preparations of plans for the establishment of a Geographical Information System (GIS) and a Cadastral Information System (CIS) have been started. Once established, both systems will form the main source of information for scientific land use planning and will combine the need of ecological and management aspects.

Introduction

Sri Lanka has a long history of maintenance of land information. Up to the end of the 18th century this information was maintained in the form of registers. Systematic mapping activity commenced at the beginning of the 19th century. By 1925, a complete set of topographic maps in the scale one inch to one mile (1: 63,360) was available. Investigation and mapping of the state commenced in 1840 and has continued since. The marking of land surveyed on the ground for statutory purposes commenced in 1910. Large tracts of land reserved under different statutory provisions of various types of reserves or reservations for relevant natural and cultural features have been earmarked since that time. These survey activities have contributed considerably to better management of the landscape of Sri Lanka. Since 1977 several studies were conducted with a view to embark on an appropriate land policy. One such study helped form the main concepts for natural resources management along the following lines: "(1) that the resources of the natural environment must be seen to belong ultimately to the whole nation and must be devoted to the national welfare, (2) that there is an obligation on the social democratic state to create an institutional structure by virtue of which such resources may be located, evaluated, conserved and distributed, so that they can be utilized on a sustainable basis and to the greatest national advantage, (3) that as land provides the conceptual and operational plane of contact between nation and environmental resources, this institutional structure should be framed in terms of land policy and land use planning, (4) land policy and planning should be rooted in scientific knowledge of biophysical processes and in a deep understanding of economic progress and of sociopolitical change; that they should be supported by reliable, qualitative and quantitative data; that they should have a positive development orientation and that they should be comprehensive and closely integrated, but sufficiently flexible to permit and promote the operation of state, corporate or private sectors in a mixed economy, (5) that the objectives must be that the nation should learn to live in production equilibrium with natural resources, that access to resources should be widely and equitably distributed and that basic needs should be safeguarded for all citizens"(Ministry of Lands and Land Development, 1983).

After a comprehensive study, the Presidential Land Commission of 1985 recommended concepts along these lines: "...the problem of land degradation has reached serious proportions in certain critically important watershed areas of the island, particularly in the hill country. If this trend continues unchecked, irreparable damage to the land and water resources of the island would result. Therefore, effective and meaningful steps should be taken to arrest this trend by the government as a matter of urgency".

Land Use Planning Project

Concepts and Cooperating Agencies

The Land Use Planning Project was formulated by the Ministry of Lands, Irrigation and Mahaweli Development in order to introduce scientific land use planning in Sri Lanka. Land use planning not only requires the participation of several disciplines but also of different agencies. Formulating a land use policy and land use plans is a challenge in planning and has to be handled from that perspective. This encompasses planning activities at different levels, i.e. national, regional and local. Finally, it has to be implemented at the plot level. Thus the required data will have to be made available from the plot level upwards, the upper level data being obtained by aggregating plot level data. The variety of data required for land use planning will be very wide. It will extend from physical data such as topography, soil condition and current land use patterns to environmental data such as hydrology and climatic conditions and further extend to socioeconomic factors such as population distribution and demographic patterns, employment and marketing. It also covers legal aspects such as ownership and land rights. It is necessary to collect these data and inventories to enable their aggregation and study in suitable and necessary combinations. In view of the very large volume of data to be collected and analyzed and in order to achieve the desired degree of efficiency in the processes of acquisition, processing and presentation of data or to produce desired plans it was necessary to avail of the advances in technology that are being made elsewhere. This meant an automation of a variety of activities utilizing advances made in computer technology. The agencies identified for cooperation as a core group for this purpose are the Survey Department for the supply of topographic, land use and cadastral survey information and for the formation and maintenance of a data base incorporating these aspects, the Irrigation Department for the supply of information on soils, the Land Use Policy Planning Division of the Ministry of Irrigation and Mahaweli Development to overlay other relevant data on data drawn from the above data bases and to formulate land use plans, the District Land Use Planning Committees, with representatives from a variety of district level agencies to carry through the above planning process to the local levels. The information is maintained in a computerized Geographical Information System in order to achieve efficiency in the maintenance, processing and presentation of information.

The Survey Department

The Survey Department has the following responsibilities for the successful operation of the Land Use Planning Project: the establishment and operation of the data bases incorporating topographic, current land use and cadastral survey information, the provision of the above data to the relevant agencies and the support for the operations of a system of registration of title to land.

Present Activities - An Overview

The Survey Department is presently carrying out a project with the aim of producing two series of topographic maps, the 1: 50,000 series and the 1: 10,000 series. The production of 1: 10,000 series is expected to be expedited by the introduction of analytical photogrammetry. The data in the 1: 50,000 series will be digitized and incorporated into the data base. A similar approach will be applied to the 1: 10,000 topographic sheets, which have already been published. Since analytical photogrammetry will be used for the production of the remaining sheets in the 1: 10,000 series, these data can be incorporated into the data base directly after field revision and editing. This will form the Geographic Data Base.

Manual digitizing is a slow process. In Sri Lanka there is a limitation on the number of units of digitizing equipment that is available for this purpose. Although it would be fast in the initial acquisition of data, it is also found that scanning would involve a heavy work load at the editing stage. Thus, in order to meet the basic needs of the Land Use Planning Project, it may be necessary to restrict the manual digitizing of the 1: 50,000 series to the most important data required for land use planning only, e.g. drainage patterns, communication networks, settlements and main contours. This will be attempted only in the initial stages. In order to maintain a Geographic Data Base on the lines mentioned above, it is expected to enhance the map production capability of the Survey Department by introducing automation. This will supplement the facilities provided by the information system. There is also a project for land use mapping series on the scale of 1: 100,000. This series will be used for the input of current land use data into the Geographic Data Base. Here too, only the main categories may be considered in the initial stages.

Cadastral survey data are expected to be maintained in a separate data base, called a Cadastral Data Base closely linked to the Geographic Data Base. The acquisition of data for this base will be partly from the cadastral plans already available in Sri Lanka and partly from new surveys of previously unsurveyed land. As already mentioned, the cadastral plans presently available differ in scales and degrees of preservation. The level of preservation causes problems in converting these to digitial forms by scanning, because this activity is expected to be handled by manual digitizing. The field survey activity will be handled partly in digital mode using total station theodolites or theodolite and EDM and partly following the conventional techniques of theodolite and tape. This activity will be carried out mainly by the district offices of the Survey Department. Thus each district survey will maintain a Cadastral Data Base relevant to the district and also transmit the data in digital form to the headquarters of the Survey Department (Surveyor General's Office) for input into the main Cadastral Data Base. The Geographic Data Base and Cadastral Data Base maintained in the Surveyor General's Office and the District Cadastral Data Bases maintained in the district survey offices will be open to all interested persons.

Much thought has been given to the adoption of a suitable parcels identifier. In addition, the production of a unique reference system, the ability to use it for aggregating data and the possibility of it serving as a link to the data bases in other institutions are important aspects of this system. On this basis, an eleven digit number was decided upon for this purpose comprised of different components to indicate location. After the input of data into the District Cadastral Data Base, digital data for input into the Cadastral Data Base in the Surveyor

General's Office will be sent in disc form. This procedure of physical data transfer will be adopted until the telecommunications network in Sri Lanka is upgraded.

The structuring of data in the data bases or the data files has not yet been finalized although the concepts have been agreed upon. The Geographic Data Base and the Cadastral Data Base in the Surveyor General's Office will maintain the following data: topographic features (several files), elevation (one file), current land use (several files), property boundaries and parcel numbers (one file), attributes of parcels (name, land use, legal rights reference to title documents, extent, boundary parcel identifiers (one file) and coordinates (x, y, z) of boundary points (one file) The updating of the 1: 100,000 land use and 1: 50,000 topographic map series will be carried out with the help of satellite images. The 1: 10,000 topographic series will be updated by air photography; hence it is not realistic to expect this series to be updated at intervals of less than 10 years. The cadastre map series are to be updated by the operation of the registration of title procedures.

Hardware, Software, Liveware

Since the project was formulated in 1987, it has envisaged the provision of two mainframe (or mini) computers from the initial stages. However, after further discussions with the national body responsible for computer applications in Sri Lanka, the Computer and Information Technology Council of Sri Lanka (CINTEC), the approach has been slightly modified to start with a few isolated workstations, networked together and supported by a large disc storage, for the acquisition of data. This facility is to expand when the necessity arises (Survey Department). The software requirements for this project include the normal Geographical Information System (GIS) capabilities together with survey software which is capable to produce cadastral maps based on data from data recorders or surveyors' field books. These should cover activities such as data acquisition and input, data storage, data retrieval, data manipulation and analysis, data output and system management.

Liveware support is one of the most important aspects in a project of this nature. The Geographical Information System/Land Information System (GIS/LIS) and digital mapping activities are comparatively new to Sri Lanka, although a few professionals have been exposed to these in their periods of training overseas. Thus the training of staff takes on a new dimension. A program of education has been started to create an interest in computer applications among staff with a view to identifying the staff to be engaged in the project and to receive further training.

Future

The Survey Department is conscious of its responsibility in its new role as an agency maintaining a wide data base in addition to its functions as a national survey and mapping agency. It is engaged in a pioneering role in this field of activity in Sri Lanka, and it has a responsibility to maintain the information system efficiently. Steps will be taken to get in contact with other agencies which are not linked with the data base in its first stage, and who could benefit from such linkage. The data base systems referred to above are in the initial stages of formation. In its widest form this data base will facilitate the maintenance, processing and presentation of data vital for land management purposes. The individual organizations who are entrusted with the task of the planning or the implementation of ecological and landscape management projects can benefit considerably by linking this data base to data use. This will permit them to overlay their specialized information onto the information in the data base.

Conclusion

The GIS/LIS that is being established for the purpose of the Land Use Planning Project under the Ministry of Lands, Irrigation and Mahaweli Development will function as an efficient tool to serve the information requirements of the organizations responsible for landscape management aspects in Sri Lanka. Such organizations should link their data collection and processing systems to the GIS/LIS in order to achieve optimum results.

Proceedings of the International and Interdisciplinary Symposium
ECOLOGY AND LANDSCAPE MANAGEMENT IN SRI LANKA
W. Erdelen, C. Preu, N. Ishwaran, C.M. Madduma Bandara (eds.)
Colombo, Sri Lanka, 12-26 March 1990
© 1993
Margraf Scientific Books, D-97985 Weikersheim
ISBN 3-8236-1182-8

Long-Term Discharge Trends in the Upcountry of Sri Lanka

A Case Study of Three Adjacent Catchments

K. BRAND

Abstract

Evaluation of discharge data from Sri Lankan catchments have been mainly related to and based on the "classical" climatic zonation of the island. Although they belong to the same climatic zone, the discharge data from the catchments of Upper Mahaweli, Kotmale Oya and Uma Oya indicate contrary long-term discharge trends for even adjacent parts of the catchments within a period of 30 years. The discharge of Upper Mahaweli and Uma Oya has increased, whereas that of Kotmale Oya has decreased. Moreover, these opposite trends are more significant during the period of NE monsoon than during the remaining seasons. These different discharge characteristics seem to result from relief structure and soil conditions within the catchments rather than from climatic changes, particularly from changes in rainfall patterns. A detailed study of runoff data from the Kotmale Oya Catchment indicates that changes in land use patterns not only affect the soil-water balance of the catchment but also contibute to the decrease in surface runoff and dry weather flow in the catchment's upper river courses.

Introduction

As the central highlands of Sri Lanka function as an orographic barrier for the monsoonal air masses, they control the seasonally differing climatic conditions and, thereby, the discharge patterns of the island's catchments. Moreover, on the one hand, the central highlands cause luff-lee effects especially along their margins, and, on the other hand, the highland's interior relief features varying even within small areas result in striking differences in the amount of rainfall within the catchments. As, in addition, intermonsoonal rainfall, which principally originates from convective air mass movements, is substantially caused by the transformation of solar radiation, which differs interdependently with the slope exposure and steepness, the central highlands, especially their western parts, receive more rainfall than the remaining island.

Since early times the western parts of the central highlands have due to their climatic conditions been used for cultivation, in particular for plantation systems and paddy fields. Since then, however, the population of the upcountry provinces has rapidly increased and hence the demand for drinking water of high quality and agricultural land has increasingly grown. During the last ten years, a new kind of "water exploitation" has been added that will probably continue in the near future: large reservoirs that use water for the production of hydroelectricity. Therefore, the growing demand for water requires water resource management and documents the need for integrated planning processes and the special importance of investigations on discharge variability and water balance changes in subcatchments. This especially applies to large areas in the upcountry which are to be converted from "old" tea plantations into new kinds of land use patterns.

The catchments of the Upper Mahaweli Ganga, Kotmale Oya and Uma Oya which all belong to the Mahaweli Ganga River System have been selected in order to carry out investigations into discharge variability and water balance changes. The study is confined to the period from 1950 to 1980 because reliable and continuous data are available only for those years. The Kotmale Reservoir was constructed after this period, and therefore discharge data collected at gauge stations located downstream from the dam cannot be applied. In all study areas, changes in the water balance arising downstream from the reservoirs resulting from the reservoir's storage capacity and evaporation from the reservoir's water surface are not included in this study.

After an overview on the general discharge characteristics the long-term discharge trends for the catchments are presented and whether they relate to changes in climate and/or land use patterns that have occurred during the time period concerned is analyzed. Based on the analysis of daily discharge data from the Kotmale Oya Catchment, we attempt to quantify how land use changes have contributed to the long-term discharge trend of the catchment.

Location and Climatic Patterns of the Study Area

The study area (80°28'-80°81'E and 06°47'-07°15'N) is located in the center of the upcountry and ranges from 463 m (Peradeniya) to 2524 m (peak of Pidurutagala) in altitude. From west to east, the area can be subdivided into the three main catchments of (1) the Upper Mahaweli Ganga (upstream Peradeniya) with an area of 612 km^2, (2) Kotmale Oya (upstream Morape) with an area of 555 km^2 and (3) Uma Oya (upstream Talawakanda) with an area of 520 km^2 (Fig. 1).

The mean annual rainfall which decreases from west to east reaches its highest at Watawala (5000 mm) and its lowest at Welimada (1350 mm). Apart from during the second intermonsoon, the catchments of Upper Mahaweli and Kotmale receive the highest rainfall during the SW monsoon. As the lee effect caused by the central highlands increases to the east, SW monsoonal rainfall decreases, and hence highest rainfall is reached here during the NE monsoon. Due to its topographical characteristics and high rainfall the study area is very suitable for the construction of water reservoirs.

Discharge Patterns - A General Overview

As it is generally assumed that the patterns of discharge closely correlate with the patterns of rainfall, the discharge data of gauge stations were converted into the catchment's areal discharge (mm/m^2). In addition, this enables us to compare the amount of water yield from the individual catchments.

As the western and southwestern parts of Upper Mahaweli and Lower Kotmale Oya Catchments receive the highest amount of rainfall with the highest rainfall intensity (Wickramasinghe and Premalal, 1988), those areas are expected to have the highest discharge rates. Based on mean annual discharge data for the period 1957-1976, however, the amount of of discharge from those areas has not reached significantly higher values either in the Upper

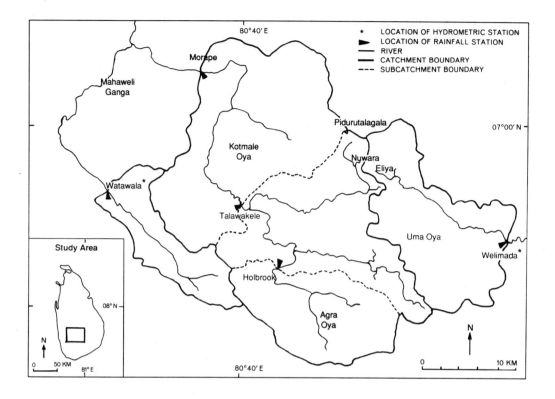

Figure 1. Catchment boundaries of the study area.

Mahaweli Catchment (at Watawala) or in the Uma Oya Catchment (at Welimada) than in the remaining parts of the study area (Fig. 2). A contrary tendency can even be recognized in the Uma Oya Catchment (at Welimada). In 1967 and 1969, its mean annual discharge reached higher rates than the Upper Mahaweli (at Watawala), although the Uma Oya Catchment received only half the rainfall with a lower rainfall intensity than the Upper Mahaweli Catchment. Similar differences between the amount of rainfall and discharge also become apparent in the subcatchments of the Kotmale Oya (Fig. 2). Although the amount of discharge generally increases simultaneously with the amount of mean annual rainfall and its intensity downstream from Holbrook over Talawakele to Morape, some years do not show this parallelism.

From this, it may be inferred that there are dominant factors such as the soil water capacity and the water consumption of the vegetation, the effects of which control the water balance within the catchments. In addition, however, considerable variations in rainfall patterns contribute to changes in the catchment's water balance. This is proved by the short-term interannual rainfall variations that have taken place when geoecological conditions are comparable among all catchments. Continuous changes in the discharge patterns, however, point to continuous changes such as changes in land use patterns and soil water capacity. But it has to be considered that the calculation of areal discharge amounts based on water level measurements in rivers may lead to inaccurate results. Therefore, the catchments can only be compared under the proviso that the conversion especially of high water levels may have resulted in incorrect data.

465

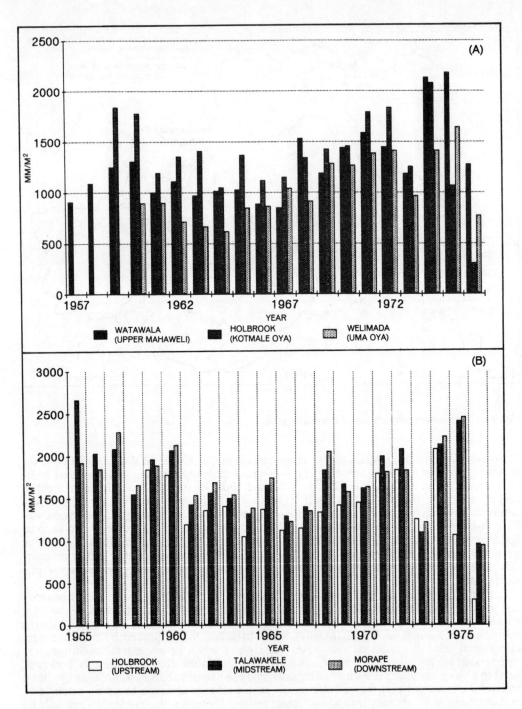

Figure 2. Runoff amounts from the different catchments. (A) Comparison between Watawala and Welimada. (B) Comparison between the upper and the downstream catchment of the Kotmale Oya.

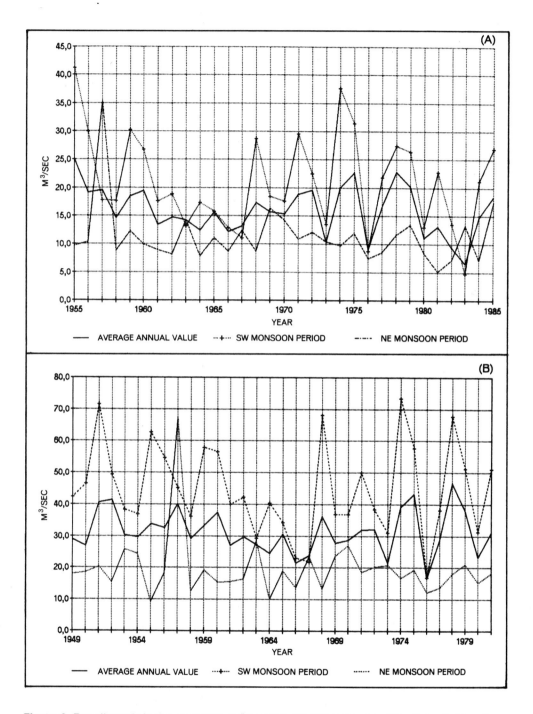

Figure 3. Runoff trends in the upcountry of Sri Lanka. (A) Upper course of the Kotmale Oya at Talawakelle. (B) The main catchment of the Kotmale Oya at Morape.

Long-Term Discharge Trends

The discharge trend within a period of time results from changes in conditions within an area and may be caused by variations in the macroclimate and/or by changes in land use patterns. This study proceeds on the assumption that the trend is linear and its degree is represented by the standard regression coefficient.

As a first step, the trends of the mean annual runoff are calculated for each individual catchment. In contrast to the hydrological standard, the beginning of the year has been fixed to 1 March, as this date represents the end of the driest season in the upcountry and none of the other seasons has to be interrupted. In addition, any deviations in the calculation of the rainfall-runoff ratio can be minimized.

As the calculation results for the catchments of Kotmale Oya at Talawakelle and Morape (Fig. 3), Upper Mahaweli at Watawala and Uma Oya at Welimada (Fig. 4) show, the trends of their mean annual runoff differ from area to area. Even in neighboring subcatchments, the trends differ in direction, gradient and statistical significance. But only a statistical significance of over 95% can be used as a reliable result for a change in runoff taken place.

The catchments of Upper Mahaweli located in the western study area and the Uma Oya located in its eastern part show increasing trends, whereas the catchment of Kotmale Oya located inbetween shows a slightly decreasing trend for both gauge stations at Talawakelle as well as Morape. As a result it is assumed that the runoff trends are influenced to a greater extent by changes taking place within the catchments rather than changes in climate which would affect the upcountry as a whole. The trends, which have a statistical significance of more than 99.9% in these subcatchments, diminish further downstream in gradient and statistical significance. This may result from the areal increase downstream, so that the factors affecting the water balance can neutralize each other's influence.

Compared to the mean annual runoff of the catchments over a period of 20 years, the runoff increase of 6.7% in the Uma Oya Catchment is much higher than in the Upper Mahaweli Catchment at Watawala with only 1.6%. In contrast, the runoff decreased by 4.2% with a statistical significance of less than 95% in the catchment of Kotmale Oya at Holbrook. The Uma Oya Catchment shows the most distinct increasing runoff trend. This corresponds to the drier climate of the eastern study area that causes a more sensitive reaction between the catchment's runoff and land use changes.

As a second step, the runoff data of each catchment have been subdivided into the four climatic seasons for which an individual trend analysis was calculated. This enables us to study the intercorrelation between external or internal catchment changes and their impact on changes in runoff patterns in more detail. The main result is that the trends of each particular season do not differ from the trends calculated for the mean annual runoff (Figs. 3, 4). Therefore, climatic changes are not the factor that cause runoff changes as this factor would mainly affect the period of the particular rainy season and its rainfall patterns. This is confirmed by the statistical significance level, which is at its highest during the period of dry season, e.g. over 99.9% in the Upper Mahaweli at Watawala during the period of NE monsoon. In the western and eastern catchments, the increase of runoff trends results specifically from land degradation and the clearing of forests, and it is caused by an increased density in the top soil interconnected with a decreased water consumption and degradation of the vegetation cover.

Long-Term Changes in Direct Surface Flow in the Kotmale Oya Catchment

As the trend analyses of both the mean annual and mean seasonal runoff data do not give sufficient results about the causes of runoff changes, runoff data from the Morape gauge station (Kotmale Oya Catchment) were analyzed daily. Trend analyses based on mean annual and/or mean seasonal data reflect changes in the total amount of runoff for the period concerned, but neither the form nor peak level of the individual runoffs can be considered and studied. The

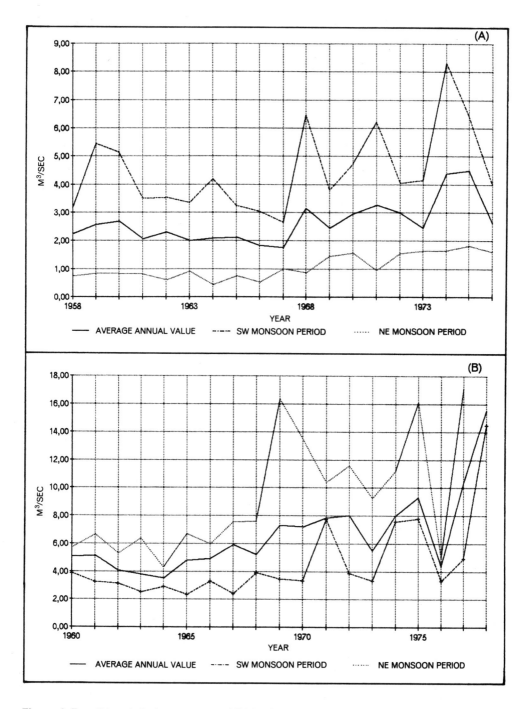

Figure 4. Runoff trends in the upcountry of Sri Lanka. (A) Upper Mahaweli at Watawala. (B) Upper Uma Oya at Welimada.

study of the direct surface runoff and the base flow, however, allows both the analyses of the change's tendency and its causes.

For that purpose, direct surface flow and base flow have been split from the total runoff. The methodological approach applied is based on the visual study of the hydrograph's form and enables us to seperate easily runoff peaks from the total runoff. It is, however, proceeded on the assumption that the amount of runoff at the runoff peak results directly from the surface flow. The point in time when the direct surface flow starts running is determined as the point in time when the runoff obviously increases. Because the peak's end in contrast to the transition from the direct over the intermediate to the base flow cannot always be easily identified, this point in time is determined by means of a logarithmic diagram (Dyck und Peschke, 1989). The line interconnecting the point of the peak's start and end has a straight course and seperates the direct surface flow above from the base flow below. As other influencing factors, such as relief and geological setting, can be assumed to have been constant within the period concerned, the results derived enable conclusions on the water storage capacity and the soil permeability under the given land use patterns of the catchment. A study that considers a longer time period provides data about changes in both soil surface infiltration rates and land use patterns.

The analyses at the Morape gauge station indicate that the amount of direct surface flow has dropped and consequently the amount of subsurface flow has increased in the period between 1951 and 1980 (Fig. 5). The annual decrease of 0.02% and the decrease of 11.7% within the 30-year period correlate with the results above which are based on the assumption that runoff changes may relate to changes within the catchments. The decrease of the surface flow may result from (a) increasing interception rates of the vegetation, or (b) increasing infiltration rates of the soil that may be caused either by high humus contents in the top soil or by roots loosening the soil surface.

Looking at the land use changes between 1965 and 1981 the areas of natural forest and tea plantations have been reduced on the one hand, and on the other, the areas of homesteads, forest plantations, crop cultivation, grasslands and built-up areas have been extended (Madduma Bandara and Kuruppuarachchi, 1989). However, if even increased soil infiltration rates and higher water deficits than in marginal tea growing areas are considered, the decrease in the surface flow cannot result from those land use changes, as a reduction of natural forests by only 6% would cancel this effect. Another land use change, however, has taken place, the impact of which has not yet been considered: the conversion of "old" seedling tea areas into vegetatively propagated tea areas (VPT) with contour drains. In areas under this kind of tea cultivation, there is a much higher content of biomass and, hence, there are much higher water consumption rates, much higher interception rates and a deep rooting of the soil up to some meters in depth (Fuchs, 1989).

Surface flow studies for individual seasons confirm these results. Although the decrease in direct surface flow can be observed in all seasons, its intensity and statistical significance diminish during periods of high rainfall, i.e. during the SW monsoon and first intermonsoon. This effect results from heavy rainfall during those periods. On the one hand, the interception rates of the plants' leaves are extremely reduced and, on the other hand, the infiltration capacity of soils has been reached, so that the process of direct surface flow can start.

Long-Term Dry Weather Flow in the Kotmale Oya Catchment

As demonstrated above, the runoff decrease can hardly be determined using mean monthly runoff data. Therefore, the patterns of dry weather flow were studied, because the effects of changes in land use lead to more marked changes in these runoff patterns than those identified in mean monthly data. Moreover, these data are of particular interest for the planning of irrigation schemes and hydroelectricity plants.

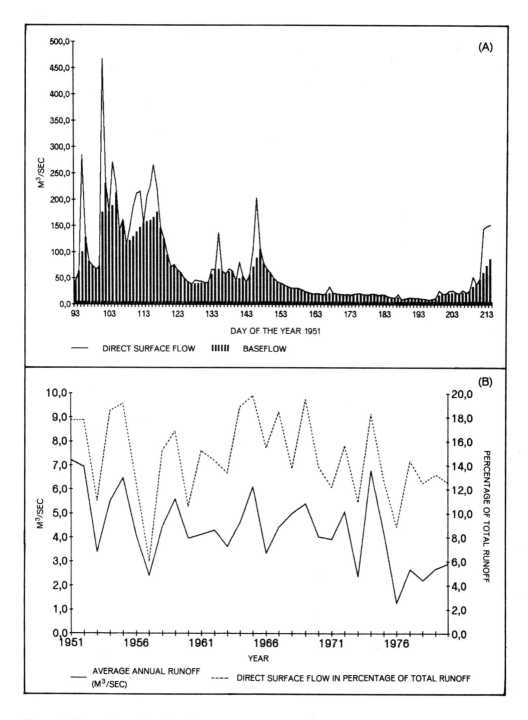

Figure 5. Separation of the direct flow and the base flow for the Kotmale Catchment at Morape. (A) Example of the method. (B) Long-term trend in direct surface flow

The long-term dry weather flow graph has been calculated according to the methodological approach recommended by IHP/OHP (1985) for small catchments. Here, the runoff data which have been registered for a particular period of the year after the setting on of a dry period are used. Afterwards, the dry weather flow data covering a particular period of years are averaged. The resulting graph represents the long-term storage capacity of a catchment for the period of time concerned.

The study of the long-term dry weather flow for the 30-year period indicates that a water deposition took place in the period between 1960 and 1980 (Fig. 6). This result, however, seems to contradict the results of the long-term changes in direct surface flow whose decrease results from increased infiltration rates of the soil within the same period. Therefore, this 'water deposition' can only result from an increased water consumption by the vegetation cover, that has used the increased soil water supply. Thus, it is demonstrated that catchments can subject changes in their water balance, although their mean monthly runoff does not show any significant trends of runoff changes which result from water deficit in dry periods.

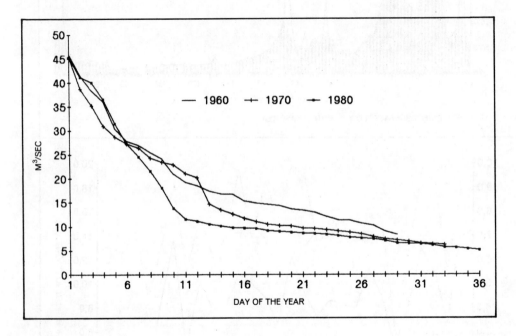

Figure 6. Dry weather flow in the Kotmale Catchment.

Conclusions

In summarizing these results it can be stated that the changes in the runoff patterns can be generally correlated with the changes in land use patterns. The dimension of the runoff changes, however, depends on the kind of land use change as well as on the regional climate, rainfall patterns and the geomorphological and pedological setting of the catchment. The runoff in the catchments of Upper Mahaweli and Uma Oya increased over a period of 30 years and relates to processes of land degradation; similar results are available from other tropical countries. In contrast, the slight decreasing runoff and increasing soil infiltration rates in the catchment of Kotmale Oya within the same period of time show an unexpected result. This long-term runoff trend, however, may be mainly related to the introduction of VPT tea plantations, but it is also caused by reafforestation and cultivation of vegetables on terraced slopes. From this it is evident that land use planning has to be conducted in close correlation with the catchment's water resources management to avoid conflicts among the different "water using groups".

Recommendations for Land Use Planning in the Upcountry of Sri Lanka

Based on the examination of the state of art and own experinces, I see the need for further and scientifically sound data in the following fields: (1) development of an appropriate methodological approach for the correct calculations of areal rainfall patterns in catchments located in mountainous areas with marked varying relief features, (2) the setting up of "research catchments" with an area of only some hectares to study the water consumption of different types of land use, (3) development of an detailed soil information system to enable a land suitability classification (Alwis *et al.* 1981), and (4) the preperation of large-scale topographical maps for planning purposes; a particular program was set up but should be continued.

Based on this, an integrated concept for water resource management of catchments should be developed and can serve as a basis for long-range planning. Moreover, this concept would enable us to implement land policy decisions in an early planning phase and to arrange land use patterns within a catchment in a sustainable way. The land suitability classification could enable us to connect the types of land use implemented and the main demands in land use planning, which are (1) the protection of nature reserves, (2) supply of unpolluted water for settlements, (3) agricultural land under consideration of soil property and agroclimatic patterns, (4) irrigable land and water reservoirs, (5) forests, (6) protection of areas affected by soil erosion and slope instability, and (7) areas for settlements and homesteads with suitable topography and infrastructure.

Land use types in unsuitable areas should be changed because they cause irreversible damage to the soil and lead to a durable loss of the area for any other kind of land use. In addition, it is recommended to start an improved farm cultivation in which both soil conservation measures are taken.

Literature Cited

Alwis K. A. De, N.S. Jayawardane and S. Dimantha. 1981. *Land suitability evaluation and land use study of Nuwara Eliya District.* Vol. 3. Summary report. IRDP, Nuwara Eliya.

Dyck, S. 1989. *Grundlage der Hydrologie.* VEB, Berlin.

Fuchs, H.J. 1989. *Tea Environments and Yield in Sri Lanka.* Tropical Agriculture Vol. 5. Margraf Scientific Publ. Weikersheim

IHP/OHP. 1985. *Empfehlung für die Auswertung der Messergebnisse von kleinen hydrologischen Einzugsgebieten.* IHP/OHP report.

Madduma Bandara, C.M. and T.A. Kuruppuarachchi. 1989. *Land use change and hydrological trends in the Upper Mahaweli Basin.* Unpubl. report. Institute of Fundamental Studies, Kandy.

Wickramasinghe, L.A. and R. Premalal. 1988. Development of a rainstorm erosivity map for Sri Lanka. *5th International Soil Conservation Conference, Bangkok* 1988: 1-8.

Proceedings of the International and Interdisciplinary Symposium
ECOLOGY AND LANDSCAPE MANAGEMENT IN SRI LANKA
W. Erdelen, C. Preu, N. Ishwaran, C.M. Madduma Bandara (eds.)
Colombo, Sri Lanka, 12-26 March 1990
© 1993
Margraf Scientific Books, D-97985 Weikersheim
ISBN 3-8236-1182-8

Suitability of Satellite-Borne Remote Sensing Techniques for Coastal Studies

A Case Study of the Southeast Coast of Sri Lanka near Hambantota

F. WIENEKE

Abstract

The suitability of satellite-borne remote sensing techniques for studying and monitoring the southeastern coast of Sri Lanka was examined. Technical improvements have led to increased spatial and spectral resolution of remote sensing systems. Yet there are limits to the use of this modern research tool set by technical characteristics of the remote sensing systems used or specific conditions of the area investigated. Natural and artificial coastal phenomena combine in a characteristic manner to form terrain patterns which may correspond to typical image patterns whose quality is strongly influenced by region-specific weather conditions. Such problems are analyzed with respect to the spatial, temporal and electromagnetic dimensions of remote sensing data collection and interpretation. The conclusions derived from the results of such an analysis are illustrated by an analysis and interpretation of a SPOT image covering the coast, near the town of Hambantota, in southern Sri Lanka.

Introduction - Coastal Studies

Coasts are triple interfaces between land, sea and the atmosphere. Therefore, coasts are effected by changes in those spheres and their interactions. The monitoring of coasts meets the need to identify their actual status, to detect changes between different registrations and to predict future changes.

Classical coastal studies developed from a description of coastal landforms which aimed at their classification to the elaboration of morphogenetic phases such as sea level changes, tectogenetical and climatic geomorphological approaches or the connection between marine-litoral and terrestrial denudation chronologies. In these fields of research, remote sensing from space can be used for preparing inventories of global or regional coastal landforms and types of coasts and for the elaboration of hypotheses (Wieneke and Rust, 1972). In later studies a process-oriented coastal geomorphology developed in order to meet the practical requirements of coastal protection preventing the silting of river mouths and harbor inlets and monitoring island displacement. Such investigations, on the one hand, aim to analyze the scheme of interactions and on the other aim to measure the material displacement. Human impact on coasts may be easily incorporated in this system and in process-oriented coastal geomorphological studies. Since prehistoric times coasts have been centers of settlements and economic activities. In modern times human influence has increased greatly and irreversibly due to extremely high population densities and because of increasing construction activities. Satellite-borne remote sensing contributes to detecting changes and monitoring the coasts in coastal geomorphical studies.

Satellite-Borne Remote Sensing

The term "remote sensing" refers to the registration of information on distant objects, especially by means of electromagnetic radiation from parts of our planet's surface. The development of space technology has led to remote sensing from space. This is done mostly from unmanned satellites. A certain section of the earth's surface is registered with all its objects within a very short period of time taking into account radiation and electromagnetic properties. The spatial pattern of objects on the earth's surface thus is transformed into an image pattern of radiation intensities. These may be digital numbers or analogous grey tones and/or colors. All remote sensing data, photographic or non-photographic, possess spatial, temporal, and electromagnetic dimensions; thus these are special types of geographical data (Curran, 1985). While non-photographic satellite remote sensing is used for the monitoring of changes because of its regular, nominal repeatability, the rarer photographic satellite remote sensing data have served mainly for thematical and topographical mapping. This is because spatial accuracy and spatial resolution of photographic satellite remote sensing data are better than those of non-photographic images.

Suitability of Data Qualities for Coastal Studies

Scale, extent or size, position and resolution describe the spatial dimension of remote sensing data. The extent of the terrain registered is determined by the scale and the size of the image. Spatial resolution determines the lower limit. Many coastal objects, natural or anthropogenetic, are small and therefore are close to the limit of being recognizable. The size and extent of several objects in association generate a pattern in the image, which corresponds to a pattern on the ground. This pattern is called structure or texture, depending on its size. Thus the specific pattern of coastal landforms from the open sea to the firm land is transformed into a specific image pattern. The absolute or relative position of objects in the image is translated by mapping from the position of the terrain objects. Object position provides information for image analysis and is fundamental for the cartographic representation of remote sensing data and for the interpretation of results.

In general, photographs are taken within a very short time and are synchronous. Therefore, the whole area is photographed at the same time. Images need some time to be registered - up to 25 minutes with meteorological satellites. However, this time interval is normally very short, but it may be of some importance for registering very rapid processes, such as wave propagation and coastal currents. Photographs document a momentary situation and images document a quasimomentary one. It is the geographer who has to use his general and regional knowledge to estimate and judge the images' representation of the actual situation on land and/or water. Since the satellite orbits are known mathematically and because differences between real and nominal positions are generally small, the temporal accuracy of the calculated

476

registration time is very high. Temporal resolution is conditioned by the image repeatability of a certain area. Image repeatability only nominally corresponds to orbit repeatability, because it is not possible to take images every time the spacecraft passes a certain terrain.

The electromagnetic dimension of remote sensing data involves spectral properties and radiometric properties. In general, spectral sensitivity of remote sensing systems depends on atmospheric windows. It is possible to take just one image at a certain moment of a certain terrain (monospectral), or to take several ones simultaneously in different sensitivity ranges, i.e. electromagnetic wavelength intervals (multispectral). Spectral resolution is determined by the number and the width of bands used simultaneously. Modern techniques (e.g. Landsat or spectroscopy) aim at higher spectral resolution. Nonphotographic data are numerical, therefore spectral accuracy is high. For the same reasons, radiometric resolution is rather high with non-photographic scanner systems using a dynamic range of 256 steps. Perhaps the most significant influence of the electromagnetical dimension in coastal studies is the strong dependence on penetration of water and absorption of the radiation by water bodies on the wavelength of the spectral range used. Short-wave radiation (blue light) is able to penetrate clear water and to register features of the bottom. Long-wave radiation (near infrared light) is totally absorbed and gives no reflection registering even shallow water as black. Thus, a very sharp and precise water line is registered when using infrared radiation.

Since the resolution power of a remote sensing system is a very important limiting factor, it is worthwhile to consider both the spatial and the temporal resolutions of space remote sensing. Until now a high temporal resolution had only been possible with operational non-photographic systems, e.g. NOAA satellites and Meteosat, which operate with a very low spatial resolution. As coastal objects are very often small, and coastal processes are very fast no space remote sensing technique is ideally suited for coastal studies. The recognizability and even the detectability of small objects depend both on the spatial resolution power of the remote sensing system and on the contrast, which is dependent upon differences between the reflectivity of the objects and their environment.

While aerial missions can be planned and postponed according to the weather, space missions circulate around the earth in determined orbits and pass areas at precisely calculated times and intervals (repeatability). At the particular moment in time when the spacecraft passes, the weather may be fair and allow good registration conditions, or it may be unfavorable for registration, e.g. cloudy and rainy, or extremely foggy. But each region has its own mean weather calendar, from which recommendations for favorable registration times may be deduced.

The SPOT Products Used

Two SPOT-HRV scenes, namely K226/J 337 and 338, both registered on April 12th, 1987, were processed by the Company of Applied Remote Sensing (GAF) in Munich, Germany, using panchromatic (P) and multispectral (XS) registrations. The preprocessed P-mode image was contrast-enhanced, and then a high-pass filter was applied. The XS-mode image was IHS-processed (all three spectral bands) and then merged with the P-product. Both products, the enhanced P-version and the P/XS-merge version were visualized on transparencies. Hardcopy enlargements were produced reprotechnically from these transparencies at scales of 1: 100,000 and 1: 50,000. In addition, 1986 aerial photographs of the study area were used.

The Study Area

The southern coast of Sri Lanka is a "bay and headland" coast (Swan, 1971), the headlands being remnants of inselbergs and the bays having been formed by spits with dune wall and beach ridge systems, often enclosing river mouths or lagoons. The Hambantota-Yala part of Sri Lanka belongs to the "dry zone" of the southeast. Here, often rather steep-sloped inselbergs, partly covered with dry forest and scrub and partly barren, dominate a peneplain which lies very low (< 100m) and is flat. The peneplain consists of bedrock, covered by lateritic sediments and reddish soils. Broad, flat valleys dissect the peneplain. There is dry field agriculture and silviculture on the interfluves. Valleys have been landscaped by man into a sequence of watertanks or reservoirs and paddy fields.

Table 1. SPOT System and Images Parameters (from various sources); HRV = Haute Resolution Visible, IFOV = Instantaneous Field of View, FOV = Field of View.

Orbit Parameters

Averaged altitude	832 km
Period	102 min
Orbits per day	14.5
Repetition	26 days
Inclination	98.7°
Orbit type	polar, sun-synchronous
Equatorial distance of two neighboring orbits	108 km
Equator crossing time (descending)	10.30 LMT (local mean time)

Satellite parameters

Launch date	22.2.1986
Start of operation	5.1986
Mass	1750 kg
Sensor equipment	HRV 1, HRV 2 (equal)
Stabilization	3-axes-stabilization

Sensor parameters (HRV - Haute Résolution Visible)

Sensor type	opto-electronical scanner, CCD
Spectral modes	P panchromatic, XS multispectral
Spectral sensitivity (optional)	P 510 - 730 nm XS 500 - 590 nm, 610 - 680 nm, 790 - 890 nm
IFOV	$1.2*10^{-5}$rad P, $2.4*10^{-5}$rad XS
Ground pixel size	10 m P, 20 m XS
FOV	4.13°
Scene size	60 km * 60-80 km
Swath width (both sensors)	117 km (3 km overlap)
Viewing angle (optional)	0° to +/-27° by 45 steps of 0.6°
Dynamic range	8 bit (P and XS)
Repetition by tilt	3-5 days
Focal length	1000 mm

Image parameters

Date	12 April 1987, 10.30 LMT
Scene no.	K 226 J 337, 338
Cloud coverage	0000, all quadrants <10%
Viewing angle	12.1° W (P and XS)
Spectral mode	P, XS 1-3

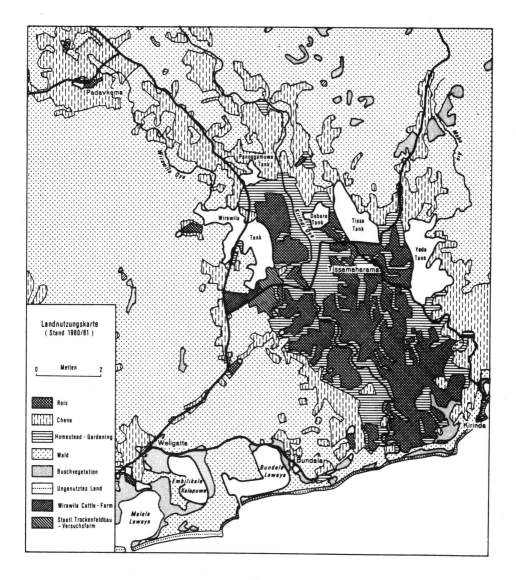

Figure 1. Land use sketch map 1960/61 of the study area (from Zaun-Axler, 1977). Legend from the top to the bottom: paddy fields, chena fields, homestead gardening, forests, bushes, unused land, Wirawila cattle farm, dry farming experimental farms.

Near the coast there are several inselbergs. They form cliffed headlands and rock outcrops in the water. East of Hambantota, the bigger river systems, all allochthonous, reach the beach in a small rivulet, because their discharge changes according to season and much of these rivers' water is used for irrigation. For example, the Kirindi Oya no longer discharges into the sea, its river mouth being closed off by the beach. The short autochthonous rivers are dammed permanently by large and broad dune wall systems and/or by the beach and form lagoons. These coastal lagoons have a changing water level, forming broad whitish salt seams at their margins during the dry season. Some of them are used for the production of salt. The

479

Figure 2. Section from the enhanced Panchromatic Hardcopy Version of the SPOT image, showing the coast east of Hambantota, enlarged to 1: 100,000. Copyright CNES, France, 12-04-1987. Processed by GAF, Munich, Germany.

vegetation near the coast consists of (a) dense evergreen forest with bushes and high trees, (b) shrub and thornbush secondary forest and (c) grassy patches near the lagoon or the dune system. The dunes are devoid of vegetation in some parts and covered with dune grass or dense bushes in others. On the beach side, the dunes are cliffed. At several sites these cliffs show bedrock cores inside the dunes, which were covered by the eolian sedimentation.

Close to the roads new villages and settlements develop often showing a regular pattern of houses and gardens. The dry fields are somewhat irregularly shaped and fenced by hedges. The broad alluvial plain of the Kirindi Oya river downstream of Tissamaharama consists of two distinct levels, only some meters apart in altitude. The lower level is almost exclusively occupied by paddy fields, the higher level contains roadside settlements with coconut trees and home gardens. Bordering the alluvial plain a step of several meters in height separates the plain itself from the peneplain with shrub forest, thornthickets and "permanent chena" agriculture.

Analysis of the SPOT Image

Natural and anthropogenic coastal objects were analyzed and measured from virtual and real enlargements on positive paper prints. The 1 inch to 1 mile map and the paper prints of the 1956 aerial photographs (1: 40,000) were also analyzed for purposes of comparison. Different types of coastal objects were studied in the scale of 1: 100,000 and 1: 50,000 in both the panchromatic black-and-white image as well as in the pan-multispectral color composite merge according to their detectability, recognizability and measurability. The photographic images were analyzed visually, measurements were performed directly, using magnifying glasses or the Interpretoskop Zeiss Jena. This process led to a rating of the objects catagorized according

Table 2. Rating of coastal objects according to their level of detection in different scales and image products; nd = not detectable, d = detectable, s = supposable, i = identifiable, e = estimable, m = measurable.

Coastal object/ coastal landform	B/W-Pan paper print	B/W-Pan paper print	XS/P-color merge paper print	XS/P-color merge paper print	B/W aerial photo paper print
	1: 100,000	1: 50,000	1: 100,000	1: 50,000	1: 40,000
Wave pattern	nd	nd	nd	nd	s
Dry beach	s	s	i	i to m	i to m
Wet beach	s	s	s	s	i to m
Beach cusps	i to e	m	i to m	e	s to m
Breaker zone	i to m	m	m	m	m
Dune cliff	nd	nd	i	i	nd to s
Rock outcrops	s	s	s	s	s to i
Inselberg	nd	s	i	i	non ex.
Bare dunes	nd	nd to s	i	i	s
Grass dunes	nd to i	nd to i	i	i	i
Bush dunes	i	i	i	i	i
Inner bush line	i	i	m	i	i to m
River mouth bar	i	i	e	e	m
Lagoon mouth bar	m	m	m	m	m
Tracks	m	m	s to m	s to m	i to m
Salt work dam	e	m	e	m	m
Surface salt	s to i	s to i	i	m	e
Grassy patches	i	m	m	m	m
Shrub	i	i	s to i	i	i
Dense forest	i	i	i	i	m
Village houses	i	i to m	i	s to i	m
Hotel	s	s	nd	s	non ex.
Tanks	i	i	i to m	i to m	m
Chena	m	m	i to m	i to m	??
Gangoda	s to i	i	s to i	i	m
Water holes	s	i to m	m	m	s

to the level of their registration: not detectable, detectable, supposable, identifiable, estimable, and measurable (Tab. 2). The rating cannot be totally objective as the images were examined visually, the objects often were only bearly visible and their recognition was dependant on contrast and because this kind of analysis is never entirely free from prior information of the area.

This analysis was done in comparison with ground truth from two field trips in September 1985 and in late March 1988, and with information from van der Zee and Cox (1988), who studied the same image and had done their fieldwork in April 1987, which was also the date of the registration of the image. The date on which the image was registered, i.e. April 12th, 1987, was at the beginning of the short rainy season following an unusually long dry period from October 1986 to February 1987 (Fig. 3). Therefore, this image shows a more arid situation than that expected and explains why so many paddy fields are barren or fallow.

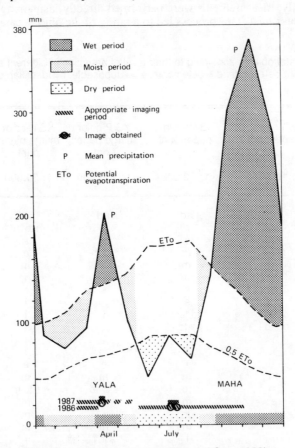

Figure 3. Climate diagram of the study area (van der Zee and Cox, 1988).

Evaluation of the Arguments

In judging the suitability of SPOT data for studies of the Sri Lankan coast it ought to be stressed that the advantages lie in the quasisynchronous registration of a large area (60 km x 60 km) and in the fact that SPOT is an operational and not an experimental system. Image data are numerical-digital, and processing is done operationally. Disadvantages include (a) a relatively coarse spatial resolution, (b) the rigid acquisition times depending on orbital parameters, (c) relatively poor repetition rate of about 3 to 5 days and (d) the spectral bands available. These are not optimal for coastal remote sensing. From the images analyzed it was impossible to obtain any information on the water bodies or on the sea bottom.

The solution to the problems seems to lie with a multistage, multitemporal approach. We require more image data from different remote sensing systems, but agree that recent developments have produced solutions which now reach the necessary range of spatial resolution.

Acknowledgments

The Company for Applied Remote Sensing (GAF, Munich, Germany) processed the SPOT images and I am very thankful for their help and advice. The figures and tables were produced at the Department of Geography, University of Munich, Germany. C. Engelbrecht, Augsburg, read the contribution at Colombo and helped with the preparation of the manuscript.

Literature Cited

Curran, P.J. 1985. *Principles of Remote Sensing.* Longman, London and New York.

Swan, S.B.St.S. 1971. Coastal geomorphology in a humid tropical low energy environment: the island of Singapore. *J. Trop. Geogr.* 33: 43-61.

Wieneke, F. and U. Rust. 1972. Das Satellitenbild als Hilfsmittel zur Formulierung geomorphologischer Arbeitshypothesen. *Wiss. Forschung Südwestafrika* 11: 1-16.

Zaun-Axler, G. 1977. *Der Reisanbau im unteren Kirindi Oya-Becken.* Steiner Verlag, Wiesbaden.

Zee, D. van der and J. Cox. 1988. Monitoring in Moneragala District, Sri Lanka, with SPOT images. *ITC-Journal 1988* 3: 260-271.

Proceedings of the International and Interdisciplinary Symposium
ECOLOGY AND LANDSCAPE MANAGEMENT IN SRI LANKA
W. Erdelen, C. Preu, N. Ishwaran, C.M. Madduma Bandara (eds.)
Colombo, Sri Lanka, 12-26 March 1990
© 1993
Margraf Scientific Books, D-97985 Weikersheim
ISBN 3-8236-1182-8

An Environmental Atlas of the Mahaweli Valley

P.G. COORAY

Abstract

The Mahaweli Ganga is characterized by a variety of different geologic and morphologic features, different climatic conditions, different soils, various agricultural practices, industries, land use systems and human settlements. Maximum benefit from proper use of natural and human resources depends on long-range resource planning, management and monitoring. But this has to be based on fundamental data which can best be provided by environmental geologic maps, such as (1) a record of the existing state of the different environments within the valley, and the processes going on within them, (2) a base for the continued monitoring of the processes of erosion, earth movements, pollution, human modification and exploitation, by continous mapping and revision of mapping, (3) a means of communication between scientists involved in the integration and application of necessary technology in the valley, and (4) information for the use of economists, planners, electrical engineers, water use managers, sanitary engineers, local and regional administrative bodies, and the many other individuals, organizations and institutions that are involved, one way or another, in the life of the valley. The valley may be divided into five sections, and for each section there will be maps showing surface and subsurface geology, landforms and substrate conditions, current land use, topography, active processes and energy resources, rainfall, stream discharge and water systems, slopes and slope stability and environmental geochemistry. Descriptive texts and statistical tables will accompany each atlas section.

Introduction

This paper is not an original contribution to the scientific literature on ecology nor is it a philosophical discourse of great importance. It is rather a practical suggestion of one way in which we can make sure that "Ecology and Landscape Management in Sri Lanka" becomes a compromise and not a conflict in the years to come.

But first permit me to indulge in what has become a standard practice of mine, namely, to define terms so that there can be no ambiguity in what follows. "Ecology", as Webster defines it, is (a) the science dealing with the interrelationship of organisms and their environment and

(b) the totality or pattern of that relationship. Both definitions apply, I think, in the present context. "Landscape" in the same dictionary is (a) the landforms of a region in the aggregate and (b) a portion of territory that the eye can comprehend, i.e. see in a single view. Here we need the second definition, I think. To "manage" is to handle, to direct, to alter something or to treat with care, so "management" is the art of doing any of those things. I like to think, therefore, that in this symposium we are seeking ways and means of treating, with care, the landscape of this island in such a way that the interrelationships between man and environment do not continue to exist in a state of antagonism (conflict) as they have in the past. Rather, we are seeking the settlement of differences by consent reached by mutual concession (compromise) in the years to come.

I am reminded here of two sayings. One is by Francis Bacon in his Nova Organum of 1640 where he said: "Nature to be commanded must be obeyed." The other is by Peres de Quellar, the UN Secretary General, who talked about finding a "balance between humanity and nature." What Bacon meant was that if we are to make the best use of the natural resources that surround us, we must understand the laws of nature and live within those laws. To do otherwise would lead to conflict - as we see happening now. And Peres de Cuellar stresses what we know we have to do in order to survive - to find a compromise between the demands of man and the laws of nature. I submit that in order even to understand the problem, we need to know what the landscape and its resources are, and the aim of my talk is to suggest one way of doing so for a small part of this island.

This paper is about the Mahaweli Valley itself, or rather, a strip of land limited to seven or eight kilometers on either side of it. In what follows, I try to answer the questions "why?", "what?", "how?", "when?" and "how much?" in respect of an Environmental Atlas of the Mahaweli Valley.

Why an Environmental Atlas?

The natural landscape of any region is a megasystem involving land, water and air, and the interplay of these three elements results in the landforms, natural vegetation and soils of the region. Each of these is a subsystem, governed by natural laws, but the natural interaction between the subsystems and the delicate balance existing between them is often disrupted by man's interference, generally without much regard for the laws of nature. For example, extensive deforestation in watershed areas can lead to soil erosion as well as to changes in rainfall patterns; and intensive cultivation of steep slopes without due attention to adequate drainage often leads to landslides. These are just two examples of how human activity can damage the environment. We can consider the environment as the sum total of the physical and social resources available at any time in any region, and it is within this environment that human beings involve themselves in so-called "development" processes in order to improve their well being, or their "quality of life". However, as a UNEP document puts it, "there can be no development without conservation." But there can be no conservation without constant monitoring and assessment of the development processes and their effects upon the environment. And the best way of recording the nature and the rate of processes as well as responses to them is through the visual means of maps.

The Mahaweli Ganga is the longest river in Sri Lanka and the one with the largest catchment area. It flows through all three main climatic zones in the island, rising in the wet zone of the southwest quadrant of the island, flowing through the intermediate zone of the central region, and it finally debouches into the sea through the dry zone of the northeast quadrant. Its sources are in the highest erosion levels of the central hill country, its middle course is through the middle peneplain, and its lowest course is through the coastal peneplain. The river's course changes direction several times, beginning in a northwesterly direction, then flowing north-northeasterly, then southeasterly, then easterly, then northerly and finally north-northeasterly. It is clear, therefore, that the Mahaweli flows through several environments during its course, and the length of its valley is characterized by a variety of geological and geomorphological features, climatic conditions, soils, agricultural practices, industries, land uses and human

486

settlements. There are, throughout the length of the valley, environments at different stages of development, with resulting problems of land use, water management, pollution and conservation.

Originally there would have been a delicate balance between the various subsystems in these environments through which the river flowed. Then in the first half of this century, when the Minipe Anicut Scheme was reconstructed and there was little settlement along the right bank, the balance was hardly affected. However, this delicate balance has, without doubt, been upset since the Accelerated Mahaweli Project was initiated. This is the largest development program in Sri Lanka in modern times, and it affects almost all aspects of the national economy and the lives of the people, in terms of the extent of land involved, the amount of money and resources spent and the number of people affected.

The building of dams and reservoirs at Kotmale, Polgolla, Victoria, Randenigala and Rantambe has resulted in extensive deforestation, vast areas of cultivation, the inundation of large numbers of villages and thousands of acres of valuable agricultural land, soil erosion, landslides, microseismics, migration of large numbers of people and salination of soils.

These are continuous processes going on all the time, and in order to obtain the maximum benefits from the proper use of lands and of natural and human resources there must be long-range planning and management of the entire river valley. But such utilization can only be based on adequate knowledge and understanding of the local and regional variations of the environment, variations which themselves impose constraints on the nature and extent of development. In other words, fundamental data on the environment are essential for proper long-term resource development and management - but it is also absolutely necessary to monitor the continuous natural and man-induced processes in the valley in order to protect and conserve the environment of the Mahaweli Valley. And this, after all, must be a priority consideration of our nation before it is too late. Hence, this proposal for an "Environmental Atlas of the Mahaweli Valley" which will provide a large part of the data required for development, management and conservation.

What is an Environmental Atlas?

The proposal for an Environmental Atlas of the Mahaweli Valley is for the production of a series of maps depicting a variety of features from the source of the river to the vicinity of Polonnaruwa. In order to do this, the chosen length of the river will be divided into nine areas, which will be grouped into four sections, each of about 400 km². Each area is a strip of land 20 km long and 10 km wide on either side of the river. The proposed sections are shown in Table 1 and in Figure 1.

Table 1. Sectional subdivisions of the Mahaweli Valley as suggested for the Environmental Atlas.

Section/Name	Area No.	Extent	Area (km²)
A. Kotmale Reservoir Section	1 & 2	Nawalapitiya-Peradeniya	350
B. Victoria Reservoir Section	3 & 4	Kandy-Victoria	400
C. Randenigala Reservoir Section	5 & 6	Randenigala-Weragantota	400
D. Wasgomuwa-Polonnaruwa Section	7, 8 & 9	Wasgomuwa-Polonnaruwa	600

The atlas consists of the following maps for each section (the list is tentative and subject to modification): (1) Environmental Geology Map showing surface and subsurface geology, mines and quarries, and sources of rock, sand, and gravel, (2) Physical Properties Map showing characteristics of substrate and landform conditions for specific uses, e.g. engineering construction, waste disposal, based on such properties as permeability, fluid transmissibility, water-table position, load strength and potential for earthslips, (3) Current Land Use Maps, an inventory of land use patterns in the area, including agricultural land, forests and grasslands, recreational, residential and urba, (4) Topography, Active Processes, Energy Resources showing areas of active erosion, sedimentation, flooding, power-generation plants, power transmission lines, (5) Rainfall, Stream Discharge, Water Systems showing data collected for a representative period (e.g. 3 years), also positions of reservoirs, lakes, irrigation channels, and (6) Landforms, Slopes and Slope Stability, Environmental Geochemistry showing classification of landforms and slopes, geochemistry of soils, of surface waters and of ground water.

Sri Lanka is extremely fortunate in having an excellent series of topographical and land use maps covering the whole island on the scale of 1 inch/1 mile and large parts of it on 1 inch : 2 miles, 1: 50,000 and 1: 10,000. It also has excellent aerial photo coverage at 1: 40,000 and larger scales. The data to be used in constructing the maps will be plotted on 1: 10,000 scale, and the final maps will be on 1: 50,000 or 1: 25,000 scales. Each section will be accompanied by a descriptive text, statistical tables, figures and plates.

How will such an Atlas be Produced?

Preparing an atlas of this nature is a major undertaking of an interdisciplinary nature. Much data of various kinds are available and the first step would be to begin with that section about which most data are available. The preparation of an atlas for section X would involve the plotting of all available data on base maps, the filling in of gaps or gathering new data by fieldwork, the interpretation of aerial photographs and satellite images, and all other available means and the writing of descriptive texts. Once the atlas for section X is prepared, we would extend outwards on both sides from section X in order to make sure that all boundaries at margins of the maps correspond and that there are no anomalies.

The preparation of such an atlas demands expertise in a number fields, some of which we may not have. Such expertise is to be found in neighboring countries, and I would have no hesitation in asking for assistance and for cooperation in such a venture. Such cooperation would, without doubt, be mutually beneficial to both parties.

The Who, When and How Much of such an Atlas?

This is not the place to go into the detailed requirements of such a project, but it might be useful to make an appropriate estimate of what would be required. The staff requirements would be a coordinator, 2 senior scientists, 3 research assistants and 2 field assistants, to cover the fields of geology, geomorphology, land use and biogeography, climatology, hydrology, engineering geology, environmental geochemistry, photointerpretation, remote sensing and sampling. There would also be a need for a senior cartographer and a couple of experienced draughtsmen and typists. Requirements of equipment would be jeeps, maps, aerial photos and satellite images, stereoscopes, drafting and computer facilities as well as use of engineering geology, geology and pedology laboratories and workshop facilities. At a very rough guess, 25 to 30 man-years would be required for the entire project, at a cost of approximately Rs. 5-6 million, possibly more, taking into account inflation over the period.

The penultimate question is, who would foot such a bill? In neighboring Kerala (India), where much work of a similar nature is being undertaken by the Centre for Earth Science Studies at Trivandrum, specific projects have been commissioned by various agencies. As examples I may quote the Environmental Atlas of the Kerala Coastal Zone, Department of

488

Environment, Government of India and a comparative study of land use patterns in two river basins, Western Ghats, Kerala; both commissioned by the Department of the Environment, Government of India; and the formulation of VIIIth Plan: District Kasaragrad - Resource Mapping: commissioned by the State Committee on Science, Technology and Environment.

What are the Benefits of such an Atlas?

If I were asked, finally, what would be the ultimate results of having an Environmental Atlas of the Mahaweli Valley, I would say there are four main benefits. Firstly, the atlas would contain a record of the different resources and environments within the valley and the various processes going on within the environments. Secondly, the atlas would produce a base for the continued monitoring of the processes of erosion, earth movements, pollution, human modification and exploitation by continuous mapping and updating. Thirdly, the atlas would provide (a) a means of communication between scientists involved in the integration and application of necessary technology in the valley, and (b) information for use by economists, planners, electrical engineers, water-use managers, sanitary engineers, local and regional administrative bodies and the many other individuals, organizations and institutions that are involved, one way or another, in the life of the valley. Fourthly, it would, when completed, provide a model as well as a pool of expertise for similar atlases in other parts of Sri Lanka. An ideal candidate for a second Environmental Atlas would be the coastal zone from Colombo to Galle, probably the most developed and most densely populated part of Sri Lanka.

Conclusions

This then is the proposal I have to put before you, who constitute a solid body of opinion on the alternatives between conflict and compromise in the management of our environment. Will the compilation of the Environmental Atlas of the Mahaweli Valley contribute towards the preservation and conservation of the environment of the valley in the face of rapid and intensive development? And if so, who will commission the compilation of such an atlas and who will undertake the actual compilation? Any takers?

Proceedings of the International and Interdisplinary Symposium
ECOLOGY AND LANDSCAPE MANAGEMENT IN SRI LANKA
W. Erdelen, C. Preu, N. Ishwaran, C.M. Madduma Bandara (eds.)
Colombo, Sri lanka, 12-26 March 1990
© 1993
Margraf Scientific Books, D-97985 Weikersheim
ISBN 3-8236-1182-8

The Hydrogeochemical Atlas of Sri Lanka

Applications in Environmental Studies

C.B. DISSANAYAKE

Abstract

The Hydrogeochemical Atlas of Sri Lanka produced by the author and his team may have a variety of applications in environmental studies. The water quality in river basins necessary for agricultural projects, background chemical data for epidemological studies such as distribution of dental diseases, cancer etc. can be provided by the atlas.

Introduction

The necessity for availability of background geochemical information is evident in a variety of environment related disciplines. One of the prime requirements for the effective study of environmental geochemistry on a regional scale is the compilation of multi-element atlases illustrating the distribution of elements and other chemical parameters. Even though geochemical atlases do not solve problems by themselves, they are invaluable in selecting target areas for detailed study and also for providing background chemical information. In general the sampling media used are rock, soil, water, lake and stream sediments and vegetation. The information obtained can be used in the investigation of a variety of problems, including those concerned with mineral resources, public health, land use, epidemology and agriculture. The data are not influenced by subjective factors (other than those involved in the selection of sampling analytical and processing techniques) and the maps provide positive baseline information and also highlight anomalies in metal distribution that might otherwise remain unsuspected. Geochemical atlases, apart from their practical value have important fundamental

491

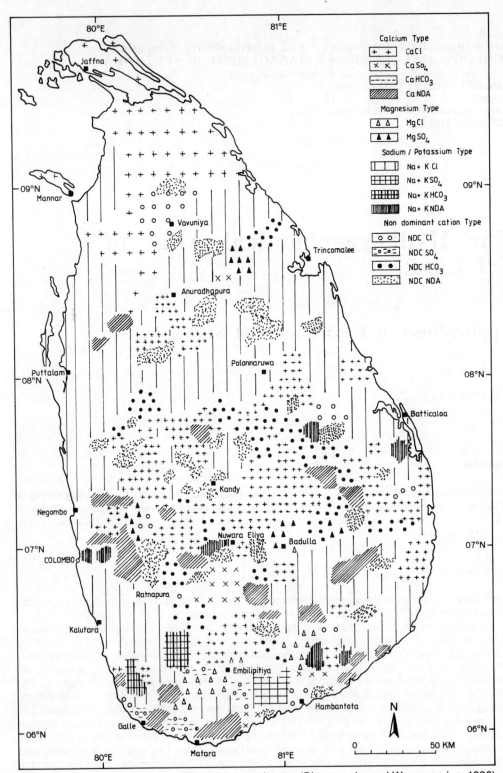

Figure 1. Geochemical classification of the ground water (Dissanayake and Weerasooriya, 1986).

significance in regional geology and in any research area where knowledge of the geographical distribution of the elements is a relevant factor (Webb *et al.* 1979). Many countries, therefore, consider the compilation of geochemical atlases as a national cartographic requirement.

In a Royal Society discussion on environmental geochemistry and health held in 1978, it was stated that the trace element toxicities and deficiencies in man can be related to the environment in developed countries only with difficulty. In the words of Underwood (1979): "In my view there is an urgent need for more combined epidemiological and geochemical studies in developing countries. These are parts of the world which because they are not yet highly industrialized, motorized and urbanized would be expected to reveal a more direct relation between human health and the geochemical environmental characteristic of the Western World."

Sri Lanka affords an almost ideal opportunity to the researchers on environmental geochemistry and health in view of the fact that the vast majority of the population of Sri Lanka lives in intimate association with the actual physical environment, depending on the soil, water, vegetation and on the immediate environment for their sustenance. This study illustrates some of the applications of the Hydrogeochemical Atlases of Sri Lanka, particularly in environment related problems.

The Hydrochemical Atlas of Sri Lanka

The Hydrochemical Atlas of Sri Lanka was prepared by the author and his team of the Environmental Geochemistry Research Group (Dissanayake *et al.* 1986). Water was collected from dug wells covering the entire island and a random sample of 465 was chosen with the help of a standard random number table for the classification and for the illustration of the spatial variations of ground water in Sri Lanka. In preparing the contour maps for 15 water quality parameters, the concentration values of each parameter were placed separately on a 1: 1,192,660 scale map of Sri Lanka which was divided into 145 square grids of 4 cm^2 ($\approx$ 568.9 km^2) so that each square contained a number of sampling locations. The average value of the concentration of each parameter in each square was assigned to the respective grid mode. This procedure eliminates the spurious values of the observed results to a great extent. It must be emphasized that the processed data are located at regular intervals rather than at irregularly spaced actual observation points. Their smoothed values were then placed in a frequency table from which it was possible to obtain a frequency distribution curve to identify the number of groups of each population studied. These group intervals are subsequently used as the contour intervals in producing the hydrogeochemical maps. For the classification of water, piper diagrams were employed to categorize the different types of water. The Hydrogeochemical Atlas of Sri Lanka contains distribution maps of TDS, total hardness, NO_3^-, NO_2^-, NH_4^+ Cl$^-$, F$^-$, total dissolved silica, Fe, Mn, V, Cr, Cu and Zn.

The Chemistry of the Ground Water of Sri Lanka

Figure 1 illustrates the chemistry of the ground water of Sri Lanka. A more detailed study of the distribution patterns of the ground water types in Sri Lanka reveals that the underlying geology and the climate affect the chemical quality of water to a great extent. Disanayake *et al.* (1985) classified the ground water of Sri Lanka into the following four main water types; (1) calcium type, (2) magnesium type, (3) sodium/potassium type, and (4) non-dominant cation type. The wet zone of Sri Lanka consists for the most part of non-dominant cation types, of calcium HCO_3 and non-dominant anion types. In contrast, the dry zone has predominantly Na/K type, and in this type of water the Cl subtype covers vast areas. The presence of Cl type in the dry zone is attributed to evaporation under the prevailing strong drought conditions which results in the accumulation of halides in the soil layer. The effect of the underlying geology on the chemistry of the ground water is clearly seen in the case of the Jaffna Peninsula which is underlain by sedimentary limestones. As expected, calcium type of water predominates in these parts of Sri Lanka. Salinity also increases in areas adjacent to shorelines, and salt water intrusion is particularly well observed in areas where fresh ground water has been extracted in excessive quantities. The effect of climate and topography is evident in the variation of water quality from the Ca-HCO$_3$ type in the highlands to the Na/K type in the lowlands. A Ca → NDC → Na/K type of sequence is apparent with decreasing elevation from highlands to lowlands. Various physicochemical factors, which clearly govern the geochemical mobility of chemical elements and the general distribution of water quality in the ground water of Sri Lanka, provide a good example of how the natural environment affects the chemistry of ground water. The delineation of areas of different water chemistry may have applications in studies pertaining to human health and epidemiology. The effect of ground water chemistry on health of the population in Sri Lanka is of paramount importance due to the fact that the vast majority of the people use ground water directly for drinking and cooking purposes. Since the water may contain an excess or a deficiency of vital chemical elements, long-term usage of water of a particular chemistry will undoubtedly have health effects both positive and negative.

Water Quality of the Mahaweli Ganga Drainage Basin

The Mahaweli Ganga Basin which covers approximately one sixth of the island, cuts across different geological formations, climatic zones and soil types. Therefore, the water quality is a result of the complex interactions of the hydrocycle with the lithosphere and biosphere within the basin. The general water quality of the Mahaweli Ganga Drainage Basin varies from the Ca-HCO$_3$ type at the source of the river through Na + K - HCO$_3$ type, Na + K - Cl type, non-dominant cation type to Na + K - Cl type at the mouth. The prevalence of the Na + K - Cl type in most substantial areas of the basin is of particular significance for agriculture. The increase in salinity is common in downstream regions where rivers have been dammed. It is of interest to note the progressive increase of chloride ions concentrations in the Mahaweli Basin from the source area towards the mouth (Fig. 2). This type of background chemical data is of great use in the planning of agricultural projects.

The progressive increase of manganese ions in the ground water of Sri Lanka (Fig. 3) is also of special importance for water quality and agriculture. Since the two elements are redox sensitive in the environment and can act as potential sinks for other trace elements, iron and manganese compounds are of particular significance. The sorption and co-precipitation phenomena of transition metals by colloidal compounds of iron and manganese are largely controlled by pH and Eh value of the media. Apart from those redox sensitive reactions of iron and manganese, organic matter, chiefly humic and fulvic acids may exert a positive influence on the complexing of Fe and Mn in water. These elements therefore, exert considerable influence on the availability of micronutrients and which in turn will affect the growth of crops. The physical and chemical properties of water are mainly dependent on the total dissolved solids (TDS) content. Water containing more than 1000 ppm of TDS (WHO, 1982), is generally not recommended for drinking purposes. In irrigation practices the TDS content of water is an extremely important water quality consideration. The water uptake relation of plants is mainly controlled by the osmotic pressure differential between soil and plant. This osmotic effect is generally related to the total dissolved solids concentration rather than to the individual concentration of specific ionic constituents.

In the Mahaweli Basin, the total dissolved solids concentration increases from the source towards Mahaweli Delta. There is a distinct salinity found around the deltaic environment (Fig. 4), and this information is particularly useful in the planning of settlement schemes, water supply schemes and also in agriculture. As in the case of salinity, the TDS contents show a relative increase in the dry zone. Here the high annual temperatures promote high evaporation, which reduces the amount of water through evaporation and which increases the TDS contents of the remaining water. The increase of TDS due to evaporation, however, is pronounced in ground water at shallow depths like in the case of the Jaffna Peninsula. The climatic effect therefore has a marked control in the TDS contents in the ground water of Sri Lanka.

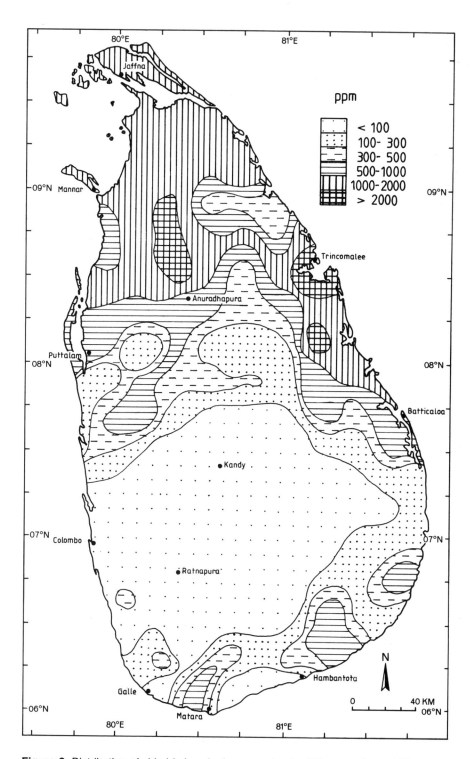

Figure 2. Distribution of chloride ions in the ground water (Dissanayake and Weerasooriya, 1986).

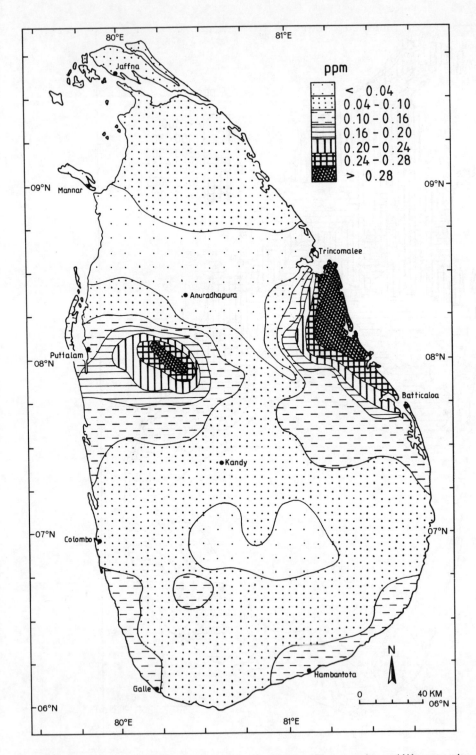

Figure 3. Distribution of manganese in the ground water (Dissanayake and Weerasooriya, 1986).

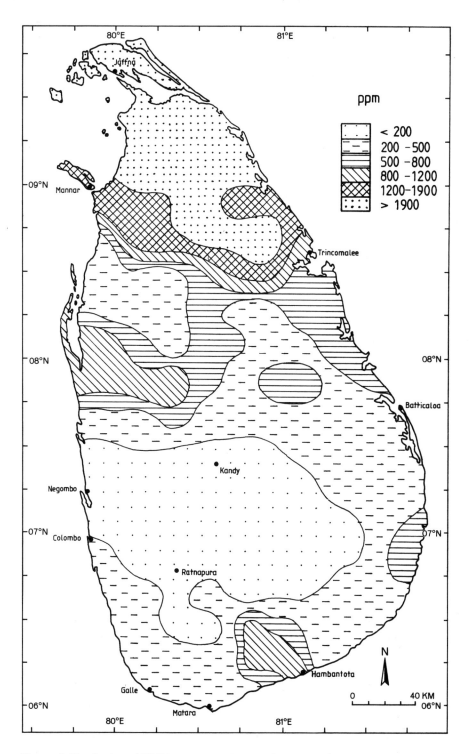

Figure 4. Distribution of TDS in the ground water (Dissanayake and Weerasooriya, 1986).

The total dissolved solid contents in the drinking water has a bearing on human health and detailed epidemiological studies may reveal an association between the TDS and the incidence of certain geographically distributed diseases in Sri Lanka.

Environmental Geochemistry and Health

Environmental geochemistry is developing into a very useful tool for investigations in regional health problems. Even though there is much emphasis laid on the pollution of the physical environment by man, the effect of the chemistry of the natural environment on the health of a population is also of equal importance. There is a clear need to differentiate between health hazards due to the natural distribution of elements and those caused by man's activities. It would for example be useful to know if there is any risk in living on a serpentine mass with a few hundred micrograms of chromium, nickel or copper per gram or on granite with 30 micrograms of uranium per gram, or in a lead mining district with a few hundred micrograms of lead per gram in the soil. What levels of lead could be expected to be taken up by plants grown on such soils compared to the lead contents in plants grown in a market garden close to a major road? These comments of Bowie (1979) clearly indicate the need for the availability of background chemical data as supplied by geochemical atlases. In Sri Lanka, there are many interesting geochemical situations that are worthy of detailed investigation.

Hydrogeochemistry of Fluorides and Dental Diseases

A well-known association between a chemical element in the environment and human health is that of fluorine with dental and bone diseases. The outer layer of the crowns of teeth is enamel, the hardest tissue of the human body. Beneath it is the dentine, the main tooth component. The principal component of enamel is microcrystalline hydroxyapatite set in a protein matrix. When fluoride is present in excess in the water, some of the ingested fluoride ions are incorporated into the apatite crystal lattice of tooth enamel during its formation and cause the enamel to become harder and possibly discolor. Even though food forms, the main source for a large number of essential trace elements required by man, fluorides are mainly derived from water. The hydrogeochemical distribution of fluoride is therefore of great importance in delineating areas in which dental and bone diseases caused by deficiency or excess of fluorides are prevalent. In Sri Lanka, it has been shown that certain areas have excess fluorides in the ground water (Fig. 5). High fluoride concentrations are found in the north central, eastern and parts of the southeastern sector of the island. Warnakulasuriya *et al.* (1987) observed that dental fluorosis is indeed common in some of those areas. As indicated by the presence of large concentrations of fluorides in some recently drilled tube wells, particularly in the Anuradhapura, Monaragala and Uda Walawe regions (Dissanayake, 1990), dental fluorosis may well turn out to be an environmental disease which is worth serious investigation. The hydrogeochemical atlas could provide the baseline data.

Cancer as an Environmental Disease

Nitrates are often linked with cancer in view of the fact that nitrates on reduction yield nitrites which can react with other substances, such as amines, in the stomach or lungs to yield nitrosamines, which are thought to be carcinogenic (Magee and Barnes 1967, Bogovski 1972). The impact of nitrates, nitrites and nitrosamines on human health therefore remains a question in the forefront of scientific research priorities. This is particularly so in developing countries considering the extreme contamination of water that can be caused by poor sanitation, improper location of pit latrines near drinking water wells and use of nitrogeneous fertilizer.

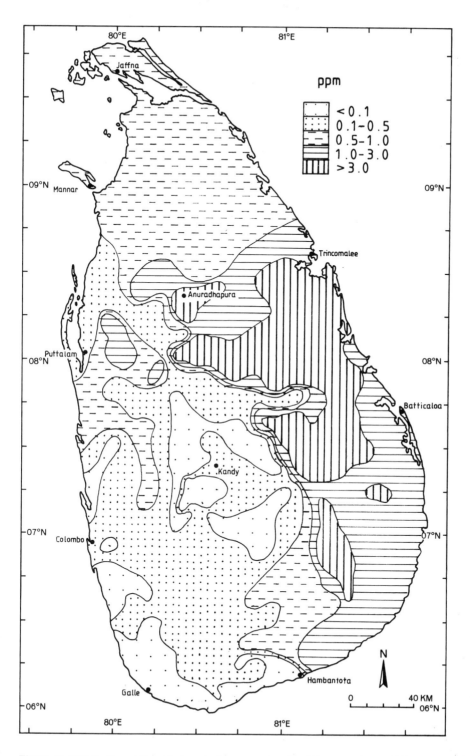

Figure 5. Distribution of fluoride ions in the ground water (Dissanayake and Weerasooriya, 1986).

Panabokke (1984) carried out a five-year study on the geographical pathology of malignant tumour in Sri Lanka. He presented data on investigations of 24,029 biopsy specimens (Tab. 1). Accordingly, the Northern Province showed the highest incidence (184 of malignant tumours per 100,000 population) in biopsy material among the nine provinces of Sri Lanka. In the Southern Province the incidence was low (37 per 100,000 population). The most common malignant tumours that arose were those of the esophagus, the buccai region and the breast. Studies by Dissanayake and Weerasooriya (1987) have revealed a strong correlation between nitrate concentrations of ground water and the incidence of cancer. The Northern Province, for example, has the highest nitrate levels in the ground water of Sri Lanka (Fig. 6). The nitrate concentrations in the ground water of Sri Lanka appear to show a marked increase in areas of high population density, extensive fertilizer usage and also in areas of the wet zone where atmospheric electric discharges are frequent.

Table 1. Incidence of human cancer per 100,000 population in Sri Lanka (Panabokke, 1984).

Province	Benign tumours	Malignant tumours	Bladder	Kidney	Small intestine	Stomach	Esophagus	Liver
Northern	92	184	0.90	0.30	1.30	5.80	37.40	3.30
Northwestern	61	63	0.40	0.40	0.30	1.20	4.60	0.78
Northcentral	35	24	0.20	0.20	0.00	0.90	1.26	0.36
Eastern	24	350	0.00	0.30	0.70	0.50	1.20	1.60
Central	114	84	1.00	0.50	0.10	2.20	13.50	1.90
Western	184	156	5.80	1.70	0.70	4.50	24.10	2.60
Sabaragamuwa	40	57	0.07	0.10	0.30	1.60	12.80	0.60
Uva	46	58	2.40	0.50	0.60	3.00	10.60	1.80
Southern	52	37	1.20	0.80	0.12	0.50	1.30	0.70

The type of farming practice and fertilizer use is another important facet in any research study concerning the regional distribution of nitrates. Further, drinking water wells located close to septic tanks, as in the case of Jaffna Peninsula also results in the increase of nitrate levels in the drinking water. Even though the relationship of nitrate levels in the ground water to the geographical distribution of cancer is yet to be firmly established, regional hydrogeochemical data on nitrates will aid the environmental geochemists and epidemiologists in their efforts at understanding the etiology of human cancer.

Problems of Iron Toxicity

Excessive iron in drinking water imparts an unpleasant taste making the water very often undrinkable. The presence of excessive quantities of iron in the soil and ground water also affects the crops as exemplified by severe iron toxicity in the paddy fields in the southern parts of Sri Lanka. The occurrence of iron in the ground water of Sri Lanka is largely controlled by the natural environment, the rocks and soils playing a significant role in the hydrogeochemical distribution of iron. Figure 7 illustrates the distribution of iron in the ground water of Sri Lanka and it is clearly observed that there are anomalously high concentrations of iron in the southwest sector of the island. As noted by Herath (1975), extensive bodies of laterites occur in

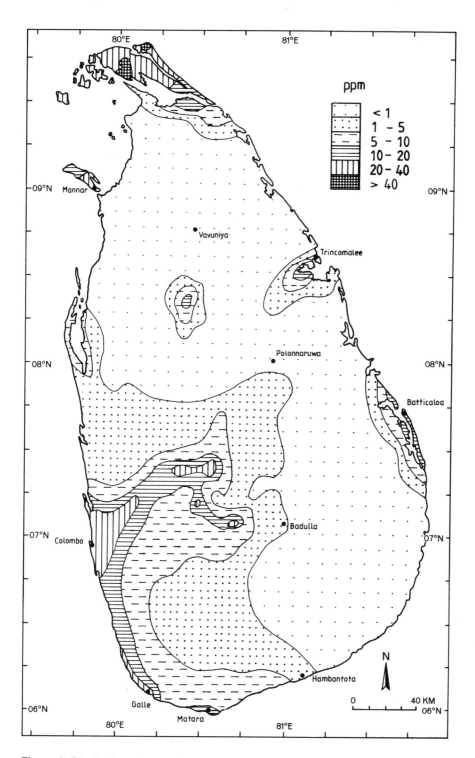

Figure 6. Distribution of nitrate ions in the ground water (Dissanayake and Weerasooriya, 1986).

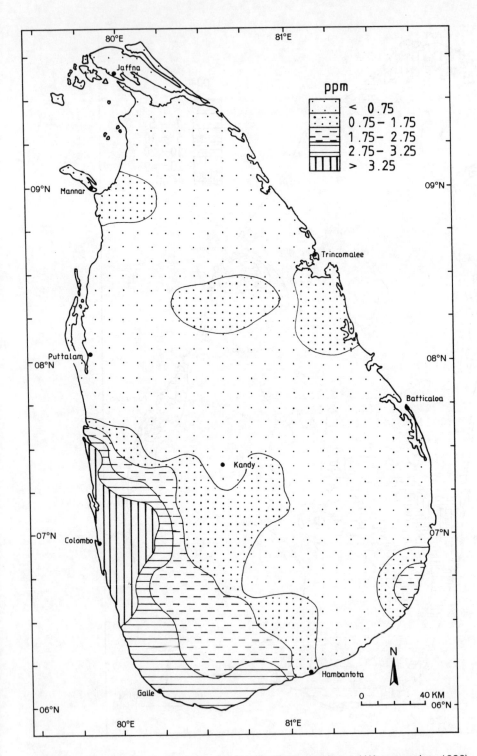

Figure 7. Distribution of iron in the ground water (Dissanayake and Weerasooriya, 1986).

502

in the district of Colombo and along the southwest coast up to Tangalle. Iron is a very common constituent of the laterites and it may accumulate in the ground water as a result of extensive leaching, since it is geochemically mobile under acidic conditions. Further, in the lateritic terrains there is a relatively shallow water table fluctuating markedly. Rain water may have an impact on ground water by its own composition as well as by liberation of components from the soil. Since, as in the case of most trace elements, the geochemical mobility is pH dependent, the slightly acidic nature of wet zone lateritic soils and the intensive rainfall favor the accumulation of iron in the ground water. In contrast, the water table in the dry zone is very deep - more than 50 m under surface. The alkaline soils in the dry zone largely immobilize the iron which form colloidal oxides and hydroacids. Maps showing the regional distribution of iron in the environment is of particular benefit in planning water supply schemes and plantations.

Conclusions

Even though geochemical atlases do not directly provide solutions to environmental problems, they can be of extreme use in providing baseline chemical data necessary for many environmentally related projects. The Hydrogeochemical Atlas of Sri Lanka is of use in a variety of disciplines, particularly in hydrology, epidemiology, river basin studies as exemplified by the Mahaweli project as well as in town and country planning.

Literature Cited

Bogovsky, P. 1972. The importance of the analysis of N-nitroso compounds in international research. *In* R. Bogovski, R. Preussman and E.J. Wackes, eds. *N.-nitroso Compounds Analysis and Formation,* Publication No. 3: 1-5. Lyon Intern. Agency for Research on Cancer.

Bowie, S.H.U. 1979. Introductory remarks to "Environmental Geochemistry and Health". *Phil. Trans. Roy. Soc. London* 288: 3-5.

Dissanayake, C.B. and S.V.R. Weerasooriya. 1985. A geochemical classification of ground water in Sri Lanka. *J. Nat. Sci. Counc. Sri Lanka* 13: 147-186.

Dissanayake, C.B. and S.V.R. Weerasooriya. 1986. *The Hydrogeochemical Atlas of Sri Lanka.* Natural Resources, Energy and Science Authority of Sri Lanka, Colombo.

Dissanayake, C.B. and S.V.R. Weerasooriya. 1987. Medical geochemistry of nitrates and human cancer. *Sri Lanka. Int. J. Env. Studies* 30: 145-156.

Dissanayake, C.B. 1991. The fluoride problem in the ground water of Sri Lanka - environmental management and health. *Int. J. Env. Studies* 38: 137-156.

Herath, J.W. 1975. *Mineral Resources of Sri Lanka.* Geo. Surv. Dept. Sri Lanka.

Magee, P. and J. Barnes. 1967. Carcinogenic nitroso compounds. *In* A. Haddow and S. Weinbourse, eds. *Advances in Cancer Research* 10: 163-246. Academic Press, New York.

Panabokke, R.G. 1984. The geographical pathology of malignant tumours in Sri Lanka - a five-year study. *Ceylon Med. J.* 29: 209-224.

Underwood, E.J. 1979. Trace elements and health, an overview. *Phil. Trans. Roy. Soc. London* 288: 5-14.

Warnakulasuriya, K.A.A., S. Balasuriya and P.A.J. Perera. 1987. Prevalence of denta-fluorosis in 4 geographic areas in Sri Lanka. *Soc. Med.* 10: 26-27.

Webb, J.S. and R.J. Howarth. 1979. Regional geochemical mapping. *Phil. Trans. Roy. Soc. London* 288: 81-93.

WHO (World Health Organizaton). 1982. *Guidelines for Drinking Water Quality*. Vol. 1. WHO, Geneva.

PAPER PRESENTATIONS

IV. MANAGEMENT ASPECTS
AND
ORGANIZATIONAL FRAMEWORK

Proceedings of the International and Interdisciplinary Symposium
ECOLOGY AND LANDSCAPE MANAGEMENT IN SRI LANKA
W. Erdelen, C. Preu, N. Ishwaran, C.M. Madduma Bandara (eds.)
Colombo, Sri Lanka, 12-26 March 1990
© 1993
Margraf Scientific Books, D-97985 Weikersheim
ISBN 3-8236-1182-8

Land Policy and Landscape Management in Sri Lanka

C.M. MADDUMA BANDARA

Abstract

Landscape management in Sri Lanka has been intimately associated with the evolution of land policy, particularly since the conquest of the hill country by the British, in the early part of the nineteenth century. The ecological implications of colonial land policies are relatively less well known compared with their economic and social consequences. It is argued that the continuation of the broad policy orientations of colonial times, even after national independence, has been a major cause of land degradation witnessed today in many parts of the country. The land policy of successive governments reflected in legislative enactments, such as the Encroachment Upon Crown Lands Ordinance (1840), the Land Development Ordinance (1935), the Crown Lands Ordinance (1947), the Paddy Lands Act (1958) and the Land Reform Law (1972, 1975) are examined with particular reference to their impact on ecology and landscape management in Sri Lanka. The low priority accorded to environmental concerns such as soil and forest conservation, in the implementation of relevant acts and ordinances, are highlighted. Problems and constraints in pursuing a long-term policy in resource management is examined in the context of a developing country like Sri Lanka where poverty and unemployment directly or indirectly lead to land degradation. In this regard attention is focused on areas prone to earthslips and coastal erosion as well as to encroachment by settlers.

Introduction

The term "land policy" is used to denote "major lines of public action designed to improve the use of land resources and the conditions of property rights under which people live and work on land" (Timmons, 1972). The question arises then; in whose domain lies the subject of land policy making? It also raises the issue of demarcating the roles and responsibilities of different groups actively involved in this vital area. Ours is a technobureaucratic world piloted by the politician. The scientists profess that they seek the truth and indicate only the options and potentials of their discoveries where necessary. It is generally thought that the politicians who claim to represent people make choices and set priorities. The bureaucrats maintain that once the directions are given from above they carry them out faithfully, often maintaining a golden silence before the public whom they are supposed to serve. This, however, is only a simplistic perception of roles and responsibilities of different groups involved in policy making, and the picture is much more complicated and mixed in real situations. Very often "priorities" also exist among scientists for research, and some politicians at least occasionally prefer to use facts. The bureaucrats not only serve their masters but often manipulate their thoughts and activities with a "yes minister" approach. In our model of democracy, therefore, policy making can often become everybody's responsibility but sometimes nobody's concern. In Sri Lanka, however, one of the more formal ways in which land policy had been directed in the past was through periodic Land Commissions. Thus the Land Commissions of 1927, 1958 and 1985 had considerable impact on the evolution of land policy in Sri Lanka.

Landscape Management

In the definition and clarification of the concept of landscape management, we owe a great debt to classical German scholarship in general and in particular to persons such as Alexander von Humboldt, Siegfried Passarge and Carl Troll. Landscape is an old word much popularized by Humboldt in his descriptions of the scenic landscapes in South America. Carl Troll (1968) who introduced the term "Landscape Ecology" gave a theoretical foundation for this concept. When Troll was asked what he meant by landscape ecology at an academic congregation in Holland, he said, it is not something really new. "It is just an attitude, an approach, a state of mind." Zonneveld (1981) maintained that landscape ecology is "considering the landscape from a conservation point of view." Landscape management is therefore very broadly the application of the findings of landscape ecology to meet the needs of society. In this context it essentially becomes an integral part of land policy. It is therefore obvious that any scientist, politician or entrepreneur who has the frame of mind to visualize the environment holistically to include all its abiotic and biotic components as a coherent system, and not treating them as separate components, could be a landscape ecologist or a landscape manager.

Sri Lanka's Land Policy - A Historical Perspective

Land policy at a given period of time in history reflects the attitude of mind of the different regimes in power. It is therefore possible to summarize the evolution of land policy in Sri Lanka to a few episodes which were dominated by different policy paradigms. The first is the period of sovereign rule during which a traditional land holding system operated under a monarchy. The vestiges of this system are still seen in the customary laws of inheritance and land tenure as in the case of temple lands. The king himself had the honorific titles of Bhupati, Bhumissara or Patavipati indicating his overlordship over the land. However, most historians agree that the role of the king which itself did not remain static was more of a trustee of land than its sole proprietor. With the spread of the doctrine of ahimsa (non-violence) the king and the country were generally guided by the words of Arhant Mahinda who brought buddhism to Sri Lanka in the third century B.C. In his first sermon he addressed the king and said "O great king! The animals who live on this land and the birds who fly over it have the same liberty as you enjoy to live and move freely over this land." Over the centuries this attitude towards nature became so entrenched in society that it was widely believed that those who establish forests and sanctuaries and provide water to the thirsty lands were on their way to the heavens.

The "age of conquest" which followed the indigenous rule, began to change the attitudes of people by subjecting them to alien values and norms. With the fall of the Kandyan Kingdom, the British introduced the concept of "crown lands" and enacted legislation to bring vast extents of lands under their control. The underlying attitude of the colonial regime was an exercise of the "right of conquest". Thus the Crown Lands Encroachment Ordinance of 1840 established the principle that "all forest, waste, unoccupied or uncultivated lands shall be presumed to be the property of the crown until the contrary thereof be proved." This legislation had the effect of bringing under direct Government control over 90% of the total land area of the country. The British knew at that time that land meant power.

The adverse social impacts of the enforcement of this legislation on the villages of the hill country are better known than its ecological impacts arising from denudation of the hills to aquire lands for plantation agriculture. It has been claimed, that over 4000 elephants were killed in the process by colonial sport-hunters. Tennent (1859) described the pre-plantation environment in the hills vividly: "The first ardent adventurers pioneered their way through pathless woods, and lived for months in log-huts whilst feeling the forest. The new life in the jungle was full of excitement and romance, the wild elephants retreated before the axe of the forester; the elk supplied their table with venison, the jungle fowl and the game were within call and abundant."

The policy of exploiting the riches of the land of Sri Lanka through plantation agriculture did undoubtedly bring much economic prosperity but its devastating ecological impacts were beginning to be felt within a few decades. Thus by 1873, the colonial government had to enact legislation for the preservation of the forests above an elevation of 1500 metres. Even with the introduction of such measures, and the development of many forest reserves and sanctuaries and the soil conservation efforts in the plantation sector, the hill country was never fully ecologically rehabilitated. The problems of landslides, soil erosion, siltation and social pressures generated by this land policy were demanding a change of mind of the colonial regime by the turn of the century. It contributed greatly to the historical phase of seeking roads to freedom by the indigenous leadership. The struggle for independence was therefore intimately associated with the need for change in land policy. Perera (1927), the Member for Kalutara in the State Council, in summarizing his motion to establish a select committee of the Council to review the colonial land policy predicted that "we shall once again have a land where the peasant and the freeman shall till his own lands." Sir Hugh Clifford then Governor of Ceylon taking note of such sentiments urged the Land Commission, established in 1927, to "devise effective means of enabling the peasants to gratify an ambition to own and till their own land."

The Land Commission of 1927 which represented the emerging local leadership had essentially become an instrument for the translation of the vision of "a prosperous, self respecting and self-supporting multitude of peasant proprietors" into reality. Its recommendations led to the enactment of the Land Development Ordinance of 1935, which guided a vigorous policy of colonization and village expansion, and even the emergence of a strong political movement. Today, nearly 30% of the people in this country live on land alienated through the procedures that can be traced back to the first Land Commission.

It may be argued that the concept of "crown land" or "crown property" which was essentially a colonial invention based on the "right of conquest" also had positive impacts on landscape management in Sri Lanka. The presence of a vast crown estate which was jealously guarded by the colonial regime left many areas outside the hill country and wet zone relatively undisturbed. The Crown Lands Encroachment Ordinance of 1840 in its preamble reflected the rigid attitude of the colonial regime towards any unlawful use of crown land. It stated that "diverse persons without any claim or pretence of title have taken possession of lands in this colony belonging to Her Majesty." During the passage to freedom this concept of "crown property" has transformed itself to a "crown trust". The Land Commission of 1927 thus observed that "crown land is held in trust for the whole community inhabiting this Island - that community which exists as well as generations yet unborn." They went on to say that "any government would therefore be falling grievously short of its duty if it neglected such a trust. Crown land is the invaluable capital of the community and as such must be conserved and administered by any government worth the name as a trust." There is hardly any doubt that these words are still as relevant and important today as it was in the 1920s. The land administration which came into existence in 1935, with the Land Commissioner as the custodian of all crown lands, carried this concept even to the extent of delaying the granting of freehold titles to generations of peasant farmers through fears of "improvident alienation".

The last episode in the evolution of land policy which covers the period after national independence in 1948, may appropriately be called an "age of politics". The first four decades of Independence witnessed a rapid politicization of the electorate and a series of changes of governments with the political pendulum swinging violently to the left and the right - a situation rarely experienced in many social democracies of the world. Ordinary politics had permeated into every aspect of national life, and land policy had also become part and parcel of political manipulation. A tendency to pursue policies which were perceived as bringing quick political returns that would give a "better political mileage" to parties seeking or in power, and an inclination to shy away from policies which were perceived to be less popular, however important they were to the long-term interests of the country, constituted the characteristic features of the "age of politics". On one hand, the State monopoly of land with over 80% of the total extent under the ultimate ownership of the State, continued to remain despite the accelerated land alienation programs. The nationalization of the plantation sector in the 1970s under the Land Reform Law added another 6% of private lands to the State ownership. Out of the total extent of nationalized lands only about 12% were eventually passed on to the landless peasants. On the other hand, landlessness among the peasantry continued to increase due to increasing population and the lack of access to available state lands and avenues of alternative employment. This resulted in large-scale encroachment of state lands by people mainly in search of land for housing and agriculture.

The State Land Encroachment Survey of 1979 revealed some startling figures indicating the magnitude of encroachments. It indicated that nearly 6% of the total area of the island had been encroached upon by well over half a million persons (Tab. 1, annexed). Some 24% of the encroached lands had permanent crops and buildings making it almost impossible to revert such lands back to State ownership, even if it was considered necessary. The largest extents of encroachments were in the dry zone districts such as Anuradhapura, Kurunegala and Moneragala, where State lands were readily available. In these districts village forests and other crown forests which came under the administration of Government Agents suffered most and have almost disappeared. The tank reservations for which there were hardly any customary legal definitions applied, were freely encroached. The chena cultivation, for which most of these encroachments were made, covered nearly 15% of the land area of the country by the early 1960s (Land Utilization Committee, 1967). Despite the restrictions imposed by the government on chena cultivation, the recent estimates of land under chena indicate that it has remained static or slightly increased.

It may be noted that a large proportion of lands that came under the Mahaweli Project were forest lands degraded by encroachments and illicit timber extraction before the project activities were commenced. Some of these areas, as in system B and C, are better protected under the project now than ever before. The most important process of land degradation through deforestation is encroachments for chena cultivation. The spread of encroachments is, on the one hand, a reflection of the increasing pressure of population on land and landlessness. On the other hand, it is facilitated by the sympathetic attitude towards the encroacher developed mainly during the "age of politics". Compared with the strict attitude during the colonial period towards

Table 2. Extents of land alienated by the State 1935-1985 (in hectares).

Major Colonization	175,941	21.17%
Village Expansion	357,239	42.99%
Highland Settlement	13,565	1.63%
Youth Settlement	7,964	0.95%
Regularization of Encroachments	205,762	24.76%
Middle Class Allotments	55,019	6.62%
Land Grants (Special Provisions)	9,980	1.20%
Rainfed Farming Settlements	5,363	0.64%
Total	830,833	100.00%

the encroacher as a violator of the law, he is now considered as a "pioneer" and an "enterprising" person even by the land administration which often chooses to follow the "path of least resistance". It might be noted that one of the three most important categories of land alienated by the government was encroachment regularization (others being major colonization schemes and village expansion) which, by 1985, accounted for 200,000 hectares (Tab. 2).

As the Secretary to the Ministry of Lands and Land Development in his adminstrative report for 1982 stated: "By 1977 the unauthorized occupation of state lands had reached gigantic and unmanageable proportions, the magnitude of which was such that even law abiding citizens preferred to believe that encroachment on state lands was the regular process to lay claim to a block of land." The suspension of the Land Kachcheri Procedure in the 1970s, aggravated the widening gap between supply and demand for land. The illicit occupation of state land by such large numbers of people invariably led to serious problems of landscape management.

Findings of the Land Commission - 1987

The third Land Commission having analyzed the land question up to the 1980s made the following major recommendations:

1. Over 80% of the total land area of Sri Lanka is under the ultimate ownership of the orientated to ensure a more realistic equilibrium in land
2. An extent of 2.5 million hectares, or nearly 40% of the land area could be developed but is virtually lying idle. The bulk is rainfed and in the dry zone. A new and pragmatic strategy is necessary to develop these lands.
3. Over 60% of the volume of litigation in our civil courts are related to land disputes. A program of registration of title to land will ease this situation considerably.
4. There is a need for allocation of land rationally among different users to increase productivity, to minimize landlessness and for the purposes of conservation.
5. The national urban system is a relic of the colonial past which was not intended to benefit the majority. It should be re-modelled to create a network of small towns rather than a smaller number of larger towns.
6. Many existing state-aided settlement schemes have become pockets of poverty and hot-beds of social discontent. Programs should be developed to attain a healthy mix of settlers with poor as well as not so poor persons.
7. the Land Kachcheri Procedure in alienating land for the needy should be strenghtenened.
8. A review the Agrarian Services Law is needed to safeguard the interests of agricultural laborers and small land owners so as to re-establish peace and harmony in the rural sector.
9. Ceilings on the ownership of private lands established by the Land Reform Law should continue.
10. Freehold status should be conferred to all residential lands provided by the State.

The present government has already taken action to follow up some of these recommendations of the Land Commission, indicated in 1, 2, 3, 4, 7 and 10 above. The establishment of the current "National Task Force on Land Alienation and Distribution" is a step taken to relieve social pressures generated by land hunger in an expeditious manner, particularly in the rural areas.

The Current Program of Land Alienation

The program of the National Task Force on Land Alienation and Distribution concerns ten major categories of land and services associated with their use:

1. Alienation of unused State land through divisional secretaries (approximately 200,000 ha)
2. Land vested in the Land Reform Commission (7000 ha)
3. Land belonging to plantation boards and corporations
4. Paddy lands vested in the Land Reform Commission (7500 ha)
5. An out-grower system in future commercial plantations.
6. Underutilized private land as per section 36 of the Agrarian Services Act (around 40,000 ha)
7. Above command land in the Mahaweli downstream areas
8. Regularization of encroachments
9. Lands that are voluntarily surrendered
10. Extension, input supplies, credit and other support services for the alienated lands.

Environmental Safeguards

The mandate for the establishment of the task force specifically provides for maintaining "environmental safeguards" in the land distribution program. Environmental safeguards indicate precautions that should be taken to prevent any harmful impacts on the environment. In practical terms this means the avoidance of certain environmentally sensitive or fragile areas from being allocated for agriculture or housing or other development purposes. Accordingly stream reservations, land with steep slopes and ecologically sensitive areas of the coastal zone are avoided from being alienated. The existing laws provide to a considerable extent the necessary legal backing for the preservation of such environmentally sensitive areas although their enforcement has not always been satisfactory.

There are also areas where the written or customary laws do not clearly provide satisfactory definitions for the land surveyors involved in identifying reservation lands on ground. An example is provided by the tanks in the dry zone which are faced with increasing problems of siltation due to deforestation and agricultural activities in the watersheds. But then there appears to be hardly any practical definition of areas that should be reserved as watersheds for the reservoirs, as in the case of tank-bund reservations.

Many tanks in the dry zone are organized into cascades within micro-catchments (Fig. 1; Madduma Bandara, 1985). The preservation of their watersheds is therefore of vital importance to their lifespan and efficiency. In the past, the remaining natural forest cover in the catchments, as seen from early aerial photographs provided adequate protection. However, the increasing incidence of chena cultivation, encroachments and unplanned alienation of lands to the public led to deforestation of watershed areas. The tavalu (or tank-bed cultivation) which had become a permanent feature in some areas had encroached into the jala gilma (or inundation area at the full supply level), and in most villages the yaya (paddy tract) of an upper village runs into the water-spread of the downstream tank.

The irrigation authorities try to maintain a narrow reservation belt below the bunds for their protection. This is reported to be 15 times the height of the bund. However, not much attention has been paid to the protection of the tank catchment area above the water-spread. In order to protect the tanks from excessive siltation, it is necessary to reserve and leave under forest cover at least the area below the contour equivalent to the elevation of the crest of the bund. The irrigation authorities have obviously failed to preserve this area from encroachment, tavalu or chena cultivation, and even from haphazard land alienation exercises. Unless some effective action is taken to restore tank reservations, dry zone tanks will cease to perform a useful role in times to come.

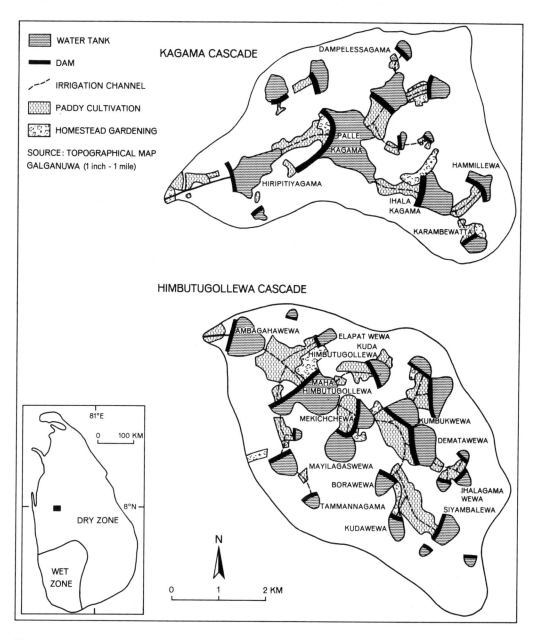

Figure 1. Cascades of village irrigation tanks in the dry zone.

The same situation prevails regarding the stream reservations provided for under the Crown Lands Ordinance. It has been observed that many recent landslides in the hill country are linear in form along streams indicating the inevitable consequence of neglect of establishing and maintaining stream reservations (Land Commission, 1989).

Challenges for the Future

The greatest challenge for landscape management in Sri Lanka lies in the formulation of a rational land use policy. Such a policy should aim at optimizing the use of available land resources by not only ensuring a high level of productivity but also at maintaining their sustainability and conserving a substantial portion of them for the generations yet unborn. In a rational land use policy each type of use has to justify its use in terms of the greatest national advantage. The questions of what proportion of land should be reserved for natural forest or what should be devoted to wildlife conservation have to be addressed in a rational rather than a political or parochial way.

A second challenge lies in the reconciliation of short-term needs with long-term planning, which is often necessary in the case of natural resources management. Economic and social development planning is predominantly "present-orientated" and tends to discount the future at too high a rate. The medium-term investment programs in Sri Lanka clearly bring out the short-term nature of development planning implicitly based on the average lifespan of governments and the low priority accorded to environmental considerations. One of the encouraging features of the present system of government is the placing of the Central Environmental Authority within the Ministry of Policy Planning, which would hopefully make possible the incorporation of environmental considerations into national policy making. However, different functions related to different aspects of the environment continue to be handled by a plethora of other departments and corporations.

A continuing challenge for landscape management in Sri Lanka is the ineffective enforcement of available legislation and the lukewarm attitude of the authorities to environmental issues. In a critique of the management of natural disasters under the title "Wrath of gods or the responsibility of men", the author stressed the failure of State authorities in developing long-term strategies to combat such problems (Madduma Bandara, 1989). Thus the destruction of forest reserves and illicit timber felling goes on unabated. Very often there are hardly any parliamentarians to raise these issues in the legislature. In these circumstances, I often wondered whether the time has come for the emergence of a "Die Grünen" or an ecological party in Sri Lanka, to safeguard the interests of the environment. Let us leave it for the new generation to decide.

Literature Cited

Clifford, H. 1927. *Some Reflections on the Ceylon's Land Question*. Address to the Second Annual Agricultural Conference. Govt. Press, Colombo.

Crown Lands Encroachment Ordinance of 1840. Govt. Press, Colombo.

Crown Lands Ordinance of 1947. Govt. Press, Colombo.

Land Commissions. 1927, 1955, 1985. *Interim and Final Reports*. Govt. Press, Colombo.

Land Development Ordinance of 1935. Govt. Press, Colombo.

Land Utilization Committee 1967. Sessional Paper No. XI of 1968. Govt. Press, Colombo.

Madduma Bandara, C.M. 1985. Catchment ecosystems and village tank cascades in the dry zone of Sri Lanka. *In* J. Lundqvist, U. Lohm and M. Falkanmark, eds. *Strategies for River Basin Development*, pp. 99-113. Reidel Publishing Company, Germany.

Madduma Bandara, C.M. 1989. Recent Natural Disasters - Wrath of Gods or Responsibility of Men. *Econ. Rev.* 2: 1-5.

Ministry of Lands and Land Development. 1983. Administrative Report of the Secretary. Govt. Press, Colombo.

Perera, E.W. 1927. Legislative Council Debates, 3rd March, 1927. Govt. Press, Colombo.

Troll, C. 1968. Landschaftsökologie. *In* R. Tüxen, ed. *Pflanzensoziologie und Landschaftsökologie,* pp. 1-21. Junk Publ. The Hague.

Timmons, J.F. 1972. Building a land policy. *In* J.F. Timmons and A.W. Murray, eds. *Land Problems and Policies.* Arno Press, New York.

Zonneveld, I.E.S. 1981. Land(scape) ecology: A science or a state of mind. *In* S.P. Tjallingi and A.A. de Veer, eds. *Perspectives in Landscape Ecology.* Centre for Agricultural Publishing and Documentation, Wageningen, The Netherlands.

Table 1. Survey of encroachments on State lands in 1979. Data from MILD (1983) Resource Development 1978-1982.

Province	Number of Encroachments	Extent of land encroached	Land Use in Encroachments					
			Extent under Paddy Cultivation	Extent under Other Crops	Extent Uncultivated	Extent with Buildings	Extent under Other Crops Permanent Cultivation	Extent of Reservations Encroached
Western	28,136	8,973	646	1,207	1,125	132	5,674	2,065
Central	34,543	15,953	2,732	6,668	3,229	257	1,848	4,979
Southern	74,665	31,128	3,780	7,646	8,798	349	43,712	5,960
Northern	47,903	42,214	10,811	13,955	14,921	707	1,005	4,251
Eastern	92,641	71,779	39,239	8,597	14,690	1,306	2,420	8,009
North Central	107,656	70,105	22,772	18,881	24,460	621	3,014	12,601
Northwestern	111,868	78,688	11,343	30,697	21,655	544	14,221	10,283
Sabaragamuwa	37,299	16,603	1,069	7,477	3,565	278	6,447	3,402
Uva	70,600	45,918	6,578	19,892	11,852	896	6,890	4,124
Total	605,302	381,361	98,970	115,020	104,295	5,092	85,231	55,674

Proceedings of the International and Interdisciplinary Symposium
ECOLOGY AND LANDSCAPE MANAGEMENT IN SRI LANKA
W. Erdelen, C. Preu, N. Ishwaran, C.M. Madduma Bandara (eds.)
Colombo, Sri Lanka, 12-26 March 1990
© 1993
Margraf Scientific Books, D-97985 Weikersheim
ISBN 3-8236-1182-8

Management Strategy for a Relatively Undisturbed Coral Reef System in Sri Lanka

A. DE ALWIS AND A. RAJASURIYA

Abstract

During the past few years impacts of several coastal development activities have led to a growing awareness of the economic importance as well as the vulnerability of the reefs around Sri Lanka. Many reefs, fringing a major part of the southern coastline, have been subjected to heavy damage by the tourist industry, destructive fishing methods, coral mining for lime production and pollution from land-based industries. Strategies and plans for the sustainable use of coral reef areas and their resources are urgently needed. In 1940, the Hikkaduwa rocky islets, situated approximately 500 m offshore, together with the Ambalangoda rocky islets, were declared sanctuaries under the Fauna and Flora Protection Ordinance with the intention of protecting seabird colonies nesting on these islets. In 1961 and subsequently in 1979, the coral reefs off Hikkaduwa were also brought under the protection of the same ordinance. These protection measures have not been successful in protecting the reef, particularly after the area was developed as a tourist resort. The concept of strict protection cannot be strictly applied to reefs around Sri Lanka. The management of those coral reefs will necessarily have to involve coastal communities and supply their resource needs at a sustainable level. Recent reef investigations carried out in the southern coastal region by the National Aquatic Resources Agency (NARA) indicate that the fringing reefs of Unawatuna Bay, a coastal indentation which is located adjacent to the Port of Galle, are relatively pristine and could be one of the last nearshore reefs remaining more or less "natural". A high diversity of marine organisms, fish and coral species makes this bay a unique ecosystem. However, Unawatuna Bay has been utilized for generations for commercial purposes such as small-scale fishing and, more recently, for tropical fish collection and tourism. Therefore, such an area cannot be converted into a strict marine sanctuary without considerable opposition from the users of the area. Instead, the resources of the sea and the land area of the bay should be maintained through effective management so that the ability of resources to renew themselves is never jeopardized. This can be achieved by converting the area into a "Multiple-Use Marine Reserve", under the supervision of a Reserve Authority.

517

Introduction

During the past few years there has been a growing awareness of the economic importance as well as a deep concern about the vulnerability of coral reefs in the wake of coastal development activities. Many coral reefs fringing a major part of the southern coastline of Sri Lanka have been subjected to heavy damage due to coral mining, removal of marine organisms for export, tourist related activities and destructive fishing methods. In addition, pollution from land-based sources and cottage industries such as retting coconut husks in lagoons have taken a heavy toll on the coral reefs in the southern part of the island (De Silva 1985a, Premaratne 1984, De Silva 1987).

Reef investigations carried out by the National Aquatic Resources Agency (NARA) in the southwestern coastal region have indicated that the coral reefs of Unawatuna are still in a comparatively undisturbed state, and that these reefs are some of the last nearshore coral reefs that need conservation. Observations of marine animals such as dolphins, turtles and whale sharks in the shallow areas of the bay and the occurrence of diverse populations of fish and corals in the area also makes this a very unique ecosystem. However, the reefs of Unawatuna have been utilized by the people of the area for generations for commercial purposes and for sustenance. Therefore, this coastal sector cannot be converted into a strict marine sanctuary without encountering considerable opposition from the people living in the area. Instead, the resources of the reef and the adjacent land area of Unawatuna should be maintained through effective management so that the resources retain their ability to renew themselves. It may be possible to achieve this by converting the area into a "Multiple-Use Marine Reserve" (De Silva 1985a, Anon. 1986).

A Multiple-Use Marine Reserve at Unawatuna will not only serve the primary conservation objectives such as maintaining a sample ecosystem and conserving genetic resources but will also be a replenishment area for the region providing facilities for education, research and environmental monitoring. Moreover, such a reserve can also produce protein and animal products on a sustainable basis, and it will also be an asset to recreation and a major attraction to tourists as plans are already underway by the Government to develop the Galle District, to which the Unawatuna Coral Reefs belong.

The present survey of the Unawatuna area aims at formulating guidelines for a "Multiple-Use Marine Reserve" with the primary aim of conserving the marine life. The surveys have been carried out to assess the quality of the coral reef and its resource potential, to assess and predict the effects of both natural and human-induced activities on the resources of the Unawatuna area, to establish limits for the use of the reef by humans, to identify priorities for management needs, to determine the boundaries of the reserve and a buffer zone and to formulate a management plan.

Materials and Methods

Initial Surveys

Between January and February 1988, initial surveys were carried out to obtain data about the land features and the bathymetric situation of the respective areas. These surveys conducted with the assistance of the National Hydrographic Office of NARA should provide background information for the determination of both the boundaries of the planned marine reserve and the surrounding buffer zone.

Reef Surveys

During regular visits (once a month) in the non-monsoonal period investigations were carried out along the coastal sector within and outside the reef lagoon up to Mihiripenna. Snorkel

518

diving was used in waters less than 3 m deep. In areas of deeper water (up to 29 m) scuba diving equipment was used. In addition, surface tows with a diver on a tow rope were employed for quick observations in areas with a depth of 10-12 m. Fish, coral and other dominant organisms were observed and recorded.

Socioeconomic Surveys

Data on touristic activities and the situation of fisheries as well as on general socioeconomic patterns related to the Unawatuna reef area were obtained from field observations and from interviews of officials of the Ministry of Fisheries, fishermen, villagers, tropical fish collectors and owners of hotels, restaurants and guest houses. Between October 1987 and August 1988, activities of the "area users" were monitored once a month (except for November, April, May and June) for a continuous period of 3-5 days including weekends. During these periods the number of foreigners and Sri Lankans indulging in recreational activities such as swimming, snorkeling, scuba diving, fishing and sunbathing were observed between 8 am and 5 pm and recorded at intervals of two hours.

Observations and Results

Reef Condition

The major reef areas, particularly nearshore as well as the rocky outcrops of Godagala, Deumbagala and the submerged Bellows Reef, are subjected to strong wave action, currents and frequently changing sea conditions throughout the year. As the areas of good coral growth are located close to or well within the wave zones or in areas where strong currents prevail, it was not possible to apply transect or quadrat methods to estimate living and dead coral cover. The area was therefore divided into 10 sections on the basis of reef type and experience gathered from other surveys. In each section the reef condition, particularly the area covered by coral and the status of a particular reef section, was estimated visually. Subsequently, these qualitative results were listed on an arbitrary scale ranging from 0%, i.e. dead reef, to 100%, i.e. reef in optimal condition, and subdivided into the categories as shown in Table 1: very poor (0%-10%), poor (11%-25%), fair (26%-50%), good (51%-75%), and excellent (76% -100%).

Table 1. Living coral cover (in %) in the study area (see text for details).

Reef sector	Coral	On sandstone reefs	On rocky reefs	Sandstone /rock
1	76-100			
2	0-10			
3	51-75			
4				0-10
5			0-10	
6		11-25		
7				0-10
8			11-25	
9	11-25			
10			0-10	

Reef Structure

The reef structures of Unawatuna can be divided into the categories viz. coral reefs, sandstone reefs and crystalline rock reefs referred to hereafter as boulder reefs (Fig. 1). Coral reefs are found only in reef sections 1, 3 and 9. Sandstone reefs are found in section 6 and 8. Boulder reefs occur in section 5 and 10. Sandstone structures wedged among crystalline rocks are found in section 4 and 7. Section 2 contains coral rubble (mainly dead *Acropora*). (Fig. 1). The percentage of live coral cover in each section is given in Table 1, and the sedimentology of the reef area is shown in Figure 1.

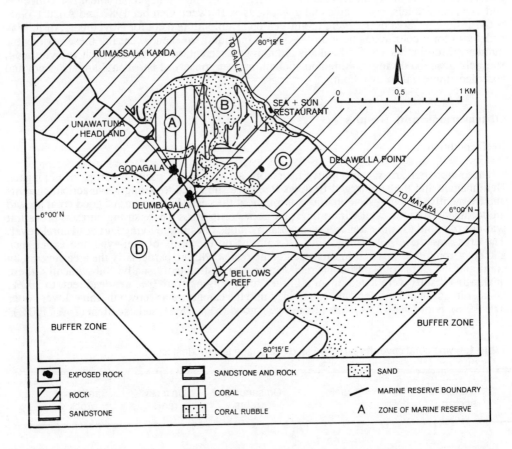

Figure 1. Sedimentology and zonation of the marine reserve (southwest coast of Sri Lanka).

Distribution of Corals

In the nearshore area, living coral reefs are found at the eastern and western ends and are built of a variety of different coral species. Massive rounded species such as Favids and branched types *Pocillopora* and *Acropora* dominate the reef crest. On the outer slope of these areas many finely branched and foliaceous species of corals such as *Echinopora* and *Montipora* predominate. The area between these reefs constitute dead corals, mainly coral rubble (*Acropora*) which support small live coral colonies indicating coral recruitment on dead corals.

In the reef lagoon, massive coral reefs of species such as *Favia* and *Favites* prevail in addition to large colonies of fire coral (*Millepora*). Coral reef growth is relatively good in the areas northwest of the rocky outcrops of Godagala and Deumbagala and is comparable to the nearshore coral reefs at the western end of the study area. Extensive sandstone reefs stretching as far as Habaraduwa are found on the eastern side of the rocky outcrops. These sandstone reefs are mostly covered with different species of soft corals as well as hard corals. In addition, several varieties of Antipatharians including black corals and sea whips, are found in the area. Beyond the rocky outcrops only a few hermatypic corals have been found. This area is characterized by debris, mostly large boulders, and covered only partly by a few coral colonies.

Distribution of Flora

The area between the rocky outcrops of Godagala and the nearshore coral reef contains an area of calcareous algae species of the genus *Halimeda*. Sea grasses as well as small patches of *Halimeda* are found in the inner reef area at the eastern end in front of the Sun and Sea Restaurant.

Faunal Diversity

The faunal diversity of the area is very high. 52 species of hard corals assignable to 41 genera were recorded. Two groups of soft corals have also been recorded belonging to the genera *Sarcophyton* and *Dendronephthya*. Fish diversity in the area was as high as 192 species assignable to 102 genera. In addition to fish and corals, 12 species of echinoderms, 22 species of molluscs and 12 species of crustaceans were recorded. Within the reef lagoon large schools of bluestripe herrings (*Herklotsichthys quadrimaculatus*) were frequently observed during the months of October, December, March and July. The occurrence of these fish in the study area seems to differ seasonally.

Fishing Activities

Various fishing activities are known to this area which concentrate on the catching of fish and lobster and the collecting of ornamental fish. Not only traditional techniques such as netting, fishing with hook and line or stilt fishing are applied, but also nearly one hundred mechanized and non-mechanized fishing crafts, i.e. wooden or fibreglass catamarans and fibreglass boats, operate from Unawatuna. Angling with hook and line and the use of cast nets is carried out in nearshore areas. The fishermen beach their catamarans and boats in the bay and they operate between the nearshore reefs of the bay and the open sea in areas up to 10 km from the coast. The gear utilized in deep waters of more than 40 m is a gill net (drift type). Net fishing is practiced only between October and April.

Both ornamental fish collecting and lobster fishing have become profitable industries in the area, and nearly 50 persons are engaged in these two activities. In shallow waters, tropical fish and lobsters are caught by snorkel divers, whereas scuba divers operate in deeper waters. Additionally, a small type of cast net termed "moxy" is used which should be prohibited because these nets destroy the coral patches and reefs. The divers of Unawatuna operate mainly in the study area. However, problems of encroachment occur when they dive in adjacent areas where divers from those areas operate.

Table 2. Monthly distribution of the average numbers of foreigners and Sri Lankans engaged in recreational activities in the study area.

Month	Foreigners	Sri Lankans
October	68	100
December	120	215
January	115	200
February	150	180
March	188	113
July	70	32
August	40	25

Tourist Dependent Facilities at Unawatuna

The number of both foreigners and Sri Lankans visiting the study area and their engagement in different kinds of touristic activities varied from month to month in the study area during the monitoring period (Tabs. 2, 3). The highest pressure on the study area deriving from recreational activities was recorded in the period between December and March. There is a great number of tourist facilities available in the coastal area of Unawatuna (Tab. 4). There may be discrepancies between the figures given here and those of the Ministry of Tourism, as different criteria are used to define the establishments. In addition, a large number of people are employed to service these tourist facilities and about 20-25 vendors work in the area selling batiks, curios, costume jewellery, etc, to tourists on the beach.

Table 3. Monthly distribution of the average numbers of people engaged in touristic activities in the study area.

Month	Tourist activities					
	Swimming & Bathing	Snorkeling	Scuba diving	Wind Surfing	Sunbathing	Fishing
October	86	16	6	3	40	-
December	118	15	10	8	120	12
January	92	80	12	4	70	3
February	122	45	4	5	135	6
March	142	30	-	7	108	1
July	35	10	-	-	52	-
August	23	8	-	-	29	2

Table 4. Number of tourist facilities in the area.

Tourist facility	Number
Guest houses	15
Restaurants	9
Hotel Resorts	1
Hotels	3
Rooms	4
Cabanas	6
Batik shops	6
Jewellery shops	8
Others (curio shops, grocery)	6

Occurrence of Rare Marine Animals

During the reef surveys a mixed pod of dolphins (common and striped) were observed about 500 m off the beach well within the area between Bellows Reef and Dalawella Point. A small whale shark (*Rhiniodon typus*) with a length of 5-6 m was also sighted. In addition, turtles were encountered frequently in the reef lagoon.

Additional Observations

Collection of coral fragments for lime production in kilns was observed in two places. Small-scale coral mining occurs at Mihiripenna where a lime kiln operates within the coastal zone. Removal of coral from the reef to be sold as souvenirs was observed at Dalawella.

A place for retting coconut husks was found close to Dalawella Point, however, this was not carried out on a large scale. Apart from those areas where the vegetation was removed for the construction of hotels, restaurants, and other tourist facilities, coastal vegetation seems to be still intact along most of this coastal stretch. The canal reaching the reef lagoon at its western corner collects freshwater during the non-monsoonal period when its mouth is closed and retting of coconut husks in parts of the canal leads to major pollution of this water body. A steady runoff of this stagnant freshwater debouches directly into the reef lagoon when the mouth of the canal is opened during the period of the heavy SW monsoonal rain polluting the reef lagoon.

Recommendations for the Establishment of a "Multiple Use Marine Reserve"

The area of Unawatuna has been utilized by the villagers for generations in various ways for fishing, beaching of boats and collecting of marine organisms, etc. Therefore, it is not practical and advisable to establish a strict marine sanctuary, as a total prohibition of certain activities would deprive the users of their livelihood. Therefore, the establishment of a "Multiple-Use Marine Reserve" is more prudent and realistic and at the same time would have a number of advantages. As an area protected in such a way, Unawatuna could be a potential attraction to tourists. An effective public awareness program should be carried out using the protected area as an "outdoor classroom". This site could also be used as a training center for scientists interested in coral reef ecosystems. People presently involved in collecting ornamental fish, lobster catching, destroying coral reefs or carrying out any other activities that harm the natural ecosystem, could be employed as tour guides, park wardens, boat operators, etc.

Zonation of the Marine Reserve

Based on the present investigation, the proposed marine reserve should be divided into four zones in which different activities are permitted (Fig. 1, Tab. 5). A buffer zone should surround the marine reserve and should extend landwards up to 300 m from the mean landward boundary of the coastal zone according to Sri Lankan law. Fishing activities that are harmful to the marine life of the reserve such as the use of drift nets, bottom set nets and certain types of commercial establishments should not be allowed in the buffer zone.

Zone A with its living corals and *Halimeda* banks east of the Godagala reef can be used for research and education. Zone B, covering the area between Unawatuna Beach Resort, the Sun and Sea Restaurant at the eastern end of the bay, the eastern end of the Godagala Reef and the eastern end of Deumbagala consists of sandstone reefs, living corals and a considerable amount of dead corals in the center. Boats should be permitted in this area of the bay and are also allowed over the sandy area at the center of Zone B. Zone C covers the area between the Sun and Sea Restaurant and Dalawela Point. The seaward limit is from the eastern tip of Deumbagala Reef to Bellows Reef. Sandstone and rock boulders are the major sediment types of this zone. The limits of this zone conform to the boundaries of the reserve excluding Zones A, B and C. The substrate consists mainly of sand, sandstone and rock boulders.

Table 5. Permitted and prohibited activities for the proposed "Multiple-Use Marine Reserve" (# = banned, P = permit needed, X = allowed, - = allowed under supervision).

Activities	Zone A	Zone B	Zone C	Zone D	Buffer Zone
Hook and line	#	P	P	P	P
Cast nets	#	P	P	P	P
Bottom set nets	#	#	#	#	#
Spear fishing	#	#	#	#	#
Rod and reel	#	P	P	P	P
Collection of spiny lobsters (pots)	#	#	#	P	P
Collecting of lobsters by hand	#	#	#	P	P
Tropical fish collecting	#	#	P	P	P
Recreational Swimming and Bathing	X	X	X	X	X
Wind Surfing	#	X	X	X	X
Snorkeling	-	-	-	-	-
Scuba diving	-	-	-	-	P
Glass-bottom boat	#	P	P	P	P

Proposed Boundaries of Marine Reserve and Buffer Zone

The northwest landward boundary of the marine reserve should be about 100 m northwest of the Unawatuna Headland at the southeastern tip of the Rumassala Kanda Cliffs and should extend as far as Mihiripenna Point as the landward boundary to the southeast. The seaward boundary forming a quadrat should stretch about 1 km in a southwesterly direction to 06°00'N and 80°14'E in the northwest and about 3 km in a southwesterly direction to 05°59'N and 80°15'E in the southeast. In the northwest, the boundary of the surrounding buffer zone should be located at Watering Point and should be extended from here about 2.5 km in a southwesterly direction to 06°00'N amd 80°13'E. In the southeast, this boundary should stretch from Talpe about 4.2 km to 05°58'N and 80°15'E. However, a land strip extending from high water sea level landwards with a width of 300 m between Watering Point and Talpe should be included in the buffer zone (Fig. 2).

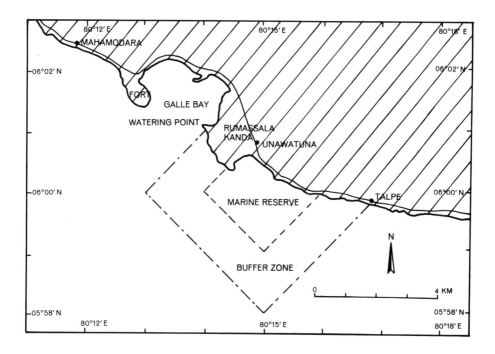

Figure 2. Location of marine reserve and buffer zone (southwest coast of Sri Lanka).

Immediate Measures

The following immediate measures in establishing the proposed marine reserve should be taken on a priority basis; (1) the declaration of the "Unawatuna Multiple-Use Marine Reserve" and the establishment of an authority for its management, (2) zoning of the "Multiple-Use Marine Reserve" based on the guidelines suggested above, (3) establishment of the Marine Reserve Headquarters, (4) conduction of a public awareness program in the area to educate people in aspects such as value of resources and their managed exploitation, (5) stopping of any further commercial construction activities in the coastal zone, (6) immediate prohibition of destructive fishing methods such as dynamiting, etc. (7) banning of coral mining and of the removal of coral to be sold as souvenirs, (8) construction of artificial reefs (tyres, old barges, etc.) in the eastern sector of the buffer zone for the development of alternative fishing grounds within and outside the buffer zone.

Marine Reserve Regulations

1. The administration of the proposed marine reserve should be invested in an authority established for the purpose. The administrative authority should necessarily consists of the

Table 6. Extractive uses.

Present activities	Impacts	Remedial measures
1. Fishing (hook and line)	Not known	Needs to be controled and allowed only in designated areas with permit
2. Fishing (rod and reel)	Not known	Needs to be controled and allowed only in designated areas
3. Spear fishing (snorkeling and scuba diving)	Depletion of large fish numbers	Should not be allowed within the reserve boundaries or in the buffer zone
4. Collection of live marine organisms for export	Damage to reef structure depletion of reef fish and other organisms	Should be discouraged, needs careful control and to be carried out only in designated areas under supervision and only under permit
5. Collection of spiny lobsters (snorkeling and Scuba diving, mainly night diving)	Severe depletion of stocks	Should be discouraged, needs careful control and to be carried out under supervision and with permit in designated areas only
6. Collection of spiny lobster lobster (pots).	Not noticed in the area	This method should be used instead of hand collecting
7. Fishing with explosives around the perimeter of the buffer zone for pelagic stocks.	Not known	Complete ban
8. Collection of corals and shells to be sold as souvenirs	Severe damage to reef in certain areas and depletion of stocks	Complete ban
9. Coral mining (live coral and beach washed) for construction	Damage to reef and loss of beach material mainly at Dalawella and at Mihiripenna	Complete ban

following: Ministry of Fisheries and Aquatic Resources, National Aquatic Resources Agency, Department of Wildlife, Department of Coast Conservation, AGA Office, Habaraduwa village committee consisting of fishermen, marine organism collectors, hoteliers, etc, and the Tourist Board.

2. The permitted and banned activities identified for each zone (Tabs. 5-7) should be strictly adhered to. All assistance should be provided to the reserve rangers to implement the regulations.
3. The entry of any boats into the lagoon reef may be allowed through all zones other than zone A. However, mooring buoys need to be provided for boats at locations away from coral areas.
4. Issue of permits for various activities (Tabs. 6, 7) has to be done by the authorities. Priority should be given to people who are already involved in the activities and who utilize resources of the marine reserve area.

Table 7. Non-extractive uses.

Present activities	Impacts	Remedial measures
1. Construction (tourist establishments)	Encroachment onto beach	Unauthorized structures to be removed
2 Diver damage due to underwater recreational diving	Some minor damage	Underwater tours to be conducted under supervision
3. Reef walking	No damage observed	Prohibit walking in protected reef areas
4. Damage by boats and their anchors	Minimum damage by boat anchors	Boat moorings to be provided and boats to operate only in permitted areas

Acknowledgments

The authors wish to thank the Chairman and the Director General of NARA. We also wish to thank the members of the coral reef research unit of NARA, Mr. P. Weerakkody, Mr. L. Ginige and Mr. C. Meedeniya for assisting in the reef surveys and the National Hydrographic Office NARA for mapping the reef areas.

Literature Cited

Anon. 1986. *The management of coastal habitats in Sri Lanka.* Report of a workshop held at the Sri Lanka Foundation Institute: 4-7.

De Silva, M.W.R.N. 1985a. Status of the coral reefs of Sri Lanka. *5th International Coral Reef Congress, Tahiti, 27th May-1st June 1985.*

De Silva, M.W.R.N. 1985b. A strategy for the management of coral reefs. *Proc. Symp. Endangered Marine Animals and Marine Parks* 1985: 440-447.

De Silva, M.W.R.N. 1987. *Effect of the tourist industry on coral reefs at Hekkaduwa, Sri Lanka.* Report submitted to IDRC.

Premaratne, A. 1984. *Socioeconomic survey of the coral mining industry on the southeastern coast of Sri Lanka.* Report of the Coast Construction Department, Sri Lanka.

Proceedings of the International and Interdisciplinary Symposium
ECOLOGY AND LANDSCAPE MANAGEMENT IN SRI LANKA
W. Erdelen, C. Preu, N. Ishwaran, C.M. Madduma Bandara (eds.)
Colombo, Sri Lanka, 12-26 March 1990
© 1993
Margraf Scientific Books, D-97985 Weikersheim
ISBN 3-8236-1182-8

Some Alternative Land Use Plans for Sri Lanka's North Central Dry Zone

C.D. GANGODAWILA

Abstract

Modern technology, related to all aspects of man's exploitation of natural resources, has now advanced to a point that man's potential to indiscriminantly disrupt environmental processes and degrade their 'quality' is increasing. Such a situation is clearly evident in Sri Lanka's north central dry zone where the traditional agricultural production systems have been increasingly disturbed due to rising population pressure, changing socioeconomic and poltitical conditions and promotion of inappropriate technology for land development and "settled" agriculture. Indicators and trends point to environmental degradation and overutilization of the scarce physical resource base. A conceptional basis for an alternative land use planning approach for these areas is suggested, emphasizing the need to integrate traditional wisdom and modern thinking in the overall development and use of land resources.

Introduction

With regard to its role as a major area of food production in the country, the north central dry zone of Sri Lanka presently faces more challenging problems than ever before. During the past few decades numerous land use policies and associated land development programs have been introduced to increase production. The area's inherently fragile agricultural resource base appears to have been subjected to increasing pressure, and this has been reflected in indicators of environmental degradation. These may suggest that the area has reached or passed the safe limits for the extensification of agricultural production.

In fact, the response of the area to the twin problems of land scarcity and population pressure during the past few decades has been to extend agricultural production on a more or less fixed resource base. The vital question now is whether this growth in agricultural production, and even the resource base itself can be maintained in a sustainable and environmentally sound manner in the face of emerging land degradation.

529

Agricultural scientists presently experimenting on farming systems for the non-irrigable highlands of the north central dry zone have increasingly begun to recognize the ecological and agronomic strengths of traditional practices, since they often exemplify careful management of soil, water and nutrients which are precisely the methods required to make modern high input farming practices sustainable. The sustainability of many traditional farming practices is well known to be linked to the "ecological models" they follow, viz. intercropping, agroforestry, shifting cultivation and crop rotations, mimic natural ecological processes (Wolf, 1987). The use of such natural analogues served as a conceptual basis in the formulation and design of alternative land use plans or spatial land use models for the north central dry zone.

Methods

A number of methods have been applied during the investigations in order to examine the current basic structure, the spatial and temporal characteristics of land use change as well as the factors affecting them. In order to relate the present situation to that of the past, a thorough literature survey was undertaken, so that past trends regarding land use and environmental impacts were well understood at the onset of these investigations. The mapping of land use and land degrading features has been carried out with the help of the aerial photographic coverage available for the area between 1956 and 1982, and have been supplemented with field studies undertaken between 1983 and 1988.

Empirical studies have been carried out based on importance and magnitude of the problem. In this respect, "bench-mark" soil salinity surveys within the Mahaweli 'H' area were carried out with a view to understanding the nature and intensity of salinity and alkalinity increases in these newly irrigated lands. Of particular interest were the sites of old tank beds that had been eventually converted to lowland rice land, in order to increase the irrigated land area for the large-scale irrigation technology introduced there. Such surveys were also extended to cover areas under the traditional small-scale irrigation systems by considering the Nachchaduwa Tank Catchment located within the Malwatu Oya Basin. Laboratory investigations of soil salinity were done using the techniques and definitions of the US Salinity Laboratory Staff (USDA, 1969).

Results

The results are presented as maps and sketches (Figs. 1-7, annexed). They show the results of the present investigations on spatial changes that occurred over the past few decades in the north central dry zone landscape. Table 1 and Table 2 (annexed) summarize the results of in-depth studies that have been carried out in order to understand the nature and intensity of salt build-up, apparently caused by poor soil drainage conditions. The results indicate that the salt build-up consisting mostly of excessive soluble salts and exchangeable sodium under waterlogged conditions, placed them in the saline-alkali soil category (Gangodawila 1988; Fig. 8, annexed).

During field studies, attempts were made to evaluate past changes from the present structure of the general land use mosaic of the area, in terms of the utilization of its available natural resource base. On the basis of this exercise, only some of the more obvious degrading trends in the environment were documented and highlighted. Within the scope of these investigations, it was not possible to consider the knowledge and understanding of all aspects of the environment in sufficient detail. In fact, many inferences had to be supported by available background information from other data sources. This proved more difficult due to the fact that agricultural development programs implemented during the past few decades have had considerable impact on the environment of the north central dry zone.

Discussion

The results suggest that the absence of an ecological approach in the exploitation of the available physical agricultural resource base has inadvertently contributed to a slow and steady deterioration of the north central dry zone environment during the past few decades. Disturbances in the ecosystem are presently evident as indicators or degrading processes. Significant among them are the twin problems of salinity and waterlogging in and around the earlier village tank cascade systems, that were eventually demolished in order to accomodate modern irrigation networks and their extended irrigated areas.

The most crucial ecological questions as well as challenges facing the area today would thus revolve round the issues of present and future land use planning, which is bound to determine the productivity of the arable land, both in the short and long term. This means that the choice of different land uses which are technologically and socioeconomically feasible for this area has to be decided carefully, based on sound ecological principles.

A major consideration in this respect has to be given to the ecological (biophysical) characteristics of land, particularly the improvement and maintenance of soil fertility. This is because such land qualities can be related to the crop requirements, productivity declines and serves as indicators of to the type of ameliorative (conservation) measures that may be regularly needed in these areas, where arable lands will continue to be exploited for agricultural production in the future.

Since decisions on land use are presently biased towards state agencies or authorities who pursue their own goals through their large-scale irrigated-related agricultural development programs, it is inevitable that conflicts of interests between such agencies and the traditional farming community in the area frequently arise. Lacking any form of institutional support at local level, the farmers continue to struggle for a livelihood trying to make the most of the remnants of a once flourishing and efficient agricultural system (Madduma Bandara, 1984). Often, the state agencies tend to preempt the most productive and convenient lands leaving the inaccessible, infertile and drought-ridden areas for the continuation of traditional farming. This disparity in sharing the available physical resource base is neither ecologically nor sociopolitically sound, as it invariably contributes to both ecological and social instability. However, a satisfactory compromise would have to be to integrate the two systems to mutually benefit each other, both in terms of technology and sociocultural development (Fig. 6, annexed).

On the basis of new insights from these investigations, land use alternatives are proposed through a spatial model or plan (Fig. 7, annexed) on restructuring the existing land use mosaic for the small-scale irrigation systems in the area. It is thought that the proposed land use readjustment based on natural drainage basins has the best potential for effective implementation of farming systems that have been suggested for the area from time to time by many agricultural scientists.

Acknowledgments

I am deeply indebted to Prof. C.M. Madduma Bandara of the Geography Department, University of Peradeniya, who inspired me to engage in this research and actively helped me to complete the study. During the period when the fieldwork for this study was done, a large number of project and field staff of the Mahaweli 'H' Area were very helpful in providing data and assistance in the research, which is greatly appreciated. I am very grateful to Mr. W.L.A.D. Jayatilaka of the Publications Division, Department of Agriculture, for skillfully drawing the maps and diagrams and for suggesting improvements to the design of a number of figures.

Literature Cited

Gangodawila, C.D. 1988. Environmental degradation and socioeconomic impacts under major irrigation development programmes in Sri Lanka - A review. *5th ISCO Conf. Bangkok*: 247-257.

Madduma Bandara, C.M. 1984. Catchment ecosystems and traditional village tank cascades in the dry zone of Sri Lanka. *In* J. Lunquist, M. Falkenmark and U. Lohm, eds. *Strategies for River Basin Management,* pp. 99-113. The Geo Journal Library, Dortrecht.

UDSA (United States Salinity Laboratory Staff). 1967. Diagnosis and Improvement of Saline and Alkali Soils. USDA, Washington DC.

Wolf, E.C. 1987. Mimicing nature: traditional farming practices and their ecological models. *Ceres* 20: 20-24.

Table 1. Mean salinity values for blocked riceland at sites of former tank beds in the Mahaweli 'H' irrigated system, based on "bench mark" salinity surveys conducted in 1985/86 in specific locations in Block 403 of the 'H' irrigated area of the Mahaweli Project, that had the twin problems of salinity and waterlogging, and identified for investigations by settlers themselves. Transect locations are as follows: 1 = TO34 Ac No. 8 Unit 5 (R_1), 2 = TO34 Ac No. 8 Unit 5 (R_2), 3 = TO34 Ac No. 8 Unit 5 (R_3), 4 = TO34 Ac No. 5 Unit 5 (R_1), 5 = TO34 Ac No. 5 Unit 5 (R_2), 6 = TO34 Ac No. 5 Unit 5 (R_3), 7 = Ac No. D_2 FC 57 (R_1), 8 = Ac No. D_2 FC 57 (R_2), 9 = Ac No. D_4 FC 57 (R_3), 10 = Ac No. D_3 FC 52 (R_1), 11 = Ac No. D_3 FC 52 (R_2), 12 = Ac No. D_3 FC 52 (R_3).

				CATONIC COMPOSITION					
Transect	Depth (cm)	pH	EC mmohs/cm at 25°C	Ca^{2+} meq/100g	Mg^{2+} meq/100g	Na^+ meq/100g	K^+ meq/100g	CEC meq/100g	ESP
1	15	9.0	2800	9.57	6.06	4.79	0.07	20.0	31.4
	30	7.8	1700	5.20	4.20	3.10	0.10	11.0	39.2
2	15	8.6	4000	9.20	5.20	2.20	0.81	20.5	26.5
	30	7.4	2200	8.20	2.00	2.12	1.10	11.0	23.8
3	15	7.5	5000	10.21	4.80	4.10	0.09	15.0	27.0
	30	7.8	3000	12.85	4.16	4.34	0.08	21.0	26.0
4	15	7.7	2500	8.21	3.26	4.98	0.08	16.0	45.2
	30	7.2	2000	8.20	2.10	2.20	0.12	13.0	20.3
5	15	7.2	1700	7.91	2.91	2.18	0.09	12.9	30.7
	30	7.3	2500	9.72	3.10	2.00	0.12	15.1	26.6
6	15	7.5	2600	8.92	3.51	5.01	0.07	16.2	40.3
	30	7.4	2400	8.51	2.98	2.32	0.08	15.1	26.6
7	15	8.8	1600	6.20	0.73	8.30	1.20	25.2	49.1
	30	8.3	1100	5.12	0.69	8.10	1.10	23.9	75.7
8	15	8.9	1550	5.35	1.33	10.39	1.03	24.5	73.6
	30	9.0	3100	8.80	1.50	14.13	0.09	25.3	126.0
9	15	7.3	1700	7.13	1.02	11.10	1.17	25.2	107.0
	30	8.5	1550	5.82	1.30	5.20	1.08	24.9	93.0
10	15	7.5	4300	10.10	8.30	4.82	-	-	24.1
	30	8.2	3900	12.50	3.61	4.82	-	-	-
11	15	8.0	3800	30.00	5.59	13.04	-	50.0	35.0
	30	7.3	2000	15.00	2.25	4.34	-	35.5	13.9
12	15	7.9	2600	8.40	2.25	6.22	-	25.5	32.2
	30	7.5	2200	15.00	4.00	5.21	-	25.0	25.8

Table 2. Mean soil salinity values for valley bottom lands in the Toruwewa tank cascade system, based on "bench mark" salinity surveys conducted in 1985/86 by the author in specific locations in the north central dry zone, e.g. Toruwewa tank cascade that had previous history of the problem and identified by farmers as to their locations.

Sample Transect	Depth (cm)	pH	EC mmohs/cm at 25°C	CATONIC COMPOSITION				CEC meq/ 100g	ESP
				Ca^{2+} meq/ 100g	Mg^{2+} meq/ 100g	Na^+ meq/ 100g	K^+ meq/ 100g		
Attawirawewa-Puranwela	0-15	8.6	2200	13.10	5.55	11.30	1.020	57.39	24.0
	15-30	8.7	2000	9.02	1.95	14.47	2.010	57.40	33.7
Attawirawewa-Akkarawela (upper part)	0-15	8.6	3000	2.55	2.31	19.17	0.055	21.96	68.5
	15-30	9.2	1750	5.76	0.05	17.10	0.955	25.66	20.6
Attawirawewa-Akkarawela (lower part)	0-15	8.6	3550	7.02	0.52	11.26	0.066	17.83	17.6
	15-30	8.7	2100	4.03	4.73	3.74	1.750	18.40	22.8
Ihala Nochchikulama (upper part)	0-15	8.3	4500	11.70	6.90	17.84	2.070	53.40	50.5
	15-30	8.4	4300	7.97	10.30	18.00	2.010	54.00	50.0
Ihala Nochchikulama (lower part)	0-15	8.2	3300	13.40	9.39	15.47	1.890	53.65	41.9
	15-30	8.2	2400	10.3	13.29	11.52	2.310	54.70	26.6
Ihala Nochchikulama (lower part)	0-15	9.6	1600	11.21	3.27	4.98	0.830	19.20	35.0
	15-30	9.7	1500	3.35	3.45	12.34	0.078	19.50	23.1
Kahatagaswewa	0-15	9.1	3600	5.85	1.90	16.79	0.050	25.00	110.9
	15-30	9.6	2300	7.77	3.88	12.75	0.037	25.00	105.0

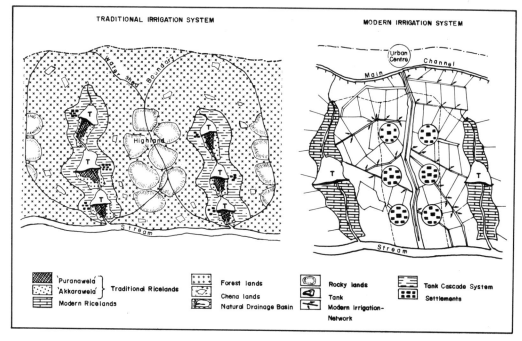

Figure 1. Land use mosaics in the north central dry zone.

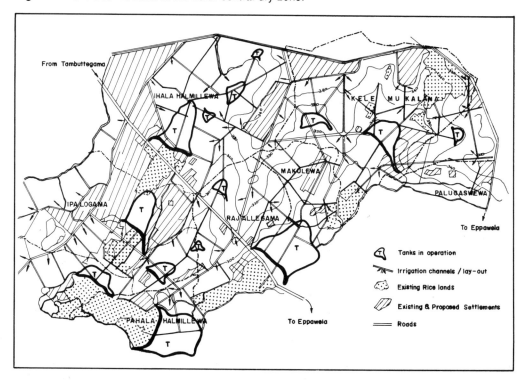

Figure 2. Map of land use during planning phase of Mahaweli 'H' area (Block 403).

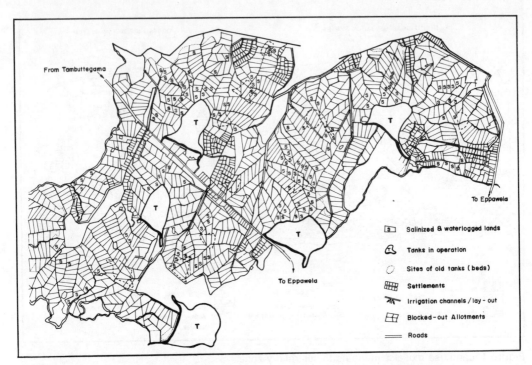

Figure 3. Map of salinized and waterlogged lands of the Mahaweli 'H' area (Block 403).

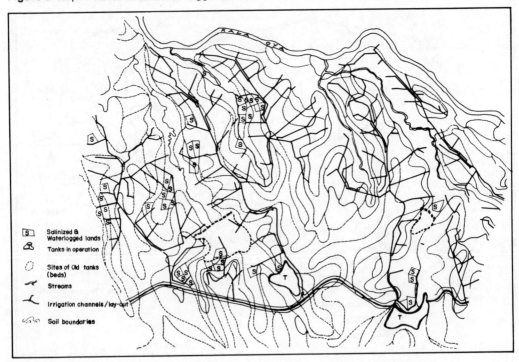

Figure 4. Map of land use during planning phase of the Mahaweli 'H' area (Block 302).

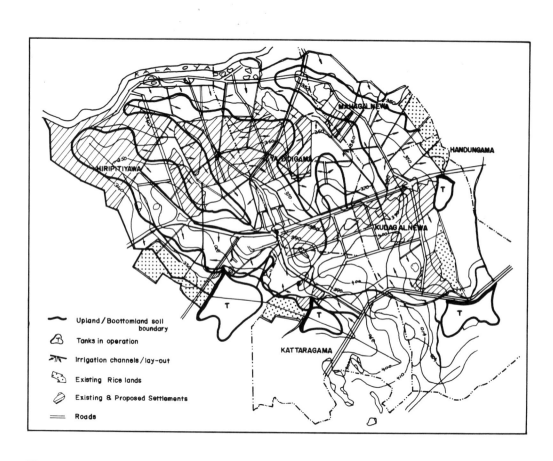

Figure 5. Map of salinized and water logged lands of the Mahaweli 'H' area (Block 302).

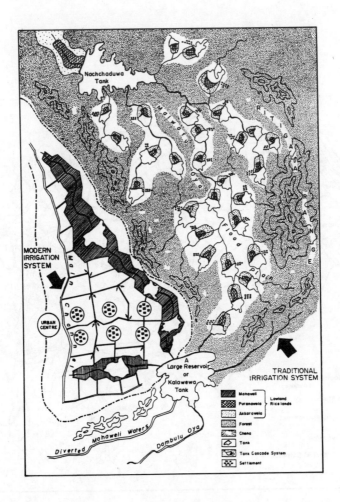

Figure 6. A conceptual plan of action for the integration of large- and small-scale irrigation systems for agricultural land and water use in the north central dry zone.

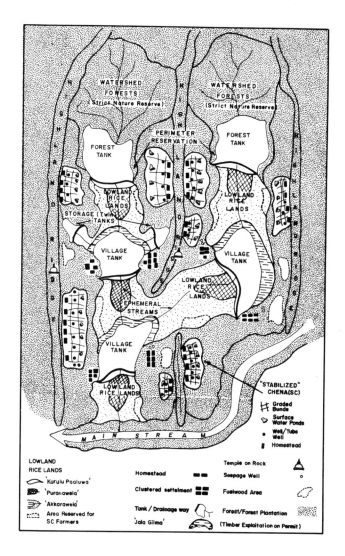

Figure 7. Idealized land use plan with small-scale irrigation system for the north central dry zone.

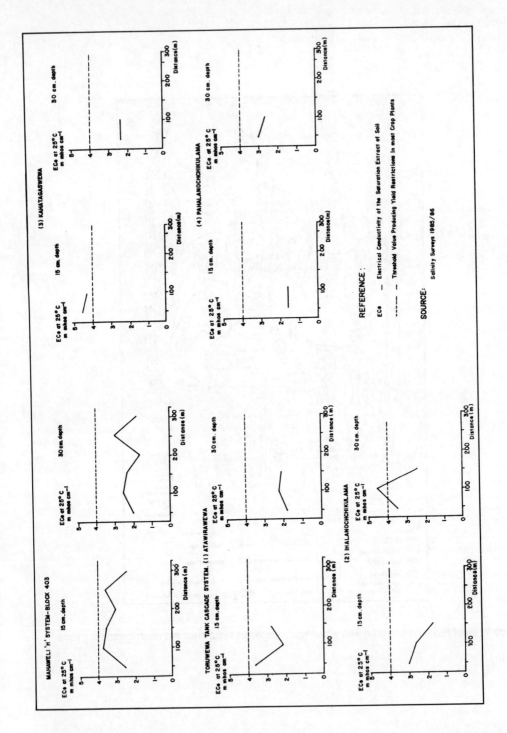

Figure 8. Vertical and horizontal variation of salt within profiles for low humic gleys in valley bottom lands under irrigated agriculture.

Proceedings of the International and Interdisciplinary Symposium
ECOLOGY AND LANDSCAPE MANAGEMENT IN SRI LANKA
W. Erdelen, C. Preu, N. Ishwaran, C.M. Madduma Bandara (eds.)
Colombo, Sri Lanka, 12-26 March 1990
© 1993
Margraf Scientific Books, D-97985 Weikersheim
ISBN 3-8236-1182-8

Interest Conflicts and Management of Protected Areas in Sri Lanka

N. ISHWARAN

Abstract

Internationally, protected area management concepts, during the last two decades, have evolved to accommodate and contribute towards the socioeconomic development of local people living in and around national parks and similar reserves. This trend has also been evident in Sri Lanka. Efforts to incorporate the interests of local people into objectives of protected area management on the island have changed from *ad-hoc* measures to systematically planned strategies. In the future, interest group conflicts could occur at the management-operations, management-concept and systems-planning levels. An open consultative approach, involving all interest groups from the earliest stages of the decision-making process is probably the best way to resolve conflicts. Such an approach would ensure that the technical and financial support necessary for implementing management plans for protected areas are obtained from a wide range of interest groups.

Introduction

The modern practice of conserving species and ecosystems in legally designated areas, such as national parks, nature reserves, wildlife and game sanctuaries, is now nearly a century old in Sri Lanka. The first game sanctuary in Sri Lanka was established in 1900 (Crusz, 1973) in Yala, southeastern Sri Lanka. Since then several other protected areas have been established, and those established during the early part of the century have been extended to include additional areas. Currently about 10%-12% of the island's area is reserved in strict nature reserves, national parks, nature reserves, sanctuaries, biosphere reserves and World Heritage Sites.

The legal designation of an area for nature, species and ecosystem conservation prioritizes long-term benefits over short-term ones that may be derived from the immediate exploitation of resources within that area. Conflict of interests in the management of protected areas need not be confined to that between groups which promote non-consumptive (nature protection, training, education, research and tourism) and consumptive (forestry, farming and fisheries)

541

uses. "In-house" conflicts often occur among conservationists, nature-lovers and scientists regarding management approaches to protected areas. Protected area managers in Sri Lanka have so far opted for a "laissez-faire" approach to managing national parks and similar reserves. However, the pressures from a growing population with rising socioeconomic aspirations and the need to conserve populations of wide-ranging species, such as the elephant, in relatively small reserves, could compel future managers in Sri Lanka to adopt interventionist policies and strategies.

In this paper, some global trends in the evolution of protected area management concepts are briefly reviewed. This is followed by an analysis of the trends in the resolution of conflict between local people and management in selected protected areas of Sri Lanka. Such conflicts are being increasingly resolved by accommodating the interests of local people as one of the goals of protected area management. In outlining a framework for resolving conflicts among interest groups in the future establishment and management of protected areas in Sri Lanka, three probable levels of conflict are recognized, and possible solutions discussed.

Evolution of Protected Area Management Concepts - Some Global Trends

Since the origin of the national park concept in the nineteenth century, managers of national parks and similar reserves have emphasized the exclusion of people for the sake of protecting undisturbed nature. Even the international definition of national parks, adopted in New Delhi in 1969, recommended the elimination of settlements and resource exploitation within such protected areas (Miller, 1982). In several developing countries, however, a variety of tribal, indigenous and rural people were already inhabiting areas of declared and proposed national parks. The need for an alternative concept became evident during the 1970s, and the conservation unit (Lusigi, 1981) and UNESCO's Biosphere Reserve (Batisse 1982, 1986) were attempts to meet this need. These alternative concepts proposed that protected areas be zoned to incorporate a variety of uses, including subsistence level resource extraction by people who had been dependent on the resources of the area for long periods of time.

During the last two decades zoning schemes have been developed and applied to the management of all types of protected areas, and multiple use is now increasingly a characteristic of most such areas. Some types of uses, for example tourism and scientific research, could be accommodated even within the conventional national park concept. However, permitting resource extraction by local people in a national park and managing such use for the overall benefit of the area is a more challenging task. One example comes from the Royal Chitwan National Park of Nepal where villagers are allowed to collect thatch grass (primarily *Imperata cylindrica* but also several other tall grasses) for a nominal fee of 1 Nepali Rupee (US $ 0.04). Nearly 130,000 people enter the park during each cutting season and remove as much grass as they can carry away. Cutting of these tall grasses stimulates regeneration which improves the usefulness of these grasslands to the community of grazing mammals in the park (Lehmukl *et al.* 1988). Many mammalian grazers do not feed upon mature stages of tall grasses such as *Imperata cylindrica* (Edroma 1981, Ishwaran 1984).

Multiple-use management regimes which emphasize benefits to local people were characteristic of protected areas considered as "promising reserves" for the future (Gradwohl and Greenberg, 1988). While providing benefits to local people is increasingly an objective of management in many protected areas, there are a few sites which have successfully incorporated the participation of local people in the management process itself. The Sian Ka'an Biosphere Reserve of Mexico and the Community Baboon Reserve of Belize were both established through the initiatives of local people who continue to play a major role in the management of those areas (Gradwohl and Greenberg, 1988). Globally, therefore, both the principles and practice of protected area management are evolving towards attempts to link benefits of conservation with socioeconomic development of local people more closely.

Local People and Protected Areas in Sri Lanka

The present distribution of protected areas in Sri Lanka is skewed towards the dry zone (Ishwaran and Erdelen, 1990). Given the "laissez-faire" approach which has characterized the management of these areas since their establishment, most of them support vegetation which is the climatic climax (Ceylonese Monsoon Forest; Udvardy 1975) for the dry zone of Sri Lanka. Thus it is not surprising that the remaining natural forests of Sri Lanka are also largely confined to the dry zone (Gunatilleke and Gunatilleke 1984, Ishwaran and Erdelen 1990).

The economy of the British colonial government centered on the plantations of tea, rubber and coconut which were concentrated predominantly in the wet and intermediate zones of Sri Lanka. Game sanctuaries and reserves during colonial times in the early part of this century were set up mainly in the dry zone. After Sri Lanka gained its independence in 1948, however, successive governments launched large-scale river-valley development schemes in the dry zone. Incentives were provided to people by way of land, loans, fertilizer subsidies, etc, to move into the dry zone, settle and develop irrigated agriculture there. Today, densely populated settlements border most protected areas of the dry zone, and encroachments and illegal use of protected area resources pose major threats to nature conservation in Sri Lanka.

Since 1948, conflicts of interest between local people and the management of protected areas have always been recognized by managers. Steps taken by managers to resolve these, however, have evolved from "unwritten" common sense responses to that of planned and organized efforts. The following four cases drawn from my own field experience in Sri Lanka between 1975 and 1986 are intended to illustrate this point.

Gal Oya National Park

The Gal Oya National Park (25,900 ha; Fig. 1) was established in 1954 (DWLC, 1990) to protect parts of the catchment of rivers which fed into Senanayake Samudra, a reservoir constructed in connection with the Gal Oya (a river) Valley Development Project. The park is still an ideal site for viewing elephants (*Elephas maximus maximus*), spotted deer (*Axis axis ceylonensis*) and a variety of species of birds which inhabit the reservoir area. With this man-made lake as its center, this park has an excellent potential for tourism and recreation development.

Fishermen camped along the shores of the reservoir often raised cattle. Their activities led to dry season fires and poaching of game (predominantly spotted deer, sambur (*Cervus unicolor*) and wild boar (*Sus scrofa*). The fishermen were, however, not local people but came from regions outside the immediate vicinity of the park. Even the villagers who are legally resident in areas adjacent to the park came from various parts of Sri Lanka and were settled in colonization schemes established as part of the Gal Oya Valley Development Project.

Local people who were dependent on the resources of the park before its establishment included a group of "veddahs", a hunter-gatherer tribe, resident in the village of Rattugala and surrounding areas bordering the northern parts of the park. Between 1975 and 1977, when they were already in the midst of a process of acculturation, the veddahs lived outside the park but often collected medicinal plants, honey and firewood inside park boundaries. The veddahs performed various traditional dances and other acts for the tourists who visited the park. The tourists had to spend at least one half of a day to visit the veddah areas since the route to those areas was not the same as the route into the park for viewing wildlife. Tourist access to the veddahs was, however, made possible by private tour operators and their local contact-persons, but not by the park management. Income to the park came from entrance fees charged to visitors and, at times, through motor-boat hire for a ride in the reservoir to view wildlife. Conflict between park authorities and the veddahs erupted occasionally when the latter were

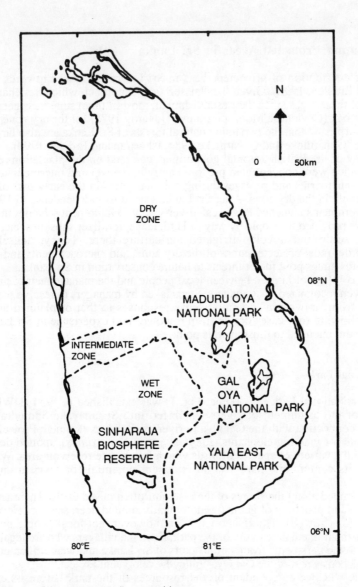

Figure 1. Location of national parks discussed here.

prevented from collecting honey or medicinal plants, or caught poaching inside the park. The park lacked a management plan and the situation continued to remain unmanaged. The larger share of the tourism benefits accrued predominantly to private hotels, tour-operators and their local agents than to the veddahs or to the management of the park.

Yala East National Park

The Yala East National Park (18,148.2 ha; Fig. 1) established between 1969 and 1970 (DWLC, 1990) is an important site for resident and migratory species of birds. As a site contiguous with Sri Lanka's oldest national park, i.e. the Yala National Park, this site also shares the latter's faunal, esthetic and cultural features, making it an important site visited by locals and foreigners.

Kumana is a village inside the Yala East National Park, and villagers have co-existed with park authorities since the declaration of this site as a protected area. The villagers practiced fishing and hunting prior to the establishment of the park and probably continue to do so on a small scale. Although not having a management plan, the Department of Wildlife Conservation authorities recognized the long-term implications of sustaining the village within the boundaries of the park and provided some incentives for the village youth to move out of the park. Several people from the Kumana village have become guards or rangers within the Department of Wildlife Conservation and subsequently have been posted for service in other reserves of Sri Lanka.

Maduru Oya National Park

The Maduru Oya National Park (51,468.5 ha; Fig. 1) was established in 1983 and an eastern extension (7381.3 ha) was added to the park in 1985 (DWLC, 1990). The conflict between the group of veddahs resident in the village of Dambana bordering the southwestern parts of this park, and park planners and managers, is probably the most publicized conflict in the history of protected area management in Sri Lanka.

The "Dambana veddahs", as compared with the "Rattugala veddahs" described in the case of the Gal Oya National Park, were popularly believed to be a group representative of the traditional hunter-gatherer culture of the veddahs. Furthermore, global awareness and recognition of the importance of accommodating the interests of such indigenous people into protected area management had grown stronger during the 1970s and the 1980s. Thus, incorporating the traditional needs of the Dambana veddahs was a consideration of greater importance in setting up the Maduru Oya National Park in the 1980s than that of accomodating the needs of the Rattugala veddahs in the establishment of the Gal Oya National Park in the 1950s. In fact, the highway between the towns of Mahiyangana and Padiyatalawa which improved visitor access to the residence of the Dambana veddahs and along which the latter often waited to attract tourists, was constructed during the implementation of the Gal Oya Valley Development Project in the 1950s and the 1960s. Access to villages of the Rattugala veddahs even during the late 1970s remained difficult, restricted to jeep-tracks which could be impassable during heavy monsoonal rains. Easy accessibility to major highways and the tourist boom in the 1970s probably contributed towards the chieftain of the Dambana veddahs becoming a public figure, and association with him had considerable symbolic value to politicians and to other important leaders of the country.

Lands traditionally used by the Dambana veddahs for hunting and slash-and-burn (chena) agriculture were earmarked for inclusion into the Maduru Oya National Park during 1979 and 1980. There were widespread protests and pressure from various sympathetic groups to release the lands for the benefit of the tribal people. The Maduru Oya National Park was established to protect the catchments of three reservoirs which were constructed in connection with the Mahaweli Development Project, the largest river valley development project undertaken by any Sri Lankan government. The Dambana veddahs were provided with alternative land outside the protected area into which several of them moved, but many returned to their traditional homelands after a few months. The chieftain and the older members of the tribe have continued to remain and use their traditional homelands, parts of which are inside the Maduru Oya National Park.

Sinharaja Biosphere Reserve

The Sinharaja Biosphere Reserve (8864 ha; Fig. 1) was declared an international biosphere reserve in 1978 and has subsequently been extended to include an additional 2450 ha to the east of the original site. It is also Sri Lanka's first National Wilderness Heritage Area and, to date, the only natural site of Sri Lanka inscribed in UNESCO's World Heritage List (Ishwaran and Erdelen, 1990).

Nationally, Sinharaja was originally declared as a forest reserve. In theory, such forest reserves in Sri Lanka could be released for sustained yield production of timber. Despite the fact that the initial legislative framework of this reserve, in comparison to those of national parks, was considered insufficient for its protection, Sinharaja has become the first area in Sri Lanka where the potential for linking conservation with the socioeconomic development of the local people is tested in a systematic manner (Ishwaran and Erdelen, 1990). Its declaration, in 1988, as the island's first National Wilderness Heritage Area has elevated its status similar to that of a national park. This is partly due to the international recognition this site has enjoyed since the early 1970s for protecting the last patch of tropical humid forest in the biogeographical province of the Ceylon (Sri Lankan) wet zone (Udvardy, 1975).

A conservation (management) plan for Sinharaja was prepared in 1985 (Forest Department, 1986). In the implementation of the plan, the development of buffer and transition zones of the reserve for the socioeconomic benefit of people resident within the reserve and in surrounding areas is assigned a high priority. Several schemes, e.g. giving preferential treatment to local people for employment opportunities within the Forest Department, and providing alternative land for resettling people resident within the reserve, used as *ad-hoc* measures in cases described earlier, have been incorporated as recommended actions and as part of an overall management strategy which also attempts to (a) create plantations of species useful to local people, (b) develop an infrastructure of roads and schools for their benefit, and (c) improve the flow of government and international assistance to these rather remote villages. One benefit which such planned action in Sinharaja has already generated is financial and technical assistance from international sources for the implementation of the plan (IUCN, 1989). This plan was prepared via a consultative process which incorporated a variety of interest groups, such as foresters, wildlife conservationists, academics, research scientists, voluntary workers from non-governmental organizations and representatives of international agencies. Such a process prevented "in-house" conflicts from surfacing after the plan had already been prepared and from delaying the implementation of the plan. Despite the fact that Sinharaja had never been a national park, the process adopted in the preparation and implementation of a management plan for this site is likely to be imitated in the future management of other national parks and similar reserves of Sri Lanka.

Interest Group Conflicts at Different Levels and their Resolution

Modern concepts of protected area management (IUCN/UNEP, 1986a) advocate the development of a management strategy and plan for each individual protected area unit. It is evident from the four cases described above that managers have recognized the usefulness of certain tactics, e.g. providing preferential consideration for employment in the park services for people who are dependent on the resources of the park, minimizing conflicts with local people and improving the chances for the long-term survival of the park. However, what has been practice for a long time is now being assigned the status of a principle in protected area management. Application of this and other such principles at the very early stages of establishing a protected area in order to develop a management plan could facilitate and guide the resolution of conflicts in a manner that might otherwise be difficult to sustain. In Sri Lanka, groups with conflicting interests occur at least at three different levels of a process common to the establishment and management of all protected areas.

The Management-Operations Level

Conflict at this level centers around the protected area itself and would involve (a) officers of the management authority responsible for the site, (b) officers of other government agencies with whom there are disagreements regarding the boundary of the reserve and the types of land uses permissible within it, (c) absentee landowners and resource users dependent on the protected area, (d) local people dependent on the resources in and around the protected area, and (e) other groups, particularly non-governmental organizations and voluntary groups, whose interests, e.g. environment, protection of the rights of tribal people, reform of land-tenure, etc. might overlap with the objectives of protected area management.

Local people resident around most protected areas in Sri Lanka today are rural people who are aware of the modern needs of socioeconomic development and are eager to have access to them. Hence, managers of national parks and similar reserves in Sri Lanka, as in the case of the Sinharaja Biosphere Reserve, are likely to be increasingly compelled to incorporate the needs of socioeconomic development of local people into their management plans.

The Management-Concept Level

The development of concepts for a management plan for a protected area involves groups who are physically distant from the site and whose interests with regard to the management of the site might be of a technical or intellectual nature. Conflicts and disagreements regarding concepts for a management plan often occur among academics, research scientists, leaders of non-governmental organizations, and planners and managers from the agency responsible for the administration of the protected area system. In Sri Lanka, such conflicts had revolved around changes in the boundaries of protected areas, use of exotic species in boundary or buffer zone plantations, and strategies used for managing populations of certain species of mammals such as the elephant.

An example of an issue which might become a source of conceptual level conflict in the future is the relative importance given to the protection of natural vegetation, conservation of elephant populations and the interests of local people in the management of various national parks and similar reserves in the dry zone of Sri Lanka. In all these reserves the protection of the natural vegetation (forests) has been the most important objective until now. This, however, limits the availability of grazing sites for elephants which raid croplands around most protected areas of Sri Lanka. Creating grasslands inside reserves by removal of forests has been considered undesirable (Seidensticker, 1984) and action to conserve elephant populations has been confined to defensive tactics such as capture and translocation, driving of elephants into sanctuaries and removal of elephants which had become persistent cropraiders. While farmers suffer crop damage in many parts of the dry zone where agricultural land and elephant ranges are adjacent to each other, compensation schemes are rare or lacking. This issue will have to be addressed when management plans for protected areas in the dry zone are prepared (DWLC, 1990).

System-Level Conflicts

The biogeographical basis for the development of protected area systems in the Indo-Malayan realm was developed during the 1970s (Udvardy, 1975) and has since been further refined (IUCN/UNEP, 1986b). Representation of protected area units in the wet zone is far below desirable levels and the Sri Lankan (Ceylon) wet zone is a biogeographic province where urgent action is needed for setting up new units (MacKinnon, 1988). Given the fact that the Sri Lankan wet zone is a densely populated area, setting up new protected areas is likely to be difficult and to conflict with other land-use interests. Even in the dry zone where establishment of protected areas in connection with major river valley development projects has been practice since the 1950s, the ratio of new land cleared for agriculture to new land established under protected areas decreased substantially from the Gal Oya Valley (1950s) to the Mahaweli (1980s) Development Projects (Ishwaran, 1984).

System-level conflicts could also arise when decisions need to be taken regarding the future of some of the protected areas, which have been reserves only on paper. Sri Lanka has several sanctuaries (Tab. 1) and quite a few of them are less than 1000 ha. Small protected areas which may have been encroached or otherwise degraded could be exchanged for other areas which still retain natural ecosystems in a relatively undisturbed condition but are not yet legally protected. Small, degraded reserves may also become experimental sites for the establishment of plant species of value to local people or for breeding endangered animal species (Ishwaran, 1991). Any change in the prevailing status of a protected area, despite the fact that it has been degraded, might be resisted by the conventional pro-conservation lobbies. Exchanging degraded sites for better sites, particularly in the wet zone where availability of land is already scarce, could be opposed by interest groups promoting development and seeking short-term economic profits over long-term conservation benefits.

Table 1. Numbers and coverage of protected area categories of Sri Lanka: *WZ = wet zone, IZ = intermediate zone, DZ = dry zone. Several protected areas of the dry zone have parts that are in the intermediate zone. Hence, representation in the intermediate zone has been underestimated. Biosphere reserves are: Sinharaja (8,864 ha) and Hurulu (512 ha). Sinharaja biosphere reserve is also a natural World Heritage Site, and together with an eastern extension (an additional 2,450 ha), constitutes the National Wilderness Heritage Area (DWLC, 1990).

Protected Area Category	Number			Area (ha)
	WZ	IZ	DZ	
1. National Parks	1	-	10	460,070.2
2. Strict Nature Reserve	1	-	1	31,575.4
3. Nature Reserve	-	-	2	32,548.5
4. Sanctuary	5	4	40	255,236.7
5. Biosphere Reserve	1	-	1	9,376.0
6. National Wilderness Heritage Area	1	-	-	10,314.0
7. World Heritage Site (Natural Site only)	1	-	-	8,864.0

While the conceptual separation of these different levels of conflict is possible, in reality they are often linked. Alliances are formed between different interest groups involved with the different levels of conflict. Academics and research scientists working in the field might sympathize with local people who have been dependent on the resources of the area and have used them in a "sustainable" manner until outside commercial users arrived at the scene. Managers might be compelled to maximize the financial return from a protected area to meet targets set by their employer but scientists, nature-lovers and local non-governmental organizations may emphasize the negative socioeconomic and cultural impacts of over-use of the site, for example by unregulated tourism.

The solution to conflict at any level could be greatly enhanced by drawing up a list of the different interest groups involved and incorporating their participation in the decision-making process from the earliest possible stages. Decisions drawn up through a process of consensus tend to be implemented without undue delays. On the other hand, when decisions are taken by the management agency without adequate consideration of the views of other interest groups, implementation could well be delayed by protests and disagreements which are expressed only after the decisions are publicized.

Resolving conflicts at the systems level might be more time consuming than at other levels and therefore the process of consultation to discuss systems level changes needs to be more continuous than at other levels. In the Sri Lankan wet zone where the establishment of additional protected areas is an urgent requirement, candidate sites, i.e. remaining patches of natural areas as well as sites where regeneration has been in progress for sufficiently long periods of time (Gunatilleke and Ashton 1987, DWLC 1990), are under the jurisdiction of the Forest Department, and not the Department of Wildlife Conservation which is responsible for most protected areas of the island. The legal framework within which these two agencies implement their policies are not the same and there are likely to be members of academic and non-governmental communities who will also have opinions regarding suitable sites for the establishment of new protected areas and priority objectives for their management. Even in the dry zone, where protected area coverage is more representative than in the wet zone (IUCN/UNEP, 1986b), new protected areas would have to be established in some ecosystems, e.g. the coastal zone. Proposals in this regard, too, require cooperation between the Department of Wildlife Conservation and several governmental and semi-governmental agencies responsible for the management of coastal resources of Sri Lanka. Since the coastline of Sri Lanka is also important to fisheries, tourism and several rural industries, setting up coastal parks would require consultations with many governmental and non-governmental interest groups allied to those industries.

Resolution of conflicts at management-concept and management-operations levels are closely linked and consultations among groups will often be required both within and between these levels. Nevertheless, the process of conflict-resolution is likely to achieve realistic results if solutions are sought on a "bottom-up" rather than a "top-down" basis. In developing concepts for a management plan for a protected area, it will be desirable to bring together interest groups at the operations-level first, in order to identify major problems and issues. Subsequently, groups at the concept-level could be presented with these problems and issues and requested to find suitable strategies for managing the site. Ideally, some individuals belonging to academia, research institutions and/or international conservation organizations might participate in the discussions at both levels to ensure continuity and coherence between decisions taken at operational and conceptual levels. In developing the strategies for a management plan for the Sinharaja Biosphere Reserve, a one-day workshop was initially convened in the reserve itself, to bring together officers of several government departments and representatives of local people. This was later followed by a five-day workshop to develop concepts for the management plan. There were quite a number of field and technical persons who participated in both meetings to ensure that the same major issues and problems were discussed at both events.

In several less-developed countries like Sri Lanka, development of protected areas to meet modern conservation objectives cannot be achieved without adequate input from international sources. Involvement of technical specialists from recognized international agencies in the consultative processes mentioned above improves the chances that the outcome of plans and strategies developed attract financial and technical support from bi- and multi-lateral donors. Involving all relevant interest groups in resolving conflicts at the various levels discussed above may be time-consuming and reaching consensus on issues and problems on divergent opinions might be difficult. These disadvantages, however, are outweighed by the fact that decisions taken on the basis of such broad-based consultative processes have better chances of being fully implemented and attracting the technical and financial support necessary for their implementation from a wide range of interested parties.

Summary

Internationally, conflicts between local people and protected area management are being increasingly resolved by incorporating the promotion of the interests of such people as one of the goals of management. This trend has also been evident in Sri Lanka. While the response of protected area managers in Sri Lanka to problems involving local people has been *ad-hoc* in the past, in recent times they have been incorporated into management plans and strategies in a systematic manner. This approach is likely to continue in the future. In future establishment and management of protected areas in Sri Lanka, problems may occur at the management-operation, management-concepts and systems-planning levels. At all levels adopting an open, consultative approach to resolving conflicts would not only increase the chances that decisions taken are implemented without undue delays, but would also ensure that the technical and financial input necessary for the implementation of plans and programs are obtained from a wide range of interested parties.

Literature Cited

Batisse, M. 1982. The biosphere reserve: a tool for environmental conservation and management. *Env. Conserv.* 9: 101-11.

Batisse, M. 1986. Developing and focussing the biosphere reserve concept. *Nature and Resources*. XXII: 1-11.

Crusz, H. 1973. Nature conservation in Sri Lanka (Ceylon). *Biol. Conserv.* 5: 199-208.

DWLC (Department of Wildlife Conservation, Sri Lanka). 1990. *A five-year development plan for the wildlife conservation and protected area management sector of Sri Lanka.* DWLC, Sri Lanka.

Edroma, E. L. 1981. The role of grazing in maintaining high species composition in *Imperata cylindrica* grasslands in Rwenzori National Park, Uganda. *Afr. J. Ecol.* 19: 215-224.

Forest Department. 1986. *A Conservation Plan for the Sinharaja Forest.* Forest Department, Sri Lanka and WWF/IUCN, Gland, Switzerland.

Gradwohl, J. and R. Greenberg. 1988. *Saving the tropical forests.* Earthscan Publ. London.

Gunatilleke, C.V.S. and P.S. Ashton. 1987. New light on the plant biogeography of Ceylon. II. The ecological biogeography of the lowland endemic tree flora. *J. Biogeogr.* 14: 295-327.

Gunatilleke, C.V.S. and I.A.U.N. Gunatilleke. 1984. *National Conservation Strategy.* Sector paper on natural forests. Unpubl. mscript. Central Environmental Authority, Sri Lanka.

Ishwaran, N. 1984. *The Ecology of the Asian Elephant (Elephas maximus L.) in Sri Lanka.* Ph.D. Thesis. Michigan State University, East Lansing, USA.

Ishwaran, N. 1991. The role of protected area systems in a growing environmental sector in less-developed countries. *In* W. Erdelen, N. Ishwaran and P. Muller, eds. *Tropical Ecosystems: Systems Characteristics, Utilization, Destruction and Conservation Concepts,* pp. 151-160. Verlag Josef Margraf, Weikersheim.

Ishwaran, N. and W. Erdelen. 1990. Conserving Sinharaja-an experiment in sustainable development in Sri Lanka. *Ambio* 19: 237-244.

IUCN/UNEP. 1986a. *Managing Protected Areas in the Tropics.* Compiled by John and Kathy MacKinnon, Graham Child and Jim Thorsell. IUCN, Gland, Switzerland.

IUCN/UNEP. 1986b. *Review of the Protected Area System in the Indo-Malayan Realm.* Compiled by John and Kathy MacKinnon. IUCN, Gland, Switzerland.

IUCN. 1989. Sinharaja project launched. *Tropical Forest Program Newsletter*, No. 3, Nov. 1988. IUCN. Gland, Switzerland.

Lehmukl, J.F., R.K. Upreti and U.R. Sharma. 1988. National parks and local development: grasses and people in Royal Chitwan National Park, Nepal. *Env. Conserv.* 15: 143-148.

Lusigi, W.J. 1981. New approaches to wildlife conservation in Kenya. *Ambio.* 10: 87-92.

MacKinnon, J. 1988. How complete is the system? Conservation biological assessments of the protected areas of Africa and Asia. Paper presented at the workshop *"New challenges to the world's protected area systems"* IUCN General Assembly, Costa Rica, 1988.

Miller, K.R. 1982. *Planning national parks for ecodevelopment.* School of Natural Resources, Univ. Michigan, Ann Arbor, USA.

Seidensticker, J. 1984. *Managing elephant depredations in agriculture and forestry projects.* A World Bank Technical Paper. World Bank, Washington DC.

Udvardy, M.D.F. 1975. *A classification of biographical provinces of the world.* IUCN Occasional Paper No. 18, Gland, Switzerland.

PAPER PRESENTATIONS

V. SPECIAL EVENING LECTURES

Proceedings of the International and Interdisciplinary Symposium
ECOLOGY AND LANDSCAPE MANAGEMENT IN SRI LANKA
W. Erdelen, C. Preu, N. Ishwaran, C.M. Madduma Bandara (eds.)
Colombo, Sri Lanka, 12-26 March 1990
© 1993
Margraf Scientific Books, D-97985 Weikersheim
ISBN 3-8236-1182-8

Tropical Ecology in Practice
- The Wau Ecology Institute in
Papua New Guinea

F. GÖLTENBOTH

Abstract

The Wau Ecology Institute (WEI) is located in the mid-montane area at Wau, Morobe Province of Papua New Guinea. The institute was established in 1972 as a non-profit, non-governmental corporation for study and education in the fields of ecology and conservation, rural development and environmental protection in Papua New Guinea. Visiting scientists are offered the institutional facilities while carrying out studies in Papua New Guinea. Activities at the institute consist of basic research and improvement of subsistence agriculture systems. With the use of an appropriate tropical gardening system, the traditional practice of "slash and burn" may be altered into a site-stable gardening system. New methods developed proved adaptable to the needs of the village people, thus preventing further cutting and burning of primary rain forest. The institute aims at making local people aware of ecological facts and showing them how to appropriately handle their own environment by offering training courses and publishing books and pamphlets about the fauna and flora. Thus the institute has initiated a change of thinking which may be summarized as "development should not mean forced consumption of natural resources but adequate use of them."

Introduction

Since the first humans were expelled from the peaceful Garden of Eden, man has learnt not only to live with wars, crimes, and other assaults, but also to experience increasing pressures on his environment. Although the reasons may be very different, the motive, however, is mainly greed for economic, social or political power. This human attitude has caused an increasing ecological destruction of the environment. Available disaster records prove the extent of the present ecological and social crises throughout the world. Only some of the most serious environmental problems may be listed here: water pollution has resulted in "lifeless" rivers and lakes, air pollution has caused smog in urban areas, application of chemicals and deposition of toxic industrial wastes have entailed unfruitfulness (sterility) and contamination of land, and the negligence of people's living conditions in squatter settlements and remote rural areas as well as the indifference to terror and the irresponsible inhumane threat to individuals and peoples have resulted in social pollution.

Presently, the major components of man's life-supporting systems are slowly and steadily being changed. The increasing concentration of carbon dioxide and other gases in the atmosphere changes the climates in an unpredictable way and has disastrous effects for all organisms. This process is supported by the deforestation of large rain forest areas in South America along the River Amazon, in the Malayan and Indonesian parts of Kalimantan, in Irian Jaya and Sumatra, in the Philippines and Sri Lanka, in the Himalayan mountains of Nepal, the Ivory Coast, in the Kongo Basin of Equatorial Africa, and in Papua New Guinea. Previously about 14% of the earth's surface was covered with tropical rain forest, half of which man has already destroyed. The last 40 years have been the most destructive period in this respect.

Demand for wood has increased twofold in the tropical countries since 1950, but in the industrialized nations, led by Japan, demand is now sixteen times greater than it was in 1950. This wood is needed not only for timber production but more and more for woodchips to be used as raw material in the paper industry. After selective or clear felling a given patch of rain forest ends up in a dramatic state of existence; soil erosion, river floods, climatic drought, destruction of the genetic resources of many useful plants such as medicinal plants, loss of dignity of the inhabitants living in and off the rain forest, local and global climate changes, and the impoverishment of the rain forest population (Tab. 1, annexed).

Also in Papua New Guinea, massive human interference in the unique ecological system has destroyed huge parts of rain forest areas. There are two main reasons for the extraction of wood from these areas; the need for food and fuelwood and the excessive greed of people mostly in industrialized nations. While the former cause of deforestation resulted from shifting cultivation practices by local people in order to grow the food they needed, the latter aims at the extension of land for the production of crops, which are mostly for export, such as coconut, cacao, coffee, rubber, pineapple or banana, and in some areas of the world aims at the extension of pasture land for breeding.

However, the natural resources, which are presently under stress, are very often vital to tomorrow's economic development and to the growth of the tropical countries. Recognizing and considering this problem, the Wau Ecology Institute in Papua New Guinea started a program which may contribute to the improvement in subsistence farmers' lives and, at the same time, to the conservation of the natural environment of the mid-montane areas of Papua New Guinea which are already under stress.

Conservation and Ecology - The Approach of the Wau Ecology Institute

Papua New Guinea is richly endowed with a great variety of natural resources. Both the terrestrial and marine environment consist of ecosystems with a great diversity of species, individual plants and animals (Figs. 1-3, annexed). Due to the exploitation of its rich resources present developments in Papua New Guinea characterize a great pressure on the natural environment through both foreign companies and countries, the so-called developers (Figs. 4-6, annexed), as well as the native population (Figs. 7-8, annexed).

But limited and insufficient knowledge about the general ecological situation, particularly the more abundant forms of life, has led to a dramatic threat and serious upset of functions and balances within the natural environment. However, wise steps towards conservation may help to avoid mistakes caused by many foreign countries before ecology was adequately appreciated (Gressitt et al. 1976). Both study of the environment as well as environmental education must be carried out hand in hand. However, information about ecological principles are needed not only at the lower levels but also at the decision-making levels in the villages. Moreover, the ecological consequences of different land use practices should be demonstrated on particular sites.

In the traditional agricultural land use system, a patch of forest is cut for temporary gardens and when the soil is depleted a new patch is cut (Figs. 9-10, annexed). Since about 82% of Papua New Guinea's population lives in villages, "slash-and-burn" cultivation is a very common and important subsistence agricultural system in the country. Formerly, when the population was low, this cultivation method was adequate and posed no threat to the environment. But due to the present rapid population growth, particularly in coastal and mid-montane areas, this land use system affects the forests. In areas with steep slopes the forest is affected to a much greater extent (Gressitt, 1982). In forest areas which are sparsely populated, farmers practice a long fallow period (Fig. 11, annexed), whereas the fallow period in the anthropogenic grassland areas is much shorter, and various enrichment techniques are applied to regenerate the soil. In addition, however, large areas of primary forest have been converted into single crop farming systems while the villagers' needs and the effects on flora and fauna have been totally neglected; species diversity has decreased, some species are already extinct and the soil has been eroded. This particularly applies to areas where large timber production projects have been set up (Fig. 14, annexed).

Since the impact of extensive farming systems on tropical forests and the resulting degradation of the natural environment was recognized and that the food resources of the subsistence farmers had to be improved, the Wau Ecology Institute initiated a research program in 1976 in order to investigate how shifting cultivation may be transformed and intensified without environmental destabilization (Gagne 1979, 1980). Based on the results of these studies the project activities, which were started in 1982, aimed at combining traditional and appropriately improved gardening techniques and at demonstrating this cultivation method to other villagers, officials and individuals who are expected to teach and propagate this method (Göltenboth, 1990).

The "slash-and-burn" cultivation technique is a kind of subsistence agriculture involving the growing of local food crops by local people in their own gardens for their own consumption (Figs. 15-17, annexed). Very simple working methods and tools are used, for which only material from the natural environment is used. Crops such as banana, taro (*Colocasia esculenta*), sweet potato (*Ipomoea batata*), cassava (*Manihot esculenta*), sugar cane (*Saccharum officinarum)* (Fig. 18, annexed) and corn (*Zea mays*) are planted without any specific soil preperation.

This cultivation technique is only applicable and suitable as long as population densities are low. It is only then that the forest areas are not reduced and fauna is not affected. However, because population conditions have changed, this cultivation technique must also be changed and adjusted. Therefore, the Wau Ecology Institute started the "Subsistence Agriculture Improvement Project" in which many aspects of the traditional cultivation technique are considered and included, but modified towards an agroecological system which is environmentally beneficial. People involved should not only know the practical handling of the particular techniques, but should also bear in mind the following principles at all times (Dalpadado, 1984):

- Go to the village and live with the people
- Search for the leading people in the village
- Learn from the people
- Plan together with the people and not for them
- Serve the people
- Begin your progagation (extension work) with what the villagers already know
- Build with local materials and tools
- Love the people

Methods and Tools of the Improved Subsistence Garden System

A fundamental rule is to produce all tools and other basic equipment from local material, if and when possible. Furthermore, available knowledge and skills of villagers and trainees as well as local land use practices are integrated in the project. In order to avoid chemicals but to give the soil back what has been used up in form of crops and fruits, the production of compost is necessary for the improvement of the system (Figs. 19-22, annexed). Depending on individual requirements, different compost stockades can be constructed.

In some villages, nurseries with seedbeds for vegetables and tree seedlings on fertile soil are required (Figs. 21-22, annexed). The nursery roof is constructed in such a way that it can be easily modified and rearranged according to the requirements of the growing conditions of the plants and the people working there. Each tree seedling is planted in a seperate pot to prevent any disturbances through repeated replanting. As banana fibres are preferably used as raw material for the pots (Figs. 23-25, annexed), which can be produced by the people themselves and therefore are cheap, the pot can rot and function as compost for the plant. Moreover, while the tree seedling grows, the small pot can be put in another bigger one without disturbing root development. Vegetables such as tomatos, capsicum, lettuce and cabbage compost bricks are recommended as these plants have small seeds and germinate relatively slowly. Most of the other crops cultivated only require composted soil and compost bricks are not required.

Compost bricks (Figs. 26-27, annexed) are made of a soil-compost mixture which is sterilized in a soil-steamer drum constructed from an old petroleum barrel (Figs. 28-29, annexed). The sterilization process is completed when starchy fruits, such as English potatos, sweet potatos, cassava, taro or yams, which are wrapped in banana leaves and placed in the upper third of the soil mixture, are cooked.

Because of steep terrain, soil erosion measures are necessary on most subsistence farms. The detrimental effects of soil erosion can be largely reduced when the garden beds are laid out either on leveled terraces or on ridges running parallel to the contour lines. However, the question is how a uniform altitudinal level on a slope can be determined using local materials and techniques. As a solution, an A-shaped wooden frame with a piece of string fixed at the upper end of the frame as a free swinging pendulum with a stone functioning as weight and some sharpened sticks was constructed and is needed for the following procedure (Figs. 30-31, annexed):

1. A stick is placed in the ground where the first garden bed or terrace is to be positioned.
2. One flank of the frame is put next to the stick while the second flank is turned around until the pendulum has reached exactly the central point of the frame's crossbeam. The point on the second frame flank should be marked with a stick: this is of the altitude as the other flank.
3. From here, the measurements are repeated in the same manner until the other end of the terrace or contour ridge is reached.
4. Finally, the sticks marking the same level on the slope are connected with a line.

After this procedure, a wall of stones, logs or plants such as sugar cane or any other nitriferous tree is constructed to stabilize the contour ridge (Fig. 32, annexed). Another helpful measure preventing soil erosion is the digging of ditches in which the soil washed off the surface by the water run off can be trapped (Fig. 33, annexed). In addition to these measures, many other methods and techniques can contribute to improving the subsistence garden system.

In a number of other tropical countries, the cultivation method mentioned above or some of the following alternatives have been adopted according to their suitability for the specific way of life:

- Paddy cultivation in irrigation plants to produce stable food for the people
- Substituting grazing or grass fallow between the cultivation periods
- Increasing use of animal and human manure as well as compost as fertilizer
- Crop rotation and application of crop hygiene methods to control pests and disease

558

- Use of nitriferous plants in crop rotation or application of green manure to improve the nitrogen level of the soil
- Improvement of soil conservation measures
- Various agroforest or agroecological methods including the application of compost, green manure, mulching, crop rotation, mixed cropping, contour and strip planting (Fig. 34, annexed)

In any case, all kinds of action should be taken to prevent any further destruction of the remaining natural forests and to decrease pressure on forests caused by subsistence farmers' requirements. However, it is a necessity to train villagers in the principles of soil conservation and in the improvement of the subsistence gardening system through practicing appropriate methods and techniques in their own gardens. Only then can the gardening system be used as an alternative in order to prevent a further shift in cultivation, and it is only then that this system will have good chances of success in the future.

Measures Counteracting Destruction of Rain Forest by Logging

De Ath's (1980) study on "The Throwaway People: Social impact of the Gogol Timber Project, Madang Province," which was sponsored by the United Nations' MAB Program (Man and the Biosphere Program) shows what happens to the rain forest wherever big companies are involved. For example, after the Honshu Paper Ltd (Japan) in cooperation with its subsidiary Japanese and New Guinea Timber Company (JANT) had completely cut down an 50,000 ha area of virgin rain forest (Fig. 35, annexed), they left behind a so-called clear-felled area of mud, and not a single tree nor shrub was left (Fig. 36, annexed). The trees felled were chopped to woodchips (Fig. 37, annexed) and converted into paper and cardboard boxes, and sold as Japanese goods on the world market. However, the area continues to exist in a state of devastation as its reforestation, promised by the Japanese company, is too slow to prevent the complete loss of the top soil caused by surface water run off. At present only some 3000 ha of the 50,000 ha cleared have been reforested with fast growing trees such as *Eucalyptus* sp. or other softwood species, and the people involved were paid "mere peanuts." For instance, the village of Bacu receives an amount of about US $ 300 annually for their part in the sale of their forest and a further US $ 300 in royalties. This is a total of US $ 22 per year for each villager, next to nothing for the loss of his forest, his independence, his dignity and in many cases for the loss of the village itself (Fig. 38, annexed). Now, the villagers have to cope with a changed environment created by the logging company and a new dimension of problems such as soil erosion and extinction of wildlife including fish, because the suspension load and siltation of creeks and rivers have increased due to soil erosion. As a result, clear fresh water is no longer available, and the people have lost their source of building materials, their basis for growing medicinal plants and fruit trees and their source of materials needed for traditional social events.

The Wau Ecology Institute recognizing these problems has started a so-called "exposure program". Villagers requested to give their piece of forest to a logging company have the opportunity to visit an area already logged and to see what consequences they have to expect. In workshops and seminars, the public has been informed of the environmental impacts of logging and the methods undertaken by international logging companies to collect the "gold of the forest".

In contrast to the wonderful benefits of this kind of development envisaged by the international logging companies, the reality is totally different. The great hopes of the people for construction of roads and development of large-scale agricultural schemes such as cattle farms, paddy fields, small holder plantations and timber plantations based on reforestation are only impressive project proposals and planning maps. The Wau Ecology Institute produces information material, booklets and books and organizes seminars, workshops and excursions to sites logged in order to contribute to initiating better development and introducing relevant changes.

However, the government of Japan has declared that Papua New Guinea will not receive any further aid if its activities are restrained. Therefore, the Japanese logging companies, backed in such a way by their government, will continue what they are doing at the moment: skinning the land.

Literature Cited

Behrend, R.W.P. 1990. *Raubmord am Regenwald.* Rowohlt Verlag, Hamburg.

D'Ath, C. 1980. *The Throwaway People: Social Impact of the Gogol Timber Project.* Monograph 13. Madang Province. Inst. of Applied Social and Economic Research, Port Moresby, Papua New Guinea.

Dalpadado, V. 1984. Principles for a coworker in the Subsistence Agriculture Improvement Project of the Wau Ecology Institute. *In* F. Göltenboth, ed. *Subsistence Agriculture Improvement Manual,* pp. 214-215. Handbook 10. Wau Ecology Institute, Wau, Papua New Guinea.

Gagne, W. 1979. *Natural Control of Insect Pests in an Organic Garden.* Leaflet 3. South Pacific Commission Workshop on Biological Control, Noumea. Wau Ecology Institute, Wau, Papua New Guinea.

Gagne, W. 1980. The transformation and intensification of shifting cultivation: past and present practices. *In* L. Moranta, J. Gernetta and W. Heaney, eds. *Traditional Conservation in Papua New Guinea: Implications for Today.* Monograph 16. Inst. of Applied Social and Economic Research, Port Moresby, Papua New Guinea.

Göltenboth, F. 1985a. Clear felling: A case study. *Catalyst* 15: 129-136.

Göltenboth, F. 1985b. Umweltschutz und Subsistenzlandwirtschaft im Tropenwald. Praktische Beispiele aus dem biologischen Landbau. *Entwicklung und Ländlicher Raum* 19: 19-21.

Göltenboth, F. 1989. Pencemaran Lingkungan dan Social. *J. Bina Darma* 26: 66-76.

Göltenboth, F. ed. 1990. *Subsistence Agriculture Improvement. Manual for the Humid Tropics.* Handbook 10. Wau Ecology Institute, Wau, Papua New Guinea.

Gressitt, J.L. and K.P. Lamb. 1976. *Ecology and Conservation in Papua New Guinea.* Pamphlet 2. Wau Ecology Institute, Wau, Papua New Guinea.

Gressitt, J.L. ed. 1982. *Biogeography and Ecology of New Guinea.* Junk Publ. The Hague.

Lee, D. 1980. *The Sinking Ark.* Heinemann Publ. Co, Singapore.

Annex

Table 1. Forest clearance and agricultural development (Lee 1980).

Cost	Benefits
Labor and equipment for cutting forest	Cutting and selling of timber
Labor and materials for developing plantations	Temporarily increased employment from rapid timber harvest
Fertilizer costs	
Pesticide costs	Interim crops such as tapioca, eventual profits, from rubber, oil palm and cocoa
Labor and materials for building towns, schools, hospitals, etc	Increased employment from plantations and related industries
Fuel costs	New town sites for an expanding population

Other costs
   Flood damage and costs of flood
   Loss of future forest timber revenues
   Loss of minor forest products, such as
      wildlife, rattan bamboo
   Loss of homes and way of life for
      indigenous people
   Change in local climate
   Agricultural pollution
   Loss of revenue from wildlife
   Extinction of animals and plants due to
      habitat destruction
   Loss of recreation
	Intensively cultivated vegetable gardens, poultry and livestock near the towns

Figure 1. Mid-montane landscape in the Morobe Province, Papua New Guinea.

Figure 2. Flowering liana in the lower story of a primary rain forest.

Figure 3. Tree climber marsupial Cuscus (*Phalanger ursinus*).

Figure 4. Freshly cleared area in front of a primary forest in the mid-montane Bulolo Valley, Morobe Province, Papua New Guinea.

Figure 5. Terraces of a gold mine in the Bulolo Valley, Papua New Guinea.

Figure 6. Cocao tree with fruit in a cash crop plantation.

Figure 7. Modern cash cropping.

Figure 8. Typical subsistence garden with important plants such as sugar cane, banana, papaya, sweet potatos and taro, surrounding the self-constructed house of the subsistence farmer.

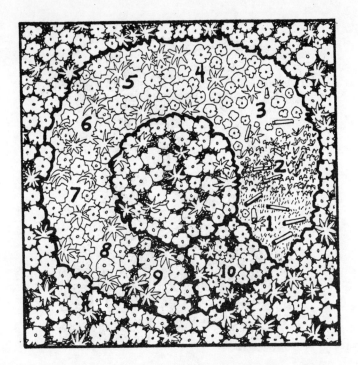

Figure 9. Drawing showing the first type of bush-fallowing rotation in the shifting cultivation system of Papua New Guinea. 1. Newly prepared garden area. 2-5. Garden areas in use. 6-8. Areas of regrowing secondary forest. The village is located in the center (Göltenboth, 1990).

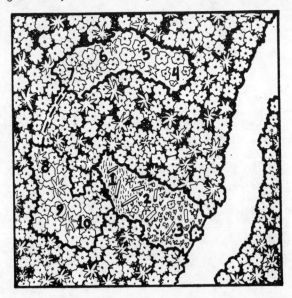

Figure 10. Drawing showing the second type of bush-fallowing rotation in shifting cultivation system of Papua New Guinea. 1. Newly prepared area. 2-5. Garden areas in use. 6-8. Areas of regrowing secondary forest. 9-10. Fully established secondary forest. The village is not necessarily located nearby (Göltenboth, 1990).

566

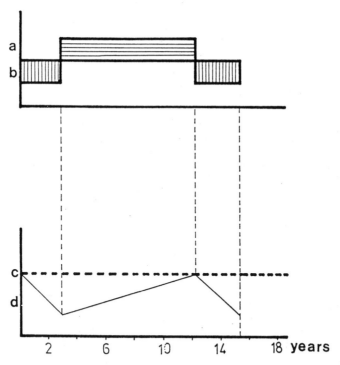

Figure 11. Land use rotation and changes in soil nutrient level in the cultivation system with long fallow period (Göltenboth, 1990).

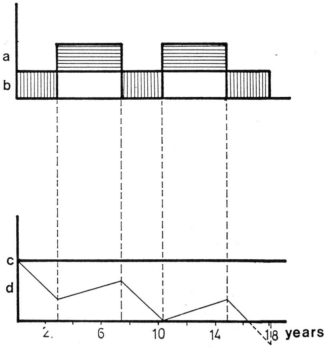

Figure 12. Land use rotation and changes in soil nutrient level in the cultivation system with short fallow period (Göltenboth, 1990).

Figure 13. Coconut plantation near Finchhafen, Pacific coast of the Morobe Province, Papua New Guinea.

Figure 14. A klinki pine stand in a reforestation area of a plywood factory.

Figure 15. Area cleared for a subsistence garden. To kill the taller trees they are "ringed" not felled.

Figure 16. Subsistence farmer with a digging stick in a freshly burned subsistence garden.

569

Figure 17. Terraces and moulds (ditches) in an improved subsistence garden growing sweet potatos (*Ipomoea batata*).

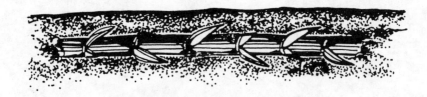

Figure 18. Sugar cane planting technique. The "eyes" of the sugar cane piece are in a horizontal position to allow for optimal growth (Göltenboth, 1990).

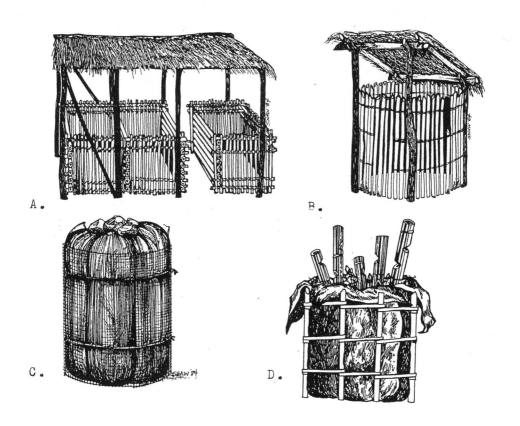

Figure 19. Tyes of compost stockades. A. Tripartite stockade for production of large quantities of compost. B. Fence stockade for production of small quantities for the individual farmer's use.
C. Movable mesh stockade. D. Plastic-shed stockade in which hollow bamboo canes are put providing ventilation for the compost during rotting. Types A, B and C are lined with banana leaves which are also used to cover the compost mixture during rotting.

Figure 20. Materials used in the production of high quality compost within a short period of time. 1. Organic material such as banana leaves, grass, etc. 2. Banana trunks. 3. Leaves and small tree branches. 4. Animal manure which is only necessary to initiate the rotting process if no other material is available. 5. Organic waste from households and/or markets. 6. Two or three shovels of old compost to start the rotting process (Göltenboth, 1990).

Figure 21. Vegetable nursery with sawdust or sand bottom to prevent weed growth and roof to protect the soil or compost bricks from heavy rain and bright sun (Göltenboth, 1990).

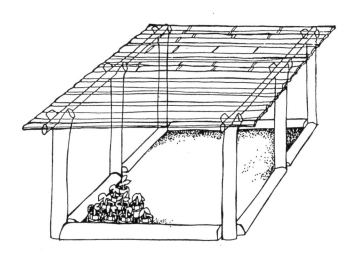

Figure 22. Tree seedling nursery where the soil is covered with sawdust or sand to prevent weed growth (Göltenboth 1990).

Figure 23. Setting for the manufacture of banana-fibre pots.

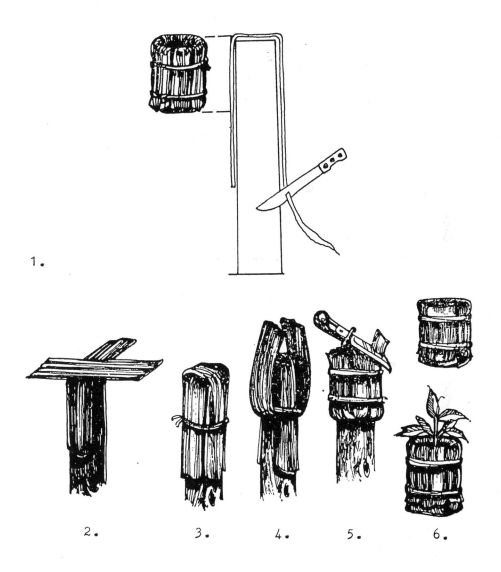

Figure 24-25. Stages of banana-fibre pot production (Göltenboth, 1990). 1. Marking the pot size by bending dried banana-stem fibres over a post. 2. Bending the fibres over the post. 3. Tying the fibres in the center with a small banana-fibre rope. 4. Bending the lower parts up while keeping the fibres in position. 5. Tying of the upper end (near the upper rim) and of the lower end and the subsequent cutting of the remaining banana fibres.

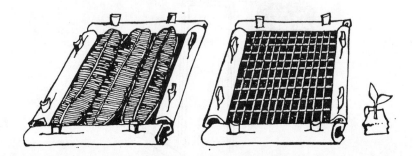

Figure 26. The production and application of compost bricks in a vegetable nursery surrounded by trunks made of the pseudo-stem of banana plants and covered with banana leaves to keep the soil moist during germination of the seeds (Göltenboth, 1990). The bricks are produced by cutting the moist layer of soil with a bushknife. About 2 seeds are planted in one small square.

Figure 27. Compost brick with plant seedling.

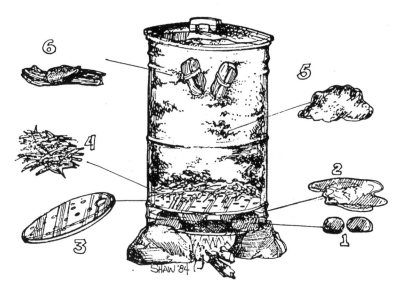

Figure 28. Construction and operation system of a drum-steamer to sterilize soil and compost mixture (Göltenboth, 1990). 1. Stones at the bottom of the drum on which to place the perforated lid. 2. Water. 3. Perforated drum lid. 4. Grass on top of the drum lid to prevent the soil-compost mixture from falling through the holes in the lid. 5. Soil-compost mixture. 6. Potatos (wrapped in banana leaves and placed in the upper third of the soil-compost mixture) serving as an indicator of when the steaming process to sterilize the soil-compost mixture is finished.

Figure 29. Soil sterilization drum in operation.

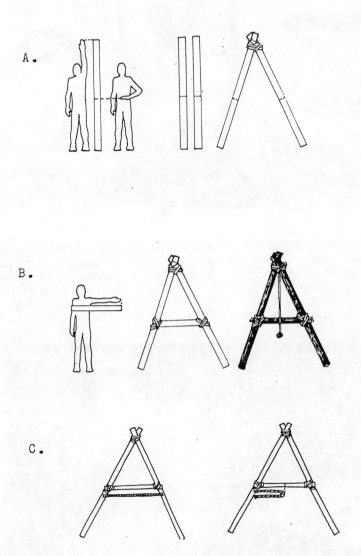

Figure 30. Construction of an A-shaped frame using body measurements (A, B) and the technique to determine the exact center of its crossbeam (C).

Figure 31. Application of the A-shaped frame in a sloping area.

Figure 32. Mixed planting system in a terraced sloping garden area. To stabilize the contour ridges cassuarina, leucena, fruit trees, sugar cane or other cane species may be used.

Figure 33. Silt traps between garden beds (Göltenboth, 1990).

Figure 34. Strip planting in a forest area (Göltenboth, 1990).

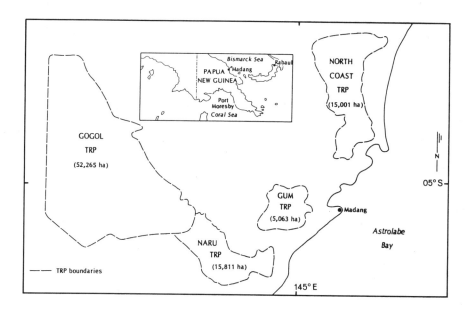

Figure 35. The Timber Purchase Rights areas (TRP) of the Japanese and New Guinea Timber Ltd (JANT), a subsidiary company of Honshu Paper Ltd near the Pacific coast in the Madang Province, Papua New Guinea (D'Ath, 1980).

Figure 36. The "frontline" of a clear felling project, Gogol near Madang on the Pacific coast of Papua New Guinea.

Figure 37. The JANT complex in the harbor of Madang, Papua New Guinea, where about 20,000 tons of woodchips are piled to be shipped to Japan.

Figure 38. Village in the Gogol Clear-Felling Project of the Honshu Paper Ltd and her subsidiary company Japanese and New Guinea Timber Company (JANT).

Proceedings of the International and Interdisciplinary Symposium
ECOLOGY AND LANDSCAPE MANAGEMENT IN SRI LANKA
W. Erdelen, C. Preu, N. Ishwaran, C.M. Madduma Bandara (eds.)
Colombo, Sri Lanka, 12-26 March 1990
© 1993
Margraf Scientific Books, D-97985 Weikersheim
ISBN 3-8236-1182-8

The Application of Remote Sensing Techniques for Surveys on Forest Damage

The German Experience

W. KIRCHHOF

Abstract

Since forest damage was recorded from all over Germany, the Ministry of Research and Technology of the Federal Republic of Germany has been supporting cooperative research projects for the development of methods for the detection, classification and mapping of forest damage using multispectral data from remote sensing systems. For surveys on forest damage of fir, pine, beech and oak stands, ten test areas were selected varying in environmental parameters such as topography, stand of trees, etc. Eight institutions cooperate using aerial CIR photos and multispectral scanner data from airborne and satellite platforms. Different image correction and processing methods were applied, including spectral signature analysis and additional spectroradiometer measurements on the ground. Results obtained indicate that the use of supervised classification, based on spectral differences of healthy and damaged classes, gives good and reliable results for larger homogenous stands using airborne data. Non-uniform spectral behavior which has been caused, for instance, by the relief of the area analyzed, the mixture of tree species or the statistical distribution of damage, are still causing confusion.

Introduction

Over the last decade, forest damage has become a serious environmental problem in Germany and adjacent European countries where severe forest damage has been observed in various regions. Investigations reveal that this present forest damage occurs in industrial areas as well as in areas with "clean air". In addition, forest damage seems neither to be caused by natural hazards, such as storms or climatic anomalies, nor by so-called "classic" biotic or abiotic factors. In general, the damage is optically visible as leaves and needles change color and turn yellow, the trees lose their leaves and needles, the crowns thin out and branching becomes anomalous. However, the symptoms vary from tree to tree. Some are typical for specific species and change seasonally. Anomalous branching often indicates the early stage of degradation, sometimes more than one decade before "real" damage occurs. Since symptoms of damage become visible in the crown section first, damage measuring systems should focus on data from the treetops. Aerial photos or multispectral scanner data from airborne or satellite platforms can meet these requirements. When forest damage was first noted, mainly fir and spruce trees were affected (Hermann *et al.* 1988), but increasing damage has been recorded for deciduous trees since 1983 (Landauer and Voss, 1989). According to the forest damage statistics of the Federal Republic of Germany for 1988, 63.4% of beech and 61.6% of oaktrees were already damaged. 39% of the forests were deciduous and 61% coniferous. The total damage amounted to 50.2% in 1984, 52.3% in 1987 and 52.4% in 1988 (Tab. 1, annexed).

Methods

The most common method for surveying and inventorying forest damage is the interpretation of color infrared (CIR) aerial photographs. With the use of standard evalution methods and a new forest damage classification key, comparable data could be obtained from sample areas located in different regions at variable data acquisition times. At the beginning, the main information about damage or disease of trees was derived from the color, but color may vary rather widely depending on factors such as film type, processing and flight mission. However, it was one of the major findings of a group of experts using this photo interpretation technique to detect forest damage (Kenneweg, 1989), to work out a general interpretation key applicable in different regions at different flight times and that "structural elements of tree crowns and their reproduction in aerial photographs rather than colors are used as the main source of information for identifying different damage classes." The degree of discoloration resulting from forest damage can play an important role for the preparation of a classification. For the results under discussion, the UN-ECE forest damage classification scheme was used as an European standard, but structural elements have not yet been considered (Tab. 2). The fundamental differences in the evaluation of visual features for damage classification, in particular the loss of leaves or needles and the discoloration on one side and the additional consideration of structural elements on the other side, indicate a general problem of photo interpretation techniques. The changes in tree crowns and branching of beech is illustrated in Runkel and Roloff (1985a, 1985b, 1985c).

Table 2. UN-ECE forest damage classification scheme for trees, used as an European standard. Class definition: 0 = healthy, 1 = low damage, 2 = medium damage, 3 = heavy damage, 4 = dead.

Loss of leaves/ needles	Yellowing		
	11%-25%	26%-60%	61%-100%
<10%	0	1	2
11%-25%	1	2	2
26%-60%	2	3	3
>60%	3	3	3
Dead trees	4	4	4

Multispectral Scanner Data

Research Objectives of the Cooperative Forest Damage Project

The investigation of forest damage demanded inventories of the spatial distribution of forest damage and its change over large areas in support of further studies. The final goal was to find out the reasons for this damage. Therefore, the German Ministry of Research and Technology (BMFT) in Bonn supported a cooperative research project between 1987 and 1989 to develop

Table 3. Cooperating partners, test areas and main research tasks of the project "Investigation and mapping of forest damage by means of remote sensing" See Figure 1 (annexed) for location of test areas.

Cooperating Partners	Research Subjects
Dr. Landauer DLR, German Aerospace Research Establishment, Oberpfaffenhofen	For all test areas Project coordination, data acquisition, preprocessing and distribution, radiometric correction including atmospheric effects Test areas: Black Forest, Fichtelgebirge and Stadtwald Frankfurt Optimization of feature selection and classification of forest damage, measurement and analysis of spectral signatures
Prof. Akca Universität Göttingen	Test area: Ith-Hils Tree species: spruce Signature analysis, combination of multispectral information and thematic information in a geographic information system (GIS), ecology
Prof. Albertz Techn. Universität Berlin	Geometric rectification including the use of flight attitude data, digital terrain models (DTM)
Prof. Ammer	Test areas: Haunstetten, Reichswald, Höglwald Universität Munich Tree species: pine, spruce Signature measurement and analysis, damage classification and mapping
Dr. Haydn GAF Gesellschaft für Angewandte Fernerk.	Test area: Schluchsee Tree species: spruce Processing of multispectral data and CIR film, GIS implementation for damage mapping
Prof. Hildebrandt Universität Freiburg	Test areas: Black Forest and Vogelsberg Tree species: spruce, fir, beech, oak Damage classification and multitemporal analysis
Prof. Kenneweg Techn. Universität Berlin	Test area: Harz Tree species: spruce Signature analysis, damage classification and mapping, feature analysis
Dr. Schramm ifp-Institut für Planungsdaten, Offenbach	Test area: Stadtwald Frankfurt Tree species: beech, oak, pine Damage classification and mapping of larger areas with mixed stands, signature analysis, close collaboration with DLR

methods for (1) the detection, (2) classification and (3) mapping of forest damage in larger areas of Germany with the use of remotely sensd multispectral data. The project started in late 1985 and was terminated at the end of 1989. The final report was issued in December 1989 by Landauer and Voss (1989).

The main research objective was the development and the verification of new multispectral scanner techniques including image processing and mapping. However, this approach required a new understanding of the information content of multispectral remote sensing data from forests with respect to damage classes of the same species in both single and mixed speies forest stands. Five institutes of German universities, two private firms and the German Aerospace Research Establishment (DLR) participated in the project. Among the participating specialists were experts in different fields such as forestry, landscape ecology, landscape planning, remote sensing and image processing. The test areas were selected in such a way that investigations could cover fir, spruce, pine, beech and oak tree stands. Different approaches for the detection of damage and its classification were applied by different working groups (Tab. 3) Each cooperating partner carried out his specific research programs in selected test sites. Between 1986 and 1988, the DLR which conducted the overflights at different altitudes and flight times, gathered airborne multispectral scanner data from altitudes between 300 m and 4000 m above the ground, normally taken at noon in a north to south flight direction. In addition, bands of Landsat MSS and TM as well as of SPOT image data were procured, distributed and processed.

Characteristics of Multispectral Scanner Data

The analysis of multispectral scanner data is different from the interpretation of aerial photographs. The spatial resolution of scanners is defined by the instantaneous field of view (IFOV) in respect to the size of the image element. The size of the image element is determined by the IFOV of the sensor and the flight altitude. The sensor field of view (FOV) defines the total scan angle (Fig. 2).

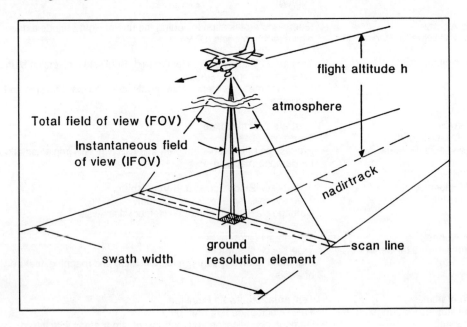

Figure 2. Principle of airborne scanner data acquisition.

The FOV is defined by the scanning motion of the optical system, which is a rotating mirror scanning the surface perpendicular to the flight direction. The scanner produces the across-track-scan-motion and scans the surface line by line. The along-track-motion of the sensor is provided by the velocity of the platform such as satellite, aircraft or balloon. A multispectral scanner, while detecting the surface, produces radiance related signals, each belonging to a defined spectral band and location. These data and specific calibration measurements are processed and transmitted to the ground receiving station, or they are directly recorded on magnetic tape or film on the platform. These data may undergo further preprocessing such as calibration and geometric rectification before they are presented and processed as raster images. For each image element, the integral spectral radiance is recorded. In this application, the integral reflected spectral radiance may be produced by the forest cover of one single species and, hence, may generate a so-called "pure pixel", or may be produced by surface elements, which may also contain portions of other plant communities, as well as road network, gravel, etc, and hence generate so-called "mixed pixels", which obviously influence the spectral analysis.

Table 4. Comparison of color infrared (CIR) film and multispectral scanner data performance for evaluation of forest damage.

	CIR film	Multispectral scanner data
Source	Kodak "Aerochrome infrared 2443" Scale 1: 3000/10,000 Kodak "High definition aerochrome" Scale above 1: 10,000	Daedalus ATM 1268 Landsat-TM
Spatial resolution	High	Low
Spectral region	Small: 0.5 - 0.9 µm	Large: 0.4 - 14 µm
Spectral resolution	Low	High
Dynamic radiometric range	Low	High
Available products	Aerial photographs	Digitial imagery on CCT or film copies
Reproduction	Degraded copies	No degradation from CCT
Radiometric fidelity	Dependent on: emulsion, illumination/turbidity, storage and handling; film processing	Calibrated radiances/ reflectances
Image processing/ evaluation	Subjective, time consuming, tedious, trained personnel required	Objective, computerized processing need for geometric and radiometric processing
Application status	Operational	Experimental
GIS application	Conversion of data/results in digital form necessary, information loss possible	Data/results directly available in digital form for further processing

In photographic systems, the data are recorded simultaneously from a central point of view, whereas scanner images present a view perpendicular from the center line or nadir and the data are gathered in a sequential fashion. The applicability of these systems, i.e. CIR film and multispectral scanner data for investigating forest damage is different as a consequence of data acquisition geometry, spatial, spectral and radiometric resolution and radiometric range and further influencing fators as indicated in Table 4.

Data Aquisition

For airborne measurements, the 11-channel multispectral line scanner Daedalus ATM 1268 was used. Its channel allocation, band width and compatibility with Landsat Thematic Mapper (TM) spectral channels is described in Figure 3 (Amann, 1986). Flying at an altitude of 1000 m above ground, the resulting swath width is 1860 m. For each scan line 716 image elements are recorded. This corresponds to an instantaneous scan angle of 2.5 mrad and an image element size of 2.5 m x 2.5 m at the nadir (subpoint). Since multispectral scanner data were gathered from altitudes between 300 m and 4000 m above the ground the pixel sizes range from 0.75 m x 0.75 m to 10 m x 10 m. For comparison and interpretation purposes such as definition and verification, the aerial camera of the type Zeiss RMK A 30/23 was used to cover the same scene with color infrared photos simultaneously with the scanner. A Kodak CIR film 2443 or the high spectral resolution film SO 131, mainly for higher altitudes, was used.

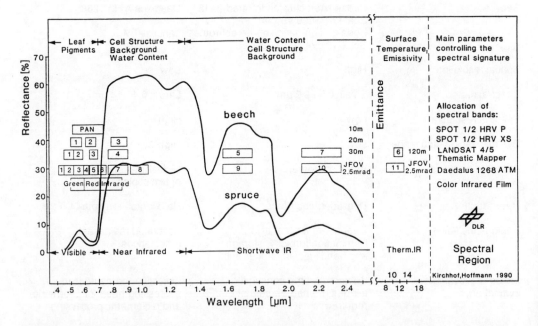

Figure 3. Spectral band allocation and bandwidth of SPOT 1-2, Landsat TM, Daedalus 1268 ATM and color infrared film. Main parameters controling the spectral signature of vegetation are indicated in addition the spectral reflectance of five stacked green branches of beech and spruce in the reflective portion of the solar spectrum.

Data Analysis

Multispectral scanner data cover a wider spectral range than CIR photos. For interpetation purposes, the spectrum of vegetation can be divided into three rather distinct ranges (Johnson 1969, Sinclair *et al.* 1971, Walter 1981 and Rock *et al.* 1986; see Fig. 3). In the visible range (400-700 nm) the main part of the radiation energy is absorbed by the plant pigments of the upper leave or the needle layer. Reflection and transmission is rather low. In the near infrared range (NIR; 700-1300 nm) the reflection of green vegetation is high, but depends on the species and number of layers. Reflectance is mainly influenced by cell structure, background and water content. In the short wave infrared range (SWIR; 1300-4000 nm) reflectance can be attributed to water content, cell structure and background.

Spectral reflectance depends on plant species and age, form and orientation of leaves or needles, branches, stem, background and health status (Koch 1987, Hermann *et al.* 1988, Kirchhof *et al.* 1988, Hoffmann and Kirchhof 1989a, 1989b). In addition, conditions of the ground such as soil cover, surface roughness, relief, mineral supply, humidity and heavy metal content are main parameters, influencing the optical behavior (Collins *et al.* 1983, Kronberg 1985). Hildebrandt (1976) and Tanner *et al.* (1981) found that the spectral signature of beech and spruce is spectrally stable in the period from mid-July to the end of August in the study areas. Therefore, airborne data acquisition was restricted to this period of time.

In systematic overflights at different flight altitudes, the spectral reflectance of single crowns and larger assemblies such as forest stands and their state of damage was investigated. Complementary to airborne cartography of only selected areas with respect to damage, a large-scale mapping of the Bavarian forests was conducted by means of satellite images. For this purpose thematic maps at a scale 1: 200,000 were produced, each covering an area of 90 km x 95 km. The main objective was the separation of deciduous forest, coniferous forest and mixed forest in preparation of further damage identification at the single species level.

Image Processing

Acquisition and processing of multispectral scanner data are determined by the users' needs, spectral, temporal and spatial characteristics, the quality of the scene and the data processing capabilities, including output devices. Depending on the evaluation goal and the level of interest, image processing includes the following steps; (1) data acquisition, (2) image preprocessing and processing, (3) image classification and interpretation, and (4) modelling approaches. For this project, aircraft and satellites served as observation platforms (Fig. 4). Airborne multispectral data were mainly applied for research and development of application, whereas satellite data were used for more operational oriented investigations. The data flow mentioned above shows a sequence in which operations and products for the generation of information about tree species and forest damage were successfully applied.

General Results of Forest Damage Classification

In the test areas the characteristics of healthy and damaged vegetation varied largely in size, form and attributes. In some areas, damage patterns are statistically distributed single-tree-wise. In other parts, patterns are uniform in homogeneous stands. The degree of damage can often be correlated with the age of trees. Forest damage can be attributed to three damage classes 0/1, 2, 3, provided that the specific signature can be defined and extracted from the mixed spectral signature - or better - from the stand characteristics. The spectral separation of damage requires a profound understanding of the primary and secondary effects of the particular damage class on the behavior of the spectral signal. The accuracy of damage classification using airborne scanner data could be greatly improved and the usable angular range could be extended by a factor of two, if radiometric and atmospheric corrections (empirical approach) are combined

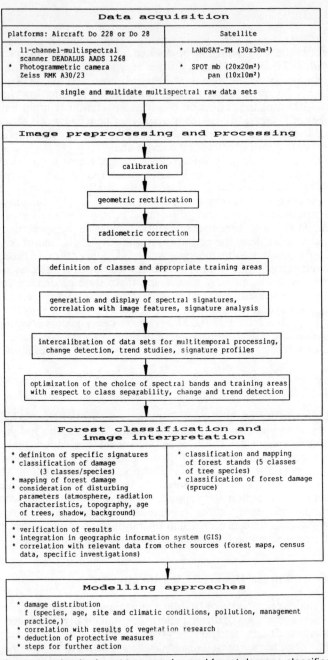

Figure 4. Information generation for forest tree species and forest damage classification and mapping of larger areas with the use of multispectral image data: data acquisition and image preprocessing and processing (top); forest classification and image interpretation and modelling approaches (bottom).

(Kritikos *et al.* 1988). By optimizing the choice of spectral bands and verification in training areas, the error rates of automatic classification could be reduced considerably (Reinartz, 1989).

The results of different image processing methods indicate that with supervised classification, based on spectral differences between healthy and damaged classes, good and reliable results can be obtained for larger homogenous stands. A large amount of non-uniform spectral behavior, caused, for instance by terrain relief, mixtures of tree species or statistical distribution of damage classes, is still a source of confusion or makes the separation of damage classes from the spectral information impossible.

The tendency to underestimate damage when using scanner techniques in comparison to CIR-film interpretation is confirmed. Photointerpretation is done tree by tree; only information from the tree surface is accounted for. Scanner data represent the average spectral radiance of the image element concerned. It includes not only surface portions of trees but also their environment.

Therefore, if only crown portions of different degrees of damage are recorded, the mean value will tend to a medium value. Landsat TM data renders spectral separation in different object classes of deciduous and coniferous forest as well as mixed forest possible (Keil *et al.* 1990). In the Regensburg area, five forest classes could be identified by means of supervised multispectral classification (Tab. 5). The test area covering about 96 km x 89 km with quite varied "growth zones" amd "growth districts". For the multitemporal approach, two sets of Landsat TM data, one for 20 April 1984 and one for 9 July, 1984, were processed. These data did not permit the classification of damage classes in the Regensburg test areas. However, in the Harz test area, three different damage classes for spruce trees could be separated using a threshold technique (TM channels 4 and 5). In a larger area near Nuremberg, which was severely affected by an insect calamity (*Lymanatria monacha*), different damage gradients were detected, correlated with soil types and mapped (Landauer and Voss, 1989).

Table 5. Classification of damage(%) in 211 training areas and 238 control areas for five tree classes of the map TÜK 200, Regensburg.

	Deciduous	Spruce/ Pine	Pine	Mixed Deciduous/ Coniferous	Blanks/ Cultures	Non- Forest	Sum of Classified Pixels
Deciduous	85.9	1.5	-	11.9	0.1	0.6	2899
Spruce/ Pine	0.1	88.5	9.5	1.6	0.3	0.2	8256
Pine	-	17.8	80.0	1.5	0.6	-	3441
Mixed Deciduous/ Coniferous	11.5	16.9	2.0	69.1	-	0.5	2217
Blanks/ Cultures	10.3	0.2	-	2.7	74.5	10.3	224

Spectral Measurements

Measurement Philosophy

Spectral analysis of forest stands in the Stadtwald Frankfurt test area revealed that primary and/or secondary effects of damage influence the spectral signatures (Guttmann *et al.* 1987). More detailed information could not be derived from multispectral scanner data with a pixel size ranging from 5m x 5m to 10m x 10m (Kirchhof *et al.* 1988). Therefore, spectroradiometric measurements became necessary.

The primary effects resulting from damage were (1) a change in the spectral signature of tree components, i.e. the branches, leaves, needles, barks and lichens, (2) the discoloration of leaves and needles, (3) a loss of leaves, needles and biomass, (4) the orientation of branches, leaves and needles as well as the roll of leaves, and (5) a change of crown structure and texture including anomalous branching. These lead to changes in the course of the sprectral signature of the trees.

The secondary effect is caused by an increase in background radiation, due to the loss of biomass, the change of crown structure and anomalous branching which leads to an increase in optical transparency and shadow. To improve our understanding of spectral signature changes resulting from tree damage, a measurement program of tree components was developed to improve the understanding of spectral signature changes resulting from tree damage. The central theme of this program is the understanding of the reflectance behavior from tree components in different compositions (layers) and its application in the selection of spectral bands and image processing algorithms for multispectral classification, and to optimize damage identification and separation at an early stage.

Table 6. Measurement configuration and instrument data for the simulation of multispectral scanner data acquisition (nadir looking at noon).

Bidirectional Reflectance Measurements	
Instrument	Iris Mark IV Spectroradiometer, double beam design for two targets
Sample, reference spectral range	0.49-2.50 µm
Spectral resolution	2 nm at 0.49-1.06 µm, 2 xSi 4 nm at 1.04-1.88 µm, 2 x PbS 6 nm at 1.84-2.50 µm, cooled 243 K
Viewing angle	0°
Illumination angle	30° laboratory measurement
Sample measurement	3-5 continuous scans
Reference measurement	White standard, Halon G-80 parallel to each sample scan, before and after sample change on the sample beam
IFOV (Instantaneous Field of View)	12 x 4 cm^2 at 140 cm distance
Laboratory illumination source	Quartz-halogene 1000 W,180 cm above sample

Simulations of a multispectral scanner data acquisition, i.e. nadir looking at noon, were carried out (Tab. 6). The high resolution spectral measurements were conducted in one continuous scan. The spectra of the vegetation sample and the reference sample (white standard) were measured simultaneously so that variations in illumination intensity and spectrum could be corrected automatically. The signal level was monitored for gain and scan time selection. Both these sets of data were stored and recorded for processing at a later stage either as two separate spectra calibrated for radiation or as a single ratio spectrum calibrated in terms of percentage reflectance.

Results from Spectral Measurements of Beech and Spruce Branches

The reflectance of single branches as well as stacked branches (up to 7) of beech (*Fagus sylvatica*) and spruce (*Picea abies*) was measured with the IRIS Mark IV spectroradiometer at a wavelength range from 0.49 μm to 2.50 μm. Each sample was measured several times; five times in 1988 and 3 times in 1989. For each measurement the branches were rearranged, and a mean value was calculated. The background reflectance in every case was less than 10%. In 1988, the measurements focused on spectral signatures of beech, but spruce branches were also measured for comparison. In 1989, the main objective was the measurement of the spectral signatures of branches from damaged beech and spruce trees.

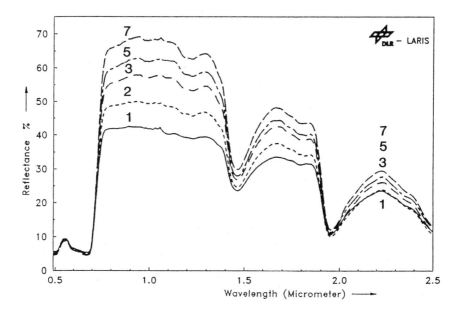

Figure 5. Reflectance of beech branches with shadow leaves for single and up to seven stacked branches. The numbers indicate the quantity of branches piled up.

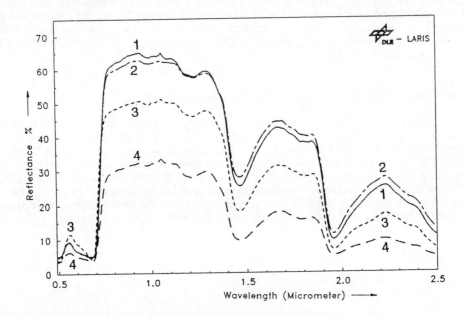

Figure 6. Reflectance of five stacked branches of 1 = beech with sun leaves, 2 = beech with shadow leaves, 3 = beech with discolored leaves and 4 = spruce.

When healthy beech branches were stacked, the most obvious change in reflection occurred in the infrared range (IR). Reflection increases with any additional branch and reaches its maximum when 5-7 branches are stacked (Fig. 5). Reflection remains relatively unchanged in the visible (vis) and the water absorption region of 1900 nm.

This result verifies that the pigments of the highest surface layer determine the spectral response in this wavelength range. In the infrared range, reflection is influenced by the contribution of multiple transmitted and scattered radiation as well as water and/or carbon dioxide absorption. For the measurement configuration, optical thickness was reached for 5-7 stacked branches.

Results of the reflectance measurements of five stacked branches of (1) beech with sun leaves (2) with shadow leaves, (3) with discolored leaves (yellowing) and (4) spruce indicate that differences in species and color determine the course, mainly the level of the near infrared plateau in addition to minor variations in reflectance of sun leaves and shadow leaves of beech (Fig. 6). The curves show the general shape of spectral signatures of green vegetation. In the visible range, the course of discolored beech branches differs considerably from those of green beech. Yellowing results in (1) an increase of reflectance in the green-red range, (2) a "red shift" of the reflection peak at about 10 nm and (3) a change of its course at the red edge, which may be caused by decreasing chlorophyll absorption near to 680 nm.

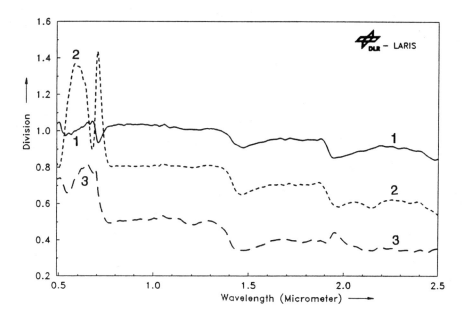

Figure 7. Ratio spectra, each spectrum of five stacked branches of 1 = beech with sun leaves, 2 = beech with yellowing and 3 = spruce divided through the corresponding spectrum of beech with shadow leaves.

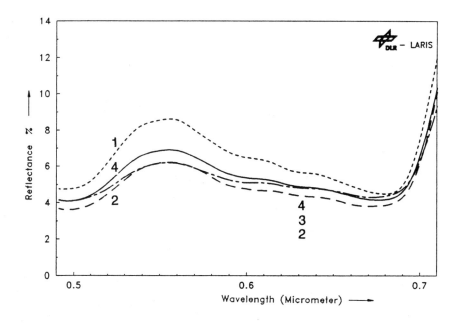

Figure 8. Reflectance spectra of spruce, measured at a branch with 1 = current year's needles, 2 = 1 year old needles, 3 = 2-4 year old needles, 4 = total sample.

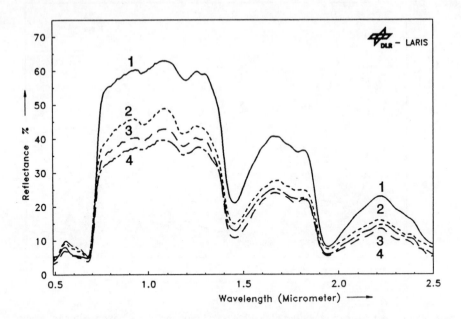

Figure 9. Reflectance of beech branches of different damage classes, 5 branches piled up from trees of 1 = damage class 0/1; 2,3 = damage class 2/3; 4 = damage class 3.

The calculation of the ratio spectra shows these effects clearly (Fig. 7). The double peaked feature in the division spectrum of the yellowed beech sample is most prominent. The first maximum is caused by the increase and "red shift" of the reflectance peak in the visible range of the sun spectrum. The second maximum located at the "red edge" is caused by the preceded rise of the spectral curve of branches with yellowing in contrast respect to green branches with shadow leaves.In the visible range, the age of needles influences their spectral reflectance (Fig. 8). Measurements of the current year's young needles from branches collected on 20 July 1988 show that a high amount of sprouts increases reflectance in the visible and near infrared stage, whereas reflectance decreases on the short-wave-infrared range (SWIR). If this effect is not considered, classification errors may occur.

In the infrared range, spectral reflectance of beech branches decreases with the increase of damage (Fig. 9). Spectral analyses of multispectral scanner data gathered by the airborne Deadalus scanner at flight altitudes of 2000 m and 4000 m from beech and oak stands in the Stadtwald Frankfurt on 9 September, 1986, proved this spectral behavior for areas detected with 5 m x 5 m or 10 m x 10 m seized image elements (Guttmann *et al.* 1987, Kirchhof *et al.* 1988). These results led to the hypothesis that primary and secondary effects resulting from damage to the same species and the same age should result in a decrease of reflectance in the infrared range provided there is no other significant change in the surface layer vegetation. If there is no discoloration of leaves the same tendency should apply for the visible range.

The variation in spectral reflectance in the visible range is rather important for branches of the damage class 2/3 (Fig. 10). Although only primary effects of damage are considered within the frame of these measurements, they are superimposed by secondary effects with varying magnitudes of nature. Branches of the same damage class showed yellowing of different degrees leading to spectral variation. The higher spectral values for damage class 3 are caused by intensive yellowing.

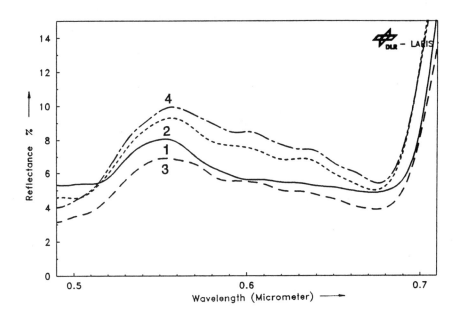

Figure 10. Reflectance in the visible of five piled up beech branches from trees of 1 = damage class 0/1; 2,3 = damage class 2/3; 4 = damage class 3.

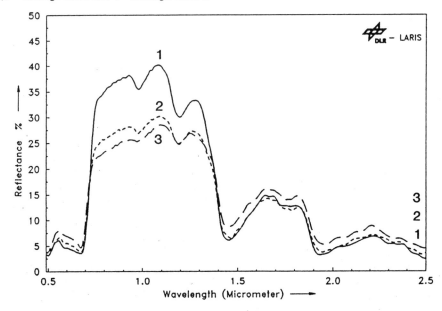

Figure 11. Reflectance of spruce branches of different damage classes for five branches piled up from trees of 1 = damage class 0/1, 2 = damage class 2 and 3 = damage class 3.

The calculation of the ratio spectra shows these effects clearly (Fig. 7). The double peaked feature in the division spectrum of the yellowed beech sample is most prominent. The first maximum is caused by the increase and "red shift" of the reflectance peak in the visible range of the sun spectrum. The second maximum located at the "red edge" is caused by the preceded rise of the spectral curve of branches with yellowing in contrast respect to green branches with shadow leaves.

In general, the course of reflectance of spruce branches fits the spectral reflectance curve of a drying up damaged pine stand in the Stadtwald Frankfurt (Guttmann *et al*. 1987, Kirchhof *et al*. 1988, Fig. 11). In the visible range, reflectance increases with increasing damage class as a consequence of discoloration or yellowing of needles (Fig. 12).

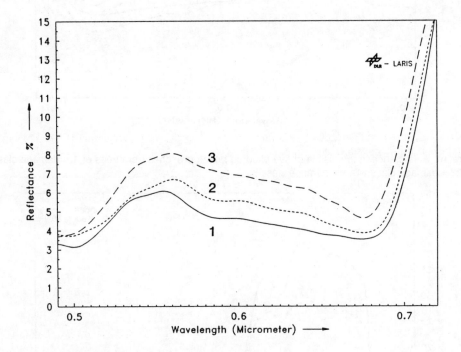

Figure 12. Reflectance of five piled up spruce branches in the visible for different damage classes; 1 = damage class 0/1, 2 = damage class 2 and 3 = damage class 3.

This effect is also proved by studies of Hoque *et al*. (1990) in a multilevel experiment of DLR and GSF. With increasing damage the minimum, before the curve raise up the NIR plateau, shifts to shorter wavelenghts and the curve gradient and the height of the plateau of the NIR decrease. Moreover, the water absorption in the NIR decreases with increasing damage level. Therefore, higher damage causes an increase of reflectance in NIR.

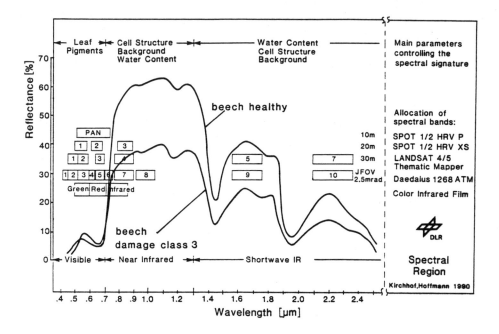

Figure 13. Spectral reflectance of five stacked healthy and heavily damaged beech branches in the visible region, near and shortwave infrared.

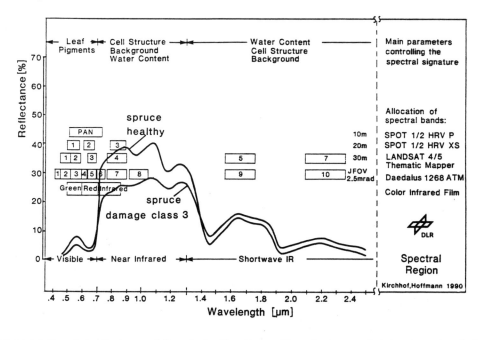

Figure 14. Spectral reflectance of five stacked healthy and heavily damaged spruce branches in the visible region, near and shortwave infrared.

Conclusions from Spectral Measurements of Beech and Spruce Branches

Measurements carried out (Figs. 5-14) show that the spectral behavior of tree components as a function of biomass, number of branches of the same species stacked up, the influence of species and the yellowing of healthy and damaged trees lies in the spectral range between 0.49 μm and 2.50 μm. Data from this spectral range are normally used in multispectral classification of vegetation. But further studies on the separability of forest and forest damage classes (Reinartz 1989, Kritikos *et al.* 1988, Kirchhof *et al.* 1986) confirm the results of our spectral measurements. The separation of tree species and degrees of yellowing is possible either by means of the spectral bands TM2 or TM3, TM4, TM5 and TM7 of the Landsat Thematic Mapper or the corresponding bands 3 or 5, 7, 9 and 10 of the Daedalus ATM scanner. But the best results in damage separation of the same species were obtained from the spectral signature ratios TM2/TM4 or TM3/TM4.

Recommendations for Investigations in the Future

For further project investigations a number of suggestions may be made. Multispectral scanner data recorded from planes flying at high altitudes (10 km) may result in pixel sizes of 15-30 m (Daedalus), and are comparable with data from existing earth resources satellites (Landsat, TM and SPOT). Larger areas can be covered by two or more overflights. High quality data can be obtained with flexiblilty regarding time acquisition and the choice of area. In addition, weather and illumination conditions should be selected according to their favorability for particular study targets in order to enable an optimized mission. Atmospheric, radiometric and geometric corrections have to be improved further as a matter of routine.

The implementation of geographic information systems, mainly their capability to combine information from different sources in modeling approaches, should become an essential element in the successful use of remote sensing techniques. In the future, imaging sensor systems with selectable spectral bands and high spectral and radiometric resolution should be adapted to the user's needs. The main demands from the forestry point of view are an improvement of spatial and radiometric resolution and the selection the optimal spectral bands. A mathematical model for the generation of spectral signatures from trees and tree stands in different conditions of health should be developed. Only a few input parameters such as leaf reflectance, canopy geometry, and ground (soil) reflectance, needed for the prediction and understanding of spectral reflectance and their variations by environmental impact would be required. This approach should be applicable to the main tree species and mixed forest. The spectral reflectance measurements of beech and spruce branches may be considered as a first step towards this direction.

Acknowledgments

The author is grateful to H. Hoffmann, DLR, for his close cooperation in spectral measurements and for the technical assistance and advice provided by his DLR colleagues and E. Hoque and P.J.S. Hutzler from GSF.

Literature Cited

Amann, V. 1986. *Multispectral Linescanner 'Daedalus AADS 1268 (ATM)*. Interne Mitteilung DLR, Operpfaffenhofen.

Collins, W., S.H. Chang, G. Raines, F. Canney and R. Ashley. 1983. Airborne Biogeophysical Mapping of Hidden Mineral Deposits. *Econ. Geol.* 78: 737-749.

Guttmann, S., W. Kirchhof, M. Lamberty, T. Roth, M. Schramm and I. Zwenger. 1987. Multispektrale Auswertung und Klassifikation von Flugzeug-Scanner-Daten im Untersuchungsgebiet Frankfurter Stadtwald, 2. *DLR Statusseminar*. DLR, Oberpfaffenhofen.

Hermann, K., B.N. Rock, U. Ammer and H.N. Paley. 1988. Preliminary assessment of airborne imaging spectrometer and Thematic Mapper data acquired for forest decline areas in the Federal Requblic of Germany. *Remote Sensing of the Environment* 24: 129-149.

Hildebrandt, G. 1976. Die spektralen Reflexionseigenschaften der Vegetation. Proc. XVI IUFRO World, Oslo.

Hoffmann, H. and W. Kirchhof. 1989a. Vergleichende reflexionsspektroskopische Vegetationsmessungen im Labor und Gelände an Rotbuchen- und Fichtenzweigen, Teil 1: Versuchsaufbau, Labormessungen, Modellierung. *DLR-JB* 552: 50.

Hoffmann, H. and W. Kirchhof. 1989b. Vergleichende reflexionsspektrokopische Vegetationsmessungen im Labor und Gelände an Rotbuchenund Fichtenzweigen, Teil 2: Geländemessungen, Vergleich mit Labordaten. Eignungstests verfügbarer Spektralbänder. *DLR-JB* 552: 56.

Hoque, E., P.J.S. Hutzler and H. Hiendl. 1990. Studies on reflective features of Norway spruce and their possible applications in remote sensing of forest damage. *Toxicol. Environ. Chem.* 27: 209-215.

Johnson, P.L. 1969. *Remote Sensing in Ecology*. University of Georgia, Athens.

Keil, M., M. Schardt, A. Schurek and R. Winter. 1990. Forest mapping in Bavaria, using satellite imagery and integrating additional map information: results in the three map sheets 1: 200,000 Regensburg, Nuremberg, Augsburg. *JSPRS symp. 1990,* Victoria B.C.

Kenneweg, H. 1989, Remote sensing approaches to assessment and diagnosis of forest decline. *In* I.B. Bucher and I. Bucher-Wallin, eds. *Air pollution and forest decline*, pp. 217-221. Birmendorf.

Kirchhof, W. and H. Hoffmann. 1990. The change of spectral signatures of beech and spruce by forest damage. *JSPRS Symp. 1990,* Victoria BC.

Kirchhof, W., S. Guttmann, M. Schramm, I. Zwenger and M. Lamberty. 1988. Spectral characterisation of forest damage in beech, oak and pine stands. *ESA SP* 284: 623-624.

Kirchhof, W., W. Mauser and H.J. Stibig. 1986. Investigation of the information content of Landsat Thermatic Mapper and SPOT multiband image data using simulated multispectral image data of the Freiburg region. *ESA TT* 975: 138.

Kuoch, B. 1987. *Quantifizierung von Schäden an Waldbäumen auf der Grundlage spektraler Rückstrahlungseigenschaften.* FB LMU München, Lehrst. Landschaftstechnik.

Kritikos, G., R. Mueller and P. Reinarzt. 1988. Optimization for classification of forest damage classes. *Proc. Spectral Signatures of Objects, ESA IPISP 287*:

Kronberg, P. 1985. *Fernerkundung der Erde.* Enke, Stuttgart.

Landauer, G. and H.H. Voss, eds. 1989. *Untersuchung und Kartierung von Waldschäden mit Methoden der Fernerkundung, Teil A,* DLR, Oberpfaffenhofen.

Reinartz, P. 1989. Untersuchungen zur multispektralen Klassifizierung von schwer trennbaren Klassen mit Beispielen aus Waldschadensgebieten. *DLR-FB* 89/55: 180.

Rock, B.N., I.E. Vogelmann, D.L. Williams, A.F. Vogelmann and T. Hoshizaki. 1986. Remote detection of forest damage. *Bioscience* Vol 36, No 7.

Runkel, M. and A. Roloff. 1985a. Schadstufen bei der Buche im Infrarotfarbluftbild. *AFZ* 30: 789-792.

Runkel, M. and A. Roloff. 1985b. Schadstufen bei der Buche im Infrarotfarbluftbild. *AFZ* 31: 789-792.

Runkel, M. and A. Roloff. 1985c. Schadstufen bei der Buche im Infrarotfarbluftbild. *AFZ* 32: 789-792.

Sinclair, T.R., R.M. Hoffer and M.M. Schreiber. 1971. Reflectance and internal structure of leaves from several crops during a growing season. *Agron. J.* 63: 864-868.

Tanner, V. and B.M. Eller. 1981. Veränderungen der spektralen Eigenschaften der Blätter der Buche (*Fagus sylvatica*) von Laubaustrieb bis Laubfall. *Allgem. Forst- u. Jagd Ztg.* 157: 108-117.

Waldzustandsbericht 1988. *Schriftenreihe des BML, Reihe A: Angewandte Wissenschaft*, Heft 364. Landwirtschaftsverlag, Münster-Hiltrup.

Walter, H. 1981. Optical Parameters of Leaves of Crops and Weeds. *Proc. Int. Coll. Spectral Signatures of Objects in Remote Sensing*, pp. 225-232. INRA, Versailles.

Annex

Table 1. Distribution of forest damage and main tree species affected in the Federal Republic of Germany in 1988 (Waldzustandsbericht, 1988).

Tree species	Surface portion		Damage portion			
			Damage classes 2-4		Damage classes 1-4	
	mill. ha	% of total forest area	mill. ha	% of total tree species area	mill. ha	% of total tree species area
Spruce	2.883	39.0	0.420	14.6	1.404	48.8
Pine	1.469	19.9	0.178	12.2	0.784	53.4
Fir	0.173	2.3	0.077	44.6	0.127	73.0
Other conifers	0.356	4.8	0.020	5.5	0.094	26.5
Beech	1.259	17.0	0.213	16.9	0.799	63.4
Oak	0.622	8.5	0.151	24.2	0.433	69.6
Other deciduous trees	0.626	8.5	0.062	9.9	0.232	37.0
Total	7.388	100.0	1.121	15.1	3.873	52.4

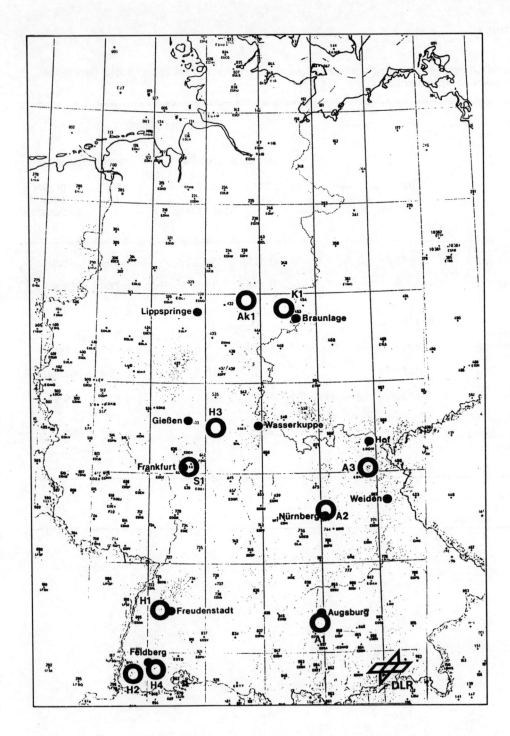

Figure 1. Location of the test areas and the nearest weather stations in the German forest damage research project.

SUMMARIZING REMARKS

Proceedings of the International and Interdisciplinary Symposium
ECOLOGY AND LANDSCAPE MANAGEMENT IN SRI LANKA
W. Erdelen, C. Preu, N. Ishwaran, C.M. Madduma Bandara (eds.)
Colombo, Sri Lanka, 12-26 March 1990
© 1993
Margraf Scientific Books, D-97985 Weikersheim
ISBN 3-8236-1182-8

Landscape Management in Sri Lanka: Meaning and Problems.

W. ERDELEN AND C. GANS

Abstract

The conference summarized in this volume allows one to characterize some situations noted in the title. However, the observations during the excursion also provided the potential for practical solutions to at least some of the practical problems faced. Most important, they let one note the components that would have to be incorporated in a working plan for landscape management. Such a plan will have to take into account the needs of the local populations and the resources that can be devoted to current management.

Introduction

The subtitle of this conference on the subject of ecology and landscape management, i.e. "Conflict or Compromise" raised the potential for conflict, and several of the contributions and demonstrations did offer examples of potential conflict. However, claims for the inevitability of conflict do not contribute to progress in any human endeavor. It may be more significant to establish areas containing the potential for agreement on issues of landscape management and to characterize paths that may achieve resolution of potential conflicts.

This conference generated at least the potential for the recognition of the ecological problems faced by Sri Lanka. It clearly disclosed that Sri Lanka is an ecological microcosm. One can travel from mountain peak to coral reef in a single day. One can see a diversity of natural but also of human impacted elements of the landscape. The papers presented provide clues to the issues that require resolutions specific to Sri Lanka. Also, they show that the island can serve as a model for geographically larger tropical areas. On the other hand, it became apparent that some of the problems observed also characterize other tropical countries, and that potential solutions to these problems obtained elsewhere may be applied to Sri Lanka. The availability of these data makes it desirable to discuss a framework here within which problems may ultimately be resolved.

Definitions

Webster's New World Dictionary defines "landscape", as among other things, "an expanse of natural scenery seen by the eye in one view" (Guralnik, 1984). More important, it also refers to "landscaping" as "to change ... to make it more attractive." Whereas it does not list "landscape management", "management" by itself is defined as the "act, art ... of controlling, [and] directing". Hence, landscape managers presumably motivate others to match human creations to the natural features of the original environment among which they are placed. The definition of ecology may be seen as much simpler and more encompassing. Thus, dictionaries agree that ecology is that field of biology that characterizes the relations between living organisms and their environments, with the environment encompassing both biotic and abiotic factors. Recently, the combined term "landscape management" has taken on further implications among which may be the control of environmental resources. Thus, one talks of landscapes as including several diverse components, parts of more or less natural ecosystems and parts of zones such as farm areas and woodlots undergoing human exploitation (Simmons 1979, Risser 1987). Their management is intended both to maintain a pleasing, esthetically appealing appearance of the land and to limit its ecological degradation. This incorporates the idea that exploitation will be on a sustainable basis, which implies that the land, as an ultimate resource, maintains certain structural features or essential processes, for instance its productivity. The esthetic aspect is probably inherent because the term landscape derives from the Dutch "Landschap" and was initially a descriptor of a school of painting (Zonneveld, 1988). Also inherent is the concept that landscapes are rarely purely wild, but rather include various levels of domestication. In adducing arguments involving esthetic aspects, one should be cognizant of the fact that these are culturally loaded and differ markedly with time and space. For instance, the writings of the early settlers in North America include many aspects suggesting that clearing of forest was meritorious; a byproduct of the common feeling enshrined in the literature of the period, that open areas were more appealing than the "oppressive" forest environment and that they were easier to make a living in (Kaplan and Kaplan, 1989). In other areas, forests incurred natural protection, perhaps because of superstitions regarding environments in which the eye could encompass only a very limited aspect. Furthermore, natural landscapes may incorporate elements inimical to those who enter them, such as leeches, tsetse flies, poisonous snakes, nematodes and viruses.

However, protection of particular species and patches of natural environments is intrinsic in many advanced religions and cultures, particularly in Asia (Callicott and Ames, 1989). Hence, there are sacred forest groves and trees, and the trees and animals adjacent to the grave sites of marabouts are often protected. Such trends may be contrasted with the perhaps apocryphal stories about the destruction of Byzantine orchards to "make sheep pasture" and with the effects of waves of human settlers in New Zealand who erased the native biota and engaged in concerted attempts at the introduction of familiar Polynesian, Asian and European forms. Certainly, the protectionist trends seen in various human cultures provide a base for the retention of parts of the natural heritage rather than letting environmental modification continue to be driven largely by need and greed.

Why is Management Now Critical?

Management of landscapes, as well as management of ecosystems, has become more and more essential since the last century. In the past, the process of environmental modification proceeded relatively slowly; unfortunately it has reached spectacular rates in the last few centuries (Richards, 1986). Even more important is that destructive practices were restricted geographically, sometimes due to a lack of technological capacity. Although major groups of species became extinct due to human activity (Martin, 1984), growth of the human population was limited by disease; the capacity of agricultural practice to facilitate widespread monoculture was limited by the inevitable rise of predators and pest species soon associated therewith. Also, many environments were intrinsically inhospitable to humans. The fear of tropical forests was presumably based on the associated disease conditions and the fact that it provided reservoirs for species that competed with humans and with domesticated species. These conditions have changed. Modern medicine now permits humans to live in almost all formerly uninhabitable areas. Domesticated species can similarly be protected. Modern technology allows rapid modification and destruction of vast landscapes. The destruction of every patch of the original landscape and of every residual element of the original biotas is claimed to be economically advantageous as it avoids the reseeding of the original vegetation. Areas once unproductive can be made to generate crops by modifying the natural texture of the soils and supplementing their available nutrients, but generally only for a few years. Most critical is the threat posed by genetically engineered organisms, which may soon be tailored to fit environments that now permit only limited occupation or that are totally unsuitable for domesticated species. It may well be that introduced organisms, whether plant or animal, will not survive long in such degraded sites; however, this represents a cold comfort for environmentalists. Once the original organisms have disappeared, they will be gone forever.

There are many reasons why organismic diversity should be preserved (e.g. Ehrlich and Wilson 1991, McNeely 1988, McNeely *et al.* 1990, Wilson 1988, 1992), and we hope to document some of them below. However, the need for management transcends even these, important as they are. First of all, there is the need to develop landscapes for their esthetic components, there being substantial evidence that these are related to human health. Secondly, nowadays agriculture is exploitative. This is based on the underlying premise that new crops, new pesticides and new fertilizers will be developed and will be affordable by the time the present practices become counterproductive. By the time the topsoil has disappeared, new parasites will have been developed and particular crops and farm species will no longer be desirable. It assumes that land will not become limiting to the maintenance and exponential growth of human population.

No aspect of history suggests that this optimism is well founded. Whereas we may be feeding more people than ever before, it is unclear whether their mean economic status (even if only measured in terms of nutrients and access to other resources) has been improving; there is other evidence that the maintenance of an acceptable economic standard is unlikely unless present practices change. Directed change of practice (intended to lead to improvement) represents management and improvement, and even the maintenance of the human condition has made management imperative now.

The implementation of landscape management will receive an independent discussion. However, one aspect needs immediate mention. This is the common claim made by some politicians that we cannot "afford" to concern ourselves with the environment; the cost would be too high both in terms of funds expended and jobs potentially associated with development lost. This is the argument one still hears, even in the richest and most developed nations. It is paralleled by the never-ending argument that "poor" countries must "first" provide for their population before attending to the "luxury" of engaging in environmental concerns.

Both arguments are specious. Naturally, we cannot do everything simultaneously. Of course, management must be cost effective. However, delays incur the costs of accelerating environmental and human degradation and even greater potential costs for restoring the degradation. Even in purely economic terms, waiting does not make sense; restoration, even if possible or if seen as important, involves costs which exceed the benefits derived from the initial destruction many times. Recent developments regarding joint analyses of environmental and ecological issues have brought both disciplines closer together, a shift that has long been overdue. For instance, management of protected areas and of biodiversity have recently been analyzed in economic terms (e.g. Dixon and Sherman 1990, 1991, McNeely 1988).

Some Problems Observed

The key agricultural problems encountered during the presentations in this conference, and pointed out during the excursions, are of three types: (1) the destruction of the initial vegetation, with loss of organismic diversity, (2) the topographic modification leading to ever-increasing erosion and silting, and (3) agricultural practices that produce obvious soil degradation, suggesting that they will only be tolerated on a short-term basis. These three problems are actually interrelated and are exacerbated by a fourth, which is the combination of local poverty and population growth, and which inevitably requires more and more substantial resources for its amelioration. The loss of diversity is sufficiently critical at this moment that we treat it independently in the following section. The second problem is a common byproduct of major and minor agricultural and industrial projects. During the construction of dam sites and roads, soil is exposed and stripped of its intrinsic cover; the leaching action of the tropical rains and oxidation of organic matter reduces the binding organic components, thus particulate matter gradually silts downward.

The basic pattern is exacerbated by the steep hillsides; however, the problem also exists in lower regions and exhibits a variant at the edge of the sea and on the fringe reef where mining of recent and fossil corals has exposed the shores to erosion (Preu, 1991). Topographic modification affects runoff, causes silting of hydrodams and modifies the flood patterns and sedimentation dynamics of rivers and coastal waters. All of these factors have deleterious effects on the many levels of aquatic productivity.

Various agricultural practices also contribute to topographic modification. The construction of unpaved roads in agricultural areas exposes much free surface. Indeed, the annual amount of road repair and ditch maintenance required in coffee, tea and cardamom plantations provides a simple but powerful indicator of the amount of topsoil being shifted per year. Too commonly, burning is used as a weed control tool. This practice destroys the mass of roots which binds the topsoil and supports the sponge-like effect of the mass. The uncovered topsoil is exposed to the pounding effects of rain and to the wear of rivulets of muddy water. Repeated burning then facilitates extremely rapid erosion and consequent loss of the most nutritive fractions of the soil.

Also of concern is the planting of crops that are known to poison soils, as indicated by the loss of most other species, for instance, the absence of seedlings and other understory in many *Eucalyptus* plantations. Another kind of poisoning occurs when the crops selected require various pesticides and fertilizers; these compounds are often selected without much concern for their long-term stability and the accumulation of their degradation products in the food chain.

Whereas, weather is not ordinarily included under the heading of "landscape", the percentage of vegetation cover and amount of evaporation may have substantial effects on this (Henderson-Sellers *et al.* 1988). Certainly, the presence of adjacent forests influences the local microclimates. Like all of the preceding items, absence of attention to this topic inevitably forces shifts to more destructive agricultural practice.

The Importance of Diversity

Biologists have discovered that the world contains an enormous number of discrete kinds (species) of animals and plants (e.g. Barnes 1989, Erwin 1982, May 1988) that differ in subtle and profound ways. Substantial, but hardly known, fractions of this biota often survive in the remnant natural areas (e.g. McCloskey and Spalding, 1989, for an overview). The enormous and interlocked complexity of biological systems is commonly underestimated. Studies in the forests of Costa Rica, which in some ways are analogous to those of Sri Lanka, show that populations of some tree species require large mammals as seed dispersers (Janzen 1984, Janzen and Martin 1982). Also several large and seemingly separate forest zones share certain invertebrate species; thus it has recently been shown that many kinds of butterflies migrate for hundreds of miles from the east to the west coast of Costa Rica, crossing the central mountains in the process (Janzen, pers. comm.).

The implication of these studies transcends the findings that the organisms are diverse, so that one particular kind of tree is not like other trees, and wild cats are not like domesticated cats. An even more important implication of diversity is that the biota is interlocked. For instance, the disappearance of the western lowland forest of Sri Lanka would cause loss of much of the fauna and flora of the eastern part, even if this remained otherwise untouched.

610

Another example reported is the interdependence between processes such as soil erosion in the highlands and productivity in the coastal or near-coastal zone of Sri Lanka (Preu 1991, Preu and Erdelen 1992). Hence, random destruction of local populations, and general human impact may have far-reaching effects in causing not only a local loss of diversity but also severe environmental problems in ecosystems far from where the anthropogenic disturbances actually take place. The potential for such loss is important because the diversity of inhabitants provides a very significant resource for the occupants of a region, and knowledge of the ecosystem characteristics remains a key factor in sustainable land use. Plant and animal species that have evolved in and/or now occupy a region have unique histories. Mostly they differ from those of other regions in obvious aspects of their life history and in the ways they deal with predators and parasites, i.e. in essential ecological characteristics. In short, they represent the results of millions of years of biological experimentation; their adaptation to local circumstances should be of critical importance to people now occupying the same area.

Beyond the esthetics of observing organisms and the human responsibility not to destroy the world we share, these organisms provide resources for medicine, agriculture and human nutrition. We are beginning to be able to amplify complex chemical compounds; this makes it even more critical to obtain access to the models that are locked up in the genotypes of diverse plants and animals. The many drugs and nutrients that we now use and have derived from animals and plants are but a tiny fraction of those likely to benefit us in the future (e.g. Farnsworth 1988, Plotkin 1988). However, we can only hope to use them if they and their gene pools survive. Furthermore, the many still undescribed agriculturally significant species such as the new lowland cardamom of the Sinharaja forest will not be able to benefit agriculture once their seed stocks have disappeared. However, there are several limits to the usage of such organisms, even after the preservation of these species has been assured. The key element is that we have a most inadequate view of what organisms now occur in Sri Lanka. Whereas some groups of biologists have been working for centuries and decades to describe and catalog the fauna and flora, the number of such specialists have been few in relation to the number of species involved. For many groups of organisms, the available studies represent the efforts of amateurs and hobbyists who volunteered their services; however, their efforts represent only a beginning. Estimates for Sri Lanka are that fewer than 80% of the large and showy vertebrates have so far been identified; this percentage is likely to be less than 50% for many common invertebrates and lower still for members of obscure groups (Barnes 1989, for a general overview). Yet, the obscure includes animals, such as earthworms and other soil organisms, that are widely acknowledged to be key organismic elements, critical to agriculture.

Some of the reports at this conference have documented these limits of our knowledge. It is, for instance, critical for management that we know how many kinds of native trees there are; for this reason, it is most significant to hear that many of the Sinharaja species have recently been discovered to be distinct from the trees of other wet zone forests. Not only do these trees need to be characterized, but we need to know more about their reproductive and spreading patterns (Dayanandan et al. 1990), their tolerance of soil types, their rates of growth, resistance to predators, water needs and other characteristics. For most species, we lack all of this information. If we now remember that these are the largest and most obvious organisms found in Sri Lanka, we will see that the situation is much worse for smaller and less obvious but as important creatures. Whatever the mechanism, it is imperative that the diversity residual in Sri Lanka be maintained. Maintenance demands protection of samples, but more than this it requires more information about the biota, its types and the geographic distribution of its elements.

An Approach to Management

During the present conference and the following excursion, we saw many examples of inappropriate practice demanding modification and management to limit recurrence. Unfortunately, even the most cost-effective management measures will inevitably incur costs. Whereas benefits and costs may be calculated for the island as a whole, they are likely to affect different and independent portions of the population. At the very least, they tend to involve a present cost (or delayed gratification) and a future benefit. Furthermore, management practices in a democratic society must depend on the informed consent of the populace, and this requires education about the underlying concepts for the management practice. It also requires trust of the populace that the practices for which it is presumably paying are actually designed and likely to achieve the claimed effect.

Beyond trust, it is necessary to plan and manage in a way that will deal with the needs of those who may be displaced or whose livelihood will be adversely affected by the modified procedures. This is particularly important whereever management plans are to affect a community that is living close to its subsistence. Banning the "traditional gathering" of firewood from the edges, and ever closer to the centers, of reserve forests is more effectively implemented, if the villagers are provided with alternate sources of fuel. Control of fishing, coral mining, "jungle clearing" and poaching again requires economic alternatives for those who have long engaged in, and are now continuing to engage in, these practices (see Ishwaran and Erdelen 1990, for a recent analysis of the protection status of Sinharaja forest). Provision of a substitute living has to represent an early component in planning, not an afterthought.

However, the practice should have limits, so that it is not subverted to enrich the few. It should be noted in the beginning that different areas impose different tasks and that diversification of existing land use patterns is likely to be advantageous, for both esthetic and practical reasons. It avoids the difficulties of monoculture by not providing a premium for any predator or disease that is able to utilize what humans have assembled. Monoculture by its nature does not contain barriers to inimical organisms so that these may expand without limits. The very lack of environmental and genetic diversity removes defenses.

Also, landscape management must utilize a triage technique to decide on the priority of a certain action for the several sets of problems. Solutions are too important to let action wait until all evidence is in. Commonly, practical approaches based on the best currently available evidence need initially to be implemented. Often, this evidence may derive from studies on other continents, even on those faced with other climates.

However, it should be made clear to observers that the start of remedial action implies only that its selection represents the best option under current conditions. It should also be stated that a parallel program which monitors the effects of the proposed changes and addresses the theoretical bases of the phenomena is starting concurrently.

Public recognition of uncertainty will reduce the tendency of defending the initial decisions for no better reason than that they were made. As evidence is provided by the monitoring scheme, it permits regular reevaluation of the initial decisions and modification of procedures as appropriate. Hence, managers have to be selected in part for their flexibility of mind, which must be made a condition of employment.

These steps should let implementation proceed immediately. They avoid the risk of waiting but also reduce the risk of precipitate (and consequently inadequately planned) action. One must remember that it is often critical that the task be started, as the cost of waiting has become too high. It is as critical that evaluation proceed concurrently, as the cost of defending past errors is likely to be great.

A Sequence of Priorities

We should like to propose a sample sequence of priorities and a pattern of implementing them. They are offered less as a set of absolute recommendations and more as a demonstration of one kind of reasoning about choice and implementation. The sequence deals essentially with terrestrial environments and divides them into three categories based upon major aims in management. These are (1) the maintenance of diversity, (2) the enhancement, amelioration and gradual improvement of apparently effective land use patterns and, finally, (3) the restoration and reclamation of areas that have lost productivity or are in imminent danger of doing so or are where management imposes major problems on other areas. It is important to consider that management contains an intrinsic bias towards non-natural aspects. The residuals of natural environments keep shrinking and it is critical that they be protected.

Diversity - Parks

Maintenance of diversity means protecting some portion of the original flora and fauna. This cannot occur species by species, but must proceed ecologically group by group. We must maintain some patches of the environment in their original state. This is normally achievedthrough the establishment of protected areas such as national parks and forest reserves (see Anon. 1990, Ishwaran this volume, for an overview of the Sri Lankan situation).

However, it is not enough to draw lines on a map and assume that all will be well. The borders of protected areas need to be patrolled, to see that theft of trees and animals is limited. To facilitate this, buffer zones, which also ameliorate edge effects, have commonly been established. Uses of parks for tourism need to be controlled so that they do not interfere with the aim of maintaining perpetuity. There is an apparent need for biomonitoring as it is impossible to determine whether something has changed if one does not know its original status (Izrael and Munn, 1986).

It is also important that management considers the control of wild organisms. The effects of temporal fluctuations in the number of animals such as the elephant, buffalo and wild pig may be buffered by large regions; however, population explosions or mass migration may be devastating to the rest of the environment (particularly to adjacent agricultural areas) should the preserve prove to be too small. It should be explicit that park and landscape management implies the management of animal populations as well.

Some attention needs to be paid to those who are expected to handle the process of protection. Forest and park guards should be paid reasonable wages, sufficient to permit them to consider the position an attractive one and to reduce the need for supplementation of income by avoiding enforcement. Too often these positions have received most inadequate payment. Whenever guards are required to protect the natural environments adjacent to their native villages, they will be exposed to potential conflict of interest. Still local guards are needed, as they are the only ones with the knowledge to recognize potential problems and conflicts. It remains absolutely essential that management be accompanied by local education assuring that the overall projects and their guards are viewed as a desirable enterprise by those portions of the population most immediately affected.

Associated with the maintenance of existing parks is the question whether they have been well designed in the beginning. Design criteria have been repeatedly discussed among conservation biologists (e.g. Diamond 1975, Diamond and May 1981, Margules et al. 1982, 1988, Saunders et al. 1987, 1993, Saunders and Hobbs 1991). One of the most famous debates involves the so-called SLOSS issue (single large or several small reserves; e.g. Simberloff, 1988). This issue centers around the question as to whether protected areas are large enough in relation to the home ranges of the species to be maintained. Many landscapes are ever more fragmented, although there may be corridors that allow some formerly wide-ranging species to utilize their totality. Are there buffer zones to limit edge effects and assure that the effect of local incursions be limited (Schoenewald and Bayless, 1986)? Are the buffer zones large enough to assure that organisms emerging from the central reserves will not be inimical to human occupants of adjacent areas? Throughout one must remember that destruction of the original vegetation represents a ratchet phenomenon as it always proceeds in a single direction. In most parts of the world, it had best be curtailed or stopped; the environments previously modified should be sufficient for feeding and supplying human populations.

Diversity - Restoration

Not all desirable organisms survive in the present parks. Some native species may not occur there or may occur only incidentally, having most of their biologically important range (zones of feeding and reproduction) outside these regions. Such species may not now be endangered. However, they may be considered to be threatened because their status is likely to be unknown: minor, perhaps otherwise desirable, local modifications of the environment may produce sudden extinctions. Furthermore, it is likely that each change in land utilization will reduce the original biota further.

The difficulty lies in knowing rare native forms and the areas in which they still occur. Even more important from the viewpoint of cost effectiveness is the need to identify patches of presently occupied environment that contain many such species. Such areas might form the nuclei for miniparks in which a grouping of rare organisms might be protected. It has been proposed elsewhere (Gans, this volume) that burrowing reptiles and amphibians might form indicators of ecological zones that might otherwise be difficult to define. Thus, the ranges of natural areas might be identified, and suitable sites within these characterized as candidates for partial or total protection. As such zones are likely to be small, some of their diversity will have been lost at the time they are established. Addition of marginal areas, and plantations of natural species therein, may increase the likelihood that populations of some animal and smaller plant species will survive. Naturally such efforts should proceed with the informed consent of the local community. The benefits of maintaining diversity, such as the income from tourism, should be shared with those living in the regions under protection. If the community is kept advised of the reasons for the reserve, if they can see and benefit from its merits, it becomes more likely that they will take pride in the restoration of diversity and help maintain it.

Agriculture - Overview

Usage of land may be of several types, from the intrinsically destructive, such as most mining, to possibly self-sustaining, such as some kinds of agriculture (Redclift, 1987). Control of land usage furthermore is likely to be limited by political and other social considerations; much of what is deemed desirable is likely to have to proceed through education rather than fiat. As the several kinds of agriculture (including silviculture) are likely to affect most of the island's landscapes, they are emphasized here. However, attention should also be paid to the management of wetlands and zones occupied by mangroves.

The agricultural land use patterns need to be surveyed and may be subdivided into three categories. The first concerns regions in which productivity is high and appears to be stable, suggesting that the observed patterns may continue at least for the present. The second represents areas in which the practices involve obvious risk of rapid deterioration with the probability that the land cannot sustain the observed pattern for another generation or even less. Research will be needed to determine how the pattern may be modified before a catastrophe occurs. The third includes areas already degraded to the point at which there is no chance of maintaining former land use patterns. A need for the restoration of topography, fertility and diversity most likely exists within these areas. Naturally, the absolute area undergoing each practice and the number of people affected bear on the priority given to improvement. Minor patches of the third category may well be tolerated; however, major areas may demand current investment in management.

Agriculture - Watching Brief

Some agricultural practices are relatively old and appear to combine diversification of product and area with effective yield. Examples might be the "garden" patterns seen, in which single family holdings involve plantations of several tree and shrub species in combination with small vegetable patches and a limited number of domestic animals (Altieri, 1990). These kinds of holding appear to maintain or even enrich the soil and promise long-term stability. Current management might well be restricted to the encouragement of such practices (perhaps by taxation associated benefits) involving the search for additional garden species, inclusion of which might yield temporary or more permanent cash crops, and perhaps involving the improvement of some of the tree crop species now grown (Vandermeer, 1989). Areas identified to represent stable advantageous practice should be subjected to a watching brief, but designated for fine tuning rather than for major change.

Agriculture - Modification

The second category involves those areas that are now profitable and productive but at a significant cost to the environment. For these areas, one can justify major research efforts leading to modification of practice. An example is the growing of vegetables in the N'Eliya area. Reports presented to us noted massive use of pesticides and fertilizers, in spite of (or because of) which new pests are continuously threatening productivity. The agricultural practice with rapid replacement of crops also keeps much land surface exposed to rainfall and continuous artificial irrigation. This generates substantial destruction of topsoil; some reports talked of initial losses of more than 30 cm a year. Clearly, the system only survives due to substantial input of chemicals and labor; even then, the lifetime of the land is limited.

Management of such an exploitative system, involving as it does high current productivity and manpower, would seem to justify a substantial research effort. Possible research avenues might include study of the effects of separation of plots and diversification of crops to limit pest build-up, and of changing the moisture and fertilizer application patterns to reduce erosion. Temporary application of plastic barrier material to reduce evaporation, and hence salt build-up, might be one such approach which might also limit erosion due to direct impact of rain on exposed soil (Levins and Vandermeer, 1990); another approach might be the inclusion of additional plant species that would assure more continuous plant covering of the surface.

Land Recovery

Certain agricultural areas have suffered substantial erosion. An example that might be cited is the generation-long period of neglect in some tea estates. Then there are forests that have been subjected to selected logging over a long period of time which has removed the "valuable" timber, but has destroyed much of the intermediate zones: such practice has often allowed invasion of "weedy" plants and creepers which reduce or even arrest natural succession (Poore 1976, Poore and Sayer 1987, Westoby 1987). In some cases, deforestation followed by repeated burning has caused most of the top soil to disappear leaving granite and clay substrates that no longer support significant vegetation.

Such situations represent the need for a concerted effort at evaluation of what may arrest degradation and possibly restore such areas to productivity. The process may involve several stages, as there may be an initial need to provide ground cover, followed by a gradual increase in the suitability of the zone for tree and bush species, nitrogen fixers and soil accumulators. Limitation of grazing and elimination of burning are often key initial steps.

One important consideration is the matching of the successional stages to each other. There are common arguments for the use of fast-growing grasses, eucalypt and coniferous tree species. However, use of such exotic forms probably represents a stopgap measure, as they may have a deleterious effect on the local fauna and severely limit the plants with which they can co-exist. Some tree species gradually produce forest monocultures and modify environmental conditions. The efforts of local botanists at identifying Sri Lankan species that are suitable for the stages of land reclamation are consequently extremely important. The residuals of tropical forest diversity likely contain species that share many of the beneficial attributes of the exotics without their disadvantages.

Discussion

The preceding discussion has noted our views of what landscape management might be, why it is now critically important and what a schedule of attack for the observed problems might be. The examples given are just cases that came to mind and are neither complete lists nor do they represent a true priority rating. The latter would most likely require much more study and evaluation of the substantial evidence that already exists in the files of many Sri Lankan institutions and in the minds of their specialists.

A critical aspect that has to be kept in mind throughout is that these aspects are all interrelated, not only in ecological, but also in human terms. Soil erosion in the highlands not only reduces the availability of food for the region, but also displaces some marginal farmers. This, in turn, imposes pressure on the landscape in other regions. For instance, highland erosion is linked to wetland and coastal productivity.

The most important aspect then is not whether landscape management is in "conflict" with ecology, as one cannot be in conflict with nor can one compromise with a scientific descriptive discipline. Instead, it is necessary to ask about the kinds of ecological circumstances under which the people of the region will live in future generations. Management can make these circumstances acceptable. However, without some level of management, the future looks grim.

Acknowledgments

We thank David Allen, Tom Langton, Brad Moon, John Vandermeer, Earl Werner and Mudiyanselage Wijeyaratne for their trenchant comments on aspects of this essay. However, the opinions expressed are naturally those of the authors and not necessarily congruent with the suggestions of the reviewers. The work of C. Gans is supported by the Leo Leeser Foundation.

Literature Cited

Altieri, M.A. 1990. Why study traditional agriculture? *In* C.R. Carroll, J.H. Vandemeer and P. Rosset, eds. *Agroecology,* pp. 551-564. McGraw Hill, New York.

Anon. 1990. *IUCN Directory of South Asian Protected Areas.* IUCN, Gland, Switzerland.

Barnes, R.D. 1989. Diversity of organisms: how much do we know? *Amer. Zool.* 29: 1075-1084.

Callicott, J. B. and R.T. Ames, eds. 1989. *Nature in Asian Traditions of Thought: Essays in Environmental Philosophy.* State University of New York Press, Albany.

Dayanandan, S., D.N.C. Attygalla, A.W.W.L. Abeygunasekera, I.A.U.N. Gunatilleke, and C.V.S. Gunatilleke. 1990. Phenology and floral morphology in relation to pollination of some Sri Lankan dipterocarps. *In* K.S. Bawa and M. Hadley, eds. *Reproductive Ecology of Tropical Forest Plants,* pp. 103-133. UNESCO, Paris.

Diamond, J.M. 1975. The island dilemma: Lessons of modern biogeographic studies for the design of nature reserves. *Biol. Conserv.* 7: 129-146.

Diamond, J.M. and R.M. May. 1981. Island biogeography and the design of natural reserves. *In* R.M. May, ed. *Theoretical Ecology: Principles and Applications,* pp. 163-186. Blackwell Scientif Publ. Oxford.

Dixon, J.A. and P.B. Sherman. 1990. *Economics of Protected Areas. A New Look at Benefits and Costs.* Island Press, Washington DC.

Dixon, J.A. and P.B. Sherman. 1991. Economics of protected areas. *Ambio* 20: 68-74.

Ehrlich, P.R. and E.O. Wilson. 1991. Biodiversity studies: science and policy. *Science* 253: 758-762.

Erwin, T.L. 1982. Tropical forests: their richness in Coleoptera and other arthropod species. *Coleopt. Bull.* 36: 74-75.

Farnsworth, N.R. 1988. Screening plants for new medicines. *In* E.O. Wilson, ed. *Biodiversity,* pp. 83-97. National Academy Press, Washington DC.

Gans, C. This volume. Fossorial Amphibians and Reptiles: Their Distributions as Environmental Indicators.

Guralnik, D.B. ed. 1984. *Webster's New World Dictionary of the American Language.* 2nd College Edition. Prentice Hall Press, New York.

Henderson-Sellers, A., R.E. Dickinson and M.F. Wilson 1988. Tropical deforestation: important processes for climate models. *Climat. Change,* 13: 433-67.

Ishwaran, N. This volume. Interest Conflicts and Management of Protected Areas in Sri Lanka.

Ishwaran, N. and W. Erdelen. 1990. Conserving Sinharaja - an experiment in sustainable development in Sri Lanka. *Ambio* 19: 237-244.

Izrael, Y.A. and R.E. Munn. 1986. Monitoring the environment and renewable resources. *In* W.C. Clark and R.E. Munn, eds. *Sustainable Development of the Biosphere,* pp. 360-377. Cambridge Univ. Press, Cambridge.

Janzen, D.H. and P.S. Martin. 1982. Neotropical anachronisms: fruits the gomphotheres ate. *Science* 215: 19-27.

Janzen, D.H. 1984. Dispersal of small seeds by big herbivores: foliage is the fruit. *Am. Nat.* 123: 338-353.

Kaplan, R. and S. Kaplan. 1989. *The Experience of Nature: A Psychological Perspective.* Cambridge Univ. Press, Cambridge.

Levins, J.A. and J.H. Vandermeer. 1990. The agroecosystem embedded in a complex ecological community.*In* C.R. Carroll, J.H. Vandemeer and P. Rosset, eds. *Agroecology,* pp. 341-362. McGraw Hill, New York.

Margules, C.R., A.O. Nicholls and R.L. Pressey. 1988. Selecting networks of reserves to maximise biological diversity. *Biol. Conserv.* 43: 63-76.

Margules, C., A.J. Higgs, and R.W. Rafe. 1982. Modern biogeographic theory: are there any lessons for nature reserve design? *Biol. Conserv.* 24: 115-128.

Martin, P.S. 1984. Prehistoric overkill: the global model. *In* P.S. Martin and R.G. Klein, eds. *Quaternary Extinctions: A Prehistoric Revolution,* pp. 354-403. Univ. Arizona Press, Tuscson.

May, R. M. 1988. How many species are there on earth? *Science* 241: 1441-1449.

McCloskey, J.M. and H. Spalding. 1989. A reconnaissance-level inventory of the amount of wilderness remaining in the World. *Ambio* 18: 221-227.

McNeely, J.A. 1988. *Economics and Biological Diversity: Developing and Using Economic Incentives to Conserve Biological Resources.* IUCN, Gland, Switzerland.

McNeely, J.A. , K.R. Miller, W.V. Reid, R.A. Mittermeier and T.B. Werner. 1990. Strategies for conserving biodiversity. *Environment* 32: 16-20, 36-40.

Plotkin, M. J. 1988. The outlook for new agricultural and industrial products from the tropics. *In* E.O. Wilson, ed. *Biodiversity,* pp. 106-116. National Academy Press, Washington DC.

Poore, D. 1976. *Ecological Guidelines for Development in Tropical Rain Forests.* IUCN Books, Morges, Switzerland.

Poore, D. and J. Sayer. 1987. *The Management of Tropical Moist Forest Lands: Ecological Guidelines.* IUCN Tropical Forest Programme Ser. 4.

Preu, C. 1991. Human impact on the morphodynamics of coasts - A case study of the SW coast of Sri Lanka. *In* W. Erdelen, N. Ishwaran and P. Müller, eds. *Tropical Ecosystems. Systems Characteristics, Utilization Patterns, and Conservation Issues,* pp. 121-138. Verlag Josef Margraf, Weikersheim, Germany.

Preu, C. and W. Erdelen. 1992. Geoecological consequences of human impacts on forests in Sri Lanka. *In* J.G. Goldammer, ed. *Tropical Forests in Transition,* pp. 147-164. Birkhäuser Verlag, Basel, Switzerland.

Redclift, M.R. 1987. *Sustainable Development: Exploring the Contradictions.* Methuen, New York.

Richards, J.F. 1986. World environmental history and economic development. *In* W.C. Clark and R.E. Munn, eds. *Sustainable Development of the Biosphere,* pp. 53-74. Cambridge Univ. Press, Cambridge.

Risser, P. G. 1987. Landscape ecology: state of the art. *In* M.G. Turner, ed. Landscape Heterogeneity and Disturbance. *Ecol. Studies,* 64. Springer, New York.

Saunders, D.A. and R.J. Hobbs. 1991. *Nature Conservation 2: The Role of Corridors.* Surrey Beatty & Sons Pty Ltd. Chipping North, NSW, Australia.

Saunders, D.A., G.W. Arnold, A.A. Burbridge and A.J.M. Hopins. eds. 1987. *Nature Conservation: The Role of Remnants of Native Vegetation.* Surrey Beatty & Sons Pty Ltd. Chipping North, NSW, Australia.

Schoenewald-Cox, C.M. and J.W. Bayless. 1986. The boundary model: a geographical analysis of design and conservation of nature reserves. *Biol. Conserv.* 38: 305-322.

Simberloff, D. 1988. The contribution of population and community biology to conservation science. *Ann. Rev. Ecol. Syst.* 19: 473-511.

Simmons, I.G. 1979. *Biogeography: Natural and Cultural*. Edward Arnold, London.

Soulé, M.E. 1991. Conservation tactics for a constant crisis. *Science* 253: 744-750.

Vandermeer, J.H. 1989. *The Ecology of Intercropping*. Cambridge Univ. Press, Cambridge.

Wilson, E.O. ed. 1988. *Biodiversity.* National Academy Press, Washington DC.

Wilson, E.O. 1992. *The Diversity of Life*. Harvard Univ. Press, Cambridge.

Zonneveld, I.S. 1988. Landscape ecology and its application. *In* M.R. Moss, ed. *Landscape Ecology and Management,* pp. 3-15. Poliscience Publishers Inc. Montreal.

TAJ SAMUDRA DECLARATION

TAJ SAMUDRA DECLARATION

The international and interdisciplinary sypmosium "Ecology and Landscape Management in Sri Lanka" took place at the Taj Samudra Hotel, Colombo, Sri Lanka 12 March to 26 March 1990. This symposium was a pioneering and unique effort to bring together scientists and specialists, both Sri Lankan and foreign, from institutions related to the ecology and landscape management of Sri Lanka. Among these were universities, departments, ministries and non-governmental organizations (NGOs). It was the first event to expose participants to problems in the field both in respect to natural landscapes as well as to landscapes altered drastically by man. As a result of the combination of both theory (paper presentations, 13-16 March 1990) and field experiences (excursions, 18-24 March 1990) the following conclusions were drawn together in the final session on 26 March 1990.

1. It is imperative that scientific input should be channelled into decision-making processes which would contribute to solving the problems of ecology and landscape management in Sri Lanka in an organized manner.
2. There is data, information and scientific expertise available in Sri Lanka for solving these problems, but significant gaps do exist.
3. Available information is "discipline-bound". There are very few studies which are interdisciplinary, i.e. which synthesize concepts of at least the relevant natural science disciplines. The interaction between natural and social sciences is even less developed. Where teams are involved in conducting research the work is more "multidisciplinary" than "interdisciplinary".
4. It became apparent that there is a need to develop an organizational structure (here tentatively termed "commission") which would enable the Sri Lankan scientific community to contribute to policy planning and decision-making processes in matters related to the environment and landscape management in the future. The commission will be permanently in contact with the representatives in Sri Lanka of donor countries and topic-related organizations. It will have the general tasks of (a) identifying urgent issues that require interdisciplinary research and study, (b) coordinating national and international research and monitoring programs, (c) establishing an effective communication link between policy planners, decision makers and the scientific community, (d) establishing additional links and further collaboration with international agencies, scientific and technological societies, (e) maintaining a documentation unit including publications, the production of a data base, the establishment of awareness programs and the creation of an information center, and (f) coordinating national and international training and exchange programs.
5. As a first step, a steering committee was set up among the Sri Lankan participants covering a wi wide spectrum of scientific and technological expertise. It has the tasks of (a) negotiating with governmental (e.g. NARESA) and non-governmental (e.g. SLAAS) organizations with regard to collaboration with the commission, the definition of the organizational structure of this commission and the clarification of the organizational affiliation of the commission, (b) holding regular meetings of its members, and (c) forming the commission itself. In addition, an associate group of overseas members was formed to coordinate international activities.

The three organizational elements of the symposium, i.e. the paper presentations, the excursions and the final session, which successfully established a new organizational framework, as mentioned above, may be considered an innovative mode of "scientific politics" related to environmental issues in the tropics. The question of conflict or compromise is rhetorical only, as compromise is the only way forward, especially when quality of life is concerned.

Colombo, 26 March 1990